INTERNATIONAL ECONOMICS

SECOND EDITION

PARVIZ ASHEGHIAN

California State University San Bernardino

2000

DAME

Thomson Learning™

Australia • Canada • Denmark • Japan • Mexico • New Zealand • Philippines
Puerto Rico • Singapore • South Africa • Spain • United Kingdom • United States

International Economics—Second Edition, by Parviz Asheghian
Desktop Publishing: Sonda Frament
                             Sheryl New
Artist: Pamela S. Porter
        Jan Tiefel
Cover Design: Andrea P. Leggett
Cover Photos: © Corel Professional Photos. Images may have been combined and/or modified to produce final cover art.
Printer: Sheridan Books – Braun-Brumfield

Printed in the United States of America
1 2 3 4 5 02 01 00 99

For more information contact Thomson Learning Custom Publishing, 5101 Madison Road, Cincinnati, Ohio, 45227, 1-800-355-9983 or find us on the Internet at http://www.custom.thomsonlearning.com

For permission to use material from this text or product, contact us by:
• telephone: **1-800-730-2214**
• fax: **1-800-730-2215**
• web: **http://www.thomsonrights.com**

Library of Congress Cataloging-in-Publication Data: 99-74614

ISBN 0-87393-888-7

This book is printed on acid-free paper.

TABLE OF CONTENTS

Preface xvii

Chapter 1 INTRODUCTION 1

1.1 THE GLOBAL ECONOMY 1
1.2 WHAT IS INTERNATIONAL ECONOMICS? 3
   GLOBAL INSIGHTS CASE 1.1 - The Global Factory 3
1.3 INTERNATIONAL VERSUS DOMESTIC TRADE 4
   1.3a Factor Mobility 4
   1.3b National Currencies 4
   1.3c National Policies 5
   1.3d Cultures 5
1.4 THE WORLD IN TRANSITION 5
   1.4a Newly Industrialized Countries 5
   1.4b The Soviet Union and Eastern Europe 6
   1.4c The Unification of Germany 6
   1.4d Europe after 1992 6
   1.4e North American Free Trade Agreement 7
   1.4f The International Debt Crisis 7
   1.4g Multinational Corporations 7
   1.4h Transborder Data Flow 7
1.5 THE SIGNIFICANCE OF INTERNATIONAL TRADE IN THE WORLD ECONOMY 8
   GLOBAL INSIGHTS CASE 1.2 - Is IBM All-American? 8
   GLOBAL INSIGHTS CASE 1.3 - U.S. Exports More than Peanuts 10
   GLOBAL INSIGHTS CASE 1.4 - Economic Linkages among G-7 Countries 12
1.6 SUMMARY 13
   Review Questions 14
   Problems 14
   Notes 15
   Suggested Readings 15

Part I THEORIES OF INTERNATIONAL TRADE 17

Chapter 2 DEVELOPMENT OF INTERNATIONAL TRADE THEORIES: SUPPLY 19

2.1 INTRODUCTION 19
2.2 THEORY OF MERCANTILISM 19
2.3 THEORY OF ABSOLUTE ADVANTAGE 20
   GLOBAL INSIGHTS CASE 2.1 - Hornick and Mercantilism 20
2.4 THEORY OF COMPARATIVE ADVANTAGE 22
2.5 AN EMPIRICAL TEST OF COMPARATIVE ADVANTAGE 22
2.6 PRODUCTION POSSIBILITIES FRONTIER 24
   2.6a The Production Possibility Frontier under Constant Costs Assumption 24
   2.6b The Basis for and the Gains from International Trade under Constant Costs Assumption 25

    Consumption Gains from Trade. 26
    Production Gains from Trade 27
  2.6c Production Possibility Frontier under Increasing Costs Assumption 27
  2.6d The Basis for and the Gains from International Trade under Increasing Costs Assumption 28
2.7 COMPLETE VERSUS PARTIAL SPECIALIZATION 30
  2.7a The Case of a Small Country 30
2.8 SUMMARY 31
  Review Questions 32
  Problems 33
  Notes 34
  Suggested Readings 34

Chapter 3 MODERN THEORIES OF INTERNATIONAL TRADE: DEMAND 35

3.1 INTRODUCTION 35
3.2 INDIVIDUAL INDIFFERENCE CURVES 35
3.3 COMMUNITY INDIFFERENCE CURVES 39
3.4 COMMUNITY INDIFFERENCE CURVES AND INTERNATIONAL TRADE 40
  3.4a Equilibrium in Autarky 40
  3.4b Basis for and Gains from Trade under the Increasing Costs Assumption 41
3.5 TRADE BASED ON TASTE DIFFERENTIALS 43
  GLOBAL INSIGHTS CASE 3.1 - Export and Import Price Indexes and Terms of Trade 45
3.6 OFFER CURVES 45
  3.6a Derivation of Offer Curves 46
  3.6b Equilibrium Relative Commodity Price with Offer Curves 46
3.7 MEASUREMENT OF TERMS OF TRADE 47
  3.7a Commodity Terms of Trade 48
  GLOBAL INSIGHTS CASE 3.2 - Oil Shocks and Terms of Trade 50
  3.7b Income Terms of Trade 51
  GLOBAL INSIGHTS CASE 3.3 - Growth in Advanced Nations' Terms of Trade 51
  3.7c Single Factoral Terms of Trade 52
  3.7d Double Factoral Terms of Trade 52
3.8 SUMMARY 52
  Review Questions 53
  Problems 53
  Suggested Readings 54

Chapter 4 MODERN THEORIES OF INTERNATIONAL TRADE: APPLICATIONS AND NEW APPROACHES 55

4.1 INTRODUCTION 55
4.2 HECKSCHER-OHLIN THEORY 55
  4.2a Assumptions and Implications of the Heckscher-Ohlin Theory 56
  4.2b Graphical Illustration of the Heckscher-Ohlin Theory 57
4.3 FACTOR-PRICE EQUALIZATION THEOREM AND INCOME DISTRIBUTION 58
  4.3a Factor-Price Equalization Theorem 58
  4.3b Income Distribution Effects of International Trade 59
  GLOBAL INSIGHTS CASE 4.1 - Global Resource Endowments and Trade Patterns 60
4.4 EMPIRICAL STUDIES OF THE HECKSCHER-OHLIN THEORY 61
  4.4a Leontief Paradox 61

4.4b Other Empirical Studies 62
4.5 EXTENSIONS OF AND ALTERNATIVES TO THE HECKSCHER-OHLIN THEORY 62
   4.5a Increasing Returns to Scale as the Basis for Trade 62
     Graphical Analysis of Increasing Returns to Scale as the Basis for Trade 63
   4.5b Theory of Overlapping Demand (Linder Thesis) 64
   4.5c Technological Gap Theory 64
   4.5d Product Life Cycle Theory 65
     GLOBAL INSIGHTS CASE 4.2 - Product Life Cycle of the Pocket Calculator 67
4.6 EFFECTS OF TRANSPORTATION COSTS ON TRADE 68
4.7 REAL-WORLD RELEVANCE OF INTERNATIONAL TRADE THEORIES 69
4.8 SUMMARY 70
   Review Questions 70
   Problems 71
   Notes 72
   Suggested Readings 72

Part 2   NATIONAL POLICIES, INTERNATIONAL ORGANIZATIONS AND AGREEMENTS, AND RECENT POLITICAL EVENTS AFFECTING INTERNATIONAL TRADE . . . 73

Chapter 5 TARIFF BARRIERS 75

5.1 INTRODUCTION 75
5.2 DEFINITION OF A TARIFF 75
5.3 CLASSIFICATIONS OF TARIFFS 75
   5.3a Protective and Revenue Tariffs 75
   5.3b Specific, Ad Valorem, and Compound Tariffs 76
5.4 EFFECTIVE RATE OF PROTECTION 77
   GLOBAL INSIGHTS CASE 5.1 - Tariff Wars in the 1930s 78
5.5 WELFARE EFFECTS OF A TARIFF 79
   5.5a Consumer Surplus and Producer Surplus 79
   5.5b Effect of Tariffs on Consumers 80
   5.5c Effect of Tariffs on Producers 83
   GLOBAL INSIGHTS CASE 5.2 - Offshore Assembly Provisions 84
   5.5d Effect of Tariffs on Government Revenue 85
   5.5e Net National Loss from Tariffs 85
5.6 SUMMARY 87
   Review Questions 87
   Problems 88
   Suggested Readings 88

Chapter 6 NONTARIFF TRADE BARRIERS 93

6.1 INTRODUCTION 93
6.2 QUOTAS 93
   6.2a Import Quotas 93
   GLOBAL INSIGHTS CASE 6.1 - "Nontrade" Policies Can Cause Trade Disputes 94
   6.2b Export Quotas 94
   6.2c Welfare Effects of a Quota 95
6.3 VOLUNTARY EXPORT RESTRAINTS 96
   GLOBAL INSIGHTS CASE 6.2 - U.S. Sugar Quotas and the Global Sugar Market 97

6.3a Welfare Effects of Voluntary Export Restraints 98
6.4 COMPARISON OF TARIFFS AND QUOTAS 100
6.5 SUBSIDIES 100
  6.5a Welfare Effects of a Subsidy 101
    Domestic Production Subsidy 101
    Export Subsidy 102
6.6 TAXES 104
6.7 DUMPING 104
  6.7a International Price Discrimination 106
6.8 OTHER NONTARIFF TRADE BARRIERS 107
  6.8a Government Purchasing Policies 107
  6.8b Administrative and Technical Regulations 107
    Government Health and Safety Standards 107
    Marketing and Packaging Standards 107
  GLOBAL INSIGHTS CASE 6.3 - Trade and Intellectual Property Rights 108
    Customs Procedures and Valuation 108
  6.8c Intervention in the Foreign Exchange Market 108
6.9 SUMMARY 109
  Review Questions 110
  Problems 110
  Notes 111
  Suggested Readings 112

Chapter 7 ARGUMENTS FOR PROTECTION 113

7.1 INTRODUCTION 113
7.2 THEORY-BASED ARGUMENTS 113
  7.2a Terms-of-Trade Argument and Optimum Tariff 113
    Graphical Illustration of the Optimum Tariff and Retaliation 114
  7.2b Domestic Distortion Argument 116
  7.2c Strategic Trade Policy Argument 116
  GLOBAL INSIGHTS CASE 7.1 - The Semiconductor Accord 118
7.3 ERRONEOUS ARGUMENTS 118
  7.3a Domestic Production Argument 118
  7.3b Prevent-Money-Outflow Argument 119
  7.3c Wage Protection Argument 119
  7.3d Equalization of Production Costs Argument 120
7.4 QUESTIONABLE ARGUMENTS 120
  7.4a Antidumping Argument 120
  7.4b Balance of Trade Argument 121
  7.4c Employment Protection Argument 121
7.5 QUALIFIED ARGUMENTS 122
  7.5a Infant Industry Argument 122
  7.5b National Security Argument 122
  7.5c Diversification Argument 123
  7.5d Infant Government Argument 124
  GLOBAL INSIGHTS CASE 7.2 - Trade Promotion Coordinating Committee (TPCC) . . . 124
7.6 OTHER ARGUMENTS 125
  7.6a Environmental Protection Argument 125
  7.6b Political Argument 126

7.7 SUMMARY 127
    Review Questions 129
    Problems 129
    Notes 130
    Suggested Readings 130

Chapter 8 INTERNATIONAL ORGANIZATIONS AND AGREEMENTS AFFECTING INTERNATIONAL TRADE 133

8.1 INTRODUCTION 133
8.2 INTERNATIONAL CARTELS 133
    8.2a Centralized Cartels 134
    GLOBAL INSIGHTS CASE 8.1 - Erosion of OPEC's Power in the Global Market ... 136
8.3 ECONOMIC INTEGRATION 136
    8.3a Preferential Trade Arrangements 137
    8.3b Free-Trade Areas 137
    8.3c Customs Unions 137
      Static Welfare Effects of a Customs Union 137
      Trade-Creating Customs Unions 137
      Trade-Diverting Customs Unions 139
    8.3d Dynamic Welfare Effects of a Customs Union 141
      Empirical Investigations of a Customs Union 142
    8.3e Common Markets 142
    8.3f Economic Union 143
8.4 MAJOR TRADE ASSOCIATIONS AMONG DEVELOPING COUNTRIES 143
    GLOBAL INSIGHTS CASE 8.2 - The Oilseed Disputes 144
8.5 ORGANIZATION FOR ECONOMIC COOPERATION AND DEVELOPMENT 145
    GLOBAL INSIGHTS CASE 8.3 - U.S.–Chinese Standoff over MFN Status 146
8.6 GENERAL AGREEMENT ON TARIFFS AND TRADE 147
8.7 STATE TRADING 151
8.8 SUMMARY 152
    Review Questions 153
    Problems 153
    Notes 154
    Suggested Readings 155

Chapter 9 RECENT FREE TRADE AGREEMENTS AND POLITICAL EVENTS AFFECTING THE GLOBAL ECONOMY 157

9.1 INTRODUCTION 157
9.2 EUROPE AFTER 1992 157
    GLOBAL INSIGHTS CASE 9.1 - The EU in Action 158
    GLOBAL INSIGHTS CASE 9.2 - The EU and the European Currency Crisis 160
9.3 RECENT FREE TRADE AGREEMENTS AFFECTING THE GLOBAL ECONOMY 161
    9.3a United States—Canada Free Trade Agreement 161
    9.3b North American Free Trade Agreement (NAFTA) 162
    9.3c Asian-Pacific Economic Cooperation (APEC) 165
    GLOBAL INSIGHTS CASE 9.3 - Regional Trade Agreements: Building Blocks or Stumbling Blocks for Multilateral Process? 166
    GLOBAL INSIGHTS CASE 9.4 - APEC Tariff Reductions and Other Initiatives .. 167

9.4 RECENT POLITICAL EVENTS AFFECTING THE GLOBAL ECONOMY 167
   9.4a Eastern European Countries Economic Reforms 168
   9.4b Unification of Germany 168
   9.4c Demise of the Soviet Union 170
   GLOBAL INSIGHTS CASE 9.5 - Bilateral Investment Treaties 171
9.5 SUMMARY 172
   Review Questions . . . . : 174
   Problems 174
   Notes 174
   Suggested Readings 176

Part 3 INTERNATIONAL MONETARY RELATIONS 179

Chapter 10 THE BALANCE OF PAYMENTS 181

10.1 INTRODUCTION 181
10.2 DEFINITION OF THE BALANCE OF PAYMENTS 181
10.3 BALANCE OF PAYMENTS ACCOUNTING 181
   10.3a Debit and Credit Items 182
   10.3b Major Accounts in the Balance of Payments 183
   10.3c Double-Entry Bookkeeping 183
   GLOBAL INSIGHTS CASE 10.1 - Major U.S. Merchandise Exports and Imports in 1996 185
10.4 THE UNITED STATES' BALANCE OF PAYMENTS 186
   10.4a Significance of the United States' Balance of Payments 186
   10.4b The United States' Balance of Payments Statistics 186
   10.4c Major Accounts in the United States' Balance of Payments 189
   GLOBAL INSIGHTS CASE 10.2 - The Chief Trade Partners of the United States 190
10.5 MEASURES OF BOP DEFICITS AND SURPLUSES 191
10.6 INTERNATIONAL INVESTMENT POSITION 192
   GLOBAL INSIGHTS CASE 10.3 - Countertrade 194
10.7 USEFULNESS OF THE BALANCE OF PAYMENTS 195
10.8 SUMMARY 195
   Review Questions 196
   Problems 196
   Suggested Readings 197

Chapter 11 THE FOREIGN EXCHANGE MARKET 199

11.1 INTRODUCTION 199
11.2 DEFINITION OF THE FOREIGN EXCHANGE MARKET 199
11.3 FUNCTIONS OF THE FOREIGN EXCHANGE MARKET 199
11.4 FOREIGN EXCHANGE INSTRUMENTS 200
   11.4a Cable Transfers 200
   11.4b Commercial Bills of Exchange 200
   11.4c Bank Drafts 201
   11.4d Letters of Credit 202
   11.4e Other Means of Payment 202
11.5 EXPORT SHIPMENT PROCESS 202
11.6 FUNCTIONS OF COMMERCIAL BANKS IN THE FOREIGN EXCHANGE MARKET 204
11.7 FOREIGN EXCHANGE RATE DETERMINATION 204

11.7a The Freely Fluctuating Exchange Rate System 204
11.7b The Fixed Exchange Rate System 206
11.8 FOREIGN EXCHANGE TRANSACTIONS 206
   GLOBAL INSIGHTS CASE 11.1 - Oil and Deindustrialization in Britain 207
11.8a Foreign Exchange Risks 208
11.8b The Spot Market 210
11.8c The Forward Market 211
11.8d Hedging 212
11.8e Speculation 212
   GLOBAL INSIGHTS CASE 11.2 - Turmoil in Asian Economies 213
11.8f Swaps 214
11.8g Arbitrage 216
11.9 THE EUROCURRENCY MARKET 216
11.9a Growth of the Eurodollar Market 216
11.9b Financial Activities of the Eurocurrency Market 217
11.10 INTERNATIONAL BANKING 217
11.11 SUMMARY 218
   Review Questions 220
   Problems 220
   Suggested Readings 221

Chapter 12 THE INTERNATIONAL MONETARY SYSTEM 223

12.1 INTRODUCTION 223
12.2 THE GOLD COIN STANDARD 223
12.3 THE GOLD BULLION STANDARD 224
12.4 THE BRETTON WOODS SYSTEM AND THE GOLD EXCHANGE STANDARD 225
12.5 THE INTERNATIONAL MONETARY FUND 226
   GLOBAL INSIGHTS CASE 12.1 - The Role of the IMF in Economic Reform 227
12.5a Special Drawing Rights 227
12.6 THE WORLD BANK 229
12.7 DEMISE OF THE BRETTON WOODS SYSTEM 229
12.8 THE SMITHSONIAN AGREEMENT 230
12.9 THE PRESENT INTERNATIONAL MONETARY SYSTEM 230
12.10 THE EUROPEAN MONETARY SYSTEM 232
12.11 ALTERNATIVE EXCHANGE RATE SYSTEMS 233
   GLOBAL INSIGHTS CASE 12.2 - Latin American Exchange Rate Systems 234
12.11a Crawling Pegs 234
12.11b Target Zone Approach 235
12.12 FIXED VERSUS FLEXIBLE EXCHANGE RATES 235
   GLOBAL INSIGHTS CASE 12.3 - Pegged Exchange Rates and Disinflation in Argentina 236
12.13 SUMMARY 237
   Review Questions 238
   Problems 238
   Notes 239
   Suggested Readings 239

Chapter 13 BALANCE OF PAYMENTS AUTOMATIC ADJUSTMENT MECHANISMS 241

13.1 INTRODUCTION 241
13.2 AUTOMATIC PRICE ADJUSTMENT MECHANISM 241

13.2a Adjustment with Fixed Exchange Rates 242
13.2b Adjustment with Flexible Exchange Rates 243
13.3 AUTOMATIC INCOME ADJUSTMENT MECHANISM 244
13.3a Income Determination in a Closed Economy 244
Graphical Determination of Equilibrium in a Closed Economy 245
The Closed Economy Multiplier 247
13.3b Income Determination in an Open Economy 248
Graphical Determination of Equilibrium in an Open Economy 249
The Open Economy Multiplier 251
13.3c Foreign Trade Repercussions 253
13.4 AUTOMATIC MONETARY ADJUSTMENT MECHANISM 254
GLOBAL INSIGHTS CASE 13.1 - Economic Links among G-7 Countries 255
13.5 DISADVANTAGES OF AUTOMATIC ADJUSTMENT MECHANISMS 256
13.6 PURCHASING-POWER-PARITY THEORY 256
13.6a Absolute Version of the Purchasing-Power-Parity Theory 257
13.6b Relative Version of the Purchasing-Power-Parity Theory 257
GLOBAL INSIGHTS CASE 13.2 - An Empirical Test of Purchasing-Power-Parity 259
13.7 SUMMARY 260
Review Questions 261
Problems 262
Notes 263
Suggested Readings 263

Chapter 14 BALANCE OF PAYMENTS ADJUSTMENT POLICIES 265

14.1 INTRODUCTION 265
14.2 EXPENDITURE-ADJUSTING POLICIES 265
14.2a Evaluation of Monetary-Fiscal Policy Mix 267
14.3 GENERAL EXPENDITURE-SWITCHING POLICIES 268
14.3a Devaluation and Revaluation 268
14.3b Approaches to Devaluation 269
The Elasticity Approach 269
Example 1: Improving the Balance of Trade 270
Example 2: Worsening the Balance of Trade 271
Estimates of import and export demand elasticities 272
J-Curve Effect 272
The Absorption Approach 275
The Monetary Approach 276
14.4 SELECTIVE EXPENDITURE-SWITCHING POLICIES OR DIRECT CONTROLS 276
14.4a Trade Controls 276
14.4b Capital Flow Controls 277
14.4c Exchange Controls 277
GLOBAL INSIGHTS CASE 14.1 - Japanese Capital Flow Controls 278
GLOBAL INSIGHTS CASE 14.2 - IMF Foreign Exchange Controls 279
GLOBAL INSIGHTS CASE 14.3 - Black Market Premium/Discount for the Dollar 280
14.4d Other Direct Controls 281
14.5 SUMMARY 281
Review Questions 282
Problems 283
Notes 283
Suggested Readings 284

Part 4 INTERNATIONAL ECONOMICS AND DEVELOPING NATIONS 285

Chapter 15 INTERNATIONAL TRADE AND ECONOMIC DEVELOPMENT 287

15.1 INTRODUCTION 287
15.2 PROFILE OF DEVELOPING COUNTRIES 287
15.3 TRADE THEORY AND ECONOMIC DEVELOPMENT 288
  GLOBAL INSIGHTS CASE 15.1 - Economic Development Strategies of East and Southeast Asia 289
  15.3a Dependency Theory 289
    Criticism of Dependency Theory 290
  15.3b Theory of Immiserizing Growth 291
    Graphical Illustration of Immiserizing Growth 292
  15.3c Prebisch Theory 293
15.4 EXPORT INSTABILITY 294
  15.4a Factors Giving Rise to Export Instability 294
    Price Variability 294
    High Degree of Commodity Concentration 295
  15.4b Empirical Studies of Export Instability in Developing Countries 295
  15.4c Policies to Stabilize Export Prices or Revenues 297
    Domestic Marketing Boards 297
    International Commodity Agreements 297
    International Buffer Stock Agreements 297
    International Export Quota Agreements 298
    Multilateral Agreements 299
15.5 TRADE LIBERALIZATION IN DEVELOPING NATIONS 300
15.6 DEMANDS FOR A NEW INTERNATIONAL ECONOMIC ORDER 302
15.7 NEWLY INDUSTRIALIZED COUNTRIES 304
  GLOBAL INSIGHTS CASE 15.2 - U.S. Policy on Trade with Developing Countries 305
15.8 SUMMARY 306
  Review Questions 307
  Problems 307
  Notes 308
  Suggested Readings 308

Chapter 16 DEVELOPING COUNTRIES AND THE DEBT CRISIS 311

16.1 INTRODUCTION 311
16.2 MAGNITUDE OF THE DEBT CRISIS 311
16.3 ORIGIN OF DEVELOPING COUNTRIES' DEBT CRISIS 313
  16.3a Tight Monetary Policies of Advanced Countries 313
  16.3b The Second Oil Shock 313
  16.3c Poor Public Sector Investment in Developing Countries 314
  16.3d The World Wide Recession 315
  16.3e Capital Flight from Developing Countries 316
  16.3f Appreciation of the Dollar 318
  16.3g Excess Loanable Funds in Advanced Countries 318
16.4 THE MEXICAN DEBT CRISIS 319
  GLOBAL INSIGHTS CASE 16.1 - Debts of Transitional Economies 320
16.5 DEBT CRISIS IN OTHER DEVELOPING COUNTRIES 321
16.6 SOVEREIGN DEFAULT 322

16.7 THE INTERNATIONAL MONETARY FUND AND THE DEBT CRISIS 322
16.8 THE UNITED STATES AND THE DEBT CRISIS 323
16.9 SOLUTIONS TO THE DEBT CRISIS 324
   16.9a Debt-Equity Swap 324
   GLOBAL INSIGHTS CASE 16.2 - Trade Liberalization and the Debt Crisis 325
   16.9b The Baker Plan 325
   16.9c The Brady Plan 326
   GLOBAL INSIGHTS CASE 16.3 - Tied-Aid Agreements 326
16.10 PHASES OF THE DEBT CRISIS 327
16.11 THE CHALLENGE AHEAD 327
16.12 SUMMARY 328
   Review Questions 329
   Problems 329
   Notes 330
   Suggested Readings 330

Part 5 FOREIGN DIRECT INVESTMENT AND MULTINATIONAL CORPORATIONS . . . 333

Chapter 17 NATURE AND SCOPE OF MULTINATIONAL CORPORATIONS 335

17.1 INTRODUCTION 335
17.2 DEFINITION OF MULTINATIONAL CORPORATION 336
17.3 THE WORLD'S MAJOR MULTINATIONAL CORPORATIONS 336
17.4 FOREIGN DIRECT INVESTMENT AND PORTFOLIO INVESTMENT 338
17.5 CHANNELS OF ENTRY INTO INTERNATIONAL BUSINESS 340
   17.5a Exporting 340
   17.5b Licensing 341
   17.5c Franchising 342
   GLOBAL INSIGHTS CASE 17.1 - Pizza Hut Goes to Brazil 342
   17.5d MNC-Owned Foreign Enterprise 343
      Joint Venture 343
      Wholly Owned Subsidiary 344
   17.5e Management Contract 345
   17.5f Turnkey Operation 345
17.6 APPROPRIATE TECHNOLOGY AND TECHNOLOGY TRANSFER 345
   17.6a Technology Transfer 346
   GLOBAL INSIGHTS CASE 17.2 - Gillette's Blunder 347
      Home Countries' Reactions to Technology Transfer 347
      Host Countries' Reactions to Technology Transfer 347
      Reconciling Host and Home Countries' Reactions 348
   17.6b Modes of Technology Transfer 349
      Sophistication of the Technology 349
      Home and Host Countries' Environments 349
      Characteristics of the Multinational Corporation 349
   GLOBAL INSIGHTS CASE 17.3 - Matsushita's Forecast of the Growth of Electronics and
      Related Technologies 350
      Characteristics of Domestic Firms 350
   17.6c Pricing of Technology Transfer 350
      Transfer Pricing 350
17.7 SUMMARY 351

Review Questions 353
Problems 353
Notes 354
Suggested Readings 354

Chapter 18 THEORIES OF INTERNATIONAL FACTOR MOVEMENTS AND MULTINATIONAL CORPORATIONS

Chapter 18 THEORIES OF INTERNATIONAL FACTOR MOVEMENTS AND MULTINATIONAL
   CORPORATIONS 357

18.1 INTRODUCTION 357
18.2 THEORIES OF INTERNATIONAL CAPITAL MOVEMENTS 357
   18.2a Theory of International Portfolio Investment 358
   18.2b Market Imperfections Theory 358
   GLOBAL INSIGHTS CASE 18.1 - Investment Climate in Poland 360
18.3 THEORIES OF THE MULTINATIONAL CORPORATION 361
   18.3a Internalization Theory 361
   18.3b Appropriability Theory 361
   18.3c Eclectic Theory of International Production 362
18.4 MARXIST THEORY 363
   GLOBAL INSIGHTS CASE 18.2 - McDonald's in Russia 364
18.5 INTERNATIONAL LABOR MOBILITY AND IMMIGRATION 365
   18.5a Causes of International Labor Migration 365
   18.5b Effects of International Labor Migration 367
   The Output Effect 367
   GLOBAL INSIGHTS CASE 18.3 - The Push and Pull of U.S. Immigration Policy 368
   Income Distribution Effect 370
   Other Effects 371
18.6 SUMMARY 372
   Review Questions 373
   Problems 373
   Notes 374
   Suggested Readings 374

Chapter 19 CONFLICTS SURROUNDING MULTINATIONAL CORPORATIONS

Chapter 19 CONFLICTS SURROUNDING MULTINATIONAL CORPORATIONS 377

19.1 INTRODUCTION 377
19.2 MAJOR CRITICISMS OF MULTINATIONAL CORPORATIONS 377
19.3 SOURCES OF CONFLICTS 378
   19.3a Multinational Corporations' Objectives 378
   19.3b Home Countries' Objectives 378
   Economic Goals 378
   GLOBAL INSIGHTS CASE 19.1 - Fears and Facts about Foreign Direct Investment . . . 379
   Noneconomic Goals 380
   19.3c Host Countries' Objectives 380
   Economic Goals 380
   Economic Growth Goal 380
   Distributive and Allocative Goal 381
   Balance of Payments Goal 381
   Noneconomic Goals 381
   GLOBAL INSIGHTS CASE 19.2 - Historical Evidence Against Multinational Corporations 382
   Colonialism 383

  Income Distribution Effect 383
  Environmental Effect of Multinational Corporations 384
  Transborder Data Flow 384
 GLOBAL INSIGHTS CASE 19.3 - The Role of Copyright in an Electronic Global Economy 385
19.4 HOST COUNTRIES' REACTION TO MULTINATIONAL CORPORATIONS 385
 19.4a Joint Venture Arrangements 386
 19.4b Controlling Entries and Takeovers 387
 19.4c Excluding Foreigners from Specific Activities 387
 19.4d Controlling the Local Content and Local Employment 388
 19.4e Export Requirements 388
 19.4f Controlling the Local Capital Market 388
 19.4g Debt Equity Requirements 389
 19.4h Taking the Foreign Investment Package Apart 389
 19.4i Requiring Disinvestment 389
 19.4j Controlling Remittances, Rates, and Fees 390
 19.4k Other Policies 390
19.5 WHO IS RIGHT? 390
 GLOBAL INSIGHTS CASE 19.4 - U.S. Tobacco Exports; A Health-trade Controversy 391
19.6 SUMMARY 392
 Review Questions 393
 Problems 393
 Notes 394
 Suggested Readings 395

Part 6 COMPREHENSIVE CASES
. . . . 399

Case 6:1 CHINA OPENS ITS DOORS TO THE WEST
. . . . 401

INTRODUCTION 401
 History 401
 International Arrangements 402
 Joint Venture 402
 Cooperative Enterprise 403
 Compensation Trade 403
CHINA'S MAIN TRADING PARTNERS 403
 Japan 403
 The United States 404
 Western Europe 404
BALANCE OF PAYMENTS 405
LOOKING INTO THE FUTURE 405
CONCLUDING REMARKS 405
QUESTIONS 405
 Notes 406
 Suggested Readings 406

Case 6:2 TO PROTECT OR NOT TO PROTECT: THAT IS THE QUESTION?
. . . . 409

INTRODUCTION 409
QUESTIONS 410
 Notes 410
 Suggested Readings 410

Case 6:3 DOLEFIL 411

INTRODUCTION 411
OPERATIONS 411
EMPLOYMENT PRACTICES 412
COMMUNITY RELATIONS 412
QUESTIONS 413
    Notes 413
    Suggested Readings 413

Case 6:4 ALUMINUM INDUSTRY OF JAMAICA AND REYNOLDS METALS COMPANY 415

INTRODUCTION 415
THE ALUMINUM INDUSTRY IN JAMAICA 415
THE JAMAICAN BUSINESS ENVIRONMENT 416
REYNOLDS METAL COMPANY 417
QUESTIONS 418
    Notes 418
    Suggested Readings 418

Case 6:5 THE SONY CORPORATION 419

INTRODUCTION 419
COMPANY HISTORY 419
INDUSTRY DESCRIPTION 420
COMPANY DESCRIPTION 421
SONY GOES MULTINATIONAL 421
QUALITY 421
LIFETIME EMPLOYMENT SYSTEM 422
DIVERSIFICATION 423
LOOKING INTO THE FUTURE 423
QUESTIONS 423
    Notes 424
    Suggested Readings 425

Case 6:6 POLAROID: THE INSTANT IMAGE AND THE SUN CITY 427

INTRODUCTION 427
THE PROBLEM 427
THE SOLUTION 428
RECURRENCE OF THE PROBLEM 429
QUESTIONS 429
    Notes 429
    Suggested Readings 430

Case 6:7 THE INGERSOLL-RAND CORPORATION 431

INTRODUCTION 431
HISTORY 431
    Company Description 432

INTERNATIONAL OPERATIONS 433
QUESTIONS 434
  Notes 434
  Suggested Readings 434

Case 6:8 CITICORP 435

INTRODUCTION 435
INTERNATIONAL OPERATIONS 435
LATIN AMERICAN OPERATIONS 436
UNITED KINGDOM'S OPERATIONS 436
ADAPTATION 437
QUESTIONS 437
  Notes 437
  Suggested Readings 438

Case 6:9 FORD: "QUALITY IS JOB ONE" 439

INTRODUCTION 439
THE HISTORY OF FORD 439
LEGAL ACTIONS 440
FORD OVERSEAS OPERATIONS 441
QUESTIONS 444
  Notes 444
  Suggested Readings 445

Case 6:10 UNION CARBIDE AND THE BHOPAL ACCIDENT 447

INTRODUCTION 447
HISTORY 447
OPERATIONS 447
UNION CARBIDE IN INDIA 448
THE BHOPAL ACCIDENT 448
  The Problem 448
  The Company's Reaction 448
  Bhopal's Reaction 449
  The Carbide Strategy of Containment 449
  Settlement Talks 449
  India Settles Lawsuit 450
CONCLUSION 451
QUESTIONS 451
  Notes 452
  Suggested Readings 453

Glossary 455
Index 475

PREFACE

Since the early 1970s the world has witnessed a steady sequence of events that has significantly changed the global economic picture. The fixed exchange rate system of the early 1970s has given way to the managed floating exchange rate system. The erratic changes in exchange rates have increased the demand for revision of the international monetary system. The immense growth in computer and telecommunications industries has given rise to the transborder data flow problem. Eastern European countries have switched to a market-oriented economic system, and the collapse of the Soviet Union and the unification of Germany have changed the world political and economic climates. On January 1, 1999, European Union (EU) members finally achieved complete economic integration which was supposed to be implemented by 1992. The United States has entered into two significant free trade agreements, the U.S.—Canada Free Trade Agreement and the North American Free Trade Agreement. The immense debt of developing countries, especially those in Latin America, and their inability to service their debt on time, has continued to endanger the stability of the world banking system. Newly industrialized countries have emerged as an important economic force, capturing a significant share of the world export market for manufactured goods from advanced nations. Multinational corporations have expanded their operations around the globe, becoming an important force in shaping the world economy. The booming global capital markets have given rise to new financial instruments and practices that have further deteriorated governments' supervision of internal monetary affairs. The successful completion of the Uruguay Round of negotiations has renewed the prospect of freer international trade.

These changes have contributed to the importance of international economic courses in undergraduate curriculums, resulting in greater demand for a textbook that addresses the most recent developments in the world economy. Unfortunately, most existing textbooks do not deal adequately with these issues. Instead, they confront students with elaborate models and assumptions that are difficult for most undergraduates to comprehend without sufficient real-world examples. This textbook attempts to remedy the problem.

The idea of writing this textbook came from my experience in teaching international economics to undergraduate students over the last two decades. My belief is that the best way to motivate students and to teach a theory is to show how it is used in practice. This textbook reflects this tenet by presenting international economic theories with abundant examples, followed by thought-provoking questions, problems, and case studies.

To challenge students even more, they should be required to do supplemental reading. To this end, each chapter provides a list of suggested readings that includes many diverse and current publications in the field.

All the materials in this textbook have been classroom tested in international economic classes at California State University, San Bernardino, and St. Lawrence University, Canton, New York. Students' feedback has been incorporated to improve the presentation.

DISTINCTIVE TEXT FEATURES

Several features distinguish this textbook from others in the field.

Coverage of the Contemporary Issues

Given recent world events, it is easy for a textbook to become out of date. Unfortunately, many textbooks are concerned mainly with theoretical models and are either completely lacking or inadequate in their coverage of current events. This textbook provides more complete coverage of contemporary issues than other textbooks in international economics. Topics discussed include:

✦ Newly industrialized countries (Chapter 15)
✦ Europe after 1992 (Chapter 9)

- ✦ Europe after 1992 (Chapter 9)
- ✦ The unification of Germany (Chapter 9)
- ✦ The transborder data flow problem (Chapter 19)
- ✦ The economic reforms of Eastern European countries (Chapter 9)
- ✦ The demise of the Soviet Union (Chapter 9)
- ✦ Strategic trade policy (Chapter 7)
- ✦ Economic sanctions (Chapter 7)
- ✦ Developing countries' debt crises (Chapter 16)
- ✦ The nature and scope of multinational corporations (Chapter 17)
- ✦ Theories of multinational corporations and foreign direct investment (Chapter 18)
- ✦ Conflicts surrounding multinational corporations (Chapter 19)

Application of Theories

Theories are discussed with numerous real-life examples and case studies to illustrate their relevance and application to real-world situations. For example, the discussion of the product life cycle theory is followed by a case demonstrating the life cycle of a pocket calculator (Chapter 4), and the theory of customs unions is followed by a discussion of trade creation and trade diversion in the European Union (Chapter 8). Further, currency devaluation and the J-curve effect are presented with a discussion of the depreciation of the U.S. dollar in September 1985 (Chapter 14). Our discussion of mercantilism is illustrated with the example of "high-tech mercantilism" that is practiced in France today (Chapter 2), and the presentation of the purchasing power parity theory is followed by a case testing its predictability for the United States (Chapter 13). Finally, the presentation of the Prebisch theory includes a demonstration of its usefulness in studying the import substitution policies practiced by Latin American countries such as Colombia, Peru, and Chile (Chapter 15).

Depth of Coverage

The presentation of often-ignored theories, including theories of foreign direct investment and multinational corporations, the technological gap theory, and the theory of overlapping demand, make this textbook more comprehensive than most. Because of the increasing importance and attention given to foreign direct investment and multinational corporations, a complete and separate section is devoted to this topic. A comprehensive treatment of debt crisis is presented separately in Chapter 16, elaborating on the elements that gave rise to this issue and discussing different solutions to resolving this problem. Finally, Chapter 9 is devoted to recent free trade agreements and political events affecting global economy.

IMPORTANT FEATURES OF THE SECOND EDITION

I have tried to keep the flavor of the first edition while updating the materials therein. The following is a list of the most important features incorporated into this edition:

1. All the existing tables have been updated to provide the students with up- to- date information on various issues discussed in the text.
2. Some of the Global Insights cases have been eliminated, and replaced by new cases that are more relevant to the most recent events in the global economy. All the cases presented are updated. New Global Insights cases include topics such as "Turmoil in Asia (Chapter 11), Latin American Exchange Rate System," (Chapter 12), "Japanese Capital Flow Control (Chapter 14), U.S. Tobacco Exports: A Health Trade Controversy," and "Pegged Exchange Rate and Disinflation in Argentina." (Chapter 12).
3. Whole new section (VI) is added to the textbook. This section contains ten comprehensive case studies and includes questions for discussion at the end of each case.

ORGANIZATION OF THE TEXT

The text consists of six parts composed of 19 chapters and 10 case studies. Part I focuses on the theories of international trade. It discusses the historical development of modern theories, from both the demand side and the supply side. It also presents applications of theories and explains new theoretical approaches to international trade.

Part II deals with national policies, international organizations and agreements, and recent political events affecting international trade. Topics include tariff and nontariff trade barriers, arguments for protection, international organizations and free trade agreements, and recent political events. Included in this part are some current events that have been subject to much attention in academic circles: the EU after 1992, the U.S.—Canada free trade agreement, the North American Free Trade Agreement, the economic reforms of Eastern European countries, the unification of Germany, and the demise of the Soviet Union.

Part III elaborates on international monetary relations. Topics include balance of payments, the foreign exchange market, the international monetary system, balance of payments automatic adjustment mechanism, and balance of payments adjustment policies.

Part IV covers international economics and developing nations. It includes the international trade and economic development, and the developing countries' debt crisis.

Part V draws attention to foreign direct investment and multinational corporations. Topics discussed are the nature and scope of multinational corporations, theories of foreign direct investment and multinational corporations, conflicts between host and home countries, and the transborder data flow problem. Given the economic and noneconomic implications of this last problem, its importance to economic study is crucial.

Part VI contains ten comprehensive case studies and includes questions for discussion at the end of each case. These real cases describe situations faced by an individual or organization whose identities are known. They typically include a chronology of significant events, summaries of important financial and nonfinancial data, and information about competitors and industry. Cases provide students with an opportunity to use the principles and theories presented in the text in decision-making situations.

PEDAGOGY

Each chapter begins with a set of main learning objectives and concludes with a detailed summary, review questions, thought-provoking problems, and a list of suggested readings. Each chapter also includes two to five global insight cases that apply theories to real-world situations.

The text concludes with a complete glossary for easy access to the terminology used in international economics.

SUPPLEMENTARY MATERIALS

To aid instructors and students we have developed a comprehensive support package that includes the following materials.

Instructor's Manual. For each chapter this manual includes learning objectives, answers to the end-of-chapter problems, and lecture notes. Additionally, a list of sources for research in international economics is included in the manual. These lecture notes may be transformed to transparencies and used as a summary of key points in presenting different chapters to the class.

Test Bank. The test bank has been classroom tested. Each chapter contains 30 multiple-choice questions, 30 true/false questions, and 30 completion questions, with answers provided.

ACKNOWLEDGMENTS

A comprehensive textbook on international economics could not be written without the help of individuals who offer their valuable time and talents. My students at California State University, San Bernardino, and St. Lawrence University have been instrumental in providing feedback and contributing to some of the cases presented in this book. I am grateful to all of them.

I owe a deep debt of gratitude to reviewers who read the manuscript of the first edition at different stages and provided me with constructive criticism and useful suggestions. These reviewers include:

Jafar Alavi
East Tennessee State University

Basudeb Biswas
Utah State University

Jen-Chi Cheng
Wichita State University

Addington Coppin
Oakland University

William W. Davis
Western Kentucky University

Yoonbai Kim
University of Kentucky

Robin Klay
Hope College

Evan Kraft
Salisbury State University

Chyi-Ing Lin
University of Missouri, Columbia

Thomas K. Lowinger
Washington State University

James McCoy
Murray State University

Ali Moshtagh
Eastern Illinois University

Dipankar Purkayastha
California State University, Fullerton

Matiur Rahman
McNeese State University

N. N. Reddy
University of Michigan, Flint

John J. Reid
Memphis State University

Donald G. Richards
Indiana State University

Gerald Scott
Florida Atlantic University

Robert R. Sharp
Eastern Kentucky University

Russell E. Smith
Washburn University

Richard L. Sprinkle
University of Texas, El Paso

Rebecca Summary
Southeast Missouri State University

Victor Ukpolo
Austin Peay State University

John Wade
Western Carolina University

I would like to thank Professor Ali M. Kutan (Southern Illinois University at Edwardsville) for his through review of the first edtion. I am indebted to Professor Bahman Ebrahimi (University of Denver), who contributed to a part of Chapter 17 and wrote one of the cases included in this textbook. I would like to thank Professor Reza Saidi (Catholic University of America) who provided me with a link to Washington, DC, helping me with data collection and library research. I would like to thank Professor Michael LeMay (California State University San Bernardino), who wrote a case on the subject of immigration.

I would also like to thank the professional staff of Dame Company for working with me at different stages of the development of this second edition.

My deepest thanks go to my family who had to sacrifice on so many occasions so that I could work on this project. My love and thanks to my wife, Dorothy Thurman, who read every page of the manuscript and provided me with valuable comments, and my children, Daniel Thurman Asheghian and Laila Thurman Asheghian, for their understanding, support, and tolerance throughout the whole project.

Parviz Asheghian
California State University
San Bernadino

Chapter 1

INTRODUCTION

1.1 THE GLOBAL ECONOMY

The world economy has changed drastically during the last two decades. The international monetary system has been completely restructured. The immense growth in the computer and telecommunications industries has contributed significantly to the flow of information across national boundaries. The volumes of world trade and investment have expanded significantly. The United States' relative share in the world export market continuously declined over the decades preceding the late 1980s, losing ground to countries such as Germany and Japan. Newly industrialized countries, such as Taiwan and South Korea, have captured a significant share of the world market for manufactured goods. The collapse of the Soviet Union and the Eastern European reforms have added to the list of countries that operate under a market-oriented economic system. Many developing countries, especially those in Latin America, have been struggling with the debt crisis that hit the world in the early 1980s.* Unable to service their debt on time, they have faced staggering unemployment, rampant inflation, and a lower standard of living. The debt crisis also threatened several U.S. banks with bankruptcy, emphasizing the need for a solution to the situation. Multinational corporations have expanded their operations around the globe, emerging as an important force in shaping the world economy.

These changes have contributed to the importance of international economics in a world in which the competition for goods and services has gone far beyond national boundaries. We have entered a new age of global competition that is characterized by a one-world market. In this market, just as manufacturers "go global," so must suppliers of raw materials, distributors, bankers, accountants, lawyers, and brokers. Successful corporate managers increasingly are treating the whole world as their domain of operation for securing sources of supply as well as demand. It is estimated that the sales between foreign subsidiaries of the same company account for roughly 25 percent of global trade. Such estimates stress the fact that, in this age, competitiveness is beyond the grasp of any purely domestic company. In such a competitive environment, the life cycles of different products are getting shorter, and it is costlier and more difficult to develop a new product. This makes today's corporate managers' jobs more challenging. To turn these challenges into opportunities, managers need to develop products and bring them to global markets much faster than before.

Although globalization is not a new phenomenon, what is different today is the speed and the extent of growth in global markets. Two major factors have contributed to this growth. First, advances in communication technology and transportation methods have greatly expanded international trade and investment. As a result, the percentage of gross national product (GNP) absorbed by foreign trade for major developed (advanced) countries has roughly doubled since 1960. Second, long-term increases in the GNP per capita coupled with higher life expectancies and education levels have increased the role of some developing countries in global markets. For example, Brazil, Hong Kong, Singapore, and South Korea now rank among the top 20 exporters of manufactured goods, whereas in 1965 no developing country was even included in the top 30. The increasing importance of developing countries in global markets has decreased the capacity of developed countries to dominate these markets.[1]

Just as a country's business operations have global implications, so do its overall economic activities. No country operates in an economic vacuum. A nation's production, consumption, inflation, interest rates, investment, technology, and all other variables affecting its economic system are influenced by the economies of other nations.

---

* As we explain in detail in Chapter 15, developing countries are primarily identified by relatively low standards of living, high rates of population growth, low levels of per capita income, high illiteracy rates, and general economic and technological dependence on advanced nations. The classification schemes used to define developing countries differ, depending on the scheme's source (United Nations, World Bank, Organization for Economic Cooperation and Development).

1

For example, the U.S. budget deficit, running at an annual rate of about $200 billion in the 1980s, gave rise to a chain of events that affected the economies of many other countries. The high budget deficit fueled inflationary expectations and forced the U.S. government to pursue tighter monetary policies. It also meant a higher demand for credit by the U.S. government to finance the deficit. These changes caused the nation's interest rates to rise. The higher interest rates, compared to those in other industrial nations, encouraged the movement of short-term funds from those countries to the United States. The increase in the inflow of short-term funds to the United States caused the dollar to appreciate, that is, the prices of foreign currencies in terms of the U.S. dollar decreased.* This, in turn, increased U.S. imports and restrained U.S. exports, leading to an annual trade deficit of more than $100 billion in the 1980s. This series of events raised protectionist sentiments in the United States and put pressure on the federal government to use measures to restrict imports. These measures in turn further intensified the debt problems of developing countries.[2]

Because of the global implications of these events and the desire to mollify U.S. protectionist sentiments, the major industrial nations (the United States, Japan, Germany, Great Britain, and France) collectively decided to depreciate the dollar (that is, to decrease the price of the dollar in terms of other currencies) in September 1985. However, the cheaper dollar made Japanese and European exports to the United States more expensive, causing these countries to retaliate by decreasing the price of their own currencies.[3] The possibility that the United States might respond by further depreciating the dollar shook foreign investors' confidence in the U.S. market. They feared that with the depreciating dollar the value of their investment, measured in terms of their home currency, would continue to decline.**[4] This caused some foreign investors to pull out of the U.S. stock market, while others who had large U.S. investments were effectively paralyzed. They found themselves "too deeply invested to pull out, yet too worried to resume buying."[5]

The chain of events that started with the U.S. budget deficit contributed to the crash of the U.S. stock market on October 19, 1987. On this so-called "Black Monday," the Dow Jones industrial average fell nearly twice as far as it did on the "Black Friday" of 1929, wiping out $500 billion in wealth in a few hours. Within hours of the collapse of the U.S. stock market, the European and Asian markets were falling fast, experiencing an unprecedented decline in stock prices and losing billions of dollars.[6] Following this event, financial markets revamped their trading and payment systems to better deal with the pressure. For example, one of the immediate post-crash reforms established special phone connections between New York City, Chicago, Washington D.C., and overseas markets to ensure that in a crisis, markets could be in instant communication.[7]

As a less dramatic example of the interrelationship between nations' economies, cheaper labor costs in developing countries such as Brazil, China, Hong Kong, India, Mexico, the Philippines, South Korea, Taiwan, and some Southern African countries, have caused many multinational corporations in developed countries to move their plants to these developing nations. This has caused labor unions in developed countries to resist foreign imports because union members fear the loss of jobs or lower wages. Such a fear is not without basis. For example, when General Electric moved its plant from Ashland, Massachusetts, to Singapore, 1,100 jobs were lost in Ashland. In another instance, 4,000 jobs were lost when RCA closed its Memphis, Tennessee, facilities and moved to Taiwan.[8]

Such events are expected to drastically change the nature of international trade and have a profound impact on corporate strategy, leading to a new global business environment. The global environment is more complicated, more dynamic, and more unpredictable than the domestic environment. It calls for managers and government policy makers who are able to cope with the challenges of complex political, economic, social, technological, and competitive elements. It also demands better training in the field of international economics and requires a thorough comprehension of the many factors that shape our global environment. Our exploration of international economics starts with a review of some of the basic concepts needed for a better understanding of this subject.[9]

---

* The concepts of appreciation and depreciation is explained in Chapter 14.

** The depreciation of the U.S. dollar makes the foreign investor's home currency relatively more expensive. As a result, each dollar invested before depreciation commands smaller amounts of domestic currency after depreciation.

1.2 WHAT IS INTERNATIONAL ECONOMICS?

Like other economics subjects, **international economics** is the study of the allocation of scarce resources to satisfy humans' alternative wants. However, the distinctive feature of international economics is that it approaches this basic economic problem at the international, as opposed to the national, level. Its objective is to explain how international

---

GLOBAL INSIGHTS CASE 1.1

The Global Factory

Today, globalization of world trade and investment has pushed specialization beyond the old pattern of production in which one country produced all components for a chosen good. Production of a single good now involves several nations, with each nation in this "global factory" producing only the components in which it has a cost advantage. The table illustrates the production components for the Ford Escort (Europe). The production of this U.S. automobile in Europe involves the participation of 15 different nations producing parts that are finally assembled in Halewood (Great Britain) and Saalouis (Germany).

Component Network for the Ford Escort (Europe)

Country	Parts
Austria	Tires, radiators and heater hoses
Belgium	Tires, tubes, seat pads, brakes, trim
Canada	Glass, radio
Denmark	Fan belt
France	Alternator, cylinder head, master cylinder, brakes, underbody coating, weatherstrips, clutch release bearings, steering shaft and joints, seat pads and frames, transmission cases, clutch cases, tires, suspension bushes, ventilation units, heater, hose clamps, sealers, hardware.
Germany	Locks, pistons, exhaust, ignition, switches, from disc, distributor, weatherstrips, rocker arm, speedometer, fuel tank, cylinder bolt, cylinder head gasket, front wheel knuckles, rear wheel spindle, transmission cases, clutch cases, clutch, steering column, battery, glass
Italy	Cylinder head, carburetor, glass, lamps, defroster grills
Japan	Starter, alternator, cone and roller bearings, windscreen washer pump
Netherlands	Tires, paints, hardware
Norway	Exhaust flanges, tires
Spain	Wring hamess, radiator and heater hoses, fork clutch release, air filter, battery, mirrors
Switzerland	Underbody coating, speedometer gears
Sweden	Hose clamps, cylinder bolt, exhaust down pipes, pressings, hardware
United Kingdom	Carburetor, rocker arm, clutch, ignition, exhaust, oil pump, distributor, cylinder bolt, cylinder head, flywheel ring gear, heater, speedometer, battery, rear wheel spindle, intake manifold, fuel tank, switcher, lamps, front disc, steering column, glass weatherstrips, locks
United States	EGR valves, wheels nuts, hydraulic tappet, glass

Source: The World Bank, *World Development Report 1987* (New York: Oxford University Press, 1987), 39.

economic interactions influence the allocation of scarce resources both within and between nations. The subject matter of international economics includes all transactions that cross national boundaries, including trade in goods and services, capital and labor movements, and transactions in financial assets.

1.3 INTERNATIONAL VERSUS DOMESTIC TRADE

International trade is an outgrowth of domestic trade. In fact, most major corporations that are active in the international scene today, started their operations in domestic markets. For example, major Japanese automobile manufacturers, such as Toyota, Nissan, and Honda, started their operations in Japan. With the expansion of their domestic market, they started to export to other countries. As the magnitude of their operations grew, they found it profitable to set up their plants and equipment in countries such as the United States.

Although international trade is an extension of domestic trade, it is significantly different from the latter, mainly due to the environment in which it takes place. The variables that shape this environment include: factor mobility, national currencies, national policies, and cultures.

1.3a Factor Mobility

In distinguishing international trade from domestic trade, nineteenth-century classical economists maintained that factors of production—land, labor, capital, and entrepreneurship—moved freely within a nation but not between nations. Even land was considered to be domestically mobile in the sense that it could be used to produce different products, depending on market prices. For example, the same land could be used to produce rice instead of wheat if the price of rice was higher than the price of wheat in the domestic market.

With the passage of time, the classical assumptions about domestic factor mobility and international factor immobility became questionable. Neoclassical economists noted that factors of production did not move freely from one region to another region within a country. They also observed that a significant movement of capital was emanating from Europe to the rest of the world. As a result, they agreed that factor mobility was not a good criterion to clearly distinguish domestic trade from international trade since both were subject to various degrees of factor immobility.

Today, it is believed that the two classical assumptions of domestic factor mobility and international factor immobility are too rigid. At the international level, there is some factor mobility between nations. For example, immigration has been a significant source of labor supply for countries like the United States, Canada, and Israel, just to name a few. At the domestic level, there is a considerable degree of immobility within a nation.

It is reasonable to conclude that in the absence of government-imposed obstacles to free movement of factors of production, domestic factor mobility is greater than international factor mobility due to the traditions, customs, and dialects that exist within the regions of a country.

1.3b National Currencies

One of the significant factors that makes it necessary to differentiate between international trade and domestic trade is the existence of different currencies. In domestic transactions, only one currency is used. For example, the dollar is used in the United States, while the deutsche mark, dinar, franc, pound, and yen are the currencies of Germany, Kuwait, France, Great Britain, and Japan, respectively. In international transactions, however, two or more currencies are involved. For example, an American importer who wants to purchase French wine usually possesses dollars, whereas the French exporter who makes the sale wishes to be paid in francs. Because of the difference in currencies, some mechanism must exist to allow for the settlement of this international transaction so that both parties' requirements are met. Such a mechanism is provided in the form of the foreign exchange market. The fluctuations in the foreign exchange rate make international trade relatively more risky than domestic trade and provides opportunities for speculators and arbitragers to profit from these fluctuations.

Because the international monetary system changes continuously, we need to understand the major events that have shaped its present form. The evolution and workings of the international monetary system are explained in detail in Chapter 12.

1.3c National Policies

Because each sovereign nation has its own specific needs, various nations may follow policies that are incompatible with the free flow of goods, services, and capital between countries. Some of these policies are wholly international in nature and may be pursued specifically to interfere with the free flow of international trade. As we explain in Chapters 5 and 6, such policies include tariff and non-tariff trade barriers. Other policies may be purely domestic in nature. Those regarding taxes, investment, competition, wages, prices, and business regulation significantly affect international trade and investment. For example, variations in interest rates, inflation rates, and tax laws have important effects on the profitability of a firm operating in a foreign country. If the firm is borrowing and investing in a foreign country, higher interest rates, taxes, or inflation rates in that country mean a higher cost of operations and lower profitability. On the other hand, if a firm is only investing financially in a foreign country, that country's higher interest rate means a higher return on investment.

There is sometimes a conflict between a country's domestic and international goals. To keep its economy in tune with the rest of the world, a country must, for example, keep its wage rate down in order to be competitive with other countries. Although this may be a wise policy for strengthening the country's international position, it may be opposed by labor unions. In countries with strong, politically powerful labor unions, conflict is often resolved in favor of labor through the imposition of trade barriers. However, as we explain in Part Two, when nations adopt protectionist policies, all trading countries generally suffer from a loss of welfare.

1.3d Cultures

A **culture** consists of a set of beliefs, values, attitudes, and practices of a group of people who live in a given environment. Because international trade takes place between sovereign nations with distinct cultures, it requires an understanding of the cultural variables that affect the trading partners. Managers in a company involved in international trade must know acceptable and unacceptable modes of behavior for the societies in which the company operates. For example, drinking alcohol at social or business occasions may be acceptable behavior in Western cultures; however, it is outlawed in most Islamic countries. Similarly, kissing a girlfriend or wife in public is admissible in Western cultures, but it is unacceptable in many Islamic nations such as Saudi Arabia and Iran.

1.4 THE WORLD IN TRANSITION

As we mentioned at the beginning of this chapter, the world economy has changed drastically during the last two decades. Some of these changes have presented the world with new economic opportunities and also have intensified international competition for goods and services. In the following section, we introduce several of these issues and elaborate their importance to international economics.

1.4a Newly Industrialized Countries

The spread of industrialization and industrial innovation is leading the world economy into a new era. Significant economic and technological considerations are forcing the movement of traditional industries to developing countries and creating newly industrialized countries (NICs).

Many companies from developing countries (such as Hong Kong, South Korea, and Taiwan) have been engaged in foreign direct investment, mainly in manufacturing in other developing countries. Because of their scaled-down, relatively labor-intensive technology and their lower managerial and overhead costs, these companies have been able to produce relatively low-cost products. These products have competed successfully in the world market, based mainly on their low prices.

This situation has triggered a reallocation of resources in industrial nations from the traditional "capital-intensive" industries, such as automobiles, steel, and consumer electronics, to the new "knowledge/service-intensive" industries, such as semi-conductors, information processing, and telecommunications. Such changes are causing various economic problems, such as unemployment and corporate bankruptcy, for many developed nations.

The NICs have demonstrated that they are a significant competitive force with which firms in developed countries must learn to compete. We discuss NICs' development and their significance to the world economy in Chapter 15.

1.4b The Soviet Union and Eastern Europe

In the mid-1980s, Mikhail Gorbachev came to power as leader of the former Soviet Union and launched new reforms that pushed the nation toward a market-oriented economy. His reforms, referred to as "perestroika" (restructuring) and "glasnost" (openness), called for major changes in Soviet economic policies. These changes affected U.S.-Soviet relations on both economic and political grounds. They also laid the foundation for Eastern European countries to assert their political independence from the Soviet Union and to switch to more open, market-oriented economies.

The unsuccessful military coup of August 1991 opened a new chapter in the former Soviet Union's economy by making Gorbachev rethink his commitment to the Communist party. Although he started his reform by insisting that he would not violate the basic communist philosophy, he abandoned the party following the coup. Declarations of independence by different republics followed the military coup, leading to the collapse of the Soviet Union as a communist superpower and to the birth of the new Commonwealth of Independent States (CIS).* Russia, comprising 51.3 percent of the former Soviet Union's population and 75 percent of its land mass, has especially attracted the attention of the Western world and is being closely watched by Western leaders.

In Chapter 9, we discuss the collapse of the Soviet Union and elaborate on its economic implications for the world.

1.4c The Unification of Germany

In the early 1990s, the world witnessed many extraordinary economic and social events, one of which was the unification of Germany. East and West Germany merged their economies in the summer of 1990, a move that had economic implications for Germany and the rest of the world. The absorption of the relatively poor and decaying East German economy by West Germany was expected to cost West Germany an estimated $1 trillion in the next decade. West Germany's benefits from the unification widen as its firms' investments in East German industry continue to expand. In the short run, East Germany is expected to experience hard economic times, but in the long run it will do better. Given the huge size of a united German market and the inability of German companies to satisfy its demand, the rest of the world is offered the incredible opportunity to export more to this vast market. The United States, Japan, Great Britain, the Netherlands, Belgium, Australia, and especially France, which were already doing the most business with West Germany, are among the countries most likely to benefit first. We discuss the economic implications of the German unification in more detail in Chapter 9.

1.4d Europe after 1992

At the 1985 summit in Milan, the European Union (EU) members endorsed the **"White Paper,"** which established a detailed legislative program for complete economic integration by 1992.** The basic thrust of the White Paper is the removal of a whole series of trade barriers. The dismantling of these trade barriers, resulting in a single EU home

---

* The republics that initially declared independence included Moldavia, Byelorussia, Ukraine, Estonia, Latvia, Lithuania, Georgia, Armenia, and Uzbekistan.

** The European Community changed its title to the European Union in 1994. Discussions throughout the rest of this text will refer to the European Union (EU), regardless of the date or event discussed.

market, is not only challenging and rewarding for Europeans; it also has global economic implications. We discuss this topic in more detail in Chapter 9.

1.4e North American Free Trade Agreement

In 1990, U.S. and Mexican officials agreed to negotiate a free trade area between the two nations. Canada later declared that it would participate in talks, setting the stage for the formation of the largest free trade union in the world. With a combined population of over 350 million people and an annual GNP of $6 trillion, the potential economic power of this union surpasses that of EU, which in 1992 consisted of 320 million people and had an annual GNP of $4 trillion.[10]

Negotiation between the American trading partners was concluded on August 12, 1992. The U.S. Congress, the U.S. Senate, and the Mexican Senate approved the North American Free Trade Agreement (NAFTA) in November 1993; the Canadian government approved NAFTA on December 2, 1993, clearing the way for the creation of a free-trade area that stretches from the Yukon to the Yucatan.[11] We discuss this topic in more detail in Chapter 9.

1.4f The International Debt Crisis

The international debt crisis—made worse by the tighter monetary policies of developed countries, the second oil shock of the late 1970s, and poor public sector investment in developing countries—hit the world in 1982. In that year, the total debt of Argentina, Brazil, and Mexico (the countries with the three biggest debts) reached the level of $220 billion. Since then the external debt of developing countries has continued to grow, surpassing $1,918 billion in 1999. To resolve the debt crisis, lenders and borrowers have been forced to enter multilateral negotiations through the International Monetary Fund (IMF). This has resulted in the imposition of severe measures on the debtor countries. Some of these measures require debtor nations to reduce inflation, decrease imports, use more efficient monetary restraints, and decrease government expenditures.

The debt crisis has a significant impact on both international commercial banks and debtor nations. Although no widespread default has erupted yet, the debt problem is by no means over. We discuss this topic in detail in Chapter 16.

1.4g Multinational Corporations

With the movement of the former Soviet Union and Eastern European countries toward more market-oriented economies, the significance of multinational corporations as the dominant force in shaping the world economy continues to increase. These corporate giants have been the subject of heated debates in academic and political circles and have raised nationalistic fervor in developing countries. At one extreme, they have been praised as the chief instrument for abolishing poverty in developing countries; at another extreme, they have been accused of being the main device used by developed countries to achieve "economic imperialism." Due to the significance of this topic, a whole section is devoted to its coverage. In Chapter 17, we study the nature and scope of multinational corporations. In Chapter 18, we review theories of international factor movements and multinational corporations. Finally, we discuss host-home countries' conflicts in Chapter 19.

1.4h Transborder Data Flow

Transborder data flow refers to the flow of electronically transmitted information across national boundaries. The immense growth in the computer and telecommunications industries in the 1970s tremendously facilitated the international storage and transmission of massive amounts of information. This enabled multinational corporations to collect information in different host countries and transmit it to their home countries for use in worldwide operations. A country's ability to store and process information has both economic and noneconomic implications. Given the increasing importance of this issue, a separate discussion is included in Chapter 19.

1.5 THE SIGNIFICANCE OF INTERNATIONAL TRADE IN THE WORLD ECONOMY

The importance of international trade in the world economy can be viewed from three different angles. First, international trade activities provide us with a variety of goods and services from many countries. In this context, we become citizens of the world and are no longer confined to the products produced in our own country. As Americans, for example, we can buy a Japanese car or video cassette recorder, French mineral water, Italian olive oil, Canadian beer, and so on. More importantly, international trade allows us access to raw materials that we need for our industries. For example, the United States lacks deposits of chromium, tin, and tungsten, which are important for certain industrial processes.

Second, as a result of international trade and specialization, the world's production efficiency increases. This allows countries that are relatively more efficient in the production of certain commodities to concentrate their efforts on the production of such goods. They can then export what they cannot consume and import from other nations what they cannot produce. In this way, larger quantities of better-quality goods are produced at lower prices. Thus, products such as French wines, Persian rugs, and tropical fruits and nuts from all over the world can be enjoyed at relatively lower prices than domestic firms would charge.

Third, international trade provides a source of income and employment for the countries involved. In the United States, for example, exports account for 9.5 percent of national income and generate 1 out of every 11 jobs.[12]

GLOBAL INSIGHTS CASE 1.2

Is IBM All-American?

As a major U.S. corporation, one might assume that IBM is all-American. However, most of the parts and components of IBM personal computers that are sold in the U.S. market are produced abroad. As the table indicates, out of the $860 cost of producing an IBM personal computer in 1985, $625 (about 72.5 percent) was spent on parts and components manufactured outside the United States. The remaining $235 (about 27.5 percent) was spent on American-owned plants. It is also interesting to note that in 1992 IBM produced its new PS/55 laptop completely in Japan.

Allocation of Manufacturing Costs of IBM Personal Computers Abroad and at Home

Components	Country	Manufacturing Costs		
		Abroad	Home	Total
Monochrome monitor	South Korea	$ 85		$85
Semiconductors	Japan	105	105	
	United States		105	105
Power supply	Japan	60	60	
Graphic printer	Japan	160	160	
Floppy disk drive	Singapore	165	165	
Assembly of disk drive	United States		25	25
Keyboard	Japan	50	50	
Case and assembly	United States		105	105
Total manufacturing costs		$625	$235	$860

Source: "America's High Tech Crisis: Why Silicon Valley is Losing Its edge" Business Week, 11 March 1985, 56—62; "Selling Now in Tokyo: Thinnest IBM Portable," The New York Times, 11 March 1991, D1.

As a rough measure of the importance of international trade in a country's economy, we can compare the percentages of exports and imports to the gross national product (GNP) of the country in question. Also, to recognize the real significance of a country's trading position in the world, we can measure the ratios of its exports and imports to the world's total exports and imports.* Table 1-1 portrays the trade positions of the major industrialized countries in the world. As this table indicates, in 1995, the United States held a 11.49 percent share of the world export market (the largest share), followed by Germany (10.29%), Japan (8.71%), France (5.63%), Great Britain (4.75%), Italy (4.54%), Netherlands (3.85%), and Canada (3.78%).

Until the late 1980s, the United States' relative share in the world export market continuously declined over the years, losing ground to countries such as the former West Germany and Japan, as shown in Table 1-2. This table indicates that the U.S. share in the world export market declined from 17.15 percent in 1960 to 10.64 percent in 1987. During the same period, Japan's share rose from 3.38 percent in 1960 to 9.83 percent in 1987. Beginning in 1988, the United States' share of the world export market started to increase, reaching 11.49 percent in 1995.

TABLE 1-1
Trade Positions of the World's Major Industrial Countries In the World , 1995

Country	Exports (billions of U.S.$)	Imports (billions of U.S.$)	X/W_X (%)	M/W_M (%)
United States	584.743	770.852	11.49	15.02
Germany	523.743	464.220	10.29	9.05
Japan	443.116	335.882	8.71	6.55
France	286.738	275.275	5.63	5.36
Great Britain	242.042	263.719	4.75	5.14
Italy	231.336	204.062	4.54	3.98
Netherlands	195.912	176.420	3.85	3.44
Canada	192.197	168.426	3.78	3.28

X = Exports, M = Imports; W_X = World Exports; W_M = World Imports

Source: International Financial Statistics, Vol. 50, No. 5, February 1997, p.8.

TABLE 1-2
Relative Shares (By Percentage) of Major Industrial in the World Export Market, 1960-1996

Country	1960	1975	1984	1986	1987	1988	1990	1995
United States	17.15	13.15	11.86	10.91	10.64	11.97	11.89	11.49
Canada	4.84	4.14	5.07	4.53	4.17	4.33	3.98	10.29
Japan	3.38	6.79	9.86	10.58	9.83	9.83	8.69	8.71
France	5.72	6.46	5.65	6.27	6.30	6.23	6.54	5.63
Germany	9.50	10.96	10.18	12.22	12.50	12.00	12.39	4.75
Italy	3.04	4.25	4.27	4.90	9.94	4.75	5.15	4.54
Netherlands	3.55	4.26	3.79	4.04	3.92	3.84	3.98	3.85
Great Britain	8.83	5.28	5.63	5.38	5.58	5.39	5.60	3.78

X = Exports; M = Imports; W_X = World Exports; W_M = World Imports

Source: International Financial Statistics, Vol. 50, No. 5, February 1997, p.8.

---

* This procedure is recommended instead of comparison of the percentage of exports and imports to GNP, which may overlook the role of illegal trade.

The decrease in the United States' relative share prior to 1988 can be attributed to three factors. First, countries such as Germany and Japan captured a great share of the world market.* Second, U.S. firms concentrated their activities in foreign direct investment. Third, a stronger dollar made U.S. goods more expensive abroad, causing a decrease in the nation's exports and an increase in its imports.** The increase in the United States' share of the world export market can be attributed to the depreciation of the dollar in September 1985, the U.S. government's increasing efforts to promote exports, and the rise in the United States' manufacturing productivity.[13]

GLOBAL INSIGHTS CASE 1.3

U.S. Exports More than Peanuts

In 1992, American service firms exported to nonaffiliates abroad:

- Over two-thirds as much in passenger fares ($17.4 billion), such as seats on U.S.-flagged air carriers, as the United States exported civilian aircraft ($24.5 billion).
- More educational services ($6.1 billion) than the United States exported corn ($5.7 billion).
- More financial services ($5.4 billion) than the United States exported wheat ($4.6 billion).
- More equipment installation and repair services ($2.8 billion) than the United States exported agricultural machinery ($2.1 billion).
- More information services, including computer and data processing and database services ($2.6 billion), than the United States exported aluminum ($$1.2 billion).
- More legal services ($1.4 billion) than the United States exported vegetable oils ($1.0 billion).
- More management consulting services ($0.78 billion) than the United States exported milled rice ($0.72 billion) or peanuts ($0.21 billion).

Source: U.S. Government Printing Office, *Economic Report of the President*, (Washington, D.C: U.S. Government Printing Office, February 1994), 209.

---

* The United States was slower in boosting its capital stock and skills per unit of labor than countries such as Germany and Japan. As a result, the United States' relative export position declined in technology- and capital-intensive goods.

** The "stronger dollar" means the price of the U.S. dollar, measured in terms of foreign currencies, increased. This made the value of U.S. exports, measured in terms of foreign currencies, more expensive, causing these exports to fall. The higher dollar price also meant that the cost of U.S. imports was less, causing imports to rise.

Table 1-3 provides data on the direction of world trade. As this table indicates, the bulk of world exports is made by the developed countries: Shares of the world's total exports are 71.99 percent for developed countries, 26.91 percent for developing countries, and 1.1 percent for other countries. Additionally, of the total dollar amount exported by developed countries, 74.82 percent went to developed countries themselves, 23.31 percent went to developing countries, and 1.87 percent went to other countries. This means that in general, developed nations are the major trading partners for most internationally traded goods and services. However, we must not underestimate the importance of developing countries in providing export markets for developed countries. For example, until the increase in their debt-service ratios, Latin American countries provided the highest growth market for U.S. exports. Mexico, a developing country, is the third most important trading market for the United States.

TABLE 1-3
Shares of World Exports (By Percentage) by Destination, 1991

| | Destination of Exports | | | |
Origin of Exports	Developed* Countries	Developing* Countries	Other Countries	Total
World	71.99	26.91	1.10	100.00
Developed Countries*	74.82	23.31	1.87	100.00
Developing Countries**	61.19	34.36	4.45	100.00

* Developed countries include the following nations: the United States, Canada, Australia, Japan, New Zealand, Austria, Belgium—Luxembourg, Denmark, Finland, France, Germany, Greece, Ireland, Italy, the Netherlands, Norway, Portugal, Spain, Sweden, Switzerland, and Great Britain.

** Developing countries include the following nations: (Africa) Algeria, Cameroon, Cote d'Ivoire, Gabon, Ghana, Kenya, Morocco, Nigeria, Senegal, South Africa, Sudan, Tanzania, Tunisia, Zaire, and Zambia; (Asia) China, Taiwan, Hong Kong, India, Indonesia, Korea, Malaysia, Pakistan, the Philippines, Singapore, and Thailand; (Europe) Hungary, Poland, Romania, Turkey, Yugoslavia, and the Netherlands; (Middle East) Bahrain, Egypt, Iran, Iraq, Israel, Kuwait, Libya, Saudi Arabia, and the Syrian Arab Republic; (Western Hemisphere) Argentina, the Bahamas, Brazil, Chile, Colombia, Ecuador, Jamaica, Mexico, Panama, Peru, Trinidad, Tobago, and Venezuela.

Source: International Monetary Fund, Direction of Trade Statistics (Washington, DC: International Monetary Fund, June 1993).

GLOBAL INSIGHTS CASE 1.4

Economic Linkages among G-7 Countries

Given the increasing globalization of the world economy, the economic interdependence among nations continues to rise. In an empirical study, Roy C. Fair examined the linkages among nations in terms of price, interest rate, trade, and output. The table demonstrates the estimated final result of a sustained and autonomous increase of 1 percent in the U.S. GNP, on the country's short-term interest rate, GDP deflator (a price index), exports, and imports. It also presents the effects that these changes have on the same variables in Great Britain, Canada, France, Germany, Italy, and Japan, 18 months after the change in GDP takes place. As the table shows, the 1-percent rise in the U.S. GNP, working through the multiplier process, causes its GNP to rise further (1.39 percent) 18 months after the change occurs. Short-term interest rates rise by 0.89, and GDP deflator by 0.55 percent. Finally, exports increase by 0.65 and imports by 2.49 percent.

The rise in the U.S. exports reflects the increase in the GNP of other countries, which is stimulated by the increase in the U.S. imports. As the table indicates, the 1 percent rise in the United States GNP leads to an increase of 0.10 in Britain's GNP, 0.55 percent in Canada's GNP, -0.07 percent in France's GNP, 0.14 percent in (the former) West Germany, 0.21 percent in Italy's GNP, and 0.12 percent in Japan's GNP. It is interesting to note that the largest increase occurs in Canada. This reflect the relatively high interdependence of the Canadian and the United States economies. The increase in the U.S. GNP also results in an increase in short-term interest rates, exports, and imports of most other countries.

The Impact of a 1 percent Increase in the United States GNP (in percentage)

Nation	Real GNP Interest Rate	Short-Term Deflator	GDP	Exports	Imports
United States	1.39	0.89	0.55	0.65	2.49
Britain	0.10	0.02	-0.11	0.20	0.23
Canada	0.55	0.60	0.56	2.66	1.14
France	-0.07	0.29	-0.14	0.20	0.25
Italy	0.21	-0.27	-0.42	-0.43	0.39.
Germany*	0.14	0.41	0.10	0.35	-0.60
Japan	0.12	0.12	-0.10	0.92	1.04

*Denotes the former West Germany

Source: Ray C. Fair, "Estimated Output, Price, Interest Rate, and Exchange Rate Linkages among Countries," *Journal of Political Economy* (June 1982): 507-535.

In conclusion, we must emphasize that in today's world no nation, whether developed or developing, can live in isolation. Because the global economy is profoundly affected by international trade and investment activities, we are, in a sense, citizens of the world. As informed citizens we need to understand the elements that affect international economic relationships and trade and, hence, our own economic well-being. A prerequisite for this understanding is familiarity with the institutions and theoretical frameworks necessary for analyzing global economic issues. These are the subjects of forthcoming chapters.

1.6 SUMMARY

1. The objective of international economics is to explain how international economic interactions influence the allocation of scarce resources both within and between nations.

2. The subject matter of international economics includes all transactions that cross national boundaries. These include trade in goods and services, capital and labor movements, and transactions in financial assets.

3. Although international trade is an extension of domestic trade, it is significantly different from the latter, mainly due to the environment in which it takes place. The variables that shape this environment include factor mobility, national currencies, national policies, and cultures.

4. In distinguishing international trade from domestic trade, nineteenth-century classical economists maintained that factors of production—land, labor, capital, and entrepreneurship—moved freely within a nation but not between nations.

5. It is reasonable to assume that when obstacles to free movement of factors of production are absent, domestic factor mobility is relatively higher than international factor mobility.

6. A culture consists of a set of beliefs, values, attitudes, and practices of a group of people who live in a given environment; a culture can determine the nature and scope of international trade.

7. Newly industrialized countries have demonstrated that they are a significant force with which firms in the developed countries must learn to compete.

8. Gorbachev's reforms, "perestroika" (restructuring) and "glasnost" (openness), called for major changes in Soviet economic policies. These reforms led to the eventual collapse of the Soviet Union and the creation of the Commonwealth of Independent States.

9. In the early 1990s, the world witnessed several extraordinary economic and social events, one of which was the unification of Germany. East and West Germany merged their economies in the summer of 1990.

10. At a 1985 summit in Milan, European Union members endorsed the "White Paper," which established a detailed legislative program for complete economic integration by 1992. The basic thrust of the White Paper was the removal of a series of trade barriers.

11. The international debt crisis—fueled by the tighter monetary policies of developed countries, the second oil shock of the late 1970s, and poor public-sector investment in developing countries—hit the world in 1982.

12. Multinational corporations have been the subject of heated debates that have raised nationalistic fervor in developing countries. These corporations have been praised as the chief instrument for abolishing poverty in developing countries, but, they have also been denounced as the main device used by developed countries to achieve "economic imperialism."

13. Transborder data flow refers to the flow of electronically transmitted information across national boundaries. This has become an important issue in current international trade and investment relations.

14. The importance of international trade in the world economy can be viewed from different angles. First, it provides us with a variety of goods and services from many countries. Second, it results in greater product specialization, causing greater efficiency in worldwide production and higher consumption levels. Third, international trade provides a source of income and employment for the countries involved.

15. The importance of international trade in a country's economy can be measured by comparing the percentage of the country's exports and imports to its GDP.

16. To determine a country's relative significance in world trade, we can measure the ratio of its exports and imports to total world exports and imports.

17. International trade is dominated by the world's major industrialized countries. In 1995, the United States held the largest share of the world export market, followed by Germany, Japan, France, Great Britain, Italy, the Netherlands, and Canada.

18. The United States' relative share in the world export market declined prior to the late 1980s, losing ground to countries such as the former West Germany and Japan. This can be contributed to three factors. First, countries such as West Germany and Japan captured a large share of the world market. Second, U.S. firms concentrated their activities in foreign direct investment. Third, a stronger dollar made U.S. goods more expensive abroad, causing an increase in imports and a decrease in exports.

19. The increase in the United States' share of the world export market, beginning in 1988, was due to the depreciation of the dollar in September 1985 and the U.S. government's increased efforts at export promotion.
20. Overall, developed nations are the major trading partners for internationally traded goods and services. However, we must not underestimate the importance of developing countries in providing export markets for these developed countries.

Review Questions

1. Why does international economics exist as a separate field of study in economic science? What is the objective of international economics? What transactions are included in the study of international economics?
2. Why is an understanding of international trade important to you?
3. What major events have contributed to a drastic change in the world economy during the last two decades? What general impact have these changes had on the world economy?
4. What is the distinctive feature of international trade? What are the differences between international trade and domestic trade? Explain.
5. Which countries are the major trading nations? What factors contributed to the deterioration of the United States' trade position prior to the late 1980s? Explain.
6. What factors have contributed to the growth of global markets in recent years? What is the impact of globalization on developed and developing countries? Explain using some examples.
7. What is the significance of international trade to the world economy?

Problems

1. Explain the changing pattern of the United States' overall international trade position in the last two decades. Include a discussion of the growth of international trade in European countries and Japan in your answer. What do you think the patterns of international trade will look like in the future?
2. How do you think the recent movements toward more market-oriented economies will affect global welfare? Discuss.
3. Go to your library and find the latest edition of *International Financial Statistics (IFS),* published by the International Monetary Fund. Choose seven developed countries and seven developing countries, and use the *IFS* data to calculate the ratio of imports to GDP for each of your countries. Compare the imports/GDP ratios of developing countries to developed countries. In general, is the imports/GDP ratio lesser or greater for developing nations as compared to developed nations? Explain your findings.
4. Choose a newspaper from your library and select an event of international significance. Given your choice, answer the following questions:
    (a) What are the global economic implications of this event?
    (b) What is the major impact of this event on the economy of your country?
5. Go to your library and find the latest edition of *International Financial Statistics Yearbook,* published by the International Monetary Fund. Using this book, update Tables 1-1 and 1-2 in this chapter and answer the following questions:
    (a) What country accounts for the largest share of the world export market?
    (b) Examine the trade position of the United States over the years, elaborating on factors that have contributed to its position.

Notes

1. "Entering A New Age of Boundless Competition," *Fortune,* 14 March 1988, 40-48.
2. Franklin R. Root, "Some Trends in the World Economy and Their Implications for International Business," *Journal of International Business Studies* (Winter 1984): 19-23.
3. "Big-Five's Attempt to Deflate the Dollar Is Losing Steam; Can They Win the War?" *The Wall Street Journal,* 12 December 1985, 34.
4. "The Plunge in Stocks Has Experts Guessing about Market's Course," *The Wall Street Journal,* 19 October 1987, 1.
5. "Anguish Abroad: Foreign Ardor Cools toward U.S. Stocks after Market's Dives," *The Wall Street Journal,* 26 October 1987, 1.
6. "How Bad? The Economy Will Have to Struggle to Avoid a Recession," *Business Week,* 2 November 1987, 42-43; "How The Bull Crashed Into Reality," *Business Week,* 2 November 1987, 48-50.
7. "Taking Stock: Changes since Crash Can't Prevent a Repeat But Might Soften One," *The Wall Street Journal,* 17 October 1992, 1, A16.
8. California Newsreel, *Controlling Interest: The World of Multinational Corporation* (San Francisco: California Newsreel, 1978). Video tape.
9. Root, 19-23.
10. "Economic Outlook: Free Trade with Mexico Will Boost America's Economy," *U.S. News and World Report,* 13 May 1991, 58; "A Giant Marketplace: Bush Starts Free Talks with Mexico," Maclean's, 25 June 1990, 21.
11. "Canadian Government Approves Trade Pact, Claims Improvements," *The Wall Street Journal,* 3 December 1993, A2, A4.
12. Percentages calculated by the author from data derived from U.S. Department of Commerce, *Statistical Abstract of the United States, 1993* (Washington DC: U.S. Bureau of Census, 1993), tables 621, 1348, 1352.
13. "U.S. Intensifies Effort to Urge Small Firms to Export," *The Wall Street Journal,* 16 June 1989, B2; "U.S. Competitiveness Wins New Respect from Leading Players in Global Market," *The Wall Street Journal,* 16 July 1993, A6; "Age of Angst: Workplace Revolution Boosts Productivity at Cost of Job Security," *The Wall Street Journal,* 10 March 1993, 1, A8.

Suggested Readings

Abernathy, William J., Kim B. Clark, and Alan M. Kantrow. "The New Industrial Competition." *Harvard Business Review* 59 (September-October 1981): 68-81.

Adams, J. *The Contemporary International Economy.* New York: St. Martin's Press, 1985.

Baldwin, R. E., and J. D. Richardson. *International Trade and Finance: Readings.* Boston: Little Brown, 1986.

Blake, David H., and Robert S. Walters. *The Politics of Global Economic Relations.* Englewood Cliffs, NJ: Prentice-Hall, 1987.

Bosworth, Barry P., and Robert Z. Lawrence. "America in the World Economy." *Brookings Review* 7 (Winter 1988/1989): 39-52.

Cassing, James H., and Steven L. Husted, eds. *Capital, Technology, and Labor in the New Global Economy.* Washington DC: American Enterprise Institute, 1988.

Culbertson, J. M. *International Trade and the Future of the West.* Madison, WI: 21st Century Press, 1984.

"Entering A New Age of Boundless Competition." *Fortune,* 14 March 1988, 40-48.

Fieleke, Norman S. *The International Economy Under Stress.* Cambridge, MA: Ballinger, 1988.

Frieden, Jeffry, and David A. Lake, eds. *International Political Economy: Perspectives on Global Power and Wealth.* New York: St. Martin's Press, 1987.

Hafer, R. W., ed. *How Open Is the U.S. Economy?* Lexington, MA: D. C. Heath, 1986.

Root, Franklin R. "Some Trends in the World Economy and Their Implications for International Business." *Journal of International Business Studies* (Winter 1984): 19-23.

Spero, Joan Edelman. *The Politics of International Economic Relation.* New York: St. Martin's Press, 1985.

Stewart, M. *The Age of Interdependence.* Cambridge, MA: MIT Press, 1984.

World Bank. *World Development Report 1993.* New York: Oxford University Press, 1994.

Part I

THEORIES OF INTERNATIONAL TRADE

The world of international trade is extremely complicated. It includes many nations with different cultural, economic, and social backgrounds. Such complexity is further amplified by the fact that all nations are economically related to each other in one way or another. For example, the increase in oil prices by the Organization of Petroleum Exporting Countries (OPEC) in 1973, from $2.59 per barrel to $11.65 per barrel, was felt by almost everyone in the world. In the United States, this resulted in an increase in oil prices and fueled inflation for years to come. As a consequence, the entire economic picture of the United States took on a new dimension. Foreign trade, investment, consumption, and government spending were all affected.

In the area of foreign trade, for example, the demand for fuel-efficient Japanese cars increased, whereas the demand for U.S.-manufactured automobiles ("gasguzzlers") declined. This contributed to the gloomy picture of the U.S. automobile industry in the 1970s evidenced by the financial crisis of one of its major manufacturers, Chrysler Corporation, which the federal government finally "bailed out" of bankruptcy. In the area of investment, U.S. automobile manufacturers were forced to retool their industry in order to respond to the ever-increasing demand for smaller, more fuel-efficient cars. In the area of consumption, many consumers changed their driving habits and rebudgeted their income to account for the higher fuel cost. Other industrialized nations in the world experienced similar problems, facing what was then the deepest recession since the depression of the 1930s. Oil-producing nations, however, became richer overnight and found themselves confronted with a whole range of opportunities that set the stage for both new prosperity and the host of economic problems that could accompany it.

The decline in oil prices, starting in the early 1980s, once again changed the world economic picture. Some oil-producing nations faced one of the most serious economic crises they had ever experienced. For example, Mexico found itself on the brink of bankruptcy, unable to pay its huge debt; Iran and Iraq, in need of additional funds to finance the Iran—Iraq war (1980—1988), were badly hurt by shrinking oil revenues. In desperation, both countries kept cutting their oil prices in order to capture a larger portion of the market, worsening their economic conditions in the long run.

In the industrial nations, lower oil prices in the early 1980s allowed some countries, like the United States, to enjoy one of the lowest inflation rates they had ever experienced. Both consumption and investment increased. Yet, the United States kept struggling to resolve its balance of trade deficit (excess of merchandise imports over merchandise exports), especially with Japan, which continues to capture a large percentage of the U.S. market, mainly because of its high-quality products.

The global economic picture changed once again when the threat of a war in the Persian Gulf led to a surge in oil prices, adversely affecting the world economy and contributing to the U.S. recession in the early 1990s. The military defeat of Iraq, which ended the Gulf crisis, led to the collapse of oil prices, thus contributing to U.S. economic recovery (by March 1991 the economy was slowly emerging from recession).

As these examples indicate, a change in the price of one commodity, such as oil, creates such an enormous chain of events that the analysis of all the causal relationships is virtually impossible. In this situation one finds a mass of data that is difficult to manage or understand without an appropriate theoretical framework. To be able to use these data and to discover an orderly relationship between different economic variables, it is necessary to develop a theory. A **theory** is an abstraction from reality and is based on certain simplifying assumptions. In our example of the oil price change, rather than trying to examine all the variables involved, we may concentrate on a few of them. For instance, we may ask what happens to the quantity of oil demanded as a result of a change in the price of oil, assuming that all other things affecting the price and quantity of oil demanded stay constant. Such an assumption allows us to simplify and abstract from the myriad data. In fact, every theory, whether in the biological, physical, or social sciences, uses the same approach in simplifying reality. Such a methodology allows the development of a theory that, if it holds up under empirical testing, provides us with an understanding of diverse empirical data. It allows us to predict the future course of events with a reasonable degree of certainty.

In summary, theories are used to arrive at conclusions about the real world. Theory is an abstraction from reality and is based on certain simplifying assumptions. The test of the usefulness of a theory is its power to predict. We continue to use a given theory until certain events falsify it. In this case, a new theory replaces the old one.

Having emphasized the importance of theory, Part I is devoted to a discussion of international trade theories. Chapter 2 presents the historical development of modern international trade theories, discussing a country's production or supply considerations. Chapter 3 explains modern theories of international trade, focusing on the demand side. Finally, Chapter 4 extends the discussion of modern international trade theories by elaborating on their applications and discussing new theoretical approaches to international trade.

Chapter 2

DEVELOPMENT OF INTERNATIONAL TRADE THEORIES: SUPPLY

2.1 INTRODUCTION

International trade theories have been developed to explain various issues that are encountered in trade among nations. Some of the most important questions raised in international trade are as follows:

1. Why do nations trade?
2. What are the gains from trade?
3. How are relative prices of goods determined in international trade?
4. What factors determine the direction of trade (who exports what)?
5. What are the welfare effects of restricting trade?

This chapter examines these questions. First, we review the historical development of modern theories. The writings of the mercantilists and classical economists, including Adam Smith and David Ricardo, have been crucial in shaping the foundation of modern trade theories. Second, we present the theoretical principles that are employed in analyzing the impact of international trade among nations.

2.2 THEORY OF MERCANTILISM

The systematic study of international trade started in the era of mercantilism that prevailed in Europe between the sixteenth and eighteenth centuries. This period marked the beginning of the development of modern states. The basic idea of **mercantilism** was that wealth is a necessary condition for national power. National power is in turn enhanced by the increase in specie, that is, gold and silver coins. Thus, for a country without gold and silver mines, the only means of acquiring gold and silver is by encouraging exports and discouraging imports.

The problem with mercantilists ideas was that they confused the concept of wealth with precious metal. Because they assumed that wealth was limited, they concluded that one nation's gain from trade was achieved only by another nation's loss.

David Hume, the eighteenth-century British economist, essayist, historian, and philosopher, criticized mercantilism and showed that there is a self-correcting mechanism (called the price-specie-flow mechanism) that makes mercantilists policies self-defeating. He explained that as a nation increases its exports and accumulates more gold and silver coins, the money supply in the economy increases. An increase in the money supply creates an inflationary effect and increases domestic prices. The increase in domestic prices makes domestic goods more expensive for other countries to buy, resulting in a decrease in exports. On the other hand, an increase in domestic prices makes foreign-produced goods relatively cheaper than domestic ones, causing imports to increase.[1] When exports fall and imports rise, the country's money supply (precious metals) declines.

Although mercantilism continued to be criticized by later economists, such as Adam Smith and David Ricardo, some of its teachings are still practiced today, though to a lesser degree. For example, in an attempt to take away some of the United States' world economic power and leadership, General Charles De Gaulle adopted policies to increase French exports and discourage imports, particularly from the United States. Additionally, he demanded that the United States settle its payments deficit with France in gold. De Gaulle's mercantilists policy is still followed by his successors, although in a less extreme fashion.[2] Today, socialists have created a France in which key industries and banks are nationalized. As a result, about one third of France's productive capacity and 70 percent of its high-tech industries are under the government control. Today, government intervention in France has reached the same level practiced in the seventeenth century, prompting some authors to call the present government's policy "high-tech mercantilism."[3]

2.3 THEORY OF ABSOLUTE ADVANTAGE

The theory of **absolute advantage** was developed by Adam Smith. Smith, a leading advocate of free trade, recognized the significance of specialization and division of labor. His theory of absolute advantage states that two countries can benefit from trade if, due to natural or acquired endowments, they can provide each other with a product made more cheaply than they can be produced at home. This means that the total resource cost to produce a good in one country is absolutely less than the resource cost to produce the same good in another country. Thus, according to this theory, each country should specialize in the production of goods in which it is most efficient, that is, the goods it can make most cheaply.

GLOBAL INSIGHTS CASE 2.1

Hornick and Mercantilism

Phillip Von Hornick (1638-1712) wrote a widely read tract called *Austria Over All, If She Only Will in 1684.* His writings provided one of the clearest explanations of mercantilists policy. One section reads:

> *To inspect the country's soil with the greatest care, and not to leave the agricultural possibilities of a single corner or clod of earth unconsidered . . . all commodities found in a country, which cannot be used in their natural state, should be worked up within the country . . . attention should be given to population, that it may be as large as the country can support . . . gold and silver once in the country are under no circumstances to be taken out for any purpose . . . the inhabitants should make every effort to get along with their domestic products . . . [foreign commodities] should be obtained not for gold or silver, but in exchange for other domestic wares . . . and should be imported in unfinished form, and worked up within the country . . . opportunities should be sought night and day for selling the country's superfluous goods to these foreigners in manufactured form . . . no importation should be allowed under any circumstances of which there is a sufficient supply of suitable quality at home.* *

Hornik's writing reflects the basic mercantilists policies of nationalism, self-sufficiency, and national power which were employed in differing scales by all European nations between the sixteenth and eighteenth centuries. More specifically, these policies included the following:

1. Promotion of manufacturing by subsidies, special privileges, patents, and monopolies.
2. Encouragement of foreign trade by seizure of colonies and attempts to keep wages down and regulated by tariffs, navigation laws, and trade limitations.
3. Fostering of agriculture by a variety of policies. For example, to keep foreigners out of the domestic competitive market, food imports were taxed in England. To support domestic production, agricultural products were taxed in France.

We should not assume that mercantilism was practiced in the same fashion everywhere in Europe. In fact there were great differences between nations. In France, for instance, where goods such as wine, silks and linens had a high demand, the government imposed regulations to monitor the quality of such goods. Contrast this with England where the regulation of domestic industry was not emphasized because the government was not effective enough to enforce it. Instead, English mercantilism concentrated essentially on the expansion of trade and promotion of manufacturers.

The Age of the Economist, Daniel R. Fusfeld (Glenview, IL: Scott, Foresman and Company, 1966), 9. Reprinted by permission of Harper-Collins College Publishers.

Absolute advantage might be the result of natural endowment or acquired endowment. Natural endowment includes factors that are related to climate, soil, and mineral resources. For example, some nations, such as Saudi Arabia and Iran, have petroleum, but most do not. Bananas can be grown relatively cheaply in Central America because of the tropical climate. The soil and climate conditions are conducive to the production of wine and lumber in France and Sweden, respectively. Acquired endowments include special skills and technology, such as those used by the United States to produce AWACS planes and those used by Japan to produce electronic robots. Thus, according to the theory of absolute advantage, the U.S. should export AWACS to Saudi Arabia, and Saudi Arabia should export petroleum to the United States. France should export wine to Sweden and Sweden should export lumber to France. Japan should export electronic robots to Iran, and Iran should export petroleum to Japan.

The concept of absolute advantage can be explained numerically by a simple example. Let us assume that: 1) the United States and France are both able to produce two goods, cotton and wine; 2) there are no transportation costs between these countries; 3) competitive conditions prevail; 4) labor is the only factor of production and thus the only cost of production; 5) labor is freely mobile within countries but not between countries; and 6) there is no government intervention. Table 2-1 shows the production resulting from one day (eight hours) of labor.

TABLE 2-1
Production from One Day of Labor at Full Employment

	Cotton Output (Bales/Day)	Wine Output (Gallons/Day)
United States	10	5
France	5	10

According to Table 2-1, France has an absolute advantage in the production of wine because one day of labor produces 10 gallons of wine in France compared to 5 gallons of wine in the United States. The United States has an absolute advantage in the production of cotton because one day of labor produces 10 bales of cotton in the United States compared to 5 bales in France. Thus, it is sensible for the United States to specialize in the production of cotton, export the cotton to France, and import French wine. The reverse is true for France.

We may now introduce the concept of opportunity cost to show the extent by which each country benefits from trade. **Opportunity cost** is the value of the benefit foregone when choosing one alternative rather than another. This simply means what a nation would have to give up of one good in choosing to produce another good. For example, the opportunity cost of 1 gallon of wine in the United States is 2 bales of cotton, because 1 day of labor can produce either 5 gallons of wine or 10 bales of cotton.

In our example, both countries can gain from trade, if they specialize and exchange wine for cotton at a relative price ratio of 1:1, that is, by trading 1 gallon of wine for 1 bale of cotton. As a result, the United States can employ all of its resources to produce cotton, and France can use all of its resources to produce wine. The United States can import 1 gallon of wine for 1 bale of cotton, as opposed to sacrificing the production of 2 bales of cotton to make 1 gallon of wine at home, thereby saving 1 bale of cotton. In the same manner, France can save 1 gallon of wine in trade with the United States.

In summary, the theory of absolute advantage suggests that:

1. The higher the level of a country's specialization, according to its absolute advantage, the more potential gain from trade.
2. Both trading parties gain from trade. These points are in contrast to mercantilists thought, which implies one country's gain from trade is achieved by another country's loss.

2.4 THEORY OF COMPARATIVE ADVANTAGE

The theory of absolute advantage showed the effects of trade when each trading partner had an absolute advantage in the production of only one commodity. A more complicated situation emerges when a country has an absolute advantage in producing both goods; that is, it can make both goods at a lower cost than the other country. David Ricardo first demonstrated this case in his theory of **comparative advantage.** He showed that both trading nations can benefit from trade even when one of the nations has an absolute advantage in the production of both commodities. In terms of our previous example with two countries (the United States and France) and two goods (cotton and wine), Ricardo's theory can be explained using Table 2-2.

TABLE 2-2
Production from One Day of Labor at Full Employment

| | Cotton Output (Bales/Day) | Wine Output (Gallons/Day) | Opportunity Costs | |
			Bales of Cotton/ Gallons of Wine	Gallons of Wine/ Bales of Cotton
United States	180	90	1W = 2.0C	1C = 0.5W
France	40	80	1W = 0.5C	1C = 2.0W

As the table indicates, the United States has an absolute advantage in the production of both commodities. One day of labor produces 180 bales of cotton or 90 gallons of wine in the United States as compared to 40 bales of cotton or 80 gallons of wine in France. This might lead one to think that trade is not advantageous for the United States. Yet trade is profitable to both countries because the relative cost of production in both countries is different. The opportunity costs column reveals how cotton (C) and wine (W) are exchanged in each country before trade takes place. According to these numbers, 2 bales of cotton can be exchanged for 1 gallon of wine in the United States. In other words, 1 bale of cotton commands 0.5 gallons of wine in the United States. In France, on the other hand, 1 bale of cotton is exchanged for 2 gallons of wine. This shows that cotton is relatively cheaper in the United States, whereas wine is relatively cheaper in France. If the United States exports 1 bale of cotton to France, it can receive 2 gallons of wine, as opposed to 0.5 gallons at home. If France exports 1 gallon of wine to the United States, it can receive 2 bales of cotton, as opposed to 0.5 bales at home. Therefore, the United States should export cotton to France, and France should export wine to the United States.

However, as France exports wine to the United States, the supply of wine in the United States increases and the price falls. Similarly, in France, cotton imports from the United States increase the supply, decreasing its price. This process continues until the price ratios in the United States and France become equal to each other. In other words, trade equalizes the relative prices in both countries. At this new price, it pays for both countries to specialize in the production of the commodity in which they have a comparative advantage—the United States in cotton and France in wine. In this way, both countries export the surplus of domestic production over domestic demand and import the excess of domestic demand over domestic production.

Thus, according to the theory of comparative advantage, if one country can produce two goods more efficiently than another country and can produce one of these goods more efficiently than the other, it should specialize in and export that commodity in which it is comparatively more efficient, that is, the commodity in which it has the greatest absolute advantage. The less efficient nation should specialize in and export the commodity in which it is comparatively less inefficient, that is, the commodity in which its absolute disadvantage is least.

2.5 AN EMPIRICAL TEST OF COMPARATIVE ADVANTAGE

One of the earliest empirical studies of the theory of comparative advantage was done by the British economist, G. D. A. MacDougall, in 1950. The theory of comparative advantage postulates that a nation will have a comparative advantage in those commodities in which its labor is more efficient than other commodities and other nations. MacDougall wanted to know if export performance was consistent with relative labor productivities and wage rates in the United States and Great Britain. He hypothesized that in those industries in which labor productivity was relatively higher in the United States, U.S. exports should be higher than British exports after adjusting for wage differentials.

The idea behind MacDougall's empirical study is the realization that the unit labor cost of each commodity is determined by two factors—labor productivity and wage level. Thus, when comparing two countries' exports, both of these factors should be taken into consideration.

If two countries, A and B, have the same wage level but country A has a relatively higher labor productivity, country A can produce the same product more cheaply than country B. This is because an hour of labor in country A produces more output than an hour of labor in country B. This in turn causes the cost per unit of the product to decrease.

Even a country that has both higher wage levels and higher labor productivity can still produce a certain good more cheaply than another country if the overall difference in productivity can more than offset the overall difference in wage rates. For example, suppose countries A and B are producing a commodity that requires only labor. Country A pays $10 an hour for labor and spends 1 hour to produce one unit of the commodity. Country B pays only $5 an hour but takes 3 hours to produce one unit of the same commodity. Although the wage rate is higher in the more efficient country (country A), the cost of production ($10 x 1 = $10) is lower than in country B ($5 x 3 = $15).

To carry out his experiment, MacDougall chose a sample of 25 separate industries in the United States and Great Britain and compared their labor productivities and wage rates. His analysis showed that

1. Labor productivity in the United States was greater than in Great Britain (see Table 2-3).
2. On average, U.S. wage rates were twice as high as British rates.

TABLE 2-3
U.S. and British Pre-War Output per Worker and Quantity of Exports, 1937

U.S. output per worker more than twice the British:			
Wireless sets and valves	U.S. exports	=	8 times U.K. exports
Pig iron	U.S. exports	=	5 times U.K. exports
Motor cars	U.S. exports	=	4 times U.K. exports
Glass containers	U.S. exports	=	3.5 times U.K. exports
Tin cans	U.S. exports	=	3 times U.K. exports
Machinery	U.S. exports	=	1.5 times U.K. exports
Paper	U.S. exports	=	1 times U.K. exports
U.S. output per worker 1.4 to 2.0 times the British:			
Cigarettes	U.K. exports	=	2 times U.S. exports
Linoleum, oilcloth, etc.	U.K. exports	=	3 times U.S. exports
Hosiery	U.K. exports	=	3 times U.S. exports
Leather footwear	U.K. exports	=	3 times U.S. exports
Coke	U.K. exports	=	5 times U.S. exports
Rayon weaving	U.K. exports	=	5 times U.S. exports
Cotton goods	U.K. exports	=	9 times U.S. exports
Rayon making	U.K. exports	=	11 times U.S. exports
Beer	U.K. exports	=	18 times U.S. exports
U.S. output per worker less than 1.4 times the British:			
Cement	U.K. exports	=	11 times U.S. exports
Men's/boy's outer clothing of wool	U.K. exports	=	23 times U.S. exports
Margarine	U.K. exports	=	32 times U.S. exports
Woolen and worsteds	U.K. exports	=	250 times U.S. exports

Exceptions (U.S. output per worker more than twice British, but U.K. exports exceeded U.S. exports): Electric lamps, rubber tires, soaps, biscuits, matches.
Source: G. D. A. MacDougall, "British and American Exports: A Study Suggested by the Theory of Comparative Costs." Reprinted in Richard E. Caves and Harry G. Johnson, eds., Readings in International Economics (Homewood, IL: Richard D. Irwin, 1968), 554. Reprinted by permission.

Given these results, we would expect the United States' share of the world export market to be greater than Great Britain's share in those industries where U.S. labor productivity was more than two times greater than British labor productivity. We would also expect Britain to have a higher share of export markets in those industries where its labor was more than half as productive as U.S. labor.

According to the data presented in Table 2-3, out of the 25 industries MacDougall investigated, 20 followed the expected outcome. The U.S. share of the export market was largest when its labor productivity was at least twice that of British productivity.

By relating export patterns to wage levels and productivity, MacDougall added a new dimension to the theory of comparative advantage. However, his test is not without its limitations. One of these limitations is that it relates the export patterns to labor, ignoring the impact of other factors of production. Another problem is that it does not account for differences in product quality that exist between countries. For example, one reason Japanese cars are popular in the United States is their superior quality compared to similar American cars. Thus, in using the theory of comparative advantage, we should incorporate these additional factors in determining a country's comparative advantage.

Similar studies supporting MacDougall's early findings were carried out by Stern (1962) and Balassa (1963). All of these studies were based on data for Great Britain and the United States from 1937 (MacDougall), 1950 (Balassa), and 1950 and 1959 (Stern).

2.6 PRODUCTION POSSIBILITIES FRONTIER

The law of comparative advantage can be illustrated by the **production possibilities frontier (PPF),** or curve, also known as the transformation curve. This curve shows all possible combinations of two products that a country can produce with available technology and full employment of all resources. The shape of the curve depends on the underlying assumptions regarding the costs of production. The two assumptions that may be used in construction of this curve are (a) constant opportunity costs, and (b) increasing opportunity costs. We can explain this curve by examining the Ricardian principles of comparative advantage under each of these two assumptions.

2.6a The Production Possibility Frontier under Constant Costs Assumption

Under the **constant opportunity costs** assumption, the relative cost of one product in terms of another product is considered to be constant. The constant opportunity costs assumption holds if both of the following are true:

1. Factors of production or resources are either perfect substitutes for each other or are employed in fixed proportion in the production of both goods.
2. The units of each factor of production employed are homogeneous, that is, they have precisely the same quality.

As a result, when a nation transfers resources from one product to another, say from wine to cotton, it does not have to utilize resources that are less suitable to the second product (cotton), no matter how much of that product has already been produced. Thus, costs remain constant in the sense that the same amount of one commodity should always be sacrificed to produce an additional unit of another commodity. Although the assumption of constant opportunity costs may not hold in the real world, it is helpful in developing the skills to analyze international trade issues and in understanding the more realistic case of increasing costs.

Using the data presented in Table 2-2, we reach the graph shown in Figure 2-1. Lines AB and A`B` depict the PPF of cotton and wine for the United States and France, respectively. The constant opportunity costs assumption gives rise to a straight-line PPF. This indicates that the relative cost of one commodity in terms of the other commodity stays constant, regardless of a country's position on its PPF. As Figure 2-1 shows, for the United States, the relative cost of each gallon of wine produced is 2 bales of cotton. For France, the cost of producing each gallon of wine is 0.5 bales of cotton, regardless of the country's position on its PPF. The opportunity cost of each product is given by the absolute value of the slope of its PPF. The (absolute) slope of the PPF is also referred to as the

marginal rate of transformation (MRT). Assuming that prices are equal to the costs of production and that each nation produces some of both commodities, the opportunity cost of a product is equal to the price of that product relative to the price of another product, or its **relative commodity price.** For example, in Table 2-2 the opportunity cost of wine in the United States, measured by the price of wine (P_W) divided by the price of cotton (P_C), is equal to 2 ($P_W/P_C = 2/1$). Conversely, the opportunity cost of cotton in the United States, measured by the price of cotton (P_C) divided by the price of wine (P_W), is equal to 0.5 ($P_C/P_W = \frac{1}{2}$). As Figure 2-1 indicates, P_C/P_W for each country is also measured by the absolute value of the slope of that country's PPF. It must be noted that, according to the law of comparative advantage, relative prices are determined only by production, or supply, conditions in each country. In other words, in determining relative commodity prices, demand conditions are not taken into consideration at all. The difference in relative commodity prices (determined by the slope of PPFs) between the two countries provides the only basis for international trade.

<h1 style="text-align:center">FIGURE 2-1</h1>
<h2 style="text-align:center">Production Possibilities Frontier under Constant Opportunity Costs</h2>

The U.S. and French PPFs are drawn by plotting the data in Table 2-2. The curves have negative slopes, showing that as each country produces more cotton, it has to give up some wine. The straight-line PPF reveals the constant opportunity costs assumption. Given this assumption, the relative cost of producing one commodity in terms of another stays constant regardless of the nation's position on its PPF.

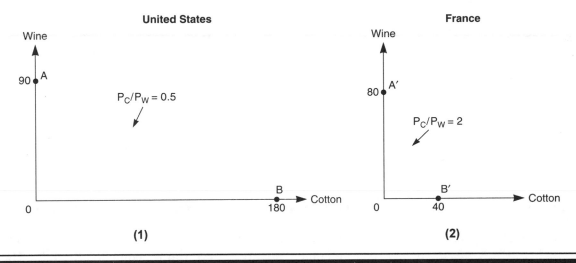

2.6b The Basis for and the Gains from International Trade under Constant Costs Assumption

In the absence of trade (**autarky**), a country's PPF depicts the possible points at which the nation chooses to produce and consume. All points along the PPF are possible production and consumption points, since in autarky a nation can consume only what it produces. To illustrate the gains from trade, we construct Figure 2-2 from Figure 2-1. Point A in the first panel of Figure 2-2 indicates the position of the United States on its PPF before trade. At this point, the United States is producing and consuming 40 gallons of wine and 100 bales of cotton per day. The pretrade position of France is shown by point A′ (second panel of Figure 2-2) on its PPF. At this point, France is producing and consuming 20 gallons of wine and 30 bales of cotton.

According to Figure 2-2, the MRTs for both the United States and France are different, as indicated by the slopes of their respective PPFs. As we explained earlier, the MRT (the absolute value of the slope of the PPF) gives the relative cost of one product in terms of another product. According to the theory of comparative advantage, the relative cost differential provides a basis for mutually advantageous trade. With regard to the direction of trade, the United States specializes in and exports cotton to France, while France specializes in and exports wine to the United States.

The gains from trade can be divided into consumption and production gains.

FIGURE 2-2
Trading under the Constant Opportunity Costs Assumption

In autarky, the United States produces and consumes at point A, and France produces and consumes at point A'. With international trade, the United States specializes in the production of cotton and produces at point B, whereas France specializes in the production of wine and produces at point B'. By exchanging 50 bales of cotton for 50 gallons of wine, the United States ends up consuming at point C, gaining 10 gallons of wine and 30 bales of cotton. Similarly, France ends up consuming at point C', and gains 10 gallons of wine and 20 bales of cotton.

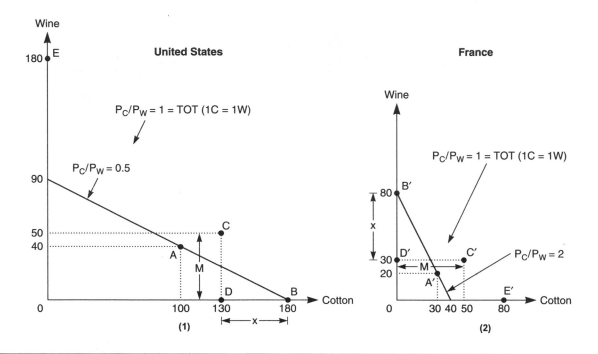

Consumption Gains from Trade. In the absence of trade, the consumption in both the United States and France is restricted by their PPFs. For each country, consumption alternatives are given by points on the PPF. The exact location of each country on its PPF is determined by tastes and preferences in that country.

According to the theory of comparative advantage, with international trade each nation will find it profitable to specialize in the production of the commodity in which it is comparatively more efficient. This allows each country to reach points outside its PPF. These points are determined by each country's **terms of trade** (TOT), or the international price ratio. The TOT are the relative prices at which two products are traded in the international market.[*]

Given our previous example in Figure 2-2, assume that the United States and France reach a 1:1 TOT ratio. At this rate, 1 gallon of wine is exchanged for 1 bale of cotton. Lines BE and B'E' both have slopes with an absolute value of 1, representing the TOT for the United States and France, respectively.

Now assume that the United States wants to export 50 bales of cotton to France. Starting from specialization point B in the first panel of Figure 2-2, the United States moves along its TOT line (BE) until it reaches point C. At this point, 50 gallons of wine are exchanged for 50 bales of cotton, leaving 130 bales of cotton for domestic consumption. As the comparison of point C (posttrade consumption point) and point A (autarky point) shows, free trade results in a net consumption gain for the United States of 10 gallons of wine and 30 bales of cotton. The U.S. exports and imports are depicted on the triangle BCD as X and M, respectively. The absolute value of the slope of this triangle, also referred to as the trade triangle, shows the TOT.

---

[*] Terms of trade are measured by the ratio of the index price of a nation's exports to index price of imports.

For France, the specialization point and posttrade point are shown by points B' and C', respectively. Starting at point B', France moves along its TOT line (B'E') until it reaches C'. At this point, France exports 50 gallons of wine for 50 bales of cotton, leaving 30 gallons of wine for domestic consumption. A comparison of points C' (posttrade consumption point) and point A' (autarky point) shows that France enjoys a net consumption gain of 10 gallons of wine and 20 bales of cotton. These data are repeated in Table 2-4.

TABLE 2-4
Consumption Gains from International Trade

	Autarky		Posttrade		Net Gain/Loss	
	Wine	Cotton	Wine	Cotton	Wine	Cotton
United States	40	100	50	130	10	30
France	20	30	30	50	10	20
Total	60	130	80	180	20	50

Production Gains from Trade. With free international trade, each country specializes in the production of the commodity in which it is relatively more efficient. Looking at the first panel of Figure 2-2, U.S. production moves from the autarky point A (producing 40 gallons of wine and 100 bales of cotton) to specialization point B (producing 180 bales of cotton and no wine). Similarly, France moves from autarky point A' in the second panel of Figure 2-2 (producing 20 gallons of wine and 30 bales of cotton) to specialization point B' (producing 80 gallons of wine and no cotton.)

As Table 2-5 indicates, adding up the results reveals that both countries together realize a net total gain of 20 gallons of wine and 50 bales of cotton.

TABLE 2-5
Production Gains from International Trade

	Autarky		Specialization		Net Gain/Loss	
	Wine	Cotton	Wine	Cotton	Wine	Cotton
United States	40	100	0	180	-40	80
France	20	30	80	0	60	-30
Total	60	130	80	180	20	50

2.6c Production Possibility Frontier under Increasing Costs Assumption

The previous section described the theory of comparative advantage under the assumption of constant opportunity costs. As we mentioned earlier, this assumption is unrealistic because in the real world a commodity's opportunity cost increases as its production is enhanced. **Increasing costs** may arise whenever factors of production are imperfect substitutes for each other. As a result, as the production of one commodity, such as cotton, is increased, factors that are less and less suitable in the production of another commodity, such as wine, are released into the production process. Thus, for each additional unit of cotton produced, more wine has to be sacrificed. Graphically, this leads to a PPF that is concave to the origin, depicting the law of increasing costs. Figure 2-3 illustrates a PPF for a hypothetical country that is producing wine and cotton.

FIGURE 2-3
PPF of Increasing Costs Assumption

Increasing costs assumption results in a PPF that is concave to the origin. The marginal rate of transformation (the absolute value of the slope) increases with the movement from point A to point B, indicating that the opportunity cost of cotton keeps growing in terms of wine.

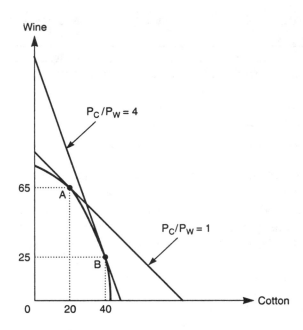

Under the increasing costs assumption, the slope of the PPF changes as a country moves along this curve. Because the MRT is equal to the (absolute) slope of the PPF, the MRT also changes as a nation assumes different points on the curve. This is illustrated in Figure 2-3 by a movement along the PPF from point A to point B. A comparison of these points shows that the absolute value of the slope increases with the movement from point A to point B, indicating that the opportunity cost of cotton keeps growing in terms of wine.

2.6d The Basis for and the Gains from International Trade under Increasing Costs Assumption

Figure 2-4 demonstrates trading under the assumption of increasing costs. Using our previous example, assume the U.S. pretrade (autarky) location is point A. At this point, the United States is producing and consuming 50 gallons of wine and 10 bales of cotton. France is located at point A′ producing and consuming 10 gallons of wine and 45 bales of cotton. At these points, the relative price of cotton for each country is shown by the absolute value of the slope of the line tangent to each point. For the United States, this line is labeled R_{US} and shows that 1 bale of cotton is equal to 0.44 gallons of wine ($P_C/P_W = 0.44$). For France, this line is labeled R_F and indicates that 1 bale of cotton is equal to 2.5 gallons of wine ($P_C/P_W = 2.5$). Because line R_{US} is flatter than line R_F, cotton is relatively cheaper in the United States and wine is relatively cheaper in France. According to the law of comparative advantage, the United States exports cotton to France and imports wine; France exports wine to the United States and imports cotton.

FIGURE 2-4
Trading under the Increasing Costs Assumption

In the absence of trade, the United States produces and consumes at point A, and France produces and consumes at point A'. With trade, the U.S. production moves from point A to point P. By exchanging 30 bales of cotton for 30 gallons of wine with France (see triangle CDP), it ends up consuming at point C. Thus, the United States gains 10 gallons of wine from trade (compare points A and C). In the same manner, France's production moves from A' to P'. By exchanging 30 gallons of wine for 30 bales of cotton, it ends up consuming at point C'. Thus, France gains 10 bales of cotton from trade with the United States.

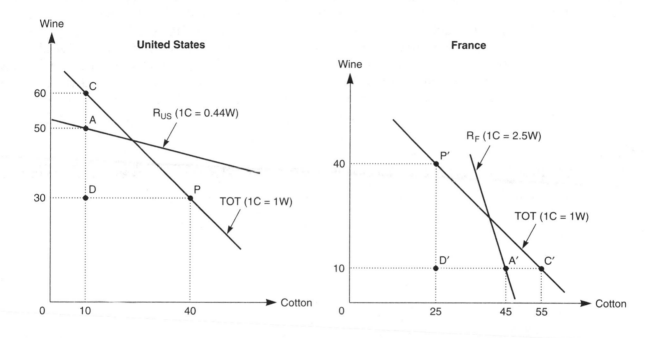

This process continues until the relative costs of producing wine and cotton are equal in both countries. In Figure 2-4 it is assumed that the relative cost equalization occurs at the TOT of 1C = 1W, whereby 1 gallon of wine is traded for 1 bale of cotton. As the figure shows, these terms are beneficial to both countries. This is because TOT line is steeper than R_{US} for the United States, indicating that wine has become cheaper in that country following trade. For France, TOT line is flatter than R_F, showing that cotton has become cheaper in that country following trade.

Given the TOT of 1C = 1W, production in the United States moves to point P. If the United States continues to consume 10 bales of cotton after trade, as it did before trade, consumption is at point C. The trade triangle CDP shows that at this point it will export 30 bales of cotton for 30 gallons of wine. A comparison of points C and A indicates a consumption gain of 10 gallons of wine for the United States.

In the same manner, France's production is shown at point P', where the TOT line is tangent to the PPF. Assume that France continues to consume 10 gallons of wine after trade, as it did in autarky. This will put France's consumption at point C'. The trade triangle C'D'P' shows that at this point France will export 30 gallons of wine for 30 bales of cotton. As a comparison of points C' and A' shows, this results in a consumption gain of 10 bales of cotton for France. These results are summarized in Table 2-6.

2.7 COMPLETE VERSUS PARTIAL SPECIALIZATION

In the preceding graphical analysis of trade, the constant costs assumption led to complete specialization in production (see points B and B' Figure 2-2), whereas increasing costs assumption gave rise to partial specialization (see points P and P', Figure 2-4).

Partial specialization usually occurs under the assumption of increasing costs. This is because under this assumption, unit costs increase as both countries produce more of their export goods. Increasing costs give rise to a mechanism that equalizes costs in both countries. Thus, after cost differentials cease to exist, the basis for continued specialization is eliminated.

Complete specialization generally takes place under constant costs assumption. Using our previous example, this happens because if it is advantageous for the United States to exchange one bale of cotton for one gallon of French wine, it is also beneficial for the United States to acquire all the French wine it needs in exchange for cotton because the U.S. opportunity cost of cotton in terms of wine remains constant. The only exception to complete specialization under constant costs assumption is in the case of a small country trading with a large country. In this situation, only the small country specializes completely in the production of the commodity in which it has a comparative advantage. The large nation continues to produce both goods, even with international trade. The following section discusses the case of a small country under the constant costs assumption.

TABLE 2-6
Gains from International Trade Under Increasing Costs Assumption ▬▬▬▬▬▬

	United States		France	
	Wine	Cotton	Wine	Cotton
Pretrade				
Consumption	50	10	10	45
Production	50	10	10	45
Posttrade				
Consumption	60	10	10	55
Production	30	40	40	25
Exports	—	30	30	—
Imports	30	—	—	30
Gains from trade	10	—	—	10

2.7a The Case of a Small Country

If a country is too small, it is not able to satisfy all the demands of its trading partner. In our example (Figure 2-2), if France were too small to meet the entire U.S. demand for 50 gallons of wine, then France would specialize completely in the production of the commodity in which it has a comparative advantage (wine). The United States, on the other hand, would continue to produce both commodities, even with international trade. However, the TOT between the two countries would be equal to the U.S. pre-trade ratio of $P_C/P_W = 0.5$. As a result, France would capture the entire gain from trade. Figure 2-5 illustrates this case.

In Figure 2-5, it is assumed that France is half as large as it was in Figure 2-2. Given this assumption, its PPF crosses the axes at 40W and 20C, and the autarky location is assumed to be at A', where the country is producing and consuming 10 gallons of wine and 15 bales of cotton. The U.S. pretrade position is given at point A, where, as before, it is producing and consuming 40 gallons of wine and 100 bales of cotton. Because the relative price ratio in France is $P_C/P_W = 2$, as it was in Figure 2-2, France specializes completely in the production of wine, moving to point P' on its PPF. Then, by exchanging 10 gallons of wine for 20 bales of cotton with the United States, France ends up consuming at point C'. At this point, France gains 20 gallons of wine and 5 bales of cotton (compare points A' and C'). With international trade in place, the United States moves to point P, producing 30 gallons of wine and 120 bales of cotton. Then, by exchanging 20 bales of cotton for 10 gallons of wine with France, the United States ends up consuming at point A, as it did before trade. In this scenario, the United States does not gain from trade.

FIGURE 2-5
Small-country Case with Constant Opportunity Costs

In the absence of trade, the United States produces and consumes at point A, and France produces and consumes at point A'. With trade, the U.S. production moves from point A to P. France specializes completely in the production of wine, moving to point P'. Then by exchanging 10 gallons of wine for 20 bales of cotton with the United States, it ends up consuming at point C'. Thus, France gains 20 gallons of wine and 5 bales of cotton from trade (compare points A' and C'). The United States moves to point P, producing 30 gallons of wine and 120 bales of cotton. Then by exchanging 20 bales of cotton for 10 gallons of wine with France, the United States end up consuming at point A, as it did before trade.

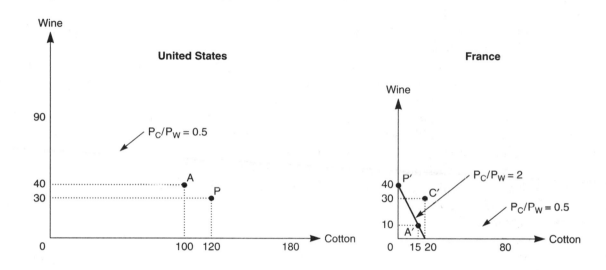

Why would the United States engage in trade if it did not gain anything? This question can be answered only if we look at a more realistic picture, that is, assuming that there is at least one other large nation, such as Canada, that has a comparative advantage in cotton production. If this were the case, the TOT would be determined by supply and demand considerations in the United States and Canada, resulting in net gains for both countries. France then would enter the market, trading at the prevailing TOT. In this process, France, as the small nation, would have no impact on the TOT and would reap all the benefits from its own trade. However, there would be a cost attached to these benefits. That is, by relying on a larger nation for its economic survival, France would run the risk of possible curtailment of demand for the only commodity that it produces and supplies to the market. The difficulties that a nation may encounter in such a situation are discussed in Chapter 7.

2.8 SUMMARY

1. The basic idea of mercantilism is that wealth is a necessary condition for national power. National power is in turn enhanced by the increase in specie. Thus, a country lacking gold and silver mines can only acquire gold and silver by encouraging its exports and discouraging its imports.
2. The theory of absolute advantage states that each country should specialize in the production of the goods in which it is more efficient, that is, the goods it can produce at the least cost.
3. According to the theory of comparative advantage, if one country can produce two goods more efficiently than another country and can produce one of these goods more efficiently than the other, it should specialize in and export that commodity in which it is comparatively more efficient, that is, the commodity in which it has the

greatest absolute advantage. The less efficient nation should specialize in and export the commodity in which it has the least disadvantage.

4. The idea behind MacDougall's study is the realization that the unit labor cost of each commodity is determined by two factors—labor productivity and wage level. Thus, according to MacDougall, both of these factors should be taken into consideration when comparing two countries' exports.

5. Opportunity cost is the value of the benefit foregone when choosing one alternative over another.

6. A production possibilities frontier (PPF) shows all possible combinations of two products that a country can produce with the given state of technology at full employment.

7. The shape of the PPF depends on the underlying assumption regarding the costs of production. The two alternative assumptions that can be used in construction of this curve are (a) constant costs, and (b) increasing costs.

8. Under the constant opportunity costs assumption, the relative cost of one product in terms of another product is considered to be constant.

9. The constant opportunity costs assumption holds if (a) factors of production or resources are either perfect substitutes for each other or are employed in fixed proportion in the production of both goods, and (b) the units of the same factor of production employed are homogeneous.

10. According to the law of comparative advantage, relative commodity prices are determined only by the production, or supply, conditions in each country. In other words, demand conditions are not taken into consideration in determining relative commodity prices.

11. The opportunity cost of each product for a nation is given by the absolute value of the slope of its PPF. This (absolute) slope is also referred to as the marginal rate of transformation (MRT).

12. The terms of trade (TOT) are defined as the relative prices at which two products are traded in the international market.

13. Under the increasing costs assumption, the slope of the PPF changes as a country moves along this curve.

14. Partial specialization usually occurs under increasing costs assumption. Complete specialization generally takes place under constant costs assumption. The only exception to complete specialization under constant costs assumption is in the case of a small country.

Review Questions

1. Define the concept of a production possibilities frontier and explain the factors that determine its shape.
2. Define the concept of opportunity cost and explain the following:
    (a)   Under what conditions are opportunity costs constant?
    (b)   Assuming constant opportunity costs, what happens to the relative price of one commodity in terms of another commodity?
    (c)   How is the opportunity cost of each product measured for a nation?
    (d)   Under what assumption does complete specialization occur?
    (e)   Under what assumption does partial specialization occur?
3. Compare the theories of comparative advantage and absolute advantage.
4. Briefly discuss the mercantilists' ideas with regard to international trade. How do these ideas differ from Adam Smith's view? Give an example of the application of the theory of mercantilism as it exists today. What are some fallacies of this theory?
5. Explain the concepts of constant opportunity costs and increasing opportunity costs. Under what conditions does a nation experience either of these costs?
6. What determines the shape of the PPF? Why do the PPFs of different countries have different shapes? How is the slope of the PPF determined?

Problems

1. Assume that a nation produces two goods, apples (A) and bananas (B).
   (a) On one set of axes draw a linear production possibility curve, measuring A on the horizontal axis and B on the vertical axis. Pick a point near the middle of the curve and explain what happens as you move the point along the curve in either direction. Does the slope of the curve change with these movements? Explain.
   (b) On another set of axes draw a concave to the origin PPF, measuring A on the horizontal axis and B on the vertical axis. Pick a point near the middle of the curve and explain what happens as you move the point along the curve in either direction. Does the slope of the curve change with these movements? Explain.
   (c) Which of these curves is more realistic?
2. A nation can produce 120 million bales of cotton if it employs all of its resources in the cotton industry or 180 million bushels of wheat if it uses all of its resources in wheat production.
   (a) Assuming constant opportunity costs, sketch the PPF for this country.
   (b) Assume in the absence of trade the country consumes 90 million bushels of wheat. How much cotton will the nation be able to produce/consume?
   (c) In the absence of trade, what is the nation's relative commodity price ratio?
   (d) Assume trade takes place at the TOT of 1 bale of cotton for 1 bushel of wheat. Explain what happens to the allocation of resources as the result of trade.
   (e) Assume the country consumes 110 bushes of wheat after trade takes place. How much cotton does the country consume?
   (f) What is the nation's gain from trade?
3. Assume a two-country trading world consists of France and Costa Rica. The following table explains the amount of output produced by each country.

Country	Labor Input (Days)	Output of Wine (Gallons)	Output of Beef (Pounds)
France	2	140	70
Costa Rica	2	20	60

   (a) Assuming constant opportunity costs, sketch the PPF for each country.
   (b) Which country, if any, has an absolute advantage in production? A comparative advantage? Explain.
   (c) In what commodity does each country specialize?
   (d) What are the gains from trading at a 1:1 ratio?
4. Assume a two-country trading world that consists of Columbia and Ecuador, both of which produce coffee and oil. Suppose labor is the only factor of production, and the relative cost of producing one product in terms of another product is constant in both nations. The available supply of labor in Colombia and Ecuador is 2,400, and 1,600, respectively. The following table shows the unit labor requirements in coffee production and oil production in both countries.

Country	Unit Labor Requirement	
	Oil(Gallons)	Coffee(Pounds)
Ecuador	6	4
Colombia	10	2

   (a) Graph the PPF for each country.
   (b) Calculate the opportunity cost of coffee in terms of oil for each country.
   (c) In the absence of trade, what is the relative price of coffee in terms of oil for each country? Explain.
   (d) Assuming free trade, in what commodity should each nation specialize? Explain.
   (e) What is each country's gain from trading at a 1:1 ratio?

Notes

1. David Hume, "Of Money," *Essays* (London: Green and Co., 1912), vol. 1, 319; see also, Eugene Rotwein, *The Economic Writings of David Hume* (Edinburgh: Nelson, 1955).
2. Alan M. Rugman, Donald J. Lecraw, and Laurence D. Booth, *International Business: Firm and Environment* (New York: McGraw-Hill Book Company, 1985), 26—27.
3. Donald A. Ball and H. Wendell McCulloch, Jr., *International Business: Introduction and Essentials,* 2nd ed. (Plano, TX: Business Publications, Inc., 1985), 61.

Suggested Readings

Balassa, B. "An Empirical Determination of Comparative Cost." *Review of Economics and Statistics* 44 (1963): 231-238.

Bhagwati, J. *International Trade: Selected Readings.* Cambridge, MA: MIT Press, 1981.

————. "The Pure Theory of International Trade: A Survey." *Economic Journal* (March 1964).

Chipman, J. S. "A Survey of the Theory of International Trade." *Econometrica* (July 1965).

Ellis, H. S., and L. M. Metzler. *Readings in the Theory Of International Trade.* Homewood, IL: Irwin, 1950.

Haberler, G. *The Theory of International Trade.* London: W. Hodge and Co., 1936, chs. 9, 10, 12.

Johns, R. A. *International Trade Theories and Evolving International Economy.* New York: St. Martin's, 1985.

Jones, R. W., and P. B. Kenen, eds. *Handbook of International Economics.* New York: North Holland, 1984.

Krauss, M. B. A. *A Geometric Approach to International Trade.* New York: Halsted-Wiley, 1979.

McDougall, G. D. A. "British and American Exports: A Study Suggested by the Theory of Comparative Costs." *Economic Journal* 6 (1951): 697-724.

Meade, J. E. *A Geometry of International Trade.* London: Allen and Unwin, 1952.

Ohlin, B. G. *Interregional and International Trade.* Harvard University Press, 1935, part 2.

Ricardo, D. *The Principles of Political Economy and Taxation.* Homewood, IL: Irwin, 1963, ch. 7.

Shutt, H. *The Myth of Free Trade.* New York: Basil Blackwell, 1985.

Smith, A. *The Wealth of Nations.* New York: The Modern Library, 1937, book 1, ch. 3; Book 4, chs. 1-3, 6-8.

Stern, R. M. "British and American Productivity and Comparative Costs in International Trade," *Oxford Economics Papers* 14 (1962): 275-296.

Chapter 3

MODERN THEORIES OF INTERNATIONAL TRADE: DEMAND

3.1 INTRODUCTION

In reviewing the historical development of international trade theories in Chapter 2, we discussed a country's production, or supply, considerations as portrayed by its PPF. However, quantities of goods purchased and sold cannot be determined by supply alone. In either the domestic or international marketplace, these variables are determined by both demand and supply.

We devote this chapter to an analysis of demand, examining the way in which demand affects (a) the basis of international trade; (b) the composition of the goods consumed; and (c) the gains from international trade.

In discussing these topics, we first introduce individual and community indifference curves and then turn our attention to the role of demand in establishing equilibrium terms of trade. Finally, we introduce offer curves to show how a country's offer of exports for imports depends on relative commodity prices. Offer curves provide the same information as a nation's supply of exports and demand for imports. Demand and supply curves illustrate the relationship between price and quantity. Offer curves focus on exports supplied in return for imports at different relative commodity prices. The continuous use of offer curves by theorists has made them a significant analytical device in international economic theory.

3.2 INDIVIDUAL INDIFFERENCE CURVES

Recall from microecnomic theory that demand curves can be derived from indifference curves (ICs) which portray an individual's tastes or demand preferences. An **indifference curve** is the locus of points representing combinations of two goods that give the same level of satisfaction to the individual consumer. Figure 3-1 shows an IC for a consumer of two goods, wine (W) and cotton (C).

All the points on an IC represent the same level of satisfaction to the individual. The individual is just as satisfied consuming 8 gallons of wine and 3 bales of cotton (point A) as he or she is consuming 5 gallons of wine and 5 bales of cotton (point B) or 2 gallons of wine and 9 bales of cotton (point C). Thus, movement along the indifference curve does not change the individual's level of satisfaction.

Indifference curves for two goods have the following properties:

1. They are negatively sloped, that is, slope downward to the right.
2. They are convex to the origin (concave upward).
3. They do not intersect.

The negative slope of an IC for two goods is based on the assumption of nonsatisfaction. This means that the individual always prefers more to less. More of one good must be obtained to compensate for the reduction in the availability of another good if the consumer is to remain indifferent or maintain the same level of satisfaction. If ICs had positive slopes (see Figure 3-2), it would mean that as the individual moves from point A to point B, giving up some wine and some cotton, he or she would still enjoy the same level of satisfaction. This clearly violates the assumption of nonsatisfaction; thus, ICs cannot have positive slopes.

FIGURE 3-1
Indifference Curve for Cotton and Wine

All points on an indifference curve represent the same level of satisfaction to the individual. The individual is just as satisfied consuming 8 gallons of wine and 3 bales of cotton (point A) as he or she is consuming 5 gallons of wine and 5 bales of cotton (point B) or 2 gallons of wine and 9 bales of cotton (point C). Thus, movement along the indifference curve does not change the individual's level of satisfaction.

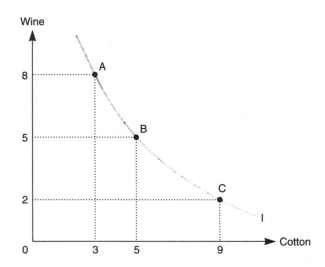

FIGURE 3-2
Implications of an Upward-Sloping Indifference Curve

An individual whose indifference curve is shown here would accept less cotton and less wine and still be equally satisfied (indifferent). In other words, point A and B give equal levels of satisfaction, although at point B less wine and cloth are acquired. This violates the assumption of nonsatisfaction, that is, more is always preferred to less.

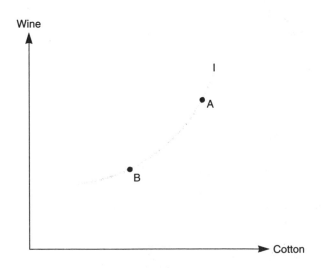

Indifference curves are convex to the origin, reflecting the law of diminishing marginal rate of substitution (MRS). The **marginal rate of substitution** is the rate at which commodities are substituted for each other by an individual while keeping the level of satisfaction unchanged. In our example, the MRS shows the rate at which the individual is willing to substitute cotton for wine (or vice verse) and still enjoy the same level of satisfaction. In other words, MRS shows the amount of wine that a consumer is willing to give up for an additional unit of cotton and still remain on the same indifference curve. Algebraically, the MRS of cotton for wine is expressed as:

$$\text{MRS}_{CW} = \Delta W / \Delta C.$$

The MRS is equal to the absolute value of the slope of the indifference curve. The slope of the indifference curve at each point is defined by the slope of the line tangent to that point. The implications of the convexity of the IC can be seen in Figure 3-3. As we move downward on the IC, for each additional unit of cotton that is gained, less wine must be given up. In other words, the MRS_{CW}, as shown by the absolute value of the slope of the tangent at each point on the IC, diminishes. As the figure shows, the MRS_{CW} decreases from 2 to 0.5 as the individual moves from point A to point D, substituting cotton for wine. This is because as cotton becomes more available, wine becomes less available. With less wine and more cotton, each additional unit of wine becomes more valuable to the individual. As a result, the individual is willing to give up a smaller amount of wine in order to obtain an additional unit of cotton. This means that the MRS_{CW} decreases. This happens in all convex indifference curves because of the diminishing MRS.

FIGURE 3-3
Implications of the Convexity of the Indifference Curve

The implications of the convexity of the indifference curve (IC) can be seen in this diagram. As an individual moves down along the curve, for each additional unit of cotton that is gained, less wine must be given up. In other words, MRS_{CW}, shown by the absolute value of the slope of the tangent at each point on the IC, diminishes. As the figure shows, MRS_{CW} decreases from 2 to 0.5 as the individual moves from point A to point D, substituting cotton for wine.

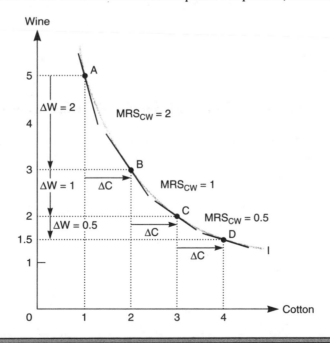

Indifference curves do not intersect. Consider indifference curves I and II in Figure 3-4. By definition, the individual is indifferent between consumption at points A and C, located on indifference curve I. Also by definition, he or she is indifferent between consumption at points A and B, which lie on the same IC (II). As we know from microeconomics courses, the assumption of transitivity (consistency) requires that the individual be indifferent between points B and C.* However, point B represents more wine and more cotton than does combination C. Because more is always preferred to less (the nonsatisfaction assumption), it is impossible for the individual to be indifferent between points B and C. Thus, ICs cannot intersect.

FIGURE 3-4
Intersecting Indifference Curves

Consider indifference curves I and II. By definition, an individual is indifferent between consumption at points A and C on indifference curve I. Also by definition, he or she is indifferent between consumption at points A and B, which lies on the same IC (II). The assumption of transitivity (consistency) requires that the individual be indifferent between points B and C. However, point B represents more wine and more cotton than does combination C. Because more is always preferred to less (the nonsatisfaction assumption), it is impossible for the individual to be indifferent between points B and C. Thus, ICs cannot intersect.

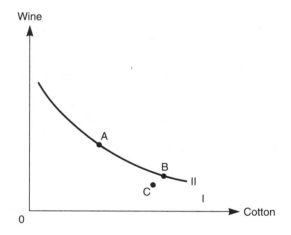

An entire set of ICs forms an indifference map. Higher ICs indicate a higher level of satisfaction; lower ICs show lower levels of satisfaction. Figure 3-5 (page 39) illustrates an indifference map. Although only three ICs are shown in this figure, an infinite number can be drawn.

---

* According to the transitivity (consistency) assumption, if the individual is indifferent between points A and C and is also indifferent between points A and B, then he or she must be indifferent between points B and C.

FIGURE 3-5
Indifference Map

An entire set of ICs forms an indifference map. Higher ICs indicate a higher level of satisfaction; lower ICs show lower levels of satisfaction. Although only three ICs are shown in this figure, an infinite number can be drawn.

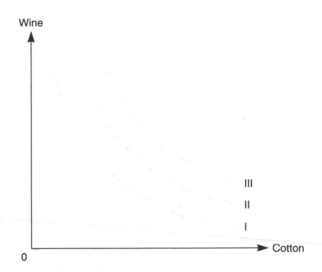

3.3 COMMUNITY INDIFFERENCE CURVES

A community indifference curve (CIC) is analogous to an individual indifference curve. A **community indifference curve** indicates different combinations of two commodities that give the same level of satisfaction to a community or nation. The major difference between an individual indifference curve and a community indifference curve is that the former portrays an individual's preferences, whereas the latter shows a nation's preferences.

Theoretically speaking, difficult questions could be raised about CICs because each particular set or map of CICs is based on a given income distribution. As a country enters international trade or enhances its existing level of trade, exporters benefit at the expense of the domestic (import-competing) producers. The rise in exports increases the income of exporters; however, the increase in imports depresses the prices of import-competing goods, leading to a decline in the income of domestic producers. This process disturbs the existing pattern of income distribution and leads to a new set of CICs that might intersect the old set. As we already know, this violates the assumption of nonsatisfaction which requires indifference curves to be nonintersecting.

Despite the aforementioned difficulties, economists continue to use CICs, albeit cautiously. One basis for their use is the "**compensation principle.**" According to this principle, we assume that the persons who could benefit from trade could fully compensate the losers and still retain some of their gains. As a result, the nation as a whole would be better off after trade. Alternatively, by making a number of other assumptions, we can again use CIC to reach conclusions about the effect of trade on a nation's welfare. For instance, we can assume that (a) the community's tastes can be represented by the tastes of one individual; (b) tastes are constant from period to period; and (c) the pattern of income distribution does not change.

COMMUNITY INDIFFERENCE CURVES AND INTERNATIONAL TRADE

n Chapter 2, we examined the production possibilities frontier (PPF), which depicts a country's production, or supply, conditions. In the previous section, we discussed CICs, which portray a country's tastes or preferences. In this section, we show how the interaction of supply and demand defines the autarky equilibrium that maximizes welfare for a nation. We then employ PPFs and CICs to restate the basis for and gains from trade under the increasing opportunity costs assumption.

3.4a Equilibrium in Autarky

In autarky (the absence of trade), a country's production and consumption coincide; it can consume only what it produces. Assuming that the nation would like to achieve the maximum social welfare, given its community indifference map, it tries to reach the highest possible CIC. Although achieving the highest CIC is what a nation would like to do, its choice is limited by the availability of resources and existing technology. These constraints are given by the nation's PPF. In other words, a nation's PPF shows what a nation can do. In autarky, given the constraint set by the PPF, a nation tries to reach the highest possible CIC. This occurs at a point where the highest attainable CIC is tangent to the nation's PPF.

Figure 3-6 shows the PPF and community indifference map for a hypothetical country that produces wine and cotton. In the absence of international trade, equilibrium is achieved at point B, where community indifference curve II is tangent to the nation's PPF. Any point below community indifference curve II, such as point A or C, does not yield the maximum satisfaction because the consumer can easily move along the existing PPF to reach a higher level of satisfaction on community indifference curve II. Any point outside the PPF, such as point D, puts the nation on a higher CIC. However, such points are not attainable with the existing resources and state of technology. Thus, point B represents the autarky equilibrium at which social welfare is maximized.

FIGURE 3-6
Autarky Equilibrium

In the absence of international trade, equilibrium is achieved at point B, where community indifference curve II is tangent to the nation's PPF. Any point below community indifference curve II, such as point A or C, does not yield the maximum satisfaction because the nation can easily move along the existing PPF to reach a higher level of satisfaction on curve II. Any point outside the PPF, such as point D, puts the nation on a higher community indifference curve. However, such points are unattainable with existing resources and state of technology. Thus, point B represents the autarky equilibrium at which social welfare is maximized.

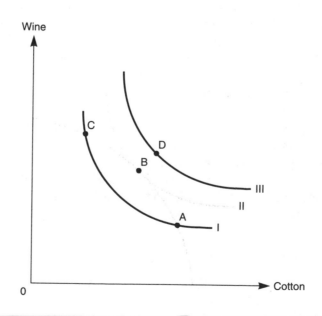

3.4b Basis for and Gains from Trade under the Increasing Costs Assumption

In the previous section, we discussed autarky equilibrium using the PPF and CIC curves. Now we employ these curves to restate the basis for and gains from international trade under the increasing costs assumption. Using our previous example of wine and cotton, assume that the autarky equilibria for Greece and France are given by points A and A', respectively, in Figure 3-7.

At point A, Greece maximizes its welfare by producing and consuming 25 gallons of wine and 20 bales of cotton. At this point, Greece's PPF is tangent to its community indifference curve (I). Similarly, France maximizes its welfare at point A', where it produces and consumes 15 gallons of wine and 35 bales of cotton. At this point, France's PPF is tangent to community indifference curve I'.

FIGURE 3-7
Basis for Trade under the Increasing Costs Assumption

At point A, Greece maximizes its welfare by producing and consuming 25 gallons of wine and 20 bales of cotton. At this point, Greece's PPF is tangent to its community indifference curve I. Similarly, France maximizes its welfare at point A', where it produces and consumes 15 gallons of wine and 35 bales of cotton. At this point, France's PPF is tangent to community indifference curve I'. The equilibrium relative commodity prices for Greece and France are given by the absolute value of the slope of the tangent at points A and A'. At point A, the equilibrium relative price of cotton in terms of wine (P_C/P_W) is 0.25 (1C = 0.25W) for Greece. At point A', France's relative price of cotton in terms of wine (PC/PW) is 4 (1C = 4W). Because the relative price of cotton is lower in Greece than in France, Greece has a comparative advantage in the production of cotton and France has a comparative advantage in the production of wine.

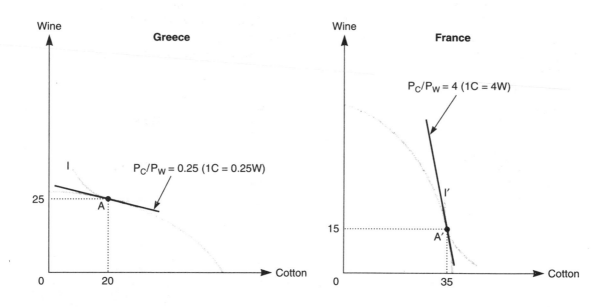

The equilibrium relative commodity prices for Greece and France are given by the absolute value of the slope of the tangent at points A and A', respectively. At point A, the equilibrium relative price of cotton in terms of wine (P_C/P_W) is 0.25 (1C = 0.25W) for Greece. At point A', France's relative price of cotton in terms of wine (P_C/P_W) is 4 (1C = 4W).

ecause in autarky relative commodity prices are different, the stage is set for international trade. Greece has a comparative advantage in the production of cotton and France has a comparative advantage in the production of wine. Thus, according to the theory of comparative advantage, Greece should specialize in the production and export of cotton in exchange for wine from France. Similarly, France should specialize in the production and export of wine in exchange for cotton from Greece. Assuming that there are no obstacles to trade, Figure 3-8 illustrates this process. Starting from the autarky equilibrium, point A, Greece specializes in the production of cotton by moving down its PPF. Similarly, starting from point A', France specializes in the production of wine by moving up its PPF. The process of specialization in production continues until the relative commodity prices, measured by the absolute value of the slope of PPF, becomes equal in both Greece and France. The common relative commodity price (international terms of trade [TOT]) should fall between pretrade prices of 0.25 and 4. In our example, assume that this common price is equal to 1 (1C = 1W). With these TOT in place, Greece moves its production point from A to B, where the common relative commodity price (P_C/P_W) line is tangent to the PPF. At point B, Greece produces 10 gallons of wine and 65 bales of cotton. To reach its highest possible indifference curve, Greece exchanges 30 bales of cotton for 30 gallons of wine (see trade triangle BCD), consuming at point C, where the P_C/P_W line is tangent to community indifference curve II. A comparison of points A (autarky point) and C shows that Greece gains 15 gallons of wine and 15 bales of cotton as a result of international trade with France.

FIGURE 3-8
Gains from Trade under the Increasing Costs Assumption

With trade, Greece moves from point A to point B in production. Then, to reach its highest possible indifference curve Greece exchanges 30 bales of cotton for 30 gallons of wine (see triangle BCD), consuming on point C, where P_C/P_W line is tangent to community indifference curve II. Thus, Greece gains 15 gallons of wine and 15 bales of cotton as a result of international trade with France (compare points A and C). Similarly, France moves from point A' to point B' in production. Then, to reach its highest possible indifference curve, France exchanges 30 gallons of wine for 30 bales of cotton (see triangle B' C' D'), consuming on point C', were P_C/P_W line is tangent to community indifference curve II'. Thus, France gains 15 gallons of wine and 15 bales of cotton as a result of international trade with Greece (compare points A' and C').

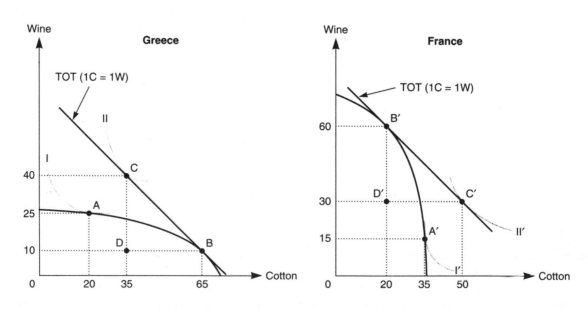

Similarly, France moves from producing at point A' to point B', producing 60 gallons of wine and 20 bales o cotton. To reach its highest possible indifference curve, France exchanges 30 gallons of wine for 30 bales of cotton (see trade triangle B'C'D'), consuming at point C' on community indifference curve II'. A comparison of points A' (autarky point) and C' shows that France gains 15 gallons of wine and 15 bales of cotton as a result of international trade with Greece. Table 3-1 summarizes these results.

TABLE 3-1
Gains from Trade under Increasing Costs Assumption

	Greece		France	
	Wine	Cotton	Wine	Cotton
Pretrade (autarky):				
Production	25	20	15	35
Consumption	25	20	15	35
Posttrade:				
Production	10	65	60	20
Consumption	40	35	30	50
Exports	—	30	30	—
Imports	30	—	—	30
Gains from specialization in production and trade	15	15	15	15

3.5 TRADE BASED ON TASTE DIFFERENTIALS

In our discussion of the basis of trade, we showed that the relative commodity price differentials, determined by the two nations' respective PPFs, set the stage for international trade. This leads to specialization in production and mutually advantageous trade for both nations.

Under increasing costs assumption, taste differentials or consumption preferences alone could give rise to mutually advantageous trade. Figure 3-9 illustrates this case. Using the example of France and Greece, we assume that the two nations' PPFs are identical. Given this assumption, a single curve can be used to represent the PPF of both countries. Greece's autarky position is shown at point A', where indifference curve I is tangent to the PPF. At this point, Greece is producing and consuming 80 gallons of wine and 20 bales of cotton. In the same manner, the France's autarky position is shown at point A', where indifference curve I' is tangent to the PPF. At this point, France is producing and consuming 20 gallons of wine and 80 bales of cotton. As Figure 3-9 indicates, the slope of the relative commodity price (P_C/P_W) line at point A is flatter than the slope of the P_C/P_W, line at point A'. This means that cotton is relatively cheaper in Greece than in France. In other words, Greece has a comparative advantage in the production of cotton and France has a comparative advantage in the production of wine.

With international trade, Greece specializes in the production of cotton by moving down the PPF and France specializes in the production of wine by moving up the PPF. The process of specialization continues until the relative commodity prices are equal for both nations. In Figure 3-9, this happens at point P, where $P_C/P_W = 1$. Given this production point for both nations, Greece exchanges 30 bales of cotton for 30 gallons of French wine (see triangle PBD) and reaches consumption point D on indifference curve II. A comparison of points A and D shows that Greece gains 10 gallons of wine and 10 bales of cotton as the result of trade. Similarly, France exchanges 30 gallons of wine for 30 bales of Greek cotton (see triangle P'B'D') and reaches consumption point D' on indifference curve II'. A comparison of points A' and D' indicates that France gains 10 gallons of wine and 10 bales of cotton from trade. Thus, both countries reach higher levels of satisfaction as indicated by their CICs. Table 3-2 summarizes these results.

FIGURE 3-9
Trade Based on Taste Differentials

Given the assumption of identical PPFs in both nations, a single curve is used to represent the PPF of both nations. In autarky, Greece produces and consumes at point A and France at point A'. Because P_C/P_W line at point A is flatter than the slope of the P_C/P_W at point A', Greece has a comparative advantage in the production of cotton and France has a comparative advantage in the production of wine. With international trade, Greece specializes in the production of cotton and produces at point P, whereas France specializes in the production of wine and produces at point P' which coincides with point P. By exchanging 30 bales of cotton for 30 gallons of wine with each other (see triangles PBD and P'B'D') Greece ends up consuming at point D, (gaining 10 gallons of wine and 10 bales of cotton from trade [compare points A and D]), whereas France ends up consuming at point D' (gaining 10 gallons of wine and 10 bales of cotton from trade [compares points A' and D']).

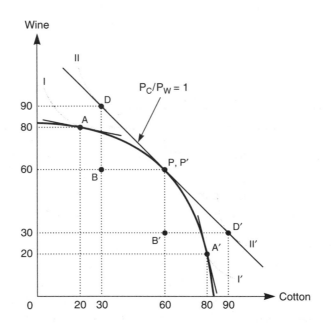

TABLE 3-2
Gains from Trade under Taste Differential Assumption

	Greece		France	
	Wine	**Cotton**	**Wine**	**Cotton**
Pretrade (autarky):				
Production	80	20	20	80
Consumption	80	20	20	80
Posttrade:				
Production	60	60	60	60
Consumption	90	30	30	90
Exports	—	30	30	—
Imports	30	—	—	30
Gains from specialization in production and trade	10	10	10	10

GLOBAL INSIGHTS CASE 3.1

Export and Import Price Indexes and Terms of Trade

Export and import price indexes can be used to calculate a nation's commodity terms of trade (TOT), allowing it to assess, on average, the amount of goods exported per unit imported (or the amount of goods imported per unit exported) in a given year. A comparison of the TOT between two different years reveals the relative improvement or deterioration in terms of trade of the nation.

Columns two and three of the table show the export and import price indexes of selected countries. The fourth column shows the ratio of export to import price indexes or the terms of trade, for these nations. With 1985 as a base year (equal to 100), the terms of trade for each country are calculated by dividing the export price index by the import price index and multiplying the result by 100. For example, the table shows that by 1992 Greece's export price index rose to 211.7, a 111.7-percent increase from its 1985 level. During the same period, Greece's import price index rose by 179.9 percent to 279.9 percent. Accordingly, Greece's terms of trade ([211.7/279.9] x 100 = 75.6) declined by 24.4 percent over the 1985—1992 period. This means that to buy a given quantity of imports, on average, Greece had to forego 24.4 percent more exports, or, for a given quantity of exports, Greece could acquire 24.4 percent fewer imports.

A comparison of countries listed in the table reveals that Japan ranks number one with regard to improvement in its terms of trade, experiencing a 38.8-percent rise. It is followed by Germany, Portugal, and Korea. The table also shows that Greece ranks first in deterioration in its terms of trade, followed by Poland and the United States.

Export and Import Price Indexes and Terms of Trade of Selected Countries, 1992 (1985 = 100)

Country	Export Price Index	Import Price Index	Terms of Trade
Japan	70.5	50.8	138.8
Germany	104.8	78.5	133.5
Greece	211.7	279.9	75.6
Korea	123.4	108.4	113.8
Poland*	6,991.9	7,241.9	96.5
Portugal**	132.3	110.0	120.3
United States	115.0	116.5	98.7

*1991 data.
**1992 data.

Source: International Monetary Fund, *International Financial Statistics* (Washington, DC: International Monetary Fund, May 1993).

3.6 OFFER CURVES

In Figure 3-8, we assumed that the equilibrium relative commodity price was established at 1 (1C = 1W). This TOT was determined by trial and error; that is, different prices were tried until a relative commodity price at which trade was balanced was reached. A more accurate way of handling this is to use a theoretical approach, that is, to use offer curves.

An **offer curve,** also referred to as a **reciprocal demand curve,** indicates the relationship between a nation's exports and imports at different relative commodity prices. Each point on an offer curve shows the maximum amount of export commodity a nation is willing to offer in exchange for a certain amount of import commodity at a given relative commodity price level. Alternatively, each point on an offer curve portrays the minimum amount of import commodity that a country will be willing to accept in return for a certain amount of export commodity at a given relative commodity price level.

A nation's offer curve can be derived from its PPF and its indifference map, as described in the next section.

3.6a Derivation of Offer Curves

In Figure 3-8, the equilibrium for each country (points C and C′) was set on the basis of a relative commodity price that was equal to 1. If the price changes, a new equilibrium is obtained. In other words, the posttrade equilibrium point depends on the relative commodity price at which the two nations trade. This provides a basis for the derivation of an offer curve which traces the posttrade equilibrium points at different relative commodity prices. Using our previous example of Greece and France, we will demonstrate how offer curves are derived.

In panel (a) of Figure 3-10, assume that before trade Greece is in equilibrium at point A on indifference curve I. If trade takes place at $P_C/P_W = 1$, Greece moves to point B on its PPF. It then exchanges 30 bales of cotton for 30 gallons of wine, ending up at point G on indifference curve III (also shown as point G in panel [b]). If trade takes place at $P_C/P_W = 0.5$, Greece moves to point D on its PPF. It then exchanges 20 bales of cotton for 10 gallons of wine, ending up at point E on indifference curve II (also shown as point E in panel [b]). If we connect the origin with points G and E and other points derived in the same manner, we obtain Greece's offer curve as illustrated in panel (b). Note that Greece's offer curve is convex toward the x-axis, measuring the export commodity (cotton). This shows that in order to induce Greece to export more cotton, the relative commodity price must rise. There are two explanations for this phenomenon. First, as more of the import commodity (wine) becomes available, it becomes increasingly less desirable. Second, as Greece increases the production of cotton, its opportunity cost rises, making cotton relatively more expensive. As a result, Greece will demand more gallons of wine per bale of cotton traded.

In panel (a) of Figure 3-11, page 48, assume that before trade France is in equilibrium at point A′. If trade takes place at $P_C/P_W = 1$, France moves to point B′ on its PPF. It exchanges 30 gallons of wine for 30 bales of cotton, ending up at point G′, on indifference curve III′ (also shown as point G′ in panel [b]). If trade takes place at PC/PW = 2, France moves to point D′ on its PPF. It then exchanges 20 gallons of wine for 10 bales of cotton, ending up at point E′ on indifference curve II′ (also shown as point E′ in panel [b]). If we connect the origin with points G′ and E′ and other points derived in the same manner, we obtain France's offer curve, as illustrated in panel (b). Note that France's offer curve is convex toward the y-axis, which measures the export commodity (wine). This shows that to induce France to export more wine, the relative commodity price must fall. The explanations for this phenomenon are similar to those for the Greek situation. First, as more of the import commodity (cotton) becomes available, it becomes increasingly less desirable. Second, as France increases the production of wine, its opportunity cost rises, making wine relatively more expensive. As a result, France will demand more bales of cotton per gallon of wine traded.

3.6b Equilibrium Relative Commodity Price with Offer Curves

To find the equilibrium relative commodity price for international trade, we put Greece's offer curve (panel b of Figure 3-10) and France's offer curve (panel b of Figure 3-11) together in Figure 3-12, page 49. Point G of Figure 3-10 and point G′ of Figure 3-11 now join to define equilibrium at $P_C/P_W = 1$. At this point, Greece offers 30 bales of cotton for 30 gallons of wine and France offers 30 gallons of wine for 30 bales of cotton. Thus, trade is in equilibrium.

FIGURE 3-10
Offer Curve for Greece

In panel (a), before trade, Greece is in equilibrium at point A on indifference curve I. If trade takes place at $P_C/P_W = 1$, Greece moves to point B on its PPF. It then exchanges 30 bales of cotton for 30 gallons of wine, ending up at point G on indifference III (also shown as point G in panel [b]). If trade takes place $P_C/P_W = 0.5$, Greece moves to point D on its PPF. It then exchanges 20 bales of cotton for 10 gallons of wine, ending up at point E on indifference curve II (also shown as point E in panel [b]). If we connect the origin with point G and E and other points derived in the same manner, we obtain Greece's offer curve. Each point on this curve shows the minimum amount of wine that Greece will be willing to accept in return for a certain amount of cotton at various relative commodity prices.

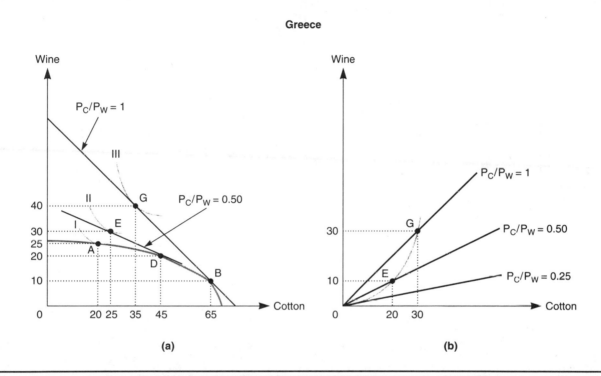

If we pick any other point we would see that trade is not in equilibrium. For example, at $P_C/P_W = 0.5$, Greece would like to export 20 bales of cotton (see point E in Figure 3-12), whereas France's demand for import is 60 bales of cotton (shown by point F, where the price line crosses the extended offer curve). France's excess demand for cotton leads to an increase in the relative commodity price. This higher price induces Greece to produce more cotton and causes France to reduce its import demand for cotton. Thus, Greece moves up its offer curve, while France moves down its offer curve. This process continues until the supply of export and demand for import are equalized at point G (G′), where $P_C/P_W = 1$.

3.7 MEASUREMENT OF TERMS OF TRADE

In Chapter 2 we defined terms of trade as the relative commodity price at which two commodities are traded in the international market. Alternatively, TOT can be defined as the ratio of the price a country's export goods to the price of its import goods. There are four different measures of TOT: commodity, or net barter terms of trade; income terms of trade; single factoral terms of trade; and double factoral terms of trade.

FIGURE 3-11
Offer Curve for France

In panel (a), before trade, France is in equilibrium at point A′ on indifference curve I′. If trade takes place at $P_C/P_W = 1$, France moves to point B′ on its PPF. It then exchanges 30 gallons of wine for 30 bales of cotton, ending up at point G′ on indifference III′ (also shown as point G′ in panel [b]). If trade takes place at $P_C/P_W = 2$, France moves to point D′ on its PPF. It then exchanges 20 gallons of wine for 10 bales of cotton, ending up at point E′ on indifference curve II′ (also shown as point E′ in panel [b]). If we connect the origin with points G′ and E′ and other points derived in the same manner, we obtain France's offer curve, shown in panel (b). Each point on this curve shows the minimum amount of cotton France will be willing to accept in return for a certain amount of wine at various relative commodity prices.

France

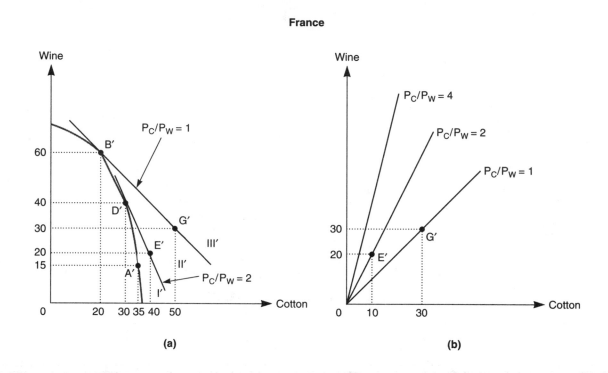

(a)   (b)

3.7a Commodity Terms of Trade

Commodity, or **net barter terms of trade** (C_{TOT}) are the most frequently used measure of TOT. This ratio portrays the relationship between the prices a nation pays for its imports and the prices it receives for its exports. Commodity terms of trade are calculated by dividing a nation's export price index (P_X) by its import price index (P_M). This ratio is usually multiplied by 100 to express the terms of trade in percentages:

$$C_{TOT} = (P_X/P_M)100$$

For example, if we define 1970 as the base year ($C_{TOT} = 100$) and learn that by the end of 1990 a country's P_X rose from 100 to 115 (a 15-percent increase) and its P_M declined from 100 to 95 (a 5-percent decrease), then we have

$$C_{TOT} = (115/95)100 = 121.05$$

Given these results, we conclude that during the period from 1970 to 1990 the country's C_{TOT} improved. More specifically, export prices rose by about 21 percent relative to import prices.

From this peak value, oil prices declined sharply in subsequent years, reaching $12 per barrel in 1986. This deteriorated the TOT of oil-producing nations. A tremendous increase in oil prices in 1987 caused significant improvements in the TOT; however, oil prices declined in 1988, leading to a negative annual percentage change in the C_{TOT}.

3.7b Income Terms of Trade

Income terms of trade (I_{TOT}) indicate a country's export-generated capability to import:

$$I_{TOT} = (P_X/P_M)Q_X,$$

where Q_X is the export volume index.

Using our previous example, if Q_X declined from 100 in 1970 to 90 in 1990, then we would have

$$I_{TOT} = (115/95)90 = 108.94$$

Given these results, we would conclude that during the period from 1970 to 1990 the country's I_{TOT} improved, despite the fact that the volume of its exports declined. More specifically, the nation's capability to import, based on income generated by its exports, increased by 8.94 percent.

The change in I_{TOT} is an especially useful measure for developing countries because these countries depend to a large degree on the importation of capital goods for their development process.

GLOBAL INSIGHTS CASE 3.3

Growth in Advanced Nations' Terms of Trade

The table shows the rate of growth in terms of trade for advanced nations from 1975 to 1992. As the last row of this table indicates, taken as a whole, advanced nations experienced a negative growth rate during the 1975—1984 period. This negative growth is partially explained by the two oil crises that occurred in 1973—1974 and 1979—1980. Following 1985, advanced nations' terms of trade remained positive, except during 1989 and 1990.

It is interesting to note that in 1992, Japan ranked first in terms of trade growth with a rate of 8.3 percent. This position was followed by Germany (3.1 percent) and Italy (1.2 percent).

Terms of Trade of Leading Developed Nations (Annual Percentage Change)

Country	1975—1984 (average)	1985	1986	1987	1988	1989	1990	1991	1992
United States	0.5	0.6	-1.6	-3.8	1.2	-0.7	-2.5	2.1	0.8
Japan	-2.9	4.4	34.6	0.7	3.1	-4.4	-6.1	9.0	8.3
Germany	-1.3	1.3	15.1	3.7	—	-2.7	1.4	-0.7	3.1
France	0.2	2.9	11.8	0.7	0.5	-0.9	-0.1	-0.1	0.4
Italy	-0.4	0.4	16.6	2.8	0.8	-1.2	2.8	3.4	1.2
Great Britain	1.6	0.9	-5.1	1.9	0.7	3.0	0.3	3.0	0.4
Canada	0.5	-1.2	-2.4	3.2	1.8	2.0	-2.1	-1.5	0.2
Other advanced nations	0.3	0.3	4.4	2.1	1.6	1.0	-0.3	-0.5	0.2
All advanced nations	-0.1	1.1	8.7	1.5	1.3	-0.6	-0.7	1.6	1.8

Source: International Monetary Fund, *World Economic Outlook* (Washington, DC: International Monetary Fund, May 1993), 155.

3.7c Single Factoral Terms of Trade

Single factoral terms of trade (S_{TOT}) show the amount of imports a country acquires for each unit of domestic factors of production contained in its exports:

$$S_{TOT} = (P_X/P_M)E_X,$$

where E_X is the export productivity index (that is, the productivity index of the country's export sector).

Given our previous example, if the country's export productivity declined from 100 to 85, then we would have

$$S_{TOT} = (115/95)85 = 102.89$$

On the basis of these results, we would conclude that the nation's S_{TOT} improved during this period. More specifically, in 1990, the country received 2.89 percent more imports for each unit of domestic factors of production contained in its exports.

Like I_{TOT}, S_{TOT} is important for developing countries because productivity growth plays an important role in the process of economic development.

3.7d Double Factoral Terms of Trade

Double factoral terms of trade (D_{TOT}) is defined as the S_{TOT} divided by an import productivity index, that is, the index of productivity in the trading partners' export industries. It is written as:

$$D_{TOT} = (P_X/P_M) (E_X/E_M)100,$$

where E_M is the import productivity index.

Double factoral terms of trade indicate how many units of foreign factors of production contained in a country's imports are exchanged per unit of domestic factors of production contained in its exports.

Returning to our previous example, if E_M fell from 100 in 1970 to 90 in 1990, then we would have

$$D_{TOT} = (115/95) (85/90)100 = 114.32$$

This means that D_{TOT} improved during the 1970—1990 period. More specifically, there was a 14.32-percent rise in the number of units of foreign factors of production contained in the country's imports exchanged per unit of domestic factors of production contained in its exports. This means that the "exchange of factors" between trading partners became more advantageous to the home country.

3.8 SUMMARY

1. An indifference curve is the locus of points representing combinations of two goods that give the same level of satisfaction to the individual consumer.
2. Indifference curves have the following properties: (a) they are negatively sloped; that is, they slope downward to the right; (b) they are convex to the origin; and (c) they do not intersect.
3. The negative slope of an indifference curve for two goods is based on the assumption of nonsatisfaction.
4. Indifference curves are convex to the origin, displaying the law of diminishing marginal rate of substitution.
5. The marginal rate of substitution (MRS) is the rate at which commodities are substituted for each other by an individual while keeping the level of satisfaction unchanged. It is equal to the absolute value of the slope of the indifference curve.
6. Indifference curves do not intersect due to the transitivity (consistency) assumption.

7. A community indifference curve indicates different combinations of two commodities that give the same level of satisfaction to a community or nation.

8. In the absence of trade (autarky), a country's production and consumption coincide.

9. Under increasing costs assumption, taste differentials or consumption preferences alone could give rise to mutually advantageous trade.

10. An offer curve, also referred to as a reciprocal demand curve, indicates the relationship between a nation's exports and imports at different relative commodity prices.

11. Terms of trade (TOT) can be defined as the ratio of the price of a country's export goods to the price of its import goods.

12. There are four different measurements of terms of trade: commodity, or net barter terms of trade; income terms of trade; single factoral terms of trade; and double factoral terms of trade.

13. Commodity, or net barter terms of trade (C_{TOT}) are the most frequently used measure of terms of trade. This ratio portrays the relationship between the prices a nation pays for its imports and the prices it receives for its exports.

14. Income terms of trade (I_{TOT}) indicate a country's export-generated capability to import.

15. Single factoral terms of trade (S_{TOT}) show the amount of imports a country acquires for each unit of domestic factors of production contained in its exports.

16. Double factoral terms of trade (D_{TOT}) indicate how many units of foreign factors of production contained in a country's imports are exchanged per unit of domestic factors of production contained in its exports.

Review Questions

1. What is an indifference curve? What are the properties of indifference curves?

2. Why does an indifference curve slope downward? What does its slope measure? Why is this curve convex to the origin?

3. Differentiate between an individual indifference curve and a community indifference curve.

4. Theoretically speaking, what problems occur in the utilization of community indifference curves? Given these problems, on what basis do economists continue using these curves?

5. What is an offer curve? How is an offer curve derived? How do offer curves define the equilibrium relative commodity price for trading nations?

6. Differentiate between marginal rate of substitution and marginal rate of transformation.

7. What are terms of trade (TOT)? What are different measures of TOT? Which one of these measurements is most frequently used?

Problems

1. Community indifference curves are extensions of individual indifference curves. Just like individual indifference curves, community indifference curves are subject to three restrictive assumptions. Given these restrictions, they could be used without reservation.

    Do you agree with this statement? Discuss, elaborating on the three restrictive assumptions.

2. Select a country; go to your library and gather the data required to calculate the following TOT: commodity, income, single factoral, and double factoral. Given your data, calculate these terms of trade and interpret your results.

3. A country's offer curves provide us with basically the same information as its import demand or export supply curve. They add nothing to what is already contained in PPF and CIC. Thus, the offer curve is not a useful device in international trade theory.

    Do you agree with this statement? Explain.

4. Assume nation A's offer curve has a greater curvature than that of its trading partner, nation B.
    (a) Graphically demonstrate these offer curves.
    (b) Do both nations benefit equally from trade? Explain.
5. Draw five community indifference curves. Make the bottom three indifference curves nonintersecting, and the top two indifference curves intersecting.
    (a) Elaborate on the slopes of these indifference curves. What does the slope of each indifference curve measure? Why are they convex to the origin?
    (b) Prove that the top two indifference curves are invalid by definition.
6. Countries A and B produce two commodities, X and Y. Country A has a comparative advantage in the production of X; country B has a comparative advantage in the production of Y.
    (a) Using production possibilities frontiers and community indifference curves, graphically demonstrate the pretrade position of each country.
    (b) If the slope of the relative commodity price line is the same in both countries would there be a basis for mutually beneficial trade between the two countries? Explain.
7. If two nations have identical PPFs, there would be no basis for mutually beneficial trade between them.
    Do you agree with the above statement? Explain.
8. Suppose country A and country B have identical PPFs and are operating under increasing cost conditions.
    (a) Graphically demonstrate the PPFs for these countries.
    (b) Assuming that tastes and preferences are similar in these countries, graphically demonstrate that trade is not advantageous to both countries.
    (c) Assuming that tastes and preferences are not similar in these countries, graphically demonstrate that trade is advantageous to both countries.
9. Assume the world is made up of two countries, A and B. Suppose both of these countries produce two commodities, X and Y. For each country, draw a set of axes, measuring X on the horizontal axis and Y on the vertical axis. On country A's axes, sketch a community indifference curve that is tangent to a concave PPF near the horizontal axis. On country B's axes, sketch a community indifference curve that is tangent to the concave production possibilities frontier near the vertical axis. Sketch the relative commodity price line, showing the autarky equilibrium in each country.
    (a) In which commodity does each nation have a comparative advantage?
    (b) What happens if the relative commodity price line has the same slope in both countries?

Suggested Readings

Bhagwati, J. N. "The Pure Theory of International Trade." *Economic Journal* 74 (March 1964): 1-84.
Haberler, G. *The Theory of International Trade*. London: W. Hodge and Co., 1936, ch. 11.
Krauss, M. B. *A Geometric Approach to International Trade*. New York: Halsted Wiley, 1979.
Leontief, Wassily W. "The Use of Indifference Curves in the Analysis of Foreign Trade." *Quarterly Journal of Economics* 47 (May 1933).
Lerner, A. P. "The Diagrammatic Representation of Demand Conditions in International Trade." *Economica* (1934); reprinted in Lerner, A. P. *Essays in Economic Analysis*. London: Macmillan, 1953.
Meade, J. E. *A Geometry of International Trade*. London: George Allen and Unwin, 1952, chs. 1-4.
———— *Trade and Welfare*. London: Oxford University Press, 1955.
Meier, G. *The International Economics of Development*. New York: Harper and Row, 1968, ch. 3.
Samuelson, Paul A. "Social Indifference Curves." *Quarterly Journal of Economics* 70 (February 1956): 584-585.
Viner, J. *Studies in the Theory of International Trade*. New York: Harper and Brothers, 1937, ch. 9.

Chapter 4

MODERN THEORIES OF INTERNATIONAL TRADE: APPLICATIONS AND NEW APPROACHES

4.1 INTRODUCTION

In our discussion of international trade theories so far, we have seen that the relative price differential between two nations gives rise to international trade. In this chapter, we extend our analysis by first explaining the Heckscher-Ohlin theory. Second, we examine the impact of international trade on factor payments and income distribution of the trading parties. Third, we present the major empirical studies that tested this theory. Finally, we analyze transportation costs and evaluate their impact on free international trade.

4.2 HECKSCHER-OHLIN THEORY

Ricardo's theory of comparative advantage assumes that domestic differences in natural or acquired endowment give rise to different factor productivities that provide the basis for trade among nations. This implies that the primary basis for trade is differences in factor productivity.[*]

Eli Heckscher and Bertil Ohlin, two Swedish economists, argued that international differentials in supply of factors of production explain the direction of international trade. They explained that supply includes not only factor productivities but factor endowments as well.[**] Their ideas gave rise to the development of a theory that considers factor endowment as the primary cause of international trade.

According to this theory, price differentials among nations are related to two factors:

1. Differences in relative endowments of the factors of production that exist among countries
2. Differences in the intensity of factor usage in the production of different commodities

Given these conditions, the Heckscher-Ohlin (H-O) theory states that each country should export those commodities that use its abundant factor most intensively and import goods that use its scarce factor most intensively.[***] This means, for example, that countries with an abundance of labor, such as India or Hong Kong, should export commodities such as cloth, which require labor-intensive technology. On the other hand, a capital-abundant country like the United States should export commodities such as airplanes and electronic computers, which require capital-intensive technology.

---

[*] The term *factor productivity* refers to the productivity of the factors of production. For example, labor productivity is measured as output per day in Table 2.1.

[**] The term *factor endowment* refers to the relative abundance of factors of production in a country. For example, some countries have more capital relative to labor (they are capital abundant); other countries have more labor relative to capital (they are labor abundant).

[***] The term *factor* here refers to the factors of production, for example, capital and labor. A factor of production can be abundant (cheap) or scarce (expensive).

4.2a Assumptions and Implications of the Heckscher-Ohlin Theory

Like all economic theories, the H-O theory is based on a number of simplifying assumptions. The theory assumes the following:

1. There are two countries using two factors of production, capital and labor, to produce two goods.
2. Identical production functions exist in both countries.
3. Production functions in both countries display constant return to scale.
4. One of the commodities is capital intensive at all input prices; the other is labor intensive.
5. Perfect competition in both commodities and factor markets, as well as full employment of resources exists in both nations.
6. Both nations have identical tastes.
7. There are no transportation or similar costs and no barriers to free international trade.
8. Perfect factor mobility exists within each nation but not between nations.
9. Neither country has complete specialization in production.

The meaning of assumption 1 is clear. It allows us to simplify the presentation of the theory in a two-dimensional graph.

Assumption 2 means that input-output relationships are the same in both countries. In other words, if factor prices were the same in both countries, producers in both nations employ precisely the same amount of capital and labor in the production of each unit of a given good.

Assumption 3 means that doubling all factor inputs (capital and labor) used in the production of a commodity will result in doubling the output of that commodity for both nations.

Assumption 4 means that, given two commodities, one commodity requires relatively more capital to produce than the other commodity in both nations. In other words, the capital/labor (K/L) ratio is relatively higher for one commodity than for the other in both nations. For example, the K/L ratio is relatively higher in the production of steel than in the production of cloth in both countries.

Assumption 5 implies that for both nations: (a) Sellers and buyers of the two goods are too small to have any impact on the prices of these goods; (b) sellers and buyers of factors of production are too small to have any impact on their prices: (c) in the long run, the prices of the two goods are equal to the cost of their production; and (d) sellers and buyers of the goods and factors of production have perfect knowledge of their prices.

Assumption 6 implies that demand preferences, as revealed by the shape and location of community indifference curves, are identical in both countries. As a result, when relative commodity prices are equal in the two countries, both consume the two goods in the same proportion.

Assumption 7 implies that, with free international trade, specialization in production will continue until prices are equal in both nations. In the absence of this assumption, specialization in production will continue until the price differential between the two nations is equal to the costs of transportation and the tariff on each unit of the good traded.

Assumption 8 implies that factors of production move within the country from industries or areas with lower payments to those with higher payments. This movement will continue until the payments to the same factors of production are equal within the nation (in other words, until payments to the same type of capital and labor are the same in all industries and regions of the country). However, factors of production are not mobile between nations. As a result, in the absence of international trade, factor payment differentials will continue to exist between the two nations.

Assumption 9 means that, even with international trade, both countries still continue to produce both goods.

4.2b Graphical Illustration of the Heckscher-Ohlin Theory

Given the assumptions of the H-O model, suppose that in Figure 4-1: steel (S) and cloth (C) are produced in both England and India; capital and labor are the only two factors of production; and England is the capital-abundant country, and India is the labor-abundant country. Panel (a) shows the production possibilities frontiers (PPFs) of the two nations before trade. England's PPF is skewed along the horizontal axis because steel is the capital-intensive commodity and England is the capital-abundant nation. Similarly, India's PPF is skewed along the vertical axis because cloth is the labor-intensive commodity and India is the labor-abundant country. Given the assumption of identical tastes in both nations, they share the same indifference map. The pretrade positions of England and India are shown at points A and A′, respectively. At these points their common indifference curve I is tangent to their respective PPFs. As the slopes of the tangencies at these points show, steel is relatively cheaper in England and cloth is relatively cheaper in India. Thus, England has a comparative advantage in the production of steel, whereas India has a comparative advantage in the production of cloth.

FIGURE 4-1
Heckscher-Ohlin Model

The pretrade positions of England and India are shown at points A and A′, respectively. Given the assumptions of equal tastes, at these points their common community indifference curve I is tangent to their respective PPFs. As the slopes of tangencies at these points show, steel is relatively cheaper in England and cloth is relatively cheaper in India. Thus, England has a comparative advantage in the production of steel, whereas India has a comparative advantage in the production of cloth. With international trade (see panel b) England produces at point F and by exchanging 15 pounds of steel for 20 yards of cloth (see trade triangle FDE) reaches point E in consumption. India produces at point F′ and by exchanging 20 yards of cloth for 15 pounds of steel (see triangle F′D′E′) reaches point E′, which is the same as point E. Because point E (E′) is located on community indifference curve II, both nations have reached a higher level of satisfaction relative to their pretrade positions on community indifference curve I.

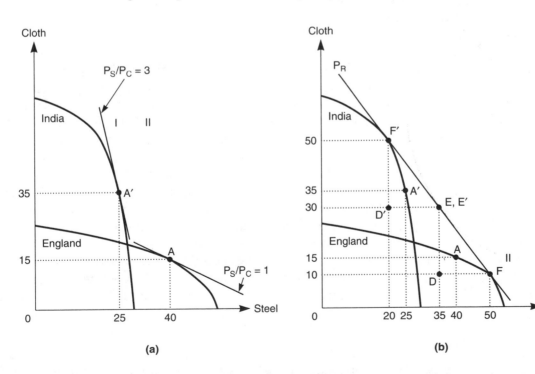

(a)   (b)

With free international trade possible, England specializes in the production of steel and India specializes in the production of cloth. Panel (b) shows that specialization in production proceeds until England reaches point F and India reaches point F′, where each country's PPF is tangent to the common relative price ratio (P_R). England will then export 15 pounds of steel in exchange for 20 yards of cloth (see triangle FDE) and consumes at point E. Similarly, India will export 20 yards of cloth in return for 15 pounds of steel (see triangle F′D′E′) and consumes at point E′, which is the same as point E. Thus, England's export of steel is equal to India's import of steel. Similarly, India's export of cloth is equal to England's import of cloth. If the price of steel relative to cloth (P_S/P_C) is greater than P_R, then England wants to export more steel than India wants to import at this relatively high price. As a result, P_S/P_C declines to P_R. Similarly, if P_S/P_C is less than P_R, then England wants to export less steel than India wants to import. As a result, P_S/P_C rises to P_R. This movement of P_S/P_C toward P_R can also be explained in terms of cloth. Because point E (E′) is located on community indifference curve II, both nations have achieved a higher level of satisfaction relative to their pretrade positions on community indifference curve I.

4.3 FACTOR-PRICE EQUALIZATION THEOREM AND INCOME DISTRIBUTION

The factor-price equalization theorem is deduced from the H-O theory. In other words, it is a proposition that follows directly from the H-O theory and holds true only if the H-O theory is maintained. In this section, we present the factor-price equalization theorem and study the related issue of international trade's impact on the distribution of income for each of the trading partners.

4.3a Factor-Price Equalization Theorem

The **factor-price equalization theorem** was proved by the 1976 Nobel prize winner in economics, Paul Samuelson. As a result, it is sometimes referred to as the Heckscher-Ohlin-Samuelson (H-O-S) theorem. According to this, free international trade leads to equalization of not only goods prices but also factor prices.[*] In this manner, international trade is a substitute for international factor mobility.

With free international trade in place, each country's output expands in its comparative-advantage industry. In other words, each country increases the production of the commodity that uses its abundant (cheap) factor most intensively. This causes the demand for the abundant factor to rise and, hence, its price to increase. As the demand for the abundant factor increases, the scarce (expensive) factor will be released from the comparative disadvantage industry. Producers will not hire this factor until its price declines. Because this process takes place simultaneously in both countries, the price of the abundant factor increases and the price of the scarce factor decreases in each nation. As a result, free international trade leads to equalization of relative factor prices in both nations.

Returning to our previous example of England and India, England's demand for cheap Indian cloth leads to an increased demand for India's abundant factor, labor. This causes the price of labor (wage rate) to rise in India. As England's production of cloth decreases, its demand for labor declines. This leads to a fall in the price of labor. This process continues until the wage rates are the same in both countries. Similarly, India's demand for inexpensive English steel leads to an increased demand for capital in England. This causes the price of capital (interest rate) to rise in England. As India's production of steel decreases, its demand for capital declines. This leads to a fall in the price of capital. This process continues until interest rates are the same in both nations.

Although the implication of factor-price equalization is simple and appealing, factor-price differentials persist in the real world. In general, hourly wages in advanced countries, such as the United States, Canada, England, France, Germany, and Japan, are higher than in developing countries, such as Mexico, Greece, Taiwan, and Korea.[**]

---

[*] The idea that free international trade leads to equalization of factor prices was first suggested by Heckscher. Ohlin, however, believed that there would only be a tendency toward factor-price equalization. The proof of this theory was left to Samuelson, "International Trade and Equalization of Factor Prices," *Economic Journal* 58 (1949), 165-184. After Samuelson's article was published he was informed that Abba Lerner, an economist, had already written a paper proving the theory when he was a student in England in 1933.

[**] *Developing countries* were defined in Chapter 1 and are explained further in Chapter 15.

Why has free international trade not led to an equalization of returns on factors of production in accordance with the H-O-S theory? The reasons are as follows:

1. Many of the H-O-S theory's simplifying assumptions do not hold in reality. For example, countries do not employ the same technologies. As a result, a nation with superior technology might end up with both a higher wage rate and a higher interest rate than a country that employs inferior technology.
2. The presence of transportation costs and barriers to free international trade may prevent product prices from becoming equal in different countries.
3. Perfect competition and constant returns to scale are not prevalent in many industries. The existence of such imperfections in the market may inhibit the degree to which commodity prices and factor prices are equalized in different nations.

Given these conditions, the more appropriate question is whether international trade has mitigated, rather than eliminated, the international factor-price differentials. Although it is difficult to give a clear-cut answer to this question due to the many other variables that affect factor prices, indications are that international trade has helped to reduce factor-price differentials between different nations. For example, in the United States, the competition from the Japanese automobile manufacturers has forced the United Auto Workers (UAW) union to accept a wage cut. This has contributed to the decline in the wage rate in the U.S. auto industry, bringing it closer to the lower wage rate in the Japanese auto industry. In other words, the United States' trade with Japan has mitigated the wage differentials between the two countries.

4.3b Income Distribution Effects of International Trade

In the previous section, we analyzed the impact of international trade on factor-price differentials between trading partners. In this section, we examine the effect of trade on income distribution.

From our discussion of the H-O-S theory we know that international trade leads to an increase in the demand for a country's abundant (cheap) factor of production and a decrease in the demand for its scarce (expensive) factor of production. This causes the price of the abundant factor to increase and the price of the scarce factor to decrease. Because the prices of factors of production determine factor incomes, international trade causes the income of the abundant factor to rise at the expense of the scarce factor. In our previous example of England and India, the price of labor fell and the price of capital rose in England. As a result, the incomes of the owners of capital rose at the expense of labor. The reverse is true for India; the wage rate increased and the interest rate decreased. As a result, the income of labor rose at the expense of the owners of capital.

Because advanced countries are capital abundant, international trade serves to increase the income of owners of capital and decrease the income of labor. On the other hand, since developing nations are labor abundant, international trade tends to increase the income of labor and decrease the income of the owners of capital. As we explain in Chapter 7, this is one of the arguments used by labor unions in advanced countries to support trade restrictions. However, such restrictions seem to be counterproductive because the income loss that accrues to labor is less than the gain acquired by capital. If a government is worried about the income distribution effects of trade, the appropriate action is a redistribution of income rather than trade restrictions. An appropriate redistribution policy could be to tax owners of capital and subsidize workers, thus mitigating the undesirable impact of international trade on income distribution. We examine the impact of trade restrictions in more detail in our discussion of tariff and nontariff barriers to trade in Chapters 5 and 6.

GLOBAL INSIGHTS CASE 4.1

Global Resource Endowments and Trade Patterns

The relative abundance of factors of production in a nation determines its role as an importer or exporter in the global market. Table A shows six leading advanced nations' resource endowments as percentages of the world's total resources in 1980. The United States, for example, has 33.6 percent of physical capital, 50.7 percent of research and development scientists, 29.3 percent of arable land, 27.7 percent of skilled labor, 19.1 percent of semiskilled labor, and 0.19 percent of unskilled labor. These amount to 28.6 percent of all resources combined. As shown, the United States has a greater relative share of world resources in physical capital, research and development scientists, and arable land than any other country. Given this data, according to the Heckscher-Ohlin theory, the United States should export capital- and technology-intensive products, as well as agricultural products.

Table B shows export-import ratios for the same nations. An export-import ratio greater than one indicates that the nation is a net exporter of a specific product. On the other hand, an export-import ratio less than one means that the nation is a net importer of that product. As these data indicate, the United States is a net exporter of technology-intensive products and services, a pattern that reflects U.S. technological expertise and past accumulation of physical capital.* Although the data are from 1979, circumstances are not very different today and still hold true for the United States. These results are in accord with the Heckscher-Ohlin theory.

TABLE A
Relative Resource Endowments of Leading Developed Nations*
(As a Percentage of World Total)

Country	Physical Capital	R & D Scientists	Arable Land	Skilled Labor	Semi-Skilled Labor	Unskilled Labor	All Resources (1982 GDP)
United States	33.6	50.7	29.3	27.7	19.1	0.19	28.6
Great Britain	4.5	8.5	1.0	5.1	4.9	0.09	5.1
Canada	3.9	1.8	6.1	2.9	2.1	0.03	2.6
France	7.5	6.0	2.6	6.0	3.9	0.06	6.0
Japan	15.5	23.0	0.8	8.7	11.5	0.25	11.2
West Germany	7.7	10.0	1.1	6.9	5.5	0.08	7.2

*Shares are computed from a group of 34 nations that account for more than 85 percent of GDP among market economies.

Source: John Mutti and Peter Morici, *Changing Patterns of U.S. Industrial Activity and Comparative Advantage* (Washington, DC:\E National Planning Association, 1983), 8; World Bank, *World Development Report 1984* (New York: Oxford University Press, 1984), 222-223.

Global Insights Case 4.1 Continued

TABLE B
Export/Import Ratios of Leading Advanced Nations

Country	Product Technology-intensive	Labor-intensive	Services	Standardized	Primary
United States	1.52	0.38	1.47	0.39	0.55
Great Britain	1.39	0.71	1.19	0.76	0.81
Canada	0.77	0.20	0.50	1.38	2.21
France	1.38	0.86	1.32	1.03	0.52
Japan	5.67	1.04	0.73	1.09	0.44
West Germany	2.40	0.59	0.80	0.84	0.29

Source: John Mutti and Peter Morici, *Changing Patterns of U.S. Industrial Activity and Comparative Advantage* (Washington, DC: National Planning Association, 1983), Dominick Salvatore, International Economics 4th ed. (New York: MacMillan, 1993), 121; P. Morici, *Meeting the Competitive Challenge: Canada and the United States* (Washington, DC: Canadian-American Committee, 1988), 49.

*In spite of its comparative advantage in agriculture, the United States is a net importer of other primary products, especially petroleum.

4.4 EMPIRICAL STUDIES OF THE HECKSCHER-OHLIN THEORY

Empirical studies are undertaken to test the validity of a theory. If a theory is contradicted by empirical evidence, it must be rejected and an alternative theory devised. In this section, we study some of the major empirical studies that have attempted to test the H-O theory. First, we elaborate on the work of Wassily Leontief, who used the United States as a case study. Second, we present other empirical studies that have tried to assess H-O theory's validity for other countries.

4.4a Leontief Paradox

In 1953, Wassily Leontief made the first major attempt to empirically examine the H-O theory. Using an input-output table with data for 1947, he analyzed the capital-to-labor ratio for some 200 export industries and import-competing industries in the United States.* He found that the capital-to-labor ratio for U.S. export industries was lower than that for U.S. import-competing industries. In other words, his results suggested that the United States exported goods that were relatively labor intensive and imported those that were relatively capital intensive. Given that the United States was considered to be a capital-abundant, labor-scarce country at the time of the study, Leontief's results seemed to contradict the H-O theory (which predicted that a capital-abundant country exports relatively capital-intensive goods). To further examine the H-O theory, Leontief did another study using 1951 data and again found that U.S. exports were relatively less capital intensive than U.S. imports. To explain the paradox, Leontief argued that the United States was about three times more efficient than other countries. If we multiply the U.S. labor supply by three and compare this figure to the availability of the nation's capital, the United States could be considered a labor-abundant nation. Thus, it is only correct that the U.S. exports should be labor-intensive. However, Leontief later withdrew this proposition. His logic was that although U.S. labor was more productive than foreign labor, so was U.S. capital. Hence, both U.S. labor and U.S. capital should be multiplied by three. As a result, the relative abundance of capital and labor remains basically unaltered.

---

* The input-output table portrays the origin and destination of each good in the economy. Leontief pioneered input-output analysis and was awarded the Nobel Prize in 1973 for his contribution.

4.4b Other Empirical Studies

Leontief's paradoxical conclusion gave rise to similar studies for other countries. For example, a case study of Japan, by Tatemoto and Ichimura in 1959, suggested that Japanese exports were capital intensive and its imports relatively labor intensive. Because Japan was believed to be a labor-abundant country at the time of the study, the paradox was repeated. However, a more careful analysis of the Japanese export patterns revealed that exports to developing countries tended to be relatively capital intensive, whereas exports to advanced countries—the United States and Western countries—tended to be labor intensive. This explanation seems to conform to the H-O theory because Japan is a relatively labor-abundant country compared to the United States, and it is relatively capital-abundant in comparison to its developing country trading partners.

Another study by D. F. Wahl of Canada in 1961 showed that Canada exported capital-intensive commodities. Because Canada's major trading partners the United States, which is relatively more capital abundant, the results were in contrast to the H-O model.

A 1962 study of India by R. Bharadwaj showed that India, a labor-abundant country, exported labor-intensive goods and imported capital-intensive goods. These results supported the H-O theory. However, in another 1962 study the same author found that in trade with the United States, India exported capital-intensive commodities rather than labor-intensive commodities, contrary to the H-O theory.

4.5 EXTENSIONS OF AND ALTERNATIVES TO THE HECKSCHER-OHLIN THEORY

The overall conclusion of the empirical studies described here and numerous other tests of the H-O theory is that the theory cannot be proved or refuted. As a result, although this theory is provisionally maintained, efforts are being made to either extend or provide alternatives to it. However, because the alternative theories are not comprehensive enough and explain only certain facets of international trade, some economists view them as complements to the H-O theory. In this section, we review these alternative theories and elaborate on their implications for the real world.

4.5a Increasing Returns to Scale as the Basis for Trade

One of the underlying assumptions of the H-O theory (assumption 3 in our list) is that production functions in both countries display constant returns to scale. However, in the real world, a production function may display increasing return to scale (IRS), that is, the doubling of all inputs may result in more than double the output. In this section, we elaborate on factors that give rise to IRS and, using graphs, show that mutually beneficial trade can occur under IRS.

Several factors might give rise to IRS:

1. *Specialization.* As the scale of operation expands, opportunities for specialization are enhanced, leading to an increase in labor productivity.
2. *Productive equipment.* Large-scale operation allows the use of more productive, specialized equipment that would not be possible with small-scale operation.
3. *Reduced unit costs of inputs.* A larger firm, buying in large quantities, can obtain "quantity discounts" from its suppliers.
4. *The use of by-products.* In some industries, large-scale operation allows the use of by-products that otherwise would be wasted by small-scale operation. For example, a large-scale meat-packing plant could use cattle hooves to produce glue.
5. *Development of ancillary facilities.* In some cases, one firm's large-scale operation encourages other firms to develop ancillary facilities, such as a transportation system and warehousing, resulting in cost savings for the growing firm.

It recently has become apparent that IRS in advanced countries is the outcome of firms concentrating their efforts on producing only one or, at most, a few varieties and styles of the same product rather than many different types of goods. This has been a significant strategy in holding costs down. It has contributed to the development of more efficient equipment, facilitating the operation of large-scale production processes. For example, the establishment of the European Union (EU) resulted in the elimination of tariff barriers among its members. This caused trade to expand within the EU, allowing each European plant to specialize in the production of only a few varieties and styles of a product. As a result, unit costs fell significantly. *

Graphical Analysis of Increasing Returns to Scale as the Basis for Trade. Assuming that two nations are identical in all aspects, mutually beneficial trade can occur under IRS.

Let's assume that the United States and Canada are identical in every aspect and produce wheat and bicycles, as shown in Figure 4-2. Given this assumption, we can use a single PPF and a single community indifference map to represent both countries. The existence of IRS causes the PPF to be convex to the origin, showing that the relative cost of producing each unit of one good decreases in terms of the other good. Point A shows the common pretrade equilibrium positions of both countries. At this point, the equilibrium relative commodity price ratio is equal to the absolute value of the slope of the common tangent to the PPF. Both countries are producing and consuming 20 bushels of wheat and 20 bicycles.

FIGURE 4-2
Increasing Return to Scale as the Basis of Trade

Given that two countries are identical in every aspect they share the same PPF which is convex to the origin, due to the assumption of IRS. Point A shows the common pretrade equilibrium positions of both nations. At this point, the equilibrium relative commodity price in the two nations is identical and is given by the absolute value of the slope of the common tangent to the PPF. With trade, the United States specializes completely in the production of bicycles by moving to point B on the PPF. Canada, on the other hand, specializes completely in the production of wheat moving to point W on the PPF. By trading 30 bicycles for 30 bushels of wheat, both nations end up at point C on indifference curve II, thus gaining 10 bushels of wheat and 10 bicycles (compare points A and C).

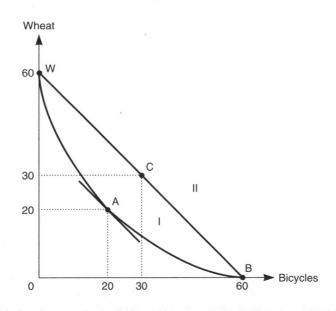

---

* The EU is explained in more detail in Chapter 8.

Suppose with the opening of international trade that the United States specializes completely in the production of bicycles by moving to point B on the PPF, producing 60 bicycles. Canada, on the other hand, specializes completely in the production of wheat by moving to point W on the PPF, producing 60 bushels of wheat.* By trading 30 bicycles for 30 bushels of wheat, both countries end up at point C. Because point C is located on a higher community indifference curve (II), both countries achieve a higher level of satisfaction. A comparison of points A and C shows that as the result of international trade, both countries gain 10 bushels of wheat and 10 bicycles.

4.5b Theory of Overlapping Demand (Linder Thesis)

The thrust of the H-O theory, as we explained earlier, is based on the premise that trading partners are dissimilar with regard to their factor endowments. It is this dissimilarity on the supply side that gives rise to trade between different nations. Thus, in applying this theory to the real world, we would expect the bulk of international trade to be between the labor-abundant developing countries and the capital-abundant industrialized countries. However, the empirical evidence presented since World War II provides results that are contradictory to the H-O theory. The bulk of international trade involves the industrialized nations trading manufactured goods with each other. This finding casts further doubt on the validity of the H-O theory and its ability to explain the trade in manufactured goods. Given these conditions, the stage was set for the development of a new theory by Swedish economist Staffan Linder in 1961.

Linder argues that for trade in primary commodities, factor endowment has significant importance. For trade in manufactured products, however, the importance of factor endowments is insignificant. This is because the primary force influencing trade in manufactured products is domestic demand conditions. Given that most international trade involves manufactured goods, it follows that domestic demand is the key variable explaining the flow of products among countries. The production and sale of a product starts in a domestic market where the demand and market conditions are familiar to the producer. Domestic demand gives rise to production and allows the producer to grow large enough to be able to compete in foreign markets.

Because the decision to produce is initially based on local demand conditions, it is reasonable to assume that trade would take place between countries that have similar demand conditions for their manufactured goods. In other words, the entrepreneur tries to minimize the risk of unknowns by operating in countries where demand patterns are similar to the domestic market. Thus, according to Linder, trade in manufactured goods is mainly attributed to the existence of overlapping demand conditions among the trading partners.

Linder also regarded income as the main variable that gives rise to demand. He explained that tastes and preferences for certain commodities only materialize when they are supported by income. It follows that, according to the overlapping demand theory, international trade in manufactured goods would be undertaken by countries with similar income levels. Thus, the more similar two countries are with respect to income, the greater the potential for trade in manufactured products.

4.5c Technological Gap Theory

The H-O theory's inability to explain trade in manufacturing was first noticed by Irving Kravis. His 1956 work, along with that of other authors, underlined the empirical importance of technology in explaining the patterns of trade between countries.

We explained earlier that, according to the H-O theory, each country should export the commodity that uses its abundant factor most intensively. Thus, a labor-abundant country, paying relatively low wages, should export labor-intensive commodities. However, Kravis' empirical investigation of the H-O theory provided contradictory results. He learned that in virtually every country studied, the exporting industries were those that paid the highest wages. To explain this contradiction, Kravis maintained that each country would, in essence, export the commodity that its entrepreneurs could develop. If a country has cheap labor to produce pocket calculators, but lacks the innovators, entrepreneurs, and skilled labor to develop the calculator, production and exportation of the product would not take

---

* From an analytical standpoint, it does not matter which of the two countries specializes in which product.

place. In other words, what counts for a country that wants to export a technically advanced product is its technological superiority over its trading partners.

The pioneering work of Kravis was followed by a number of writers, giving rise to the technological gap theory. In 1961, Posner introduced the concept of **imitation lag** to elaborate on the possibility of international trade between countries. He divided the lag into two components: the demand lag and the reaction lag. When new products are imported into a country, it takes time for a demand to develop because the new foreign goods may not be a perfect substitute for domestic goods or consumers may not be familiar with the product. The **demand lag** is the time needed for the demand for newly exported goods to develop. The **reaction lag** refers to the time it takes for the local entrepreneur to react to competition from abroad by starting local production. The difference between these two lags causes international trade to take place. A manufacturer might export a commodity to a nation when the demand lag is shorter than the reaction lag.

Gordon Douglass used the concept of imitation lag in 1963 to explain the export patterns for U.S. motion pictures. He argued that once a country was a leader in a given product, it would have a continuing advantage in related products. The United States pioneered innovations in the film industry and was able to continue its exportation with success by incorporating product innovations, such as talkies, color, and wide-screen movies, which were not yet available in other countries. After a lag, when the technology became commonplace, the volume and direction of U.S. trade was indeterminate.

In his 1966 study, Gary Haufbauer used the concept of imitation lag to explain the pattern of trade in synthetic materials. He found that a country's share of synthetic-material exports could be explained by the imitation lag and the market size.

Ranking countries according to their imitation lags, he learned that new synthetics were introduced rather consistently in countries at the top of the list and exported down to countries with longer lag times. The spread of technology caused the movement of the production down the list, displacing top countries' exports. Top countries, however, then moved into the development and exportation of new products.

In summary, the empirical studies of the technological gap theory support the view that technology is the most significant element in explaining the pattern of international trade. As these findings suggest, the production and exportation of a product starts in a technologically advanced country like the United States. As the technology becomes commonplace and the country starts losing its export market for that product, a new product is developed, following the same pattern as the old product.

The technological gap theory is similar to the product life cycle theory, which is explained in the next section. These two theories are consistent with each other, both referring to the element of technology as the most significant factor in explaining patterns of international trade.

4.5d Product Life Cycle Theory

This theory, initially known as "product cycle," (1966) was pioneered by Raymond Vernon. The theory was further developed by Louis Wells who applied it to marketing using the term "product life cycle." According to this theory, manufactured goods (products) pass through a life cycle. During this cycle, a country like the United States that is initially an exporter eventually loses its export market for a product and becomes an importer of the same product. On the basis of this theory, we can divide the life of a product into five stages: introduction, expansion, maturity, sales decline, and demise. Figure 4-3 illustrates the stages of a product life cycle. In both panels, time is measured on the horizontal axis. Panel (a) shows how the U.S. sales volume, measured on the vertical axis, changes over time.

Panel (b) shows the net exports, measured on the vertical axis, of different countries over time. At the first stage, a firm in an advanced country (we will use the United States for this example) innovates a product at time T_0 and begins its production and sale in the local market. At this stage, the firm has a virtual monopoly over the new product in the world market. As the firm's operation and foreign demand expand, the firm takes advantage of its economies of scale and exports the product to other nations at time T_1. By the time the product enters its third stage at time T_2, the product's income and familiarity abroad have increased. Higher overseas demand for the product induces some entrepreneurs or companies in other industrialized nations (Canada, the European nations, and Japan) to take advantage of the higher demand and start production of the same product. In some cases, some of the U.S.

FIGURE 4-3
Life Cycle of a Product

In stage 1 (introduction), an advanced country innovates a product at Time T_0 and starts producing the product for domestic consumption. In stage 2 (expansion) firms in the innovating country take advantage of their economies of scale and start exporting the product to other nations at time T_1. In stage 3 (maturity), other advanced nations take advantage of the higher demand and start their own production at time T_2. In stage 4 (sales decline), other advanced nations become net exporters of the product at time T_3. In stage 5 (demise), the innovating country becomes a net importer of the product at time T_4 and developing nations become net exporter of the product at time T_5.

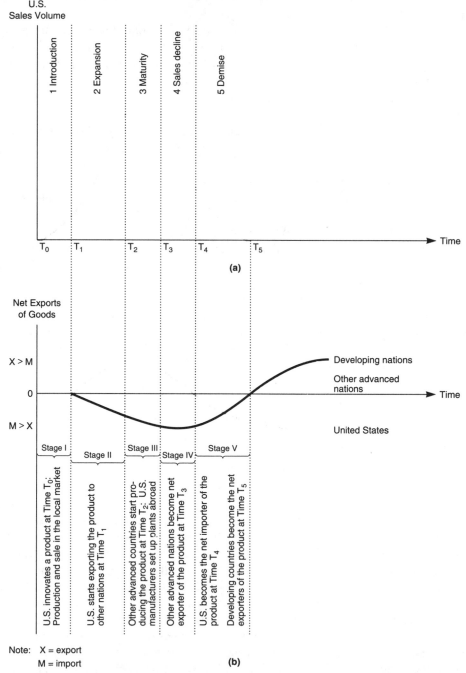

Note: X = export
        M = import

(b)

Adapted from Louis T. Wells, Jr. ed. *The Product Life Cycle and International Trade (Boston: Division of Research, Harvard Business School, 1972), 15; Raymond Vernon, "International Investment and International Trade in the Product Life Cycle," Quarterly Journal of Economics,* 80 (May 1966): 199; and Charles P. Kindleberger and Peter H. Lindert, *International Economics* 6th ed. (Homewood, IL.: Richard D. Irwin, 1978), 77.

manufacturers may start building their production facilities abroad to protect their share of the market against loss due to tougher competition in the foreign market. As foreign producers become larger and their ability to produce at a lower cost increases, they become net exporters of the product at time T_3. This brings the product to its fourth stage, at which point its production becomes increasingly standardized. Firms in other nations take advantage of the scale economies that were previously available to the U.S. manufacturers. This enables them to cut their costs and lower prices. This in turn causes the United States to lose its competitive advantage and become a net importer of the product at time T_4. At the final stage, the product is so commonplace that it is exported from low-income developing countries to higher-income advanced countries at time T_5. This happens because the lower wage rate in developing countries outweighs the advanced countries' superior technology.

The product life cycle theory provides a convincing explanation of the pattern of world trade in manufactured goods and foreign direct investment for the early post—World War II period. During this period, U.S. research and development activities led to innovation and production of new products, such as the computer and ball-point pens. Later, as the market expanded, these products were exported to other countries. Eventually, demand for these products increased to a level sufficient to support local production facilities. At this stage, as competition in foreign markets became tougher, the U.S. share in the exports market was threatened with decline. In response, U.S. multinational corporations (MNCs) either shifted their production facilities to low-cost countries or allowed local firms to take over production. This resulted in some products being produced by low-wage developing countries and then exported back to advanced countries.

Much of the production by MNCs is not initiated by innovation, as the product life cycle theory leads us to believe, but rather due to a cost advantage. The theory does not explain why MNCs invest abroad instead of, for example, engaging in a contractual agreement or licensing. Additionally, much of the foreign investment by MNCs, especially in the raw-materials industries, does not seem to follow a product life cycle.[1]

GLOBAL INSIGHTS CASE 4.2

PRODUCT LIFE CYCLE OF THE POCKET CALCULATOR

A standard pocket calculator—the battery-operated device that performs the four simple functions of addition, subtraction, multiplication, and division—was invented by scientists at Sunlock Comptometer Corporation in 1961. It was marketed the same year and sold for $1,000. At that price, the calculator (in its introductory phase) was considered cheap compared to mechanical calculators and large computers which were then used to provide the same simple calculations. Within eight years of the introduction of pocket calculators, several other firms, including Hewlett-Packard, Texas Instruments, and Casio, penetrated the market, making the onset of the calculator's expansion phase. Each of these firms developed a similar product and added to the intensity of competition in the United States and other countries. The greater competition, in turn, led to a 60-percent drop in the price of pocket calculators, from $1,000 to $400. These introduction and expansion stages lasted for about six years.

More firms entered the market during the early 1970s, signaling the onset of the calculator's maturity stage. Several of these firms started to produce their calculators overseas in locations such as Taiwan and Singapore. Fierce competition resulting from more firms entering the market, caused a continuous and significant drop in the price of the calculators signaling the onset of sales decline stage. For example, in 1971, Bowmar Corporation, a U.S. firm, marketed a four-function calculator at $240. By 1975, when the product technology was widely available, the same calculator sold for about $10. Given that the product technology was commonplace in 1975, we could argue that the calculator entered its demise stage, completing its life cycle. In other words, the life cycle of the standard calculator was completed in less than one and a half decades.

Source: Robert Grosse and Duane Kujawa, *International Business: Theory and Managerial Applications*, 2d ed. (Homewood, IL: Richard D. Irwin, Inc., 1988), 77-78.

4.6 EFFECTS OF TRANSPORTATION COSTS ON TRADE

One of the assumptions of the H-O theory is that transportation costs are zero. However, in the real world the economic impact of distance on international trade cannot be overlooked. Transportation costs include freight charges, insurance premiums, interest charges, and handling charges. In this section, we relax the H-O assumption of no transportation costs and use the standard supply and demand curves to demonstrate international trade between two countries.

Using the United States and France, the vertical axis in Figure 4-4 measures the dollar price of cotton in both countries, and the horizontal axis measures the quantity of cotton. The supply (S) and demand (D) curves for both the United States and France are consistent with the assumption that the United States has a comparative advantage in cotton production. This can be seen by comparing points A and A′ which show the autarky equilibria for the United States and France, respectively. In the absence of trade, the price of cotton in the United States is $2.00 per bale compared to $4.00 per bale in France. For the United States, an increase in the amount of cotton is shown by a movement to the left along the supply curve from the origin (0). For France, an increase in the amount of cotton

Figure 4-4
TRADE EFFECTS OF TRANSPORTATION COSTS

In the absence of trade, the United States is producing and consuming 20 bales of cotton at the equilibrium price of $2.00 per bale at point A. France is producing and consuming 20 bales of cotton at the equilibrium price of $4.00 per bale at point A′. With trade and no transportation cost, both nations reach the common equilibrium price of $3.00 per bale of cotton. If we introduce transportation costs of $1.00 per bale of cotton into our analysis, trade is in equilibrium when both nations share the transportation costs equally. This happens when the price of 1 bale of cotton is equal to $2.50 in the United States and $3.50 in France. At $2.50 per bale, the United States produces 25 bales of cotton at point E, consumes 15 bales at point F, and exports 10 bales. At $3.50 per bale, France produces 15 bales of cotton at point E′, consumes 25 bales at point F′, and imports 10 bales.

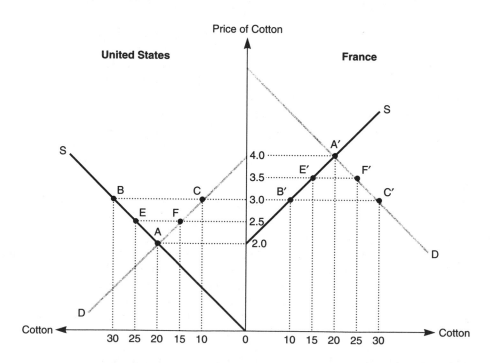

is shown by a movement to the right along the supply curve from the origin. At point A, the United States is producing and consuming 20 bales of cotton at the equilibrium price of $2.00 per bale. At point A', France is producing and consuming 20 bales of cotton at the equilibrium price of $4.00 per bale. With the opening of trade, the United States moves toward greater specialization in cotton production, exporting cotton to France. On the other hand, France reduces its cotton production, importing it from the United States. This causes the price of cotton to rise in the United States and to fall in France. If we assume that the transportation cost is zero, further growth in international trade is halted when the two nations reach the common price of $3.00 per bale of cotton. At this price, the United States produces 30 bales of cotton at point B, consumes 10 bales at point C, and exports 20 bales (compare points B and C). On the other hand, France produces 10 bales of cotton at point B', consumes 30 bales at point C', and imports 20 bales (compare points B' and C'). Thus, $3.00 per bale of cotton is the equilibrium price for both nations because the excess supply of cotton is equal to the excess demand.

Now let us introduce transportation costs into our analysis by assuming that the transportation cost of 1 bale of cotton between the two countries is $1.00. This causes the U.S. export price (production cost plus transportation cost) to rise by $1.00. In other words, the price of cotton in the United States exceeds the price of cotton in France by $1.00. According to Figure 4-4, trade is in equilibrium when both nations share the transportation costs equally.[*] This happens when the price of 1 bale of cotton is equal to $2.50 in the United States and $3.50 in France. At $2.50 per bale, the United States produces 25 bales of cotton at point E, consumes 15 bales at point F, and exports 10 bales (compare points E and F). On the other hand, at $3.50 per bale, France produces 15 bales of cotton at point E', consumes 25 bales at point F', and imports 10 bales (compare points E' and F').

As the comparison of trade with and without transportation costs shows, these costs lead to a lower level of specialization in production and diminish the gain from trade. Additionally, because the price of cotton with transportation costs is not the same in both countries, factor-price equalization will not take place.

4.7 REAL-WORLD RELEVANCE OF INTERNATIONAL TRADE THEORIES

Trade theories have important implications for real-world business. These theories have been developed in response to a need, that is, a desire to predict the future course of events with a reasonable degree of accuracy. Understanding these theories helps to explain the rationale for different nations' pursuit of different trade policies over time. For example, the theory of mercantilism, developed in the sixteenth century, is practiced in less extreme terms today by France.

Trade theories are useful in providing a framework to assist businesses or government authorities in formulating international trade policies. For instance, a business may use the product life cycle theory as a framework to scrutinize products that are likely candidates for export. As the theory suggests, a newly developed product, such as a personal computer, that has a high technological base is more apt to be marketable in a high-income advanced country than in a developing country. Trade theories can also help government authorities in a developing country by providing them with guidelines regarding the direction their trade should follow. For example, if a labor-abundant developing country plans to enhance its exports, it should concentrate on the production of standardized products because, according to the product life cycle theory, these products will generate more exports than other products.

In summary, trade theories are useful in assisting an international manager, or a government authority, in formulating policies with regard to international trade. These theories are also helpful in understanding the hows and whys of different policies that are undertaken by people involved in international trade. It is important to keep in mind that theories are abstractions from reality, and as such they provide us with a framework to help in the analysis of international trade. To be useful, such a framework should be applied for a given problem along with information gathered from the real world.

---

[*] Figure 4-4 is drawn to allow for the transportation costs to be shared between two countries. In general, the steeper the slopes of the supply and demand curves for the United States relative to France, the higher the percentage of transportation costs paid by the United States.

4.8 SUMMARY

1. According to the H-0 theory, each country should export those commodities that use its abundant factor most intensively and import goods that use its scarce factor most intensively.
2. According to the factor-price equalization theorem, free international trade leads to equalization of not only goods prices but also factor prices.
3. International trade causes the price of the abundant factor of production to increase and the price of the scarce factor of production to decrease.
4. Leontief's Paradox provided the first major test of the H-O theory. His study suggested that the United States exports goods that are relatively labor intensive and imports commodities that are capital intensive.
5. The overall conclusion of empirical studies described in this chapter and numerous other tests of the H-O theory is that the theory cannot be proved or refuted.
6. The following factors might give rise to increasing returns to scale: (a) specialization, (b) productive equipment, (c) reduced unit costs of imports, (d) the use of by-products, and (e) development of ancillary facilities.
7. The theory of overlapping demand states that international trade in manufactured goods is undertaken by countries with similar demand and income levels.
8. The technological gap theory relates the trade between nations to the technological gap among them. According to this theory, it is a country's technological superiority that gives it an advantage in securing export markets.
9. According to Posner, the possibility of international trade between nations could be explained by the imitation lag, which is composed of the demand lag and the reaction lag. The demand lag is the time needed for the demand for a newly exported good to develop. The reaction lag refers to the time it takes for the local entrepreneur to react to competition from abroad by starting local production. The difference between these two lags causes international trade to take place.
10. According to the product life cycle theory, manufactured goods pass through five different stages: introduction, expansion, maturity, sales decline, and demise. During the life cycle, an advanced country that is initially an exporter eventually loses its export market for a product and becomes an importer of the same product.
11. Transportation costs lead to a lower level of specialization in production and diminish the gains from trade. Additionally, when transportation costs are present, factor-price equalization will not take place.
12. Trade theories have important implications for international trade. Understanding these theories is important because (a) they explain the rationale for different nations' pursuit of different trade policies over time; and (b) they are useful in providing a framework to assist businesses or governments in formulating international trade policies.

Review Questions

1. Explain the difference between the H-O theory and the theory of comparative advantage.
2. Explain the H-O theory by answering the following questions:
   (a)   What does the theory state?
   (b)   What are the assumptions underlying this theory?
   (c)   What are the implications of the assumptions underlying the theory?
3. Explain the Leontief Paradox.
4. Explain the factor-price equalization theorem by answering the following questions.
   (a)   What is the basis of this theorem?
   (b)   What does the theorem state?
   (c)   Has factor-price equalization occurred in the real world?

5. Graphically illustrate and then explain the product life cycle theory. Explain the usefulness of this theory for the manager of a multinational corporation. Give examples of nations that have gone through stages of the product life cycle.
6. Discuss the usefulness of trade theories for businesses and governments using real-world examples.
7. What is meant by constant returns to scale and increasing returns to scale? What factors give rise to the latter?
8. How does Staffan Linder explain international trade patterns for manufactured goods as opposed to primary goods?
9. Explain the technological gap theory by answering the following questions.
   (a)   What does the theory state?
   (b)   What is meant by "imitation lag," "demand lag", and "reaction lag?"

Problems

1. Assume that a two-country world is composed of the United States and Mexico, and that the capital/labor ratio for the United States is higher than for Mexico. Given these assumptions, answer the following questions.
   (a)   What kind of commodities would you expect each country to export? Explain.
   (b)   What would you expect to happen to wages and interest rates in both countries as a result of free international trade? Explain.
2. Choose a capital-abundant advanced country and a labor-abundant developing country, then select a capital-intensive good and a labor-intensive good. Given the assumptions of the H-O theory, complete the following problems.
   (a)   Graphically demonstrate the pretrade positions of both countries on their PPFs, and show that potential for trade exists between the two nations.
   (b)   With the opening of trade, in what commodity does each nation specialize and why? Demonstrate your answer on the graph.
   (c)   Explain how factor mobility between the two nations leads to factor-price equalization.
   (d)   Explain what happens to the real income of labor and the real income of owners of capital in each nation as a result of international trade.
3. Choose two countries and a good that is being traded between them. Using the two countries as an example, complete the following problems.
   (a)   Assume that the slopes of both countries' demand curves are equal and that their supply curves have equal slopes as well. Given this assumption, graphically demonstrate that transportation costs are equally shared between the two countries.
   (b)   Assume that the slopes of one country's demand and supply curves are steeper than those of the other country. Given this assumption, graphically demonstrate and then explain that the nation with the steeper demand and supply curves pays a higher percentage of the transportation costs than the other nation.
4. In Chapter 1, we used Table 1-5 and stated that " . . . developed nations are the major trading partners for most internationally traded goods and services."

   Which of the theories explained in this chapter agrees with this statement? Explain this theory and elaborate on its implications for developing countries.
5. Assume that the world consists of two nations that use two factors of production to produce two goods. Given these assumptions, answer the following questions.
   (a)   What elements cause nations' PPFs to have different shapes?
   (b)   What assumption(s) gives rise to different PPFs for the two trading nations in the H-O model?
   (c)   What elements give rise to different relative commodity prices in the two nations?
6. Assume that a two-nation trading world consists of the United States and Great Britain, using two factors of production—capital (K) and labor (L)—to produce two goods—steel and cloth. Consider the H-O model and assume that all of its assumptions hold true, but suppose that the production functions of both commodities (not just both countries) are identical. Given these assumptions, answer the following questions.

(a)   What does the identity of production functions between cloth and steel imply about the shape of the PPFs of Great Britain and the United States?

(b)   Is there a basis for trade between the United States and Great Britain?

(c)   What are the implications of the identical production functions between steel and cloth for the H-O theory and the factor-price equalization theorem?

Notes

1.   H. Ian Giddy, "The Demise of the Product Cycle Model in International Business Theory," *Columbia Journal of World Business,* (Spring 1978), 90-97.

Suggested Readings

Bharadwa, J. R. "Factor Proportions and the Structure of Indo—U.S. Trade." *Indian Economic Journal* (October 1962).

Brecher, R. A., and E. U. Choudri. "The Leotief Paradox, Continued." *Journal of Political Economy* (August 1982): 820-823. Das, S. P. "Economies of Scale, Imperfect Competition, and the Pattern of Trade." *Economic Journal* (September 1982).

Deardorff, A. A. "The General Validity of the Heckscher-Ohlin Theorem." *American Economic Review* (September 1982).

Douglass, G. K. "Product Variation and International Trade in Motion Pictures." Ph. D. diss., Massachusetts Institute of Technology, 1963. Giddy, I. H. "The Demise of the Product Cycle Model in International Business Theory." *Columbia Journal of World Business* (Spring 1987).

Grubel, Herbert G. *International Economics.* Rev. ed. Homewood, IL: Richard D. Irwin, 1982.

Heckscher, E. "The Effects of Foreign Trade on Distribution of Income." *Economisc Tidskrift* 21 (1919): 497-512.

Hufbauer, G. C. *Synthetic Materials and the Theory of International Trade.* Cambridge, MA: Harvard University Press, 1966.

Kravis, I. B. "Availability and Other Influences on the Commodity Composition of Trade." *Journal of Political Economy* 64 (April 1956): 143-155.

Leontief, W. "Domestic Production and Foreign Trade: The American Capital Position Reexamined." *Proceedings of the American Philosophical Society* 97 (September 1953).

Linder, S. B. *An Essay on Trade and Transformation.* New York: John Wiley and Sons, 1961, ch. 3.

Markausen, A. *Product Cycles, Oligopoly, and Regional Development.* Cambridge, MA: MIT Press, 1985.

Mullor-Sebastian, A. "The Product Life Cycle Theory: Empirical Evidence." *Journal of International Business Studies* (Winter 1983).

Ohlin, Bertil. *Interregional and International Trade.* Cambridge: Harvard University Press, 1933.

Posner, M. "International Trade and Technical Change." *Oxford Economic Paper* 13 (October 1961): 323-341.

Salvatore, D. *Theory and Problems of International Economics.* New York: McGraw-Hill, 1984, ch. 4.

Samuelson, P. A. "International Trade and the Equalization of Factor Prices." *Economic Journal* (June 1984).

Tatemoto, M., and S. Ichimura. "Factor Proportions and Foreign Trade: The Case of Japan." *Review of Economics and Statistics* (November 1959).

Vernon, R. "International Investment and International Trade in the Product Life Cycle." *Quarterly Journal of Economics* 80 (May 1966): 190-207.

Vernon, R., ed. *The Technology Factor in International Trade.* New York: NBER, 1970.

Wahl, D. F. "Capital and Labour Requirements for Canada's Foreign Trade." *Canadian Journal of Economics and Political Science.* (August 1961).

Wells, L. T. "A Product Life Cycle for International Trade." *Journal of Marketing* 32 (July 1968): 1-6.

Wells, L. T., ed. *The Product Life Cycle and International Trade.* Boston: Division of Research, Graduate School of Business Administration, Harvard University, 1972.

Part 2

NATIONAL POLICIES, INTERNATIONAL ORGANIZATIONS AND AGREEMENTS, AND RECENT POLITICAL EVENTS AFFECTING INTERNATIONAL TRADE

The discussion of international trade theories, presented in Part I led us to the conclusion that free trade is the most efficient way of allocating the world's scarce resources. We learned that if countries specialize according to the theory of comparative advantage, not only do they benefit as participants of trade, but world output is maximized as well. However, in spite of the convincing arguments for free trade, governments have always interfered with the free flow of goods and services by imposing tariff and nontariff barriers.

Today, although the majority of economists favor free trade and oppose any kind of trade barriers, they carefully discuss the exceptional cases that might warrant trade restrictions.

The purpose of Part II is to explain national policies that affect the free flow of goods and services across national boundaries. This provides us with a deeper understanding of the benefits of free international trade. We also study the arguments in favor of trade restrictions. Some of the major questions that are answered in this part are as follows:

1. What are tariff barriers?
2. What are nontariff trade barriers?
3. Are trade barriers beneficial to the nation imposing them? Are they beneficial to the world as a whole?
4. What are the arguments for protectionism? Are these arguments valid?
5. What international organizations affect international trade?
6. What international agreements affect international trade?

Part II, therefore, is designed to provide a detailed perspective on the elements that restrict free international trade and their welfare implications on national and international levels. Chapter 5 discusses tariffs; Chapter 6 explains nontariff trade barriers. Chapter 7 elaborates on arguments for protection, and Chapter 8 presents international organizations and agreements affecting international trade. Finally, Chapter 9 elaborates on recent trade agreements and political events affecting the global economy.

Chapter 5

TARIFF BARRIERS

5.1 INTRODUCTION

The argument for free trade is based mainly on economic analysis showing that there are usually net gains associated with free trade on both national and global levels. We introduced some of this analysis in Part I, demonstrating that free international trade leads to the most efficient allocation of the world's scarce resources. The major objective of this chapter (and the subsequent chapters of Part Two) is to compare free international trade policies with a wide range of policies calling for trade restrictions. Using an analysis of trade policies, we will gain a better understanding of why most economists generally favor free international trade and oppose any kind of trade restriction. Having understood this analysis, we will be in a better position to comprehend what divides the majority of economists from the group that supports trade restrictions. In this chapter, we first introduce the concept of a tariff and elaborate on its purpose; second, we explain the classification of tariffs according to the way they are calculated; third, we discuss the welfare effects of a tariff and analyze the net national losses that result from its imposition; and fourth, we elaborate on the effective rate of protection.

5.2 DEFINITION OF A TARIFF

Tariffs are the most commonly used form of trade restraint. A **tariff** is a tax, or a custom duty, imposed on the importation or exportation of a product that is crossing national boundaries. Import duties are more prevalent than export duties because most countries would like to restrict their imports and expand their exports, thereby increasing their foreign earnings. In some cases, however, when a nation has a monopoly on a commodity, it may benefit from export tariffs. A higher export tariff raises the price of a commodity, but it is not very effective in decreasing demand by foreigners who are dependent on goods from an exporting nation. To put it in more technical terms, the nation with a monopoly on a product faces a relatively inelastic demand for its exports. As a result, the higher export price leads to a higher revenue. For example, Burma and Thailand have taxed rice exports to other south Asian nations to raise government revenues. In the United States, the taxation of exports is prohibited by law. As a consequence, the goal of U.S. export restrictions is achieved by another device known as export quotas, as we explain in Chapter 6.

5.3 CLASSIFICATIONS OF TARIFFS

Tariffs can be classified into two major categories, depending on either their purpose or the way they are calculated. In this section, we study the two major categories of tariffs and provide examples of their real-world applications.

5.3a Protective and Revenue Tariffs

Depending on a tariff's purpose, it may be classified as a protective tariff or a revenue tariff. **Protective tariffs** are levied to protect a home industry from foreign competitors. By imposing a tax on the importation of a foreign product, a protective tariff increases the price of that product. The increase either brings the price of the imported good in line with or makes it relatively more expensive than the similar domestically produced good. This weakens the imported good's competitive position in the domestic market. As a result, the demand for the domestic product may increase.

Governments sometimes impose **revenue tariffs** to raise tax revenues. These tariffs are most often used by developing countries, such as Thailand and Burma, to provide a source of income for these countries. In advanced countries, tariffs are employed primarily as a protective device rather than as an income-generating tool. However, the use of revenue tariffs in advanced countries is not unusual. For example, the United States has imposed tariffs on the importation of commodities such as bananas and coffee to raise tax revenues.

5.3b Specific, Ad Valorem, and Compound Tariffs

Depending on the way tariffs are calculated, they can be classified as specific tariffs, ad valorem tariffs, or compound tariffs. A **specific tariff** is expressed in terms of a fixed amount of money per unit of the imported product, such as $0.02 per chicken or $500 per automobile. An **ad valorem** tariff is expressed in terms of a percentage of the total value of a commodity; for example, 10 percent of the value of baseball gloves or 20 percent of the value of plywood imported. Finally, a **compound tariff** is a combination of specific and ad valorem tariffs. For example, as Table 5-1 indicates, in 1997 the compound tariff imposed by the United States on the imported heat meters included a specific portion, that is, $0.296 per unit, and an ad valorem portion, that is 4.6 percent of the value.

Because a large and increasing number of goods are traded internationally every day, they make the job of tariff administration difficult. To deal with this difficulty, most countries use two major lists in their tariff systems. These are (a) a list of those goods that can enter the country free of duty, and (b) a list of goods that are subject to custom duties. Each country has its own tariff schedule, which lists all its import duties. Tariff schedules may have a single column or multiple columns. A single column schedule provides a single tariff for a given good, irrespective of the exporting country in question. A multiple column schedule tariff, however, differentiates between countries by applying lower rates to countries with which treaty agreements have been arranged.

Table 5-1
The Selected Tariffs of the United States, 1997

Product	Rates of Duty
Glass fiber	5.4%
Human hair	1.2%
Wigs	1.1%
Golf shoes	8.5%
Heat meters	$0.296 each + 4.6%
watch cases and parts thereof	$0.13 each + 4.6%
Button	1.4%
Pipe & pipe bowls	Free
Escalator & moving walkways	0.8%
Steam turbines and other vapor turbine & parts	7.2%
Parts of nuclear reactors	5.2%
cheese & curd, processed	15%
Tulip bulls	$1.15 per 1000
Hyacinth bulls, without solid attached	0.492 per 1000
Mushroom spawn	0.08 per kg.
Garlic	0.0107 kg.

Source: *Harmonized Tariff Schedule of the United States*, Annotated for Statistical Reporting Purposes (Washington, D.C.: U.S. International Trade Commission, 1997).

Although specific and ad valorem tariffs basically serve the same goal, they have their own advantages and disadvantages. Because a specific tariff is calculated as a certain amount of money per unit of the imported product—for example, $0.07 per pound—it is easy to measure and administer. However, a shortcoming of this tariff is that the level of protection it gives to domestic goods changes negatively with variation in the prices of imported products. In other words, the lower the prices of imported products, the higher the level of protection. For example, if we impose a specific tariff of $10 per bicycle imported, then imports valued at $200 would be discouraged more than imports valued at $250. This is because $10 is a higher percentage of $200 (5%) than it is of $250 (4%). As a result, during a business recession abroad, when the value of imported goods declines, the amount of protection provided by a specific tariff increases. However, in the case of inflation abroad, when the value of imported products increases, the protective power of the specific tariff decreases.

In comparison to a specific tariff, an ad valorem tariff has the advantage of distinguishing between products with different values and assigning tariffs according to those values. Thus, a 10-percent ad valorem tariff on imported bicycles assigns a tariff of $20 on a bicycle costing $200 and $25 on a bicycle costing $250.

Another advantage of an ad valorem tariff compared to a specific tariff is that the former provides a constant degree of protection for domestic products irrespective of variations in their prices over time. For example, if the tariff rate is 10 percent, the duty on an imported product costing $100 would be $10. If the price of the product increases to $200, the duty will be $20. On the other hand, if the price of the product decreases to $50, the duty will be $5. In other words, the amount of tariff paid is always equal to 10 percent of the value of the product. Thus, an ad valorem tariff has the advantage of assigning duty in proportion to the value of the product in question.

5.4 EFFECTIVE RATE OF PROTECTION

As we already know, tariffs are imposed on imported goods in order to protect domestically produced goods from foreign competition. A tariff raises the price of an imported good and makes the domestically produced good more attractive to residents of the country imposing the tariff. The level of protection provided by a tariff is a measure of the degree to which domestic prices can rise above foreign prices without forcing domestic producers out of the market.

Since tariffs may be imposed not only on final goods but also on intermediate goods, firms are affected by tariffs on their inputs into the production process as well as their outputs, that is, the goods they sell. For example, an automobile producer is affected not only by tariffs on cars but also by tariffs on steel, rubber, glass, and electronic devices used in the production of those cars. Consequently, the tariff rates published in a country's tariff schedule, referred to as the **nominal tariff,** do not always provide us with the real measure of protection afforded to the industry in question. This is because the nominal tariff rates are aimed only at the final products. It is necessary to calculate an effective rate that takes into account not only tariffs on the final product but also on the inputs used to make that product.

Consider the production of video cassette recorders (VCRs) in the United States. Assume that a foreign producer can manufacture this product in its entirety and export it for $400. However, the U.S. producer has to buy the component parts from abroad and assemble them at home. Assume that the U.S. manufacturer pays $240 for the component parts and the cost of assembly is $160; the production cost for the domestic manufacturer is $400. Since at this price the domestic manufacturer is not making any profit, assume that the government steps in and imposes a 20-percent tariff on the importation of VCRs from abroad. As a result, the price of the imported VCR would rise to $480, allowing the domestic manufacturer to sell VCRs at this price and make a profit of $80 on each VCR sold.[*] Although the nominal rate of protection is 20 percent, the domestic producer is afforded more than 20-percent protection because the component parts enter the country duty-free.

---

[*] In this example, we are assuming that all intermediaries (middlemen) receive zero profit. We are also assuming that the foreign producer does not change the price and continues to export the VCR at $400 per unit following the tariff.

TABLE 5-2
Effective Rate of Protection

Costs for Imported VCRs		Costs for Domestic VCRs	
Parts	$240	Part	$240
Assembly cost	$100	Assembly cost	$160
Profit	$60	Profit	$80
Nominal tariff	$80		
Import price after tariff	$480	Domestic price after tariff	$480

GLOBAL INSIGHTS CASE 5.1

Tariff Wars in the 1930s

During the early 1930s, global trade in general and U.S. exports in particular declined significantly. The major factors contributing to such a decline were (1) the Great Depression of the 1930s, resulting from inappropriate monetary policies in the United States and Europe and the subsequent boom and crash of the U.S. stock market; and (2) the Smoot-Hawley Tariff Act of 1930, which raised the average duty in the United States to the all-time-high of 59 percent in 1932, fostering foreign retaliation.

Originally, the purpose of the act was to assist American agriculture. However, as a results of congressional politics, large significant tariffs were imposed on manufactured goods as well. The objective was apparently "beggar-thy-neighbor" to discourage imports and encourage domestic employment. The Smoot-Hawley tariff was signed into law on June 17, 1930, despite the objections by 36 nations who claimed that the tariff would severely harm their economies and that they would adopt retaliatory measures. The tariff increased the effective rate of tariffs in the United States by about 50 percent between 1929 and 1932 and prompted retaliatory tariffs. For example, in response to tariffs on grapes, oranges, cork, and onions, Spain passed the Wais tariff. Switzerland, opposing new tariffs on watches, embroideries, and shoes, banned U.S. exports. Against tariffs on hats and olive oil, Italy retaliated with high tariffs on U.S. and French automobiles in June 1930. In reaction to high duties on many food products, logs, and timber, Canada raised tariffs by threefold in August 1932. Australia, Cuba, France, Mexico, and New Zealand also joined in the tariff wars.

These beggar-thy neighbor policies were responsible for the declining trade volume and high unemployment and low prices that prevailed in all countries. The evidence shows that as a result of these policies, all countries were hurt from idle productive capacity and low prices. The boosted domestic demand for U.S. farm products protected by high tariffs, for example, was more than offset by the loss of export markets. Exports of U.S. agricultural products declined 66 percent from 1929 to 1932. This provoked the fall in farm prices, which in turn led to agricultural bank crashes. The net result was a collapse of world trade. For example, the U.S. imports in 1932 amounted to only 31 percent of their 1929 level, and exports declined even more. The collapse of world trade, in turn, fueled the spreading and the deepening of the depression around the globe.

Source: The World Bank, The World Development Report 1987 (New York: Oxford University Press), 139; Salvatore, D.
    International Economics, 4th ed. (New York: Macmillan Publishing Co., 1993), 270-271.

As Table 5-2 shows, if free trade existed, the imported VCR could enter the country for $400. But at this price the domestic producer can only add $160 to the components' cost, making zero profit. However, the protective tariff would allow the domestic producer to add up to $240 ($160 for assembly cost and $80 for profit) to the cost of the component parts and still meet the $480 price of the imported VCR. In other words, the percentage increase in the domestic value added as a result of the tariff is (240 - 60)/160 = 0.5 = 50%.[*] This means that the domestic **value added,** or the price of the final product minus the cost of the imported inputs, could increase to a level of 50 percent over what might exist without the tariff. In our example, the value added before tariff was $160 ($400 - $240) which was raised to $240 ($480 - $240), a 50-percent increase. In other words, the nominal 20-percent tariff rate imposed on the final imported product resulted in an effective rate of protection equal to 50 percent, two and a half times the nominal rate.

Given this example, we can define the **effective rate of protection** as the percentage increase in an industry's domestic value added as the result of a tariff structure.[**]

5.5 WELFARE EFFECTS OF A TARIFF

A nation's imposition of a tariff causes some groups to gain at the expense of other groups. However, as we will show, the nation as a whole will lose. Who is likely to benefit and who is likely to lose from a tariff's imposition? Under what conditions would a nation or the world benefit from a tariff? We answer these questions by explaining the concepts of consumer surplus and producer surplus. We then analyze a tariff's impact on consumers and measure its effect on producers. Next, we determine a tariff's effect on government revenue; and finally, we put these three effects together to measure the net national loss resulting from a tariff.

5.5a Consumer Surplus and Producer Surplus

The welfare effect of a commercial policy, including a tariff, can be depicted by its effect on consumer surplus and producer surplus. **Consumer surplus** refers to the difference between the actual amount consumer pays for a specific good and the maximum amount that he or she would have been willing to pay for that good.

The concept of consumer surplus is depicted in Figure 5-1, which measures a consumer's demand for wheat. The demand curve shows that at the price of $3 per bushel, the consumer is buying 3 bushels of wheat for $9 ($3 x 3 = $9). But, as the curve also shows, he or she would have been willing to pay $5 for the first bushel, $4 for the second bushel, and only $3 for the third bushel, spending a maximum amount of $12 ($5 + $4 + $3 = $12). In this case, the consumer surplus is $3, which is the difference between what the consumer actually paid ($9) and the maximum amount that he or she would have been willing to pay ($12). Theoretically speaking, the consumer would have been willing to pay $6 for 0 bushels.[***] Also, he or she could buy infinitesimal quantities along the demand curve rather than one unit at a time. Given these considerations, the consumer surplus is mathematically equal to the area above the price line and below the demand curve (the shaded triangle in Figure 5-1). The triangular area (x base x height) is equal to $4.50 (x 3 x $3 = $4.50).

Producer surplus refers to the difference between the actual amount a producer receives for a good and the minimum amount that he or she would have been willing to accept for that good.

---

[*]   The equation used to calculate the percentage increases in the domestic value added as the result of tariff (0.5) is as follows:

$$\frac{\text{value added after tariff - value added before tariff}}{\text{value added before tariff}}$$

[**]   Generally the effective rate of protection can be calculated by the use of a formula as demonstrated in the appendix to this chapter.

[***]   In practice, because no one pays any amount of money to acquire a zero unit of a commodity, we may assume, alternatively, that the consumer is willing to pay $6 for a very small quantity above zero.

FIGURE 5-1
Consumer Surplus

Consumer surplus refers to the difference between the actual amount a consumer pays for a good and the maximum amount that he or she would have been willing to pay for that good. Consumer surplus is equal to the area above the price line and below the demand curve, as shown by the shaded area in the diagram.

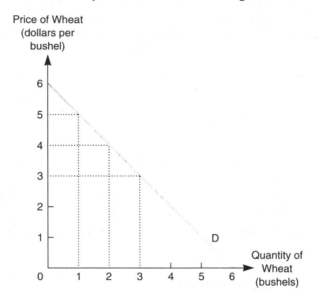

The concept of producer surplus is depicted in Figure 5-2, which measures a producer's supply of wheat. The supply curve shows that at the price of $4 per bushel, the producer is selling 3 bushels of wheat for $12 ($4 × 3 = $12). But, as the curve also shows, he or she would have been willing to accept $2 for the first bushel, $3 for the second bushel, and $4 for the third bushel, receiving the minimum amount of $9 ($2 + $3 + $4 = $9). In this case, the producer surplus is $3, which is the difference between what the producer actually received ($12) and the minimum amount he or she would have been willing to accept ($9). Theoretically speaking, the producer would have been willing to accept $1 for 0 bushels. Also, he or she could sell infinitesimal quantities along the supply curve rather than one unit at a time. Given these considerations, the producer surplus is mathematically equal to the area below the price line and above the supply curve (the shaded triangle in Figure 5-2). The triangular area (1/2 × base × height) is equal to $4.50 (1/2 × 3 × $3 = $4.50).

5.5b Effect of Tariffs on Consumers

Having explained the concept of consumer surplus, we now use this concept to determine the loss resulting from the imposition of a tariff. In Figure 5-3, S_D and D_D represent domestic supply and domestic demand for motorcycles for a hypothetical nation. In the absence of international trade, the nation is in equilibrium at point E. At this point, the nation produces and sells 25 million motorcycles at an equilibrium price of $7,000. The quantity demanded is equal to the quantity supplied. Now suppose that the nation is opened to international trade, and the world price for a motorcycle is $4,000. If we assume the existence of perfect competition in the world market for motorcycles, each

FIGURE 5-2
Producer Surplus

Producer surplus refers to the difference between the actual amount a producer receives for a good and the minimum amount that he or she would have been willing to accept for that good. Producer surplus is equal to the area below the price line and above the supply curve, as shown by the shaded area in the diagram.

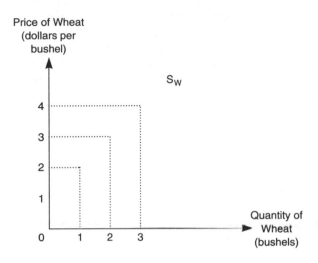

nation is a price taker, that is, no nation can influence the world price. As a result, the world supply for its import (motorcycles) is perfectly elastic (horizontal) at the price level of $4,000. This is shown by line S_W. At this relatively lower price, the quantity demanded, determined by the intersection of S_W and D_D at point A, increases to 40 million units. The quantity supplied domestically, determined by the intersection of S_D and S_W at point H, decreases to 10 million units. This excess demand of 30 million (40 − 10) is satisfied by imports (M_0). As the comparison of points A and E shows, free international trade leads to a decline in the price of motorcycles from $7,000 per unit to $4,000 per unit. It also results in an increase in the quantity of motorcycles demanded from 25 million units to 40 million units. Thus, as a result of the free international trade, consumers are definitely better off. They can buy more motorcycles at a lower price. However, domestic producers are worse off because they now have to sell fewer motorcycles (10 million instead of 25 million) at a lower price ($4,000 instead of $7,000) than they did before the opening of international trade.

Given the decrease in the price and quantity of motorcycles sold by domestic suppliers, the industry's profits will fall. As a result, some workers may lose their jobs. Assume that labor unions and management get together and decide to protect their interests by lobbying government officials. Suppose their efforts result in the imposition of a protective tariff of $2,000 per unit on motorcycle imports. Because this nation is a price taker, it cannot affect the world market price for motorcycles. Thus, the world supply of motorcycles remains entirely elastic. However, the domestic price of imported motorcycles rises to $6,000, as shown by the tariff-inclusive world supply curve (S_W+T). This curve is obtained by shifting the world supply curve, S_W, upward by the amount of the tariff (T).

The protective tariff results in a decrease in quantity demanded from 40 million units to 30 million units; an increase in domestic production from 10 million units to 20 million units; and a decrease in imports from 30 million units to 10 million units (30 − 20 = 10 M_1 in Figure 5-3). Import reduction, from 30 million units (M_0) to 10 million units (M_1), stems from a decrease in consumption and an increase in domestic production.

FIGURE 5-3
Effect of a Tariff on Consumers

S_D and D_D represent domestic supply and domestic demand for motorcycles. Point E shows the pretrade equilibrium point, at which the nation is producing and selling 25 million motorcycle at the equilibrium price of $7,000 per motorcycle. With free trade and the world price of $4,000 per motorcycles, the nation produces 10 million motorcycles, demands 40 million, and imports 30 million motorcycles. With a protective tariff of $2,000 per unit on motorcycles, the domestic price of motorcycles rises to $6,000, the domestic production increases to 20 million motorcycles, quantity demanded decreases to 30 million units and imports decline to 10 million units. Before the imposition of the tariff, consumer surplus was equal to areas a + b + c + d + e. After the imposition of the tariff, the consumer surplus was reduced to e. Thus, the tariff resulted in an overall loss of consumer surplus of areas a + b + c + d. The amount of loss can be measured by deducting area ABF (1/2 x 10 x $2,000 = $10 billion) from rectangular area ADCF ($2,000 x 40 million = $80 billion), which is equal to $70 billion.

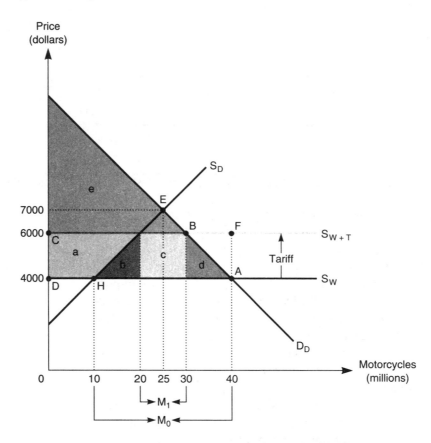

What are the effects of the protective tariff on consumer welfare? We answer this question by using the concept of consumer surplus. According to Figure 5-3, before the imposition of the tariff, consumer surplus was equal to areas a + b + c + d + e. After the imposition of the tariff, the consumer surplus was reduced to area e. Thus, the tariff resulted in an overall loss of consumer surplus of areas a + b + c + d. The amount of loss can be measured by deducting triangular area ABF (1/2 × 10 million × $2,000 = $10 billion) from rectangular area ADCF ($2,000 x 40 million = $80 billion), which is equal to $70 billion.

5.5c Effect of Tariffs on Producers

As we explained before, by imposing a tax on the importation of a foreign product, a protective tariff increases the price of that product. This weakens the competitive position of the imported good in the domestic market. As a result, the demand for the domestic product may increase, leading to additional sales and higher prices for domestic producers.

Using the previous motorcycle example, Figure 5-4 portrays the analysis of a tariff from the producer's viewpoint. As we explained before, imposing a tariff of $2,000 causes the domestic price of imported motorcycles to rise to $6,000. This higher price induces domestic producers to expand their output by moving upward along their supply curves (marginal cost curves).* They expand their output, moving from point I to point G, producing 20 million

FIGURE 5-4
Effect of a Tariff on Producers

Imposing a tariff of $2,000 causes the domestic price of imported motorcycles to rise to $6,000. This higher price induces domestic producers to expand their output from point I (10 million units) to point G (20 million units). Before the imposition of the tariff, producer surplus is equal to area f. After the imposition of the tariff, producer surplus rises to area f + a. Thus, the tariff results in an overall gain in producer surplus equal to area a. The amount of the gain can be measured by adding area IGH (0.5 × 10 million × $2,000 = $10 billion) to area CDIH ($2,000 × 10 million = $20 billion), which totals $30 billion.

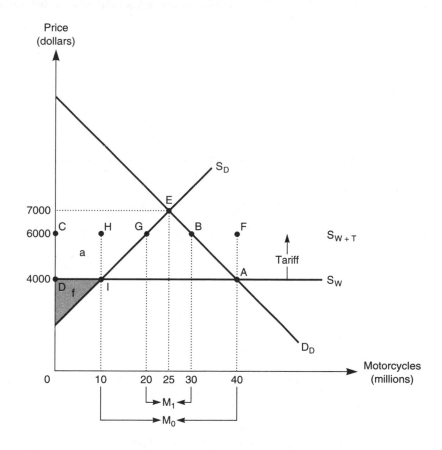

* Given the assumption of perfect competition, the firm's supply curve coincides with the rising portion of its marginal cost curve, which lies above the minimum point of its average variable cost curve.

motorcycles. At this point the cost of producing one more motorcycle, (marginal cost) shown by the supply curve, is equal to the world price after tariff ($6,000). It would not be profitable for domestic producers to expand their output beyond point G. Any further expansion would increase their marginal costs above $6,000, the competitive price.

GLOBAL INSIGHTS CASE 5.2

Offshore Assembly Provisions

Many nations, including the United States, have special provisions that grant lower tariffs on products assembled abroad from domestically produced components. Suppose a component, such as an engine, is produced in the United States and sent to Mexico to be assembled with other components to become a finished automobile. Under the offshore assembly provision (OAP) the cost of the engine is deducted from the dutiable value of the automobile. In other words, duties apply only to the value added to the product.

The OAP is used often by U.S. manufacturers to decrease manufacturing costs and become more competitive in the international market. In recent years, major products crossing the U.S. border under OAP have included office machines, television sets, and motor vehicles. These products are assembled predominately in Mexico and Germany. Semiconductors and aluminum cans are two major metal products that are assembled in countries such as Japan, Canada, and Mexico, and shipped back to the United States.

Given the abundance of cheap labor in Mexico and its proximity to the United States, that country has been a popular site for offshore U.S. manufacturing. During the last decade, many U.S. firms have invested billions of dollars to operate about 2,000 plants in Mexico. These maquila plants employ more than 500,000 Mexican laborers to assemble U.S.-made components into finished products. These finished products are sent back to the United States for sale in the U.S. market. Until recently, Mexican law confined plants to a specific area along the border. However, a change in this law now permits plants to operate farther into the country, hopefully lessening pollution and overcrowding problems.

Offshore assembly operations constitute a large percentage of manufactured imports to the United States from developing nations, especially Mexico.

The U.S. OAP applies not only to U.S. companies, but to foreign firms as well. For example, a Japanese firm that wants to export to the United States could take advantage of the U.S. OAP by buying U.S.-made components, having them assembled in a developing country like Mexico, and shipping them to the United States under the favorable OAP. In fact, many Japanese companies have used this strategy in exporting their products to the United States. A Japanese company planning to export a commodity to the United States can take the following steps:

1. Purchase the needed components from the United States.
2. Assemble the components in a maquila plant in Mexico.
3. Ship the final commodity to the United States, taking advantage of the favorable U.S. OAP provision.

Many Japanese firms have followed the above steps, assembling their components into finished goods in a number of locations in Mexico, such as Mexicali, Nogales, and Matamoros, that are close to the United States border.

Source: *U.S. News* and *World Report*, 3 August 1987, 40; P. Asheghian and B Ebrahimi, *International Business* (New York: Harper Collins, 1990), 573-575; "The Rise of Gringo Capitalism," *Newsweek*, 5 January 1987, 40.

What is the effect of the protective tariff on producers' welfare? We answer this question by using the concept of producer surplus. According to Figure 5-4, before the imposition of the tariff, the producer surplus was equal to area f. After the imposition of the tariff, the producer surplus rises to area f + a. Thus, the tariff results in an overall gain in producer surplus by area a. The amount of gain can be measured by adding triangular area IGH (1/2 x 10 million x $2,000 = $10 billion) to area CDIH ($2,000 x 10 million = $20 billion), which is equal to $30 billion.

5.5d Effect of Tariffs on Government Revenue

If a tariff is not high enough to prohibit all imports, it brings revenue to the government. In Figure 5-3, the tariff revenue collected by the government, measured by area c, is equal to $20 billion. This is found by multiplying the number of imports after tariff ($M_1 = 10$ million units) by the amount of tariff ($2,000).

The tariff revenue collected by the government may be used in various ways. For example, the government may spend it on social projects or use it to decrease other taxes. Although the way the tariff revenue is spent matters from a social welfare standpoint, the main point to keep in mind is that it represents a gain that accrues to someone in the nation, and, as such, contributes to the national welfare.

5.5e Net National Loss from Tariffs

What is the overall impact of a tariff on a nation's welfare? To answer this question, we need to combine the effects of the tariff on consumers, producers, and the government. We also need to impose a value judgment by stating how we view each dollar effect on each group. To this end, we may use the "one-dollar, one-vote yardstick." Accordingly, we consider every dollar loss or gain as significant as every other dollar loss or gain, no matter who loses or gains.*

Given the one-dollar, one-vote yardstick, the imposition of a tariff leads to a net loss for both the nation and the world as a whole. This can be seen from Figure 5-5, which is constructed on the basis of our previous motorcycle example. Adding up consumers' loss, producers' gain, and government revenue, we get the following:

		Gain (+)/Loss (−)						
Consumers' loss	Areas	−	(a	+	b	+	c	+	d)
Producers' gain	Area		a					
Government revenue	Area						c	
Net national loss	Areas	−			(b			+	d)

As the above analysis shows, the tariff brings a net national loss equal to areas b + d. Area b is referred to as the **production effect,** or **production distortion loss,** of the tariff and measures a loss to the nation imposing the tariff. This loss results from wasted resources employed to produce additional motorcycles at increasing unit costs. The tariff's imposition encourages domestic motorcycle producers to expand their output. To do this, they eventually use resources that are less appropriate to motorcycle production. In other words, resources are used less efficiently than they would have been with free international trade, which would have led to the purchase of motorcycles from low-cost foreign producers. As a result, the unit cost of producing motorcycles rises. In summary, the production effect of the tariff arises because the less efficient domestic production is substituted for the more efficient foreign production. In Figure 5-5, domestic motorcycle production rises from 10 million units to 20 million units. In the mean time, the domestic cost of producing motorcycles also rises along S_D (showing the marginal cost curve). As we already know, the same increase in motorcycle production could be achieved by foreign producers at a unit cost of $4,000 before the tariff. The welfare loss to the nation, measured by area b, is equal to $10 billion (10 million × ½ × $2,000 = $10 billion).

---

* This assumption is not acceptable to those who argue that the relative impact on poor or rich classes matter the same as absolute dollar loss or gain.

FIGURE 5-5
Net National Loss from a Tariff

Imposing a tariff of $2,000 causes the domestic price of imported motorcycles to rise to $6,000. This reduces consumer's surplus by areas a + b + c + d. Of this area, area a is redistributed to domestic producers in terms of increased producer surplus, and area c is collected by the government as tariff revenue. The remaining area (b + d = $20 billion) is a deadweight loss, representing the net national loss resulting from the tariff. Area d ($10 billion) is referred to as consumption effect, and area b ($10 billion) is known as production effect.

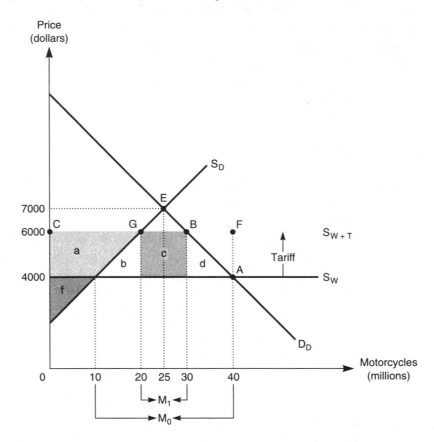

Area d is referred to as the **consumption effect,** or **consumption distortion loss,** of the tariff and measures a loss to the nation imposing the tariff. This loss results from a decrease in domestic consumption due to the rise in import price following the tariff. The tariff artificially raises the price of motorcycles, preventing domestic consumers from buying them at the lower price. Referring to Figure 5-5, following the imposition of the tariff, domestic consumption decreases from 40 million units to 30 million units, and the unit price of a motorcycle increases from $4,000 to $6,000. The consumption effect on the nation, measured by area d, is equal to $10 billion (10 million × ½ × $2,000 = $10 billion).

The total welfare loss to the nation following the tariff, measured by areas b + d, is equal to $20 billion. This is a *deadweight loss.* It represents a loss of consumer surplus that is not transferred to anyone else in the nation.

As we explained before, our analysis of the welfare effect of tariffs is based on the adoption of the one-dollar, one-vote yardstick. What if we reject this yardstick? Suppose, for example, we believe that each dollar gain for motorcycle producers is preferable to each dollar loss to consumers, perhaps because we think motorcycle producers as a whole contribute to the advancement of domestic technology. If this were the case, we would not like to accept areas b and d as the net national loss from tariff. However, the same analysis is still useful because it allows us to measure government gain (tariff-generated revenue), producers' gain, and consumers' loss. Having done this, we are able to apply some differential weight to each group's dollar stake when comparing the producers' and government's gains to the consumers' loss.[*]

In closing this chapter, we may note that the international negotiations championed by the General Agreement on Tariff and Trade (GATT) since World War II have rendered notable cutbacks in tariff rates. Nevertheless, trade in certain industries is still subject to high tariffs. During the last two decades, other types of barriers, referred to as "nontariff trade barriers," have attracted increasing attention. The welfare effects of these barriers are at least as detrimental as those of tariffs. Also, nontariff trade barriers have demonstrated that they are much less responsive to international trade liberalization attempts than tariffs. We will study nontariff trade barriers and analyze their welfare effects in the next chapter.

5.6 SUMMARY

1. A tariff is a tax, or custom duty, imposed on the importation or exportation of a product that is crossing national boundaries.
2. Depending on a tariff's purpose, it can be classified as a protective tariff or a revenue tariff. Protective tariffs are levied to protect a home industry from foreign competitors. Revenue tariffs are imposed by governments to raise tax revenues.
3. Depending on the way tariffs are calculated, they can be classified as specific tariffs, ad valorem tariffs, or compound tariffs. A specific tariff is expressed in terms of a fixed amount of money per unit of the imported product. An ad valorem tariff is expressed in terms of a percentage of the total value of the commodity. Finally, a compound tariff is a combination of specific and ad valorem tariffs.
4. The tariff rates published in a country's tariff schedule, referred to as the nominal tariff, do not always provide us with the real measure of protection afforded to the industry in question.
5. Domestic value added is the price of the final product minus the cost of the imported inputs.
6. The effective rate of protection is the percentage increase in an industry's domestic value added as the result of tariffs.
7. Consumer surplus refers to the difference between the actual amount a consumer pays for a specific good and the maximum amount he or she would have been willing to pay for that good.
8. Producer surplus refers to the difference between the actual amount a producer receives for a good and the minimum amount that he or she would have been willing to accept for that good.
9. A tariff results in an overall loss of consumer surplus.
10. If a tariff is not high enough to prohibit all imports, it will bring some revenue to the government.
11. Given the one-dollar, one-vote yardstick, the imposition of a tariff leads to a net loss for both the nation and the world as a whole.
12. A tariff's production effect measures a loss to the nation imposing the tariff. This loss results from wasted resources employed to produce additional domestic goods at increasing unit costs.
13. A tariff's consumption effect measures a loss to the nation imposing the tariff. This loss results from a decrease in domestic consumption due to the rise in import price following the tariff.

Review Questions

1. Define the concept of a tariff and name different kinds of tariffs (a) according to the purpose for which they are imposed; and (b) according to the way in which they are calculated.
2. Compare specific tariff and ad valorem tariff. Elaborate on the advantages and disadvantages of each of these trade barriers.

---

[*] This analysis ignores the fact that a tariff decreases the amount paid to foreigners, causing the total expenditures on imports to diminish. This either contributes to the balance of payments surplus or affects the exchange rate. It is also assumed that we live in a "first-best world." In such a world, the benefits and losses for individuals are considered to be society's gains and losses without tariffs. In our analysis, it is only the tariff itself that makes social costs and gains different from those of individuals.

3. Differentiate between the effective rate of protection and the nominal rate of protection, and explain how the effective rate of protection is measured.
4. Differentiate between production effect and consumption effect resulting from the imposition of a tariff.
5. Differentiate between producer surplus and consumer surplus. Elaborate on the relevance of these concepts for the consumer's welfare.
6. Discuss how a nation's imposition of a tariff leads to inefficiencies that diminish national welfare.

Problems

1. Suppose in the absence of international trade the equilibrium quantity and price for motorcycles in a hypothetical country is 50,000 units and $9,500, respectively. Now assume that the nation is opened to international trade. As a result, the total quantity of motorcycles demanded increases to 80,000 units, and the price declines to $8,000. Out of this total, 20,000 units are produced domestically, and the rest are imported. Assume that the government imposes a tariff of $1,000 on motorcycles. Given the assumption of perfect competition in the world market, analyze the tariff's impact on the welfare of this country, measuring consumers' loss, producers' loss, government revenue, and the net national loss resulting from the tariff.

2. "Tariffs are desirable because they increase government revenue and, at the same time, they provide protection for domestic industries."

   Do you agree with this statement? Discuss.

3. Consider a nation that is too small to have any influence on world prices. Assume that the demand and supply schedules for this nation's VCRs are as follows:

Price/VCR	Quantity Demanded	Quantity Supplied
$1,000	0	100
800	20	80
600	40	60
400	60	40
200	80	20
0	100	0

   On graph paper, draw the demand and supply curves for the VCRs. Given these curves, answer the following questions, using graphs to illustrate.
   (a) What are the pretrade equilibrium price and equilibrium quantity?
   (b) Determine the pretrade consumer surplus and producer surplus.
   (c) Assuming free trade, suppose the world price for VCRs is $200 per unit. How many VCRs will be supplied, consumed, and imported by this nation? By how much does consumer surplus increase and producer surplus decline following free trade?
   (d) Suppose the nation imposes a specific tariff of $100 on VCR imports. What are the tariff's effects on domestic price, domestic supply, domestic demand, and the volume of imports? By how much does the producer surplus increase and consumer surplus decrease as a result of the tariff? What are the amounts of losses associated with the consumption effect and the production effect of the tariff?

Suggested Readings

Aho, Michael C., and Jonathan D. Arouson. *Trade Talks: America Better Listen.* New York: Council on Foreign Relations, 1985.

Anjaria, S. J., et al. *Trade Policy Developments in Industrial Countries:* Washington, DC: International Monetary Fund, 1981.

Ballasa, B. "Tariff Protection in Industrial Countries." *Journal of Political Economy* (December 1965).

Ballasa, B., et al. *The Structure of Protection in Developing Countries.* Baltimore: John Hopkins Press, 1971.

Bennet, J. T., and T. J. Di Lorenzo. "Union, Policies, and Protectionism." *Journal of Labor Research* (Summer 1984).

Bergsten, Fred C., and William R. Cline. "Trade Policy in the 1980s: An Overview." In *Trade Policy in the 1980s,* edited by William R. Cline. Washington, DC: Institute for International Economics, 1983.

Blackhurst, Richard, et al. *Trade Liberalization, Protectionism, and Interdependence.* Geneva: General Agreement on Tariffs and Trade. Special Paper on International Economics, No. 7. Princeton: Princeton University Press, 1965, ch. 4.

Corden, W. M. *The Theory of Protection.* London: Oxford University Press, 1971.

————. *Trade Policy and Economic Welfare.* London: Oxford University Press, 1974.

Johnson, H. G. "The Theory of Tariff Structure with Special Reference to World Trade and Development." In H. G. Johnson and P. B. Kenen, *Trade and Development.* Geneva: United Nations, 1971.

————. *Aspects of the Theory of Tariffs.* London: Allen and Unwin, 1974.

Metzler, L. A. "Tariffs, the Terms of Trade and the Distribution of National Income." *Journal of Political Economy* (February, 1949).

Rousslang, D. and A. Sumela. "Calculating the Consumer and Net Welfare Cost of Import Relief." U.S. International Trade Commission Staff Research Study 15. Washington DC: International Trade Commission, 1985.

Salvatore, D. *The New Protectionist Threat to World Welfare.* New York: North-Holland, 1987.

————. *Theory and Problems of International Economics.* 2d ed. New York: McGraw-Hill, 1984, ch. 6.

Shutt, H. *The Myth of Free Trade.* New York: Basil Blackwell, 1985.

Yeats, A. J. "Effective Tariff Protection in the United States, the European Economic Community, and Japan. *Quarterly Review of Economics and Business* (Summer 1974).

Appendix

FORMULA FOR CALCULATING
THE EFFECTIVE RATE OF PROTECTION

The effective rate of protection can be calculated by the use of the following formula:

$$R_E = \frac{T_F - rT_M}{1 - r},$$

where

R_E = the effective rate of protection.
T_F = the nominal tariff rate on the final product.
r = the ratio of the value of the imported input to the value of the final product before tariff.
T_M = the nominal tariff rate on the imported input.

Plugging the data from Table 5-2 into the formula, we get

$$R_E = \frac{0.2 - (0.6)(0.0)}{1 - 0.6} = 0.5.$$

Problem. Assume that the production of $1,000 worth of garments in Great Britain requires $500 worth of cloth. The U.S. nominal tariff rates for importing these products are 10 percent for cloth and 25 percent for garments.

Given this data, calculate the effective rate of protection for the U.S. garment industry. Show details of your work.

Chapter 6

NONTARIFF TRADE BARRIERS

6.1 INTRODUCTION

In the previous chapter, we discussed tariff barriers and their welfare effects. But a tariff is not the only tool used to restrict trade. There are many different ways a government can restrict trade without using tariffs. In fact, many countries trade policies in recent years have called for the replacement of tariff trade barriers with nontariff barriers. Major industrial countries have taken such actions as they have progressively reduced tariff rates and eliminated quotas under the auspices of the General Agreement on Tariffs and Trade (GATT), which we explain in Chapter 8. Thus, nontariff trade barriers have emerged as the main obstacle to the benefits of free international trade. The lowering of tariff rates has been compared to the emptying of a swamp. The lower water level has disclosed all the snags and stumps (nontariff barriers) that must be cleaned up to make the swamp easy to cross.

Today, although the majority of economists favor free trade and oppose any kind of trade barriers, they carefully discuss exceptional cases that might warrant trade restrictions.

In this chapter, we first explain some of the main nontariff barriers that affect free international trade. These include quotas, voluntary export restraints, subsidies and taxes. Second, we study dumping, a form of international price discrimination that restricts free international trade. Third, we discuss other nontariff trade barriers, such as customs procedures, foreign exchange restrictions, and regulations.

6.2 QUOTAS

A **quota** is the limitation set on the number of units of a commodity that crosses national boundaries. Depending on whether a good is imported or exported, the quota is referred to as an import quota or an export quota.

6.2a Import Quotas

Import quotas are the most prevalent form of nontariff trade barriers. Like import tariffs, the purpose of import quotas is the protection of domestic industries. The imposition of a quota on a foreign product limits its supply and causes its price to rise. This makes the domestic product relatively cheaper, strengthening its competitive position in the market. Three major types of quotas can be identified: unilateral quotas, bilateral or multilateral quotas, and tariff quotas.

The **unilateral quota** is a quota imposed by an importing country without negotiation or consultation with exporting countries. Because the imposition of this type of quota does not consider the opinion of the exporting countries affected, it may result in tension in, antagonism from, or retaliation by those countries. Sugar imports into the United States provide an example of a commodity that is subject to a unilateral quota established in 1982. In another instance, the quota on peanuts "all but forbids peanut imports" to the United States, allowing only 1.7 million pounds of imports—a small fraction of the total consumption in the United States.[1]

A **bilateral** or **multilateral quota** is imposed by an importing country after consultation or negotiation with exporting countries. Because the decision to impose this type of quota is made in consultation with the exporting countries, it tends to enhance cooperation among these countries, facilitating the quota system's successful operation. Countries have used this type of quota most notably in electronics, textiles, footwear, and automobiles. For example, in 1979, the United States negotiated agreements with Taiwan and the Republic of Korea to set a limit on the number of color televisions that could be imported from these countries.[2] Also in 1979, the United States and Japan signed an agreement to limit Japanese exports of textiles to the United States. This agreement, which was amended in 1982, gradually grew to include 20 categories of textiles.[3] In yet another example, the United States and Japan agreed to increase the Japanese beef import quota by 60,000 tons annually for three years beginning in 1988. They decided to abolish the quotas and replace them with tariffs. The tariff rates started at 70 percent and steadily declined to 50 percent by 1993.[4] In 1993, Japan's government asked the nation's importers to refrain from purchasing foreign beef. Such an informal government request has added to the tension between the United States and Japan at a time when the United States is battling the Japanese government on other issues, urging that Japan abolish its restraints on apple and rice imports.[5]

A **tariff quota** combines the characteristics of both a tariff and a quota. It sets a limit on the number of units of a commodity that may enter a country at a given rate of customs duty (tariff) or at no duty. Any additional quantities imported above the limit are subject to higher customs duties.

GLOBAL INSIGHT CASE 6.1

"Nontrade" Policies Can Cause Trade Disputes

Some recent cases linking trade and nontrade concerns involve meat, cigarettes, wine, and trapped fur.

In 1989 the European Community banned all imports of meat treated with growth promotants following a Community-wide ban on nontherapeutic hormones used in livestock production. The United States believed the directive was not based on scientific evidence and that it constituted an unjustifiable restriction on trade. Bilateral consultations were eventually able to resolve a number of points of contention, but not the underlying issue of how to deal with food standards that are not based on scientific evidence.

The government of Thailand instituted a ban on cigarette advertising in addition to a ban on imported cigarettes and other restrictive practices. In response to a complaint from the United States, GATT found the import ban illegal but ruled that Thailand can prohibit tobacco advertising for health reasons.

In accordance with a U.S. law prohibiting residues in foods of chemicals not registered with the Environmental Protection Agency, the United States recently imposed a temporary ban on EC wine imports containing a fungicide called procymidone until the health risk can be adequately determined. The EC and the United States are engaged in consultations on the temporary import ban.

A possible EC ban on certain furs caught in countries that permit the use of steel leghold traps would restrict U.S. fur trade. There is widespread support in the United States as well as in Europe for the development of more humane traps. However, the U.S. Government opposes the imposition of an arbitrary deadline to meet standards that have not yet been developed and argues that trapping serves the desirable environmental goal of managing the population of fur-bearing animals

Source: U.S. Government Printing Office, *Economic Report of the President*, (Washington, D.C: U.S. Government Printing Office, February 1991), 244, reprinted.

6.2b Export Quotas

Export quotas, by imposing limitations on the number of goods that can be exported, are another way a nation can restrict the free flow of international trade. In extreme cases, export quotas can ban the exportation of a product from one country to another. The three main purposes of export quotas are as follows:

1. To ensure the availability, for domestic use, of a certain amount of a good that is in short supply. For example, during the 1980s the exportation of certain foodstuffs was banned by the Islamic Republic of Iran, which was facing food shortages due to its war with Iraq.
2. To control the supply of certain commodities at the national and international levels in order to manipulate their prices. For example, beginning in 1982, Saudi Arabia, Kuwait, Libya, and the United Arab Emirates

individually restricted their production of oil. These four members of the Organization of Petroleum Exporting Countries (OPEC) reduced their production by 60 percent from 1979 levels in order to raise the price of oil.

3. To check the exportation, to hostile nations, of goods that are significant from a strategic point of view. For example, the United States previously banned the exportation of some sophisticated electronic devices and computers to the former Soviet Union. Also, the exportation of military hardware to Iran, which is considered an unfriendly nation, is prohibited by the U.S. government.

The United States was so sensitive to the exports of strategic goods to the former Soviet block nations that it even imposed trade sanctions against foreign firms that violated this rule.* For example, in 1987, such sanctions were proposed by the U.S. Congress against Toshiba Machine Company of Japan and Kongsberg Vaapenfabrikk of Norway. These firms shipped machine tools for making ultraquiet submarine propellers to the former Soviet Union.[6]

Export quotas, like import quotas, can be classified as unilateral, and bilateral or multilateral. A unilateral export quota is established without the prior consent of importing nations. A bilateral or multilateral export quota, however, is initiated by agreements between trading nations.

6.2c Welfare Effects of a Quota

The analysis presented in Chapter 5 showed that tariffs adversely affect an economy's welfare. As we demonstrate in this section, a quota, like a tariff, leads to net national losses for the nation imposing it.

Using Figure 6-1, assume that the United States' demand and supply for motorcycles in a year are given by D_D and S_D, respectively. The world supply of motorcycles is given by S_W at the competitive price of $4,000 per motorcycle. Given this price, in the absence of a quota, U.S. producers manufacture 1 million motorcycles and U.S. consumers buy 4 million motorcycles. Thus, U.S. imports are equal to 3 million motorcycles (M_O).

Assume that the U.S. government decides to limit the number of motorcycles imported to 1 million a year by imposing an import quota (Q). Graphically, this causes the domestic supply (S_D) to shift to the right by the amount of the quota (Q) to S_{D+Q}. The intersection of S_{D+Q} and D_D at point E′ gives the new equilibrium price of $6,000. Thus, the result of the quota is to limit imports (from 3 million to 1 million) and raise the commodity's price (from $4,000 to $6,000). The reason for the rise of price to $6,000 is that only at this price does the quantity demanded (3 million motorcycles) equal the 2 million motorcycles produced domestically plus the 1 million motorcycles allowed by the import quota. At the higher price, domestic consumption decreases to 3 million units a year, and domestic production increases to 2 million units a year.

The welfare effect of the quota is the same as that of a tariff under competitive conditions, discussed in the previous chapter. Producer surplus rises by area a, consumer surplus falls by areas a + b + c + d, and the quota revenue is equal to area c. Thus, like a tariff, a quota leads to the deadweight loss of areas b + d. Area b represents the *production effect*, and area d represents the *consumption effect* of the quota.

The quota revenue can be collected by the U.S. government, U.S. importers, or foreign exporters. The quota revenue accrues to the U.S. government if it auctions off import licenses to domestic importers. The quota revenue accrues to U.S. importing companies if they organize as buyers and succeed in buying motorcycles at the prevailing world price of $4,000 per unit, reselling them to domestic consumers at the price of $6,000. Finally, the quota revenue accrues to foreign exporting companies if they organize as sellers and increase the price of motorcycles to $6,000, thereby capturing the quota's revenue. In this case, the welfare effects of a quota are not equivalent to those of a tariff.

---

* As we will explain in detail in Chapter 7, trade sanctions involve either banning a country's export to another country or imposing quotas on another country's imports.

FIGURE 6-1
Welfare Effect of a Quota

D_D and S_D represent U.S. demand and supply for motorcycles. At the world price of $4,000 per motorcycle, U.S. production is 1 million units, demand is 4 million units, and imports are 3 million units (M_0). The imposition of an import quota (Q) shifts domestic supply (S_D) to the right by the amount of quota to S_{D+Q}. The result of the quota is to limit imports (from 3 million to 1 million) and raise the commodity's price (from $4,000 to $6,000). Like a tariff, a quota leads to the deadweight loss of areas b + d. Area b represents the *production effect*, and area d represents the *consumption effect* on the quota.

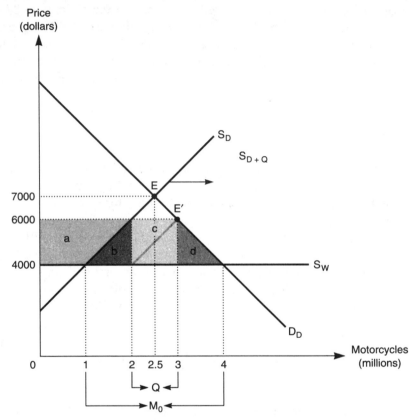

6.3 VOLUNTARY EXPORT RESTRAINTS

Because there is a general agreement between trading nations to avoid imposing quotas except in special cases, most countries are reluctant to use them. Consequently, importing nations usually request exporting countries to voluntarily restrain their exports. Exporting nations are usually reluctant to set a limit on their exports. Imposing this type of quota implies that the importing nation is threatening to impose even tougher restrictions if voluntary cooperation with a quota is not given. For example, in 1981, U.S. automakers and the United Auto Workers (UAW) asked Congress and the Reagan administration to impose quotas on Japanese automobile imports. The purpose was to limit the sales of Japanese automobiles in the U.S. market in order to allow troubled U.S. automakers to stay competitive and operate profitably. It was hoped that this would give U.S. automakers a chance to retool their factories and to produce new cars that could successfully compete with Japanese automobiles when quotas were lifted. In response to this demand, the Reagan administration came up with a compromise. Rather than imposing quotas on Japanese imports, the U.S. government got the Japanese to agree to "voluntarily" limit their exports to the United States to 1.6

GLOBAL INSIGHTS CASE 6.2

U.S. Sugar Quotas and the Global Sugar Market

The U.S. sugar quota instituted in 1982, has increasingly limited the country's sugar imports. In 1981, before the quota's imposition the United States imported approximately 4.5 million metric tons of sugar a year. In 1982, the quota limited U.S. sugar imports to about 2.62 million metric tons. As the table indicates, quotas have changed over the years, reflecting changing market conditions. In 1993, the quotas allowed only 1.38 million metric tons of sugar to be imported.

The quotas have given rise to high sugar prices in the United States. The higher prices, in turn, have stimulated the development of sugar substitutes. Industries that use large amounts of sugar, specifically the soft-drink industry, have increasingly switched to less expensive sweeteners. It has been estimated that the percentage share of the U.S. sweetener market captured by corn sweeteners rose from 4 percent to 50 percent during the 1980s.

As the analysis of quota suggests, U.S. producers have gained at the expense of consumers. According to one estimate, the annual benefit to each U.S. sugar producer is about $170,000, whereas the total cost to U.S. consumers is about $3 billion a year. These estimates do not even include industries that use sugar as an input and whose costs of production are higher as a result of sugar quotas.

The sugar quotas have hurt a number of developing countries that count on sugar exports to generate their foreign exchange needs. Among the developing countries that have been adversely affected by U.S. sugar quotas, Argentina, Brazil, Mexico, and the Philippines, have suffered most. All of these nations need sugar revenues to pay off their substantial external debts. In 1989, a GATT panel found the U.S. sugar quotas in violation of international rules, charging that such quotas unfairly limit trade. These quotas were one of the issues included in the Uruguay Round, which concluded on December 15, 1993.

Import Quotas on Raw Sugar
(Million Metric Tons)

Year Quotas	Dates	
1982-1983	10/1/82-9/30/83	2.62
1983-1984	9/26/83-9/30/84	2.88
1984-1985	10/1/84-11/30/85	2.43
1985-1986	12/1/85-12/30/86	1.68
1987	1/1/87-12/31/87	0.91
1988	1/1/88-12/31/88	0.96
1989-1990	1/1/89-9/30/90	2.83
1990-1991	10/1/90-9/30/91	2.10
1991-1992	10/9/91-9/30/92	1.38
1992-1993 through 1993-1994	10/1/92-9/30/94	2.26

Source: Foreign Agriculture Service, USDA.

Sources: Murray L. Weidenbaum, *Toward a More Open Trade Policy*, Formal Publication No. 53 (St. Louis: Center for the Study of American Business, Washington University, 1983), 10; "GATT Panel Finds U.S. Sugar Quotas Violate International Rules or Imports," *The Wall Street Journal*, 1 June 1989, A8.

million cars a year.* This agreement was extended for four years. The fourth-year quota, which set a limit of 1.85 million cars a year, expired on March 31, 1985.[7] However, on March 28, 1985, the Japanese government announced that it would continue the voluntary restraint for at least another year, but at a higher level of 2.3 million cars a year. Again, in January 1987, the Japanese government informed the United States that it would extend the restraint of 2.3 million cars to March 1988.[8] Given the U.S. recession in the early 1990s, the pressure to limit the importation of Japanese automobiles to the United States has continued to increase. For example, in 1991, former Chrysler Corporation Chairman Lee A. Iacocca called for further restraint on Japanese automakers, saying, "We just can't say the consumer is king and therefore to hell with unemployment, to hell with social costs."[9] The quota lasted until the early 1990s. As a consequence of the Uruguay Round which took effect on July 1, 1995, members of the World Trade Organization (WTO) decided to refrain from imposing any new voluntary export restraints and to phase out any existing voluntary export restraints over a four year period. It seems that the quota did not resolved the real problem, namely, the inability of the U.S. auto industry to effectively compete in the world market. According to a consumer survey taken in the 1980s, Japanese cars consistently outscored U.S. cars in terms of quality and customer satisfaction. It seems that what the U.S. auto industry really needs is a free and competitive market that forces the U.S. entrepreneur to innovate, cut costs, and improve efficiency, thereby producing high-quality cars that can compete effectively in the international market.

Manufacturers in the United States have been aware of the need to increase productivity in order to raise their shares of the world export market. Beginning in the 1990s, U.S. labor productivity started to increase significantly. In fact, according to one report, the United States' labor productivity relative to the rest of the world ranked first in 1991. This position was followed by Canada (93% of the U.S. labor productivity level), and Japan and most European countries (70% to 80% of the U.S. labor productivity level). The rise in labor productivity has helped the United States become stronger in the world market, helping U.S. corporations become extremely competitive in the world market. For example, in the automobile industry, Ford Taurus ranked first in the number of automobiles sold in the United States during 1992, replacing Honda Accord. This marks the first time that an American-made automobile was ranked as the best-selling car in the United States since 1988.[10]

6.3a Welfare Effects of Voluntary Export Restraints

The welfare effects of voluntary export restraints are similar to those of a quota. Figure 6-2 illustrates this, assuming that the United States imports automobiles from Japan.

Suppose D_{US} and S_{US} represent the demand and supply of automobiles in the United States. S_J represents Japan's supply schedule of automobiles to the United States. In the absence of any restriction on trade, the price of automobiles to the U.S. consumer is $10,000 per unit. At this price, U.S. consumers demand 40 million automobiles. However, U.S. producers supply only 10 million automobiles. This excess demand of 30 million (M_0) automobiles is satisfied by imports from Japan.

Assume that Japan imposes a voluntary export restraint (Q), limiting its automobile exports to the United States to 10 million units. Graphically, this causes the domestic supply (S_{US}) to shift to the right by the amount of the restraint (Q) to S_{US+Q}. The intersection of S_{US+Q} and D_{US} at point E' gives the new equilibrium price of $12,000. Thus, the result of the voluntary export restraint is to limit imports (from 30 million to 10 million) and raise the price of the automobile (from $10,000 to $12,000). The reason for the rise in price is that only at this price does the quantity demanded (30 million automobiles) equal the 20 million automobiles produced domestically plus the 10 million automobiles imported under the restraint. This results in a welfare loss for the U.S. economy. Table 6-1 shows that this loss is equal to areas b + c + d from Figure 6-2 and is composed of deadweight losses in production (area b), and consumption (area d). Area c denotes the quota revenue collected by the Japanese exporters. It represents a welfare loss to the United States in addition to the deadweight losses in production and consumption.

---

*   Imposing quotas on just one country, in this case Japan, would have been in violation of GATT. We elaborate on GATT in Chapter 8.

FIGURE 6-2
Welfare Effects of a Voluntary Export Restraint

D_{US} and S_{US} represent the demand and supply of automobilies in the United States; S_J represents Japan's supply schedule of automobiles to the United States. In the absence of trade, the price of automobiles is $10,000 per unit, U.S. demand is 40 million units, domestic production is 10 million units, and imports from Japan are 30 million units (Mo). Japan's imposition of a voluntary export restraint (Q) of 10 million units causes domestic supply (S_{US}) to shift to the right by the amount of the quota restraint to S_{US+Q}. This limits imports (from 30 million to 10 million) and raises the price of automobiles (from $10,000 to $12,000). The welfare loss to the U.S. economy is equal to areas b + c + d and is composed of deadweight losses in production (area b), and consumption (area d). Area c denotes the quota revenue collected by the Japanese government and represents an additional welfare loss to the United States.

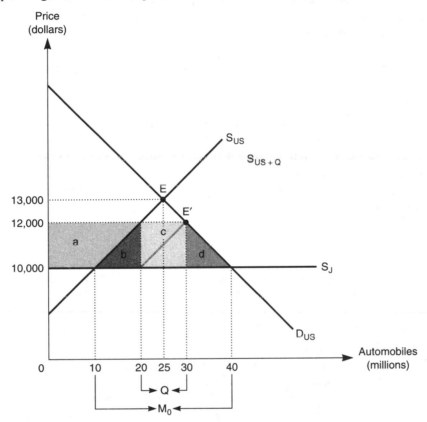

Table 6-1
WELFARE EFFECTS OF A VOLUNTARY EXPORT RESTRAINT

	Gains (+)/Loss (-)
Loss in consumers' surplus	Areas - (a + b + c + d)
Gain in producers' surplus	Area a
Net national loss	Areas - (b + c + d)

In the previous section we learned that the revenue generated from an import quota could be collected by the importing government, foreign exporters, or domestic importers. However, in the case of a voluntary export quota, the quota revenue accrues to the foreign exporter. In our example, Japanese exporters' decision to comply with their government's voluntary restraint results in a decrease in the U.S. supply of automobiles. As a result, Japanese firms can raise the price of their exports, capturing the quota revenue. The Japanese absorption of the quota revenue represents a welfare loss that is added to the deadweight losses in production and consumption experienced by the United States.

6.4 COMPARISON OF TARIFFS AND QUOTAS

Both tariffs and quotas are protectionist means used to raise the prices of foreign goods relative to domestic goods. This allows domestic producers to compete more effectively with foreign producers of similar goods. The main differences between tariffs and quotas are as follows:

1. Quotas are more effective than tariffs in restraining trade flow. An import duty raises the domestic price, but it may not limit the number of goods that can be imported into a country. Consequently, the degree of protection provided by a tariff, as the result of a higher price, is determined by the market mechanism. However, by imposing an absolute limit on the imported good, a quota entirely forecloses the market adjustment and provides us with a certain and precise restraining tool.
2. A disadvantage of quotas is that their use may lead to domestic monopoly of production and higher prices. Because a domestic firm knows that foreign firms cannot surpass their quotas, it may increase its prices. Tariffs, however, do not necessarily induce monopoly power because no limit is set on the number of goods that can be imported into the country.
3. Because quotas are more effective than tariffs in restricting trade flows, they are more effective bargaining and retaliation tools.
4. Quotas may be easier to administer than tariffs. The imposition of tariffs requires statutory legislation, which is a time-consuming process. Consequently, quotas are better suited to emergency situations.
5. Quotas are more restrictive than tariffs and suppress competition. Tariffs allow for some degree of competition.
6. Quotas may be more harmful than tariffs to an importing nation if the quotas give monopoly power to exporters. For example, in an attempt to ease U.S. protectionist sentiments in the early 1960s, the government persuaded foreign suppliers of textiles and steel products to impose voluntary export restraints to limit their exports to the United States. Accordingly, these foreign suppliers were forced to divide the limited quota of exports to the U.S. market among themselves. This led the foreign suppliers, who were previously competing with each other, to collude and charge U.S. importers the full U.S. price rather than the lower competitive world price. Consequently, the United States not only experienced the same losses it would have had with an identical tariff, but it sustained additional losses due to its inability to keep the price markup at home.[11]

6.5 SUBSIDIES

Subsidies are indirect forms of protection granted by national governments to domestic producers. Subsidies are given to either export industries or import-competing industries. The main purpose of subsidizing home industries is to improve a country's international trade position either by diminishing dependence on imports or by earning more foreign exchange by enhancing exports. Subsidies enable domestic firms to export their products at lower prices than those really needed to cover costs or provide desired profits. This allows the less efficient domestic producer to compete more successfully against the more efficient foreign producers in the international market for exported goods.

Subsidies take different forms. The simplest form is direct cash payments by the government to a domestic exporter after a sale has been completed. However, because such direct subsidies for manufactured goods are prohibited by GATT, nations may resort to other forms of subsidies to reach the same goal. These forms include special privileges, such as low interest loans, insurance arrangements, and tax concessions, granted by a government to its exporters. For example, to encourage U.S. exports, the Export-Import Bank of the United States grants direct loans and guarantees insured loans to foreign buyers of U.S. goods and services. In another example, in 1985, the Japanese government announced a plan to provide a subsidy package to small export companies that includes low-interest loans, relaxed credit rules, and loan consideration without collateral.[12]

Governments may also buy a firm's surplus products at a relatively high price and export them at a low price. This policy has been followed by the U.S. government in implementing the farm support program.

In the United States, countervailing duties can be imposed if the Commerce Department rules that subsidized imports harm domestic industry. A case in point is the example of Canadian softwood lumber. In 1992, the Commerce Department ruled that Canada had unfairly subsidized its softwood-lumber industry. To offset the alleged price advantage of Canadian softwood imports to the United States, the department set a duty rate at 6.1 percent of the imports' value.[13]

Regardless of the way a subsidy is granted, its economic effect, like that of a tariff, is the loss of economic efficiency and higher costs to consumers. Additionally, because a subsidy subverts the application of the law of comparative advantage, the gains from international specialization and division of labor also diminish.

6.5a Welfare Effects of a Subsidy

The welfare effect of a subsidy depends on whether it is granted to producers of import-competing goods (domestic production subsidy) or producers of goods that are exported (export subsidy).

Domestic Production Subsidy. Domestic production can be increased and imports decreased through the use of a production subsidy. The welfare effects of a domestic production subsidy are illustrated in Figure 6-3. Using this figure, assume that the U.S. demand and supply for bicycles are given by D_{US} and S_{US}, respectively. The world supply of bicycles is given by S_W, and it is assumed to be perfectly elastic. In other words, the United States is considered to be a small buyer of bicycles, and, as such, it cannot affect the world price of $200 per bicycle. At this price, in the absence of any restriction to free international trade, the United States demands 22 million bicycles but only produces 1 million bicycles. The excess demand of 21 million bicycles is satisfied by imports (M_0).

Now assume that the United States grants a subsidy of $75 per bicycle to its import-competing bicycle producers. This cost advantage causes the U.S. supply of bicycles to shift to the right, from S_{US} to S'_{US}. This is because the subsidy decreases the cost of production, enabling U.S. bicycle producers to sell each bicycle at a lower price. As a result, domestic production increases from 1 to 8 million bicycles, and imports decrease from 21 to 14 million (22 - 8 = 14) bicycles (M_1).

The effects of the subsidy on U.S. welfare can be seen from Figure 6-3. According to the figure, the total amount of subsidy granted by the U.S. government to the bicycle industry is equal to $600 million (the amount of subsidy per bicycle [$75] multiplied by domestic production after the subsidy [8 million bicycles]).

This $600 million is composed of two parts, denoted as areas a and b on the graph. Area a ($337.50 million) represents a gain in producers' surplus that is attributed to the more efficient domestic producers. Area b ($262.50 million) is the subsidy's *production effect* representing a deadweight loss of welfare to the United States, arising from the production of the more costly domestic output made possible by the subsidy.[*] Thus, in comparison to a tariff

---

[*]   Area a is a trapezoid. The area of a trapezoid is calculated by the following formula:

$$\tfrac{1}{2}(b)\,(h_1 + h_2).$$

In Figure 6-3, h_1 and h_2 represent the lower and upper horizontal sides of the trapezoid, respectively; b represents the vertical side. Numerically, this is equal to $337.50 million [$\tfrac{1}{2}(75)\,(1 + 8) = 337.50$].
    Area b is a triangle. The area of a triangle is calculated by the following formula:

$$\tfrac{1}{2}(b \times h).$$

Here, b and h represent base and height, respectively. In our example, this is equal to $262.50 million ($\tfrac{1}{2} \times 7 \times 75 = 262.50$).

Figure 6-3
WELFARE EFFECTS OF A DOMESTIC PRODUCTION SUBSIDY

D_{US} and S_{US} represent U.S. demand and supply for bicycles. In the absence of any restriction to free international trade, at the world price of $200 per bicycle, U.S. demand is 22 million units, domestic production is 1 million units, and imports are 21 million units (M_0). A subsidy of $75 per bicycle causes S_{US} to shift to S'_{US}. As a result, domestic production increases from 1 million to 8 million units, and imports decrease from 21 million to 14 million (22 - 8 = 14) units (M_1). Of the total amount of the subsidy ($75 x 8 million = $600 million), area a ($337.5 million) represents a gain in producer surplus, and area b ($262.50 million) represents a deadweight welfare loss to the United States.

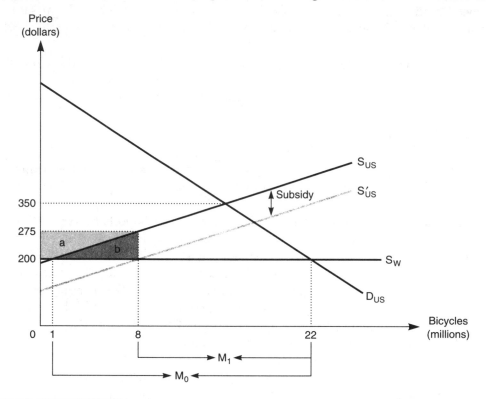

that leads to welfare-diminishing production and consumption effects, a domestic production subsidy encompasses only a production effect. As a result, a domestic production subsidy is preferable to a tariff in terms of welfare because it has a smaller deadweight loss and leaves consumption unchanged.

Export Subsidy. As we explained earlier, an export subsidy can take different forms, ranging from direct tax payment to special privileges a government may grant to its exporters, such as low interest loans, insurance arrangements, and tax concessions. For simplicity, however, we assume that the subsidy takes the form of a fixed cash payment for each unit of a commodity that is exported. In this context, the cash subsidy may be viewed as a negative export tariff. The welfare effects of an export subsidy are illustrated in Figure 6-4, which is similar to Figure 5-5. In this figure, assume that Japan's supply and demand curves for steel are given by S_J and D_J respectively. The world demand for steel is given by D_W, and it is assumed to be perfectly elastic. In other words, Japan is considered to be a small nation, and, as such, it cannot affect the world price of $300 per ton of steel. In the absence of any restriction to international trade, Japan produces 300 million tons of steel, consumes 200 million tons, and exports the remaining 100 million tons.

FIGURE 6-4
Welfare Effects of an Export Subsidy

S_J and D_J represent Japan's demand and supply for steel. In the absence of any restriction to international trade, at the world price of $300 per ton, Japan produces 300 million tons of steel, consumes 200 million tons, and exports the remaining 100 million tons. A subsidy of $50 per ton granted to Japanese exporters causes the price of steel to rise to $350 per ton. At this higher price, the quantity demanded by domestic consumers declines to 100 million tons, domestic production increases to 350 million tons, and exports increase to 250 million tons. Domestic consumers lose $7,500 (areas a + b), domestic producers gain $16,250 (area a + b + c), and the direct cost of subsidization to Japanese taxpayers is $12,500 (areas b + c + d). The net national loss—obtained by adding up consumer loss, producer gain, and the direct cost of subsidization—is equal to $37,750 (areas b + d), which comprises the consumption effect (area b; $2,500) and the production effect (area d; $1,250).

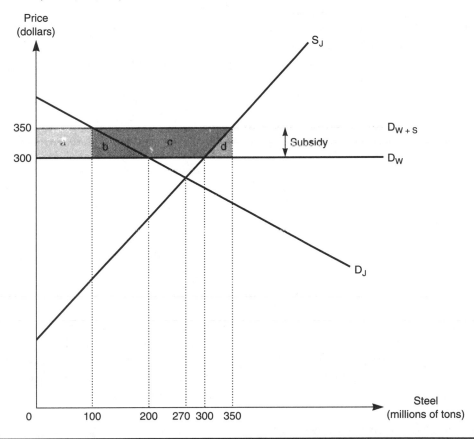

Now assume that the Japanese government grants a subsidy of $50 per ton to its exporters in order to encourage export sales. The subsidy permits Japanese exporting firms to receive revenue of $350 per ton of steel which is equal to the world price plus the subsidy ($300 + $50 = $350), as shown by ($D_W$ + S). The subsidy is not available on domestic sales. However, these firms are willing to sell to domestic consumers only at the higher price of $350 per ton. Thus, although the higher price benefits Japanese producers, it hurts Japanese consumers. Not only do they have to finance the cost of the subsidy, but they also have to pay a higher price ($350 per ton) for the same product they helped to subsidize, compared to the price paid by foreign consumers ($300 per ton). At the higher price, the quantity demanded by domestic consumers declines to 100 million tons, domestic production increases to 350 million tons, and exports increase to 250 million tons.

The welfare effects of the export subsidy on the Japanese economy can be analyzed within the context of producer and consumer surplus. Domestic consumers lose $7,500 (areas a + b), domestic producers gain $16,250 (areas a + b + c), and the direct cost of subsidization to Japanese taxpayers is $12,500 (areas b + c + d). Adding up consumers' loss, producers' gain, and the direct cost of subsidization, we get the following:

			Gains (+)/Loss (-)			
Consumers' loss	Areas	-	(a	+	b)	
Producers' gain	Areas		a	+	b	+ c
Direct cost of subsidization	Areas	-		(b	+ c	+ d)
Net national loss	Areas	-		(b	+	d)

As this analysis shows, the subsidy, like a tariff, leads to a net national loss ($3,750) that is equal to the sum of the consumption effect (area b; $2,500) and the production effect (area d; $1,250).

In this example, we assumed that the exporting country (Japan) was a relatively small nation. In the real world, an exporting nation may not be small and thus may experience a decrease in its terms of trade. This happens because in order to export more of its commodity it has to lower its price. A decline in the price of the exported good would worsen the exporting nation's terms of trade.

6.6 TAXES

The free flow of international trade and investments is disturbed not only by taxes imposed on traded goods but also by the differential tax structure of trading nations. In extreme cases, firms set up operations in foreign countries, mainly because of the lower taxes in those nations. For example, many U.S. banks have set up their offices in places such as the West Indies and Panama, which have lower tax rates than the United States, and the relatively low taxes in Hong Kong are a contributing factor in attracting foreign capital to that island.

As a protective device, taxes can be used to encourage exports or discourage imports. On the export side, exported goods may be exempted from value-added tax (VAT). **Value-added tax,** devised by French economists and used throughout the European Union (EU), is a tax imposed on the value that is added at each stage of the production of a given good. Thus, the tax paid by the producer of each stage is proportional to the value added to the product at that stage.

Another way of encouraging exports or direct investment abroad is to give a foreign tax credit to a firm to prevent double taxation of its income by both domestic and foreign governments. To achieve this goal, some countries, such as Japan, exempt the foreign earnings of the subsidiaries of their MNCs from taxes. However, other countries, like the United States, allow a firm's foreign taxes to be deducted from its domestic tax liabilities. Of course, no matter what technique is used, the granting of tax credit is like a subsidy and causes a government to give up part of its revenue to a foreign nation.

Excise taxes and processing taxes can be used to discourage the importation of certain products. **Excise taxes** are sales taxes collected when goods enter through customs. **Processing taxes,** levied on certain semifinished goods and raw materials, are duties collected when a good is first processed domestically. As protective devices, imposing these taxes on imports raises the prices of the imported goods. This causes the competitive position of domestic goods to improve, thus boosting their sales.

6.7 DUMPING

Trade restrictions may also result from dumping. **Dumping** is the practice of selling a product at below cost or at a lower price in a foreign market than in the domestic market. The practice of dumping may take three different forms, known as sporadic, predatory, and persistent dumping.

Sporadic dumping occurs when a firm with surplus inventories sells its product in a foreign market at below cost or at a price that is lower than that charged in the domestic market. This form of dumping occurs occasionally and is practiced in order to dispose of an unexpected surplus resulting from either mismanagement or unpredicted changes in supply and demand conditions. In this case, to protect its domestic industry, the importing country can impose temporary tariff duties to neutralize the impact of sporadic dumping. However, because this kind of dumping is temporary and its impact on international trade insignificant, most governments do not choose to impose tariff duties for protection purposes.

Predatory dumping is practiced when a firm temporarily sells its product at below cost or at a lower price in a foreign market, with the intention of weakening or driving its competitors out of the market. If this is successful, the firm raises the price of the product after competition has been eliminated. As a result, the firm then gains monopoly power over the product and is able to set a new price that is high enough to compensate for the losses incurred during the dumping practice. To be successful, the firm should be able to prevent possible entrants from coming into the market long enough to enjoy a monopoly profit from sales.

Persistent dumping, or international price discrimination, goes on continually. This form of dumping occurs when a firm with monopoly power consistently sells its product at below cost or at a lower price abroad than at home. The purpose of this kind of dumping is to maximize the firm's profit, and it may occur when the foreign demand for a firm's product is relatively more elastic than its domestic demand.* Persistent dumping is also practiced when an exporting firm absorbs its fixed costs at home and is able to price its exports such that the foreign price covers only its variable costs.

In summary, sporadic dumping is the *occasional* sale of a product at below cost, or at a lower price in a foreign market, to dispose of a firm's unexpected surplus. Predatory dumping is the *temporary* sale of a product at below cost, or a lower price in a foreign market, with the purpose of driving foreign producers out of the market, and then raising the price after competition is eliminated. Persistent dumping is the *continual* sale of a product at below cost, or at a lower price in a foreign market, for the purpose of profit maximization.

Over the years, many countries have been accused of dumping their products in the United States. For example, an investigation in 1970 showed that Sony was selling a particular model of its Japanese-made television sets for $180 in the United States but charging its Japanese domestic consumers $333 for the same model. Other examples of dumping in the United States include the dumping of Japanese steel and Germany's Volkswagen. Another example is the case of one Canadian firm that accused both the United States and Japan of dumping their hypodermic needles in Canada.[14]

A final example involves the 1989 case of Japanese all-terrain vehicles. An investigation by the U.S. International Trade Commission found that a number of Japanese manufacturers of all-terrain vehicles were dumping their products in the United States. As a result, the Commerce Department recommended an imposition of duties on Kawasaki Heavy Industries, Honda Motor Company, Suzuki Motor Company, and Yamaha Motor Company.[15]

Because dumping a product in a country puts that country's import-competing firms at a disadvantage, many national governments have enacted antidumping regulations that usually involve a *remedial tariff.* The purpose of this tariff is to neutralize the undesirable effect of lower prices (resulting from dumping) on domestic firms. In the United States, the Anti-dumping Act of 1921 rules that a tariff equal to the price differential (domestic price compared to the foreign price) be imposed against the dumper for as long as dumping continues.

The international antidumping code negotiated during the Kennedy round of trade liberalization (1962-1967) allows importing countries to impose a fixed duty that is high enough to offset the harm done to domestic import-competing firms by the dumper's lower prices.

In practice, when dumping charges can be proved, most accused firms usually decide to increase their prices rather than pay antidumping duties. For example, in response to dumping charges, both Volkswagen (1976) and Sony (1977) raised their prices to avoid the imposition of antidumping duties on their products in the United States.

---

* The demand for a product in a foreign market is expected to be more elastic than that in a domestic market because foreign buyers have more purchasing options than domestic buyers. Consequently, they are more responsive to price changes than domestic buyers. In other words, a one-percent increase in the price of a product would cause a relatively higher decline in the quantity demanded in the foreign market compared to the domestic market. This situation allows the entrepreneur to engage in price discrimination by charging higher prices in the less elastic (responsive) domestic market than those charged in the foreign market. The analysis of persistent dumping, or international price discrimination, is presented in the next section.

6.7a International Price Discrimination

Figure 6-5 illustrates persistent dumping, or international price discrimination, using the case of Yamaha Motor Company's 1989 dumping of all-terrain vehicles in the United States.

Figure 6-5
INTERNATIONAL PRICE DISCRIMINATION

D_J and D_{US} represent Japanese and U.S. demand for Yamaha's all-terrrain vehicles; MR_J and MR_{US} represent the corresponding marginal revenues. The total output leading to the maximization of total profit is Q_{US+J} and occurs at point E, where MR_{J+US} intersects M_C. The distribution of the total output, Q_{J+US}, between the two submarkets (domestic and foreign) and the price set in each market is shown by points E_J and E_{US}, where a horizontal line from point E intersects MR_J and MR_{US}, respectively. At point E_J, Yamaha sells Q_J units in Japan (domestic market) at the price of P_J per unit. It sells the remaining Q_{US} units in the United States (foreign market) at the price of P_{US} per unit.

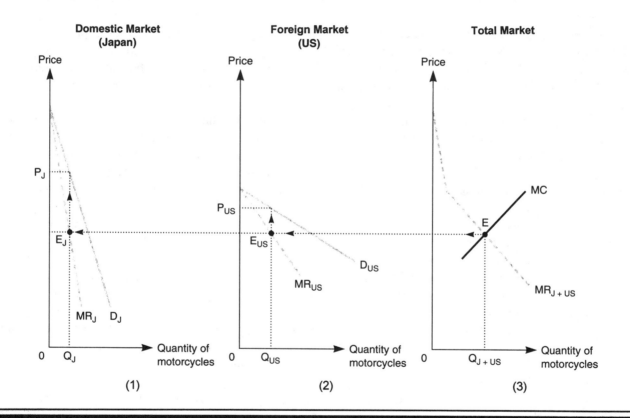

Let D_J and D_{US} represent Japanese demand and U.S. demand for Yamaha's all-terrain vehicles, respectively. Assume that the corresponding marginal revenues are given by MR_J and MR_{US}. The horizontal summation of MR_J and MR_{US} gives the total marginal revenue schedule (MR_{J+US}.) Yamaha's marginal cost of producing all-terrain vehicles is given by M_C in the third panel. Following the profit maximizing rule of $M_C = MR$, Yamaha's profit is maximized at point E, where $MR_{J+US} = M_C$. At this point, Yamaha produces Q_{J+US} units of all-terrain vehicles. The distribution of the total output, Q_{J+US}, between the two submarkets (domestic and foreign) and the price set in each of these markets is also accomplished by the $M_C = M_R$ rule. This is shown by points E_J and E_{US}, where a horizontal line from point E intersects MR_J and MR_{US}, respectively. At point E, Yamaha sells Q_J units in Japan (domestic market) at the price of P_J per unit. It will sell the remaining Q_{US} units in the United States (foreign market) at the price of P_{US} per unit. Thus, the international price discrimination results in charging a lower price P_{US} in the more elastic (foreign) market and a higher price P_J in the less elastic (domestic) market.

For price discrimination to be successful, three conditions must be met. First, the firm must have monopoly power. Second, the demand elasticities in the foreign market and domestic market must be different at any given price level. Third, the price-discriminating firm must be able to segment the two markets to prevent the purchase of the product in the cheaper market for resale in the more expensive market. This is because the purchase of the product in the cheaper market will increase the demand for the product in that market, causing its price to rise. On the other hand, the product's resale in the more expensive market will increase its supply, causing its price to fall. This process closes the price gap between the two nations.

6.8 OTHER NONTARIFF TRADE BARRIERS

Besides quotas, subsidies, taxes, and dumping, there are other forms of nontariff trade barriers, which are often well disguised and appear in the form of government policies and regulations. They may be classified into three major categories: government purchasing policies, administrative and technical regulations, and intervention in the foreign exchange market.

6.8a Government Purchasing Policies

Because governments are significant buyers in the international market, they have enormous power in affecting the flow of international goods and services. In pursuing their protectionist policies, governments usually require that preferences be given to domestic rather than foreign producers for government purchases. For example, in the United States, according to the Buy American Act, established U.S. agencies must give a 6-percent price advantage to domestic suppliers. This price advantage rises to 12 percent in the case of a business located in a small or depressed area, and to 50 percent for defense contracts. This law was still in effect during the late 1990s.

6.8b Administrative and Technical Regulations

National governments impose large numbers of administrative and technical regulations on imports. Although some of these regulations may be imposed with no intention of restricting trade, they may have the same effect as import restrictions.

Government Health and Safety Standards. An example of these standards is the U.S. pollution control standards, which call for mandatory antipollution control devices and prohibit the sale of foreign cars that do not meet these requirements. The installation of these devices makes foreign cars relatively more expensive, causing a potential decrease in foreign car imports to the United States. In another example, foreign pharmaceuticals and medical equipment imported to Japan are subject to such rigorous safety inspections that it may take months or years for a product to be tested. Usually, during the time it takes for these tests to be completed, the government gives Japanese manufacturers samples of the product. This enables them to produce their own brand of the product before the foreign brand is allowed to enter the Japanese market.[16] As yet another example, auto inspectors are so strict in Japan that they reject 80 percent of the cars that are imported from abroad.[17]

Marketing and Packaging Standards. An example of marketing and packaging standards can be seen in the Canadian regulations that require canned foods to be packed in can sizes established by the Canadian government. This means that some foreign food manufacturers, who pack their products in can sizes different from those specified by the Canadian government, cannot export their products to Canada. Consequently, the overall potential import of canned goods into Canada decreases. In another example, the Danish government requires that all soft drinks be sold in returnable bottles. This regulation discriminates against foreign exporters, such as French mineral water producers, who find it too expensive to collect the returnable bottles for refilling in France.

GLOBAL INSIGHT CASE 6.3

Trade and Intellectual Property Rights

A major nontariff barrier to U.S. exports is the lack of adequate protection for intellectual property rights (IPR) in certain countries. The nature of intellectual property has always made it vulnerable to piracy: theft of intellectual property costs U.S. exporters billions of dollars in lost sales and royalties annually. Many of the top U.S. export earners - including copyrighted products such as films, sound recordings, and computer software, and patented products such as new pharmaceuticals - are among the most vulnerable. Piracy not only reduces U.S. export earnings but also discourages the development of new products by lowering the returns to innovation. Efforts to establish strong IPR protection abroad have therefore been an essential element of the Administration's trade policy, advanced through multilateral, regional, and bilateral mechanisms.

The Uruguay Round Agreement on Trade-Related Aspects of Intellectual Property Rights (TRIPS) makes significant progress in securing stronger protection for IPR worldwide. It is the first international agreement to protect a full range of intellectual property and to provide for the establishment of the legal and judicial structures needed to enforce IPR protection. The TRIPS agreement requires all WTO members to set improved rules for the protection of copyrights, integrated circuits, patents, trademarks, trade secrets, and design. The new rules will then be subject to the WTO's improved dispute settlement system.

Source: U.S. Government Printing Office, *Economic Report of the President,* (Washington, D.C: U.S. Government Printing Office, February 1996), 236, Reprinted.

Customs Procedures and Valuation. The government of the importing country may discriminate against a product or an exporting country simply by delaying the importation process with undue inspection or by disagreeing with the invoice value of the product. For example, instead of using the invoice value of a product to calculate its duty, officials might use the domestic wholesale price, the retail price, or an estimated price based on what it might cost to produce the product at home. Consequently, they may come up with a price that is higher than the invoice price and charge the exporter a higher duty than is justified. To deal with this problem, since 1980, most industrial countries have agreed on a standard procedure for determining the value of products that cross national boundaries, in order to give foreign suppliers a fair chance.

6.8c Intervention in the Foreign Exchange Market

By intervening in the foreign exchange market, governments can help to reduce the amount of imports and/or increase the amount of exports. One method that can be used to achieve this goal is devaluation or depreciation of the national currency. Devaluation or depreciation of a national currency, as we explain in Chapter 14, makes each unit of a foreign currency relatively more expensive than the domestic currencies.* This causes import prices to rise. For example, consider the export of Beck's beer from Germany to the United States. The beer costs two German marks per bottle in Germany. If we ignore transportation costs and assume that there are no quotas or tariffs and that each German mark equals 0.5 U.S. dollar, then the value of Beck's beer in the U.S. market would be $1 per bottle. If the U.S. takes measures to depreciate the dollar so that each German mark commands only one U.S. dollar, then the value of the beer in the United States would be equal to $2 per bottle. In other words, the depreciation of the U.S. dollar

---

*   As we explain in Chapter 14, there is a subtle difference between the terms devaluation and depreciation. Devaluation implies a fixed exchange rate system, whereas depreciation implies a flexible exchange rate system. Both devaluation and depreciation lead to an increase in the price of a foreign currency relative to the domestic currency.

causes the price of Beck's beer to increase in the United States. This in turn leads to a lower quantity of Beck's beer demanded in the United States, causing the amount of beer imported to decrease.

Depreciation of the dollar may also lead to higher exports for the United States. Following a depreciation, each German mark commands more U.S. dollars, with the result that the price of American-made products decreases in terms of the German mark. This may lead to an increase in U.S. exports to Germany.

Another method that can be used to control the flow of trade is the employment of **multiple exchange rates**. As we explain in Chapter 14, with this method a country assigns separate official exchange rates for different commodities that are either imported or exported. Most developing countries today use this method to ensure that essential goods are imported and that nonessential goods are discouraged. These countries assign a high exchange rate for essential imports, such as raw materials or capital goods, and set a low exchange rate for nonessentials, such as luxury goods.*

In closing this chapter, we may note that despite the convincing theoretical arguments against tariffs and nontariff trade barriers, many nations have reverted to these protectionist tools on the basis of noneconomic considerations. In the next chapter, we elaborate on the arguments for protection. We will see that, in general, most of these arguments are rejected by the majority of economists, who support free international trade.

6.9 SUMMARY

1. A quota is the limitation set on the number of units of a commodity that crosses national boundaries. Depending on whether a good is imported or exported, the quota is referred to as an import quota or an export quota.
2. Import quotas are the most prevalent form of nontariff trade barriers.
3. The unilateral quota is a quota imposed by an importing country without negotiation or consultation with exporting countries.
4. A bilateral or multilateral quota is imposed by an importing country after consultation or negotiation with exporting countries.
5. A tariff quota combines the characteristics of both a tariff and a quota. It sets a limit on the number of units of a commodity that may enter a country at a given rate of customs duty (tariff) or at no duty. Any additional quantities imported above the limit are subject to higher customs duty rates.
6. Export quotas, by imposing limitations on the number of goods that can be exported, are another way a nation can restrict the free flow of international trade. In extreme cases, export quotas can ban the exportation of a product from one country to another.
7. Export quotas, like import quotas, can be classified as unilateral, and bilateral or multilateral. A unilateral export quota is established without the prior consent of importing nations. A bilateral or multilateral export quota, however, is initiated by agreements between trading nations.
8. The welfare effects of a quota are equivalent to those of a tariff under competitive conditions.
9. The welfare effects of a voluntary export restraint are similar to those of a quota.
10. The main difference between tariffs and quotas are as follows:
    (a) Quotas are more effective than tariffs in restricting trade flow.
    (b) A disadvantage of quotas is that their use may lead to domestic monopoly of production and higher prices.
    (c) Because quotas are more effective than tariffs in restricting trade flows, they are more effective bargaining and retaliation tools.
    (d) Quotas may be easier to administer than tariffs.
    (e) Quotas are more restrictive than tariffs and suppress competition.
    (f) Quotas may be more harmful than tariffs to an importing nation if the quotas give monopoly power to exporters.

---

* Here, the exchange rate is defined as the price of the domestic currency in terms of a foreign currency. Thus, a higher exchange rate means that each unit of the domestic currency commands more of a foreign currency.

11. Subsidies are indirect forms of protection granted by national governments to domestic producers. Subsidies are given to either export industries or import-competing industries.
12. The welfare effect of a subsidy depends on whether it is granted to an import-competing industry (domestic production subsidy) or an export industry (export subsidy).
13. The free flow of international trade and investments is disturbed not only by taxes imposed on traded goods, but also by the differential tax structure of trading nations.
14. Devised by French economists, value-added tax is a tax imposed on the value that is added at each stage of the production of a given good.
15. Excise taxes are sales taxes collected when goods enter through customs. Processing taxes, levied on certain semifinished goods and raw materials, are duties collected when a good is first processed domestically.
16. Dumping is the practice of selling a commodity at below cost or at a lower price in a foreign market than in the domestic market.
17. Sporadic dumping occurs when a firm with surplus inventories sells its product in a foreign market at below cost or at a price that is lower than that charged in the domestic market.
18. Predatory dumping is practiced when a firm temporarily sells its product at below cost or at a lower price in a foreign market, with the intention of weakening or driving its competitors out of the market.
19. Persistent dumping occurs when a firm consistently sells its product at below cost or at a lower price abroad than at home.
20. Besides quotas, subsidies, taxes, and dumping, there are other nontariff trade barriers, which can be classified into three major categories: government purchasing policies, administrative and technical regulations, and (3) intervention in the foreign exchange market.

Review Questions

1. What is meant by a quota? What are the different types of quotas? What are the welfare effects of a quota?
2. Compare tariffs and quotas, elaborating on their differences and similarities.
3. What is meant by a voluntary export restraint? What are the welfare effects of a quota compared to those of a tariff?
4. What is meant by a subsidy? What are the different types of subsidies? What are the welfare effects of a subsidy?
5. Compare subsidies and tariffs and explain the disadvantages of each.
6. What is meant by dumping? What are the different types of dumping?
7. What is meant by international price discrimination? What conditions are necessary to make international price discrimination feasible?
8. How is the free flow of trade and investment disturbed by taxes? What is meant by a value-added tax? What is the difference between an excise tax and a processing tax?

Problems

1. Consider a nation that is too small to have any influence on the world prices. Assume that the demand and supply schedules of some type of motorcycle for this nation are as follows:

Price/Motorcycles	Quantity Demanded	Quantity Supplied
$4,000	1,000	4,000
3,000	2,000	3,000
2,000	3,000	2,000
1,000	4,000	1,000
0	5,000	0

On graph paper, draw the demand and supply curves for the motorcycles. Given these curves, answer the following questions, using graphs to illustrate.

(a) What are the pretrade equilibrium price and the equilibrium quantity?

(b) Assuming free trade, suppose the world price of the motorcycle is $1,000 per unit. Given this assumption, determine domestic production, domestic consumption, and the quantity of imports.

(c) What are the amounts of losses associated with the production effect and the consumption effect of the quota that limits imports to 1000 motorcycles?

Now assume instead that the nation grants a domestic subsidy of $250 to its import-competing producers. Given this assumption, complete the following.

(a) Determine domestic production, domestic consumption, and the quantity of imports.

(b) Measure the subsidy's total cost to the nation.

(c) Determine the overall welfare loss resulting from the subsidy.

2. Tariffs are more effective as a protective device than subsidies because tariffs generate revenue, whereas subsidies require revenue.

Do you agree with this statement? Discuss.

3. Dumping is good for my country because it means some foreigners are subsidizing our consumption.

Do you agree with this statement? Discuss.

4. Suppose you are an economic advisor to a multinational corporation (MNC) with good financial position and monopoly power. You have been asked to propose a pricing strategy that maximizes the MNC's profit.

(a) Do you advise the MNC to charge a higher price in the domestic market or the foreign market? Explain, using graphs to demonstrate.

(b) What conditions are necessary for your proposed pricing strategy to be effective?

Notes

1. "Peanut Quota System Comes Under Attack for Distorting Market," *The Wall Street Journal,* 1 May 1990, 1, A12.

2. Office of the Special Representative for Trade Negotiations, Press Release #269, January 17, 1979.

3. "U.S. Is Taking a Tough Approach to Limit Japan's Textile Exports," *The Wall Street Journal,* 13 January 1986, 31.

4. "U.S. Slice of Japan Beef Market Grows, But Doesn't Sizzle, Amid Quota Accord," *The Wall Street Journal,* 16 November 1989, A14.

5. "Japan's Request to Limit Purchases of Foreign Beef Is Likely to Anger U.S.," *The Wall Street Journal,* 9 August 1993, A9.

6. "U.S. Asks Allies to Curb Exports to Soviet Union," *The Wall Street Journal,* 24 June 1987, 22.

7. "Japan's Export Increase Will Heighten Pressure on U.S. Automaker's Profit," *The Wall Street Journal,* 29 March 1985, 2.

8. "Japan to Extend Curb on Exports of Cars to U.S.," *The Wall Street Journal,* 27 January 1987, 39.

9. "Chrysler's Iacocca Calls for Limitation on Japanese Share of U.S. Auto Market," *The Wall Street Journal,* 16 October 1991, A6.

10. "U.S. Competitiveness Wins New Respect from Leading Players in Global Market," *The Wall Street Journal,* 16 July 1993, A6; "Age of Angst: Workplace Revolution Boosts Productivity at Cost of Job Security," *The Wall Street Journal,* 10 March 1993, 1, A8; "Ford Taurus Dethrones Honda Accord as Top-Selling Car in U.S. during 1992," *The Wall Street Journal,* 7 January 1993, B1.

11. Charles P. Kindelberger and H. Peter Lindert, *International Economics,* 6th ed. (Homewood, IL: Richard D. Irwin, 1978), 150-152.

12. "Japan Plans to Subsidize Small Export Companies," *The Wall Street Journal,* 2 December 1985, 24.

13. "Canada Lumber Is Ruled to Hurt Industry in U.S.," *The Wall Street,* 26 June 1992, A2.

14. "Canadians Investigate Charges of Dumping Hypodermic Needles," *The Wall Street Journal,* 11 November 1985, 32.

15. "Japan Vehicles Dumped in U.S., Agency Alleges," *The Wall Street Journal,* 27 January 1989, A16.

16. Michael Doan, "New Protectionism: A Threat to U.S. Trade," *U.S. News and World Report,* 1 February 1982, 51-52.
17. Ibid.

Suggested Readings

Aho, Michael C., and Jonathan D. Arouson. *Trade Talks: America Better Listen.* New York: Council on Foreign Relations, 1985.

Anderson, J. E. *The Relative Inefficiency of Quotas.* Cambridge, MA: MIT Press, 1988.

Anjaria, S. J., et al. *Trade Policy Developments in Industrial Countries.* Washington, DC: International Monetary Fund, 1981.

Baldwin, Robert E. *The Multilateral Trade Negotiations.* Washington DC: American Enterprise Institute, 1979.

Bhagwati, Jagdish N., and Anne Krueger. *Foreign Trade Regimes and Economic Development.* Multiple vols. New York: Columbia University for the National Bureau of Economic Research, 1973-1976.

Blackhurst, Richard, et al. *Trade Liberalization, Protectionism, and Interdependence.* Geneva: General Agreement on Tariffs and Trade. Special Paper on International Economics, No. 7. Princeton: Princeton University Press, 1965, ch. 4.

Crandall, Robert W. "Import Quotas and the Automobile Industry: The Costs of Protectionism." *The Brookings Review* 2, no. 4(Summer 1984): 8-16.

Cohen, Robert B., "The Prospects for Trade and Protectionism in Auto Industry." In *Trade Policy in the 1980s,* edited by William K. Cline. Washington DC: Institute for International Economics, 1983.

Grunwald, J., and K. Flamm. *The Global Factory: Foreign Assembly in International Trade.* Washington, DC: Brookings Institution, 1985.

Hartland-Thunberg, P., and M. H. Crowford. *Government Support for Exports.* Lexington, MA: Heath, 1982.

Krueguer, Ann O. "The Political Economy of a Rent-Seeking Society." *American Economic Review* 64, no. 3 (June 1974): 291-303.

Organization for Economic Cooperation and Development. *The Costs of Restricting Imports: The Automobile Industry.* Washington, DC: OECD Publications, 1988.

Stern, Robert M., ed. *U.S. Trade Policy in a Changing World Economy.* Cambridge, MA: MIT Press, 1987.

Stockhausen, G. L. *Threats of Quotas in International Trade.* Westport, CT: Greenwood Press, 1988.

Watson, C. M. *Blind Inspection: Policy and the Automobile Industry.* Washington, DC: Brookling Institution, 1987.

Chapter 7

ARGUMENTS FOR PROTECTION

7.1 INTRODUCTION

Our discussion of the theory of comparative advantage in Chapter 2 showed that free international trade results in the most efficient use of the world's scarce resources. Although the theory of comparative advantage and the benefits of free international trade have never been successfully refuted, many nations, under pressure from special interest groups, have reverted to protectionism. Protectionist policies have been followed by both advanced and developing countries. Examples of advanced countries that have pursued protectionist policies include Canada, Japan, France, Great Britain, and the United States. Brazil and Colombia are examples of the many developing countries that have vigorously pursued protectionist policies. The results of such policies have been higher prices for consumers and a net national loss for the society that adopts protectionism. For example, it was estimated that the 29.3-percent average tariff on U.S. apparel imports cost U.S. consumers $2.7 billion in higher prices in 1981.[1]

The history of different nations is replete with the lobbying of corporate executives, union leaders, and political groups who have sought protectionism and argued that their case was special and demanded immediate attention.

The purpose of this chapter is to elaborate on major arguments for protection. In achieving this purpose, we divide the arguments for protection into four groups: (a) theory-based arguments, (b) erroneous arguments, (c) questionable arguments, (d) qualified arguments, and (e) other arguments.

7.2 THEORY-BASED ARGUMENTS

These arguments, derived from the models of international trade theories, include the following: terms-of-trade argument and optimum tariff, domestic distortion argument, and strategic trade policy argument. The first is an argument for utilization of national monopsony power; the second is an argument for protectionism as a second-best policy when free trade (the first-best policy) is not feasible; and the third is an argument for government subsidization of high-technology firms.

7.2a Terms-of-Trade Argument and Optimum Tariff

The basic analysis of tariff, presented in Chapter 5, is based on the assumption of perfect competition. Given this assumption, each nation is considered to be too small to have any perceptible effect on the world price. In other words, each nation is a price taker. The imposition of a tariff by a small nation causes the volume of trade to decline, but it has no effect on the small nation's terms of trade (TOT). Following the imposition of a tariff, a small nation's welfare always declines.

The above assumption is often valid. Trade between countries is frequently competitive. In some cases, however, a country may have a large enough share of the world market for one of its imports to influence the world price. Large countries usually have *monopsony power* in international trade even when no individual firm has that power.* For example, the United States appears large enough in the global automobile market to be able to push exporters like Honda, Toyota, or Nissan to sell their autos to the United States at a lower price by imposing a tariff on auto imports.

The terms-of-trade argument states that a nation's restrictive trade policy can increase the ratio of export price index to import price index (P_X/P_M) and hence improve the nation's welfare. More specifically, the nation's imposition of a tariff on an import will decrease demand for that good on the world market. As a result, the world price of the

---

* A monopsony is a market structure that consists of a single buyer and many sellers of a commodity or service.

imported-good will fall and P_X/P_M will rise. Thus, a nation's imposition of a tariff has the potential of increasing that nation's welfare. However, the tariff also causes the volume of imports to fall. The decline in the volume of imports alone tends to reduce the nation's welfare because the nation's consumption of low-cost imports, which put domestic production at a disadvantage, has been reduced. Thus, there has been a gain due to the lower world price of the imported good, and a loss due to the smaller import volume of that good.

The **optimum tariff** is a tariff rate that maximizes the nation's welfare. In other words, it is the rate at which the positive difference between the gain resulting from the improvement in the nation's TOT and the loss resulting from reduction in the volume of the import is maximized. Starting from a free-trade position, as a country raises its tariff rate, its welfare increases to a maximum rate (the optimum tariff rate) and then declines as the tariff rate is increased past the optimum.[*]

As we already know, a nation's TOT are the inverse or reciprocal of its trading partner's TOT. Consequently, as the TOT of a nation imposing a tariff improve, those of its trading partner deteriorate. This reduces the trading partner's welfare and induces the partner to retaliate and impose its own optimum tariff. This action allows the trading partner to improve its TOT and thus recapture some of its losses. It also causes further reduction in the volume of the trade. The first nation may then retaliate. If this process persists, all countries may eventually lose all or most of the benefits from trade.

To be sure, even in the absence of retaliation by the trading partner, the benefits accruing to the tariff-imposing nation are less than the losses of its trading partner. As a result, the world taken as a whole is worse off than under free-trade conditions. It is in this context that free trade leads to the maximization of world welfare.

Graphical Illustration of the Optimum Tariff and Retaliation. Using a hypothetical example, suppose that France and Great Britain trade wine (W) and cloth (C). Assume that both countries have monopsony power in international trade for their import goods. Figure 7-1 portrays free trade offer curves for France (F) and Britain (B), defining equilibrium point E at $P_C/P_W = 1$.

If a nation imposes a tariff on its import good, its offer curve shifts toward the axis measuring its import good by the amount of the import tariff. This is because for any amount of the export good, importers now want more of the import good to pay for the tariff.

Assume that with optimum tariff, France's offer curve rotates to F', intersecting Britain's offer curve at point E'.[**] If Britain does not retaliate, the intersection of offer curve F' and offer curve B gives the new equilibrium point E'. At point E', France exchanges 20 gallons of wine for 40 yards of cloth so that $P_C/P_W = 1/2$ on the world market and for France. As a result, Britain's TOT deteriorate from $P_C/P_W = 1$ to $P_C/P_W = 1/2$, and France's TOT improve from $P_W/P_C = 1$ to $P_W/P_C = 2/1 = 2$.

With the optimum tariff associated with offer curve F', not only does the improvement in France's welfare due to improved TOT exceed the decline in welfare resulting from a decrease in the volume of trade, but it exemplifies the highest welfare that France can realize with a tariff and outstrips its free-trade welfare.

With deterioration in its TOT and a smaller volume of trade, Britain is certainly worse off than under free-trade conditions. This entices Britain to retaliate and impose its own optimum tariff, depicted by offer curve B'. The intersection of B' and F' establishes the new equilibrium at point E''. As Figure 7-1 shows, at this new equilibrium point, Britain's TOT ($P_C/P_W = 2/1$) are higher and France's TOT ($P_W/P_C = 1/2$) are lower than under free trade ($P_C/P_W = P_W/P_C = 1$); however, the volume of trade is much smaller. Given this situation, France is likely to retaliate, and eventually both countries may end up at point 0 (the origin of Figure 7-1), depicting the autarky position for both nations. At this point, all of the benefits from trade are lost.

---

[*] The optimum tariff rate of a country (t*) can be calculated by the use of the following formula:

$$t^* = 1/e - 1,$$

where e is the absolute value of the elasticity of the trade partner's offer curve. Proof of this relationship is beyond the scope of this textbook. For proof, see Miltides Chacholides, *International Economics* (New York: McGraw-Hill, 1990), 543-545; Peter H. Lindert, *International Economics*, 9th ed. (Homewood, IL: Richard D. Irwin, Inc., 1991), 612-617.

[**] Why the tariff associated with F' is an optimum tariff involves utilization of trade indifference curves and is beyond the scope of this book. For an explanation, see Dominick Salvatore, *International Economics*, 4th ed. (New York: Macmillan Publishing Company, 1993), 246-248.

FIGURE 7-1
Optimum Tariff and Retaliation

Free-trade offer curves for France (F) and Great Britain (B) define equilibrium point E at $P_C/P_W = P_W/P_C = 1$ in both countries. Assume that with an optimum tariff, France's offer curve rotates to F′, defining the new equilibrium at point E′. As a result, France's terms of trade improve to $P_W/P_C = 2$. Point E′ exemplifies the highest welfare that France can realize with a tariff and is better off than the free trade equilibrium at point E. However, because Britain's welfare is reduced, it will probably retaliate by imposing its own optimum tariff, as shown by offer curve B′ and equilibrium point E″. In its turn, France is likely to retaliate, and eventually both countries may end up at point 0 where all benefits of trade are lost.

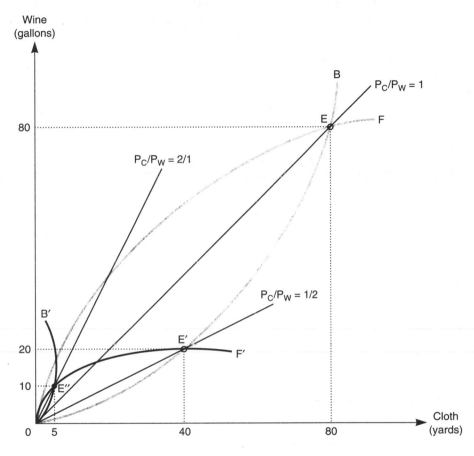

In practice, nations have engaged in retaliation either by taxing exports to their trading partners or by taxing imports from their trading partners.[*] For example, in the early and mid-1980s, as the United States imposed greater trade barriers against Asian steel and textiles, Japan, China, and other Asian nations retaliated by cutting down on their imports of U.S. soybeans and other farm products. In another instance, a tariff war broke out between France and Italy in the late 1980s, leading to serious losses for both nations.

---

[*] In our analysis, we have been tacitly discussing the optimum import tariff. However, more advanced treatises indicate that an optimum import tariff is equivalent to an optimum export tariff.

7.2b Domestic Distortion Argument

As we know from microeconomics courses, theoretically, perfect competition is **Pareto optimal**. That is, if perfect competition is achieved, no one in a society can be better off without making someone else worse off. This assertion is based on the assumption that there are no **distortions,** that is, no divergence between the marginal private benefit/cost and marginal social benefit/cost of any endeavor.[*]

In the real world, distortions are prevalent. Perfect competition is virtually never achieved. Distortions encompass the vast range of effects that economists have also named "externalities" or "spillover effects." An **externality** exists when a firm's production of a good induces effects on parties outside the firm which are not considered in the production decision. Pollution is a classic example of an externality. In the absence of antipollution regulations, a paint company may dump its waste material into a river. The resulting pollution imposes costs on third parties, that is, individuals external to the firm. However, the paint company does not take these costs into consideration. As a result, the marginal private cost (MPC) is smaller than the marginal social cost (MSC).[**] Pollution is an example of an **external diseconomy,** or an externality that imposes costs on third parties.

Production may also result in an **external economy** by inducing gains for third parties. For example, take the case of an apple grower. As a by-product of apple production, apple blossoms provide nectar for bees of a neighboring beekeeper (third party) who does not compensate the grower. In this case, the MPC of apple production is greater than the MSC.[***]

According to the theory of the second best, if the presence of distortion in an economy prevents the achievement of Pareto optimality, it may be justifiable for a government to employ policies that add more distortions (such as tariffs).

Suppose in the process of production an industry provides training for its workers that is useful in other industries. It is likely that some of these workers will leave the industry to work in other industries (third parties). Because the original industry does not reap the full benefit of its investment, the industry is likely to be underinvested. One method to aid the industry and provide society with more external economies is import restriction. This action helps the industry, but it also raises the price of the good in the domestic market. A preferable policy would be direct subsidization of the industry. Such a policy stimulates the industry but it does not lead to the consumption distortion that results from trade restriction.

One must be careful in interpreting the theory of second best. To be sure, it calls for the possible elimination of distortion-generating constraints, but it becomes appropriate only when such an elimination is considered impossible. Free trade continues to be a first-best policy.

7.2c Strategic Trade Policy Argument

A new argument for protectionism, developed in the 1980s, is strategic trade policy. This argument can be viewed as an extension of the infant industry argument (discussed later) and is advanced by industrial nations to acquire comparative advantage in high-technology industries.

According to strategic trade policy argument, high-technology industries (such as computers, semiconductors, and telecommunications) are crucial to the future growth of a nation, and thus they should be protected temporarily with subsidies, tariffs, and other forms of protection. High-technology industries have the following characteristics:

---

[*]   *Marginal private benefit/cost* refers to the benefit/cost of producing the last unit of a good from a firm's standpoint. *Marginal social benefit/cost* refers to the benefit/cost of producing the last unit of a good from society's standpoint.

[**]   This is because MPC includes only payments to the factors of production (that is, rent, wages, interest, and profit), whereas MSC encompasses payments to the factors of production plus costs imposed by pollution on individuals outside the firm.

[***]   This is because, to the apple grower, increasing production involves the marginal cost of labor, as it does to society. However, society gets more honey as a result, without additional use of resources. Thus, the MSC of apple production is the MPC minus the value of additional honey produced.

1. They are prone to high risks.
2. They need large-scale production to realize economies of scale.
3. If successful, they generate significant external economies.

Given these characteristics, the strategic trade policy argues that by promoting such industries, the nation can benefit from the large economies associated with them and augment its future growth possibilities.

The development of the strategic trade policy argument has been inspired by world economic events over the past one and a half decades. Chief among these events are

◆ The escalation of global competition
◆ A persistent U.S. trade deficit
◆ The Japanese victory in penetrating U.S. and European Union (EU) markets allegedly through Japan's strategic trade policy.

An example of successful strategic trade policy is the case of semiconductors in Japan (see Case 7.1). The development of this industry was nurtured by Japan's Ministry of Trade and Industry which provided the industry with tax advantages, promoted government—industrial cooperation, and financed research and development. Additionally, the ministry continued to protect the industry from foreign competition, especially from the United States.

Most economists attribute Japan's successful performance in the semiconductor industry to other elements, including

◆ The higher rate of investment in the semiconductor industry
◆ The Japanese management philosophy of taking a long-run view of investment rather than a short-run view of stressing quarterly profit, as in the United States
◆ Japan's approach to education, which emphasizes science and mathematics
◆ Japan's emphasis on quality control

Theoretically, strategic trade policy can enhance a country's growth and welfare in oligopolistic markets, displaying extensive economies of scale. As a result, the strategic trade policy argument seems plausible on the surface, and the success of Japanese firms in technologically oriented industries makes support of this theory tempting. However, the strategic trade policy argument suffers from the following shortcomings:

1. It assumes that the government can effectively identify the particular emerging industries that deserve public help. But history shows that politics will dominate the process and prevent the government from making the right choices.
2. It is very hard to choose an industry that will display large economies of scale in the future.
3. Even if we could successfully choose an industry, it would be very difficult to launch policies to successfully care for that industry.
4. Assuming that a country is successful in implementing a strategic trade policy, such a success comes at the expense of other nations, who are likely to retaliate.

Although there is no concrete empirical evidence to support the strategic trade policy, it continues to appeal to protectionists and is expected to strongly influence the EU and the United States in the development of their trade policies in the future.

GLOBAL INSIGHTS CASE 7.1

The Semiconductor Accord

Since the mid-1970s, Japanese industrial policy has concentrated on the promotion of high-tech industries. In pursuing such a policy, one of Japan's strategies has been to develop its semiconductor chip industry. Semiconductor chips are intricate electronic circuits used as the chief elements of many products. Until the mid-1970s, the technology for making such chips was largely monopolized by the United States. However, with government-supported research projects and some degree of domestic market protection, in the late 1970s and early 1980s, the Japanese succeeded in producing a chip called Dynamic Random Access Memory (DRAM) and capturing a large portion of that market.

With the rise in the Japanese share of the market, there have been numerous complaints by U.S. and European DRAM producers against dumping practices. The U.S. companies contended that Japanese manufacturers were engaged in predatory pricing practices. These complaints inspired negotiations that led the U.S. and Japan to sign a "semiconductor trade agreement" on July 31, 1986. According to this agreement, minimum prices were set for certain Japanese-made chips sold in any nation other than Japan. This agreement called for the cessation of all foreign market dumping of semiconductors by Japanese firms. Additionally, Japan agreed to permit U.S. microchip manufacturers to acquire a larger share of the Japanese semiconductor market. The agreement called on Japan to facilitate a rise in the U.S. market share in the Japanese market from 8.5 percent in 1986 to 20 percent in 1991.

Unfortunately, the agreement did not resolve the problem, and Japan continued to dump semiconductors into foreign countries, forcing many U.S. chip makers out of the market. As a result, in 1987, the United States imposed 100-percent retaliatory tariffs on certain Japanese electronics imports. Some of these tariffs were lifted later as a partial political reward for President Nakasone of Japan who worked hard to reach a resolution on dumping practices. The Japanese companies still dumped chips, but at a higher average price (85 percent of the fair market value) than the initial average price (59 percent of the fair market value).

Although Japan continues to claim that it has lived up to the 1986 accord, dumping charges against the country continue. In the fourth quarter of 1993, the U.S. share of Japan's chip market surged to 20.7 percent, its highest ever. This development helped to defuse some of the conflict between the United States and Japan; however, the U.S. government and American computer chip industry responded coldly and requested that Japan take additional steps to ensure that improvement in the U.S. share of the Japanese market persists.

Sources: Parviz Asheghian and Bahaman Ebrahimi, *International Business* (New York: Harper Collins, 1990), 358-366, case II:4, 367-376, Case II:5; "Semiconductor Accord With Japan Fails to Aid U.S. Firms as Intended," *The Wall Street Journal*, 12 February 1987, 1, 10; "U.S., Japan Spar Once More Over Trade Report On Semiconductors Is Expected to Criticize Tokyo," *The Wall Street Journal*, 30 July 1992, A10; "Foreign Chip Share in Japan Rises but U.S. Reacts Cooly," *The New York Times*, 19 March 1994, A39.

7.3 ERRONEOUS ARGUMENTS

Erroneous arguments for protection include those arguments that are not based on economic reasoning but that hinge on nationalistic fervor and emotion.

7.3a Domestic Production Argument

According to this argument, domestic producers have rights to the domestic market. The protection of these rights requires the reduction or abolishment of imports, allowing more domestic production and higher employment. The problem with this argument is its failure to realize that any replacement of imports with domestic production is eventually neutralized by a reduction in the production of exports. Specifically, when protection is used to increase domestic production and employment, it leads to lower exports and higher unemployment abroad. Other nations are likely to retaliate, and ultimately all nations will lose.

7.3b Prevent-Money-Outflow Argument

According to supporters of this argument, when we buy imported goods from abroad we end up with the goods but we lose the money to foreigners. When, on the other hand, we buy domestically produced goods, we end up with both the goods and the money. Because it is better to have both the goods and the money, a nation can get richer by preventing imports. To achieve this objective, a nation must resort to protectionism to replace imports with domestic production. This prevents the outflow of money and makes the nation richer.

This argument appeals to "common sense" and has been advanced by politicians such as Abraham Lincoln, who allegedly made the following remarks:

> I don't know much about the tariff. But I do know that when I buy a coat from England, I have the coat and England has the money. But when I buy a coat in America, I have the coat and America has the money.[2]

The prevent-money-outflow argument is similar to mercantilism and suffers from the same misconception that money itself is wealth. However, money is a medium of exchange which by itself has no intrinsic value. Money paid for imports eventually has to come back in terms of payments for exports or as foreign direct investment because a nation's money has no redemption value in any other nation.

7.3c Wage Protection Argument

According to this argument, high-wage countries, such as the United States or Great Britain, cannot effectively compete with low-wage countries; hence, they should impose tariffs or quotas to protect their workers from products made by low-wage workers overseas. This argument is very popular and has been endorsed by both U.S. business leaders and the U.S. labor movement, which has actively pursued protectionism since the late 1960s. Their efforts have resulted in protective controls in industries that employ a large number of people, such as the apparel, automaking, steel, sugar, and textile industries.

Opponents of the wage protection argument present the following criticisms and qualifications:

1. Cheaper labor abroad might lead only to a cheaper wage cost, not necessarily to cheaper production costs. This is because labor is not the only factor of production. Other factors of production, such as capital and land, are also significant cost components of a product. Consequently, depending on the relative proportion of resources used in the production of a commodity, products can be classified as labor-intensive, capital-intensive, and land-intensive. Thus, low-wage countries might have an advantage over high-wage countries only with respect to labor-intensive commodities, that is, products for which wages are a large percentage of total production costs.

2. Even in the case of labor-intensive products, high-wage countries could still compete effectively with low-wage countries for two reasons. First, fringe benefits and government-imposed bonuses are much higher in some low-wage nations, such as China, Chile, and Mexico. Thus, if we add these fringe benefits to the hourly wage rates, the wage differential between high-wage and low-wage countries diminishes and may become insignificant. Second, labor efficiency in high-wage countries is usually higher than in low-wage countries. Thus, the higher labor efficiency in high-wage countries might compensate for the lower wage levels in low-wage countries.

7.3d Equalization of Production Costs Argument

This argument can be viewed as an extension of the wage protection argument. The equalization of production costs argument calls for the imposition of a **scientific tariff,** that is, a tariff specifically designed to neutralize the cost advantage enjoyed by foreign producers of a tariffed product. The purpose of the scientific tariff is to equalize the costs of production between foreign and domestic producers and to offset any advantage the foreign producer may have in terms of lower wage costs, lower taxes, higher government subsidies, and so on. This argument is presumably based on "fair competition" and is not intended to eliminate imports altogether.

The irony of the equalization of production costs argument is its failure to realize that, in general, cost differentials across nations reflect comparative advantage, and if costs of production become equal, the very basis for international trade is eliminated. Additionally, in practice, the scientific tariff suffers from the following problems:

1. Because within an industry costs differ from firm to firm, the scientific tariff ends up subsidizing the most efficient firm in the industry at the expense of the consumers. Suppose that the U.S. government wants to protect all domestic firms in the electronic industry against all foreign firms in the same industry. The implementation of this policy requires setting the costs of the most efficient (least costs) foreign firm equal to the costs of least efficient (highest costs) U.S. firms. This necessitates imposing a tariff that is high enough to eliminate the extreme cost differential. Because higher costs mean higher prices, domestic prices will rise to the level of the domestic marginal producer's cost. As a result, the more efficient firms will enjoy extra monopoly profits, supported by domestic consumers' subsidization of inefficient production.
2. The implementation of such a policy involves the difficult administrative task of collecting the required cost information for tariff adjustments. Such an endeavor does not seem worth undertaking, given that it can only lead to the curtailment of imports and, if carried to an extreme, to the ultimate elimination of trade, the impairment of the nation's standard of living, and a significant decline in global welfare.

In spite of these shortcomings, a scientific tariff was, in fact, part of the U.S. Tariff Acts of 1922 and 1930. In recent years, the equalization of production costs argument has re-emerged as the "fairness" argument. The proponents of this argument claim that all they are after is fair competition, meaning the equalization of production costs between foreign and domestic firms to enable domestic firms to compete with foreign firms on a fair basis. Thus, the fairness argument is nothing more than the old equalization of production costs argument with a new name.

7.4 QUESTIONABLE ARGUMENTS

Questionable arguments for protection include those arguments that are not totally erroneous but that exemplify poor policies with abusive potentials.

7.4a Antidumping Argument

As we explained in Chapter 6, dumping is the practice of selling a product at below cost or at a lower price in a foreign market than in the domestic market. The practice of dumping can take three different forms, known as sporadic, predatory, and persistent dumping.

According to the antidumping argument, because dumping a product in a country puts that country's import-competing firms at a disadvantage, it is justifiable to impose a remedial tariff to offset the dumper's price advantage. In assessing the validity of this argument, economists distinguish between the three types of dumping and consider only predatory dumping as warranting protection.

If dumping is persistent, a firm consistently sells its product at below cost or at a lower price abroad than at home. With persistent dumping, consumers in the importing country enjoy a continuous gain resulting from the lower prices of foreign goods. Import-competing firms are in the same situation as when the lower price is the consequence of a normal cost advantage in the exporting nation. Although import-competing firms are put at a disadvantage, the argument for protection is not valid, because the country as a whole gains.

If dumping is sporadic, a firm with surplus inventories temporarily sell its product in a foreign market at below cost or at a price that is lower than that charged in the domestic market. Sporadic dumping results in temporary adverse effects on import-competing firms. However, given the short-term nature of sporadic dumping, the argument for protection is not valid.

If dumping is predatory, a foreign firm temporarily sells its product at a lower price or at below cost until competitors are driven out of the market. This gives the firm a monopoly position, allowing it to raise the price. This higher price, in turn, might attract domestic firms back into the industry, inducing the foreign firm to decrease its price once again, and so forth. Because predatory dumping results in wasteful resource movements, the argument for protection is valid.

In practice, it is difficult to distinguish between the three types of dumping. No government official has yet been able to accurately assess the intention of a firm that engages in dumping practices. As a result, the government authorities' use of antidumping measures is often questionable and reflects protectionist tendencies.

7.4b Balance of Trade Argument

As we discuss in Chapter 10, a nation's balance of trade is a statement that shows the monetary value of all merchandise imported and exported. According to proponents of the balance of trade argument, tariffs or quotas are necessary because they encourage a favorable balance of trade. It is argued that such a surplus is desirable because it means that a country is exporting relatively more products than it is importing. This in turn leads to a higher level of income, employment, and production for the domestic economy.

Although this argument seems persuasive, it ignores the following points:

1. In the long run, protectionism might lead to retaliation from another country and make the protectionist country worse off. If an industry that is threatened by imports obtains tariff protection against another country, that country might in turn impose duties against that industry's exports. If this happens, more jobs might be lost because of a decrease in exports than are gained by reducing competing imports.

    As an example of this, in 1986, the U.S. lumber industry complained that Canada was unfairly subsidizing its softwood-lumber industry. This issue gave rise to protectionist sentiment in the U.S. Congress and caused then President Reagan to impose a 35-percent tariff on imports of Canadian-made cedar shades and shingles. It was also expected that the United States would impose $2.9 billion a year countervailing duties on the Canadian softwood exports, if the subsidization charges against Canada were proven.[3] Reacting to the U. S. move, the Canadian government in turn imposed import duties on U.S. exports of books and publications, as well as certain computer parts and semiconductors. As this example indicates, protectionism did not resolve the underlying problems of either of these two nations. Its only outcome was to hinder the trading relationship of two friendly nations.

2. Import duties lead to higher prices for consumers who must pay for inefficient domestic production. From an economic standpoint, this leads to misallocation of scarce resources because, in the long run, protectionism encourages the reallocation of resources out of more productive industries into less productive (protected) industries, causing costs to increase and comparative advantage to decrease.

7.4c Employment Protection Argument

According to proponents of this argument, the imposition of tariffs or other forms of import restriction are desirable during periods of unemployment because these measures reduce imports and stimulate domestic production. Increased domestic production, in turn, leads to a reduction in unemployment.

Historically, alleged job losses to foreign competitors have been a main reason advanced by U.S. labor leaders in their pleas for protectionism. The argument was especially convincing during the Great Depression of the 1930s. However, the argument is subject to the following considerations:

1. Higher employment at home, resulting from protectionism, leads to higher unemployment in foreign countries. This happens because the reduction of imports at home means a reduction of foreign exports. As a result, foreign nations are likely to retaliate, leaving all nations worse off than before.
2. Tariffs and quotas lead to higher prices for domestic consumers, who end up supporting inefficient domestic producers. This promotes the movement of resources out of more efficient industries into less efficient, protected industries. As a result, costs are raised and comparative advantage is diminished.
3. If the objective is to increase employment, a domestic production subsidy may be a more appropriate means of protection than a tariff or a quota. This is because in comparison to a tariff, which leads to welfare-diminishing production and consumption effects, a domestic production subsidy involves only a production effect. Additionally, because subsidies are visible and must be periodically voted on by government representatives, they are less likely to provide permanent protection.

7.5 QUALIFIED ARGUMENTS

Qualified arguments for protection include those arguments that can be justified with some qualification. Their justification is based on either a noneconomic origin, such as national security, or the anticipation that long-run economic gains will more than offset the short-run protection costs.

7.5a Infant Industry Argument

The infant industry argument asserts that because a new and underdeveloped industry cannot survive competition from abroad, it should be protected temporarily with high tariffs and quotas on imported goods. It is hoped that this protectionism will allow the industry to grow and enable it to become technically more efficient, so that it can eventually compete with foreign industries without protection.

The infant industry argument can be attributed to Alexander Hamilton, the first secretary of the U.S. Treasury. In his famous *Report on Industry and Commerce,* published in 1791, he articulated the economic problems of the time and recommended the use of tariffs to enhance the development of industry and foster the growth of the U. S. economy. This report set the stage for imposing tariffs on a number of industries during the nineteenth and twentieth centuries. Because the infant industry argument pleads only for temporary protection and does not deny the validity of free trade, it is more widely accepted by economists as a theoretically sound argument. However, in practice, economists realize that there are four major shortcomings associated with this argument.

First, it is not necessarily true that an infant industry needs protection to get started. Some new industries may even displace less dynamic, older ones through effective management, marketing, and financial policies. Even if an industry is not prosperous now, it might be expected to gain sufficient profit in the future to outweigh the present costs. It should be able to borrow capital now and survive the initial rough period; thus, it does not need protection.

Second, if an industry is protected it could lose its incentive to effectively compete with the exporting nation's mature industries, and, because of this, it may never grow to maturity.

Third, this argument assumes that the government can effectively identify those industries that deserve protection. The historical evidence shows, however, that it is very difficult for a government to make the right choice in deciding which industry to protect. For example, the U.S. wool industry, which was chosen for protection by the U.S. government in the early nineteenth century, has not yet grown out of its infancy stage.

Fourth, even if the government can choose the correct infant industry to protect, it could still be argued that import protection is not a sound decision. In this case, if an infant industry must be protected from foreign competition, a domestic production subsidy may be a more appropriate means of protection than a tariff or a quota. As we explained earlier, this is due to the superiority of a subsidy over a tariff in terms of welfare.

7.5b National Security Argument

According to the national security argument, a nation that is dependent on foreign sources of essential supplies would be vulnerable in a time of war, when the flow of such supplies could be blocked by its enemies. For example, during both world wars, England's imports of food and raw materials were curtailed by the German navy. It is argued, then, that a country needs to impose tariffs on crucial goods that may be needed for war and defense in order to promote their domestic production and ensure their continued availability.

In the United States, such an argument has been used from time to time by the leaders of various industries who have appealed to the U.S. government for protection against foreign competition. For example, during the 1960s, Roger Blough, chairman of the board of the U.S. Steel Corporation, used this argument in front of a congressional committee. He argued that because a strong steel industry was necessary for modern defense, the United States could not rely on its importation of steel from countries that were close to the former Soviet Union or the People's Republic of China. For this reason, he argued that the steel industry should be protected by trade barriers.

In the late 1980s, as the U.S. economy started to slow down and head toward a recession, it triggered protectionist feelings once again. A survey of consumers' attitudes in America during the late 1980s reported that:

> ...72% of Americans consider the nation's trade imbalances a serious national security problem, and a majority see Japan as a greater threat than the Soviet Union. .... That's because a majority now believe that a country's economic power, not its military strength, must determine its influence.[4]

On the surface, the national security argument is persuasive and makes sense. However, it suffers from the following shortcomings:

1. Although this argument has many economic implications, it is a political and military argument rather than an economic one. Such an argument, therefore, should not be settled by input from those who have personal business interests at stake.
2. Because most producers consider their products essential for national security, it is difficult for the government to specify certain industries as truly warranting protection. In fact, in the United States, the producers of many ordinary products, such as plastics, electronics, umbrellas, candles, and gloves, have asked for protection on the basis of national security.
3. Apart from these considerations, if some protection is necessary, direct subsidies are preferable to tariffs and quotas (as in the case of infant industries).

7.5c Diversification Argument

Many of today's developing countries are dependent on a single commodity for their economic survival. Such single commodities include Bolivia's tin, Burma's rice, Chile's copper, Costa Rica's coffee, and Panama's bananas. Because a significant portion of these countries' incomes is based on the exportation of one product, fluctuations in the demand for that product could lead to severe economic instability. To prevent such a situation, according to proponents of the diversification argument, these countries should follow protectionist policies to encourage the establishment of different industries. Developing a number of different industries will provide for greater economic stability and growth, without reliance on a single product.

There are some elements of truth in this argument. For example, a decline in oil prices in the 1980s crippled economies that were dependent on oil production for generating most of their export revenue. A case in point was Mexico, which in the 1980s was faced with a staggering overdue international debt that brought that country to the brink of bankruptcy. The problems with the diversification argument are as follows:

1. It is not applicable to advanced countries, such as the United States, or Canada, which are already diversified.
2. It takes for granted that the government, rather than the private sector, can more effectively recognize the economy's diversification needs. Such a presumption goes against the rationale of competition and the workings of the market mechanism, and may lead to an inefficient and unnatural diversification that may be costly for the nation.
3. This argument assumes that a greater reliance on manufacturing ensures stability in export earnings. The evidence shows, however, that there has not been any significant difference between the stability of developing countries' export earnings and the stability of export earnings of advanced countries that rely on

manufacturing in generating most of their export earnings. For example, the data show that Japan's advanced economy has experienced more year-to-year instability than most developing countries have experienced since World War II.[5]

7.5d Infant Government Argument

According to this argument, a nation that is young and has no alternative means of raising the funds needed for its economic development should use import and export duties as a crucial source of public revenue.

Although this argument, like its predecessors, goes against the free-trade notion, it is widely accepted by economists on the grounds that it may contribute to the economic growth of developing countries.

For many poor, developing countries, the main impediment to economic development is their governments' inability to raise the necessary funds for essential public services, such as housing, education, road construction, and water management. Although revenue could be generated through taxes on income, property, consumption, and production, these taxes are difficult to measure and administer. Additionally, even if these taxes could be adequately measured, since the main problem of most developing countries is poverty, the amount of revenue generated would not be sufficient to launch development programs. By just patrolling the border with a few customs officials, however, revenue could be collected easily by imposing duties on imports and exports. This, in fact, is a practice that is followed by many developing countries, which get somewhere between 25 percent and 60 percent of their revenue from customs duties.

GLOBAL INSIGHTS CASE 7.2

Trade Promotion Coordinating Committee (TPCC)

One of the first initiatives under the Clinton administration was the establishment of the Trade Promotion Coordinating Committee (TPCC), which coordinates government policies affecting U.S. exports across agencies. In September 1993 the TPCC unveiled the Nation Export Strategy, which laid out 65 concrete recommendations for leveraging export promotion resources and removing government obstacles to exporting. The Administration quickly implemented the strategy, which includes opening export assistance centers around the country, providing "one-stop shopping" for new exporters, leveling the playing field for U.S. companies by countering the advocacy efforts of foreign governments, and eliminating unnecessary export controls and licenses. The National Export Strategy also includes specific initiatives for each of the "big emerging markets".

As early initiatives are successfully implemented, the National Export Strategy continues to evolve through the identification of new areas and the development of initiatives by the TPCC. For example, the TPCC concluded that the use of illegitimate practices such as bribery was far more widespread than previously known. The TPCC was able to identify $11 billion in contracts lost to U.S. exporters over a 2-year period because of bribery. And this year the TPCC is developing a strategy against the use of products standard as barriers to U.S. exports.

At the same time, the United States has continued to take steps to ensure that globalization lifts living standards in all countries, through a serious commitment to promoting labor standards through the world. In its efforts withing international organizations, the Administration has sought to establish a framework for multilateral discussion on how best to promote core labor standard; freedom of association, the right to organize and bargain collectively, nondiscrimination in the workplace, prohibition of forced labor, and elimination of exploitative child labor.

Source: U.S. Government Printing Office, *Economic Report of the President* (Washington DC.: U.S. Government Printing Office, 1997), 249-250, Reprinted.

In summary, the infant government argument is valid only when a developing country that has no other source of revenue uses import and export duties to finance its economic development programs and does not use import and export duties as a protectionist device.

7.6 OTHER ARGUMENTS

In this section, we discuss two other arguments that have attracted increasing attention in recent years. The first is an argument for the protection of the environment. The second is a political argument that uses economic sanctions against a nation to achieve a given political objective.

7.6a Environmental Protection Argument

The growing interest in recent years toward protecting the environment has made this issue a source of heated debate in international trade policymaking. Many environmentalists have called for trade restrictions on the grounds that free trade hurts the environment by encouraging firms to move to nations that have lax environmental regulations. For example, as we discuss in the next chapter, opponents of the North American Free Trade Agreement (NAFTA) argued that the agreement encourages U.S. firms to expand in Mexico where the environmental regulations are less stringent than in the United States. On the other hand, opponents of the environmental protection argument present the following counterarguments:

1. The primary determinant of demand for environmental protection is a nation's or area's level of income. Because free international trade increases the level of income, it causes demand for environmental protection to rise. This trend reverses when, given the higher income level resulting from free trade, newer and cleaner technologies are developed.*

2. Frequently, what is needed is not new environmental regulations but the alteration of existing domestic and international policies that have an unfavorable influence on environmental conditions. For example, Borneo loggers cut the tropical rain forest as fast as possible. Part of the reason is the policy of short-term logging concessions that give a firm rights to log a piece of land for 20 to 25 years. Given the lack of long-term interest in the land's productivity, loggers have little incentive to use environmentally sound methods in managing the forest. As a result, they adopt the policy of cutting as much as possible in the short-run before moving on to the next piece of land.[6]

3. The environmental protection argument might be used as an excuse by some protectionists to achieve their own self-interest. For example, South Korea recently passed the Toxic Substance Control Act, which requires firms that are selling a chemical product in Korea to provide a list of ingredients, their proportions, and the manufacturing method employed to produce that product. Foreign chemical companies are skeptical about this act. More specifically, U.S. chemical firms have asserted that this new act is a ploy used by Korean chemical companies to acquire trade secrets from foreign companies.

The General Agreement on Tariffs and Trade (GATT), an international organization created to promote freer international trade, does not have specific rules regarding environmental policy.** However, GATT keeps nations from discriminating between foreign and domestic products in applying their environmental policies. For example, a nation cannot exempt domestic car producers from installing anti-pollution devices if such devices are required for foreign cars. A case in point is Thailand's ban on imported cigarettes, presumably for health reasons. The ban was repudiated by GATT on the grounds that there were no restrictions on domestic production or sale of cigarettes in Thailand. The ban was seen as a ploy to give the government monopoly power over the production and sale of cigarettes.

---

* According to a GATT report, air pollution in cities increases with national income up to about $5,000 per head per year; beyond that income level, it declines as income rises.

** As we discuss in the next chapter, following the Uruguay Round of Negotiations, GATT was replaced by the World Trade Organization (WTO) in 1995.

According to GATT rules, imports may not be excluded on the basis of the environmental consequences of the process used to produce them. Under this rule, a nation cannot exclude a product on the grounds that the foreign plants producing the products generated air pollution that surpasses the home country's standard. Such a case was recently brought before GATT. In 1990, in response to environmentalist concerns, the United States banned the importation of tuna caught by using fishing nets that resulted in high rates of dolphin deaths. Mexico, which exports tuna to the United States, appealed to GATT, which ruled in Mexico's favor and found the U.S. ban illegal. The reasoning behind the GATT decision was that (a) the product, tuna, did not violate the U.S. environmental standard; and (b) GATT could not permit one nation to impose its regulations regarding production methods, such as fishing techniques, on other nations. This ruling understandably made environmentalists angry.[7]

Given the growing concern over environmental issues, many experts believe this issue will be a top priority in future trade negotiations.

7.6b Political Argument

The political argument for protection calls for a government to use protectionist means to reach a political goal. Governments have attempted to use **economic sanctions** to protect human rights, to reduce nuclear build up, to fight international terrorism, to set restitution for property expropriated by foreign governments, to oppose racial discrimination, and to promote fair labor practices or safe working conditions. The nation employing these sanctions hopes to hinder the economic ability of another country so that country will agree to the objectives of the sanctioning nation. Economic sanctions can take the form of either trade sanctions or financial sanctions.

Trade sanctions involve either banning a country's exports to another country or imposing quotas on another country's imports. For example, when the former Soviet Union sent its troops to Afghanistan in 1980, the U.S. government imposed a grain embargo against the Soviet Union. In another instance, four days after Iraq invaded Kuwait in August 1990, the United States, under United Nations (UN) auspices, imposed sanctions against Iraq on both its exports, primarily oil, and its imports. Also, in mid-1992, given Serbian aggression in Bosnia-Herzegovina, the UN voted a trade sanction against the rest of Yugoslavia.

For trade sanctions to be effective, the following conditions must be met:

+ A nation planning to impose trade sanctions must identify imports that are vital to the economy of the other nation and, hence, inelastic in demand.
+ The identified imports must be either unavailable in the domestic market or inadequate in supply.
+ The imposing nation must be able to control or bring into alliance all major suppliers of the identified imports.

Because of these requirements, especially the third, trade sanctions by one nation against another tend to be ineffectual. **Financial sanctions** are limitations set on official lending, aid, or flow of currency to another country. For example, the United States froze Iranian assets during the late 1970s to induce Iranian officials to release the U.S. hostages. A more recent example involves the U.S. financial sanctions against Haiti in early June 1994. This sanction called for prohibiting wire transfers, letters of credit, and other financial transactions to restrain the flow of U.S. dollar among Haitians. Although U.S. residents could still send up to $50 a month to their relatives in Haiti, such transactions were thoroughly scrutinized. The sanction was imposed to put pressure on Haiti's ruling military leaders and the elite class that supports them.

We conclude this chapter by stating that, as a general rule, protectionist policies should be avoided. Such policies fuel inflation and raise consumer costs by increasing the domestic prices of the protected products. Such policies misallocate scarce resources by encouraging producers to shift their production activities from products they produce more efficiently to those they produce less efficiently. For example, in an effort to improve its economy, Mexico, a country that has been burdened with heavy foreign loans, started to dismantle its protectionist barriers in 1985. At that time, more than 5,000 items were subject to restrictive import licenses. In 1987, there were fewer than 500 such items. During this two-year period (1985-1987), government subsidies were also reduced and tariffs were cut from as high as 100 percent to about 40 percent. As a result of these policies, the Mexican economy became more competitive. The increased competition forced Mexican producers to improve the quality of their products. These freer trade policies contributed greatly to the Mexican economic recovery which, in 1987, seemed to be moving toward "an impressive economic turn around."[8] Because about two thirds of Mexican exports go to the United States, the two economies are closely linked. Thus, the future of the Mexican economy, to a large extent, depends on the success of the North American Free Trade Agreement (NAFTA). We elaborate on this agreement in Chapter 9.

As a second example, in 1985, it was estimated that the U.S. trade barriers on manufactured goods were costing the U.S. consumers more than $50 billion a year, or $450 for every working individual. In the clothing industry alone, U.S. protectionist policies resulted in more than doubling of prices compared with what they would have been without trade barriers.[9] Under then President Jimmy Carter, protectionist price policies in the steel industry cost consumers about $100 million a year for more than three years. These policies saved, temporarily, 12,000 steel workers' jobs. However, the cost of each job saved to the consumer was more than $80,000 a year, which is more than the job actually paid.[10] Although these policies were enacted presumably to save jobs, economists believe that no job was saved on a permanent basis.

In a third example, according to critics of the U.S. peanut quota, "While the peanut program has prevented glut and propped up quota holders' income, . . .the success has come at the cost of stifled industry growth, market distortions, and higher costs to consumers".[11]

Defining competitiveness as "the ability to take advantage of opportunities in the international marketplace," a 1989 survey of 32 nations ranked the United States' economic competitiveness third, after Switzerland (second) and Japan (first).[12] Given the United States' vast human and nonhuman resources, the country definitely has the potential to continue to remain the world's number one economic power. What seems to be needed in the case of U.S. manufacturing is free trade that causes inefficient manufacturers to drop out of the market and encourages efficient producers to make high-quality products that can compete in the international market. For example, in 1987, a U.S. steel-industry executive wrote, "It is only during periods of intense competitive pressures, such as the one we have seen since 1982, that modernization accelerates, along with the closing of antiquated facilities that cannot be modernized or be environmentally acceptable. . . . The steel industry's problem is not in what steel workers are paid, but in their lack of productivity."[13] As Japanese manufacturers have demonstrated, the popularity of their automobiles in the world market is due not to their government's protectionism, but to the excellent quality of their cars, which has kept them in high demand throughout the world despite rising prices.[14]

As we enter the 2000s, there are signs that U.S. manufacturers are "on the right track." The data indicate that they have recently managed far better than their foreign counterparts in holding costs down. The existing date shows that U.S. manufacturers experienced a remarkable turnabout by showing a decline in unit costs, while most other countries faced double-digit increases. Looking into the future, U.S. manufacturers are expected to continue to improve their competitive position.[15] Given this situation, any plea for protectionist measures is unfounded, to say the least.

7.7 SUMMARY

1. Theory-based arguments, derived from the models of international trade theories, include terms-of-trade argument and optimum tariff, domestic distortion argument, and strategic trade policy argument.
2. The terms of trade argument states that a nation's restrictive trade policy can increase the ratio of exports price index to imports price index (P_X/P_M) and hence improve the nation's welfare.
3. The optimum tariff is a tariff rate that maximizes the nation's welfare.
4. According to the theory of second best, if the presence of distortion in an economy prevents the achievement of Pareto optimality, it may be justifiable for a government to employ policies that add more distortions (such as tariffs).
5. According to the strategic trade policy argument, high-technology industries are crucial to the future growth of a nation, and thus they should be protected temporarily with subsidies, tariffs, and other forms of protection.

6. Erroneous arguments for protection include those arguments that are not based on economic reasoning but that hinge on nationalistic fervor and emotion. Domestic production, prevent-money-outflow, wage protection, and equalization of production costs are conventional erroneous arguments.

7. According to the domestic production argument, domestic producers have rights to the domestic market. The protection of these rights requires the reduction or abolishment of imports.

8. According to the prevent-money-outflow argument, importing goods into a nation will result in the outflow of money from that nation. To stop such an outflow, the nation must resort to protectionism to replace imports with domestic production.

9. According to the wage protection argument, high-wage countries such as the United States or Great Britain, cannot effectively compete with low-wage countries; hence, they should impose tariffs or quotas to protect their workers from products made by low-wage workers overseas.

10. The equalization of production costs argument calls for the imposition of a scientific tariff, that is, a tariff specifically designed to neutralize the cost advantage enjoyed by foreign producers of tariffed product.

11. Questionable arguments for protection include those arguments that are not totally erroneous but that exemplify poor policies with abusive potentials. Antidumping, balance of trade, and employment-protection are typical questionable arguments.

12. According to the antidumping argument, because dumping a product in a country puts that country's import-competing firms at a disadvantage, it is justifiable to impose a remedial tariff to offset the dumper's price advantage.

13. According to proponents of the balance of trade argument, tariffs or quotas are necessary because they encourage a favorable balance of trade.

14. According to the proponents of the employment protection argument, the imposition of tariffs or other forms of import restrictions are desirable during periods of unemployment because these measures reduce imports and stimulate domestic production. Increased domestic production, in turn, leads to a reduction in unemployment.

15. Qualified arguments for protection include those arguments that can be justified with some qualification. Their justification is based on either a noneconomic origin, such as national security, or the anticipation that long-run economic gains will more than offset the short-run protection costs. Infant industry, national security, diversification, and infant government are traditional qualified arguments.

16. The infant industry argument asserts that because a new and underdeveloped industry cannot survive competition from abroad, it should be protected temporarily with high tariffs and quotas on imported goods.

17. According to the national security argument, a country needs to impose tariffs on crucial goods that may be needed for war and defense in order to promote their domestic production and ensure their continued availability.

18. According to proponents of the diversification argument, countries that are dependent on a single commodity for their economic survival should follow protectionist policies to encourage the establishment of different industries.

19. According to proponents of the infant government argument, a nation that is young and has no alternative means of raising the funds needed for its economic development should use import and export duties as a crucial source of public revenue.

20. Many environmentalists have called for trade restrictions on the grounds that free trade hurts the environment by encouraging firms to move to nations that have lax environmental regulations.

21. The political argument for protection calls for a government to use protectionist means to reach a political goal.

22. A government may use economic sanctions against other countries to achieve a given political or military objective. Economic sanctions can take the form of either trade sanctions or financial sanctions.

23. Trade sanctions involve either banning a country's exports to another country or imposing quotas on another country's imports.

24. Financial sanctions are limitations set on official lending, aid, or flow of currency to another country.

Review Questions

1. The arguments for protection can be classified into five groups. Differentiate between these groups, and name different types of arguments that are included in each group.
2. What is meant by an optimum tariff? What condition is needed for imposition of an optimum tariff?
3. Define and give examples of external economy and external diseconomy.
4. A new argument for protection, developed during the 1980s, is the strategic trade policy.
   (a) Briefly describe this argument.
   (b) Elaborate on events that gave rise to this argument.
   (c) Give an example of a successful trade strategy.
   (d) Discuss the shortcomings associated with this argument.
5. An erroneous argument is the prevent-money-outflow argument. Briefly describe this argument. What is its main flaw?
6. What is meant by a scientific tariff? Assume that all commodities in all nations are subject to scientific tariffs. Given this scenario, how do you think international trade will be affected?
7. The infant industry argument represents an old argument that dates back to the late eighteenth century.
   (a) What do proponents of this argument suggest?
   (b) What are the shortcomings of this argument?
   (c) Given these shortcomings, why do you think it is still popular?
   (d) Assume that a nation decides to protect its infant industry. Suggest a policy that accomplishes this goal at a minimum welfare loss.
8. National security represents a qualified argument for protection.
   (a) Briefly describe this argument.
   (b) Name industries that have applied this argument.
   (c) What are the shortcomings of this argument?
   (d) Is trade restriction the most efficient way of dealing with the problem? Discuss.
9. The text presents 16 arguments for protection. Which of these arguments presents the strongest case for protection? Explain.

Problems

1. Because the theory-based arguments are built on economic models, they represent legitimate cases for protection. Do you agree with this statement? Discuss.
2. Discuss the following statement: American workers are wrong to think they need protection from imports in order to save their jobs.
3. Given the United States' commitment to human rights issues, the government should impose tariffs on imported products made by underpaid workers in developing countries who are exploited in sweatshops and work in unacceptable environments.
   Do you agree with this statement? Discuss.
4. Suppose that France and Great Britain trade wine (W) and cloth (C). Assume that both countries have monopsony power in international trade for their import-goods. Given these assumptions, complete the following:
   (a) Draw a figure similar to Figure 7-1, demonstrating that with optimum tariff France will exchange 20 gallons of wine for 40 yards of cloth.
   (b) Demonstrate the effect of retaliation by England imposing an optimum tariff of its own.
   (c) What happens if both nations retaliate against each other's optimum tariffs several times?

5. The text presents 16 arguments for protection.
   (a) Give a recent example of protectionism that fits one of these arguments.
   (b) Do you think that protectionism is justifiable under the circumstances explained in your example? Explain.
   (c) Which of the arguments for protection do you think are most relevant for your country today?

Notes

1. "A Global Trade War on the Way?" *U.S. News & World Report,* March 1, 1982, 57-58.
2. Milton H. Spencer, *Contemporary Economics* (New York: Worth Publisher, 1971), 580.
3. "Lumber Probe Is Not Expected to Fuel Dispute: U.S. to Play Down Action on Trade Complaint on Canadian Softwood," *The Wall Street Journal,* 9 June 1986, 8; "Canadian Dollar Falls 1% Against U.S. Currency: Concern over Trade Dispute Pulls Down Canada Unit," *The Wall Street Journal,* 3 June 1986, 34.
4. "American First: Protectionist Attitudes Grow Stronger in Spite of Healthy Economy," *The Wall Street Journal,* 16 May 1988, 1, 7.
5. Joseph D. Coppock, *International Instability: The Experience After World War II* (New York: McGraw Hill, 1982), Ch. 4.
6. "Empires of the Chainsaws," *The Economist* (August 10, 1991): 36.
7. "Environmental Imperialism," *The Economist* (February 15, 1992): 8.
8. "Fading Prospects? Mexico's Turnaround of Sagging Economy Now Seems Imperiled," *The Wall Street Journal,* 23 November 1987, 1, 19.
9. "As Free-Trade Bastion, U.S. Isn't Half as Pure as Many People Think," *The Wall Street Journal,* 1 November 1985, 1.
10. "Protectionism Ensures Stagnation," *The Wall Street Journal,* 21 August 1987, 22.
11. "Shell Game: Quota System for Peanuts Is Attacked for Inflicting Peanut Prices, at Consumers' Expense," *The Wall Street Journal,* 1 May 1990, A12.
12. "Survey of 32 Nations Rates Japan No. 1, U.S., Third, in Economic Competitiveness," *The Wall Street Journal,* 5 July 1989, A4.
13. "Protectionism Ensures Stagnation," *The Wall Street Journal,* 21 August 1987, 22.
14. U.S. Congress, Office of Technology Assessment, *U.S. Industrial Competitiveness: A Comparison of Steel, Electronic and Automobiles* (Washington, DC: U.S. Government Printing Office, 1981), 47; "Buying Foreign: Despite Fallen Dollar, Americans Continue to Snap Up Imports," *The Wall Street Journal,* 9 February 1988, 1, 18.
15. "U.S. Competitiveness Wins New Respect from Leading Players in Global Market," *The Wall Street Journal,* 16 July 1993, A6; "Age of Angst: Workplace Revolution Boosts Productivity at Cost of Job Security," *The Wall Street Journal,* 10 March 1993, 1, A8.

Suggested Readings

Baldwin, Robert E. *Nontariff Distortions of International Trade.* Washington, DC: Brookings Institute, 1970.
"The Case Against Infant Industry Protection." *Journal of Political Economy* (May/June 1969): 295-305.
Bell, Martin, Bruce Ross-Larson, and Larry E. Westphal. "Assessing the Performance of Infant Industries." *Journal of Development Economics* (September-October 1984): 101-128.
Bergsten, Fred C., and William R. Cline. "Trade Policy in the 1980's: An Overview." In *Trade Policy in the 1980s,* edited by William R. Cline. Washington, DC: Institute for International Economics, 1983.
Bhagwati, Jagdish N. *Protectionism.* Cambridge, MA: MIT Press, 1988.
Blackhurst, Richard, et al. *Trade Liberalization, Protectionism, and Interdependence.* Geneva: General Agreement on Tariffs and Trade. Special Paper on International Economics, No. 7. Princeton: Princeton University Press, 1965, Ch. 4.

Cohen, Robert B. "The Prospects for Trade and Protectionism in Auto Industry." In *Trade Policy in the 1980s,* edited by William K. Cline. Washington DC: Institute for International Economics, 1983.

Coughlin, Cletus, K. Alec Chrystal, and Geoffrey E. Wood. "Protectionist Trade Policies: A Survey of Theory, Evidence, and Rationale." *Federal Reserve Bank of St. Louis Review* (January-February 1988): 12-29.

Crandall, Robert W. "Import Quotas and the Automobile Industry: The Costs of Protectionism." *The Brookings Review* 2, no. 4 (Summer 1984): 8-16.

Grunwald, J., and K. Flamm. *The Global Factory: Foreign Assembly in International Trade.* Washington, DC: Brookings Institution, 1985.

Hagen, E. "An Economic Justification of Protectionism," *Quarterly Journal of Economics.* (November 1985): 496-514.

Howell, Thomas R, et al. *The Microelectronics Race: The Impact of Government Policy on International Competitiveness.* Boulder, CO: Westview Press, 1987.

Hufbauer, Gary C., et al. *Trade Protectionism in the United States: 31 Case Studies.* Washington, DC: Institute for International Economics, 1986.

Krueger, A. O., and B. Tuner. "An Empirical Test of the Infant Industry Argument." *American Economic Review* (December 1982): 1142-1152.

_____. "Is Free Trade Pass;aae?" *Journal of Economic Perspectives.* (Fall 1987): 3-12.

Lawrence, Robert Z. *Can America Compete?* Washington, DC: Brookings Institution, 1984.

_____. "Protectionism: Is There a Better Way?" *American Economic Review Papers and Proceedings* (May 1989): 118-122.

Organization for Economic Cooperation and Development. *The Costs of Restricting Imports: The Automobile Industry.* Washington, DC: OECD Publications, 1988.

Robinson, Joan. "Beggar-My-Neighbor Remedies for Unemployment." In *Essays on the Theory of Employment,* 2d ed. edited by Joan Robinson. Oxford: Basil Blackwell, 1947, Part 3, Ch. 2.

Schott, Jeffrey J. "Protectionist Threat to Trade and Investment in Services." *The World Economy* 6, no. 2 (June 1983): 194-214.

Chapter 8

INTERNATIONAL ORGANIZATIONS AND AGREEMENTS AFFECTING INTERNATIONAL TRADE

8.1 INTRODUCTION

In Chapters 5 and 6, we discussed tariff and nontariff barriers to international trade. As we noted in those chapters, trade barriers enacted by individual nations lead to unilateral restriction of trade from one country to another. But trade can also be affected multilaterally by governments and firms from various nations acting in harmony. Their actions, leading to the creation of international organizations and the enactment of agreements, influence the free flow of goods and services across national boundaries.

In this chapter we study the major international organizations and agreements that affect international trade. First, we explain international cartels and describe economic integration. We then present the major trade associations in developing countries. Next, we discuss the Organization for Economic Cooperation and Development and elaborate on the General Agreement on Tariff and Trade. Finally, we discuss state trading and elaborate on trade between market-oriented economies and command economies.

8.2 INTERNATIONAL CARTELS

An **international cartel** can be defined as an organization composed of firms in the same industry from different countries (or a group of governments) who agree to limit their outputs and exports in order to influence prices of their commodities and maximize their profits.

International cartels existed in railway services and the tobacco business as early as the 1880s. The post—World War II period has witnessed international cartel arrangements in such industries as oil, steel, sugar, coffee, and farm products.

Today, the most successful international cartel is the Organization of Petroleum Exporting Countries (OPEC), which was formed on September 14, 1960, in reaction to unilateral cuts in crude oil prices by the international oil companies. The objectives of OPEC, as stated by the five original members (Iran, Iraq, Kuwait, Saudi Arabia, and Venezuela), were to stabilize oil prices and to unify petroleum policies for the member countries. During the 1960s and 1970s, this organization expanded rapidly and enrolled eight additional members (Qatar, Indonesia, Libya, the United Arab Emirates, Algeria, Nigeria, Ecuador, and Gabon). Although this 13-member international cartel won a few concessions in the 1960s and 1970s, it did not come to full power until 1971. When, according to the Tehran Agreement, OPEC countries won concessions that allowed them to participate in the process of setting the posted prices of oil. Subsequently, they succeeded in quadrupling the price of crude oil, between 1973 and 1974, setting the stage for the energy crisis of the early 1970s.

In general, the successful operation of a cartel depends on four major elements: supply, demand, price, and the degree of homogeneity among members. More specifically, for a cartel to operate effectively, it must meet the following conditions:

◆ Be able to control a large percentage of the world's supply of an essential commodity
◆ Face an inelastic demand for a commodity that has only a few substitutes
◆ Have members with similar revenue requirements, facilitating the establishment of an optimum price
◆ Have members with similar backgrounds in such areas as culture, religion, race, language, and political ideology

Because OPEC fulfills most of these requirements, it has been able to survive for four decades. However, since a cartel's power to control the market lies in the unification of its members, and since each member country has its own national objectives, it is not always easy for them to reach a common goal. Consequently, cartels are inherently unstable and are usually expected to collapse in the long run. Even in the case of OPEC, which has successfully operated for many years, there are now signs of its deterioration, evidenced by the lack of cooperation among its member countries. Today, its members do not honor the production quotas they once agreed on. As a result, the cartel members do not even know exactly how much oil they really produce.[1] During the 1980s, two of OPEC's prominent members, Iran and Iraq, engaged in a war, and the rest of the member countries could not agree on a common pricing policy. Saudi Arabia pressed for a relatively low price in order to discourage conservation efforts, substitution, and technological progress that might replace oil. Indonesia, Iran, Nigeria, and Venezuela, however, desired a relatively high price to maximize their short-run revenues.

The 1990-1991 Persian Gulf crisis that removed Iraq and Kuwait from the oil export scene opened a new chapter in OPEC history. In the wake of the war, Iran was among those countries that increased its oil production. Saudi Arabia, Venezuela, and the United Arab Emirates enhanced their production after Iraq invaded Kuwait. In January 1992, OPEC's output reached its highest production level in 10 years, leading to yet another disagreement among its members. Several OPEC members suggested Saudi Arabia reduce its production. However, Saudi officials declined to do so and refused all calls for emergency meetings to discuss the issue.

The OPEC's power in controlling the oil market was further diminished in 1993 when one of its members, Ecuador, resigned from the organization, reducing OPEC's membership to 12 nations.

Theoretically, if a cartel is successful in unifying its members, it would behave exactly like a monopoly in maximizing its total profit. The next section shows how such a monopoly (a centralized cartel) maximizes its profit.

8.2a Centralized Cartels

If all the cartel members could agree on maximizing their collective profit, they would behave as a perfectly unified profit—maximizing monopolist.

In Figure 8-1, assume that D represents the world demand for OPEC's oil, and MR is the corresponding marginal revenue curve. Given the monopoly assumption, note that D has a negative slope, and MR is twice as steep as D. The curve labelled S shows the supply schedule of exports of OPEC's oil. Recall from microeconomics courses that this curve is the horizontal summation of the individual OPEC members' marginal cost curves, and, as such, it also portrays OPEC's marginal cost (MC) curve.

Under perfect competition, international equilibrium is established at point E, where demand schedule D intersects supply schedule S. Accordingly, under perfectly competitive conditions, the cartel members as a unit export 45 million barrels of oil at the equilibrium price of $25 per barrel.

An international cartel of oil exporters (such as OPEC) acting as a monopolist will maximize its total profit by following the familiar MC = MR rule. In Figure 8-1, this is achieved at point E', where S intersects MR. This leads the cartel to export 35 million barrels of oil per day at the price of $30 per barrel (point H). Thus, in comparison to perfect competition, the centralized cartel results in a decrease in output (from 45 million to 35 million barrels a day) and an increase in price (from $25 per barrel to $30 per barrel).

The increase in the total profit of the cartel as a group is given by the shaded area (EE′F). The reason for this higher profit is that by restricting total oil exports to 35 million barrels a day, the cartel omits all exports for which MC is greater than MR. As a result, profits are greater by the sum of those differences. In Figure 8-1, at the competitive price of $25 per barrel, the cartel's marginal cost (EG) is much higher than its marginal revenue (FG). Indeed, marginal cost is higher than marginal revenue for all units between G (45 million barrels a day) and I (35 barrels a day). By reducing each unit of its exports, the cartel saves that unit's MC (additional cost associated with the production of that unit), but also loses that unit's MR (additional revenue associated with the production of that unit). Because between points G and I each unit's MC is greater than MR, the cartel's profit continues to expand by the difference between MC and MR until it decreases its oil production to 35 million barrels a day. The shaded area of EE′F simply shows the increase in the cartel's total profit resulting from restriction of exports from 45 million barrels a day to 35 million barrels a day.

FIGURE 8-1
Profit Maximization by a Centralized Cartel

D represents demand for OPEC's oil, and MR is the corresponding marginal revenue curve. Perfect competition leads to equilibrium at point E, at which 45 million barrels of oil are traded at $25 per barrel. An international cartel of oil exporters (OPEC) acting as a single profit-maximizing monopolist maximizes its total profit at point E′, where MC = MR. At this point, it exports 35 million barrels of oil at $30 per barrel. The increase in OPEC's total profit is given by the shaded area.

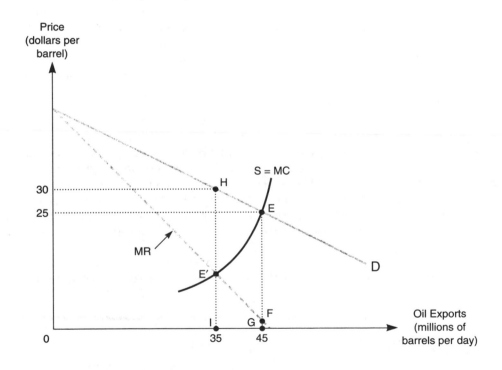

GLOBAL INSIGHTS CASE 8.1

Erosion of OPEC's Power in the Global Market

The oil crises of 1973-1974 and 1979-1980 brought OPEC to world attention and confirmed its position as a formidable power in influencing the world's financial markets. Following these shocks, OPEC members found themselves with surplus funds that were eventually "recycled" through Western banks to Latin American nations and other nations that were in desperate need of funds. This funneling of money contributed to the debt crisis, raising developing nations' debt to $500 billion. Years of austerity followed before the debt-stricken developing nations and bankers could come up with a resolution.

The prosperity of OPEC in the 1970s and 1980s did not last long. In the early 1990s, OPEC members found themselves heavy borrowers in the global financial market. For example, Saudi Arabia's debt reached $50 billion in 1993 (from zero in 1979). In the same year, Kuwait faced an external debt of $40 billion. The only exception was the United Arab Emirates, which in 1992 had a $672 million payment surplus. As a result, OPEC members, such as Nigeria, Saudi Arabia, and Venezuela, started searching for extra funds to finance their budget deficits and industrial imports. Given their financial problems, OPEC members found themselves at odds with each other. One member, Ecuador, resigned in 1993, and the rest found that recurring production ceilings were not honored.

As we pass into the new millennium, OPEC members find themselves grappling with yet another issue that threatens to further diminish their dwindling market power. The issue is whether the earth can tolerate the environmental harm from the growing use of oil, natural gas and coal. The environmentalists maintain that the emissions from burning hydrocarbons are raising global temperatures. This so called "greenhouse effect", environmentalists warn, damages the world's climate. Although not everyone agrees with the environmentalists claim and the scientific evidence is scarce and disputed, OPEC members feel pressure from shifting energy policies around the globe, and they expect such pressure to continue to rise.

These developments have significantly eroded OPEC's power in influencing the global oil market. Given the erosion of OPEC's control over oil prices, there is now a relative ease about the long-run prospect of oil supply in the international market. Nevertheless, OPEC's power in manipulating oil prices, at least in the short-run, should not be underestimated. The organization still accounts for most of the world's oil reserves, and controls about 40 percent of the world's production. It is still capable of causing significant oscillation of oil prices in the world market and continues to be a major client for a large number of banks. As such, it remains an important player in the world market; however, it no longer exercises the immense financial might that once made the world economy apprehensive.

Source: "OPEC, Once the World's Big Bad Wolf, Has Lost a Good Deal of Its Bite Lately," The Wall Street Journal, 29 January 1993, A11.; "Now OPEC Members Are the worried Ones," *The Wall Street Journal*, 23 June 1997, p. 1.

8.3 ECONOMIC INTEGRATION

Economic integration is an agreement among nations to decrease or eliminate trade barriers. Depending on the terms and the intensity of the agreement, economic integration can be classified as a preferential trade arrangement, a free-trade area, a customs union, a common market, or an economic union.

8.3a Preferential Trade Arrangements

A **preferential trade arrangement** is an agreement between participating nations to lower trade barriers among themselves. A classic example of a preferential trade arrangement is the British Commonwealth Preference scheme, which was formed in 1932. According to this agreement, Great Britain imposed a lower tariff rate if a commodity entered Britain from a nation that was a member of the British Commonwealth, such as Australia, Canada, or India.

8.3b Free-Trade Areas

A **free-trade area** is established by an agreement among nations that removes trade barriers while allowing each member nation to define its own barriers on trade with nonmembers. The European Free Trade Association (EFTA) provides the best example of a free-trade area. This association, formed in 1960, initially included Austria, Denmark, Norway, Portugal, Great Britain, Sweden, and Switzerland. Later, the Faroe Islands, Finland, and Iceland joined this association. Britain and Denmark left EFTA when they became members of the European Union (EU).

In recent years, the United States adopted free-trade area arrangements by negotiating free-trade agreements with Israel (1984), Canada (1989), and, most recently, Mexico and Canada (1993). These recent free-trade agreements are discussed in the next chapter.

8.3c Customs Unions

A **customs union** is an organization that allows the lowering or abolishing of trade barriers between member countries and adopts a unified system of tariffs against nonmembers. An example is the Zollverein, a customs union established in 1834 by a number of small sovereign German states before the political unification of Germany (1870). By removing trade barriers through much of Germany, the Zollverein was an important factor in German reunification. As we explain later in this chapter, the EU provides another example of a customs union that developed into a common market and, in 1999, evolved into an economic union.

Static Welfare Effects of a Customs Union. The static welfare effects of a customs union can be analyzed in terms of trade creation and trade diversion. Viner, who pioneered the theory of customs unions in 1950, used these concepts as the main analysis tools.

Trade creation arises when some domestic production of one customs-union member is replaced by another member's lower-cost imports. Given that all economic resources are employed before and after the customs union is established, trade creation increases the welfare of the member countries because it induces greater production specialization according to factor endowment and comparative advantage.

Trade diversion arises when lower-cost imports from a country that is not a member of the customs union are replaced by higher-cost imports from a member country. In other words, trade diversion occurs when there is a shift from a low-cost producer outside the union to a high-cost producer inside the union. Trade diversion decreases the welfare of member countries because it goes against production specialization on the basis of factor endowment and comparative advantage.

To analyze the static welfare effects of a customs union in the context of trade creation and trade diversion, we distinguish between two types of customs unions: trade-creating customs unions and trade-diverting customs unions.

Trade-Creating Customs Unions. A **trade-creating customs union** is a customs union that results only in trade creation, leading to a net increase in the social welfare of union members because it leads to greater specialization on the basis of comparative advantage. A trade creating customs union also enhances the nonmembers welfare since some of the increase in its real income, resulting from its greater specialization in production, encourages increased imports from the nonmembers.

The static welfare effects of a trade-creating customs union are illustrated in Figure 8-2. In this figure, assume that there are only three countries in the world—Belgium, Canada, and France—producing wheat. The supply and demand schedules of wheat for Belgium are given by S_B and D_B, respectively. Suppose, in comparison to France and

Canada, Belgium is a very small country that is unable to influence the foreign prices of wheat. As a result, the foreign supply curve for wheat to this country is entirely elastic. Canada's free-trade price for wheat, given by its supply curve S_{CA}, is $1.00 ($P_{CA}$ = $1.00). France's free-trade price for wheat, given by its supply curve S_F, is $1.50 ($P_F$ = $1.50).

As Figure 8-2 shows, we assume that Canada is the most efficient producer of wheat. Thus, its supply (S_{CA}) falls below France's supply curve (S_F), and it charges a lower price ($1.00 per bushel) for its wheat exports to Belgium than the price charged by France ($1.50).

Under free-trade conditions and before the formation of a customs union, France does not engage in trade because its supply price ($1.50 per bushel) surpasses Canada's ($1.00 per bushel). Belgium buys all of its imports from Canada (the cheapest source) at $1.00 per bushel. At this price, Belgium consumes 700 million bushels of wheat, produces 50 million bushels, and imports 650 million bushels (700 - 50) from Canada.

FIGURE 8-2
A Trade Creating Customs Union

The supply and demand schedules of wheat for Belgium are given by S_B and D_B, respectively. S_{CA} and S_F represent the free trade perfectly elastic supply curves of wheat of Canada and France, respectively. Under free trade conditions, Belgium produces 50 million bushels, consumes 700 million bushels and buys all of its imports (650 million bushels) from Canada (the cheapest source) at $1.00 per bushel. Belgium's imposition of a nondiscriminatory tariff of $1.00 per bushel on all imports causes S_{CA} and S_F to shift to S_{CA+T} and S_{F+T}, respectively. Given these tariff-inclusive supply curves, Belgium still continues to purchase all of its imports (250 million bushels) from Canada at the tariff-inclusive price of $2.00 per bushel, produces 250 millions bushels, and consumes 500 million bushels. After formation of a customs union with Canada, Belgium continues to buy all of its imports (650 million bushels) from Canada at $1.00 per bushel. Areas b + d ($200 million), representing the favorable welfare-augmenting trade creation effect, comprise a production effect (area b; $100 million) and a consumption effect (area d; $100 million).

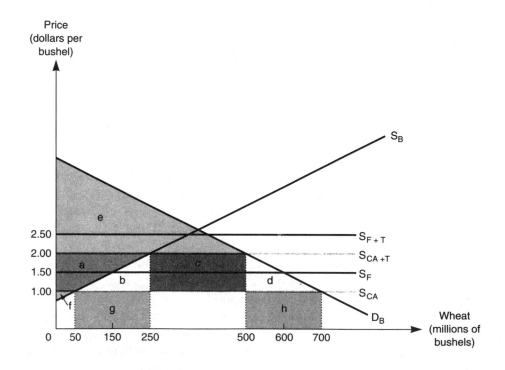

Assume that Belgium imposes a nondiscriminatory specific tariff of $1.00 per bushel on all wheat imports. The tariff-inclusive (price plus tariff) supply curves of Canada and France are shown by S_{CA+T} and S_{F+T}, respectively.[*] Given these tariff-inclusive supply curves, Belgium still continues to buy all of its imports from Canada at the tariff-inclusive price of $2.00 per bushel, which is lower than the tariff-inclusive price charged by France ($2.50). At the price of $2.00 per bushel, Belgium consumes 500 million bushels of wheat, produces 250 million bushels, and imports 250 million bushels (500 - 250) from Canada.

Now, suppose Belgium and Canada agree to form a customs union. Given this agreement, Belgium eliminates its tariff on Canadian imports, but continues to maintain its tariff against nonmember France's goods. This means that the price charged by Canada ($1.00) is still lower than France's tariff-inclusive price ($2.50). As a result, Belgium buys all of its imports, amounting to 650 millions of bushels, only from Canada and imports no wheat from France.

The welfare effect of the formation of the customs union, analyzed by using the now-familiar concepts of consumer and producer surplus, is presented in Table 8-1. The combined area of b + d represents the favorable welfare-augmenting **trade-creation effect.** As Figure 8-2 shows, trade creation (areas b + d) is composed of a production effect (area b) and a consumption effect (area d). The production effect (area b, $100 million) results from shifting the production of 200 million bushels of wheat (250 - 50) from less efficient Belgian producers (at a cost of $300 million; areas (b + g) to more efficient Canadian producers (at a cost of $200 million; area g).

TABLE 8-1
Static Welfare Effects of a Trade-Creating Customs Union

	Before Customs Union	After Customs Union	Gain (+)/Loss (-)
Consumer surplus	Area e	Areas a + b + c + d + e	Areas a + b + c + d
Producer surplus	Areas a + f	Area f	Area − a
Tariff revenue collected by Belgian government	Area c	—	Area − c
Net gain			Areas b + d

The consumption effect (area d, $100 million) results from the rise in consumption of 200 million bushels of wheat (700 - 500) in Belgium, giving a benefit of $300 million (areas d + h) with an expenditure of only $200 million (area h).

Given this analysis, the overall trade creation, representing the net static gain to Belgium as a whole, is equal to $200 million. This figure is obtained by adding the production effect (area b, $100 million) and the consumption effect (area d, $100 million).

In his analysis, Viner focused on the production effect and overlooked the consumption effect. It was left to James Meade to extend the theory of customs unions by perceiving the consumption effect. Finally, Harry Johnson added the two effects together to measure the overall static welfare effects of a customs union.

Trade-Diverting Customs Unions. The **trade-diverting customs union** is a customs union that results in both trade creation and trade diversion. The overall effects of a trade-diverting customs union on its members depends on the relative strength of the opposing effects of trade creation and trade diversion. The welfare of nonmembers, however, can be expected to decrease because nonmembers' economic resources can only be employed less efficiently than before the formation of the customs union.

Using our example of Belgium, Canada, and France, the static welfare effect of a trade-diverting customs union is illustrated in Figure 8-3. Belgium's domestic supply and demand curves of wheat are S_B and D_B, while S_{CA} and S_F are the free-trade, perfectly elastic supply curves of Canada and France, respectively. With a nondiscriminatory

---

[*] S_{CA+T} is obtained by shifting S_{CA} upward by the amount of the tariff (t). In the same manner, S_{F+T} is obtained by shifting S_F upward by the amount of the tariff.

specific tariff of $1.00 per bushel on wheat imports, Belgium imports wheat only from Canada at the tariff-inclusive price of $2.00 per bushel (exactly as in Figure 8-2). As we saw in Figure 8-2, at this tariff-inclusive price, Belgium consumes 500 million bushels of wheat, produces 250 million bushels, and imports 250 million bushels (500 - 250) from Canada.

Now suppose that Belgium and France agree to form a customs union. Given this agreement, Belgium eliminates its tariff on French goods, but continues to maintain its tariff against nonmember Canada. This means that the price charged by France ($1.50) is now lower than Canada's tariff-inclusive price ($2.00). As a result, Belgium now buys all of its imports, amounting to 450 millions of bushels (600 - 150), from France only and imports no wheat from Canada.

The static welfare effects of the formation of the customs union, analyzed by using the concepts of consumer and producer surplus, are presented in Table 8-2. Areas b + d represent the favorable welfare-augmenting trade-creation effect. Area f measures the unfavorable welfare-reducing *trade-diversion effect*. As seen earlier, the *trade-creation effect* is composed of a production effect (area b) and a consumption effect (area d).

TABLE 8-2
Static Welfare Effects of a Trade-diverting Customs Union

	Before Customs Union	After Customs Union	Gain (+)/Loss (−)
Consumer surplus	Area e	Area a + b + c + d + e	Area a + b + c + d
Producer surplus	Area a + g	Area g	Area − a
Tariff revenue collected by Belgium's government	Area c + f	—	Areas − (c + f)
Net gain			Areas b + d − f

As seen in Figure 8-2, the production effect (area b, $25 million) results from shifting the production of 100 million (250 - 150) bushels of wheat from less efficient Belgian producers (at a cost of $175 million; areas b + h) to more efficient French producers (at a cost of $150 million; area h).

The consumption effect (area d, $25 million) results from the rise in consumption of 100 million bushels of wheat (600 - 500) in Belgium, giving a benefit of $175 million (areas d + i) with an expenditure of only $150 million (area i).

Given this analysis, the overall trade-creation effect, representing the net static gain to Belgium as a whole, is equal to $50 million. This figure is obtained by adding the production effect (area b, $25 million) and the consumption effect (area d, $25 million).

Although the formation of a trade-diverting customs union can add to the world's welfare through trade creation, it also leads to a loss in the world's welfare by way of trade diversion. In Figure 8-3, the formation of the customs union between Belgium and France means that Belgium has to buy all of its imports, amounting to 450 million bushels (600 − 150), from France only and import no wheat from Canada. In this case, Belgium does not collect any tariff revenue. The importation of wheat to Belgium is diverted from the more efficient Canadian producer to the less efficient French producer because the tariff discriminates against Canadian imports. The 450 million bushels of wheat (600 - 150) could have been imported from the low-cost Canadian producers at $1.00 per bushel, rather than from the high-cost French producers at $1.50 per bushel. This would have resulted in a cost savings of $125 million (area f in Figure 8-3; 250 x 0.5) for Belgium. This cost represents not only a welfare loss to Belgium, but also a deadweight loss to the world as a whole.

Given this analysis, we need to compare the positive trade-creation effect with the negative trade-diversion effect to assess the overall welfare effect of a trade-diverting customs union. If we find that the positive trade-creation effect more than offsets the negative trade-diversion effect, we conclude that the trade-diverting customs union would increase the welfare of its members. The reverse also holds true. Because in Figure 8-3 the positive trade-creation effect is less than the negative trade-diversion effect, the formation of the customs union decreases the welfare of its members, resulting in a welfare loss of $75 million [$50 million trade creation (areas b + d) − $125 million trade diversion (area f)].

FIGURE 8-3
Trade-Diverting Customs Union

The supply and demand schedules of wheat for Belgium are given by S_B and D_B, respectively. S_{CA} and S_F represent the free trade perfectly elastic supply curves of wheat of Canada and France, respectively. With a nondiscriminatory tariff of $1.00 per bushel on all imports, Belgium buys all of its imports (250 million bushels) from Canada at the tariff-inclusive price of $2.00 per bushel, produces 250 million bushels, and consumes 500 million bushels (exactly as in Figure 8-2). Now suppose that Belgium and France agree to form a customs union. This means that the price charged by France ($1.50 per bushel) is now lower than Canada's tariff-inclusive price ($2.00 per bushel). As a result, Belgium buys all of its imports (450 million bushels) from France at $1.50 per bushel, produces 150 million bushels, and consumes 600 million bushels. Areas b + d ($50 million) represent the favorable welfare-augmenting trade creation effect, and comprise a production effect (area b; $25 million) and a consumption effect (area d; $25 million). Area f represents the welfare-diminishing trade diversion effect. Thus, the formation of the customs union results in a welfare loss of $75 million (areas [b + d] - area f).

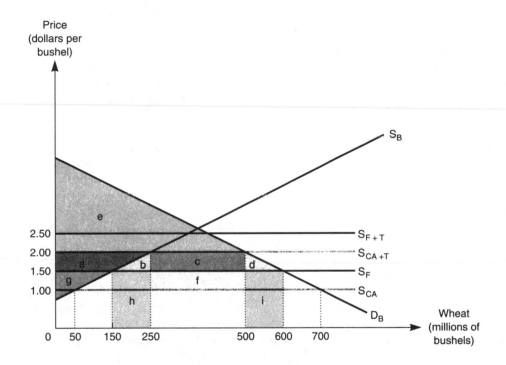

8.3d Dynamic Welfare Effects of a Customs Union

The static analysis of a customs union ignores the union's many dynamic effects. All of these effects augment welfare, and the gains associated with them may more than offset any unfavorable static effects. These dynamic effects include increased competition, economies of scale, and stimulus to investment.

Perhaps the most significant dynamic benefit of a customs union is *increased competition.* In the absence of a customs union, suppliers—especially those in oligopolistic and monopolistic markets—are most likely to grow slowly in the sheltered national market. However, when a customs union is formed and trade barriers among member nations are dismantled, firms that have grown lazy are exposed to increased competition from rivals in other member countries. Inefficient firms must either become more efficient or go out of business. The higher level of competition among firms leads to increased research and development activities, resulting in new products. This environment is likely to stimulate technological improvement and foster economic growth. A case in point is the EU, which has experienced a substantial modernization of its members' industrial plants since 1958. In fact, one of the main reasons for Great Britain's decision to become a member of the EU was the hope that competition would inspire labor and management to boost efficiency.

The second possible dynamic benefit of a customs union is *economies of scale,* that is, a decrease in a firm's long-run average costs as the size of its plant increases. Economies of scale are likely to stem from an enlarged market. Because they can enter freely the domestic markets of other member countries, firms can expand the size of their plants, taking advantage of the economies of scale that would not have happened in smaller markets confined by trade restraints. Economies of scale lead to efficiencies which in turn result in cost reductions for several reasons: greater specialization of resources (workers and equipments), reduced unit cost of inputs, use of the most efficient equipment, increased opportunities for use of by-products, and growth of auxiliary facilities.* The evidence suggests the EU has achieved economies of scale in products such as automobiles, copper refining, footwear, and steel.[2]

The third possible dynamic benefit of a customs union is *stimulus to investment.* This may stem from the larger market resulting from the formation of the customs union. The larger market promotes greater competition among producers within the union, stimulating investment. This happens because with free trade in place, domestic producers must compete with the more efficient foreign producers or face the possibility of bankruptcy. To avoid such a possibility, producers must invest in new equipment, technologies, and product lines to keep costs down and allow increased amounts of output. Establishing a customs union may also induce outsiders to set up so-called *tariff factories,* that is, to establish plants within the customs union in order to avoid the discriminatory trade barriers imposed against nonmembers' products. The United States' massive investment in Europe following 1955 provides an example of tariff factories established by U.S. firms to avoid exclusion from this rapidly growing market.

The dynamic benefits associated with the formation of a customs union seem to be much higher than the static benefits discussed earlier. This is evident from recent empirical studies, estimating that dynamic benefits are about five to six times greater than static benefits.

Empirical Investigations of a Customs Union. The EU provides an example of a customs union that developed into a common market and evolved into an economic union. Several studies have attempted to measure the probable welfare effect of the EU. One study computed that the EU's trade-creation effect for industrial products was $2.3 billion in 1967 with a trade-diversion effect of $0.9 million.[3] Several other empirical investigations of trade impacts of the EU in the 1960s acknowledge that the trade creation in manufactured goods surpasses trade diversion by about four times. In a study of trade conducted in the 1970s, McBean and Snowden found that with the exception of agriculture, there was no indication of increased trade diversion compared with the 1960s.[4] Bela Balassa, in a study of EU trade effects, found evidence of substantial trade creation in the industrial sector and significant trade diversion in the agricultural sector of the EU. In the manufacturing sector, evidence of substantial trade creation was found in the chemical, fuel, machinery, and transportation equipment industries. In the agriculture sector, trade diversion effects were especially strong in the beverage, tobacco, raw materials, and food industries. According to the study, Great Britain and the former West Germany were the two countries that felt the main impact of diversion because, before joining the EU, both countries imported a significant portion of their food from the cheapest overseas sources. After joining the EU, however, they had to import these supplies from high-cost EU sources.[5]

To be sure, any comprehensive analysis of a customs union must assess what the member nations trade flows would have been if the customs union had not been formed and then contrast these hypothetical findings with the actual trade flows. However, given the hypothetical nature of analysis and the problems in determining and quantifying dynamic effects, such an analysis is speculative at best and does not lend itself to unequivocal conclusions.

8.3e Common Markets

A **common market** is a more complete form of customs union. It combines the characteristics of a customs union with the elimination of barriers against the movement of capital and labor among member countries. As we have already shown, the EU—previously called the European Community (EC), the European Economic Community (EEC) and the European Common Market (ECM)—provides an example of a customs union that developed into a common market and finally evolved into an economic union. The EU was formed in 1958 by Belgium, France, Italy,

---

* A large-scale firm can usually purchase its inputs at a lower price per unit due to quantity discounts granted on large purchases.

Luxembourg, the former West Germany, and the Netherlands. In 1973, Denmark, Ireland, and Great Britain joined, followed by Greece in 1981, and Portugal and Spain in 1986.

The EU's first objective was to abolish all restrictions on traded goods (industrial or agricultural) and the establishment of common external tariffs against nonmember countries. The second objective was to promote free movement of labor and capital among its member countries. The first objective was satisfied within about a decade of the agreement's initial signing, giving the EU the status of a customs union. However, attempts at more economic integration in meeting the second objective were not very successful. In 1971, the EU agreed to a 10-year plan designed to reach a full economic union.

The movement toward a complete common market and economic union stumbled seriously in the 1970s and the first half of the 1980s. During this period, two oil crises hit the world, contributing to a slowdown in economic growth and high unemployment in the EU. This caused member nations to concentrate their efforts on internal problems and enact policies that precluded any advancement toward further economic integration.[*]

To recapture the push toward full economic union, EU members endorsed the "White Paper" at their 1985 summit in Milan. Accordingly, they established a detailed legislative program for complete economic integration by 1992. This development is discussed in the next chapter.

Overall, EU members have been very cooperative and have stayed together in protecting their market. For example, in response to the loss of jobs and sales in the United States and Japan, the EU announced a fivefold increase in its industrial research expenditures to boost its competitive position. Additionally, it called on Japanese automakers to voluntarily restrain their exports to the EU as a whole.[6] In 1987, at the request of its members, the EU opened up an antidumping investigation against the Japanese, who were suspected of dumping semiconductors, and against the South Koreans, who were suspected of dumping compact-disc players, on the European market.[7] In 1988, the EU barred British publishers from fixing minimum retail prices for their books.[8] In 1989, the EU Commission was given a new power that makes it, in most cases, the main authority in the EU to halt those corporate mergers and takeovers that appear to harm fair competition.[9] In 1990, the EU secured a waiver from the GATT rules on tariffs and trade for the former East Germany, the former Soviet Union, and East European countries.[10] Also in 1990, EU members reached an agreement on the reduction of subsidies and other barriers to the trade of agricultural products.[11] This actions dismantled one of the main obstacles of the Uruguay Round of negotiations.[**] In 1991, the EU called on the United States to abandon its legislation on unilateral trade retaliation as a precondition to concluding the Uruguay Round.[12] In 1992, one of the issues in talks between the United States and the EU related to the EU's failure to remove subsides given to European oilseed producers. The U.S. compiled a list of European imports that might be subject to taxes.[13]

8.3f Economic Union

An **economic union** is the most complete form of economic integration. It goes one step further than a common market and calls for the harmonization or unification of its member nations' fiscal, monetary, and tax policies. An example of an economic union is Benelux, which includes Belgium, the Netherlands, and Luxembourg. This economic union, formed during the 1920s, is now a part of the EU.

8.4 MAJOR TRADE ASSOCIATIONS AMONG DEVELOPING COUNTRIES

The triumph of the EU has inspired some developing countries to engage in economic integration with the intention of advancing their own economic development. Developing countries have embarked on this cooperative movement, in part, as a defensive reaction to the regional economic integration in Europe, which began in the late 1950s and early 1960s. This has resulted in the emergence of different trade associations among developing countries, some of which have met with scant success.

One factor that has contributed to the failure of some of these trade associations has been the uneven distribution of gains among their members. With most of the benefits accruing to the group's relatively more developed nations, other nations in the group have been discouraged and have consequently withdrawn from the association.

---

[*] The oil crises occurred in 1973-1974 and 1979-1981. As we explain in Chapter 16, these two oil crises also contributed to the debt crisis in developing nations.

[**] The Uruguay Round of negotiations is explained later in this chapter.

Another factor in the dissolution of these associations is the reluctance of many developing countries to surrender part of their sovereignty to a trade association. Also, transportation and communications among developing countries are inadequate. The natures of their economies make them compete for the same world market, discouraging trade association agreements.

GLOBAL INSIGHTS CASE 8.2

The Oilseed Disputes

In December 1987, U.S. farmers complained that exports of soybeans and other oilseeds to the EC [now the EU] were being unfairly restricted by a program that encouraged the production of oilseeds in the EC. In the 1960—1961 Dillon Round of GATT negotiations, the EC had agreed to make a concession to oilseeds exporters by setting its oilseeds tariff at zero. At that time individual EC countries had no widespread system of supports for domestic oilseed production. By the early 1980s, the EC had adopted an oilseeds support program that increased domestic supply, reduced growth in demand for imported oilseeds, and, according to international trade law, "impaired the value of the concession."

The U.S. government instituted an investigation to determine the validity of this complaint. As the investigation proceeded, the United States asked GATT to establish an expert panel and issue an opinion. In December 1989, the expert panel agreed that the U.S. complaint was justified and recommended that the EC end or modify its oilseeds program to remove the impairment. In October 1991, the EC approved substantial modifications in the oilseeds program. However, the GATT panel studied the modifications and found, in March 1992, that they were not sufficient to bring the EC into conformity with its GATT obligations.

In accordance with Section 301 of the Trade Act of 1974, the U.S. government threatened to impose tariffs on $1 billion worth of imports from the EC if the EC did not take appropriate actions. Intense negotiations between the United States and the EC continued throughout the summer and fall of 1992, but no solution could be found that would fully compensate U.S. oilseed farmers for their lost market.

On November 5, the United States announced that it would impose a 200-percent tariff on over $300 million of EC exports, primarily white wine, starting on December 5. The United States deliberately announced a retaliation for only part of the damage caused to its trade by the EC policies in order to leave the door open for further negotiations while making clear its intention to insist on its rights under GATT.

Later in November, the United States and the EC reached an agreement in principle resolving the oilseeds dispute. Among other things, the EC agreed to reduce the area on which oilseeds will be grown by reducing program payments if plantings exceed specified area limits. With the agreement in place, the United States withdrew its threat to retaliate.

Source: U.S. Government Printing Office, *Economic Report of the President* (Washington DC: U.S. Government Printing Office, 1993), 319, Reprinted.

The major trade associations among developing countries are as follows:

1. The **Andean Common Market (ANCOM)** was established by Bolivia, Columbia, Chile, Ecuador, and Peru in 1969. In 1976, Chile left the ANCOM, and Venezuela joined in 1973. This association is a subgroup of the Latin American Free Trade Agreement (listed subsequently), and its main policy is to restrict foreign-owned investment.

2. The **Association of Southeast Asian Nations (ASEAN)** was established by Indonesia, Malaysia, the Philippines, Singapore, and Thailand in 1967.

3. The **Caribbean Free Trade Association (CARIFTA)** was established in 1968 by Antigua, Barbados, Bolivia, Colombia, Dominica, Ecuador, Grenada, Guyana, Jamaica, Montserrat, Peru, St. Lucia, St. Vincent, Trinidad, Tobago, and Venezuela. In 1973, the name was changed to the Caribbean Common Market (CARICOM) and was extended to include the Bahamas, Belize, and St. Kitts-Nevis-Angullia.

4. The **Central American Common Market (CACM)** is a customs union established by Costa Rica, El Salvador, Guatemala, Honduras, and Nicaragua in 1960.

5. The **East African Community (EAC)** was established by Kenya, Tanzania, and Uganda in 1967. Due to the ideological, economic, and political upheavals in Uganda, this association lost its effectiveness and was consequently dissolved in 1977.

6. The **Economic Community of West African States (ECOWAS)** was established by the Treaty of Lagos (Nigeria), which was signed in May 1975. Its membership includes the following countries: Benin, Burkina Faso, Cape Verde Islands, Cote d'Ivoire, Gambia, Ghana, Guinea, Guinea-Bissau, Liberia, Mali, Mauritania, Niger, Nigeria, Senegal, Sierra Leone, and Togo.

7. The **Latin American Free Trade Association (LAFTA)** was established by Argentina, Bolivia, Brazil, Chile, Colombia, Ecuador, Mexico, Paraguay, Peru, Uruguay, and Venezuela in 1960. This association was relatively successful in extending tariff reductions to its members until the mid-1960s. After that, however, the nationalist views of some of its members made further tariff reductions difficult. In 1980, the members of LAFTA signed a treaty to form a new association called the **Latin American Integration Association (LAIA).** This association established new objectives for tariff reductions and other policies to be followed in integrating its members' economies.

8.5 ORGANIZATION FOR ECONOMIC COOPERATION AND DEVELOPMENT

The Organization for Economic Cooperation and Development (OECD), established in Europe in 1961, is an organization that provides an important channel for multilateral cooperation in the world today. Although most members of this organization are European, it also includes the major industrial countries of Australia, Canada, Japan, New Zealand, and the United States. The major objectives of the OECD are: (a) to assist its member countries in pursuing policies that promote economic and social welfare; and (b) to coordinate and encourage members' assistance to developing countries.

To help its members with trade issues, the OECD has organized three committees, each dealing with a specific trade issue. These committees are the Development Assistance Committee, the Executive Committee Special Session, and the Trade Committee.

The Development Assistance Committee deals with the transfer of funds to developing countries. The Executive Committee Special Session is concerned with the coordination of the economic policies of the member countries. Finally, the Trade Committee is responsible for discussing current issues and studying member countries' long-term trade policies.

An important OECD contribution to international cooperation is the issuance of a code of conduct regarding the operation of multinational corporations (MNCs). The purpose of this code is to help MNCs enhance their contributions to international cooperation, while minimizing the problems that arise from their operation. Specific provisions provided by the code specify that a MNC should:

✦ Consider national balance-of-payments and credit objectives in formulating its financial activities
✦ Advance national scientific and technological goals
✦ Disclose complete information regarding their tax liabilities
✦ Observe national standards regarding labor practices and working conditions
✦ Refrain from employment discrimination
✦ Avoid engaging in activities that might adversely affect competition by unfair practices
✦ Regularly make public important operational and financial information

Although this code of conduct is not legally enforceable, it has been publicly accepted by most MNCs and has become an increasingly important element affecting the activities of MNCs.

GLOBAL INSIGHTS CASE 8.3

U.S.–Chinese Standoff over MFN Status

Following the bloody repression of student dissent in 1989, China has been at odds with the United States over the human rights issue. Such concern has led the United States to base the granting of MFN status to China on its annual human rights record. In 1993, under the Clinton administration, China managed to win the MFN for another year. However, the administration made it clear that renewal of MFN status in 1994 would depend largely upon China's treatment of political dissenters and curtailment of advanced weapons sold to offensive governments. China has regarded such a condition as interference with its internal affairs.[1]

China, with a population of 1.2 billion and an average annual economic growth of 9 percent over the last 15 years, is now one the world's top 10 trading nations. According to China's own estimate, its trade reached the level of $200 billion in 1993. This amount is more than a third of China's GNP and accounts for the greatest share (3 percent) of world trade in this century. Additionally, China's trade continues to grow at an annual rate of 19 percent. The country's coastal regions, where electronics, garment, shoe, and toy factories occupy newly established industrial zones, experience even more rapid growth.[2]

Economically speaking, revocation of China's MFN status would hurt both the United States and China. American consumers would lose substantially because they would have to pay much more for electronics, garments, shoes, and toys imported from China. On some types of apparel, the tariff rate would increase from 15 percent to 55 percent. China has announced that if its MFN status is not renewed, it will curtail its $7.5 billion purchase of U.S.-made goods, predominantly high-technology products such aircraft and communications equipments.[3] According to one estimate, this would lead to a loss of 200,000 U.S. jobs.[4] China would also lose. In 1993, it exported $25.7 billion of goods to the United States.[5] Loss of its MFN status, according to some, would cause its average tariff rate to rise about 40 percent from the current (1994) 8 percent.[6] With higher tariffs on its exports to the United States, the price of Chinese products in the United States would rise. Higher export prices would lead to a decrease in U.S. quantity demanded of Chinese products, inducing higher unemployment, especially along China's coastal regions.

The revocation of China's MFN status would not only affect China and the United States, but other nations as well. Some European firms could gain as they rush to replace the United States in China's high-tech market, but some Asian countries might find themselves crushed between the two giants because China's demand for Asian products would shrink if its export income from the United States diminishes.[7]

Given the economic impact of revoking China's MFN status and under pressure from U.S. business, the Clinton administration finally renewed China's MFN status on May 16, 1994. While President Clinton maintains that the human rights issue remains a U.S. priority, he disassociated the issue from China's MFN status and said that "we have reached the end of the usefulness of that policy."[8]

Instead, the United States will prohibit importation of Chinese ammunition and guns and leave other sanctions in place.

Under Clinton's administration, China's MFN status has been renewed on a regular basis (every 12 months) and was still in effect in the year 2000. Clinton's decision to continue China's MFN status seems to indicate the end of the Cold War policy of employing trade as a means of promoting the human rights issue. This thought was conceived in the Jackson-Vanik amendments 20 years ago and was used to push the former Soviet Union to allow Jews to emigrate. With the post—Cold War era behind us, however, national security is increasingly interpreted as economic power. Given this fact, the United States may not be able to afford to lose China's vast market.[9]

Notes
1. "Trade Rights, as Well as Civil Rights, Will Factor into China's MFN Status," The Wall Street Journal, 4 June 1993, A8.
2. "More Trade Snags Between China, U.S. Loom Despite Renewal of MFN Status," The Wall Street Journal, 27 May 1994, A5.
3. "Who Gains and Who Loses if the U.S. Toughens Its Trade Rules for China?" The Wall Street Journal, 27 May 1993, A10.
4. "Revoking Trade Status Would Hit China Where It Hurts Most: Rising Guangdong," The Wall Street Journal, 22 April 1994, A12.
5. "U.S. Firms, Anticipating Huge Market, Worry China May Lose Its MFN Status," The Wall Street Journal, 14 May 1993, A8. President Clinton renewed China's MFN status in 1994, effectively unlinking trade from the issue of human rights.
6. "U.S., Chinese Clash Over Trade, Rights Means Worry for Smaller Asian Nations," The Wall Street Journal, 3 May 1994, A11.
7. Ibid.
8. "Clinton Renews China's Status For Trading: Ammunition, Gun Imports Are Banned as Penalty for Abuses on Rights," The Wall Street Journal, 27 May 1994, A3.
9. Ibid.

8.6 GENERAL AGREEMENT ON TARIFFS AND TRADE AND THE WORLD TRADE ORGANIZATION

In 1945, the United States, an advocate of free international trade, spearheaded the formation of an international organization to promote international trade and investment. This led to many months of negotiations in Geneva, London, and Lake Success (New York), and in March 24, 1948, resulted in the signing of the Havana Charter for the International Trade Organization (ITO) in Havana, Cuba. The charter called for a series of agreements among 53 countries and was designed to cover international trade and investment activities. Unfortunately, most nations refused to ratify the provision of the ITO, fearing that the new powerful organization might threaten their national sovereignty. As a result, the creation of such an organization was not realized at the time. However, the international negotiation led to the creation of The General Agreement on Tariffs and Trade (GATT). The formation of this organization was an attempt to combat the worldwide trade restrictions that had contributed to the post-World War II economic recession. Established in 1947 by 23 countries, including the United State, the GATT was not intended to be an international organization, but rather a multilateral treaty designed to promote freer international trade, operating under the International Trade Organization. But, because the ITO did not come into existence, the GATT emerged as the governing body for settling international trade disputes. Eventually, it developed into an institution that sponsored several successful rounds of international negotiations.

In 1994, it had 117 members from virtually all the advanced countries, many developing countries, and several former communist countries of Eastern Europe. The principle policies governing the operations of GATT are as follows:

1. *Nondiscrimination.* This principle dictates that each member country should impose the same tariff rates on all GATT members. This tariff rate is referred to as the **most-favored nation (MFN)** rate. According to the MFN principal, changes in tariff rates agreed upon between any two GATT countries must also be applied to other GATT countries as well. For example, if the United States decreases the tariff rate on Italian guitars from, say, 20 percent to 17 percent, it should impose the same rate on all other GATT countries from which it imports guitars. There are two exceptions to this principle. The first is made in regard to associations of economic integration. This means that countries belonging to customs unions, free-trade areas, or international trade associations, can impose lower tariff rates on their member countries than those levied on nonmember countries. The second exception applies to a nation's trade relationship to its former colonies. For example, British Commonwealth preferences are retained under GATT.

2. *Reduction of tariffs by negotiation.* The negotiations to reduce tariffs and nontariff barriers have been one of GATT's most important activities. These negotiations have been accomplished by GATT's sponsorship of periodic conferences referred to as "rounds." Table 8-3 (page 148) provides a summary of these rounds of negotiations. Among these, the sixth round, known as the **Kennedy Round,** represents the first major attempt at trade liberalization. This round, initiated by the United States, was formally opened in 1964 and concluded in 1967. The Kennedy Round led to an agreement to reduce tariff rates for industrial products by a total of 35 percent from their 1962 level, with the tariffs to be phased out in five years. Overall, the Kennedy Round proved to be successful and resulted in the most significant tariff reduction since GATT came into existence.

   The second major round is known as the **Tokyo Round,** which was formally opened in Tokyo in 1973 and concluded in 1979. The primary goal of the Tokyo Round was the elimination of nontariff trade barriers. Since many tariffs were either removed or significantly decreased under the previous rounds, many nations had increasingly used nontariff trade barriers to pursue their own protectionist policies. The Tokyo Round demanded tariff reductions from member countries and called for a code of conduct that would prevent legitimate domestic policies from turning into nontariff trade barriers. The round ruled that industrial countries' tariffs had to be cut by an average of 33 percent over an eight-year period. This included tariff cuts of 31 percent for the United States, 27 percent for the EU, and 28 percent for Japan. Overall, the major achievement of the Tokyo Round was unification of the international community in dismantling the nontariff barriers for the first time. Obviously, the success of the round depends on how governments follow, in practice, the agreed-upon nontariff codes.

TABLE 8-3
Rounds of Negotiations under Gatt Auspices

Rounds	Location of Negotiations	Date
First	Geneva, Switzerland	1947
Second	Annecy, France	1949
Third	Torquay, England	1951
Fourth	Geneva, Switzerland	1956
Fifth (the Dillion Round)	Geneva, Switzerland	1960—1961
Sixth (the Kennedy Round)	Geneva, Switzerland	1964—1967
Seventh (the Tokyo Round)*	Geneva, Switzerland	1973—1979
Eighth (the Uruguay Round)	Punta del Este, Uruguay	1986—1993

* The seventh round of negotiation is referred to as the Tokyo Round because the negotiations were initially launched in the Japanese capital in 1973. Source: "General Agreement On Tariffs and Trade—GATT." in The Europa Year Book, 2 Vols. (London: Europana Publications Limited, 1993): 1, 56

Since 1947, eight rounds have been completed and the eighth round of negotiation, referred to as the **Uruguay Round,** which started in 1986, is considered by far the most complex and ambitious to date. This complexity stemmed from the fact that the number of participants, as well as the number of issues under consideration, were greater than ever before. The four major issues for this round were (a) nondiscrimination, (b) a further clarification or new rules on distinguishing between "border" measures (such as taxes on international trade) and "nonborder" measures (such as subsidies), (c) the widening trade gap between advanced countries and developing countries, and (d) a determination of GATT's future role.

The Uruguay Round experienced some setbacks, when it was suspended at the Brussels Ministerial in December 1990. The suspension of negotiations was caused by the reluctance of the EU, Japan, and Korea to negotiate serious commitments to agricultural reforms. Agricultural reforms were described as the "linchpin" of the negotiation. Given that most developing countries' exports are composed of agricultural products and raw materials, these countries have demanded commitments on agriculture in return for their approval of issues important to advanced countries.

Following the suspension of negotiations, a series of consultations was undertaken with the delegations, resulting in the resumption of negotiations in February 1991.[14] In December 1991, GATT's director-general submitted a draft on the issues that were being negotiated under the Uruguay Round, including proposals designed to resolve the dispute over agricultural subsidies. However, this draft was not accepted by the EU on the basis that it would disrupt common agricultural policy. In September 1992, the United States requested GATT to rule on the amount of remuneration to be paid by the EU to states which had lost trade due to the EU's subsidization of oilseed producers. Although the oilseed problem was not formally part of the Uruguay Round, it became crucial to the United States' negotiating status. As a result, in November 1992, the EU and the United States reached an agreement on agriculture. According to this agreement, the EU agreed to reduce the production of oilseed. It also agreed to reduce both the volume and value of its subsidized exports of farm products. Following this agreement, the Uruguay Round was resumed. March 1, 1993, was set as the final deadline for agreement on the areas under discussion.[15] Nevertheless, this deadline was not met and disillusions with GATT grew.[16] However, the North American Free Trade Agreement (NAFTA) victory in November 1993 renewed the hope that the negotiators would meet a new U.S. congressional deadline of December 15, 1993.[17] This deadline was met, marking yet another significant step toward freer international trade by slashing tariffs and cutting subsidies on an international scale.[18] It also extended GATT principles both to agriculture and to services. Accordingly, certain nontariff barriers were converted to tariffs that were later to be progressively reduced. A major outcome of the Uruguay round, was to set up the World Trade Organization (WTO) along the lines envisioned 50 years earlier. By May 1997 the WTO had 131 members. Although an updated version of the GATT agreement is now part of the WTO agreements, GATT handles trade in goods, The General Agreement on Trade in Services (GATS) handles trade in services, and the

GLOBAL CASE 8-4

The WTO Dispute Settlement Process and U.S. Trade Policy

The WTO Dispute Settlement Understanding (DSU), part of the Uruguay Round package of agreements improves on GATT dispute settlement proceedings by expediting decision making and instituting an appeal process. It also establishes procedures to ensure the implementation of dispute panel rulings, one of which is the acceptance of cross-sector retaliation for countries that choose not to abide by the ruling. In the 3 years since its institution, many countries have made efficient use of the reformed dispute settlement mechanism, largely to the satisfaction of all involved.

The introduction of a strengthened multilateral dispute settlement system in the WTO, together with WTO agreements covering the protection of intellectual property rights and trade services, has brought about a shift in U.S. tactics for resolving trade disputes. During the 1980s the United States frequently restored to the bilateral negotiations and unilateral sanctions authorized in Section 301 of U.S. trade laws to resolve differences with other countries. This approach was used in particular in the areas of agriculture, intellectual property protection, and services, which GATT covered barely or not at all. Beginning in 1995, however, the DSU and new WTO rules have permitted the United States to use multilateral dispute settlement procedures to address the overwhelming majority of issues that have been the subject of Section 301 investigations. The results of 35 complaints filed by the United States suggests that the DSU process has proved very effective, with the United States prevailing in 9 out of 10 rulings to date. The United States has also reached a bilateral settlement prior to a formal ruling in eight cases. Seventeen petitions are still pending. Section 301 investigations can now more often make use of multilateral dispute settlement, at least for disputes with WTO members in areas subject to WTO commitments. All nine of the Section 301 investigations initiated during 1996, and three of the six investigations initiated in 1997, have involved resort to the WTO dispute settlement procedures; a fourth was terminated before WTO consultations were initiated. As the following chart shows, the DSU process has been used against a variety of countries, the majority of which are our major trading partners.

U.S.-Initiated WTO Dispute Settlement Cases by Target Country

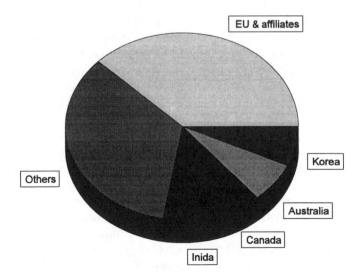

Source: U.S. Government Printing Office, *Economic Report of the President* (Washington D.C: U.S. Government Printing Office, 1998), p. 223, Reprinted.

Agreement on Trade-Related Aspects of Intellectual Property (TRIPS) handles such issues as copyright, trademarks, patents, industrial design and trade secrets.

The GATT and now the WTO has made significant contributions in ameliorating trade and investment climate around the globe. It benefits its member nations by instituting a more effective means of enforcement and clearer multilateral trading rules. Its existence makes the international trading system more predictable by facilitating international trade and investment.

3. *Forum for discussion in resolving trade disputes.* In resolving trade disputes between different nations, GATT and now WTO acts as an international court of law, and, as such, plays a significant role in the world of international free trade.* Before the establishment of WTO, trade disputes between two nations could not be resolved through a formal channel by the intervention of a third party. Consequently, trade disagreements between nations went on for years and often resulted in retaliation and trade wars. Today, if two countries cannot settle their dispute by negotiation, they can appeal to WTO for a decision. Accordingly, WTO assigns a committee of experts from different countries to investigate the problem and make recommendations to the parties involved. If these recommendations are not followed, WTO rules for countermeasures to be taken against the nation deemed to be at fault.

So far, very few disputes have been referred to WTO, and of those that were, some were never resolved. For example, mid-1962, the EU members increased their duties on poultry imports, which came mostly from the United States, resulting in a 63-percent decline in U.S. poultry exports to EU-member countries. This set the stage for what became known as the "chicken war." Since bilateral negotiations between these two parties did not resolve the problem, the case was taken to WTO. The association ruled that the United States had experienced a loss of $26 million and should be compensated by withdrawing concessions to the EU if a settlement could not be reached. Although both sides accepted the ruling, they were still unable to resolve the "chicken war." Thus, in January 1965, the United States imposed high retaliatory tariffs against the EU on imports of brandy, dextrine, potato starch, and trucks. Although in this example WTO was not effective in eliminating the EU duties on poultry, it did limit the extent of U.S. retaliation and precluded the EU from employing counterretaliatory measures.

In fact, WTO's existence has been a deterrent to trade wars between nations and has caused trading partners to try to solve their disputes rather than await WTO rulings. For example, in 1975, the United States protested the EU granting subsidies to the producers of certain cheeses. As a result, a compromise was reached when the EU chose to temporarily suspend its export rebate payments (the cash subsidies given to cheese exporters), and the United States decided not to impose countervailing duties against the EU.

Another example occurred in 1982, when the United States filed a complaint with WTO regarding the performance requirements imposed on new U.S. foreign investments in Canada. According to these requirements foreign companies had to (a) give preference to the purchase of Canadian goods over imported goods, and (b) meet certain export requirements. In the 1982 WTO ruling, it was decided to drop the first requirement but maintain the second requirement.

The United States again complained to WTO in 1987 about the EU's policy of subsidizing its soybean producers. According to the American Soybean Association, EU soybean subsidies were costing U.S. producers $1.5 billion a year in lost sales revenue. In 1989, WTO ruled in favor of the United States. Accordingly, the EU announced that it would accept the ruling, dismantling its soybean subsidies.[19]

In another instance, WTO ruled in 1989 that South Korea's restrictions on beef imports from Australia, New Zealand, and the United States should be eliminated. Accordingly, South Korea agreed to phase out its beef import quotas.[20] Also in the same year, in response to Australia's complaints, a WTO panel found the U.S. sugar quota in violation of international rules. Accordingly, the United States decided to take up this issue as part of the Uruguay Round of multilateral trade negotiation.[21]

A final example occurred when the United States complained in 1990 that Canadian trade practices discriminated against the U.S. beer market. Following WTO's criticism, all Canadian provinces except Ontario and Quebec modified their practices. The refusal of these two provinces to alter their approach led the Bush Administration to impose a 50-percent duty on beer imported from Ontario. Canada, in turn,

---

* Because an updated version of GATT is now part of the WTO, discussions throughout the rest of this text will refer to the WTO, regardless of the date or event discussed.

retaliated by imposing a 50-percent duty on beer shipped to Ontario by Helleman Brewing Company and Stroh Company—the U.S. firms that initiated the complaint against Canada.[22]

8.7 STATE TRADING

This book deals with trade among market-oriented economies, rather than among command economies or between command and market-oriented economies. In this section, we briefly examine trade between command economies and elaborate on trade between market-oriented and command economies.

In market-oriented economies, such as the United States, Canada, France, and Great Britain, the allocation and distribution of resources are carried out by the pricing system. In other words, prices perform the rationing role in a manner that reflects the actions of independent buyers and sellers who are acting in their own interests.

In command (centrally planned) economies, such as China, North Korea, Vietnam, and Cuba, the allocation and distribution of resources are performed by the government. In such a system, prices are determined by government directives and not by market forces. As a result, they do not reflect opportunity costs. The crucial economic questions, such as what to produce, how to produce, and for whom to produce, are decided by planning boards. All international transactions are controlled and decided by a number of **state trading companies,** each undertaking a certain line of products. The types and amounts of goods imported are determined on the basis of the national plan requirements over and above domestically produced products. In other words, imports are used to close the gap in the "material balance." After determining imports, the state decides what commodities to export in order to pay for its imports. In command economies, relative commodity prices and comparative advantage do not play any significant role. Given command economies' goal of self-sufficiency, they tend to consider international trade a necessary evil used to obtain those goods and services they cannot produce for themselves. In other words, they consider international trade to be an economic disturbance that interferes with the economic planning process.

Trade among command economies is usually carried out on the basis of bilateral agreements and bulk purchasing. A **bilateral agreement** usually involves barter trade, whereby one good is exchanged for another. Countries engage in barter trade due to the inconvertibility of command economies' currencies, not only among themselves, but also with respect to market economies. **Bulk purchasing** is an agreement by a state trading company to purchase a given amount of a good from another nation's trading company for a specified period (one year or several years).

In January 1949, the then Soviet Union and communist bloc countries in Eastern Europe formed the **Council of Mutual Economic Assistance (CMEA or COMECON).** Besides the Soviet Union, the original members of the council included Bulgaria, Czechoslovakia, Hungary, Poland, and Rumania. Late in 1949, Albania and East Germany joined the council. In 1962, Mongolia and Cuba joined, and Albania withdrew. The purpose of forming the council was to diver trade away from Western market economies and achieve a higher level of self-sufficiency among CMEA members. Although CMEA was successful in certain areas, trade among its members continued to be mostly bilateral, and their craving for Western technology induced them to pursue trade with Western market economies.

Historically speaking, trade between market-oriented and command economies has been subject to many political and economic obstacles that have significantly reduced the potential benefits of trade among these nations. From a political standpoint, the obstacles to trade between these nations have stemmed from their deeply rooted differences in political ideology. Economically speaking, the problems are related to the existence of the incompatibility of their economic systems. Some of the major issues that have hampered trade between the two systems are pricing practices, currency inconvertibility, and credit limitations.

As we mentioned earlier, unlike the market-determined prices of market-oriented economies, command-economy prices do not reflect opportunity costs. As a result, foreigners are not allowed to trade freely on the basis of these artificial prices. Additionally, residents are not allowed to purchase or sell commodities abroad. Such functions are carried out by the state trading companies, whose functions are hampered by their inability to compare domestic prices, defined by government action, with foreign prices that reflect opportunity costs.

Command economies' currencies are inconvertible. Accordingly, foreigners are not permitted to hold and spend domestic currencies freely. Similarly, residents are not allowed to use domestic currencies to buy foreign currencies. The restriction set on currency convertibility diminishes the scope of potential trade between the two types of economies.

The former Soviet Union and Eastern European nations (before their recent economic reforms) were faced with significant trade deficits with Western market-oriented economies. This problem was due primarily to the low quality of Soviet and Eastern European products. As a result, they were unable to generate enough exports to pay for their imports. Consequently, all of their deficit had to be financed by loans from Western banks and governments. In dealing with the United States, these countries had to turn to commercial banks for their financing requirements due to the U.S. government's refusal of granting credit. However, with legal lending restrictions on the amount of commercial bank funds that could be used to finance their imports, their trade activities with the West were hampered.

Recent world events—the collapse of the Soviet Union, the unification of Germany, and the economic reforms of the Eastern European countries—have opened up a new chapter in the world of free trade that promises to change the nature of East-West trade relations. We devote part of the next chapter to an explanation of these important events, elaborating on their implications for the global economy.

8.8 SUMMARY

1. An international cartel is an organization composed of firms in the same industry from different countries who agree to limit their outputs and exports in order to influence the prices of their commodities and maximize their profits.

2. The most successful international cartel is the Organization of Petroleum Exporting Countries (OPEC). This organization, formed in 1960, today is composed of 12 oil-producing nations.

3. An international cartel of oil exporters acting as a monopolist (centralized cartel) will maximize its total profit by following the familiar MC = MR rule.

4. Economic integration is an agreement among nations to decrease or eliminate trade barriers.

5. Depending on the terms and intensity of agreements, economic integration can be classified as a preferential trade arrangement, a free-trade area, a customs union, a common market, and an economic union.

6. A preferential trade arrangement is an agreement among participating nations to lower trade barriers among themselves.

7. A free-trade area is established by an agreement among nations that removes trade barriers while allowing each member nation to define its own barriers on trade with nonmembers.

8. A customs union is an organization that allows the lowering or abolishing of trade barriers between member countries and adopts a unified system of tariffs against nonmembers.

9. The formation of a customs union may lead to both trade creation and trade diversion. Trade creation arises when the domestic production of one customs-union member is replaced by another member's lower-cost imports. Trade diversion arises when lower-cost imports from a country that is not a member of the customs union are replaced by higher-cost imports from a member country.

10. A common market is a more complete form of a customs union. It combines the characteristics of a customs union with the elimination of barriers against the movement of capital and labor among member countries.

11. An economic union is the most complete form of economic integration. It goes one step further than a common market and calls for the harmonization or unification of its member nations fiscal, monetary, and tax policies.

12. The major trade associations among developing countries are the Andean Common Market (ANCOM), the Association of Southeast Asian Nations (ASEAN), the Caribbean Free Trade Association (CARIFTA; changed to CARICOM in 1973), the Central American Common Market (CACM), the East African Community (EAC), the Economic Community of West African States (ECOWAS), and the Latin American Free Trade Association (LAFTA; changed to LAIA in 1980).

13. The Organization for Economic Cooperation and Development (OECD) is an organization that provides an important channel for multilateral cooperation in the world today. The major objectives of the OECD are: (a) to assist its member countries in pursuing policies that promote economic and social welfare; and (b) to coordinate and encourage member's assistance to developing countries. The OECD has also issued a code of conduct for the operations of multinational corporations (MNCs).

14. The General Agreement on Tariff and Trade (GATT) is an international organization created as a forum for negotiations to promote freer international trade.

15. The principal policies governing GATT operations are as follows: (a) nondiscrimination in trade matters; (b) the reduction of tariffs by negotiation; and (c) the establishment of a forum for discussion in resolving trade disputes.

16. Since 1947, GATT and now WTO has completed eight rounds of negotiations and the eighth round, referred to as the Uruguay Round, started in 1986, was concluded on December 15, 1993, and took effect on July 1, 1995.

17. In command economies all international transactions are controlled and decided through a number of state trading companies, each undertaking a certain line of products.

18. Trade among command economies is usually carried out on the basis of bilateral agreements and bulk purchasing.

  (a) Bilateral agreement usually involves barter trade, whereby one good is exchanged for another.

  (b) Bulk purchasing is an agreement by a state trading company to purchase a given amount of a good from another nation's trading company for a specified period (one year or several years).

Review Questions

1. Define the concept of an international cartel and answer the following questions.
  (a) How does a cartel restrict trade?
  (b) What is the most successful international cartel?
  (c) What conditions are necessary for a cartel's successful operation?
  (d) What is meant by a centralized cartel?
  (e) Theoretically, how does a centralized cartel maximize its profit?

2. Define the concept of economic integration and elaborate on its different classifications, giving an example of each.

3. Explain the difference between a customs union and a free-trade association.

4. Define the concepts of trade creation and trade diversion and answer the following questions.
  (a) What are the static welfare effects of trade creation and trade diversion?
  (b) According to the empirical studies of the EU, what are the welfare effects of trade creation and trade diversion for the EU?

5. Name major trade associations among developing countries and elaborate on the major factors that inspired developing countries to engage in economic integration.

6. Describe OECD by answering the following questions.
  (a) What are OECD's major objectives?
  (b) What are the three committees set up by OECD to help its members with trade issues?
  (c) What is an important contribution of OECD to international cooperation?

7. Elaborate on GATT by answering the following questions.
  (a) What major factor gave rise to the establishment of GATT?
  (b) What are the principal policies governing GATT operations?
  (c) Since GATT's inception, how many rounds of negotiations have been completed? Among these rounds, which ones are considered major rounds?

8. What were the major accomplishments of the Kennedy Round and the Tokyo Round? Explain.

9. Differentiate between market-oriented economies and command economies and answer the following questions.
  (a) What are state trading companies?
  (b) What is meant by a bilateral agreement? Bulk purchasing?
  (c) What is CMEA?

Problems

1. Suppose you are an international economic advisor who is helping nations X and Y form a customs union. Nation X imports all of its raw materials and agricultural products, and produces only manufacturing goods.

Nation Y imports all of its manufacturing goods and produces only raw materials and agricultural products. Given these assumptions, what are the implications of the customs union on the welfare of these two countries. (Hint: Use the concepts of trade creation and trade diversion.)

2. Country A, a very small country that has no impact on the world price, has just formed a customs union with country B. Before the formation of the union, country A imported 50 billion VCRs from abroad (the world market) at $200 per unit and added a tariff of $40 per unit on each VCR imported. The per-unit cost of producing a VCR is $240 in country A and $120 in country B.

   (a) What is the cost to country A when the VCR trade is diverted to country B (the trade diversion effect)?

   (b) What amount of extra imports would country A have to buy in order to offset this trade-diversion effect?

3. Given that developing countries produce similar products, they will not gain from trade with each other.
   Do you agree with this statement? Discuss, using the concepts of trade creation and trade diversion.

4. Although OPEC was formed in 1960, it did not attain a level of world significance until the 1970s. In the 1980s, however, OPEC experienced a serious setback in its power to manipulate worldwide oil prices.
   Do you agree with this statement? Discuss.

5. Given the existence of tension between some OPEC members, it is evident that it will break up in the future.
   Do you agree with this statement? Discuss.

6. In 1986, Portugal and Spain, who import agricultural products from the United States, joined the EU. This led the United States to declare that it would impose heavy duties on luxury goods that are imported from these countries to the United States unless the EU would allow greater market entry to other U.S. goods. What do you think was the rationale behind the U.S. action? Do you think the U.S. action is justifiable? Explain.

Notes

1. "As OPEC's Members Produce Above Quota, Big Data Gap Widens," *The Wall Street Journal*, 24 November 1987, 1, 18.

2. Nicholas Owen, *Economies of Scale, Competitiveness, and Trade Patterns Within the European Community* (New York: Oxford University Press, 1983), 119-193.

3. "The Trade Effects of EFTA and the EEC," *EFTA Bulletin*, June 1972, 16-17 (Tables 10 and 14).

4. "A. I. MacBean and P. N. Snowden, *International Institutions in Trade and Finance* (London: George Allen and Unwin, 1981), 157.

5. Bela Balassa, *The Theory of Economic Integration* (Homewood IL: Richard D. Irwin, 1961).

6. "Europeans Mull Major Research Boost to Compete with U.S., Japanese Firm," *The Wall Street Journal*, 10 June 1986, 32; "Japan Concern on Autos Is Linked to German Sales," *The Wall Street Journal*, 12 June 1986, 32.

7. "EC Opens Anti-Dumping Investigations Against Japanese and South Koreans," *The Wall Street Journal*, 7 July 1987, 24.

8. "EC Bars Publishers in U.K. from Fixing Book-Export Prices," *The Wall Street Journal*, 14 December 1988, A12. 9."EC Panel Wins Power to Block Combinations," *The Wall Street Journal*, 22 December, 1989, A4.

10. "EC Secures a GATT Waiver on Trade with East Germany," *Financial Times*, 14 December 1990, 6.

11. "EC Reaches Pact on Cutting Farm Subsidies," *The Wall Street Journal*, 7 November 1990, A12.

12. "EC Seeks Removal of U.S. Trade Law as Part of Accord," *The Wall Street Journal*, 5 November 1991, A10.

13. "Risk of EC Trade War Forces Makers of Wine, Spirits to Stockpile for Holidays," *The Wall Street Journal*, 27 July 1992, C19.

14. "Uruguay Round Negotiators Overcome Stalemate," *Business America*, 25 March 1991, 26-27; "Brussels Ministerial Inconclusive: GATT Talks Suspended to Allow Countries to Reflect on Positions," *Business America*, 14 January 1991, 10-14; "Negotiators Are At Work in Geneva to Conclude the Uruguay Round," *Business America*, 23 September 1991, 12-16.

15. "General Agreement On Tariffs and Trade-GATT." In *The Europa Year Book*, 2 vols. (London: Europana Publications Limited, 1993): vol. 1: 56-57.

16. "For GATT Officials, the Talking Stops Only if Months Are Full," *The Wall Street Journal,* 8 November, 1993, A13.
17. "NAFTA Victory Keeps GATT's Chances Alive," *The Wall Street Journal,* 19 September 1993, A9.
18. "Trade Pact Is Set by 117 Nations, Slashing Tariffs, Subsidies Globally," *The Wall Street Journal,* 16 December 1993, A3.
19. "GATT Rules in Favor of U.S. in Soybean Dispute," *The Wall Street Journal,* 18 December 1989, A2.
20. "South Korea Yields to GATT Demand Ending Beef Quotas," *The Wall Street Journal,* 8 November 1989, A14.
21. "GATT Panel Finds U.S. Sugar Quotas Violate International Rules on Imports," *The Wall Street Journal,* 1 June 1989, A8.
22. "Beer Row Erupts Between U.S., Canada After Efforts to Reach Settlement Fizzle," *The Wall Street Journal,* 27 July 1992, C21.

Suggested Readings

Baldwin, R. C. *Issues in U.S.-EC Trade Relations.* Chicago: University of Chicago Press, 1988.

Cecchini, P. *The European Challenge: 1992.* Brookfield, VT: Gower, 1988.

Cox, David, and Richard Harris. "Trade Liberalization and Industrial Organization: Some Estimates for Canada." *Journal Of Political Economy* 93, no. 1 (February 1985): 115-145.

El-Agraa, Ali M., ed. *International Economic Integration, 2d ed. New York: Macmillian, 1988.*

European Community. Europe. Luxembourg Commission of European Communities (published monthly).

European Community. *General Report on the Activities of Community* (published annually).

Finger, J. M., and A. Olechowski, eds. *The Uruguay Round.* Washington, DC: World Bank, 1987.

General Agreement on Tariffs and Trade. *Focus.* Geneva, Switzerland: General Agreement on Tariffs and Trade Information Service (published monthly).

Griffin, James, and David Teece. *OPEC Behavior and World Oil Prices.* London: Allen and Unwin, 1982.

Hitiris, T. *European Community Economics: A Modern Introduction.* New York: Harvester Wheatsheaf, 1988.

Holzman, Franklyn D. "Comecon: A Trade-Destroying Customs Union?" *Journal of Comparative Economics* 9 (1985): 410-423.

Hudec, R. E. *Developing Countries in the GATT Legal System.* Brookfield, VT: Gower, 1988.

————. "An Economic Theory of Protectionism, Tariff Bargaining, and the Formation of Customs Unions." *Journal of Political Economy* (September 1965).

Kerr, A. *The Common Market and How It Works.* New York: Pergamon Press, 1977.

MacAvoy, Paul. *Crude Oil Prices: As Determined by OPEC and Market Fundamentals.* Cambridge, MA: Harper and Row/Ballinger, 1982.

Maclennan, Malcom. "European Community Development." *European Management Journal* 9, no. 1 (March 1991): 43-44.

Meade, J. *The Theory of Customs Unions.* Amsterdam: North-Holland, 1955.

Molle, W., and R. Cappellin. *Impact of Community Policies in Europe.* Brookfield, VT: Gower, 1988.

Rosenblatt, J., et al. *The Common Agricultural Policy of the European Community.* Washington, DC: International Monetary Fund, 1989.

Organization for Economic Cooperation and Development. *The Impact of the Newly Industrializing Countries on Production and Trade In Manufacturers.* Paris: OECD, 1979.

Pomfret, Richard. *Unequal Trade: The Economics of Discriminatory International Trade Policies.* Oxford: Basil Blackwell, 1988.

Rohson, Peter. *The Economics of International Integration.* London: George Allen & Unwin, 1980, Chs. 2, 3.

Swann, D. *The Economics of the Common Market.* Baltimore: Johns Hopkins University Press, 1975.

United States International Trade Commission. *Annual Report.* Washington, DC: U.S. Government Printing Office (published annually).

Viner, J. *The Custom Union Issues.* New York: The Carnegie Endowment for International Peace, 1953.

Chapter 9

RECENT FREE TRADE AGREEMENTS AND POLITICAL EVENTS AFFECTING THE GLOBAL ECONOMY

9.1 INTRODUCTION

The global economy has changed drastically in recent years, presenting the world with new economic opportunities and intensifying international competition for goods and services. Movement toward market-oriented economic systems and free international trade has exemplified itself in expanded and new free-trade agreements and the collapse of communist power, continuing to change the picture of the world economy.

In the previous chapter, we discussed the theory of economic integration and elaborated on the welfare implications of a customs union. One of the main objectives of this chapter is to study recent movements towards economic integration. First, we study Europe after 1992, elaborating on the efforts of the European Union (EU) to evolve into an economic union. Second, we elaborate on the recent free-trade agreements that have established new free-trade areas. Another main objective of this chapter is to discuss recent political events and to elaborate on their global economic impact. To this end, we discuss the Eastern European economic reforms, study the unification of Germany, and investigate the demise of the Soviet Union.

9.2 EUROPE AFTER 1992

As we explained in Chapter 8, in 1971, EU members agreed to a 10-year plan to achieve a full economic union. However, the economic conditions of the 1970s and the first half of the 1980s prevented any further progress toward economic integration.[*]

The cooperative efforts of EU members reached a zenith with the launching of their "project 1992." At its 1985 summit in Milan, the EU endorsed the **"White Paper,"** which established a detailed legislative program for complete economic integration by 1992. According to the EU Commission president, it was necessity rather than idealism that gave rise to the White Paper. Under competitive pressure from U.S. and Japanese companies in both domestic and international markets, Europe found itself struggling with persistently high unemployment. This set the stage for the development of the White Paper, the basic thrust of which was the removal of a whole series of trade barriers. These trade barriers can be separated into three major categories: (a) physical barriers, such as customs procedures and the related paperwork; (b) technical barriers, such as conflicting commercial laws and technical regulations; and (c) fiscal barriers, such as differing excise and value-added taxes. The dismantling of these trade barriers resulted in a single EU home market, and is not only challenging and rewarding for Europeans, but also has global economic implications.

For EU members, the removal of the trade barriers has stimulated both supply and demand. From the supply standpoint, this means tougher competition within the community. EU businesses, faced with the pressure of new rivals in previously protected markets, are forced to become more efficient. From the demand side, the decrease in prices that results from increased efficiency means an increase in the quantity demanded, which in turn encourages EU businesses to expand their output. The increased competition in the EU also means that businesses are forced to cut costs by using their resources more efficiently and to make products that better suit the European and global markets.

---

[*] As mentioned in the previous chapter, the EC became the EU in early 1994. For simplicity, throughout this chapter, we use the new name (the EU) in discussing events that occurred before and after 1994.

GLOBAL INSIGHTS CASE 9.1

The EU in Action

Overall, EU members have been very cooperative and have stayed together in protecting their market. For example, in response to the loss of jobs and sales in the United States and Japan, the EU announced a fivefold increase in its industrial research expenditures to boost its competitive position. Additionally, it called on Japanese auto makers to voluntarily restrain their exports to the EU as a whole.[1] In 1987, at the request of its members, the EU opened up an anti-dumping investigation against the Japanese, who were suspected of dumping semiconductors, and against the South Koreans, who were suspected of dumping compact-disk players, on the European market.[2] In 1988, the EU barred British publishers from fixing minimum retail prices for their books.[3] In 1989, the EU Commission was given a new power that makes it, in most cases, the main authority in the EU to halt those corporate mergers and takeovers that appear to harm fair competition..[4] In 1990, the EU secured a waiver from the GATT on tariffs and trade for the former East Germany, the former Soviet Union and the East European countries.[5] Also, in 1990, the EU members reached an agreement on the reduction of subsidies and other barriers to the trade of agricultural products.[6] This action dismantled one of the main obstacles of the Uruguay Round of negotiations. In 1991, the EU called on the United States to abandon its legislation on unilateral trade retaliation as a precondition to concluding the Uruguay Round.[7] In 1992, one of the issues in talks between the United States and the EU related to the EU's failure to remove subsidies given to European oilseed producers. The U.S. compiled a list of European imports that might be subject to taxes.[8] On January 1, 1999, the EU evolved into an economic union.

Notes

1. "European Mull Major Research Boost to Compete with U.S., Japanese firm,"The Wall Street Journal, 10 June 1986, 32.
2. " EC Opens Anti-Dumping Investigations Against Japanese and South Koreans," The Wall Street Journal, 7 July 1987, 24.
3. " EC Bars Publishers in U.K. from Fixing Book-Export Prices," The Wall Street Journal, 14 December 1988, A12.
4. " EC Panel Wins Power to Block Combination," The Wall Street Journal, December 1989, A4.
5. " EC Secures a GATT Waiver on Trade with East Germany," Financial Times, 14 December 1990, 6.
6. " EC Reaches Pact on Cutting Farm Subsidies ," The wall Street Journal, 7 November 1990, A12.
7. " EC Seeks Removal of U.S. Trade Law as Part of Accord," The Wall Street Journal, 5 November 1991, A10.
8. " Risk of Trade War Forces Makers of Wine, Spirits to Stockpile for Holidays, " The Wall Street Journal, 27 July 1992, C19.

Besides its impact on supply and demand, removal of the trade barriers affects the economy at large. Public deficits are expected to decrease as a result of a more prosperous European economy. The decline in prices, as explained earlier, is expected to ease inflationary pressure, thus ensuring economic growth without harming the EU's external trade status. Inflation-free growth, along with the removal of trade barriers, increases job prospects, which should decrease unemployment for EU members.

From a global standpoint, a more dynamic EU stimulates worldwide competition, and, as trade theories suggest, global welfare increases.

Not only did 1992 present EU members with a wave of opportunity, it also provided their businesses and governments with new challenges. For businesses, the removal of trade barriers signaled the end of protectionism and the beginning of tougher competition; this meant downward pressure on profits resulting from monopoly power and protectionism. It also meant that businesses would have to adopt new strategies to capitalize on the expanded market's increased opportunities for innovation and economies of scale.

For EU governments, 1992 was the deadline by which they were to have fulfilled their obligations to enact legislation supporting the White Paper's objectives. The White Paper outlines 300 items of legislation for the removal of physical, technical, and fiscal barriers within the EU.

After achieving these objectives, the governments must help to maintain them by giving clear evidence of their commitment to businesses.

The EU's success depends on cooperation among the businesses and governments involved. Such cooperation is complicated by the European community's diverse cultural and economic picture. It is composed of 12 countries, 10 cultures, 9 official languages, 12 currencies, and 12 sets of requirements on border controls.[*] All of this demands an institutional adjustment entailing a stronger European monetary system that is capable of dealing with problems that may arise.

In Europe, changes have evoked an investment boom that will affect global competition. The EU, the United States, the European Free Trade Association (EFTA), and Japan doubled their assets in the EU in 1989 and 1990 compared to their 1985 figures. With the passing of 1992, some firms have altered their strategies.[1] European companies have engaged in mergers, established joint ventures, and invested as never before in expectation of a new economic boom. It is interesting to note that some European companies are not only expanding in Europe, but are also looking for opportunities in the United States. For U.S. firms, post-1992 has meant revival of activities that had declined drastically due to trade barriers in Europe. Subsidiaries incorporated in the EU gain from the dismantling of the barriers to the same extent as do European firms. The U.S. multinational corporations (MNCs) that are already established in Europe have devised strategies to take advantage of opportunities offered by the EU. Many other firms have considered a possible future in the Union. Such concerns are shared not only by European and U.S. firms but by all non-Union countries, especially Japan. Anticipation of a unified European market has put tremendous pressure on European politicians to see that the goals of the White Paper are achieved on time.

It must be understood, however, that Europe 1992 is an ongoing process that did not start and end in 1992. In other words, there was no "big bang" prospect for 1992. Although most of the 1992 directives have been adopted by EU institutions, many of the measures have not been implemented by member countries and will not come into effect for years to come. Additionally, an important element of the project 1992, the creation of a monetary union, is still in its infancy. This union was launched in December 1991 when the 12 EU nations signed the ***Maastricht Treaty,*** compelling them to devise a single currency (new ECU[**]) and a single central bank by the end of the century (1999), long after 1992.[***] The Maastricht Treaty provided the blueprint for monetary union and closer cooperation among the member countries. The treaty was voted on by the 11 government of Euroland (Austria, Belgium, Finland, France, Germany, Ireland, Italy, Luxembourg, the Netherlands, Portugal, and Spain), leading to the creation of the European Monetary Union (EMU) on January 1, 1999.[2]

---

[*]   Added to this is resistance from some political elites who saw 1992 as a threat to their authority.

[**]   The concept of ECU will be explained in detail in Chapter 12.

[***]   As we explain in Chapter 12, when the ECU was created by EMS in 1979, it served as a common accounting unit for the EU's internal financial operations. Although the ECU still exists, its name does not appear on any banknote. It is used only for settling international accounts. However, the new ECU, issued by a new European central bank, presents a currency that has the potential to vigorously compete with the U.S. dollar in the international market.

GLOBAL INSIGHTS CASE 9.2

The EU and the European Currency Crisis

The EU's road to a unified market has not been all smooth. Denmark's unexpected rejection of the EU's treaty on economic and political union in June of 1992, jolted many observers.[1] Additionally, Germany's policy of maintaining high interest rates, has seriously hindered cooperation among EU members, fueling the currency chaos that came to a head in mid-September 1992. During the process of German unification, the former West Germany committed itself to giving a large amount of subsidies to the former East German citizens and businesses. Germany made a concurrent decision not to raise taxes to pay for these subsidies. To prevent a surge in inflation, caused by the influx of subsidies into Germany's economy, it was decided to support a higher interest rate. The higher interest rate led to a currency inflow into Germany and increased the value of the German mark relative to other major currencies, including the United States dollar. The rise in German interest rates pulled up rates in other countries, as well as in the United States, retarding economic growth. This was an especially sore issue for the United States which in the early 1990s was struggling to fight its recession with lower interest rates.[2] Given European leaders' 1987 decision to fix their exchange rates among participating currencies, some European countries like Italy and Great Britain faced a tough choice: either increase interest rates or disburse the enormous amount of money needed to support their currencies to reach the agreed-upon levels. Finally, under pressure from the international community, and as part of surprise realignment of European currencies that practically devalued the Italian lira by 7%, Germany decided to lower its interest rates. Such a decision was welcomed by Western leaders. It did not, however, deter Great Britain from following Italy by devaluing its currency and temporarily suspending its membership in the European Exchange Rate Mechanism (ERM), which fixes exchange rates among the currencies of the member countries. This event was followed by devaluation of the Spanish peseta, and a sudden rise in Sweden's one key interest rate. The Swedish authorities raised their interest rate to defend their currency (the krona) by eliminating sources of funding that could have been used for speculation against the krona. Following this event, an emergency meeting was held in Brussels.

The aforementioned chain of events in Europe, leading to devaluation of the British pound, the Italian Lira, and the Spanish Peseta, left currencies in turmoil, and threatened to kill the Maastricht Treaty that was to be voted on by the French on September 20, 1992. Fortunately, for the members, the Maastricht Treaty passed by a narrow margin.[3] The EU experienced yet another victory on May 18, 1993, when Danish voters approved the Maastricht Treaty, which they had almost defeated a year before.[4] However, Germany's support of high interest rates ignited a crisis in the currency market in summer 1993, bringing the ERM to the brink of collapse. Once again, under pressure from European allies, Germany's central bank cut its two key lending rates, precipitating a series of interest cuts throughout Europe. Other European central banks followed Germany's lead in cutting interest rates, and reviving the ERM.[5] This situation paved the road for EU members continued efforts to implement the Maastricht Treaty. Although these developments led to currency crises in Europe, the EU maintained its commitment to advance a unified market as it altered its strategy and pressed ahead with the hope of winning acceptance in all its member nations. Eventually, such persistence paid off on January 1, 1999 when the EU was successful in creating the European Monetary Unit (EMU), completing the formation of an economic union.

Notes

1. "Dane's Vote Bolsters Foes of EC Unity," *The Wall Street Journal*, 4 June, 1992, p.A8.
2. "As Central Banks go their separate ways, Global Tensions Rise," *The Wall Street Journal*, 4 June 1992, A8.
3. "Sudden German Action to Cut Interest Rates Has Broad Implications," *The Wall Street Journal*, 14 September, 1992, pp. 1 A 9; "Conflicts of Interest: Currency Turmoil, Europe Faces Chaos At Time of Unity," *The Wall Street Journal*, 17 September, 1992, pp. 1 & A 6; "Europe's Leaders Brace for French Vote; U.S., Others to Urge German Rate Cut," *The Wall Street Journal*, 18, September, 1992, p. A2; "Mark Continues to Gain in Uncertain Market," *The Wall Street Journal*, 18 September, 1992, p. C1; "Yes, but..French Vote Leaves Europeans Scrambling to Salvage Unity Plan," *The Wall Street Journal*, 21 September 1992, pp. 1 & A6;
4. "Denmark Approves European Unity Pact," *The Wall Street Journal*, 19 May 1993, p. A 10.
5. "German Stance on Rates Sends ERM to Brink," *The Wall Street Journal*, 30 July 1993, p. C3; "Currency Markets Face Continued Upheaval," *The Wall Street Journal*, 2 August 1993, C1; "German Rates Are Lowered By Central Bank," *The Wall Street Journal*, 10 September, 1993, p. A 2.

Today, the EU is faced with the challenge of preserving European unity while facing intense raids on financial markets, vast diversities in member nations' economic conditions, retribution among governments, and uncertainty in the European public. Given the magnitude of problems facing the EU, most economic observers expect that it will continue to experience, at best, slow growth in the next few years.[3]

9.3 RECENT FREE TRADE AGREEMENTS AFFECTING THE GLOBAL ECONOMY

As a strong advocate of free trade, the United States has been busy in recent years practicing what it preaches. During the 1980s, the United States negotiated two free-trade agreements. In 1985, it signed its first free-trade agreement with Israel. Although this agreement does not have a significant impact on the U.S. economy due to the relatively small size of its trading partner, it is helpful in strengthening U.S. relations with Israel, a country that is strategically important to the United States. Following the signing of this trade agreement, the United States negotiated a free-trade agreement with Canada that became effective in 1989 and is discussed in the next section. In 1990, U.S. and Mexican officials agreed to negotiate a free-trade pact between themselves. This trade agreement, which was later expanded to include Canada, creating three trading partners, is referred to as the North American Free Trade Agreement (NAFTA).

Given the significance of the U.S.-Canada free-trade agreement and NAFTA, we devote this section to a discussion of these agreements, elaborating on their economic impacts.

9.3a United States—Canada Free Trade Agreement

The U.S.-Canada Free Trade Agreement (FTA) is an old idea that existed even before the Canadian Confederation itself. The move toward the FTA started in 1854, when the United States agreed with the British North American colonies on a reciprocity treaty that provided for free navigation, reciprocal fishing rights, and free trade in natural products. Although this treaty was terminated in 1866, as Table 9-1 shows, the two nations considered the issue several more times. Finally, in 1988, the FTA was signed and went into effect January 1, 1989. The factors that contributed to the eventual achievement of the FTA include the weakening of the United States' international position and Canada's increasing dependence on the United States. The United States is Canada's principal supplier and major customer. In 1987, before the signing of the FTA, Canada exported more than 25 percent of its gross national product (GNP), and about 75 percent of its exports went to the United States.

Although the FTA did not call for the establishment of a complete free-trade zone between the two nations, it provided for the elimination of all import duties and many nontariff trade barriers over a 10-year period. The agreement also called for the following:

Table 9-1
U.S.–Canada Free-trade Agreement Chronology

1854	Reciprocity Agreement (terminated by United States in 1866)
1874	Reciprocity Agreement defeated by U.S. Senate
1911	Free Trade Agreement defeated by Canadian electorate
1947	General Agreement on Tariffs and Trade (multilateral agreement, including United States and Canada)
1948	Free Trade Agreement suspended by Prime Minister King
1965	Auto Agreement (free trade in automobiles and spare parts)
1988	Free Trade Agreement signed
1989	Free Trade Agreement put into effect
1998	All tariffs eliminated under Free Trade Agreement

Source: Department of State Bulletin, October 1989, 4.

✦ Creating a "U.S.-Canadian tribunal" to settle trade disputes between the two nations
✦ Discussing such difficult issues as trade subsidies in the two nations and Canadian domestic content rules for automobiles
✦ Modifying the 1965 U.S-Canadian agreement allowing for a form of free trade in cars and trucks
✦ Providing U.S. winegrowers greater access to the Canadian market
✦ Guaranteeing the United States nondiscriminatory access to Canadian oil, uranium, and natural gas
✦ Removing some restrictions on cross-border investment
✦ Setting up the first-ever rules governing trade in services[4]

The economic effects of free-trade areas are essentially identical to those of customs unions and can be measured in terms of trade creation and trade diversion. Some trade diversion was expected to result from the FTA. However, the extent and cost of this trade diversion was anticipated to be modest.[5] According to a number of estimates, it was expected that Canadian gains, in percentage terms, would be larger than those of the United States. For Canada, one estimate was that the FTA would raise the nation's real GNP annually within the range of 2.5 to 3.5 percent.[6] For the United States, one estimate was that: (a) The U.S. GNP will rise 1 percent annually above its existing level; (b) 75,000 new jobs will be created; and (c) consumers might save between $1 billion and $3.5 billion annually.[7]

Although these estimates supported the theoretical proposition that the FTA should be advantageous for both countries, unknown factors made the road to agreement uncertain. Such uncertainties fueled the fires of opposition to the agreement in both countries. As with any free-trade agreement, the FTA leads to a reduction in trade barriers, causing job displacement. As a result, some individuals and businesses who have benefitted from protectionism will lose, at least in the short run. Ironically, opposition to the FTA has been stronger in Canada. For example, according to a survey, about 60 percent of Canadian respondents believed the FTA had hurt the Canadian economy, whereas less than 10 percent thought the FTA had been beneficial to their country. Additionally, Canadian labor union leaders blamed the FTA for the loss of more than 100,000 manufacturing jobs.[8]

From the beginning, the trade agreement forced some multinational corporations to rethink their strategies. Many companies, both domestic and international, engaged in mergers of some kind. Some companies decided to simply halt their manufacturing in Canada. For example, in 1989, the Gillette Company declared plans to stop manufacturing in Canada within one and a half years, dismissing 590 employees. According to observers, this decision was due to the fact that Gillette had idle capacity in the United States, and that the trade agreement eliminates the tariff on razors.[9] As we explain in the next section, the integration of the United States and Canada has been extended, creating a three-country free-trade area that includes Mexico.

9.3b North American Free Trade Agreement (NAFTA)

In 1990, U.S. and Mexican officials agreed to negotiate a free-trade area between the two nations. Later, Canada declared that it would participate in talks, setting the stage for the formation of the largest free-trade union in the world. With a combined population of over 350 million people and an annual GNP of $6 trillion, the potential economic power of this union surpasses that of the EU, which in 1992 consisted of 320 million people and an annual GNP of $4 trillion.[10]

Negotiations between the trading partners were concluded on August 12, 1992. The U.S. Congress, the U.S. Senate, and the Mexican Senate approved NAFTA in November 1993. This was followed by the Canadian government's approval on December 2, 1993, clearing the way for the creation of a free-trade area that stretches from the Yukon to the Yucatan.[11]

Table 9-2 presents the highlights of NAFTA. As this table indicates, NAFTA is more than a regular free-trade area which includes only trade in goods. It encompasses trade in services and foreign direct investment. It also includes provisions for the environment, giving rise to a new ground for a free-trade agreement.

TABLE 9-2
Highlights of the North American Free Trade Agreement

General Provisions on Trade in Goods. Elimination of U.S. and Mexican tariffs and quotas on goods qualifying as North American under NAFTA's rules of origin. For most goods, trade barriers will be lifted in the next few years, others over 15 years.

Rules of Origin. Goods that are manufactured with resources from outside the NAFTA region qualify for NAFTA treatment only if they are substantially transformed within the NAFTA region (the United States, Canada, or Mexico).

Automotive Goods. Elimination of trade barriers on automotive goods after eight years. To qualify for NAFTA treatment, 62.5% of the cost of automotive goods must represent North American materials or labor. After 10 years, U.S. manufacturers will no longer have to produce their automotive goods in Mexico in order to sell them in that country.

Textiles and Apparel. Elimination of customs duties on textiles and apparel made from North American—spun yarn or from fabric made from North American fibers.

Government Procurement. Main government procurement will be open to firms from all three members. However, there will be a 10- year phaseout for Mexican restrictions for procurement by its government-owned energy industry.

Trucking. Elimination of restriction imposed on truckers driving cargo across the border by the end of 1999.

Agriculture. Elimination of approximately half of the existing tariffs and quotas upon enforcement of the agreement. Tariffs and quotas imposed on "politically sensitive" crops—such as Mexican orange juice, sugar sold to the United States, or U.S. corn sold to Mexico—will be lifted over 15 years.

Trade in Services. Establishment of a set of regulations and agreements to promote trade between the three members, excluding social programs, air, the maritime industry, governmental procurement and financial services, and telecommunications.

Financial Services. Elimination of limits on foreign investment in Mexican banks, insurers, and brokerage firms over the next 7- to 15-year period.

Investment. Treatment of NAFTA investors in the same manner as domestic investors. However, there are exceptions and various phaseout periods. Mexico will continue to limit foreign ownership of some land. Rigid limits will be imposed on U.S. airlines and radio, communications industries, Canada's cultural industries, and Mexico's energy and railroad industries.

Energy. Opening of Mexico's chemical and electric-generation sectors to U.S. investment. Exceptions are foreign investment in oil and gas exploration, production, and refining.

Development. Investment of $450 million by the U.S. and Mexican governments ($225 million each) in a new North American Development Bank. In addition to the funds generated by this $450 million investment, the bank will borrow $3 billion and loan money to assist communities harmed by the agreement and to aid cleanup of the border regions.

Environment. Establishment of an agency in Canada to examine environmental misuses by any of the three member nations and impose fines or trade sanctions on any member nation that falters in executing its own environmental laws. Together, the North American Development Bank, the World Bank, and the Inter-American Bank will commit a sum of $8 billion to be used by the U.S.—Mexico Border Environmental Commission on various environmental cleanup projects.

Labor. Establishment of an agency in Washington, DC, to examine labor mistreatment if two of the three nations agree. If a member nation fails to observe worker safety rules, child labor laws, or minimum-wage standards, that nation will be subject to the imposition of fines or trade sanctions.

Retraining. The United States will commit up to $90 million to be spent on retraining and aiding workers whose jobs will be lost due to NAFTA in the first 18 months.

Source: "The House Passes NAFTA," *The Wall Street Journal*, 18 November 1993, A12; Cladio Loser and Eliot Kalter, Mexico: *The Strategy to Achieve Sustained Growth*, Occasional Paper no. 99 (Washington, DC: International Monetary Fund, September 1992), 34—35; *North American Free Trade Agreement* (Washington, DC: Office of the U.S. Trade Representative, August 12, 1992).

The agreement is expected to have a significant effect on the three nations involved by providing each country with better access to the others' markets, expertise, labor, technology, and raw materials.[12] According to a report released by the Institute for International Economics, increases in employment and wages from NAFTA would likely be 1.0 and 0.3 percent, respectively, for the United States, 1.0 and 0.5 percent for Canada, and an astonishing 7.0 and 8.7 percent for Mexico.[13]

The Mexican economy, which has been faced with declining real wages, soaring population, high unemployment, and a huge national debt ($100 billion), desperately needs the free trade agreement. With low savings and no domestic capital-goods industry, Mexico is expected to benefit from U.S. and Canadian investment and expertise. Additionally, its proximity to the United States offers Mexico the added advantage of lower freight costs and closer access to the U.S. market.

Mexico and the United States have long been economically intertwined, even without NAFTA, which aims at eliminating many of the existing hurdles to cross-border trade. Mexico is the United States' third largest trading partner after Canada and Japan.[14] Trade between the two countries amounts to $52 billion a year. About 70 percent of Mexico's exports are sent to the United States. In 1991, Mexico provided the United States with 25 percent of the fruits and vegetables it consumes, a figure far larger than any other nation.[15]

Of the several economic ties the United States has with Mexico, the one that has attracted a lot of attention is the "maquiladoras" industry. **Maquiladoras** are manufacturing plants along the U.S.-Mexican border. These plants assemble components produced in the United States and shipped to Mexico duty-free. The assembled components are then shipped back to the United States for resale. Maquiladoras are beneficial for both the United States and Mexico. By fusing U.S. capital and Mexican labor, maquiladoras allow U.S. manufacturers to produce their products more cheaply and also provide employment opportunities for Mexican workers. In 2000, the maquiladora industry employed more than 500,000 Mexican workers in 2,000 plants along the U.S.-Mexican border.[16]

With $2.3 billion in annual trade, Mexico is Canada's seventeenth-largest market. Despite the fact that the amount of trade between the two countries is relatively small, Canada's decision to enter free-trade negotiation is partially explained by its desire to protect its market in the United States. Given the relatively cheaper labor in Mexico, Canada did not want Mexico to have an advantage. Canadian business leaders knew that if the United States signed a separate deal with Mexico, Canadian businesses would not be able to compete in the U.S. market. Additionally, as a Canadian official noted, "If the Mexican economy really takes off, the economic muscle will give it political weight. If we enter into a trilateral deal, Mexico and Canada together can be a counterweight to the United States."[17]

The U.S.-Mexico-Canada free-trade agreement is the first of its kind. Never before have advanced nations formed such a huge free-trade area with a developing nation. Because the union of a developing nation with two advanced industrial nations was unprecedented, it produced uncertainty.[18] This uncertainty was imbued by a voice of opposition from all three countries. Environmentalists claimed that U.S. and Canadian firms expanding in Mexico might take advantage of lax health and safety standards in that country, which had been accused of not doing enough to protect the environment. Organized labor in both the United States and Canada feared the loss of jobs to Mexican industry, which paid its workers much less than comparable Canadian and U.S. workers.* Many Mexicans feared that their country might become one big maquiladora at the mercy of the United States. The uncertainty was profoundly ingrained upon the Mexican psyche that had not forgiven the United States for land lost in the past and that wondered what would now stop Mexico from becoming the fifty-first state. Some Mexican industrialists were concerned that they would be swamped by big U.S. firms, unable to compete with them effectively. This would make them and their country less self-sufficient.

The arguments against the formation of NAFTA are not new. We discuss similar arguments in Chapter 7. As we mention in that chapter, the majority of economists disagree with any plea for protection and argue for free trade. For example, Gary Hufbauer and Jeffrey Schott of the Institute for International Economics estimated that expansion of trade, resulting from tariff elimination between the three countries, would create about 325,000 new jobs in the United States alone by 1995. They predicted that during this period, only 150,000 unskilled factory jobs would be lost in the United States. From a global standpoint, however, some of these jobs will be recovered by cheaper Mexican labor.[19] Thus, NAFTA could result in significant benefits for both nations.

---

* In 1990, manufacturing wages were $1.90 an hour in Mexico, compared to $14.50 an hour in the United States and $20 an hour in Canada.

The agreement could also lead to some trade diversion as the United States purchases goods from Mexico that displace exports of other developing countries. Nevertheless, the size of this trade diversion was expected to be relatively small compared to trade creation. Thus, most economists agreed that NAFTA would increase the wealth of its members. Like any other free-trade agreement, NAFTA's income distribution effect results in winners and losers. The relatively abundant factor of production wins, but the relatively scarce factor of production loses. Thus, in the United States and Canada, owners of capital (the relatively abundant factor) were expected to win and unskilled workers (the relatively scarce factor) were expected to lose. In Mexico, where the relative factor abundance is the opposite of the United States, NAFTA's income distribution effects are reversed. Labor was expected to gain, and owners of capital were expected to lose. Hence, it was not surprising that labor unions in the United States and Canada so vigorously opposed NAFTA. The agreement's provision for labor training was an attempt by the United States to compensate its losers (unskilled workers).[*]

In 1996, three years after NAFTA was signed, trade between the United States, Canada, and Mexico had grown about 33 percent. NAFTA proved to be valuable during Mexico's financial crisis in 1995. The agreement ensured that Mexico's markets would stay open to U.S. goods. This was in contrast to the 1982 Mexican financial crisis that compelled Mexico to carefully follow restrictive policies. In 1996, U.S. exports to Mexico reached record heights, encouraging the U.S. government to pursue further market opportunities in the Western Hemisphere. Building on NAFTA, the United States actively engaged in laying the foundation for the formation of a Free Trade Area of the Americas (FTAA) that called for the participation of 34 Western Hemisphere countries in a free-trade area by 2005.[20]

In closing this section we should keep in mind that customs unions and other forms of economic integration are intrinsically discriminatory, favoring member nations over nonmember nations. As such, to most economists, they represent a second-best trade policy, while global free trade remains the first-best trade policy.

9.3c Asian-Pacific Economic Cooperation (APEC)

The successful passage of NAFTA by the legislative bodies of its member countries helped to strengthen the General Agreement on Tariff and Trade (GATT) and now WTO, which was losing ground due to the slow progress in concluding the Uruguay Round. As we explained earlier, the Uruguay Round of negotiation was concluded on December, 1993, taking effect on July, 1995. The NAFTA victory puts the United States in a better position for moving the Asian-Pacific Economic Cooperation (APEC) group toward freer trade. This group includes Australia, Canada, Mexico, the United States and 12 East Asian Nations, and represents a channel through which the United States can accelerate the opening of Asian markets to U.S. products. One estimate is that freer trade with the APEC nations would create about 1.5 million U.S. jobs.

In late November 1993 the APEC members began talking about establishing a timetable for moving toward freer trade. One recommendation was to assign 1996 as a target date for engaging in negotiations, which would then take years to execute.[21] This recommendation led to a summit that was held at Subic Bay in the Philippines in December 1996. At this summit, the 18 APEC members pledged to lay the foundation for open trade and investment and a free-trade area by 2020. They also supported the U.S. initiative in creating the Information Technology Agreement (ITA) that would liberalize trade in computer and telecommunications equipment, software exports, and semiconductors. Following this summit, at the WTO's first ministerial meeting held in Singapore a few weeks later, the agreement was endorsed by 28 nations including almost all of the advanced countries, several developing countries in East and Southeast Asia, and Turkey. The ITA would encompass products amounting to $500 billion in annual global trade and over $90 billion in annual U.S. exports.[22]

---

[*]   What occurs to total welfare hinges on how the gains of winners are measured in relation to the losses of losers. Because total income increases with free trade, the winners must gain more income than the losers lose. One way of dealing with this problem is the compensation principle. According to this principle, since the winners gain more income than the losers lose, the winners can fully compensate the losers and still maintain net gains.

GLOBAL INSIGHTS CASE 9.3

Regional Trade Agreements: Building Blocks or Stumbling Blocks for Multilateral Process?

Does regionalism accelerate or slow the momentum of multilateral liberalization? Some compelling arguments suggest that the formation of regional blocs can serve as building block—or act as a stumbling block— to the multilateral process.

Perhaps the most compelling theoretical argument for protectionism—and the primary mechanism by which regionalism might act as stumbling block—is the optimal argument. Imposing tariffs may enable a country to exploit some monopsony power in its import markets, and so achieve more favorable terms of trade with the rest of the world. Moreover, a group of countries setting this optimal tariff in concert may have more success, because of their combined market power, than if each acted alone. Fortunately, Article XXIV of GATT, which governs regional trading arrangements among members, prohibits increases in tariffs against nonparticipants. (GATT now extends the same principle to services.) A regional trading arrangement may also undermine the multilateral process if special interests can manipulate the arrangement's more technical aspects (such as exemptions, phase out, and rule of origin) to their advantage, or if regional initiatives divert political capital and energy from multilateral initiatives.

On the other hand, regional arrangements can serve as building blocks for multilateralism in several ways. They can lock in countries' unilateral reforms, simplifying negotiations by reducing the number of countries involved, and set in motion a process of competitive liberalization in which reluctant countries are prodded into liberalizing by the threat of exclusion from a regional agreement.

The history of NAFTA provides an example of how regionalism can lock in reforms. By entering into NAFTA, the then-President of Mexico hoped to prevent his successors from undoing the unilateral liberalizations his government had undertaken since the mid-1980s. Mexico's reaction to the peso crisis of 1994-95 showed that this lock-in strategy worked. Unlike the 1982 debt crisis, when Mexico raised trade barriers against all its trading partners, in the 1994-95 crisis Mexico continued to reduce tariffs for its NAFTA partners (while raising tariffs against some other countries).

Negotiating with 150 other countries over dozens of sectors, as WTO negotiators must do, can be inefficient and difficult. The process can be made more efficient if countries can join into customs unions and thus negotiate as a larger unit. Also, within such a group it may be easier to test out innovative agreements in certain areas—such as services, investment, dispute settlement, and competition policy—before introducing their provisions into the multilateral negotiations.

The events of 1993 demonstrate the power of competitive liberalization. The Administration is said to have made a "triple play" that year, with the passage of NAFTA, the pathbreaking APEC summit, and the conclusion of the Uruguay Round. These not only were landmark achievements in themselves but interacted with each other in advantageous ways. By pushing NAFTA through the Congress despite strong opposition, the President revealed the political will to make free trade commitments stick. Combined with the upgrading of APEC negotiations to a high-profile leaders' meeting in Seattle, the passage of NAFTA send a strong signal to the Europeans that the United States had serious regional alternatives should the Uruguay Round of GATT negotiations fall apart. German policymakers have reportedly stated that this was part of their motivation for prevailing on their EU partners to make certain concessions that allowed the GATT negotiations to be successfully concluded in December 1993.

These examples show that there are both positive and negative links between regionalism and the multilateral negotiations. Every regional bloc will have its share of each. In the end, however, the evidence suggests that the recent growth of regionalism has served more to foster than hinder process toward liberalization. Those groups of countries that have participated in regional liberalization have often tended to reduce their barriers against nonmembers at the same time that they do so internally.

Source: U.S. Government Printing Office, *Economic Report of the President* (Washington D.C: Government Printing Office, 1998, pp.229-230, Box 7-2. Reprinted.

GLOBAL INSIGHTS CASE 9.4

APEC TARIFF REDUCTIONS AND OTHER INITIATIVES

Although APEC members have not yet engaged in formal negotiations over tariff reductions, many have already implemented dramatic reductions in their tariff levels. As the table indicates, between 1988 and 1996 the average applied tariff among APEC members fell by more than a third, from 15.4 percent to 9.1 percent.

The progressive lowering of tariff barriers is only one aspect of the APEC Action Agenda. This agenda details steps that APEC members have agreed to take to promote greater economic interaction throughout the region. Other agenda items include reducing barriers to competition in the fast-growing air transport market, and a variety of measures designed to reduce the cost of doing business in the region. These include the development of an infrastructure opportunity data base, the promotion of uniform customs classification and procedures and advances in the harmonization of standards.

Economy	1988	1996
Australia	15.6	6.1
Brunei	3.9	2.0
Canada	9.1	6.7
Chile	19.9	10.9
China	40.3	23.0
Chinese Taipei (Taiwan)	12.6	8.6
Hong Kong	.0	.0
Indonesia	20.3	13.1
Japan	7.2	9.0
Malaysia	13.0	9.0
Mexico	10.6	12.5
New Zealand	15.0	7.0
Papua New Guinea	*	*
Philippines	27.9	15.6
Singapore	.4	.0
South Korea	19.2	7.9
Thailand	40.8	17.0
United States	6.6	6.4
Average	15.4	9.1

* Not available

Source: U.S. Government Printing Office, *Economic Report of the President* (Washington DC: U.S. Government Printing Office, 1998), 232, Reprinted.

9.4 RECENT POLITICAL EVENTS AFFECTING THE GLOBAL ECONOMY

The economic reforms in Eastern European countries, the fall of the Berlin Wall and the reunification of Germany, and the demise of the Soviet Union brought an end to the Cold War. These events, which occurred in such a remarkably short time frame, surprised everyone in the world and opened a new chapter in the global economy. The purpose of this section is to explain these events and elaborate on their global economic impact.

9.4a Eastern European Countries Economic Reforms

Following World War II, the Eastern European countries (Bulgaria, Czechoslovakia, the former East Germany, Hungary, Poland, Romania, and Yugoslavia) adopted the command economy that was initiated and practiced by the former Soviet Union. The collapse of Communist power in 1989 brought an end to Soviet domination in this part of the world and laid the foundation for the transformation of Eastern European economies into market-oriented economic systems. For the global economy, as a whole, this transformation is good news, providing the free world with new markets for exports, new sources of raw materials for imports, and new investment opportunities. The economic forces that contributed to the collapse of Soviet power in Eastern Europe are related to inefficiencies that stem from a command economy. With no competition and the absence of a profit-maximization objective, firms in Eastern Europe had little or no incentive to produce efficiently, cut costs, develop new markets, improve quality, or innovate. As a result, by the late 1980s, the income growth of these countries had fallen significantly behind that of advanced market-oriented economies and newly industrial countries (NICs). Countries such as Poland and Hungary found themselves facing huge external debts, the proceeds of which had been used, for the most part, to finance unproductive investments. In their economic planning, they stressed a growth process that demanded significant increases in factor input rather than a surge in productivity. Such a growth process was not feasible, however, due to a decrease in the growth of labor input. This resulted from the virtual halt of labor migration from the agricultural sector to the industrial sector.

The integration of the Eastern European countries into the global market has created new channels for exports and has offered rich commercial opportunities for Western companies. Many manufacturing firms are now being attracted to the emerging Eastern European nations as a low-cost, conceivably high-technology zone on their borders.[23] Most of the impact on world trade volumes will result from the closing standard-of-living gap between Eastern and Western Europe. The overall trade impact of economic reform is expected to be small, accounting for an approximate 2- to 3-percent expansion of global trade. Countries directly affected by such integration are the middle-income countries.* These countries are expected to see some of their exports displaced from the EU markets. Additionally, middle-income countries are not expected to be able to compensate for the lost market by enhancing their exports to Eastern European countries.[24]

Working within the IMF and the World Bank, The United States has been very active in facilitating the transition of the Eastern Europan countries into market economic systems. In the late 1990s there were signs that the economic conditions were improving in Eastern European countries. For example, Poland's economy was booming, inflation was less than 20%. Foreign investors like Citibank referred to Poland as "Eastern Europe's tiger economy." It was even predicted by some observers that "Poland would become the regional headquarers of many companies."[25]

9.4b Unification of Germany

One significant event that took place in November 1989 was the fall of the Berlin Wall, which paved the way for German unification. On July 2, 1990, economic union of the two Germanies was achieved. East Germany agreed to scrap its currency and adopt the West German mark. It also adopted West German economic rules and laws, joining the market-oriented economic system.[26] This unification created a Germany with a population of approximately 80 million people and a land mass half the size of Texas.[27]

German unification has economic implications for both Germany and the rest of the world. In the short run, it is expected that eastern Germany will experience hard economic times. West Germany's absorption of the poor and decaying East German economy was estimated to cost $1 trillion in the next decade, a cost financed by West Germany. It was also estimated that it would take about five years for the former East Germany's economic structure to meet the level of its western counterpart. During this period, Germany was expected to experience significant social and economic problems in its eastern section. It was estimated that 70 percent of 8,000 enterprises in the East

---

* Middle-income countries include some of the Mediterranean countries, the East Asian NICs, and the more industrialized Latin American countries.

would face bankruptcy, and 75 to 100 billion West German marks would be spent annually on unemployment relief, social security, wage increases, and reconstruction in the East.

In the long run, Germany's benefits from unification are expected to widen as western investment in eastern industries continues to expand. German economic power, measured by GNP, might increase by one tenth after unification. Given the huge size of a united German market and the inability of German companies to satisfy market demand, the EU and the rest of the world are offered the incredible opportunity of exporting more goods to this vast market.

Before unification, West Germany—one of the six original founders of the EU—provided the biggest share of the EU budget (about 27 percent) and accounted for more than half of the EU's total trade. With the unification of its eastern and western sections, Germany naturally has an even greater impact on the EU. In the short run, Germany's effort to finance the development of its eastern part drains potential funds available for the EU's less developed member states. Additionally, following unification, eastern Germany started to receive $4.8 billion annually in subsidies from the EU budget. Eighty percent of this amount is contributed by western Germany. This will eventually lead to a decrease in Germany's contribution to the EU.

German unification has also made the implementation of the EU's agricultural policy difficult because the abundant agricultural products from eastern Germany have added to the existing surplus of the EU agricultural product market.

In 1991, Germany was expected to remain an economic giant, experiencing healthy economic growth (2.5 percent to 3 percent for the early 1990s) despite growing political problems at home and abroad following unification. From the global standpoint, given the need for rebuilding eastern Germany, the demand for imports was expected to increase well in excess of 10 percent a year.[28] This would benefit Germany's major trading partners: the United States, Japan, Great Britain, the Netherlands, Belgium, Australia, and especially France, which were already doing the most business with West Germany. Other countries benefiting directly from German unity include Italy, Spain, Switzerland, and Korea. However, against this optimistic forecast for Germany, 1992 was marked as the year of German "recession and helplessness."[29] In 1993, Germany experienced a number of problems, such as an escalation in "far-right" disorder, a destabilizing inflow of immigrants, and growing cynicism about Germany's construction plans for eastern Germany.

Another aspect of German unification with global implications is the country's decision to unify its currency. In order to exchange East German currency for West German money on a one-for-one basis, West Germany committed itself to giving large amounts of subsidies to East German citizens and businesses. A concurrent decision was to not raise taxes to pay for these subsidies. To prevent a surge in inflation from the influx of subsidies into Germany's economy, the country decided to support higher interest rates. As we explained earlier in this chapter, this contributed to the currency turmoil in Europe, threatening to kill the Maastricht Treaty that was to be voted on by the French on September 20, 1992. Fortunately for the EU, French voters ratified the treaty by a narrow margin, paving the way for the intensified efforts of EU members to implement that treaty. However, Germany's support of high interest rates ignited yet another crisis in the currency market in the summer of 1993, bringing the ERM to the brink of collapse. Once again, under pressure from European allies, Germany's central bank cut its two key lending rates, precipitating a series of interest cuts throughout Europe. Other European central banks followed Germany's lead in cutting interest rates, and the ERM was revived.

The impact of the Germany's reunification on the world economy has been compared to that of the OPEC price increase in 1973 and the "Reaganomics" of the 1980s. These events shocked the world's economy for years to come, significantly affecting international trade and investment flows.

In the mid-1990s, five years following the unification, German taxpayers had spent $575 billion on the former East Germany for development of an infrastructure of 14,000 state-owned companies and the overhauling the late phone system. This has resulted in soaring economic growth, reaching the level of 8.5% in 1994. It remains to be seen how soon the former East Germany can stands on its own, and whether or not growth in East Germany can be sustained.[31]

9.4c Demise of the Soviet Union

In the late 1950s, Nikita Khrushchev claimed that Soviet economic output would overtake and surpass that of the United States. He told the United States, "We will bury you." Such statements set the stage for a bitter cold war between the two superpowers. The United States and the Soviet Union fought a political battle that most observers believed would end in a final nuclear war. However, economic and political problems within the Soviet Union created an inefficient, bureaucratic system. This led to shortages of agricultural and industrial products, forcing the nation to continue to expand its imports from Western Europe and, ironically, from the United States, the country Khrushchev was supposed to bury.

The political and economic problems in the former Soviet Union set the stage for the emergence of one of the century's pivotal leaders, Mikhail S. Gorbachev, who came to power in 1985. His reforms, referred to as "perestroika" (restructuring) and "glasnost" (openness), transformed the political and economic structure of the Soviet Union and helped to end the Cold War. However, he became the victim of the very reforms that he initiated. Gorbachev's reforms, opened Soviet society to the world and ended the Communist party's seven-decade monopoly on power. He allowed the fall of the Communist regimes in Eastern Europe, introduced multiple-party and multiple-candidate elections, and strengthened the elected legislature. He stopped religious oppression, freed political prisoners, and gave Soviet citizens the freedom to travel and emigrate. In talks with the United States, Gorbachev agreed to drastic reductions in nuclear and conventional arms, thereby strengthening the world's prospect for peace. However, despite his accomplishments in reshaping his country's political and economic systems, he made some mistakes. Many observers believe Gorbachev moved too slowly on economic reforms. As a result, shortages of food, fuel, housing, and consumer goods worsened. In planning and implementing his reforms, Gorbachev did not consult sufficiently with republics, nor did he give them enough autonomy. Finally, he chose his aides unwisely, ending up with colleagues who eventually turned against him. These mistakes not only cost Gorbachev his presidency, but they paved the way for the demise of the Soviet Union and the birth of the new Commonwealth of Independent States (CIS).

Western leaders welcomed the formation of the CIS; U.S. President George Bush referred to the demise of the Soviet Union as "a defining moment in history." He said that U.S. security would be enhanced by offering aid to the region, and added that "If this democratic revolution is defeated, it would plunge us into a world more dangerous in some respects than the dark years of the Cold War."[32]

The CIS has many obstacles to overcome before becoming a modern market-oriented society. Russia, comprising 51.3 percent of the former Soviet Union's population and 75 percent of the land mass, has especially attracted the attention of the Western world and is being closely watched by Western leaders. Boris Yeltsin, the former Russian leader, faced tremendous economic and political problems that threatened his own survival. Such problems came to a head in the fall of 1993 when hard-line lawmakers took a stand against Yeltsin by encamping inside the Parliament. This standoff ended in violence and led to the dissolution of the Parliament and approval of the final draft of a new Russian constitution (written by Yeltsin) that would augment presidential powers and legally grant citizens the right to own property.[33] Russian voters' approval of the draft on December 12, 1993, gave Yelstin a significant political victory.[34] Yeltsin was successful in keeping many of the government's free-market programs on course, but the economic challenges facing him were overwhelming. Yeltsin dealt with an economic system marked by a significant drop in production. It was expected that some sectors of the economy would experience as much as a 50 percent decline in their output levels. Yelstin had to deal with a variety of other problems as well, including inflationary pressures caused by shortages and unemployment that resulted from dismantling the communist system.[35] Added to the economic problems were the political problems of keeping the CIS together and preventing the disintegration of the awesome military structure that were left by the Soviet government.[36] Following a number of health problems, finally Yeltsin stepped down on January 1, 2000. He was replaced by one of his closest allies. It remains to be seen how the new leader of Russia manages numerous problems that are facing his country.

GLOBAL INSIGHTS CASE 9.5

Bilateral Investment Treaties

For much of the last decade the United States has been actively pursuing the negotiation of bilateral investment treaties with emerging-market countries around the world. The U.S. government places priority on negotiating such treaties with countries undergoing economic reform where it believes the United States can have a significant impact on the adoption of liberal policies on the treatment of FDI. The structure of these treaties has also laid the policy groundwork for broader multicountry initiatives in the OECD (the MAI) and eventually the WTO.* The structure of our bilateral investment treaties provides U.S. inventors with the following six basic guarantees:

- treatment that is as favorable as that received by their competitors— this implies the better of national or most-favored nation treatment
- clear limits on the expropriation of investments, and fair compensation when expropriation does occur
- the right to transfer all funds related to an investment into and out of the country without delay, at the market rate of exchange.
- limits on the ability of the host government to impose inefficient and trade-distorting performance requirement.
- the right to submit an investment dispute with the host government to international arbitration
- the right of U.S. investors to engage the top managerial personnel of their choice, regardless of nationality.

In cases where national treatment is the binding standard, the treaty ensures that U.S. inventors are treated in a manner equivalent to domestic inventors; where it is most-favored nation treatment, U.S. inventors are assured treatment no worse than investors from any third country receive. As the table indicates, to date, the United States has successfully negotiated bilateral investment treaties with some countries and is actively engaged in pursuing a multilateral version of the treaty under the auspices of the OECD.

Countries with Which the United States Has Bilateral Investment Treaties

Country and date		Country and date		Country and date		Country and date	
Albania	pending	Croatia	pending	Jordan	pending	Romania	1994
Argentina	1994	Czech Republic	1992	Kazakhstan	1994	Russia	Pending
Armenia	1996	Ecuador	1997	Kyrgyzstan	1994	Senegal	1990
Azerbaijan	pending	Egypt	1992	Latvia	1996	Slovakia	1992
Bangladesh	1989	Estonia	1997	Moldova	1994	Sri Lanka	1993
Belarus	pending	Georgia	1997	Mongolia	1997	Trinidad and Tobago	1996
Bulgaria	1994	Grenada	1989	Morocco	1991	Tunisia	1993
Cameroon	1989	Haiti	pending	Nicaragua	pending	Turkey	1990
Congo (Brazzaville)	1994	Honduras	pending	Panama	1991	Ukraine	1996
Congo (Kinshasa)	1989	Jamaica	1997	Poland	1994	Uzbekistan	Pending

Note-Years are those when the treaty entered into force.

*The MAI stands for Multilateral Agreement on Investment.

Source: U.S. Government Printing Office, *Economic Report of the President* (Washington DC: U.S. Government Printing Office, 1998), 259, Box 7-6. Reprinted.

From the outset of independence, it was clear that it would be extremely difficult for the CIS to be transformed to market-oriented systems without economic aid from the West. Realizing this, Western leaders have been quick to pour economic aid to the region, contingent upon market-oriented economic reforms. On April 2, 1992, President

Bush and Allied leaders pledged to funnel a combined $24 billion of additional aid to Russia.[37] The aid was given to help Yeltsin implement market-oriented economic reform. The U.S. and European officials made it clear that "any backpedaling on economic reform could jeopardize billions of dollars in planned Western aid."[38] In July 1992, the leaders of the G-7 nations (Great Britain, Canada, France, Germany, Italy, Japan, and the United States) promised to provide debt relief to Russia. They also pledged to extend export credit to Russia, lift their trade barriers, and provide the Russians with more technical assistance.[39]

Following Bill Clinton's presidential victory over George Bush, Russia continued to receive billions of dollars in grants, credits, and special funds to sustain its demolished economy. However, the outflow of funds was just as massive as the inflow. An estimated $10 to $15 billion flew out of Russia in 1992—an amount totalling about 15 percent of Russia's gross domestic product (GDP) for the year. Capital flight is a manifestation of the malfunctioning economy and is expected to reverse itself once the Russian economy stabilizes.[40]

With focus on international trade, at their September 1994 summit in Washington, both presidents of the United States and Russia signed a Partnership for Economic Cooperation that serves as a framework for reducing barriers to expanded economic cooperation. A number of U.S. agencies, including the Overseas Private Investment Corporation, the Export-Import Bank, the Trade and Development Agency, and the Department of Commerce, have programs that are aimed at facilitating trade and investment in Russia. Since 1992, the U.S. Agency for International Development (USAID) has offered about $2 billion in assistance to helping Russia develop democratic and market institutions.[41]

We conclude this chapter by noting that movement toward a market-oriented economy and free international trade is reaching a new and unprecedented height. Recent world events, such as those explained here, open up a new chapter in the world of free trade, changing the nature of East-West trade relations. However, the transition from a command economy to a market-oriented economy is not painless. Experience has shown that the dismantling of subsidies and price controls, and the suspension of regulations regarding employment and worker dismissals may initially lead to higher unemployment and inflation. It may also worsen income inequality before economic growth and higher productivity induce an improvement in standards of living. Higher inflation, leading to a rise in the prices of domestically produced goods, may cause exports to fall and imports to rise, generating foreign exchange shortages. These factors, along with political considerations, may force some countries to move away from further openness. Given these problems, some observers have argued that a rapid transition toward a market economy is preferable to a slow one because the faster the economic reforms take place, the lower the probability of their being blocked by those who benefited from the previous system. Additionally, it is argued that public support for reform may best be achieved when tangible benefits of the reforms are felt more quickly. One thing is clear: Eastern European countries cannot achieve a successful transformation to market-oriented economic systems without help, especially financial assistance from the West. Such a transformation requires political leadership and demands global cooperation between the leaders of the advanced market-oriented economies. Aware of this fact, the United States and its allies have cooperated in easing restrictions on the sale of high-technology goods to Eastern European countries that are adopting democratic reforms.[42]

9.5 SUMMARY

1. At its 1985 summit in Milan, the EU endorsed the "White Paper," which established a detailed legislative program for complete economic integration by 1992.
2. The basic thrust of the White Paper is the removal of a whole series of trade barriers. These trade barriers can be separated into three major categories: (a) physical barriers, (b) technical barriers, and (c) fiscal barriers.
3. For EU members, the removal of the trade barriers has stimulated both supply and demand. From the supply standpoint, this means tougher competition within the community. From the demand side, the decrease in prices means an increase in the quantity demanded, which in turn encourages EU businesses to expand their output.
4. Besides its impact on supply and demand, removal of the trade barriers affects the economy at large.
5. From a global standpoint, a more dynamic EU stimulates worldwide competition, and, as trade theories suggest, global welfare increases.

6. For EU governments, 1992 was the deadline by which they were to have fulfilled their obligations to enact legislation supporting the White Paper's objectives. The White Paper outlines 300 items of legislation for the removal of physical, technical, and fiscal barriers within the EU.

7. For U.S. firms, post-1992 has meant revival of activities that had declined drastically due to trade barriers in Europe.

8. During the 1980s, the United States negotiated two free-trade agreements, one with Israel and the other with Canada.

9. The Free Trade Agreement (FTA) between the United States and Canada was signed in 1988 and went into effect January 1, 1989. According to a number of estimates, it was expected that Canadian gains, in percentage terms, would be larger than those of the United States.

10. The factors that contributed to the eventual achievement of the FTA include the weakening of the United States' international position and Canada's increasing dependence on the United States.

11. The United States is Canada's principal supplier and major customer.

12. In 1990, U.S. and Mexican officials agreed to negotiate a free-trade area between the two nations. Later, Canada declared that it would participate in negotiation, setting the stage for the formation of the largest free-trade area in the world. The agreement, referred to as the North American Free Trade Agreement (NAFTA), was concluded on August 12, 1992.

13. Of the several economic ties the United States has with Mexico, the one that has attracted a lot of attention is the "maquiladora" industry. Maquiladoras are manufacturing plants along the U.S.—Mexican border. These plants assemble components produced in the United States and shipped to Mexico duty-free. The assembled components are then shipped back to the United States for resale.

14. The collapse of Communist power in 1989 brought an end to Soviet domination in Eastern European countries and laid the foundation for the transformation of these nations' economies into market-oriented economic systems.

15. The economic forces that contributed to the collapse of Soviet power in East Europe are related to inefficiencies that stem from a command economy.

16. The overall trade impact of the economic reforms in Eastern Europe is expected to be small, accounting for an approximate 2- to 3-percent expansion of global trade.

17. On July 2, 1990, the economic union of the two Germanies was achieved. East Germany agreed to scrap its currency and adopt the West German mark. It also adopted West German economic rules and laws, joining the market-oriented economic system.

18. In the short run, it was expected that eastern Germany would experience hard economic times.

19. In the long run, Germany's benefits from unification are expected to widen as western investment in eastern industries continues to expand.

20. The impact of Germany's reunification on the world economy has been compared to that of the OPEC price increase in 1973 and the "Reaganomics" of the 1980s, which shocked the world's economy for years to come, significantly affecting international trade and investment flows.

21. The demise of the Soviet Union led to the creation of the new Commonwealth of Independent States (CIS). The CIS has many obstacles to overcome before becoming a modern market-oriented society.

Review Questions

1. Elaborate on "project 1992" by answering the following questions.
   (a) What factors gave rise to project 1992?
   (b) What is the White Paper?
   (c) What is the basic thrust of the White Paper? Explain.
2. Elaborate on project 1992's impact on the EU from the standpoint of each of the following:
   (a) Demand and supply in the EU
   (b) The EU economy at large
   (c) EU businesses
   (d) The global economy
3. What is the Maastricht Treaty? What is its major objective? What major crises have stood in the way of its approval and implementation? Explain.
4. During the 1980s, the United States negotiated two free-trade agreements.
   (a) What are these two agreements
   (b) In the context of economic integration, how would you classify these agreements?
5. Elaborate on the economic forces that contributed to the demise of Soviet power in Eastern Europe, and discuss the overall trade impact of Eastern European economic reforms.
6. Discuss the economic implications of German unification, in both the short run and the long run.
7. Who are the major beneficiaries of German unification? Explain.
8. Following unification, why did Germany support a high interest rate policy? Elaborate on the impact of this policy on the EU and the global economy.

Problems

1. Although it was estimated that Canadian gains from FTA would be larger than U.S. gains, some Canadians seemed to be skeptical of the possible benefits of this agreement. Additionally, they feared that NAFTA could hurt their country. What possible factors do you think gave rise to Canadian skepticism of the two agreements? Explain.
2. Do you think project 1992 is beneficial to the United States? Answer this question in the context of short-run and long-run effects.
3. The collapse of Communist power in Eastern Europe gave rise to the prediction that some of the Eastern European countries might become members of the EU, leading to its enlargement. What are the possible costs of such an enlargement from the stand point of each of the following:
   (a) Eastern European countries who would become members
   (b) Western European countries
   (c) Other countries
4. Some opponents of the FTA fear that the economies of scale realized by many U.S. firms might lead such firms to underprice Canadian import-competing goods as well as Canadian export products. Some Canadians also fear that NAFTA could hinder Canada.
   (a) Assuming that the economies of scale are realized by the U.S. firms, do you think Canada as a whole would lose or gain from the FTA?
   (b) How would you explain Canadians' concerns that NAFTA hampers Canada?

Notes

1. J. Michael Farren, "Opportunities and Challenges In the New European Market," *Business America,* 25 February 1991, 6.
2. "With Monetary Union Around the Corner, Europe's Doubt Grows," *The Wall Street Journal*, 29 Dec. 97 p. 1, "The Euro: A Look at What Might go Wrong," *The Wall Street Journal*, 6 January 99, P. A17.

3. "Western Europe Finds That It's Pricing Itself Out of the Job Market," *The Wall Street Journal*, 9 December 1993, 1, A8; "Making Change: As The Euro's Arrival Nears, Europe Braces for Lots of Headaches," *The Wall Street Journal*, 30 December 1998, p. 1; "Countdown: With Monetary Union Around the Corner, Europe's doubt Grow," *The Wall Street Journal*, 29 December 1997, p.1; "EMU's Outlook Hazy on the Eve of Union," *The Wall Street Journal*, 25 November 1998, A 15.

4. *U.S.-Canadian Free Trade Agreement: Summary of Major Provisions, 1987*. Washington, DC: Office of Public Affairs, Office of Trade Representative, 1987.

5. Canadian Department of Finance, *The Canada-U.S. Free Trade Agreement: An Economic Assessment* (Ottawa, 1989), 32.

6. Jeffrey J. Schott, "The Free Trade Agreement: A U.S. Assessment," *The Canada-United States Free Trade Agreement: The Global Impact,* in eds. Jeffrey Schott and Murray J. Smith (Washington DC: Institute for International Economics, 1988), Ch. 1.

7. John Yang, "U.S.-Canada Trade Pact Clears Congress on Senate Vote, Faces Hurdle in Ottawa," *The Wall Street Journal,* September 1988, 8.

8. "A Triple Threat? Canada is Pushing Ahead with Three-way Free Trade with the United States and Mexico," *Maclean's,* 8 October 1990, 48-49.

9. "Free-Trade Pact Creates Winners, Losers: Canadian Firms Forced to Adjust Their Operations," *The Wall Street Journal,* 7 February 1989, A20.

10. "Economic Outlook: Free Trade with Mexico Will Boost America's Economy," *U.S. News and World Report,* 13 May 1991, 58; "A Giant Marketplace: Bush Starts Free Talks with Mexico," *Maclean's,* 25 June 1990, 21.

11. Canadian Government Approves Trade Pact, Claims Improvements," *The Wall Street Journal,* 3 December 1993, A2, A4.

12. "Mexico and U.S. Move Closer on Free Trade," *The Wall Street Journal,* 28 July 1992, A3.

13. Douglas A. Schuler, "The Handshake or the Fist?" *International Trade Finance Report* 32 (November 1993): 1-3.

14. "A Salinas Serenade: Free Trade With the U.S." *Business Week,* April 9, 1990, 38.

15. "Mexico: The Salad Bowl of North America," *Business Week,* 25 February 1991, 70.

16. According to the data provided by The Coalition of Justice for Maquiladoras.

17. "A Giant Marketplace: Bush Starts Free Trade Talks with Mexico," *MaClean's,* 25 June 1990, 21.

18. "The Mexico Pact: Worth the Price?" *Business Week,* 27 May 1991, 32-35.

19. "Quick Reaction: Trade Pact Is Likely to Step Up Business Even Before Approval," *The Wall Street Journal,* 13 August 1992, 1, A6; "With Free-Trade Pact About Wrapped Up, The Real Battle Begins," *The Wall Street Journal,* 7 August 1992, 1, A4.

20. "U.S. Government Printing Office, *Economic Report of the President* (Washington DC.: U.S. Government Printing Office, 1997), 249.

21. "Asia-Pacific Group, at a Crossroads, May Dtermine How to Define Region," *The Wall Street Journal*, 19, November 1993, p. A.9; "Japan Attempts to Become a Mediator to Shift Focus form its Trade Surplus," *The Wall Street Journal*, 17, November 1993, p. A 18.

22. "U.S. Government Printing Office, *Economic Report of the President* (Washington DC.: U.S. Government Printing Office, 1997), 248-249.

23. "Exporting Labor: Western Europe Finds That It's Pricing Itself Out of the Job Market," *The Wall Street Journal,* 9 December 1993, 1, A8.

24. Susan M. Collins and Dani Rodrik, *Eastern and the Soviet Union in the World Economy* (Washington, DC: Institute for International Economics, May 1991).

25. "Booming Economy in Poland Brings Jobs, Wealth and Apathy, " *The Wall Street Journal*, November 1996, p.1.

26. "German Merger to Affect Economies around World," *Los Angeles Times,* 22 July 1990, B2.

27. "A Transatlantic Partnership: Germany and the United States," *Forbes,* 23 July 1990, A1.

28. "Unified Germany Likely to Remain an Economic Giant," *Los Angeles Times,* 5 May 1991, D1.

29. "Germany Faces a Year Worsening Ills: Recession Is Accented by Violence, Refugee Influx," *The Wall Street Journal,* 4 January 1993, A6.

30. Ibid.

31. "East-West Divide Lives on in Germany: Leipzing Show Progress, but no Economic Miracle," *Thw Wall Street Journal,* 3 August 1995, p. A8.

32. "Bush, Allies Pledge $24 Billion to Russia," *The Wall Street Journal,* 2 April 1992, A2

33. "Yelstin's Foes Holed up in Parliament Given a Way Out: Job, Cash to Defeat," *The Wall Street Journal,* 1 October 1993, A6; "Yeltsin Clears the Final Draft of Constitution," *The Wall Street Journal,* 9 November 1993, A19.

34. "Yelstin's Constitution Appears to Gain Thin Victory in Russia," *The Wall Street Journal,* 13 December 1993, A10.

35. "Russia's Crisis Over Reforms Seems to Ease," *The Wall Street Journal,* 15 April 1992, A15.

36. "Armed Forces of Former Soviet Union Are Fast Falling Apart, Analysts Say," *The Wall Street Union,* 13 April 1992, 18.

37. "Bush, Allies Pledge $24 Billion to Russia," *The Wall Street Journal,* 2 April 1992, A2.

38. "Russian Cabinet Offers to Quit to Save Reforms," *The Wall Street Journal,* 14 April 92, A14.

39. "G-7 Nations Offer Yeltsin Relief on Debt," *The Wall Street Journal,* 9 July 1992, A2.

40. "Russia Should Turn to Latin America for Advice as Capital Flight Worsens," *The Wall Street Journal,* 15 November 1993, A9.

41. "U.S. Government Printing Office, *Economic Report of the President* (Washington, D.C.: United States Government Printing Ofice, 1997), 258.

42. "U.S., Allies to Ease More Curbs on High-Tech Sales to East Europe," *The Wall Street Journal,* 20 February 1990, A20.

Suggested Readings

Baer, M. D. "North American Free Trade." *Foreign Affairs* (Fall 1991): 132-149.

Balassa, B., and J. Schott, eds. *European Community 1992: Implications for the World Economy.* Washington, DC: Institute for International Economics, 1989.

Black, Cyril E., et al. *Common Sense in U.S.—Soviet Trade.* Washington, DC: American Committee on East-West Accord, 1979.

Calingaert, Michael. *The 1992 Challenge From Europe.* Washington: National Planning Association, 1988.

Collins, Susan M. *Eastern Europe and the Soviet Union in the World Economy.* Washington DC: Institute for International Economics, May 1991.

Cox, David, and Richard Harris. "Trade Liberalization and Industrial Organization: Some Estimates for Canada." *Journal of Political Economy* 93, no. 1 (February 1985): 115-145.

Diebold, W., ed. *Bilateralism, Multilateralism, and Canada in U.S. Trade Policy.* Cambridge, MA: Ballinger, 1988.

Fahrholz, Bernad, and Reiner Loslein. "Buy-outs in Germany." *European Management Journal* 9, no. 1 (March 1991): 60-64.

Goldman, Marshal. *Detente and Dollars.* New York: Basic Books, 1975.

Havrylyshyn, Oleh, and John Williamson. *From Soviet Disunion to Eastern Economic Community.* Washington DC: Institute for International Economics, October 1991.

Kaiser, Karl. "Germany's Unification." *Foreign Affairs* 70, no. 1 (1990): 179-225.

Longworth, R. C. "U.S. Begins Assessing Impact of 1992 Market Deadline," *Europe* (May 1988): 14-15.

Morici, Peter. *Meeting the Competitive Challenge: Canada and the United States in the Global Economy.* Washington DC: Canadian-American Committee, 1988.

Mosetting, Michael D. "The Implication of 1992 for U.S. Business," *Europe* (December 1988): 18-20.

Paolo, Ceddhini. *The European Challenge 1992.* Brookfield, VT: Grower, 1989.

Schott, J. *Free Trade Areas and U.S. Trade Policy.* Washington, DC: Institute for International Economics, 1989.

Spellman, James D. "1992 Prompts Unprecedented Wave of Mergers," *Europe,* December 1988, pp. 35-39.

Turner, John. "There Is More to Trade than Trade." *California Management Review* (Winter 1991): 109-117.

Van Ham, Peter. "Soviet Economic Reform and East-West Relations." *Problems of Communism* 40 (Jan-April 1991): 144-149.

Williamson, John. *The Economic Opening of Eastern Europe.* Washington, DC: Institute for International Economics, May 1991.

Winham, Gilbert. *Trading With Canada.* New York: Twentieth Century Fund, 1988.

Wonnacott, Paul, and Ronald J. Wonnacott. "Free Trade Between The United States and Canada: Fifteen Years Later," *Canadian Public Policy,* supplement (October 1982).

Wonnacott, Ronald J., and Paul Wonnacott. *Free Trade Between The United States and Canada: The Political Economic Effects.* Cambridge, MA: Harvard University Press, 1967.

Part 3

INTERNATIONAL MONETARY RELATIONS

Parts I and II of this book deal only with microeconomic issues relating to the exchange of goods and services between nations. But the study of international economics also encompasses international monetary questions. Such questions arise from the interaction of international transactions with macroeconomic variables such as prices, money, and income. To consider the macro ramifications of international trade, it is essential to comprehend the fundamentals of international monetary economics and the manner by which international trade and financial flows influence and are influenced by the economy at large.

International trade occurs within the framework of an international monetary system. Such a system, composed of national monetary systems, links different nations through foreign exchange markets. Although the international monetary system is aimed at promoting the free flow of goods and services across national boundaries, nations sometimes employ it to restrain such flows.

The purpose of Part III is to present some of the basic principles of international monetary economics to provide a background for understanding the monetary implications of international economic relations. Chapter 10 elaborates on the balance of payments accounting system and explains the methodology for interpreting the different accounts included in this statement. Chapter 11 describes the foreign exchange market, elaborating on the nature and operation of this market. Chapter 12 explains the international monetary system and provides a basic knowledge of its evolution. Chapter 13 presents an in-depth view of the adjustment mechanism for correcting the balance of payments disequilibrium. Finally, Chapter 14 discusses the policy options a country has when faced with a balance of payments problem.

Chapter 10

THE BALANCE OF PAYMENTS

10.1 INTRODUCTION

Every year the residents of a country engage in numerous transactions with the residents of other nations. Such transactions—which take different forms and range from the export and import of goods, services, and assets to foreign aid and gifts—give rise to the inflow and outflow of foreign exchange (currency) between a nation and the rest of the world. Because the huge volume of such transactions, as presented by myriad accounting data, is hard to understand and interpret individually, it is necessary to classify and aggregate the data into a simple accounting statement known as the balance of payments.

In this chapter, we describe the balance of payments accounting system and explain the methodology for interpreting the different accounts included in this statement. To this end, we first define the concept of the balance of payments and present the U.S. balance of payments as an example. We then discuss the usefulness of the balance of payments from both a country's and a businessperson's standpoints.

10.2 DEFINITION OF THE BALANCE OF PAYMENTS

The balance of payments (BOP) can be defined as an accounting statement that summarizes all transactions between the residents of one nation and the residents of all other nations during a given period of time. In other words, the BOP indicates the amount of foreign currency that was pumped into and out of a nation's economic system during a given period. This definition, although straightforward, requires some clarification.

First, the balance of payments is usually prepared for a calendar year. However, the United States and some other countries also provide their BOP data on a quarterly basis. Second, the term "transactions" here refers to (a) exports and imports of goods, services, and assets for which payments are usually made, and (b) gifts and unilateral transfers for which no payments are made. Third, the term "residents" refers to individuals, business firms, and government agencies that legally reside in the country in question. By this definition, diplomats, military personnel, temporary migrant workers, and tourists are considered residents of their native countries. Similarly, a corporation is regarded as a resident of the country in which it is incorporated. However, the foreign subsidiaries of such corporations are considered residents of the countries in which they are located. Although some of these definitions are arbitrary, they do not pose a problem because the rest of the accounting items take them into account.

10.3 BALANCE OF PAYMENTS ACCOUNTING

The BOP is an accounting statement that, like other accounting statements, is based on a double-entry bookkeeping system. Each business firm prepares four major accounting statements: the income statement, the balance sheet, the statement of retained earnings (or the capital statement in the case of a proprietorship), and the statement of changes in financial position (SCFP). Among these statements, the SCFP for a business firm resembles the BOP for a nation. For a given period, a firm's SCFP presents (a) the sources of funds, that is, where the funds came from; (b) the uses of funds, that is, how the funds were spent; and (c) the net cash, that is, the difference between the first two items. In the same manner, the BOP shows where a nation's foreign exchange came from (the sources of funds in the SCFP) and where it went (the uses of funds in the SCFP).

However, the BOP is not identical to the SCFP. The major difference between them is that some transactions, mainly the exchange of different kinds of real financial assets, are included in the BOP but not in the SCFP. Additionally, while debit and credit entries are recorded simultaneously in a business firm's records, they are often entered independently in international accounting records. This results in a time lag between debit and credit items and causes discrepancies between them. Such discrepancies, included in the BOP as **errors and omissions** or **statistical discrepancy**, do not exist in a firm's statements. The inclusion of the errors and omissions causes the sum of debit items in the balance of payments becomes equal to the sum of credit items, as it should be in the case of all financial statements.

10.3a Debit and Credit Items

The BOP is an international accounting statement, and, like any other accounting statement, it is based on the concept of debits and credits. Thus, international transactions presented in this statement are entered as either debits or credits.

Credit items in the BOP involve the receipt of payments from foreigners. Thus, they give a nation more foreign currency or reduce a foreign nation's holdings of domestic currency. **Debit items,** on the other hand, involve payments to foreigners. These are transactions that use up a nation's foreign currency holdings or increase a foreign nation's holdings of domestic currency. In a nation's BOP, credit items are recorded with a positive sign (+) and debit items are entered with a negative sign (-).

To clarify the concepts of debit and credit, consider the U.S. BOP, which is a financial statement summarizing all debit and credit items between U.S. residents and the residents of the rest of the world. What happens to the U.S. BOP when U.S. residents buy cars from Japan, purchase cameras from Germany, or fly to Canada on a Canadian airline? All these transactions involve payments to foreigners, providing them with more U.S. dollars, and hence are considered debit items. What about foreigners buying U.S. automobiles, IBM computers, or flying on an U.S. airline? These transactions involve payments from foreigners, causing a decrease in foreign nations' holdings of the U.S. dollar, and hence are recorded as credit items in the BOP. What if the United States lends money to a developing country? This transaction represents a debit item, because it involves payment of U.S. dollars to foreigners. Finally, what if some British entrepreneurs invest in Chrysler Corporation by buying some of its stock? This is a credit item because it involves payments from foreigners and causes the British to decrease their dollar holdings.

In summary, imports of goods and services, unilateral transfers (gifts) given to foreigners, and capital outflows are recorded as debits because they result in payments to foreigners. However, exports of goods and services, unilateral transfers (gifts) received from foreigners, and capital inflows are recorded as credit items because they result in the receipt of payments from foreigners.

Before proceeding to the next section, it is necessary to clarify the concept of capital outflows and capital inflows as they are used in U.S. government publications.

Capital outflows are debit items in the BOP which can be defined in two ways:

1. An increase in a country's assets abroad. For example, when a U.S. resident buys a Germany company's stocks , there is an outflow of capital from the United States because it involves payments to foreigners.
2. A decrease in foreign assets in a country. For example, when a British multinational corporation (MNC) sells its subsidiary in the United States to a U.S. firm, there is an outflow of capital from the United States because it involves payments to foreigners.

Capital inflows are credits items in the BOP which can be defined in two ways:

1. An increase in foreign assets in a country. For example, when a Saudi Arabian sheik buys General Motors stock, there is an inflow of capital to the United States because it involves the receipt of payments from foreigners.
2. A decrease in a country's assets abroad. For example, when a U.S. citizen sells Triumph stock in England, there is a capital inflow because it involves the receipt of payments from foreigners.

10.3b Major Accounts in the Balance of Payments

The items presented in a balance of payments can be broken into three major categories: the current account, the capital account, and the compensating (official reserve) account.

The **current account** includes those transactions that do not result in any future obligations. The **capital account** includes those transactions that do involve future obligations. In the previous examples, the United States loan to a developing country and the British investment in the Chrysler Corporation represent capital account items. This is because both of these transactions create future obligations, that is, the developing country's loan has to be repaid, and the investment in Chrysler creates either profits or losses over time. Other examples, involving U.S. residents' purchases of goods and services from foreigners and vice versa, represent current account items because they do not create any future claims or obligations. In general, current account items are caused by (a) purchasing from and selling to foreigners and (b) unilateral transfers—remittances and grants given to or received from foreigners free of charge. Capital account items result when (a) a country invests in foreign nations or when foreign nations invest in that country; (b) a nation provides loans to foreigners or receives loans from foreigners and (c) a nation deposits money in foreign banks or foreigners deposit money in the country's local banks.

Items in the **compensating (Official reserve) account** are a nation's holdings of foreign convertible currencies, gold, and Special Drawing Rights (SDRs). These holdings are used by the nation's monetary authorities to finance its BOP deficit under a fixed exchange rate system or to influence the exchange rate in a floating exchange rate system.*

Compensating items resemble the cash or near-cash holdings of a private company, which provide it with the potential of settling its financial obligations. Because reserve transactions are undertaken only between governments, they are carried out by central banking systems such as the U.S. Federal Reserve system or the Bank of England. A nation's domestic currency does not constitute foreign exchange because it is not, by definition, included in the reserve items.

10.3c Double-Entry Bookkeeping

As we already know, modern accounting is based on the principle of double-entry bookkeeping. According to this principle, each transaction is recorded twice, once as a debit (-) and once as a credit (+). This is because every transaction has two sides that must be recorded. For example, the payment of $500 in wages to a company's workers results in a $500 increase in wages expense (the wages expense account is debited for $500) and a $500 decrease in cash (the cash account is credited for $500).

A nation's BOP is an accounting statement, so it is subject to the principle of double-entry bookkeeping employed in the preparation of all other accounting statements.

For example, assume that the United States exports $1,000 of merchandise to France and is paid with French francs equivalent to $1,000. Because the U.S. exports cause receipts from foreigners (the French), it is recorded as a credit (+) item. As we explain in Chapter 11, the payments and/or receipts for exports and imports are achieved through the foreign exchange market and involve certain documents. In this chapter, however, we ignore these details for the sake of simplicity, to better concentrate on the concepts of double-entry bookkeeping. The payment itself represents a short-term capital outflow from the United States.** This is because the receipt of francs by the United States represents an increase in U.S. claims against French goods and services. This is equivalent to an increase in U.S. assets abroad, and, by definition, it is a short-term capital outflow. This transaction is recorded in the U.S. BOP as follows:

---

*   As we explain in Chapter 12, under the fixed exchange rate system, the exchange rate (the price of a domestic currency in terms of a foreign currency) is pegged at a desired level and is allowed to fluctuate only within a narrow band. Under the floating exchange rate system, however, the exchange rate is defined by the market forces of demand and supply.

   Special drawing rights are international reserve assets devised by the International Monetary Fund (IMF) to complement other international reserves. They are allocated to the IMF's member nations in accordance with their quotas in the IMF.

** *Short-term capital* refers to financial obligations that are either payable on demand or have less than a year to maturity. *Long-term capital*, on the other hand, refers to financial obligations that have a maturity of one year or more. Examples of short-term capital include demand deposits (checking accounts), time deposits (saving accounts), short-term government securities, short-term corporate promissory notes and short-term bank loans. Examples of long-term capital are long-term government or corporate securities and commercial bank certificates of deposit.

	Debit(-)	Credit(+)
Short-term capital outflow	$1,000	
Merchandise exports		$1,000

Now assume that the United States imports $500 of merchandise from Germany and pays for it with U.S. dollars. This transaction is represented in the U.S. BOP as follows:

	Debit(-)	Credit(+)
Merchandise imports	$500	
Short-term capital inflow		$500

In this transaction, the merchandise imports are debited because they represent a payment to foreigners. The payment itself is considered as short-term capital inflow because this transaction results in an increase in Germany's holding of U.S. dollars. In other words, it represents an increase in Germany's claim against U.S. goods and services. This is equivalent to an increase in foreign assets in the United States, and, by definition, it is a short-term capital inflow.

As another example, suppose that a U.S. resident spends $3,000 while vacationing in Mexico. This transaction resembles the import of merchandise because the expenditure of $3,000 by a U.S. tourist in Mexico involves payments to foreigners. It is recorded as follows:

	Debit(-)	Credit(+)
Imports of travel services	$3,000	
Short-term capital inflow		$3,000

Merchandise imports are debited because they represent a payment to foreigners. The payment itself is credited because it represents an increase in foreign holdings of U.S. dollars.

Now assume that the U.S. State Department gives $1,500 to a developing country as a gift (unilateral transfer). This transaction is recorded as follows:

	Debit(-)	Credit(+)
Unilateral transfer	$1,500	
Short-term capital inflow		$1,500

In this transaction, the unilateral transfer is debited because it involves payments to foreigners. The payment itself is credited as capital inflow because it represents an increase in foreign holdings of U.S. dollars.

As another example, assume that a U.S. resident buys stock in Japan's Sony Corporation for $5,000 in cash. This transaction is recorded in the U.S. BOP as follows:

	Debit(-)	Credit(+)
Long-term capital outflow	$5,000	
Short-term capital inflow		$5,000

In this transaction, long-term capital outflow is debited because the purchase of stocks increases U.S. assets abroad. The short-term capital inflow is credited because the payment itself represents an increase in the foreign holdings of U.S. assets, that is, U.S. dollars.

GLOBAL INSIGHTS CASE 10.1

Major U.S. Merchandise Exports and Imports in 1996
(Billions of Dollars)

As an advocate of free international trade the United States has always been active in the global market. The table represents the value of the major goods imported and exported by the United States in 1996. The U.S. imports were dominated by automobile imports (mostly from Japan), petroleum products, computers, semiconductors, and food and beverages. The major U.S. exports were automotive parts and engine (mostly to Canada), food and beverages (a significant portion of which were grains), computers, chemicals, and civilian air crafts and parts. As the table indicates, the United States had a noticeable trade surplus in food and beverages, civilian air crafts and parts, chemicals, and telecommunications equipment. This is indicative of the competitive advantage held by the United States in recent years. The United States noticeable trade deficit in automotive and, computers signifies the eroding competitive position of the United States in high technology products, especially in comparison to Japan.

Major U.S. Merchandise Imports and Exports in 1996
(Billions of Dollars)

Imports		Exports	
Commodity	Value	Commodity	Value
Automotive, vehicle, parts, & engines	128	Automotive, vehicle, parts, & engines	65
Chemical, excluding medicine	26	Chemicals, excluding medicine	42
Civilian and air craft engines and parts	12	Civilian air crafts & parts	30
Computers, Peripherals and parts	61	Computers, peripherals and parts	43
Electrical generating machinery	24	Electric generating machinery	24
Food and Beverages	35	Food and Beverages	56
Nonferrous metals	21	Nonferrous Metals	15
Telecommunication equipment	14	Telecommunication equipment	20
Petroleum	72	Oil drilling, mining, & construction machinery	12
Semiconductors	36	Semiconductors	12
Iron and steel products	17	Energy Products	15

Source: U.S. Department of Commerce, *Survey of Current Business* (Washington, D.C.: U.S. Government Printing Office, July 1997), pp. 78-80.

Assuming that the five preceding examples are the only transactions that have taken place in the United States for a given year, we can present the U.S. BOP as follows:

	Debit(-)	Credit(+)
Merchandise imports	$500	
Merchandise exports		$1,000
Imports of travel service	$3,000	
Unilateral transfers	$1,500	
Long-term capital	$5,000	
Short-term capital		$ 9,000
Total	$10,000	$10,000

In this statement, the $9,000 for short-term capital is obtained by adding up the five short-term capital entries (-$1,000 + $500 + $3,000 + $1,500 + $5,000), and the rest of the entries are reported as they were recorded before.

Although all the debit and credit items were recorded simultaneously in this example, in practice, the BOP is prepared by reporting different items separately. However, as we mentioned before, this does not pose a problem because the equality of debits and credits is maintained by the inclusion of an account referred to as **errors and omissions,** or **statistical discrepancy.**

10.4 THE UNITED STATES' BALANCE OF PAYMENTS

In this section, we provide a detailed explanation of the U.S. BOP and explain the relationship between its different items.

10.4a Significance of the United States' Balance of Payments

The significance of the U.S. BOP, as compared with other countries, is the important role played by the United States in the world economy. Today, approximately 90 percent of the world's trade and investment is denominated in U.S. dollars. Also, under the present international monetary system (explained in Chapter 12), many countries' currencies are still pegged to the U.S. dollar. Finally, as we also explain in Chapter 12, the United States stands as the country with the highest share of SDRs in the world. As Table 12-1 of Chapter 12 indicates, the United States accounted for 18.25 percent of the market value of the total SDRs allocated by the IMF in 1996.

Given these facts, it is necessary for an international manager to understand the U.S. BOP because any change in this statement reflects a change in the U.S. economy and the value of the dollar, indirectly influencing the operation of any international firm.

10.4b The United States' Balance of Payments Statistics

Table 10-1, presenting a summary of the U.S. international transactions for 1995, provides data on the United States BOP. The complete statements of the U.S. international transactions for the years 1994 and 1995 are presented in Table 10.2.

According to Table 10-1 the United States exported (+) $969,189 million of goods and services in 1995. Out of this total, (+) $575,940 million represented merchandise exports (physical goods such as automobiles, computers, chemicals, and so forth) and (+) $210,590 million accounted for exports of services (travel services rendered by the United States to foreigners, fees and royalties received by the United States from its foreign affiliates)[*]. The remaining (+) $182,659 million included interest and dividends gained from U.S. foreign direct investment (FDI) abroad[**].

The U.S. imports of goods and services amounted to (-)$1,082,268 million. Out of this total, (-)$794,634 million accounted for merchandise imports (including different items such as automobiles, petroleum, textiles, television sets, VCRs, and so forth) and (-) $142,230 million represented imports of services (travel services purchased by the U.S. residents from foreigners, fees and royalties paid by the United States to foreigners). The remaining (-) $190,674 includes dividends and interest paid by the United States on foreign investment in the United States.

---

[*]   A debit is shown by (-), and a credit is shown by (+)

[**] Such factor income represents payments for capital services and hence is appropriate to this account

TABLE 10-1
Summary of The U.S. International Transactions for 1995 (Millions of Dollars)

Exports of goods and services	**969,189**
Goods , adjusted, excluding military services	575, 940
Services	210,590
Income receipts on U.S. Assets aborad	182,659
Imports of goods and services	**-1,082,268**
Goods, adjusted, excluding military	-749,364
Services	-142,230
Income payments on foreign assets in the U.S.	-190,674
Unilateral transfer, net	**-35,075**
U.S. government grants	-10,959
U.S. government pensions and other transfers	-3,420
Private remittances and other transfers	-20,696
U.S. assets abroad, net (increase/capital outflow [-])	**-307,856**
U.S. official reserve assets, net	-9,742
U.S. government assets, other than official reserve assets, net	-280
U.S. private assets, net	-297,834
Direct investment abroad	-95,509
Foreign securities	-98,960
U.S. Nonbank claims	-34,219
U.S. Bank claims	-69,146
Foreign assets in the U.S., net (increase/capital inflow[+])	**424,462**
Foreign official assets in the U.S., net	109,757
Other foreign assets in the U.S., net	314,705
Dircct investment in the U.S.	60,236
U.S. Treasury securities	99,340
U.S. securities other than treasury securities	95,268
Nonbank liabilities	34,578
Bank liabilities	25,283
Allocation of special drawing rights	....
Statistical discrepancy	**31,548**
Memoranda:	
Balance on goods	-173,424
Balance on services	68,360
Balance on goods and services	-105,064
Balance on investment income	-8,061
Balance on goods, services and income	-113,079
Unilateral transfers, net	-35,075
Balance on current account	-148,154

Source: U.S. Department of Commerce, Survey of Current Business (Washington, D.C.: U.S. Government Printing Office, July 1996), D-56.

TABLE 10-2
Summary of The U.S. International Transactions (1994-1995) (Millions of Dollars)

Line	(Credit +; Debit -)	1994	1995
1	**Exports of goods, services, and income**	**840,006**	**969,189**
2	Goods , adjusted, excluding military services	502,463	575,940
3	Services	195,839	210,590
4	Transfers under U.S. military agency sales contracts	12,255	13,405
5	Travel	58,417	61,137
6	Passenger fares	17,083	18,534
7	Other transportation	25,861	28,063
8	Royalties and license fees	22,272	26,953
9	Other private services	59,071	61,724
10	U.S. government miscellaneous services	880	775
11	Income receipts on U.S. Assets aborad	141,704	182,659
12	Direct Investment receipts	68,659	88,882
13	Other private receipts	68,946	89,064
14	U.S. government receipts	4,099	4,713
15	**Imports of goods, services, and income**	**-948,544**	**-1,082,268**
16	Goods, adjusted, excluding military	-668,584	-749,364
17	Services	-134,097	-142,230
18	Direct defense expenditures	-10,292	-9,820
19	Travel	-43,782	-45,855
20	Passenger fares	-12,885	-14,313
21	Other transactions	-27,983	-29,205
22	Royalties and license fees	-5,518	-6,312
23	Other private services	-30,980	-33,970
24	U.S. government miscellaneous services	-2,657	-2,755
25	Income payments on foreign assets in the U.S.	-145,863	-190,674
26	Direct investment payments	-21,230	-31,418
27	Other private payments	-77,614	-97,977
28	U.S. government payments	-47,019	-61,279
29	**Unilateral transfer, net**	**-39,866**	**-35,075**
30	U.S. government grants	-15,816	-10,959
31	U.S. government pensions and other transfers	-4,544	-3,420
32	Private remittances and other transfers	-19,506	-20,696
33	**U.S. assets abroad, net (increase/capital outflow [-])**	**-150,695**	**-307,856**
34	U.S. official reserve assets, net	5,346	-9,742
35	Gold	....	....
36	Special drawing rights	-441	-808
37	Reserve position in the international monetary fund	494	-2,466
38	Foreign currencies	5,293	-6,468
39	U.S. government assets, other than official reserve assets, net	-341	-280
40	U.S. credit and other long-term assets	-5,208	-4,640
41	Payments on U.S. credit and other assets	5,052	4,258
42	U.S. foreign currency holdings and U.S. short-term assets, net	-185	102
43	U.S. private assets, net	-155,700	-297,834
44	Direct investment abroad	-54,465	-95,509
45	Foreign securities	-60,270	-98,960
46	U.S. claims on unaffiliated foreigners reported by U.S. nonbanking concerns	-32,804	-34,219
47	U.S. Bank claims reported by U.S. banks, not included elsewhere	-8,161	-69,146
48	**Foreign assets in the U.S., net (increase/capital inflow[+])**	**285,376**	**424,462**
49	Foreign official assets in the U.S., net	40,253	109,757
50	U.S. government securities	36,822	72,547
51	U.S. Treasury securities	30,745	68,813
52	Other	6,077	3,734
53	Other U.S. Government liabilities	2,344	1,082
54	U.S. Liabilities reported by U.S. banks, not included elsewhere	3,560	32,862
55	Other foreign assets	-2,473	3,266
56	Other foreign assets in the United States, net	245,123	314,705
57	Direct Investment	49,760	60,236
58	U.S. Treasury securities	34,225	99,340
59	U.S. securities other than U.S. Treasury securities	57,006	95,268
60	U.S. liabilities to unaffiliated foreigners reported by U.S. nonbanking concerns	-7,710	34,578
61	U.S. liabilities reported by U.S. banks, not included elsewhere	111,842	25,283
62	**Allocations of special drawing rights**	....	....
63	**Statistical discrepancy (sum of above items with sign reversed)**	**13,724**	**31,548**
	Memoranda:		
64	Balance on goods (lines 2 and 16)	-166,121	-173,424
65	Balance on services (lines 3 and 17)	61,742	68,360
66	Balance on goods and services, (lines 64 and 65)	-104,379	-105,064
67	Balance on investment income (lines 11 and 25)	-4,159	-8,016
68	Balance on goods, services, and income (lines 1 and 15 or lines 66 and 67)	-108,539	-113,079
69	Unilateral transfers, net (line 29)	-39,866	-35,075
70	Balance on current account (lines 1, 15, and 29 or lines 68 and 69)	-148,405	-148,154

Source: U.S. Department of Commerce, *Survey of Current Business* (Washington, D.C.: U.S. Government Printing Office, July 1996), D-55.

In 1995, the unilateral transfer made by the United States amounted to (-)$35,075 million. Out of this total, (-)$10,959 million accounted for U.S. government grants to other countries, and (-)$3,420 million represented U.S. government pensions and other transfers. The remaining (-) 20,695 million was made up of private remittances and other transfers to foreign nations. Private remittances and other transfer, refers to gifts made by individuals and nongovernmental institutions to foreigners. Examples include monies sent back home by migrant workers and a contribution that is made by a U.S. resident to relief funds in developing countries. Because the sign of all the items of the unilateral transfers in the U.S. BOP is negative, it indicates that the U.S. residents sent more money abroad than they received.

The U.S. assets abroad increased by the net amount of (-)$307,856 million, as indicated by the negative sign (debit) of this capital outflow item. This amount included a net increase of (-)$9,742 million in the U.S. official reserve assets, a net increase of (-)$280 million in the U.S. government assets other than official reserve assets, and a net increase of (-) $297,834 million in the U.S. private assets abroad.

The (-)$297,834 million net increase in the U.S. official assets abroad itself is composed of (-)$95,509 million increase in the U.S. direct investment abroad, a (-)$98,960 increase in the U.S. holdings of foreign securities, an increase in the U.S. nonbank bank liabilities of (-)$34,219 million, and an increase in U.S. bank liabilities of (-) 69,146.

Foreign assets in the United States increased by the net amount of (+) $424,462 million, as shown by the positive sign (credit) of this capital inflow item. This amount included a net increase of (+) $109,757 million in foreign official assets in the United States, and a net increase of (+) $314,705 million in other foreign assets in the United States. The (+) $314,705 million itself is composed of a (+)$60,236 million increase in the amount of foreign investment in the United States, a net increase of (+) $99,340 million in the U.S. Treasury Securities, held by foreigners, a net increase of (+) $34,578 in U.S. nonbank liabilities, and an increase of (+) $25,283 in U.S. liabilities.

To find the overall credit balance for the U.S. international transactions, we add up all the items with the positive signs as follows:

Exports of goods and Services	(+) $ 969,189
Foreign Assets in the United States, net	(+) $ 424,462
Total Credit	(+) $1, 393,651

To find the overall debit balance for the U.S. international transactions, we add up all the items with the negative signs as follows:

Imports of goods and Services	(-) $ 1,082,268
Unilateral transfers, net	(-) $ 35,075
U.S. assets abroad, net	(-) $ 307,856
Total debits	(-) $ 1,425,199

Because the total amount of debit items, (-) $1,425,199 million, is greater than the total amount of credit items, (+) $1,393,651, by (-) $31,548 million, it is necessary to record an entry called **statistical discrepancy**. This entry is needed to ensure that the sum of debit items in the BOP is equal to the sum of credit items (including the statistical discrepancy). The reason for the existence of this statistical discrepancy, as we mentioned earlier, is that the debit and the credit entries are not recorded simultaneously, causing a time lag between debit and credit items. Also, some transactions may have been valued either incorrectly or may not have been reported at all. The rest of the items recorded in the U.S. balance of payments are discussed in the next.

10.4c Major Accounts in the United States' Balance of Payments

The balances of the three major accounts (current account, capital account, and official reserve account) can be derived from the data presented in the U.S. BOP (Table 10-1).

GLOBAL INSIGHTS CASE 10.2

The Chief Trade Partners of the United States

The value of U.S. exports and imports of goods and services, and the net balance with its 16 chief trade partners in 1996 is shown in the table. As the table indicates, the largest trade partners of the United States in 1996 were respectively Canada, Japan, Mexico, the United Kingdom, and Germany. The table also shows that the United States had trade deficit with 8 (fifty percent) of its 16 major trade partners. The largest trade deficit was with Japan, and then China, Canada, and Mexico. Interestingly about 75 percent of the United States trade deficit with Japan is related to U.S. automobile imports from Japan. This has been a sore issue with the United States and has led to trade disagreements between these two major trade partners.

U.S. Exports and Imports of Goods and Services and Net Balance With its Chief Trade Partners in 1996
(billions of dollars)

Nation	Exports	Imports	Net Balance
Austria	11.7	3.8	7.6
Belgium-Luxembourg	12.6	9.4	3.1
Brazil	12.3	8.7	3.5
Canada	134.6	158.4	-24.0
China	11.9	51.5	-39.5
France	14.5	18.6	- 4.1
Germany	22.9	38.8	-15.8
Hong Kong	13.8	9.8	4.0
Italy	8.6	18.2	-9.6
Japan	65.9	115.9	-49.2
Korea, Republic of	26.6	22.6	3.0
Mexico	56.7	75.1	-18.3
Netherlands	16.5	7.4	9.0
Singapore	16.2	20.0	-4.0
United Kingdom	30.2	28.8	1.4
Taiwan	17.5	29.9	-12.3

Source: U.S. Department of Commerce, *Survey of Current Business* (Washington, D.C.: U.S. Government Printing Office, July 1997), pp.74-76.

The memoranda section of this table presents six different balances. Each of these balances is obtained by adding up all the relevant credit (+) items and debit (-) items and reporting the results. The sixth item shows that the balance of the current account was (-) $148,154 for 1995. As we already know, the current account is the sum of all purchases and sales of goods and services and unilateral transfers. In fact, this figure can be calculated from Table 10-1 by adding up the balance of goods, services, and income [(-) $113,079 million] and the unilateral transfer [(-) $35,075].

The U.S. capital account balance can be calculated by adding up the changes in U.S. assets abroad (excluding official reserve assets) and foreign assets in the United States (excluding official reserve assets) during the year. From Table 10-1, the change in U.S. assets abroad, excluding official reserve assets, was (-) $298,114 million, which is calculated as (-) $307,856 - (-) $9,742. The change in foreign assets in the United States, excluding reserve assets, was (+) $314,705 million, which is calculated as (+) $424,462 - (+) $109,757. Thus, the U.S. capital account balance is (+) $1,691 million, which is calculated as (-) $298,114 + (+) $314,705.

Finally, the official reserve account balance is (+) $100,015 million, which is calculated by adding net U.S. official reserve assets [(-) $9,742] and net foreign official assets in the U.S. [(+) $109,757 million], as reported in Table 10-1.

10.5 MEASURES OF BOP DEFICITS AND SURPLUSES

As we explained earlier, the inclusion of a statistical discrepancy item always causes the balance of payments to balance. This means that the sum of debit items in the BOP is always equal to the sum of credit items. However, from an economics standpoint, concepts of surplus and deficit have been developed to measure disequilibrium in the BOP. The method for presenting a measure of surplus and deficit is to divide transactions in the BOP into two major groups known as autonomous and accommodating items. **Autonomous items**, referred to as **above-the-line items**, are regarded as those transactions that take place for their own sake, irrespective of the balance of payments position. These include all transactions that take place in response to business conditions at home and abroad. The rest of the items in the BOP are referred to as **accommodating items**, or **below-the-line items**. These transactions, also referred to as compensating items, are viewed as items that could be used to compensate for the BOP surplus or deficit. Depending on the type of transactions included in autonomous and accommodating items, different methods could be used for defining BOP surplus or deficit.

Before May 1976, the U.S. BOP showed different balances. These were (1) the balance on goods and services; (2) the balance on goods, services, and remittances; (3) the balance on the current account; (4) the balance on the current account and long-term capital (basic balance); (5) the net liquidity balance; and (6) the official reserve transactions balance.

The names of these balances indicates the kinds of transactions that are considered to be autonomous. For example, in defining the **balance of goods and services,** "goods and services" are considered as autonomous transactions. By this definition, the surplus or deficit measures the country's achievement as an international trader. The second item, the **balance of goods, services, and remittances**, is similar to the first item, except that it considers remittances, that is, U.S. government pensions and private remittances, as autonomous transactions as well. The third item, the current account balance, goes one step further than the second item and includes U.S. government grants as autonomous transactions. The balance presented by this account resembles the net profit of a business enterprise that results from its current operations.

The **basic balance** considers the current account items and long-term capital transactions as autonomous. The purpose of presenting this balance is to measure the underlying structural changes in a country's balance of payments. In other words, the basic balance measures the long-run trends in a nation's BOP. Such trends are not affected by short-run economic conditions such as interest rates, exchange rates, and monetary policies. However, they are influenced by long-run changes in international competition, factor productivity, factor endowment, and so forth.

The net **liquidity balance** is more complete than the basic balance, considering nonliquid short-term capital flows such as loans and acceptances as autonomous. The term **liquidity** refers to money or assets that could quickly be exchanged for money. Thus, the net liquidity balance emphasizes the international liquidity position of a country. In other words, it shows the amount of domestic currency (dollars) that have been accrued to foreigners as the result of autonomous transactions. Under the system of gold standards that existed before 1971, therefore, the holders of the U.S. dollars could demand gold in return for their dollars, and the net liquidity balance was a measure of pressure on the U.S. international reserve asset, that is, the U.S. gold reserve.

The **official reserve transactions balance (ORT)** considers all private international transactions as autonomous. This would leave only the net official reserve position as an accommodating (compensating) account. The net official reserve position includes reserve assets (gold and convertible currencies) and changes in liabilities to foreign official agencies.

Under a fixed exchange rate system, reserve assets are needed by a country to finance its BOP deficits.* The ORT was provided by the United States to reflect such a pressure on its BOP.

---

* This is because there is no *a priori* expectation that the sum of all autonomous transactions will balance, that is, add up to zero.

In 1976, three years after the United States adopted the managed floating exchange rate system, it was realized that the preparation of all of these balances were not necessary.[*] The major reason behind this decision was the recognition that under the system of managed floating, pressure on the dollar is transmitted to the foreign exchange market, causing its value to fluctuate. In this system, the official reserve is only used to set the dollar value at a desired level by intervening in the foreign exchange market. Thus, the loss of the official reserve is not an indicator of the exact size of the BOP deficit (surplus), but it is a measure of the degree of government intervention in the foreign exchange market.

As Table 10-1 indicates, the United States calculated seven partial balances that were reported in the memoranda of the BOP. These were (1) the balance on goods; (2) the balance on services; (3) the balance on goods and services; (4) the balance on investment and income; (5) the balance of goods, services and income; (6) the balance on net unilateral transfers; and (7) the balance on current account. But, for the reason discussed earlier, the official reserve transactions balance, the basic balance, and the net liquidity balance were not published. However, they could be easily derived from the BOP, and their understanding is necessary because they still appear in writings on international finance. Given the present international monetary system, these concepts should be interpreted with caution and must be supplemented with the analysis of the exchange rate.

10.6 INTERNATIONAL INVESTMENT POSITION

A country's international financial status can be further evaluated by an accounting statement known as the **international investment position (IIP)** or, as it is often referred to, the balance of international indebtedness. This statement shows the total amount and distribution of a country's assets abroad and foreign assets at home at a given point in time. The IIP is useful in providing us with information that can be used in projecting the future flow of income generated from a country's foreign investments.

In comparison to a nation's BOP, which shows the "flow" or rate of change of goods, services, and capital over a given period of time, the IIP provides us with the "stock" of a nation's foreign assets and liabilities at a given point in time (namely, the end of a year).

Although more attention is paid to the BOP, the two statements usually are interrelated and are analyzed together. In fact, the IIP provides us with the stock that corresponds to the flows given by the BOP's capital account and reserve items. Theoretically speaking, if we add a nation's capital flows during the current year to its IIP at the end of the preceding year, the sum should give the nation's IIP at the end of the current year. In reality, however, measurement problems prevent this.

Table 10-3 shows the IIP of the United States at the end of selected years, 1980-1995. The U.S. *net international investment position* (NIIP) in the United States, that is, Item A in the table, is obtained by subtracting the foreign assets in the United States (Item C) from the U.S. assets abroad (Item B). Because at the end of the year 1995 foreign assets in the United States ($3,745,880 million) were greater than U.S. assets abroad ($2,931,904 million), this gave the United States a negative number for the U.S. net international position of (-)$813,976. A negative NIIP did not occur until 1987 and still had not recovered by 1995.[**]

The decrease in the U.S. NIIP, which has been occurring for the last few years, is depicted by Item A in Table 10-3 for the years 1980 through 1995. This decrease is related to the relatively higher growth of foreign assets in the United States as compared with the growth of the U.S. assets abroad during the period 1980-1995. Foreign assets in the United States grew by 589 percent (from $543,728 million in 1980 to $3,745,880 million in 1995), whereas the U.S. assets abroad grew only by about 213 percent (from $936,275 million in 1980 to $2,931,904 million in 1995).

The increase in foreign assets in the United States is caused by several interrelated factors: (1) the relatively high yields on U.S. securities; (2) the relatively high interest rates in the United States as compared with other industrial

---

[*] We explain in chapter 12 that, as with the freely floating exchange rate system, under the managed floating exchange rate system, the exchange rate is determined by the market forces of demand and supply. However, unlike the freely floating exchange rate system, governments can intervene in the foreign exchange market to advance their national exchange rate policies.

[**] Statistics on assests and liabilities started to be complied in a systematic fasion in 1919.

nations; (3) the relatively higher economic growth in the United States as compared with other countries; and (4) the strong U.S. demand for foreign funds.

One of the factors that has contributed to the worsening of the NIIP of the United States is foreign direct investment (FDI). Although U.S. FDI abroad ($880,123 million in 1995) is still greater than the FDI in this country ($638,519 million in 1995), the latter has experienced a much faster growth. As Table 10.3 indicates, during the 1980-1995 period, the growth of the U.S. FDI abroad was 122 percent (from $396,249 million in 1980 to $880,123 million in 1995), as compared with the growth of the FDI in the United States, which was about 407 percent (from $125,944 million in 1980 to $638,519 million in 1995).

TABLE 10-3
U.S. International transactions, years 1980-1995 (Millions of Dollars)

Description	1980	1985	1990	1995
A. Net international investment position of the U.S.	392,547	139,056	-291,900	-813,976
B. U.S. assets abroad	936,275	1,252,641	1,942,780	2,931,904
U.S. official reserve assets	171,412	117,930	174,664	176,061
Gold	155,816	85,834	102,406	101,279
SDRs	2,610	7,293	10,989	11,037
Reserve position in the IMF	2,852	11,947	9,076	14,649
Foreign currencies	10,134	12,856	52,193	49,096
Government assets other than reserve assets	63,865	87,752	82,165	81,548
U.S. private assets:	700,998	1,046,959	1,667,951	2,674,296
Direct investment abroad	396,249	387,183	622,653	880,123
Foreign securities	62,454	112,839	229,279	721,749
Other private assets	242,295	546,937	816,019	1,072,424
C. Foreign assets in the U.S.	543,728	1,113,585	2,216,680	3,745,880
Foreign official assets in the U.S.	176,062	202,482	375,614	677,910
Direct investment in the U.S.	125,944	231,326	468,242	638,519
Other foreign assets in the U.S.	241,722	679,777	1,372,824	2,429,451

Source: U.S. Department of Commerce, *Survey of Current Business* (Washington, D.C.: U.S. Government Printing Office), Various Issues.

GLOBAL INSIGHTS CASE 10.3

Countertrade

A recent advance in international trade that has attracted a great deal of attention is the growth of countertrade. Countertrade was originated in the 1970s by East-West traders. However, it became internationally popular in the 1980s, encompassing much of developing nations' trade and even some of the trade among advanced nations.

Countertrade is a process by which an importing nation imposes conditions that link its imports with exports and, as a result, minimizes the net outflow of foreign exchange from its economy. Countertrade is usually practiced by nations with small reserves of foreign currencies or tightly controlled economies.

The process can take the following forms:

1. In a *simple barter,* imported goods are traded for commodities of equal value produced domestically. Simple barter is the oldest form of countertrade and is practiced when foreign exchange reserves or credit is not available for one or both of the trading nations. For example, the Russian government has arranged to swap vodka for Pepsi syrup and bottling equipment from the U.S. firm Pepsico. Volkswagen (of the former West Germany) used to sell compact automobiles to East Germany in return for canned hams. As a result, East Germany received cars plus marketing services for hams. From the countertrader's (East Germany's) point of view, imported cars and marketing services for the sale of excess ham were more cheaply obtained when bundled together.

2. *Buy-back,* or compensation trading, usually consists of the export of a technology package, the construction of an entire project, or the provision of services by a firm. In return, the buyer pays the supplier by delivering a share of the project's future output. For example, Volkswagen constructed an engine production plant in East Germany. Based on a buy-back agreement for a certain period of time, Volkswagen receives a fixed number of engines produced in that plant every year.

3. In a *counterpurchase agreement,* or parallel barter, a seller is paid partially in terms of credit that must be used to purchase products from a prespecified list. Such a purchase is subject to time and availability constraints. In addition, part of the payment may be made in hard currencies. For example, Iran increasingly uses counterpurchase. In order to keep abreast of its need for certain imported essentials, such as food, pharmaceuticals, and certain machinery, Iran has entered into counterpurchase agreements with many other nations. Accordingly, Iran pays for the purchases with a list of products, including oil.

4. A *switch trade* is used when the products received from the exporter are of no use to the importer or cannot be converted to cash. The original exporter may then barter the products received in trade for other products that may be sold for cash. This chain of transactions may be repeated a number of times. For example, in the late 1980s, Brazil exported corn to East Germany and received various products in return; the German products were then sold for hard currency.

5. *Offset trading* is contingent on an exporter procuring a portion of the raw materials or components used in its products from local sources. For example, a country purchasing equipment from the U.S. firm LTV may require that certain parts of the equipment be produced or assembled locally.

6. *Evidence accounts* are the agreements between an exporter and one or more foreign trade organizations from the importing nation. Based on this agreement, the exporter sells a prearranged amount of goods or services to the foreign trade organization and in return buys local products from the same or other organizations to balance the account. The importing country's bank of foreign trade and a bank in the exporter's country simultaneously maintain an evidence account to ensure the transaction balance. This arrangement fit well with the central economic planning systems of the former Eastern bloc countries.

In summary, countertrade is increasing in popularity. Countertrade is usually a cost-saving arrangement, and sometimes it improves the efficiency of trade. Contrary to common belief, countertrade is not detrimental to the growth of international business. Countertrade is generally a national response to environmental constraints and market imperfections. Therefore, it does not necessarily represent inefficient economic exchange.

Source: This case was written by Professor Bahman Ebrahimi of the University of Denver.

10.7 USEFULNESS OF THE BALANCE OF PAYMENTS

The information provided by the BOP is useful for both government authorities and businesspersons.

From the government standpoint, the BOP can be used in planning a country's commercial, fiscal, and monetary policies. Different items recorded in the BOP can help government authorities analyze the nation's economic relations with other countries. For example, they can look at the current account to assess the normal channels of receipts and payments from current economic activities. They also can study the long-term capital transactions inflow to assess the country's comparative advantage in investment opportunities. They can even determine the country's ability to intervene in the foreign exchange market by looking at its official reserve transactions account.

From a business standpoint, the BOP is affected by and also affects business activities. The influence of business activities on the BOP stems from the fact that the major items recorded in the BOP are generated by business. These items include imports and exports of goods and services; inflows and outflows of capital; and receipts and payments of dividends, fees, royalties, and rents from foreign operations.

Business activities are affected by the BOP because it is an indicator of a country's economic health. If a country is experiencing a BOP deficit, it is important for a businessperson to know what corrective action government authorities may use to alleviate the problem. If the government chooses depreciation or devaluation of the national currency, exports may be expected to rise and imports may be expected to fall.* However, if the government calls for the imposition of import tariffs or quotas, imports of certain raw materials and goods can be expected to fall. Because each of these policy options has different implications for business operations, it is important for the business manager to know which options might be chosen so that he or she can adjust the company's strategy accordingly.

10.8 SUMMARY

1. The balance of payments (BOP) can be defined as an accounting statement that summarizes all transactions between the residents of one nation and the residents of all other nations during a given period of time (usually a calendar year).
2. Credit items in the BOP involve the receipt of payments from foreigners. Thus, they give a nation more foreign currency or reduce a foreign nation's holdings of domestic currency. These items include exports of goods and services, unilateral transfers received from foreigners, and capital inflows.
3. Debit items in the BOP involve payments to foreigners. These are transactions that use up a nation's foreign currency holdings or increase a foreign nation's holdings of domestic currency. These items include imports of goods and services, unilateral transfers given to foreigners, and capital outflows.
4. Capital outflow can be defined as (a) an increase in a country's assets abroad, or (b) a decrease in foreign assets in a country.
5. Capital inflow can be defined as (a) an increase in foreign assets in a country, or (b) a decrease in a country's assets abroad.
6. The major accounts in the BOP are the current account, the capital account, and the compensating (reserve) account.
7. The current account includes those transactions that do not result in any future obligations. These transactions include (a) purchasing from and selling to foreigners and (b) unilateral transfers—remittances and grants given to foreigners free of charge.
8. The capital account includes those transactions that involve future obligations. These transactions include (a) investing in foreign nations, or when foreign nations invest in that country (b) providing loans to foreigners, or receiving loans from foreigners and (c) depositing money in foreign banks or foreigners depositing money in country's local banks.

---

*   As we explain in detail in chapter 13, the depreciation or the devaluation of a national currency causes its value to decrease as compared with foreign currencies. Thus, if the German mark is devalued, its value in terms of the U.S. dollar would decrease. This means that each mark commands less dollars (or each dollar commands more marks). As a result, the value of Germany's products in terms of the dollar would decrease. However, the value of its imports in terms of the dollar would increase. This may lead to higher exports and lower imports for Germany, improving its BOP deficit.

9. Compensating accounts are a nation's holdings of foreign convertible currencies, gold, and Special Drawing Rights (SDRs). These holdings are used by the nation's monetary authorities to finance its BOP deficit under a fixed exchange rate system or to influence the exchange rate in a floating exchange rate system.

10. The method for presenting measures of surplus and deficit in the BOP is to divide transactions into two major groups known as autonomous and accommodating items.

11. Autonomous items, also referred to as above-the-line items, are those transactions that take place for their own sake, irrespective of the BOP position. These include all transactions that take place in response to business conditions at home and abroad. The rest of the items in the BOP are referred to as accommodating (compensating) items, or below-the-line items. These transactions are those that can be used to compensate for the BOP surplus or deficit.

12. The United States calculated six partial balances that were reported in the 1996 BOP memoranda.

13. The international investment position (IIP), or balance of international indebtedness, is a statement that shows the total amount and distribution of a country's assets abroad and foreign assets at home at a given point in time (namely, the end of a year).

14. The increase in foreign assets in the United States has been caused by (a) relatively high yields on U.S. securities, (b) relatively high interest rates in the United States compared with those of other industrial nations, (c) relatively higher economic growth in the United States compared with that of other countries, and (d) the strong U.S. demand for foreign funds.

15. The information provided by the BOP is useful for both government authorities and businesspersons. From the government standpoint, the BOP can be used in planning a country's commercial, fiscal, and monetary policies. From a business standpoint, the BOP is useful because it is an indicator of a country's economic health, which must be considered in planning any firm's strategies.

Review Questions

1. Explain the concept of the double-entry bookkeeping system. Why does the application of this system to the balance of payments (BOP) result in an entry called "statistical discrepancy?"

2. Explain the method used for presenting a measure of surplus or deficit in the BOP.

3. What balances were presented by the United States to measure the BOP deficit prior to May 1976? What balances are presented now? Why?

4. Describe the pattern of the U.S. net international position in recent years. What factors have shaped this pattern? Explain.

5. Distinguish between capital outflow and capital inflow, providing some examples.

6. Distinguish between autonomous items and accommodating items. What types of transactions are included in each of these items? Explain.

7. What is meant by the international investment position (IIP)? How does a nation's IIP differ from its BOP? Explain.

8. Elaborate on the usefulness of a nation's IIP from the standpoint of (a) the government and (b) business.

Problems

1. Use the most recent copy of the U.S. BOP, printed in the current issue of the *Survey of Current Business,* to answer the following questions.
   (a) Does the United States have a deficit or a surplus in its current account? What is its size?
   (b) Explain how the balances shown in the memoranda section are determined.
   (c) Explain how the statistical discrepancy was determined.
   (d) Calculate the capital account balance and the official reserve balance.

2. Show how each of the following items is recorded (debited and credited) in the U.S. BOP:
   (a) The importation of $1,000 worth of goods by a U.S. resident from a German resident who has agreed to be paid in six months.

(b) The U.S. resident's payment with a check that is drawn on his or her German bank account after the six-month period has expired.

(c) The purchase of $5,000 worth of Mercedes-Benz stock in Germany by a U.S. resident.

(d) The transfer of $2,000 in cash as a gift from a U.S. resident to a relative in Germany.

(e) A U.S. resident's receipt of a $500 dividend from Mercedes-Benz in Germany.

3. What is the difference between a country's BOP and its IIP? Is it possible for a country to have a BOP deficit and, at the same time, strengthen its international economic status? Explain.

4. The following data is derived from the United States balance of payments for 1991:

Exports of goods, services and income	(+) $704,914 million
Imports of goods, services and income	(-) $716,624 million
Unilateral transfers, net	(+) $8,028 million
U.S. assets abroad, net	(-) $62,220 million
Foreign assets in the U.S., net	(+) $66,980 million

Given these data, answer the following questions.

(a) What is the overall debit balance for U.S. international transactions?

(b) What is the overall credit balance for U.S. international transactions?

(c) What is the amount of statistical discrepancy? Explain.

Suggested Readings

Asheghian, Parviz. "The Impact of Devaluation on the Balance of Payments of Less Developed Countries: A Monetary Approach." *Journal of Economic Development* (July 1985): 143-151.

Congdon, Tim. "A New Approach to the Balance of Payments." *Lloyd's Bank Review,* no. 146 (October 1982): 1-14.

Gray, Peter H. *International Trade, Investment, and Payments.* Boston: Houghton Mifflin, 1979.

Hooper, C., and C. Mann. *The Emergence and Persistence of the U.S. External Imbalances: 1980-1987.* Studies in International Finance. Princeton, NJ: Princeton University, October 1989.

Hooper, Peter, and J. David Richardson, eds. *International Economic Transactions.* Chicago: University of Chicago Press, 1991. International Monetary Fund. *Balance of Payments Manual,* 4th ed. Washington, DC: International Monetary Fund, 1977. International Monetary Fund. *Balance of Payments Yearbook.* Washington, DC: International Monetary Fund (published annually).

Johnson, Harry G. *Money, Balance of Payments Theory and the International Monetary Problem.* Princeton, NJ: Princeton University Press, 1977.

Johnson, Harry G. *The Monetary Approach to the Balance of Payments.* Winchester, MA: Allen & Unwin, 1975.

Kuwayma, Patricia H. "Measuring the United States Balance of Payments." *Monthly Review* (Federal Reserve Bank of New York) (August 1975): 183-194.

Lipsey, R. E. "Changing Patterns of International Investment in and by the United States." In M. S. Feldstein, *The United States in the World Economy.* Chicago: University of Chicago Press, 1988, 475-545.

Scholl, Russel B. Jeffrey H. Lowe, and Sylvia E. Bargas. "The International Investment of the United States in 1990." *Survey of Current Business.* Washington DC: U.S. Government Printing Office, June 1992, 42-55.

Stern, Robert M., et al. *The Presentation of the U.S. Balance of Payments: A Symposium.* Essays in International Finance Series, no. 123. Princeton, NJ: Princeton University Press, 1977.

Storm, R. *The Balance of Payments: Theory and Economic Policy.* Chicago: Aldine, 1973, Ch. 3. United States Department of Commerce, Bureau of Economic Analysis. *The Balance of Payments of the United States: Concepts, Data Sources, and Estimating Procedures.* Washington DC: U.S. Government Printing Office, May 1990.

United States Department of Commerce, Bureau of Economic Analysis. *Survey of Current Business.* Washington, DC: U.S. Government Printing Office (published monthly).

Whitman, Marina. "The Payments Adjustment Process and the Exchange Rate Regime: What Have We Learned?" *American Economic Review* (May 1975): 133-136.

Chapter 11

THE FOREIGN EXCHANGE MARKET

11.1 INTRODUCTION

One of the significant factors that differentiates international trade from domestic trade is the existence of different national currencies. In domestic transactions, usually only one currency is used.[*] For example, the dollar is used in the United States, while the deutsche mark, dinar, franc, pound, and yen are employed in Germany, Kuwait, France, England, and Japan, respectively. In international transactions, however, two or more currencies are involved. For example, a U.S. importer who wants to purchase French wine has dollars, whereas the French exporter who makes the sale demands francs in return. Thus, there are two currencies involved, necessitating the existence of a mechanism that allows the settlement of this international transaction so that both parties' requirements are met. Such a mechanism is the foreign exchange market.

The purpose of this chapter is to provide a basic understanding of the foreign exchange market. First, we define the concept of the foreign exchange market and describe the instruments used in the market and the export shipment process. Next, we elaborate on the functions of commercial banks in the market and discuss different types of foreign exchange transactions. We also describe the Eurocurrency market. Finally, we provide an explanation of international banking.

11.2 DEFINITION OF THE FOREIGN EXCHANGE MARKET

The **foreign exchange market (FEM)** can be defined as a market within which individuals, business firms, governments, and banks purchase and sell foreign currencies and other debt instruments. In this definition, the term *market* does not refer to any centralized meeting place, nor does it involve any one country. For example, the foreign exchange market for any currency, such as the U.S. dollar, consists of all locations where U.S. dollars are purchased and sold for other national currencies. These locations include Amsterdam, Frankfurt, Hong Kong, London, Milan, New York, Zurich, Paris, and Toronto. Trading among these locations is not subject to any formal requirements for participation and is usually performed using the telephone network and video screens.

11.3 FUNCTIONS OF THE FOREIGN EXCHANGE MARKET

The FEM's principal function is the provision of a mechanism by which funds in domestic currency from one nation are transferred to another nation in its currency. In this manner, the FEM performs a clearinghouse function. It brings together parties who want to exchange their currencies and enables them to clear their balances on the basis of the market exchange rate.

Participants in the FEM are commercial banks, the commercial banks' customers, and central banks. The transactions undertaken by these parties can be classified into four levels: (a) transactions between commercial banks and their customers, (b) indirect transactions between commercial banks through their brokers, (c) transactions between banks and their foreign subsidiaries, and (d) central bank transactions.

At the first level, tourists, investors, exporters, and importers purchase and sell foreign currencies from and to commercial banks. The demand for foreign currencies originates when tourists go abroad, when a firm imports goods and services from abroad, when a domestic firm invests in other countries, and so on. The supply of foreign currencies, however, stems from the expenses of foreign tourists in a country, the foreign investment in the nation,

---

[*] Some countries, including most developing nations and Russia, may accept a strong currency like the U.S. dollar in their domestic transactions.

the nation's exports of goods and services, and so on. A nation's commercial banks provide the clearinghouse that brings together those who demand and those who supply foreign currencies, allowing foreign exchange transactions to take place.

At the second level, commercial banks deal indirectly with each other through foreign exchange brokers who act as intermediaries. The purpose of these transactions is to allow commercial banks to even out the flow of foreign exchange among themselves. Whenever a commercial bank does not have its desired amount of foreign currency, it can turn to a foreign exchange broker to purchase additional foreign currency or sell its unwanted surplus. Thus, foreign exchange brokers act as wholesalers of foreign currencies, operating in an interbank market where commercial banks deal in foreign currencies.

At the third level, commercial banks deal with their overseas branches. This allows them to match the demand for foreign currencies with the supply of those currencies in their banking system. In the United States, although several banks engage in foreign exchange transactions, the major New York banks usually carry out transactions with foreign banks. Other banks in the United States maintain a correspondence relationship with the New York banks in order to meet their foreign exchange needs.

At the fourth level, the nation's central banks engage in foreign exchange transactions to control the value of their currencies. As we explain in detail in Chapter 12, under the managed floating exchange rate system, if the demand for a foreign currency in a country exceeds the supply of that currency, it causes the price of the foreign currency (measured in terms of domestic currency) to rise. To set the price at a desired level, the nation's central bank could sell that foreign currency, causing its price to decline. On the other hand, if the demand for a foreign currency falls short of its supply, its prices would decline. In this case, the central bank could buy that foreign currency, causing its price to rise to the desired level.

11.4 FOREIGN EXCHANGE INSTRUMENTS

Because residents of all countries usually want to be paid in their own currencies when dealing in international business, different financial means are needed to make such payments possible. These means, referred to as **foreign exchange instruments,** are written or printed financial documents that allow the payment of funds from one country and one currency to another country and another currency. Chief among these instruments are cable (telegraphic) transfers, commercial bills of exchange (commercial drafts), bank drafts, and letters of credit.

In the following section, we provide an explanation of these instruments and then elaborate on certain documents that must accompany these instruments in any export transaction.

11.4a Cable Transfers

The cable (telegraphic) transfer is the most important financial instrument used in international business. A **cable transfer** is an order transmitted by a bank in one country to its foreign correspondent in another country, instructing the correspondent bank to pay out a specific amount to a designated person or account. For example, consider a U.S. importer in New York who is importing £50,000 worth of Scotch whiskey from a British exporter in London. At an exchange rate of $2 = £1, the importer could pay for the whiskey by buying a cable transfer for £50,000 from a local bank and paying $100,000 (plus any bank service charges) to that bank. The New York bank then calls its correspondent bank in England to transfer £50,000 from its account into the exporter's account. The main advantage of cable transfers is the speed at which payments are made. Normally the funds are transferred within one or two days following the transaction.

11.4b Commercial Bills of Exchange

A **commercial bill of exchange** is a written order by an exporter (the drawer) to an importer (the drawee), instructing the importer to pay on demand, or on a certain date, a specified amount of money to a designated party (the payee). The payee could be either the exporter or a local bank where the exporter has an account. A bill of exchange that is payable on presentation to the drawee is referred to as a **sight bill.** A bill that is payable at some future date is known as a **time bill.** A time bill is usually expressed in terms of the days after sight, such as a "30-day sight bill," or a "60-day sight bill."

Using our previous example, if the payment for the Scotch whiskey import were to be made by a commercial bill of exchange, the British exporter (the drawer) would instruct the U.S. importer (the drawee) to transfer the stated amount (£50,000) at a given time, for example, 30, 60, or 90 days after all the whisky was delivered to New York. The transfer would be made to a designated bank in England or directly to the British exporter. An example of a 60-day time draft (the term **time draft** is synonymous with **time bill**) used in such a transaction is shown in Figure 11-1.

When a commercial bill of exchange is presented to the drawee, the willingness to honor the bill is expressed by writing "accepted" on the face of the bill, followed by the date and the signature of the drawee. The bill then becomes an acceptance and is legally binding. The accepted bill is called **trade acceptance.** The exporter may hold the trade acceptance until the maturity date or sell it at a discount to his or her local bank, to some other banks, or to an acceptance dealer.

11.4c Bank Drafts

A **bank draft** is similar to a commercial bill of exchange in the sense that it is a written order by a drawer to a drawee instructing him or her to pay, on demand or at a certain date, a specified amount of money to a payee. The major difference between these two financial instruments is that in the case of a bank draft, the drawee is a bank rather than an importer. In other words, a bank draft directs the exporter to receive payments directly from a bank designated by the importer. Usually this involves a bank in the importer's country instructing its correspondent bank in the exporter's country to pay the specified amount to the exporter. Thus, a bank draft is also a check.

Using our previous example of whisky imports, if a bank draft were used as the payment instrument, the drawee would be the U.S. importer's designated bank (that is, the London-based correspondent bank of the importer's bank in New York) rather than the importer.

As in the case of a commercial bill of exchange, the willingness of the drawee (the bank in this case) to honor the bill is declared by writing "accepted" on the face of the bill. An accepted bank draft is referred to as a **bank acceptance.** Like a trade acceptance, the bank acceptance may either be held until maturity or sold at a discount.

FIGURE 11-1

This is an example of a 60-day time draft (time draft is synonymous with time bill) used in international transactions.

£ 50,000.00   LONDON, ENGLAND,   January 1, 19 ____

Sixty days after sight-- PAY TO THE

ORDER OF The British Exporter (or its bank)

Fifty thousand and 00/100--- POUNDS

VALUE RECIEVED AND CHARGED TO ACCOUNT OF

TO The American Importer   Drawer The British Exporter

NO: 815   New York, N.Y.   London, England

11.4d Letters of Credit

A **letter of credit** is a document issued by an importer's bank declaring that payments will be made to an exporter regarding a specific shipment of commodities. The letter is accompanied by the required shipment documents. Compared to the bill of exchange, a letter of credit is a safer document in the sense that it assures payment on a certain date. With a bill of exchange, there is always the possibility that the importer will not make the payment to the exporter at the specified time. The letter of credit, however, has the guarantee of the importer's bank obliging that bank to accept the bill when it is presented.

Using our whisky example, if the British exporter were unsure of the U.S. importer's creditability, he or she could request a letter of credit. In this case, the importer would request a local bank to issue a letter of credit in favor of the British exporter. The New York bank would then inform the British exporter that it had issued a letter of credit on the exporter's behalf. This allows the exporter to draw a bill of exchange against the New York bank rather than against the U.S. importer. When the bank accepted the bill, it would become a bank acceptance. The exporter could then endorse the bank acceptance and sell it at a discount in the money market.

When the letter of credit is guaranteed by the importer's bank, the exporter still bears the risk of that bank revoking the letter of credit. There is also the risk of the importer's bank failing and the risk of nonpayment that might result from new exchange restrictions. To avoid these risks the exporter may request a confirmed, or irrevocable, letter of credit. A **confirmed letter of credit** means that the payment is guaranteed not only by the importer's bank but also by the exporter's bank. In our example, the British exporter could draw a bill of exchange on a London bank for £50,000, and this bank would be obliged to confirm the bill. If the bill were a sight bill, the exporter would be paid immediately by the London bank. However, if the bill were a time bill, the exporter would receive a bank acceptance that could easily be sold at a discount in the money market.

11.4e Other Means of Payment

In addition to payment through foreign exchange instruments, an exporter has the option of dealing with an importer either on a cash basis or on an open account basis. *Cash payment* is especially attractive when the exporter is not sure of the importer's creditworthiness and considers the transaction risky. An *open account* is usually used when a parent-subsidiary relationship exists between the exporter and importer, or when the exporter is confident of the importer's creditability. When this option is chosen, the exporter simply ships the merchandise to the importer along with the necessary documents, without any prior payment or obligation on the part of the importer.

11.5 EXPORT SHIPMENT PROCESS

The payment for an export transaction is settled through a documentary draft. A **documentary draft** is a draft that is accompanied by certain documents. An importer cannot secure the imported goods unless these documents are released to him or her. The documents are released to the importer, upon his or her acceptance or payment of the draft, giving the importer the right to claim the goods at the port of entry. Two types of documentary drafts may be used. If the exporter has no question about the importer's creditworthiness, a **documentary-acceptance (D/A) draft** is used. In this case, the documents are released to the importer upon his or her acceptance of the draft. However, if the exporter does have questions about the importer's creditworthiness, a **documentary-on-payment (D/P) draft** is used. In this case, the documents are released to the importer upon his or her payment of the draft.

Typically, documents used in an export transaction include: the commercial invoice, bills of lading, and the marine insurance certificate. The **commercial invoice** is a document showing the price of the merchandise that is being traded. The **bill of lading** is a document providing evidence of the shipment of a commodity. This is the most important document because it gives the holder the right to control the goods in question. The **marine insurance certificate** is a document showing that the shipped merchandise has insurance coverage.

To further our understanding of an export order and the way these documents are employed in the process, let us use our whiskey example and assume that payment will be made by a 60-day time draft. Given this assumption, the exportation of the whiskey and payments for it (as illustrated in Figure 11-2) involve the following steps:

FIGURE 11-2

This diagram portrays the steps involved when a hypothetical American importer in New York imports Scotch whiskey from a British exporter in London.

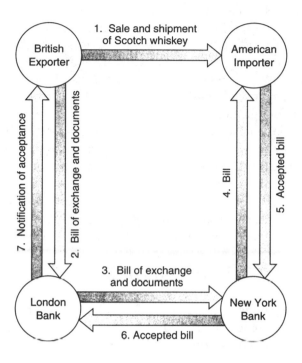

1. The British exporter sells the whiskey to the U.S. importer and ships the bottles to New York.
2. At the same time, the British exporter draws a bill of exchange, payable 60 days after sight, against the U.S. importer and sends the bill along with its supplementary documents (the commercial invoice, the bill of lading, and the marine insurance certificate) to his or her local bank in London.
3. The bank in London mails the bill and all the documents to its correspondent bank in the United States, such as the New York bank.
4. When all the whiskey is delivered, the New York bank presents the bill to the U.S. importer for acceptance.
5. The importer either pays the bill (if a D/P draft is used) or accepts the bill (if a D/A draft is used) and returns it to the bank in New York. The importer then receives the bill of lading from the bank, which gives him or her the right to claim the whiskey at the port of entry.
6. The New York bank returns the accepted bill to the London bank.
7. The London bank informs the exporter that the accepted bill has been received.

On the importer's acceptance of the bill, the exporter can endorse and sell the bill to either an investor or to the local bank (London Bank) at a discount. In this case, the bank (or the investor) assumes a financial function; that is, after 60 days it presents the bill to the U.S. importer for payment. Of course, the exporter also has the option of holding the bill until its maturity. In this case, the exporter receives the full face value of the bill rather than the discounted amount.

11.6 FUNCTIONS OF COMMERCIAL BANKS IN THE FOREIGN EXCHANGE MARKET

The parties involved in international trade seldom deal with each other directly. Rather, as our previous examples show, they usually deal with commercial banks located in their own countries. Commercial banks, therefore, are the main channels through which foreign exchange transactions take place. In performing their roles in the foreign exchange market, commercial banks render three main services through their international departments: (a) purchasing and selling foreign currencies, (b) lending, and (c) collecting.

Purchasing and selling foreign currencies are the most common tasks performed by commercial banks. The need for such transactions arises from many sources. Tourists entering and leaving a country need to exchange their currencies. Exporters generate a supply of foreign currency and a demand for local currency. Importers generate a demand for foreign currency and a supply of domestic currency. Finally, a person or firm planning to invest in a foreign country needs to purchase foreign currency.

The lending services commercial banks provide to their international customers take different forms, ranging from direct payment to a customer to discounting a customer's draft. In making such loans, banks use different lending instruments available to them, including the importer's letter of credit (discussed earlier) and a bank draft that has been discounted.

Commercial banks' collections services provide a means by which the international payments between residents of one country and residents of the rest of the world take place. Using our previous example of Scotch whiskey, payment for the sale would usually be made through a commercial bank located in either New York or London.

11.7 FOREIGN EXCHANGE RATE DETERMINATION

As we already know, the **foreign exchange rate** refers to the price of one currency in terms of another currency. Assume that the United States is the home country and Great Britain is the foreign country. Also suppose that $2 exchanges for £1. There are two ways of measuring the foreign exchange rate:

✦   The price of foreign currency (British pound) in terms of domestic currency (the dollar), or $2.00 per pound
✦   The price of domestic currency (the dollar) in terms of foreign currency, or £0.50 per dollar

Because these two exchange rates are reciprocals of each other, it is inconsequential which one we use, granted that we stay consistent. In this textbook, we use the first definition, expressing the price of foreign currency in terms of the domestic currency.

As we explain in detail in Chapter 12, under the present international monetary system, nations have a great degree of flexibility in choosing the exchange rate regimes that best fit their economic conditions. At one extreme, we have the **fixed exchange rate system**, where the exchange rate is stable and can only fluctuate within a very limited band. On the other extreme, we have the freely fluctuating exchange rate system, where the exchange rate is set by the free market forces of demand and supply. The **freely fluctuating exchange rate system** is also known as the **freely floating exchange rate system,** the **floating exchange rate system,** the **flexible exchange rate system,** and the **clean-floating exchange rate system.** Between the fixed exchange rate system and the freely fluctuating exchange rate system, we have a number of alternative methods that try to reach a compromise between the two extremes.

The purpose of this section is to provide further explanations of how exchange rates are determined under the two extremes of freely fluctuating exchange rates and fixed exchange rates.

11.7a The Freely Fluctuating Exchange Rate System

Suppose that the United States and Great Britain are the only trading partners in the world. Let us consider the United States the home country and Britain the foreign country. In a free market, the exchange rate for a foreign currency is determined by the interaction of demand and supply for that currency. Figure 11-3 depicts supply ($S_£$) and demand

(D$_£$) for the British pound. The vertical axis measures the exchange rate (ER), that is, the price of the pound in terms of the dollar (dollars per pound). The horizontal axis measures the quantity of pounds.

The demand curve for pounds corresponds to debit items in the U.S. balance of payments (BOP), arising from Americans' desire, for example, to import British goods and services or to invest in that country. This demand curve has the ordinary negative slope, indicating that the higher the ER, the smaller the quantity of pounds demanded. This is because as the exchange rate rises, each dollar commands fewer British pounds. Thus, the U.S. dollar price of British goods and services increases in the United States. As a result, U.S. residents demand fewer imports, causing the quantity of pounds demanded to decline.

The supply curve for pounds has the ordinary positive slope, indicating that the higher the ER, the greater the quantity of pounds supplied. This is because as the exchange rate rises, each British pound commands more dollars. Thus, the pound price of U.S. goods and services falls in Britain. As a result, Britons demand more U.S. goods and services. To import these goods and services, British importers exchange their British pounds for U.S. dollars, causing the quantity supplied of pounds to rise in the United States.

FIGURE 11-3

S$_£$ and D$_£$ represent supply and demand for the British pound. The vertical axis measures the exchange rate (ER), that is, the price of the pound in terms of the dollar (dollars per pound). The horizontal axis measures the quantity of pounds. With a freely fluctuating exchange rate system, the equilibrium exchange rate is established at point E, where S$_£$ and D$_£$ intersect. At the equilibrium point, ER = £1.00 = $2.50, and £2 billion is traded. At a lower exchange rate, a shortage of British pounds exists tending to raise the exchange rate toward the equilibrium. At a higher exchange rate, a surplus of British pounds exists, tending to lower the exchange rate toward the equlibrium. Suppose the exchange rate is pegged at £1.00 = $2.00. Because the par value is below the equilibrium exchange rate of £1.00 = $2.50, an excess demand for pounds, measured by line AB, exists. If demand is restricted to £1 billion, the demand curve shifts to the left to intersect S$_£$ at point B. Thus, equilibrium would be reestablished at £1.00 = $2.00. If the central bank sells £2 billion (line AB) per day at $2.00 per pound, the supply curve shifts to the right to intersect D$_£$ at point A. Thus, the surplus is eliminated, and equilibrium is reestablished at £1.00 = $2.00.

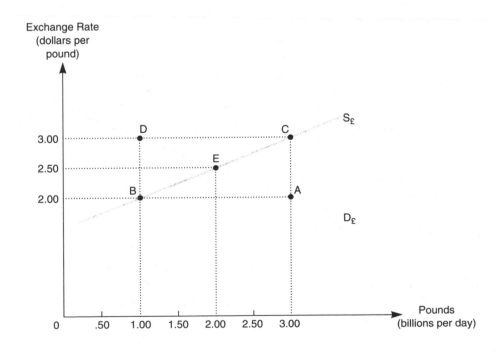

The equilibrium exchange rate is established at point E, where $S_£$ and $D_£$ intersect. At the equilibrium point, ER = £1.00 = $2.50, and £2 billion is traded. At a lower exchange rate, the quantity demanded is greater than the quantity supplied, that is, a shortage of British pounds exists. This causes the exchange rate to rise toward the equilibrium of ER = £1.00 = $2.50, eliminating the shortage. At a higher exchange rate, the quantity supplied is greater than the quantity demanded, that is, a surplus of British pounds exists. This causes the exchange rate to fall toward the equilibrium of ER = £1.00 = $2.50, again eliminating the shortage. If either $D_£$ or $S_£$ shifts, it causes the equilibrium exchange rate to fall or rise, depending on the nature of the shift. For example, if $S_£$ shifts to the right to intersect $D_£$ at point A, the equilibrium exchange rate declines to ER = £1.00 = $2.00. Because now $2.00 is needed (instead of $2.50) to buy £1.00, we say that the dollar has appreciated. In other words appreciation refers to a decrease in the domestic price of the foreign currency. As another example, if $D_£$ shifts to the right to intersect $S_£$ at point C, the equilibrium exchange rate rises to ER = £1.00 = $3.00. Because now $3.00 is needed (instead of $2.50) to buy £1.00, we say that the dollar has depreciated. In other words depreciation refers to an increase in the domestic price of foreign currency.

11.7b The Fixed Exchange Rate System

Under the fixed exchange rate system, the exchange rate is only allowed to fluctuate within a narrow band around a desired level, called *par value*. To keep exchange rate fluctuations within the prescribed band, the central bank must hold **international reserves**—gold, foreign currencies, special drawing rights (SDRs), and other assets that act as international mediums of exchange.

Given our example from Figure 11-3, suppose the exchange rate is pegged at £1.00 = $2.00. For simplicity, assume that there are no bands around the peg (par value). Because the par value is below the equilibrium exchange rate of ER = £1.00 = $2.50, an excess demand for pounds, measured by AB, exists. To maintain the equilibrium at the par value, either restrictions have to be imposed on the demand for the pound or the U.S. central bank (the Federal Reserve System) needs to fill the AB gap out of its international reserves.* If the first alternative is chosen and demand is restricted to £1 billion, the demand curve shifts to the left to intersect $S_£$ at point B. Thus, the equilibrium is reestablished at ER = £1.00 = $2.00.** If the second alternative is chosen, the central bank must sell £2 billion (AB) per day at $2.00 per pound. This causes the supply curve to shift to the right to intersect $D_£$ at point A. Thus, the surplus is eliminated and the equilibrium is reestablished at ER = £1.00 = $2.00. However, this situation cannot last forever. Eventually authorities may have to employ policy measures to shift $D_£$ and $S_£$ until they intersect at the fixed rate of £1.00 = $2.00.

If such policy measure fails to eliminate the **fundamental disequilibrium,** that is, large and persistent balance of payment deficit or surplus, the central banks may have to change the par value. If the par value is decreased, the price of foreign currency decreases in terms of domestic currency. The domestic currency is said to be *revalued*. On the other hand, if the par value is increased, the price of foreign currency rises in terms of domestic currency. The domestic currency is said to be *devalued*. Thus, **revaluation** and **devaluation** are parallel to **appreciation** and **depreciation**, respectively, of the domestic currency. The jargon is distinct to the different exchange rate systems. Revaluation and devaluation result from the deliberate action taken by the government in response to market forces. Appreciation and depreciation, however, are the result of the market forces.

11.8 FOREIGN EXCHANGE TRANSACTIONS

Foreign exchange transactions take place between commercial banks and their customers, and among commercial banks who buy and sell foreign currencies either locally or internationally. Today, foreign exchange transactions are made through a network of telephones, computers, cables, and communications satellites that allow the foreign exchange market to "follow the sun" around the globe. Consequently, commercial banks located in major financial

---

* The gap can also be closed by the central bank of Great Britain, that is, the Bank of England.

** This option does not resolve the fundamental problem, and an implicit shortage continues to exist.

centers, such as New York, London, Tokyo, and Rome, can contact each other instantly and close a foreign exchange deal verbally over the phone. What these banks exchange are, in effect, bank deposits denominated in different currencies. For example, a Chicago bank selling U.S. dollars to a German bank is, in effect, purchasing a deposit denominated in deutsche marks from that bank. This gives the Chicago bank the right to draw a check on the German bank for the amount of the deposit denominated in marks. It also gives the German bank the right to draw a check on the Chicago bank for the amount of the deposit denominated in U.S. dollars.

The speed at which these transactions take place contributes to the constant fluctuation in exchange rates. This fluctuation makes dealing in the foreign exchange market a risky business. To deal with foreign exchange risks, one may choose to do business in either the spot market or the forward market. One may also engage in either hedging or speculation.

In this section, we first explain foreign exchange risks and then discuss the choices available for dealing with these risks.

GLOBAL INSIGHTS CASE 11.1

Oil and Deindustrialization in Britain

In the 1960s and early 1970s, major oil discoveries were made in the North Sea, resulting in substantial quantities of oil production during the late 1970s and 1980s in Great Britain.[1] On the surface, it seems reasonable to assume that the impact of oil production on the British economy would be positive and that a rise in oil exports (or a decrease in oil imports) would lead to an improvement in the British balance of trade. However, the growth of North Sea oil and gas production was accompanied by a decline of manufacturing in Britain. This scenario, in which growth in an energy sector leads to deindustrialization in the form of a decrease in a nation's production of traditional export- and import-competing goods, is referred to as Dutch disease.[2]

An increase in oil production initially raises domestic income. This in turn boosts money demand and, given a fixed supply of money, exerts upward pressure on domestic interest rates. A higher interest rate at home increases the inflow of foreign capital into the economy. Given a flexible exchange rate, the higher demand for domestic currency, accompanying the foreign capital inflow, leads to an appreciation of the domestic currency. The appreciation of the domestic currency then hampers the international competitiveness of domestic products by making them relatively expensive compared to foreign products. As a result, the production of exports and import-competing manufactured goods decreases, nullifying the positive impact of the increased oil exports. In other words, the higher oil output crowds out the production of manufactured export- and import-competing goods. It does not necessarily lead to a net growth in GDP.

In Britain's case, the expansion of the North Sea production did not result in any growth in Britain's GDP. In fact, the North Sea-induced oil deindustrialization, among other factors, contributed to Britain's recession in the late 1970s and the early 1980s.[3]

Notes

1. R. E. Rowthorn and J. R. Wells, *De-Industrialization and Foreign Trade* (Cambridge; Cambridge University Press, 1987), 12.
2. W. M. Corden and J. P. Neary, "Booming Sector and De-Industrialization in a Small Open Economy," *The Economic Journal*, 92 (December 1982): 825-845.
3. C. Bean, "The Impact of North Sea Oil," in R. Dornbusch and R. Layard, eds., *The Performance of the British Economy* (Oxford: Clarendon Press, 1987); C. Beans and J. Symons, "Ten Years of Mrs. T," in O. Blanchard and S. Fischer, eds., NBER *Macroeconomics Annual*: 1990 (Cambridge, MA: The MIT Press, 1989), 15-21.

* Other factors that contributed to the recession included a reduction in money supply growth and the restrictive monetary system.

11.8a Foreign Exchange Risks

As we already know, foreign exchange rates are determined by the interaction of demand and supply in the foreign exchange market. A nation's demand and supply of foreign currencies shifts (increases or decreases) over time, causing fluctuations in foreign exchange rates. Among the factors causing the shifts are changes in different nations' relative rates of interest, different growth and inflation rates in different nations, changes in tastes for foreign and domestic products at home and abroad, changes in different nations' relative incomes, and the expectation of changes in different economic variables, such as interest rates, inflation, and so on.

For example, the higher interest rates in one nation, compared with those of other countries, may encourage the movement of short-term funds to that nation. This causes an increase in the demand for that currency, leading to its appreciation. As we explain in Chapter 1, this is, in fact, what occurred in the United States in the late 1970s and early 1980s, contributing to the U.S. trade deficit.

As another example, if Germany's taste for Japanese products increases, assuming that other things affecting demand and supply for Japanese products stay constant, Germany's demand for Japanese yen will increase (the demand curve shifts to the right). This leads to an increase in the exchange rate (the price of Japanese yen in terms of deutsche mark), or a depreciation of the deutsche mark.*

If the inflation rate is lower in Germany than in Japan, assuming other things stay constant, Germany's products are cheaper than Japanese-made products. This leads to an increase in Japan's demand for Germany's products, causing demand for deutsche marks to increase. The higher demand for the deutsche mark, in turn, leads to its appreciation.

Given the numerous economic variables that affect the world economy, great variations occur in exchange rates on a daily basis. Figure 11-4 shows the exchange rate movements for seven major industrial countries, the so-called Group of Seven (G-7), from 1986 to 1993. In this figure, with the exception of the United States, the exchange rate for each country measures the price of the dollar in terms of the domestic currency. For the United States, a trade-weighted exchange rate (TWEX) is used. This index measures the value of a given currency (the dollar) in terms of the weighted average of 17 major currencies.**

Note the sharp depreciation of the U.S. dollar until the end of 1987. The price of U.S. dollar in terms of Canadian dollars, French francs, German deutsche marks, Italian lira, Japanese yen, and British pounds, continued to rise from 1980 through 1985, indicating its appreciation. However, following the depreciation of the U.S. dollar in 1985, its price in terms of these currencies started to decline.

As Figure 11-4 indicates, large fluctuations in exchange rates occur for any currency, giving rise to **foreign exchange risk exposure.** This is the risk that one faces when dealing with different currencies, because of exchange rate fluctuations. There are three different types of foreign exchange risk exposures: transaction exposure, translation exposure, and economic exposure. **Transaction exposure** arises when individuals and institutions expect to make payments or receive funds denominated in a foreign currency. **Translation exposure** is a measure of how exchange rate fluctuations affect the recording and reporting of a company's financial position in its financial statements. This is basically an *accounting exposure.* **Economic exposure** is related to the total impact of fluctuating exchange rates on a firm's value, as measured by the present value of its expected cash flow. Economic exposure is much broader in nature than the other two exposures and is related to a firm's long-run profit performance and strategic effectiveness.

A number of techniques, described in the following sections, help to reduce foreign exchange risk exposure.

---

* The exchange rate is defined as the price of foreign currency (Japanese yen) in terms of domestic currency (deutsche mark).

** The number of countries included in the calculations of the index may vary according to the agency making the computations. For example, the Federal Reserve Bank of Cleveland includes only 10 countries (see *Economic Trends* [Federal Reserve Bank of Cleveland] [August 1987], 21). The weights take factors such as the size of trade flows and the relevant price elasticities of exchange rate changes into consideration (see *International Economic Conditions* [Federal Reserve Bank of St. Louis] [February 1994], 3).

FIGURE 11-4

With the exception of the United States, the exchange rate for each country measures the price of a dollar in terms of the domestic currency. For the United States, a trade-weighted exchange rate (TWEX) is used. Note the sharp depreciation of the U.S. dollar until the end of 1987. The price of the U.S. dollar in terms of Canadian dollars, French francs, deutsche marks, Italian lira, Japanese yen, and British pounds, continued to rise during 1980—1985, indicating its appreciation. However, following its depreciation in 1985, its price in terms of these currencies started to decline.

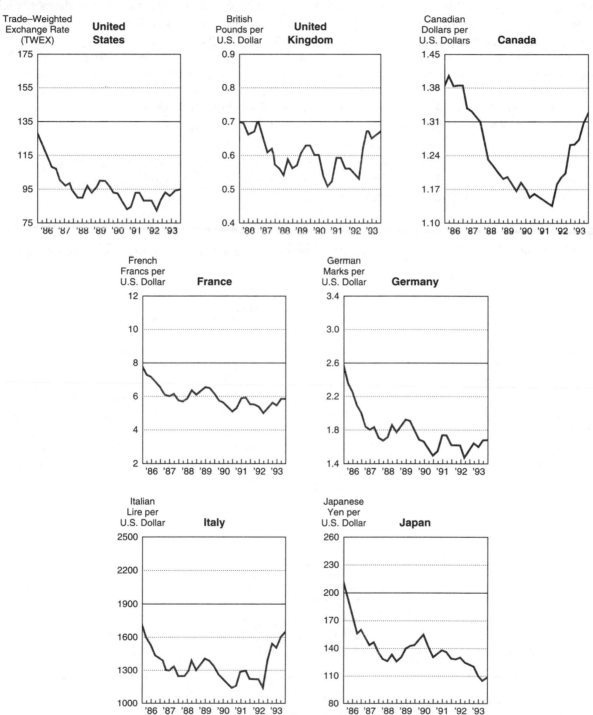

Source: The Federal Reserve Bank of St. Louis, *International Economic Conditions*, February 1994, 40-41.

11.8b The Spot Market

The **spot market** is a foreign exchange market in which foreign currencies are purchased and sold for immediate delivery, that is, within two business days after the transaction agreement. This two-day period is needed to allow the traders to instruct their respective commercial banks to make the necessary transfers in their accounts. The spot price of foreign exchange, determined by demand and supply, is subject to constant fluctuations due to appreciation or depreciation of different currencies against each other. Foreign exchange quotations are usually made in two different ways: (a) in terms of the amount of domestic currency needed to buy a unit of foreign currency; and (b) in terms of the amount of foreign currency needed to buy a unit of domestic currency.

Table 11-1 indicates the spot price (or rate) for the G-7 nation's currencies in terms of the U.S. dollar for Thursday January 14, 1999, and for Wednesday January 13, 1999. For example, next to Germany we find that the spot rate was $0.5983 = DM 1 on Thursday and $0.5963 = DM 1 on Wednesday. On the same line we find that the spot rate was DM 1.6715 = $1.00 on Thursday, and DM 1.6770 = $1.00 on Wednesday.

Today, most foreign exchange transactions take place in the spot market; the payment instruments commonly used in this market are cable transfers and "on sight" drafts.

The advantage of dealing in the spot exchange market is the immediate delivery of the foreign currency at the current exchange rate. As a result, one can avoid the risk of fluctuations in the exchange rate that may result when the foreign currency is delivered at a future date.

TABLE 11-1
Foreign Exchange Rates of the G-7 Nations

Country	U.S. $ equivalent		Currency per U.S. $	
	Thu.	Wed.	Thu.	Wed.
Britain (Pound)	1.6569	1.6480	0.6035	0.6068
30-day forward	1.6554	1.6465	0.6041	0.6073
90-day forward	1.6537	1.6448	0.6047	0.6080
180-day forward	1.6525	1.6437	0.6052	0.6084
Canada (Dollar)	0.6521	0.6563	1.5336	1.5236
30-day forward	0.6521	0.6563	1.5336	1.5236
90-day forward	0.6520	0.6563	1.5337	1.5237
180-day forward	0.6523	0.6566	1.5329	1.5230
France (Frank)	0.1784	0.1778	5.6060	5.6253
30-day forward	0.1787	0.1781	5.5975	5.6156
90-day forward	0.1792	0.1786	5.5881	5.5995
180-day forward	0.1880	0.1794	5.5483	5.5734
Germany (Mark)	0.5983	0.5963	1.6715	1.6770
30-day forward	0.5992	0.5972	1.6690	1.6744
90-day forward	0.6009	0.5990	1.6641	1.6696
180-day forward	0.6038	0.6018	1.6563	1.6618
Italy (Lira)	0.0006043	0.0006023	1654.79	1660.18
Japan (Yen)	0.008802	0.008839	113.61	113.13
30-day forward	0.008802	0.008840	113.61	113.13
90-day forward	0.008803	0.008840	113.60	113.12
180-day forward	0.008804	0.008841	113.58	113.10

Source: The Wall Street Journal, Friday January 15, 1999, p. C14.

11.8c The Forward Market

The **forward market** is a foreign exchange market in which foreign currencies are purchased and sold for future delivery. In other words, it involves an agreement between two parties to purchase or sell a given amount of foreign exchange at a specified future date at a prearranged rate. This rate is called the forward rate and is usually quoted for one month, three months, or six months. Although forward contracts for longer periods are uncommon, they can be arranged for delivery at any specified period of time up to one year and occasionally up to three years. For example, one could agree to buy DM 1,000 six months from today at DM 2 = $1. At the time this agreement is reached, the seller has to deliver only 10 percent of the marks (DM 100) to the buyer as a security margin. The rest of the marks are delivered at the agreed rate after the six-month period has elapsed. Thus, after this period, the buyer ends up with DM 1,000 for $500, regardless of what the spot rate is at that time.

Why do forward markets exist? Let us return to our previous example of a U.S. importer in New York importing $100,000 worth of Scotch whiskey from a British exporter in London. Let us assume that the British exporter and the U.S. importer have agreed to settle the payment in U.S. dollars, using a 60-day time draft. The British exporter draws a $100,000 60-day time draft against the U.S. importer. Given that the existing exchange rate is £1 = $2.00, the $100,000 is equal to £50,000. Thus, if the exchange rate does not change after the 60-day period, the British exporter receives £50,000 for the exported whiskey. However, if at the end of the 60-day period the exchange rate increases to £1 = $2.50, the British exporter loses £10,000. This is because, at the new rate, the $100,000 draft is worth only £40,000 ($100,000/$2.50 = £40,000). On the other hand, if the exchange rate decreases to £1 = $1.25, the British exporter gains £30,000 ($100,000/$1.25 = £80,000).

In this example, the British exporter takes an exchange risk in the foreign exchange market. This risk stems from payment made in a foreign currency, that is, the U.S. dollar. Therefore, the British exporter either loses or gains, depending on the exchange rate at the end of the 60-day period. In this case, the U.S. importer faces no exchange risk because the payment is made in U.S. dollars. However, if the agreement had called for payment in British pounds, the importer rather than the exporter would have faced the risk.

To avoid this risk, the forward or the future exchange market can be used. Thus, if the payment is to be made in U.S. dollars, the British exporter could sell the $100,000 for pounds forward at the time the transaction agreement is reached. To do this, he or she makes a contract with the local bank in London. Accordingly, the British exporter agrees to sell $100,000 for pounds to the London bank after six months at a forward rate set at the time the agreement is reached.

Similarly, if the payment is to be made in British pounds, the U.S. importer could avoid the risk by entering the forward market. The importer could purchase the £50,000 for U.S. dollars 60 days forward from a local bank.

As our example indicates, trading partners enter the forward market to avoid the risk of fluctuations in the foreign exchange rates. Because exporters and importers dealing in the forward market make transactions mainly through their local commercial banks, the foreign exchange risk is transferred to those banks.

Commercial banks can minimize foreign exchange risk by matching forward purchases from exporters with forward sales to importers. However, because the supply of and demand for forward currency transactions by exporters and importers usually do not coincide, the banks may assume some of the risk.

If a bank engages in speculation, as we explain in the next section, a higher level of risk is realized. Most banks do not choose to engage in speculation; instead, they prefer to make their profit on the difference between the buying and selling prices of foreign currencies they exchange. For example, a bank may buy a £50,000 bill for $100,000, sell the bill for £50,500, and make a £500 profit.

Today, forward markets exist only for the currencies of the major industrial countries. Forward contracts are not available for most developing countries' currencies. Also, it is difficult to obtain a forward contract in any currency more than a year ahead. By limiting forward contracts to only a few currencies, banks avoid the higher risk associated with dealing in the exchange of all currencies.

Table 11-1 gives the forward rate for various currencies in terms of the U.S. dollar for Thursday, January 14, 1999, and for Wednesday, January 13, 1999. For example, on the three lines under Germany, we find the 30-day forward rate ($0.5992 = DM 1), the 90-day forward rate ($0.6009 = DM 1), and the 180-day forward rate ($0.6038 = DM 1) for Wednesday.

If the forward rate is higher than the current spot rate, the foreign currency is said to be at a *forward premium* compared to the local currency. However, if the forward rate is lower than the current spot rate, the foreign currency is considered to be at a *forward discount* compared to the local currency.* Using our information about Germany from Table 11-1, because the spot rate on Wednesday is $0.5983 = 1 DM and the 180-day forward rate is $0.6038 = 1 DM, we say that the deutsche mark is at a six-month forward premium with respect to the U.S. dollar.

11.8d Hedging

Because the exchange rate changes, any future payments or receipts involve a foreign exchange risk. To avoid this risk, one could engage in hedging. **Hedging** against a foreign currency means making sure that one neither owns nor owes in that currency. Hedging can take place in either the spot market or the forward market, usually in the latter.

Using our example of whiskey exports from Britain to the United States, let us assume this time that payment has to be made in British pounds for £50,000. In this case, the U.S. importer takes the exchange risk. Thus, if the pound's present spot market rate is £1 = $2, the current dollar value of the payment is $100,000. However, if after 60 days the spot rate changes to £1 = $1.25, the dollar value of the payment becomes $62,500. If the 60-day spot rate changes to £1 = $2.50, the dollar value of the payment becomes $125,000. Thus, the importer may gain or lose, depending on the spot rate of the 60-day bill in the market. However, because the U.S. importer does not want to take such a gamble, he or she could hedge against the exchange risk by either buying or borrowing £50,000 at the present spot rate of £1 = $2, and depositing the proceeds in an interest-earning bank account for 60 days until the payment is due. If the importer chooses to borrow the £50,000, the cost involved in this transaction is the difference between the higher interest rate that must be paid on the borrowed funds and the lower interest rate that would be earned from depositing the funds in the bank for 60 days. If the importer uses his or her own money to buy the £50,000, the transaction cost is the difference between the opportunity cost of the money used and the interest rate that would be earned from depositing these funds in a bank for 60 days.**

As this example indicates, covering exchange risk through the spot market involves either a borrowing cost or the cost of tying up one's money for a period of time (60 days in the example). To avoid this risk, one could hedge in the forward market rather than in the spot market. In this way, the need for borrowing or tying up a certain amount of money for a period of time is eliminated. For example, the U.S. importer could buy British pounds in the forward market for delivery in 60 days at today's 60-day forward rate. Thus, if the 60-day forward rate is £1 = $2.20, the importer must pay $110,000 (£50,000 × $2.20) in 60 days for the £50,000. Consequently, the hedging would cost the importer $10,000 or 10 percent of $100,000 for the 60-day period.

Today, hedging usually takes place in the forward market, enabling international traders to avoid the uncertainty of the foreign exchange market and enhancing the flow of trade and investment throughout the world. Hedging is especially helpful to multinational corporations (MNCs) that have to deal in large amounts of foreign currencies of different countries every day.

11.8e Speculation

The opposite of hedging is **speculation.** In contrast to a hedger, who tries to avoid the foreign exchange risk, the speculator purposely undertakes risk with the expectation of a profit. Like hedging, speculation can occur in either the spot market or the forward market. Also, as in the case of hedging, speculators usually operate in the forward market.

---

* The forward premium or discount on a currency is indicative of the expectation that currency's appreciation (revaluation) or depreciation (devaluation).

** **The opportunity cost** is the value of the benefit foregone by depositing money in the bank account instead of using it in the best available alternative.

GLOBAL INSIGHTS CASE 11.2

Turmoil in Asian Economies

The outbreak of financial crisis in Asia was one of the most notable–and troubling–developments in the global economy during 1997. Events began in midyear as a currency crisis and intensified over the rest of the year, spilling over to the real sectors of the affected economies as well as the rest of the world.

By May 1997 Thailand was in the throes of the fourth speculative attack on its currency, the baht, since August 1996. By then the buildup of financial difficulties and balance of payments pressures had reached such a point that efforts to defend the baht could not be sustained. Pressures soon spilled over to other emerging Asian economies (especially Indonesia, Malaysia, and South Korea), most of which also had some balance of payments weaknesses, as well as to Eastern Europe. These countries difficulties shook financial market confidence elsewhere in Asia and in emerging markets around the world, even those with sounder policies and economic fundamentals, in a contagion effect.

Since June, four of the countries in the region (Indonesia, the Philippines, South Korea, and Thailand) have requested and received assistance from the International Monetary Fund (IMF). In each instance the adjustment programs developed by the domestic authorities and the IMF have included a heavy emphasis on financial and structural adjustment measures (for example, to reform bank lending practices and further liberalize the economy), as well as the more traditional macroeconomic adjustments necessary to restore financial market stability. For each of the affected economies, the question of when their financial and balance of payments situation will stabilize depends, first and foremost, on whether and how aggressively they implement their policy commitments, and second, on the easing of the contagion effect from those economies that continue to experience difficulties. In the medium terms the return of these economies' strong growth performance will depend significantly upon the degree to which structural and financial sector reforms are implemented.

Source: U.S. Government Printing Office, *Economic Report of the President* (Washington D.C: Government Printing Office, 1998, 50, Box 2-2. Reprinted.

A speculator engages in the spot market by predicting the fluctuations in the spot rate. Thus, if a speculator expects the spot rate of a foreign currency to fall, he or she will borrow that currency for, say 30 days, and immediately exchange it for domestic currency at the current spot rate. The speculator may then deposit the domestic currency in an interest-earning bank account. After the 30-day period is over, the speculator may pay off the loan by using the bank deposit of domestic currency to purchase the foreign currency at the going spot rate. At that time, if the new spot rate is lower than the previous spot rate, as the speculator predicted, a differential revenue is realized. But this speculation also involves a differential cost of the higher interest rate paid on foreign currency borrowed compared with the interest earned from domestic currency deposited in the bank. Thus, the speculator makes a profit only if the differential revenue is greater than the differential cost.

In a similar way, if a speculator expects the spot price of a foreign currency to rise, he or she may borrow domestic money, purchase the foreign currency at the current spot rate, and hold it in an interest-earning bank account for future resale. Again, if the speculator's predictions prove correct, and if the differential revenue is greater than the differential cost, a profit is realized.

As an example, assume that the current spot rate on the pound is $2.00 = £1, and a speculator believes the spot rate in one month will be $1.98 = £1. The speculator borrows £1,000 at the annual interest rate of 13 percent and immediately sells those pounds at the going spot rate of $2.00 per pound, receiving $2,000. He or she then deposits these dollars in a bank account at an annual rate of 12 percent. After one month, the speculator earns $20.00 [$2,000 x 12/100 x 1/12] interest on the account. Thus, he or she has $2,020 (principal + interest). If the speculator's prediction about the spot rate was correct, he or she may sell $2,020 at the new spot rate of $1.98 = £1, receiving £1,020.20 (2,020/1.98 = £1,020.20). Out of this amount, the speculator spends £1,010.83 to pay off the loan (£1,000 principal + £10.83 interest [£1,000 x 13/100 x 1/12 = £10.83], realizing £9.37 (£1,020.20 -£1,010.83) profit.

Thus, speculation in the spot market requires the speculator to either use his or her own funds or to borrow money. To avoid this requirement, speculation, like hedging, usually takes place in the forward market. For example, if a speculator anticipates that a foreign currency's spot rate in 60 days will be higher than its present 60-day forward rate, the speculator may purchase a certain amount of that foreign currency 60 days forward. After the 60-day period has elapsed, the speculator receives delivery of the foreign currency at the agreed forward rate. If the speculator was correct in predicting the exchange rate, the agreed-on forward rate is lower than the going spot rate. In this case, the speculator may sell the foreign currency immediately, realizing a profit. If the speculator was wrong in predicting the exchange market and the forward rate is higher than the spot rate, the speculator takes a loss.

For example, assume that the 60-day forward rate of the pound is $2.00 = £1, and a speculator expects the pound's spot rate in 60 days to be $2.05 = £1. The speculator purchases £1,000 forward for delivery in 60 days. After 60 days, the speculator takes delivery of £1,000, paying $2,000 (£1,000 x $2.00). At this time, if the new spot rate is $2.05 = £1, as the speculator predicted, he or she sells the £1,000 delivered for $2,050, making a $50 profit.

If a speculator purchases a foreign currency, in either the spot market or forward market, with the intention of selling it later at a higher spot rate, the speculator is said to be taking a *long position* in that currency. However, if a speculator borrows or sells a foreign currency forward with the intention of purchasing it at a future lower price to either pay off the foreign currency borrowed or to deliver the foreign currency sold forward, the speculator is said to be taking a *short position.*

Speculation can be either stabilizing or destabilizing. **Stabilizing speculation** refers to the purchase of a foreign currency when its domestic price (the exchange rate) is declining, in anticipation that it will soon increase and generate a profit. Stabilizing speculation also refers to the sale of a foreign currency when its domestic price is rising, in anticipation that it will soon decline. Stabilizing speculators, by smoothing changes in the foreign exchange market, perform a useful function due to the laws of demand and supply. When the domestic price of a foreign currency is falling, stabilizing speculators purchase that foreign currency, increasing the quantity demanded for that currency and causing its domestic price to increase. On the other hand, when the domestic price of a foreign currency is rising, they sell that currency, increasing the quantity supplied of that currency and causing its domestic price to decrease.

Destabilizing speculation refers to the sale of a foreign currency when its domestic price is falling, in anticipation that it will decrease even lower in the future. Destabilizing speculation also refers to the purchase of a foreign currency when its domestic price rises, in anticipation that it will increase even higher in the future. Destabilizing speculators, by magnifying the exchange rate fluctuations, disrupt the flow of international business because of the laws of demand and supply. When the domestic price of a foreign currency is falling, destabilizing speculators sell that currency, increasing the quantity supplied of that currency and causing its price to fall even further. On the other hand, when the domestic price of a foreign currency is rising, they purchase that currency, increasing the quantity demanded of that foreign currency and causing its price to rise even further.

Speculators are usually individuals or firms that undertake speculation risks in anticipation of high profit. However, banks, importers, exporters, and any other individual who expects payments in a foreign currency can engage in speculation. The speculation by exporters and importers usually involves *leads* and *lags* in payments. These refer to the few months' leeway during which one gets paid for exports or pays for imports. For example, if a U.S. exporter who is paid in British pounds expects the exchange rate to rise, he or she would try to delay the payment (a lag) by extending credit to the importer. On the other hand, if a U.S. importer who pays for goods in British pounds expects the exchange rate to rise, he or she would try to pay as soon as possible (a lead).

11.8f Swaps

A **swap** is an arrangement by which two parties exchange one currency for another and agree that, at a certain future date, each party receives from the other the amount of the original currency that was exchanged when the swap took place.

The swap was initiated by the U.S. Federal Reserve System (the Fed) in 1962. At that time, the United States was experiencing a BOP deficit, causing confidence in the U.S. dollar to diminish and short-term capital to flow out of the dollar into stronger currencies. In order to help offset this outflow of funds, the U.S. Federal Reserve System agreed with several European central banks to enter into reciprocal currency arrangements, or swap arrangements.

According to these arrangements, which are still practiced today, the central banks of different countries may swap their currencies with each other in order to help finance their temporary payments disequilibriums. For example, if the U.S. Federal Reserve System is short of British pounds, it can ask the Bank of England to provide them, with the understanding that the swap will be repaid within a given period of time, usually 3 to 12 months. In the same manner, if the Bank of England needs U.S. dollar, it can enter into a swap arrangement with the U.S. Federal Reserve System.

Swap arrangements have been used by many nations' central banking systems as a means of intervening in the foreign exchange market. For example, the U.S. Federal Reserve System uses swaps to collect the surplus of dollars from foreign central banks. These surpluses are in excess of what these banks usually hold, and if they are not collected by the Fed, they are sold in the foreign currency market, depreciating the dollar. Although a swap is a temporary arrangement that has to be repaid after a certain time period, it does buy time. This allows the Fed to make other arrangements to resolve foreign exchange disequilibrium problems.

Since the adoption of the managed-floating exchange rate system in 1973, the swap's popularity as a credit instrument, compared with the International Monetary Fund (IMF) drawing facilities, has increased.[*] This rise in popularity is due to several factors. First, swap arrangements involve minimal administrative red tape and can be executed very quickly. Second, borrowing in excess of 50 percent of a nation's quota from the IMF may require substantial justification, whereas swap arrangements are made unconditionally. Third, borrowing from the IMF is relatively costly for the borrowing nation compared to the cost of swap arrangements. Finally, if a nation borrows substantially from the IMF, the transaction is visible and may be interpreted as a symptom of an unhealthy economy, inducing destabilizing speculations.

At the corporate level, swap arrangements can be classified into currency swaps and credit swaps. A **currency swap** is an arrangement between two firms to exchange one currency for another, reversing the exchange at a future date. Currency swaps usually take place between an MNC's parent company and its subsidiary company. For example, a subsidiary of a U.S. MNC, located in Mexico and needing U.S. dollars, could enter into a swap arrangement with its parent company in the United States. Accordingly, the subsidiary could swap pesos (the Mexican currency) for U.S. dollars and agree to reverse the exchange at some future date. Because this arrangement allows the firms to avoid using the foreign exchange market, they escape the possibility of loss that might result from fluctuations in exchange rates.

A **credit swap** is an arrangement between a firm and a foreign central bank or commercial bank to exchange one currency for another, reversing the exchange at a future date. Credit swaps are often used by MNCs when one of their subsidiaries operates in a country in which either no forward exchange market exists or it is difficult to obtain local credit. For example, assume that a U.S. firm has a subsidiary in Kuwait that is in need of funds. The U.S. parent company can make a contract with a local bank in Kuwait, depositing a certain amount of dollars in the Kuwait bank for a given period of time. In return for this dollar deposit, the Kuwait bank makes a loan in an equivalent amount of dinar, at a specified rate of interest, to the U.S. subsidiary. At the end of the time period, the U.S. subsidiary pays off the dinar loan to the Kuwait local bank. The Kuwait bank, in turn, returns the original dollar amount to the U.S. parent company.

The advantage of this swap arrangement is that it does not expose the parent company to an exchange loss that might result from fluctuations in the foreign exchange market. In other words, after the loan period expires, the U.S. parent company receives the original amount of dollars deposited, irrespective of the going exchange rate.

The cost of this arrangement is the opportunity cost that accrues to the U.S. parent company as a result of depositing those dollars in a Kuwait bank at no interest. In this transaction, the parent company gains only if the opportunity cost is less than the benefit that accrues to the subsidiary. The subsidiary, its turn, benefits only if the cost of interest paid to the Kuwait bank is less than the expected rate of return on the dinars invested in the subsidiary, plus the losses or gains associated with currency fluctuations.

---

[*]   We elaborate on the IMF in the next chapter.

11.8g Arbitrage

Arbitrage refers to the simultaneous purchase of a currency in one market, where it is cheaper, and sale in another market, where it is more expensive, in order to profit from the differences in spot exchange rates. This is a riskless process that results in equalization of exchange rate quotations in different monetary centers.

For example, assume that the pound's spot price is £1 = $1.50 in New York and £1 = $1.55 in London. An arbitrager can buy pounds for $1.50 in New York, and immediately sell them for $1.55 in London, thus realizing a revenue of $0.05 per pound. Although this may seem insignificant, the revenue on £2 million would be $100,000, which can be gained from only a few minutes' work. The arbitrager also has to pay for the transfer cost—the cost of overseas phone calls and the overhead cost associated with arbitrage activities. Because these costs are small compared to the revenue gained, the arbitrager usually realizes a substantial profit.

If only two currencies are traded between two financial centers, as in the previous example, the arbitrage is referred to as **two-point arbitrage.** However, if three currencies are traded between three financial centers, the arbitrage is known as **triangular** or **three-point arbitrage.** These two forms follow the same principle; however, in practice, two-point arbitrage is more prevalent than three-point arbitrage.

As we mentioned earlier, arbitrage activities result in equalization of the exchange rates in different monetary centers. This happens because arbitragers raise demand for the foreign currency in the financial center where the currency is cheaper, causing the price of that currency to rise. At the same time, they raise the supply of foreign currency in the financial centers where the currency is expensive, causing the price of that currency to fall. Thus, arbitrage activities result in the equalization of exchange rates for currencies, leading international financial centers toward a unified market.

11.9 THE EUROCURRENCY MARKET

The Eurocurrency market is the principal international money market. This market provides an important source of debt financing for MNCs. Eurocurrencies are currencies deposited outside the country of their origin. For example, the U.S. dollars deposited in French commercial banks or in the French branch of a U.S. bank, are referred to as Eurodollars. Similarly, a British pound deposited in a German commercial bank is called a Eurosterling. Other Eurocurrencies are Dutch guilders, French francs, German deutsche marks, Japanese yen, and Swiss francs.

The Eurocurrency market is the outgrowth of the Eurodollar market. As this name implies, the dollar was initially deposited in Europe. Subsequently, however, other major currencies followed the dollar's path in being deposited outside their countries of origin, and the concept of Eurocurrency was born. Although the "Euro" prefix implies that these currencies are deposited in Europe, the market is no longer restricted to Europe. In fact, these currencies are deposited in non-European international monetary centers, such as Hong Kong, Kuwait, Singapore, and Tokyo. However, the Eurodollar is still the major form of Eurocurrency and accounts for 75 percent to 80 percent of the market.

The Eurocurrency market has a volume of roughly $6 trillion with transactions at the global level, including London and other European centers, Asia (Hong Kong and Singaporte), Canada, and Caribbean (The Bahamas and the Cayman Islands). London is the major center for this market, covering about 20 percent of all eurocurrency transactions. Brussels and Paris are the centers for Eurosterlings deposits and, Luxemburg is the center for Euromark deposits.

11.9a Growth of the Eurodollar Market

Development of the Eurodollar market started in the 1950s, when the U.S. dollar occupied a dominant position in the world economy, replacing the British pound as the leading international reserve currency. One of the main factors that contributed to the development of the Eurodollar market was the U.S. Federal Reserve System's "Regulation Q." This regulation imposed a ceiling on interest rates that U.S. banks could pay on time deposits. Because this regulation did not apply to dollars deposited in Europe, U.S. residents and foreigners deposited their dollars in London, which in the late 1950s was paying interest rates that exceeded the levels set by Regulation Q in the United States. This induced major U.S. banks to instruct their overseas branches to bid for dollars by proposing higher interest rates than those offered in the United States. The dollars collected by these branches were then sent to the parent offices in the United States, which could in turn lend such funds in the domestic (U.S.) market.

Another factor that gave rise to the Eurodollar market's growth was some depositors' fear that their deposits in the United States might be confiscated in the event of an international conflict. This was especially true of the Soviet depositors, whose dollar holdings had been confiscated by the United States during World War II. Consequently, the former Soviet Union was among the first customers of the Eurodollar market who felt that it was safe to hold dollar deposits in Europe, mainly in London, where the United States had no jurisdiction.

The growth of the Eurodollar market was also fueled by European dollar traders who found it convenient to deal in London instead of New York due to the uniformity of time zones in European countries. This made it possible to expand trading hours per day, which had been limited to only a few hours when U.S. and European banks were both open.

Finally, the growth of the Eurodollar market was accelerated in the 1970s by three main factors: (a) a sharp increase in OPEC nations' oil revenue, which caused significant BOP surpluses for these countries; (b) an expansion in the volume of world trade; and (c) the lifting of restrictions on bank transactions in Eurocurrencies.

11.9b Financial Activities of the Eurocurrency Market

As a financial center, the Eurocurrency market represents two major submarkets: the interbank market, in which banks provide credit to each other, and a market for commercial customers who seek funds from these banks in order to finance their trade and investment.

The Eurocurrency market deals in short-term and medium-term credit. A *short-term Eurocurrency loan* has a maturity of less than six months. A *medium-term Eurocurrency loan* has a maturity of three to seven years. There is also a *Eurobond market,* which handles long-term loans of 15 or 20 years. Bank loans provided through this market carry a variable rate of interest that is calculated by adding a margin to the **London Interbank Offered Rate (LIBOR).** This interest rate is used between the banks when they provide loans of Eurocurrencies to each other.

Financial activities undertaken in the Eurocurrency market have significant implications for international finance. By enabling different countries to deal with each other in one center, the Eurocurrency market increases the financial interdependence of these countries. As a result, it enhances the financial interaction between different nations, facilitating world trade and investment. However, it is argued that a country's movement of currency in and out of unregulated markets complicates the central banks' task in controlling the money supply. Thus, the Eurocurrency market may interfere with a country's plan to achieve its predetermined monetary objective.

According to a ruling enacted on December 3, 1981, U.S. banks are permitted to receive deposits from overseas and reinvest them abroad. Also, foreign deposits in the United States are exempted from the interest rate ceilings and from reserve and insurance requirements. As a result of this ruling, U.S. banks have been able to compete directly in the Eurodollar market, capturing a large percentage of that market.

11.10 INTERNATIONAL BANKING

International banking refers to those banking activities that cross national boundaries, facilitating the flow of money between different countries. These banking activities are essential elements of international business growth, without which MNCs would not have been able to expand as much as they have to date. International banks not only provide MNCs with debt financing from local and international markets, but they ensure the timely flow of existing corporate resources.

International banking developed in response to the expansion of international business operations. To meet the overseas needs of their domestic clients, commercial banks started establishing international departments. These departments arranged for reciprocal deposits with their correspondent commercial banks located in countries where the bulk of their transactions took place.

With further developments in international business activities in the correspondent commercial bank relationship appeared to be inadequate for handling MNCs' needs. Thus, many banks established branches in foreign countries or took over existing foreign banks. The first factor in the growth in international banking was the **Edge Act**, passed in the United States in 1919. This act was a reaction to the restrictions set by the Federal Reserve Board Regulations. According to these regulations, U.S. banks were not allowed to get involved in any activities abroad that are not permitted in the United States. However, the Edge Act allowed for the organization of the "Edge Act Corporations" by U.S. banks. These corporations were allowed to engage in any banking activities that were permitted in foreign countries' local markets. As a result, U.S. banks became more effective in competing against local banks in foreign countries. The second major reason for the development of international banking was the institution of various U.S. control measures in the 1960s. These measures, which were designed to control the U.S. BOP, encouraged U.S. banks to establish branches overseas. One such measure was the **Interest Equalization Tax (IET)** that was introduced in 1963 and eliminated in 1974. According to the IET, an excise tax was imposed on the purchase of foreign securities by U.S. citizens, discouraging the outflow of funds from the United States to foreigners. As a result, foreign borrowers had to look outside the United States for funds. Another control measure was the **Direct Investment Program**, which was initiated in 1968. This program set a limit on the amount of money a parent company in the United States could send to its subsidiaries overseas. As a result, U.S. firms were forced to demand more overseas assistance from their banks in transferring funds overseas.

The third major factor that was instrumental in the development of international banking was the expansion of the Eurocurrency market, which provided a large unregulated source of funds for MNCs. This was especially important to U.S. banks; They could borrow in the unregulated market and provide loans to U.S. firms that, due to the control measures already described, were forced to seek assistance overseas.

The fourth major stimulant to international banking has been the growing demand for funds from developing countries. This was especially significant when oil prices quadrupled during 1973 and 1974, exerting tremendous pressure on the world financial system. There was concern as to how non-OPEC developing countries, which had previously financed their deficits by foreign direct investment and foreign debt, would be able to survive the crisis. However, international banking came to the rescue. The surplus funds deposited by OPEC developing countries into the international banking system were loaned to the non-OPEC developing nations to finance their foreign currency needs.

The fifth major factor in the development of international banking was the U.S. Federal Reserve Board's decision in December 1981 to allow U.S. banks to set up international banking facilities (IBFs) within the United States. Before this decision, U.S. banks had to set up their IBFs in London and the Caribbean in order to take advantage of the Eurodollar market. Therefore, part of the U.S. dollar business was shifted abroad. The 1981 decision was made to increase the flow of U.S. dollar business back into the United States, free from most domestic requirements.

The pattern of international banking in the 1980s was characterized by two elements: (a) increased competition among international banks, and (b) the inability of some foreign governments to service their huge debts.

The increased competition among international banks in the 1980s can be attributed to the declining oil revenues of the OPEC nations. This decline not only reduced the funds these nations could provide to the Eurodollar market, but it encouraged OPEC nations to manage their own money instead of relying on Western international banks.

The inability of some foreign governments to meet their loan obligations can be attributed to the decline of oil prices and the general slowing of the world economy in the 1980s. A case in point is Mexico, which because of a sudden decline in its oil revenue, found itself on the brink of bankruptcy and is still unable to meet its loan obligations.

We close this chapter by noting that MNCs are among the major participants in the foreign exchange market. Their activities, along with those of some other major participants such as the central banks, fuel the constant fluctuations in foreign exchange rates. Although such fluctuations offer a range of opportunities for MNCs, they also enhance the risks of engaging in international trade.

11.11 SUMMARY

1. The foreign exchange market can be defined as a market within which individuals, business firms, and banks purchase and sell foreign currencies and other debt instruments.

2. Foreign exchange instruments are written or printed financial documents that allow the payment of funds from one country and one currency to another country and another currency. Chief among these instruments are cable (telegraphic) transfers, commercial bills of exchange (commercial drafts), bank drafts, and letters of credit.

3. A cable transfer is an order transmitted by a bank in one country to its foreign correspondent in another country, instructing the correspondent bank to pay out a specific amount of money to a designated person or account.

4. A commercial bill of exchange is a written order by an exporter (the drawer) to an importer (the drawee) instructing the importer to pay on demand, or at a certain date, a specified amount of money to a designated party (the payee).

5. A bill of exchange that is payable on presentation to the drawee is referred to as a sight bill. A bill that is payable at some future date is known as a time bill.

6. A bank draft is similar to a commercial bill of exchange because it is a written order by a drawer to a drawee instructing him or her to pay, on demand, or at a certain date, a specified amount of money to a payee. The major difference between these two major financial instruments is that in the case of a bank draft, the drawee is a bank rather than an importer.

7. A letter of credit is a document issued by an importer's bank declaring that payments will be made to an exporter regarding a specific shipment of commodities. The letter is accompanied by the required shipment documents.

8. Revaluation and devaluation are parallel to appreciation and depreciation, respectively, of the domestic currency.

9. The spot market is a foreign exchange market in which foreign currencies are purchased and sold for immediate delivery, that is, within two business days after the transaction agreement.

10. The forward market is a foreign exchange market in which foreign currencies are purchased and sold for future delivery.

11. If the forward rate is higher than the current spot rate, the foreign currency is said to be at a forward premium compared to the local currency. However, if the forward rate is lower than the current spot rate, the foreign currency is considered to be at a forward discount.

12. Hedging against a foreign currency means making sure that one neither owns nor owes in that currency. Hedging can take place in either the spot market or the forward market.

13. Speculation is the opposite of hedging. In contrast to a hedger, who tries to avoid the foreign exchange risk, the speculator purposely undertakes risk with the expectation of a profit. Like hedging, speculation can occur in either the spot market or the forward market.

14. A swap is an arrangement by which two parties exchange one currency for another and agree that, at a certain future date, each party receives from the other the amount of the original currency that was exchanged when the swap took place.

15. Arbitrage is simultaneously purchasing a currency in one market, where it is cheaper, and selling it in another market, where it is more expensive, in order to profit from the differences in spot exchange rates.

16. Eurocurrencies are currencies deposited outside the country of their origin.

17. The factors that have contributed to the growth of the Eurodollar market are (a) U.S. Federal Reserve System's Regulation Q; (b) some depositors' fear that their deposits in the United States might be confiscated in the event of an international conflict; (c) the convenience for Europeans of dealing in London instead of New York, due to the uniformity of time zones in the European countries; (d) the sharp increase in OPEC nations' oil revenue; (e) an expansion in the volume of world trade; and (f) the lifting of restrictions on bank transactions in Eurocurrencies.

18. International banking refers to those banking activities that cross national boundaries, facilitating the flow of money between different countries.

19. Factors that have contributed to the development of international banking are (a) the Edge Act of 1919, which permitted the organization of Edge Act Corporations by U.S. banks; (b) the various control measures instituted in the 1960s, which led U.S. firms to develop branches overseas; (c) the expansion of the Eurocurrency

market; (d) the growing demand for funds from developing countries; and (e) the U.S. Federal Reserve Board's 1981 decision to allow U.S. banks to set up their international banking facilities (IBFs) within the United States.

Review Questions

1. What is the foreign exchange market? What is its principal function? What are the four levels of transactions undertaken by the participants in this market?
2. What are the foreign exchange instruments?
3. What is meant by a documentary draft? What are the types of documentary drafts? What documents are used in export transactions?
4. What factors give rise to foreign exchange risk? What are the different types of foreign exchange risk exposures?
5. Compare revaluation and devaluation with appreciation and depreciation, respectively.
6. Differentiate between the spot exchange rate and the forward exchange rate.
7. Compare hedging and speculation, and explain why they usually take place in the forward market.
8. Contrast stabilizing speculation and destabilizing speculation. How can a speculator take a short position? A long position?
9. Differentiate between currency swap and credit swap, and explain why central banks use swap arrangements today.
10. Compare two-point arbitrage and triangular arbitrage, and elaborate on the impact of arbitrage activities on the exchange rates of different monetary centers.
11. What are Eurocurrencies? What factors contributed to the growth of the Eurocurrency market?
12. What is international banking? What factors have contributed to the development of international banking?

Problems

1. A U.S. exporter is expected to receive £100,000 from a British importer two months from now. The spot rate is $2.05 = £1.00, and the 60-day forward rate is $2.00 = £1.00. Given this information, how can the U.S. exporter hedge his or her foreign exchange risk? How can the British importer hedge his or her foreign exchange risk?
2. Assume that you are the manager of an MNC that is importing coffee beans from Colombia. It is expected that pesos (the Colombian currency) will change in value soon. How do you manage your leads and lags if the pesos rise in value? If the pesos fall in value?

3. Suppose you are a speculator, and the 60-day forward rate is $2.00 = £1.00. Given this information, how would you speculate in the forward market if you believed that the spot rate in two months would be $2.08 = £1.00? How much would you earn if you were correct? How would you speculate in the forward market if you believed that the spot rate in two months would be $1.98 = £1.00? How much would you earn if you were correct?
4. Suppose you are an arbitrager who is facing the following exchange rates:

   London: $2 = £1
   Toronto: Fr 15 (French francs) = £1
   Milan: Fr 6 (French francs) = $1

   Given these data, explain how you can engage in triangular arbitrage. How much profit will you make?
5. Suppose as a U.S. resident you receive £10,000 for services you rendered in Great Britain, and you would like to deposit your money in a certificate of deposit (CD) in either the United States or Britain. The spot exchange rate and the interest rates on the six-month CDs in the United States and Britain are as follows:

Spot exchange rate: $1.75 = £1
Interest rate on a six-month CD in the
United States: $i_{us} = 10\%$
Interest rate on a six-month CD in
Britain: $i_b = 8\%$.

Given this information, answer the following questions.

(a)   What action would you take if you would like to avoid the risk of the foreign exchange market? What
       would you end up with as a result of this action at the end of the six-month period?

FIGURE 11-5

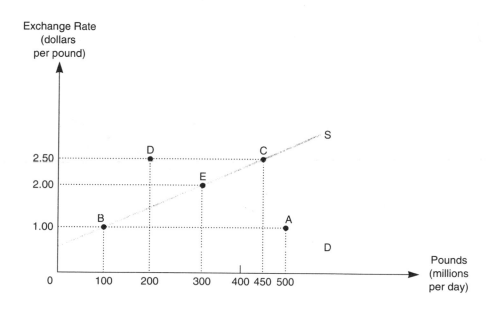

(b)   Assuming that there is no forward market, what action would you take if you would like to speculate and
       you expected the exchange rate to be $2.00 = £1 in six months? What if you expected the exchange rate
       to be $1.50 = £1 in six months? How much would you end up with in each of these cases?

6.   Assume the United States and Great Britain are the only trading partners, with the dollar as domestic currency
     and the British pound as foreign currency. Figure 11-5 above shows the demand and supply curves for the
     British pound (foreign currency) in the United States. Given this figure, answer the following questions.

(a)   Assuming a freely fluctuating exchange rate system, what would happen if the supply curve shifted to
       the left and intersected the demand curve at point D?

(b)   Assuming a freely fluctuating exchange rate system, what would happen if demand shifted to the left,
       intersecting the supply curve at point B?

(c)   Assuming a fixed exchange rate system, how could the United States maintain the exchange rate fixed
       at the level of $1.00 = £1?

Suggested Readings

Aliber, Robert Z. *The International Business Money Game.* New York: Basic Books, 1979.

————. "International Banking: Growth and Regulation." *Columbia Journal of World Business* (Winter 1975): 9-16.

Bell, Geoffrey. *The Eurodollar Market and the International Financial System.* New York: Wiley, 1973.

Booth, Lawrence D. "Hedging and Foreign Exchange Exposure." *Management International Review* (Spring 1982):
       26-42.

Eimzing, P. *The Dynamic Theory of Forward Exchange.* London: Macmillan, 1967.

Eiteman, David, and Arthur Stonehill. *Multinational Business Finance,* 3d ed. Reading, MA: Addison-Wesley, 1982.

Fieleke, Norman S. "The Rise of the Foreign Currency Futures Market." In *International Trade and Finance: Readings,* 3d ed. edited by Robert E. Baldwin and J. David Richardson. Boston: Little, Brown, 1986, 437-440.

Froot, Kenneth A., and Richard H. Thaler. "Anomalies of Foreign Exchange." *The Journal of Economics Perspectives* (Summer 1990): 179-192.

Gendreau, Brian. "New Markets in Foreign Currency Options." In *International Trade and Finance: Readings*, 3d ed., edited by Robert E. Baldwin and J. David Richardson. Boston: Little, Brown, 1986, 441-450.

Gidny, Ian H. "Measuring the World Foreign Exchange Market." *Columbia Journal of World Business* (Winter 1979): 36-48.

———. "Why It Doesn't Pay to Make a Habit of Forward Hedging." *Eurocurrency* (December 1976): 23.

Grabbe, J. O. *International Financial Markets,* 2d ed. New York: Elsevier, 1991, part II.

Jacques, Laurent L. "Management of Foreign Exchange Risk: A Review Article." *Journal of International Business Studies* (Spring/Summer 1981): 81-103.

Kubarych, R. M. *Foreign Exchange Markets in the United States.* New York: The Federal Reserve Bank, 1978.

McKenzie, G. *Economics of the Eurodollar Market.* London: Macmillan, 1976.

Melvin, Michael. *International Money and Finance.* New York: Harper & Row, 1985, Ch. 1.

Mussa, Michael L. *Exchange Rates in Theory and Reality.* Essays in International Finance. Princeton, NJ: Princeton University Press, December 1990.

Park, Yoon S. *The Euro-bond Market: Function and Structure.* New York: Praeger, 1974.

Paluls, B. Diane. "U.S. Exchange Rate Policy: Bretton Woods to Present." *Federal Reserve Bulletin* (November 1990): 891-908.

Revey, Patricia A. "Evolution and Growth of the United States Foreign Exchange Market." *Federal Reserve Bank of New York Quarterly Review* (Autumn 1981): 32.

Stockes, Houston H., and Hugh Neuberger. "Interest Arbitrage, Forward Speculation and the Determination of the Forward Exchange Rate." *Columbia Journal of World Business* (Winter 1979): 86-98.

Tavlas, G. "On International Use of Currencies: The Case of Deutsche Mark." *Princeton Essay in International Finance,* no. 181. Princeton, NJ: March 1991.

Chapter 12

THE INTERNATIONAL MONETARY SYSTEM

12.1 INTRODUCTION

Because each sovereign nation has its own currency, it is essential to maintain a workable system of international payments that facilitates trade between different countries. Ideally, such a system would be composed of an international central bank that would handle an international money accepted by all nations. Practically, however, because sovereign nations like to manage their own monetary systems rather than trust an international central bank, it has been necessary for them to engage in various cooperative arrangements. These arrangements, which involve rules, procedures, customs, instruments, and the organizational setting, are referred to as the international monetary system.

Because the international monetary system continually changes, its comprehension necessitates an understanding of the major events that have shaped its present form. The purpose of this chapter is to provide a basic knowledge of the history of the international monetary system. This will help us to understand the present institutional setting of the international monetary system and the way that it influences the foreign exchange market.

12.2 THE GOLD COIN STANDARD

In earlier times, when the volume of foreign trade was insignificant and was confined mainly to a few luxury items, international payments were made chiefly in gold and silver. Gold and silver values were determined by their market prices at the time the payments were made. With the increase in the volume of international trade in the nineteenth century, however, it became necessary to devise a unified method of international payments that could be accepted by all countries. This meant the development of a system that could not affect the free interaction of market forces and would not be subject to control by any government. The quest for such a system resulted in the development of the gold coin standard, or more simply, the **gold standard.** The essential characteristics of the **gold coin standard** were as follows:

1. A country's unit of currency (such as the U.S. dollar, the British pound, or the German deutsche mark) was defined by law in terms of a fixed weight of gold. For example, one U.S. dollar was equated to 23.22 grains of fine gold, and one British pound was equal to 113 grains of fine gold.
2. Gold itself, either in bullion or in coins, could be exported or imported without any restrictions.
3. The national currency and gold coins could be freely converted to each other at the defined rate. Also, a government was obligated to exchange gold for paper money, or vice versa, at the defined rate.
4. There were no restrictions imposed on the coinage of gold.
5. Gold coins were considered full legal tender for all debts.

Because national currencies were defined in terms of a fixed amount of gold, the exchange rate between any two currencies (the price of one currency in terms of another currency) remained stable and could only fluctuate within a very narrow limit known as the *gold export point* and the *gold import point.* To clarify, consider our example of the U.S. dollar and the British pound. Because one U.S. dollar was equal to 23.22 grains of fine gold, and one British pound was equal to 113 grains, then one British pound was equal to 4.86 U.S. dollars (113/23.22 = 4.86). Given that the cost of shipping and insurance of 113 grains of gold between New York and London was almost $0.02 in 1930, the exchange rate of one U.S. dollar fluctuated between $4.84 and $4.88 in terms of the British pound at that time.

The reason for this fluctuation was that gold could be sold at two different rates: the fixed legal rate defined by the government or the market rate defined by the demand and supply for gold. Thus, if the British pound's market rate increased to $4.89, for example, it would have been cheaper for a U.S. importer to obtain 113 grains of gold at the legal rate of $4.86 from the U.S. Treasury. The importer could then ship the gold to London to settle payments with a British exporter. Because 113 grains of gold in England was accepted as one British pound, the U.S. importer would have had to pay $4.88 for a British pound ($4.86, the legal rate, plus $0.02 shipping), instead of the higher market rate of $4.89, thus saving $0.01 on each British pound bought. Similarly, if the market rate fell to $4.83, for example, a British importer could obtain 113 grains of gold for each British pound and ship the gold to New York at a cost of $0.02 for each 113 grains shipped. Because 113 grains of gold was equal to $4.86 in New York, the importer was in effect getting $4.84 ($4.86, the legal rate, minus $0.02 shipping) for each British pound instead of the lower market rate of $4.83, thus saving $0.01 on each 113 grains of gold shipped.

In the previous example, $4.88 and $4.84 were the "gold points," $4.88 being the gold export point and $4.84 the gold import point. Thus, the gold points were equal to the legal rate, plus or minus the cost of shipping gold. These gold points set an upper and a lower limit within which the exchange rate could fluctuate. In our example, gold would be exported from the United States when the market rate rose above the gold export point ($4.88) and imported when it fell below the gold import point ($4.84). Consequently, the exchange rate remained stable within the limits set by the gold points.

The gold standard system provided an automatic adjustment mechanism that corrected for deficits or surpluses in the merchandise trade account of the balance of payments (BOP).* Because each country's money supply was composed of either gold or paper money backed by gold, a surplus in the merchandise trade account of a country's BOP meant a rise in the money supply, which resulted in higher domestic prices. This, in turn, caused exports to decrease and imports to increase, thus reducing the surplus in the BOP. A deficit in the merchandise trade account of a nation's BOP meant a decrease in the money supply. The fall in the money supply, in turn, resulted in lower domestic prices, which caused exports to increase and imports to decrease, thus reducing the deficit in the BOP.

The gold standard system prevailed mainly from 1880 to 1914. With the outbreak of World War I in 1914, the system was disrupted, but it continued on a somewhat modified basis until the early 1930s. The gold standard system is linked to classical economic theory. Consequently, the automatic adjustment in the BOP was based on the classical theory of income and employment, which assumed the following: (a) There was full employment of resources, and a rise in the quantity of money could ensure an increase in the general price level; and (b) prices and wages were flexible.

Given these assumptions, permitting the money supply to correct for BOP problems meant that a country could not employ monetary policy to attain full employment without creating inflation. This is because classical economists believed that there were automatic forces in the system that established full employment without inflation. Under these classical assumptions, no depression could be prolonged. However, the Great Depression of the 1930s proved the contrary, and Keynesian economics emerged, stating that (a) the assumption of full employment was a special, rather than a general, case; and (b) the assumption of price and wage flexibility was not valid for a modern economic system. This meant that the government had to intervene in the economic system to ensure full employment and combat depression rather than waiting for automatic forces to take effect, as classical economists recommended. Thus, although the gold standard had the desirable feature of exchange rate stability, it subjected the domestic economy to the undesirable effects of deflation or inflation. In other words, it provided external stability at the expense of internal stability. With the Great Depression, the stage was set for the abandonment of this monetary standard. As a result, it was formally abandoned by Great Britain in 1931, by the United States in 1933, and by other countries in the following few years.

12.3 THE GOLD BULLION STANDARD

Following the abandonment of the gold coin standard in the 1930s, the United States and most of the other advanced countries adopted the **gold bullion standard**.

---

*   This adjustment mechanism is the same as Hume's specie-flow mechanism, which we studied in Chapter 2.

Under this standard, a nation's unit of currency was defined in terms of a fixed weight of gold. However, unlike the gold coin standard, gold did not circulate within the domestic economy. Gold was used only to meet two purposes: (a) to meet the needs of different industries, such as dentistry and jewelry manufacturing, and (b) to settle international transactions between different nations. Thus, for the most part, the impact of gold on the monetary system was neutralized. In other words, gold was demonetized, except for any possible indirect influence that might result from transactions between national governments.

By replacing the gold coin standard with the gold bullion standard, it was hoped that countries could effectively manage their money rather than leave this management to market forces and become subservient to those forces. It was hoped that this new system would restore confidence in currencies at the national and international levels. The 1930s, however, witnessed a period of great instability in the world, as nations struggled to export their unemployment by the use of competitive currency devaluations, trade restrictions, and export subsidies. These practices resulted in declining international trade and contributed to further unemployment. Such events paved the way for the establishment of a new international monetary system known as the gold exchange standard.

12.4 THE BRETTON WOODS SYSTEM AND THE GOLD EXCHANGE STANDARD

In 1944, in response to the chaos begun in the early 1930s in the international financial system, representatives of the United States, Great Britain, and 42 other nations met at Bretton Woods, New Hampshire, to develop a new international monetary system. Their efforts resulted in the creation of the **Gold Exchange Standard** System and the establishment of two supporting institutions, known as the **International Monetary Fund (IMF)** and the **International Bank for Reconstruction and Development (IBRD)**, or the World Bank.

Under the Gold Exchange Standard System, the value of the U.S. dollar was fixed in terms of gold, that is, one U.S. dollar was equaled to 1/35 ounce of gold. This meant that the United States had to exchange dollars for gold on demand at a rate of $35 per ounce of gold, without any limitation or restrictions.* Other nations' currencies were fixed to the dollar and thus, indirectly, to gold. It was also decided that other nations should be ready to defend their currencies if their values moved 1 percent above or below their par (official) value. This meant that if a nation's currency depreciated by more than 1 percent of its par value, the nation had to sell its dollar reserves to buy its own currency in order to prevent further depreciation.** On the other hand, if a nation's currency appreciated by more than 1 percent of its par value, the nation had to purchase dollars in order to prevent further appreciation.*** Thus, the U.S. dollar served as the only intervention currency, and the system was, in fact, a gold-dollar standard.

Temporary BOP deficits had to be financed out of a nation's international reserve and by borrowing from the IMF. In the presence of a *fundamental disequilibrium,* however, a nation was allowed to repeg its currency, that is, to change its par value, up to 10 percent without permission from the IMF. Par value changes of more than 10 percent, however, required IMF approval. Although **fundamental disequilibrium** was not clearly defined, it generally referred to a large and persistent BOP disequilibrium.

The exchange rate system adopted at the Bretton Woods agreement is known as an **adjustable peg system.** Under this system, a country may change its currency's par value in order to correct its fundamental disequilibrium. This system provides for exchange rate stability in the short-run. It also allows for the possibility of exchange rate adjustment when a fundamental disequilibrium exists, that is, when the BOP moves away from its long-run equilibrium. Thus, the adjustable peg system provides exchange rate stability with some flexibility. The incorporation of such stability into the system by the Bretton Woods agreement stemmed from the participants' desire to avoid the chaotic conditions that had existed before.

Because the main rationale behind the Bretton Woods system was to prevent the recurrence of the events of the Great Depression, nations were prevented from imposing additional trade restrictions. Additionally, it was agreed that existing trade barriers had to be lifted gradually through multilateral negotiations. Restrictions on liquid capital

---

*   The U.S. government was willing to exchange dollars for gold on demand only with foreign holders of dollars; it was unwilling to do so with its own citizens.

**   Depreciation means a decrease in the price of one currency in terms of another currency.

***   Appreciation means an increase in the price of one currency in terms of another currency.

flows, however, were allowed to enable nations to protect their currencies against the instability that could result from large flows of international money.

12.5 THE INTERNATIONAL MONETARY FUND

As we noted earlier, the Bretton Woods agreement gave birth to the IMF. This institution, which started operations on March 1, 1947, with a membership of 30 countries, grew rapidly, and by 2000 included 182 members. Practically all the free world's nations have joined the IMF. Of the Eastern European countries, only Yugoslavia, Romania, and Hungary initially joined the IMF. However, following the economic reforms in Eastern Europe, most of these countries joined the IMF. Although the former Soviet Union participated in the Bretton Woods conference, it decided not to join. The reasons given for some socialist countries' reluctance to join the IMF are related to (a) the veto power granted to the United States with regard to some important decisions; (b) the reporting requirement that forces members to make statements regarding their gold and foreign exchange interests and requires them to hold part of their interest in the United States, where the IMF is located; and (c) the provisions that allow members to have access to the IMF resources.

In the mid-1980s, the Soviet Union considered joining the IMF and the World Bank. Such a move was believed to be part of the modernization policies being carried out by Soviet leader Mikhail Gorbachev. At that time, Soviet experts believed it would be years before the Soviets got a foot in the door.[1] Following the collapse of the Soviet Union and the formation of the Commonwealth of Independent States (CIS), the former communist nations started joining the IMF. In 1994, these countries included Armenia, Azerbaijan, Belarus, Estonia, Georgia, Kazakhstan, Kyrgyzstan, Latvia, Lithuania, Moldova, Russia, Tajikistan, Turkmenistan, Ukraine, and Uzbekistan. Russia, the biggest and most powerful member of the CIS, has especially attracted the attention of the IMF and Western leaders. For example, in August 1992, the IMF executive board approved a $1 billion loan to Russia. Accordingly, Russia agreed to decrease its budget deficit and control inflation. This action paved the way for the inflow of $600 million in loans from the World Bank and a $24 billion Western aid package. In June 1993, the IMF released an additional $1.5 billion to Russia; however, the IMF maintained that it would not release any more funds until Moscow resumed its faltering economic reforms.[2] In July 1999, the IMF gave $4.5 billion to help Russia stave off a debt crisis

The IMF was set up to pursue two main objectives. First, it was to ensure that nations followed the agreed-on set of rules of conduct for engaging in international trade. Second, it was to assist nations with temporary BOP deficits by providing them with borrowing facilities.

The IMF was financed by its members. Upon joining the IMF, a nation had to subscribe to a quota, which was based on its relative economic significance and the level of its international business activities. The size of members' quotas, which reflected voting ability and borrowing capacity from the Fund, has been revised several times. For example, in 1944, the United States was assigned the largest quota of 31 percent. By 1996, this quota had decreased to 18.25 percent. As Table 12-1 shows, in 1996, the quota for Great Britain was 5.10 percent; Germany, 5.67 percent; France, 5.10 percent; and Japan, 5.67 percent.

Initially, upon joining the IMF, a member country had to pay 25 percent of its quota in gold (called **gold tranche**) and the remaining 75 percent in its own currency. Beginning in 1978, the Fund no longer required the gold tranche payment; such payment could be made in "**reserve tranche**," that is, either in currencies acceptable to the IMF or in special drawing rights (SDRs), which are explained in the next section.

Under IMF rules, a member country could borrow an amount equal to 25 percent of its quota from the IMF in any given year. Any borrowing above this level required IMF approval, and it was granted only for resolving a country's BOP problems.

Today, the IMF stands as a powerful international institution whose strength stems from (a) its ability to grant or deny loans beyond the reserve tranche of its member nations; (b) the requirement that its permission be obtained for a greater-than-10-percent devaluation of a currency; and (c) the ruling that joining the IMF is a prerequisite for membership in the World Bank. Two examples of IMF activities include the approval of a $452 million loan to Nigeria to support that nation's move to trade liberalization in 1986,[3] and the approval of two loans to the Philippines in the same year.[4] In 1989, the president of the Philippines accepted an international economic plan proposed by the IMF, setting the stage for two IMF loans totaling $1.3 billion.[5] A more recent example of the IMF includes the release of $184 million to Ukraine in September 1999.

GLOBAL INSIGHT CASE 12.1

The Role of the IMF in Economic Reform

The International Monetary Fund, an organization of 154 member countries, provides technical assistance, policy advice, and financial support to countries undertaking extensive structural and macroeconomic reforms. IMF financial support is planned in conjunction with the government officials of the country itself and requires strict adherence to an agreed schedule of policy adjustments and quantitative performance targets. Disbursement of support funds is conditional on meeting these targets.

Types of Support. Standby arrangements are loans that focus on fiscal, monetary, and exchange-rate policies aimed at overcoming short-term balance of payments difficulties. Repayment is to be made in 3¼ to 5 years. Extended arrangements are loans that support medium-term (3 to 4 years) programs of macroeconomic and structural reforms. Repayment is to be made in 4½ to 10 years. Structural adjustment facility and enhanced structural adjustment facility arrangements are loans that support medium-term (3 years) structural reform programs in low-income countries.

The Compensatory and Contingency Financing Facility. This facility provides IMF loans for the following purposes. The compensatory element provides resources to members to cover temporary export shortfalls or excessive import costs of certain foodstuffs due to price fluctuations beyond their control that could otherwise jeopardize their economic performance under their IMF programs. In 1990, at the initiative of the United States, the facility was modified to allow financing for higher oil import costs and certain other losses due to the Gulf crisis.

What is conditionality? To ensure that nations with IMF financial support make consistent and substantial progress in attaining program goals, the IMF and the member country agree in advance to quarterly or semiannual target levels for a number of policy variables, such as domestic credit creation, international reserves, and government budget deficits. A country's drawings on IMF resources are conditional on attaining these intermediate targets. If these targets are not met, the IMF usually requires corrective policy actions before additional drawings may be made.

Source: U.S. Government Printing Office, *Economic Report of the President*, (Washington, D.C: U.S. Government Printing Office, February 1991), 230, Reprinted.

12.5a Special Drawing Rights

The **special drawing right** (SDR) is one of the most significant IMF inventions. During the 1960s, the world experienced an international liquidity problem.* During this period, the United States faced a BOP deficit. Confidence in the U.S. dollar, which was used as a significant international reserve (international medium of exchange), was shaken. As a result, there was widespread expectation that the dollar would not continue to supply the needed international reserve.**

At the 1967 annual meeting of the IMF Board of Governors in Rio de Janeiro, the SDR emerged as a new reserve asset to supplement the international reserves of gold and foreign exchange. Special drawing rights are IMF bank accounts. Each country can use its own money to buy SDRs from the IMF, according to its quota. In this manner, each country's bank account in the IMF is credited for the amount of SDRs purchased. The SDRs can then be used by each country to settle its accounts with other nations. In other words, SDRs entitle their holder nations to draw out any money they need to pay off their debts to other nations. Because the IMF sells SDRs to all countries, it ends

---

* *International liquidity* is the world's supply of gold, foreign exchange, and other assets that are used in settling BOP deficits among nations.

** The term *international reserve refers* to gold, foreign exchange, and other assets that act as an international medium of exchange and are set aside (reserved) by a nation in settling its BOP deficit.

up with bank accounts in all currencies that can then be sold to different countries in return for their SDRs. Thus, SDRs are not backed by gold or any other currency. All nations accept SDRs just because they have agreed to do so. Special drawing rights are employed only by nations' central banks in order to resolve countries' BOP problems; they are not used in private business transactions.

At the 1967 IMF meeting, in Rio de Janeiro, the initial allocation of SDRs, distributed to member nations according to their quotas in the IMF, totaled 9.5 billion. Table 12-1 shows the total allocation of SDRs and their distribution among major industrial countries and developing countries in 1996.

The value of one SDR was initially equal to $1.00, but following the devaluation of the U.S. dollar in 1971 and 1973, the SDR's value rose. Because the dollar's trouble was transmitted to SDRs, the IMF decided to use a weighted average of a "basket" of 16 major currencies to establish the value of the SDR beginning in 1974.

Although SDRs are not used to settle private dealings, they are used as the "money unit" in some international transactions. For example, Suez Canal tolls are stated in SDRs. However, the toll payments are not actually paid in SDRs, but in national currency. The tolls are first figured out in SDRs. Then the amount of payments in national currency is determined on the basis of the exchange rate between the SDR and the national currency.

TABLE 12-1
Quotas from IMF Members, December 31, 1996

Country	Millions of SDRs	Percentage*
All Countries	**145,318.8**	**100.00**
Industrial countries	**88,425.2**	**60.85**
United States	26,526.8	18.25
United Kingdom	7,414.6	5.10
Germany	8,241.5	5.67
France	7,414.6	5.10
Japan	8,241.5	5.67
Canada	4,320.3	2.97
Italy	4,590.7	3.16
Netherlands	3,444.2	2.37
Belgium	3,102.3	2.13
Austria	2,333.2	1.61
All others	12,795.5	8.81
Developing Countries	**56,893.6**	**39.15**
Africa	8,380.8	5.77
Asia	13,679.8	9.41
Europe	12,074.3	8.31
Middle East	11,309.4	7.78
Western Hemisphere	11,449.3	7.88

* This column was calculated by the author.

Source: International Monetary Fund, *International Financial Statistics* (February 27, 1997)

12.6 THE WORLD BANK

As we stated earlier, the IBRD, or World Bank, was established in 1944 by participating nations at the Bretton Woods conference.

Initially, the bank was set up mainly to provide loans for post-World War II reconstruction. Today, however, the bank's major function is to provide financial resources for the implementation of development projects, such as communications systems, dams, and transportation networks in developing nations. The bank has more than 180 member nations. Membership in the bank is achieved by purchasing shares of stock. The United States, having purchased about one-third of the bank's stock, represents the major stockholder of the World Bank.

The strength of the World Bank as an international financial institution stems not only from its capital stock, but from its ability to raise money through the sale of bonds. These bonds are considered very safe and are widely accepted because they are backed by the credit of all the participating nations up to a level equivalent to 100 percent of their quotas.

The expansion in World Bank activities has led to the establishment of two other institutions, the **International Finance Corporation (IFC)** and the **International Development Association (IDA)**.

The IFC was established in July 1956 to provide capital and managerial assistance to private businesses in developing nations. The IDA was created in 1960 by the World Bank to make "soft loans," that is, loans with much easier terms than the World Bank would normally make. The purpose of these loans is to help finance development projects in developing nations. Unlike regular World Bank loans, these loans are much riskier, and for this reason they may not be repaid. However, the IDA takes this risk if it believes there is a good chance that the loan would successfully stimulate the development process of the nation in question.

12.7 DEMISE OF THE BRETTON WOODS SYSTEM

The main cause of the Bretton Woods system's demise was the existence of persistent deficits in the current account of the U.S. BOP. As we explained earlier, the Bretton Woods system gave rise to the Gold Exchange Standard System that considered dollars as gold and adopted the dollar as the international reserve currency that backed the values of other world currencies. Such a strategy was feasible because the United States was in a good financial position and was ready to exchange gold for dollars at the official rate of $35 an ounce. The financial strength of the United States was reflected in its 1945-1949 current account surplus. Beginning in 1950, as the European and Japanese economies became stronger, the U.S. current account surplus turned into a deficit. However, until 1957, the deficit was relatively small and averaged only $1 billion a year. The United States could easily survive such a deficit because (a) the dollar was used as the international currency, so many nations were willing to hold on to it rather than exchange it for gold; (b) the United States had enough gold reserve and stood ready to exchange dollars for gold at the official rate of $35 an ounce; and (c) nations preferred to hold dollars instead of gold because dollars could earn interest.

Beginning in 1958, the current account deficit of the U.S. BOP, which had averaged $1 billion a year from 1950 through 1957, tripled and averaged $3 billion a year. This was followed by a huge capital outflow and high inflation, which further intensified the current account deficit. As a result, confidence in the dollar was shaken, and, beginning in 1968, the United States experienced a "dollar crisis." Foreigners, who felt that the devaluation of the U.S. dollar was inevitable, were no longer holding on to their dollars as a stable international money, but were exchanging them for gold. As a result, the U.S. gold reserve decreased to the point that it became smaller than foreign-held dollar reserves. To alleviate the problem and to discourage foreigners from demanding gold for their dollars, the United States invented **Roosa bonds**. These were interest-bearing treasury bonds with a guaranteed exchange rate. They were designed to persuade foreigners to hold on to their dollars by ensuring there would be no decrease in their value if the dollar were devaluated. This was achieved by denominating the bond in a foreign currency, such as the deutsche mark, and guaranteeing the exchange rate. This meant, for example, that a German could buy a Roosa bond for $100, and the bond would be payable (at the guaranteed exchange rate of $1.00 = DM 2.5) in deutsche marks, making it worth DM 250. Unfortunately, this scheme did not resolve the problem and the U.S. gold reserve continued to decline to the extent that, in 1970, it reached the level of one fourth of the dollar reserves held by foreigners. To deal with this problem, the United States tried to get nations with trade surpluses to revalue their currencies in 1970 and early

1971. However, such efforts proved fruitless, and the U.S. BOP deficit continued to rise, reaching the level of $12 billion in the first half of 1971. By this time, confidence in the dollar was badly shaken, forcing then President Nixon to suspend the convertibility of dollars into gold on August 15, 1971, breaking the Bretton Woods system. Concurrent with this decision, the United States launched wage and price controls and imposed a temporary 10-percent tariff on imports, to be abolished after the necessary currency realignments were made.

12.8 THE SMITHSONIAN AGREEMENT

The Nixon action of August 15, 1971, resulted in a *floating dollar*. This means that the exchange rate (price) of the dollar was determined by the market forces of demand and supply. In other words, dollars were exchanged at the rate foreign banks were willing to pay for them. However, this situation did not last for long. In December 1971, in another attempt to shape the international monetary system, the representatives of the "big ten" trading nations (the United States, Great Britain, the former West Germany, Japan, France, Italy, Canada, the Netherlands, Belgium, and Sweden) met at the Smithsonian Institution in Washington, D.C. At this meeting, it was agreed to officially devalue the dollar by changing its gold price from $35 an ounce to $38 an ounce. At the same time, the deutsche mark was appreciated by about 17 percent and the Japanese yen by about 14 percent against the dollar. Other nations' currencies were appreciated by smaller amounts. It was also decided to increase the total band of fluctuation from 2 percent (1 percent above and 1 percent below the par value), established under the Bretton Woods system, to 4.5 percent (2.25 percent above and 2.25 percent below the par value). Additionally, the United States lifted its 10-percent tariff on imports.

Because the U.S. dollar continued to be inconvertible into gold, the international monetary system was still, in principle, under the dollar standard. Nixon considered the Smithsonian Agreement the most important monetary arrangement in world history and vowed that he would never again devalue the dollar.

The Smithsonian Arrangement seemed to work well for about one year. The United States was still under wage and price controls, and the value of the dollar seemed to be under control. However, in 1972, the United States was once again faced with a huge deficit in the BOP current account amounting to $10 billion. It became obvious that the Smithsonian Agreement was not working, and another devaluation had to take place. In January 1973, Nixon relaxed the control over prices and wages, contributing to the collapse of confidence in the dollar. These situations led to another official devaluation of the dollar, which was announced in February 1973. The dollar still remained inconvertible into gold; however, its official price was changed from $38 an ounce to $42.22 an ounce.

12.9 THE PRESENT INTERNATIONAL MONETARY SYSTEM

The devaluation of the dollar in February 1973 did not succeed in resolving the dollar crisis. Given that the dollar had been devalued twice since 1971, there was speculation about the possibility of another devaluation. When such speculation reached its high point in March 1973, the major industrial nations decided to let their currencies float. Britain, Canada, Japan, Italy, Switzerland, and the United States let their currencies float independently. France, the former West Germany, and the original members of the European Union (EU) decided to maintain relatively fixed exchange rates internally, but to let their currencies float jointly against the dollar and other dollar-tied currencies. The managed floating exchange rate system was born.

Under the **freely fluctuating exchange rate system** (explained in Chapter 11), the price of a currency is defined by the interaction of the market demand and supply for it. Thus, if there is a shortage of a country's currency, the exchange rate (the price of that currency) increases. On the other hand, if there is a surplus of a nation's currency, its exchange rate declines. This free movement of exchange rates, occurring in response to the market forces of demand and supply, is what brings nations' BOP into equilibrium. In other words, a country's BOP surplus or deficit is automatically resolved by the appreciation or depreciation, respectively, of its currency. In a freely fluctuating exchange rate system, governments do not intervene in the foreign exchange market. Because in March 1973 governments did not want to surrender complete control over a variable as important as the exchange rate to market forces, a freely floating (flexible) exchange rate system seemed undesirable. As a result, the **managed floating exchange rate system** was adopted. Under this system, governments could intervene in the foreign exchange market in order to serve their national exchange rate policies.[*] To coordinate these policies, informal guidelines were established by the IMF.

Because the managed floating exchange rate system was not a planned system and was forced on the world by the demise of the Bretton Woods system, it was met with skepticism. Critics of the floating exchange rate system could not see how market forces could manage the international monetary system, when a carefully planned system had collapsed. Thus, from the beginning, serious efforts were made to design rules to govern the float. It was hoped that such rules would prevent countries from pursuing competitive exchange rate depreciation to stimulate their exports and returning the world to the chaotic conditions that existed in the 1930s. Fortunately, however, the system worked well and was formally recognized by the 1976 **Jamaica Accords**. The IMF formalized the rules of managed floating exchange rates. According to these rules, nations are allowed to intervene in the foreign exchange market in order to smooth out short-run fluctuations, without trying to change the long-run pattern of the exchange rates. The Jamaica Accords also allowed countries the option of a foreign exchange rate system as long as their activities did not disturb normal trading patterns and the operation of the world economy.

To show its determination in eliminating gold as an international reserve asset, the IMF sold one sixth of its gold holdings between 1976 and 1980. Additionally, the official price of gold was abandoned, and it was decided that the IMF would no longer engage in gold transactions among its members. Thus, the gold tranche became reserve tranche.[**] In 1974, the IMF started to measure all reserves and other official transactions in SDRs rather than in U.S. dollars.

According to Table 12-2, in 1996, eleven different exchange rate regimes were chosen by different IMF members. As the table shows, in 1996, 20 nations, or roughly 11 percent of total IMF members, pegged their currencies to the U.S. dollar. This indicates that the U.S. dollar is still considered a significant international reserve asset.

Today, nations have a large degree of flexibility and can select the exchange rate regime that best fits their economic conditions. In general, major industrial countries and countries that are faced with a relatively high inflationary strain have adopted a more flexible exchange rate regime than that chosen by the highly specialized economies of small developing nations. All countries still require international reserves in order to defend their currencies by ironing out short-run fluctuations in their exchange rates. Although most of the international reserves used to defend national monies are composed of convertible currencies, the future will call for the use of SDRs. It is expected that the number of SDRs allocated to each country by the IMF will increase in the future.

---

[*] The terms "clean-floating" and "dirty-floating" have been used by some commentators to describe floating exchange rate systems. Clean floating is synonymous with "free floating." As we have explained, in a free floating exchange rate system, exchange rates are determined by the interaction of the market forces of demand and supply. Dirty floating refers to managing a country's exchange rate system to attain goals other than just smoothing out the short-term fluctuations. For example, a country may intervene in the foreign exchange market to depreciate its currency in order to expand its exports.

[**] Although gold was abolished as an international reserve asset, the IMF decided to measure its gold asset at the pre-1971 official price of $35, or 35 SDRs, per ounce.

TABLE 12-2
Different Exchange Rate Regimes Used by IMF Members

Classification Status[a]	Number of Countries	Percentage of Countries [f]
Currency pegged to		
U.S. dollar	20	11.049
French franc	14	7.734
Russian Ruble	6	3.314
Other currency	9	4.972
SDR	2	1.104
Other currency composite[b]	20	11.059
Flexible limited vis-a-vis a single currency[c]	4	2.209
Cooperative arrangements[d]	10	5.524
Adjusted according to a set of indicators[e]	2	1.105
Managed floating	46	25.414
Independently floating	54	29.834
Total	181	100.000

[a] For members with dual or multiple exchange markets, the arrangement shown is that in the major market.
[b] Composite currencies which are pegged to various "basket" of currencies members own choice, as distinct from the SDR basket.
[c] Exchange rate of all currencies have shown limited flexibility in terms of the U.S. dollar.
[d] Refers to comparative arrangements under the European Monetary System
[e] Includes exchange arrangements under which the exchange is adjusted at relatively frequent intervals, on the basis of indicators determined by the respective countries.
[f] This column was calculated by the author.

Source: International Monetary Fund, *International Financial Statistics* 50(/February 1997): 2.

12.10 THE EUROPEAN MONETARY SYSTEM

The exchange rate instability that started with the collapse of the Bretton Woods system caused the six original members of the EU to cooperate in designing a system that would provide them with greater monetary stability. In March 1972, they decided to adopt a **joint floating exchange rate system.** Under this system, referred to as the **European Exchange Rate Mechanism (ERM),** member nations' currencies were tied closely to each other, but they were allowed to fluctuate against a given currency, such as the U.S. dollar. Thus, the currencies of the EU nations floated together in unison, in relation to the given currency (the U.S. dollar), rising or falling as a group. Actually, the EU members let their currencies float jointly against the U.S. dollar with a total fluctuation band of 2.25 percent, instead of the 4.5 percent agreed on in December 1971. This decision was referred to as the **"European Snake"** and was in effect until March 1973.

In an attempt to revive the European Snake and provide greater monetary integration among its members, the EU established the **European Monetary System (EMS)** in March 1979. The Members in this system included Belgium, Denmark, France, Ireland, Italy, Luxembourg, the Netherlands, and West Germany. Great Britain was the only EU member that decided not to join.

The objective set by the EMS members was "closer monetary cooperation leading to a zone of monetary stability in Europe."[6] To achieve this objective, the following features were incorporated into the EMS:

1. A unit of currency known as the **European Currency Unit (ECU)** was created. This currency unit, which resembled an SDR, was a weighted average of the nine EU currencies and was used for accounting purposes among the EMS members.*

2. The par value, or the central rate, of each currency was defined in terms of ECUs, and countries could intervene to prevent movements of their currencies by 2.25 percent above or below these par values. Countries whose exchange rates were previously floating against other members' currencies were allowed a greater fluctuation band of ±6 percent, instead of ±2.25 percent. Among EMS members, Italy was the only country that decided to use this option and was qualified to do so.

3. To provide short-term credit for intervention purposes, the EU members established the **European Monetary Corporation Fund (EMCF)**. This corporation allocated ECUs to member nations in return for 20 percent of their gold and dollar reserves.

Because members of the EMS are allowed to follow their own independent monetary policies, the EMS has had difficulty in achieving its objective of monetary stability. In fact, members' differential inflation rates caused the EMS to undertake seven realignments of exchange rates from its formation in March 1979 to March 1983. From 1983 until 1992, however, the EMS appeared to be more successful in achieving exchange rate stability among members' currencies. Exchange rate fluctuations of EMS currencies were, in general, smaller than the fluctuations of other major currencies. The EMS's success in maintaining relative stability from 1983 through 1992 can be largely attributed to the implementation of restrictive monetary and fiscal policies in member countries, such as France and Italy, that face high inflation rates. However, the existence of inflationary differentials between EMS members warranted another realignment of currencies during this period. This was achieved in July 1985 by depreciating the Italian lira against other member currencies by about 8 percent.[7] However, as you recall from Chapter 9, Germany's stance on high interest rates brought the ERM to the brink of collapse twice, in 1992 and in 1993. Following the 1993 upheaval in currency markets, a new structure was adopted for the European ERM. Accordingly, it was decided to increase the band of fluctuations around the par value from ±2.25 percent to ±15 percent.[8]

As we explained in Chapter 9, economic integration accelerated in Western Europe in the late 1980s, paving the way for the creation of an economic and monetary union. The Maastrich Treaty provided a framework for the shift to a common monetary policy and to a single currency administered by an autonomous European central bank. According to the Maastrich Treaty, the union was accomplished in three phases. During the first two phases, member nations tried to attain greater economic convergence gauged by four measures: inflation, interest rates, exchange rate stability, and fiscal position. During the third stage, which began in the late 1990s, member nations that satisfy the economic criteria were allowed to irreversibly fix their exchange rates and circulate a single currency.[9]

12.11 ALTERNATIVE EXCHANGE RATE SYSTEMS

As mentioned earlier, following the breakdown of the Bretton Woods system of fixed exchange rates in 1973, IMF member nations had a large degree of flexibility in choosing the exchange rate regime that best fit their economic conditions. We are already familiar with fixed exchange rates, freely fluctuating exchange rates, managed floating exchange rates, and joint floating exchange rates. Other widely discussed exchange rate regimes are **crawling pegs** and the **target zone approach.** In this section, we examine these alternative exchange rate regimes, elaborating on their advantages and disadvantages.

---

* Although Britain did not join the EMS, its currency was used in the calculation of the ECU.

GLOBAL INSIGHTS CASE 12.2

Latin American Exchange Rate Systems

Departing from the tradition of the fixed exchange rate system during the 1980s, many developing nations switched to exchange rate systems that allow greater flexibility. Some of these nations mixed fixed and floating exchange rates by using fixed rates for some international transactions and floating rates for others. Latin America represents a region that has experimented with a variety of exchange rate systems. The diversity of exchange rate regimes in this region is bewildering. Not only can we see the use of floating rates, fixed rates, and a combination of the two, but the governments' use of these systems change over time. Additionally, the currency used can change frequently. For example, during the 1980s and early 1990s, Argentina introduced at least one significant revision to its exchange rate regime about every two years. Additionally, it switched its currency from the peso to the austral in 1985 and back to the peso in 1992. Since 1980, Brazil has altered its currency several times. First, it changed from the cruzerio to the cruzado. Then, it changed from the cruzado to the new cruzado. Finally, it changed from the new cruzado back to the cruzerio again.

In the early 1990s, Nicaragua changed its currency from the cordoba to gold cordoba. In 1985, Peru changed its currency from the sol to the inti in 1985 and then to the sol nuevo (new sol) in January 1991.

These frequent changes in exchange rate systems of Latin American countries is further complicated by the fact that during the transition period, new and old currencies distribute concurrently. Additionally, residents in many Latin American nations frequently spend U.S. dollars as well as domestic money in their transactions. This frequent use of the U.S. dollar creates, in effect, a multiple currency system in these nations. For instance, it is estimated that in Argentina $5 billion circulate domestically alongside the peso.

Source: Pick's Currency Yearbook, (New York: Pick Publishing Co.), different issues reprinted.

12.11a Crawling Pegs

Under the **crawling peg system**, the par value rate changes frequently, but by very small amounts. Changes take place at clearly specified periods, such as every year, until the desired exchange rate is achieved, correcting the BOP disequilibrium. The term *crawling peg* signifies that changes in par value take place in a large number of short phases to keep exchange rate adjustment continuous. In comparison to the adjustable peg system that allows for infrequent but sudden change in a par value, the crawling peg provides for frequent changes in par values. This allows par values to crawl along in reaction to market forces. Given such characteristics, the proponents of the crawling peg system maintain that it provides the flexibility of the floating exchange rate system along with the stability of the fixed exchange rate system. It evades the problem of relatively large changes in par values associated with the adjustable peg system. Additionally, small and continual changes in par values discourage speculators.

The crawling system has been employed by a number of developing nations, mostly in Latin America, that have experienced fast and recurring inflation. These nations have realized that a pegging system can function in inflationary conditions only if there is stipulation for continual changes in the par values. Notable among these nations is Brazil, which has declared a change in the par value of its currency (the cruzeiro) several times a year. Other countries that have adopted the crawling peg include Argentina, Chile, Colombia, Israel, Peru, and Portugal.

The IMF has generally agreed that the crawling peg system is not appropriate for industrialized nations, such as the United States and Great Britain, whose currencies function as a basis for international liquidity. Today, even the most zealous advocates of the crawling peg system concede that its wide adoption is not yet warranted, and the argument over its possible virtue lingers on.

12.11b Target Zone Approach

The **target zone approach** is a relatively recent addition to the list of possible exchange rate regimes. The leading advocate of this proposal is John Williamson.[10] This approach, favored by many economists and policymakers, calls on major industrialized countries to establish mutually consistent targets for their *real effective exchange rates.** Each nation would then allow its real exchange rate to vary within a narrow band of fluctuations around the target rate, for example, 10 percent above or below the rate.** The target rate for each nation would be chosen as the exchange rate calculated to reduce conflicts between internal goals and the external goal of BOP over a medium-run period. To keep the real exchange rate within the band's limits, the participating nations would use monetary policy. The limits of the band would be "soft," that is, countries would be allowed to let their rates move outside the band in exceptional cases. In other words, there would be no absolute requirement that the rates be maintained within the limits set by the band.

Not only does the target zone approach have the advantage of reconciling internal goals and external BOP goals, but it also offers the benefit of concentrating on real exchange rates rather than on nominal exchange rates. However, real exchange rates are harder to manage than nominal exchange rates, and it is crucial to accurately estimate the target rate. As a result, some economists are not convinced that the target zone approach would be useful without additional supplementary policy tools. Nevertheless, as we mentioned earlier, this approach has continued to attract the attention of many economists and policymakers.

12.12 FIXED VERSUS FLEXIBLE EXCHANGE RATES

The breakdown of the Bretton Woods system and the 1971 Nixon action that allowed the dollar to float set the stage for the debate over fixed versus flexible exchange rates. Although a compromise was reached and the present international monetary system was born, the debate over the relative merits of these two systems continues.

The major arguments presented by advocates of the flexible (freely fluctuating) exchange rate system are as follows:

1. In general, the flexible exchange rate system is more efficient than the fixed exchange rate system because under the former only the exchange rate is required to change in order to correct the BOP disequilibrium (surplus or deficit). Although BOP equilibrium could be achieved under the classic gold standard system, discussed earlier, such a system is based on the assumption of price flexibility. This means that instead of relying on one price (the exchange rate), we should rely on all prices to bring adjustment. From an economic standpoint, this is inefficient. In addition, the assumption of price flexibility presented by classical economists is far removed from the reality of today's world.
2. Because the flexible exchange rate system automatically adjusts when BOP disequilibrium occurs, a nation does not need to worry about its external trade position. It can concentrate its resources on pursuing its internal economic goals, such as economic growth, full employment, and price stability.

---

* The effective exchange rate measures the value of a given currency in terms of the weighted average of a basket of major currencies. The rates take into consideration factors such as the size of trade flows and the relevant price elasticities of exchange rate changes.

** The real exchange rate between two currencies, such as the U.S. dollar ($) and the deutsche mark (DM), is the nominal exchange rate (DM/$) divided by the ratio of the consumer price index in one country to the consumer price index in the other country, that is, $(DM/\$)/(P_{Germany}/P_{US})$ or $(\$/DM)/(P_{US}/P_{Germany})$.

GLOBAL INSIGHTS CASE 12.3

Pegged Exchange Rates and Disinflation in Argentina

Between 1982 and 1990, inflation in Argentina averaged almost 1,000 percent annually. Three major disinflation programs based on a pegged exchange rate, announced in 1985, 1988, and 1989, all failed to achieve a lasting reduction in inflation. In each case, continued budget deficits and monetary growth forced a devaluation that set the stage for further inflation. Inflation peaked at 197 percent per month in July 1989.

After March 1990, the government reduced the fiscal deficit while allowing the exchange rate to float. The exchange rate remained relatively stable, even though monthly inflation remained above 10 percent for most of the remainder of 1990. In March 1991, following another plunge in the value of the domestic currency, Argentina passed a law fixing the exchange rate against the dollar and requiring the central bank to hold international reserves exceeding, at that exchange rate, the value of the domestic monetary base. This meant that the central bank would have sufficient reserves to support the exchange rate, even if the entire domestic monetary base were exchanged for dollars. The law prevents the central bank from financing fiscal deficits on an extended basis, since that would cause money growth to exceed the growth of the central bank's international reserves.

So far, the "Convertibility Program," as the 1991 initiative was labeled, has been successful. Annual inflation has declined below 20 percent, its lowest level since the early 1970's, while interest rates on deposits, a key indicator of inflationary expectations, have declined to around 10 percent. The interest rate is well below the rate of inflation, but, as asset holders apparently consider a devaluation of the currency to be unlikely in the near future, they are willing to accept rates of return on deposits roughly comparable to those available in international financial markets. The success of the Convertibility Program shows how a pegged exchange rate can help to lower inflationary expectations and accelerate the process of disinflation. However, the program was credible only because it was preceded by nearly a year of budget tightening and because, by requiring international reserves exceeding the monetary base, it made continued budget tightening a necessity. This aspect of the fixed exchange-rate program distinguishes it from its failed predecessors. However, Argentina's inflation remains above international levels, underscoring the continued vulnerability of the stabilization program and the need for continued responsible fiscal and monetary policies.

Source: U.S. Government Printing Office, *Economic Report of the President*, (Washington, D.C.: U.S. Government Printing Office, January 1993), 302, Reprinted.

The main arguments advanced by proponents of the fixed exchange rate are as follows:

1. Because the fixed exchange rate system is not subject to wide day-to-day fluctuations that occur under the freely fluctuating exchange rate system, it involves a lower degree of uncertainty than the flexible exchange rate system. The lower uncertainty reduces risk and increases the volume of international business and investment.

2. Speculators have a more destabilizing effect under a flexible exchange rate system than under a fixed exchange rate system because, given a flexible exchange rate system, when the price (exchange rate) of a foreign currency increases, speculators buy more of it, expecting the price to continue to rise. The speculators' higher demands push the price even higher, intensifying the price rise. Similarly, when the price of a foreign currency falls, the speculators sell their foreign currencies, pushing the price further down.

3. Fixed exchange rates are not as prone to inflationary pressures as are flexible exchange rates because, under a fixed exchange rate system, a nation's BOP deficit leads to international reserve losses and forces the nation

to control its excessive inflationary pressures.[*] The fixed exchange rate system thus gives the nation some price sensitivity. In a flexible exchange rate regime, however, where the BOP deficits are automatically corrected by changes in exchange rates, such a sensitivity does not exist. As a result, government authorities are more prone to excessively stimulate the economy in order to enhance the possibility of their reelection.

The debate over flexible versus fixed exchange rate systems continues, and the experts have not yet reached a unanimous opinion on this issue. However, the present monetary system, which represents a compromise between the two extremes of flexible and fixed exchange rate systems, seems to have served well so far. A merit of this system, as we discussed earlier, is its flexibility, which allows a nation to choose the exchange rate system that best suits its economic conditions. This has facilitated cooperation among nations and has contributed to the smooth operation of the international monetary system. Nevertheless, there are some people—notably former U.S. Secretary of Housing and Urban Development, Jack Kemp—who have argued for the return of the gold standard system and its resultant fixed exchange rate system.

12.13 SUMMARY

1. The international monetary system refers to the rules, procedures, customs, instruments, and organizational setting that provide a workable system for international payments among different countries, facilitating international trade among them.
2. The gold coin standard was a monetary standard that (a) defined a country's unit of currency in terms of a fixed weight of gold; (b) permitted gold to be exported or imported without any restriction; (c) allowed the conversion of national currency into gold and vice versa at the defined rate; (d) imposed no restrictions on the coinage of the gold; and (e) considered gold coins full legal tender for all debts.
3. The gold bullion standard was a monetary standard under which a nation's unit of currency was defined in terms of a fixed weight of gold. However, unlike the gold coin standard, gold did not circulate within the domestic economy. For the most part, the impact of gold on the monetary system was neutralized; that is, gold was demonetized.
4. The Bretton Woods agreement of 1944 resulted in the creation of the Gold Exchange Standard System and its two supporting institutions, known as the International Monetary Fund (IMF) and the International Bank for Reconstruction and Development (IBRD), or the World Bank.
5. Under the Gold Exchange Standard System (a) the value of the U.S. dollar was fixed in terms of gold; (b) other nations' currencies were fixed to the dollar and, therefore, indirectly to gold; and (c) nations were required to defend their currencies if their values moved 1 percent above or below their par (official) value.
6. The IMF was set up to achieve two main purposes. These were (a) to ensure that nations followed the agreed-on set of rules of conduct for engaging in international business; and (b) to assist nations with temporary BOP deficits by providing them with borrowing facilities.
7. Special drawing rights (SDRs) were invented by the IMF at its 1967 annual meeting in Rio de Janeiro. Special drawing rights are IMF bank accounts and are allocated among member nations according to their quotas. These SDRs allow holder nations to draw out any money they need to settle a country's balance of payments problem.
8. The World Bank was initially set up by the IMF to provide loans for post-World War II reconstruction. Today, the bank's major function is to provide financial resources for the implementation of development projects in developing nations.
9. The managed floating exchange rate system has been in effect since March 1973. Under this system, the exchange rate of a currency is determined by the market forces of demand and supply. However, a nation is allowed to intervene in the market in order to smooth out short-term fluctuations, without trying to change the long-term pattern of the exchange rate.

---

[*] The control of inflation amounts to a lowering of domestic prices compared with foreign prices. The lower prices of domestic goods and services causes their foreign demand to increase. This leads to more foreign exchange earnings for the country and thus improves its BOP deficit.

10.   The present international monetary system gives nations a large degree of flexibility in choosing the exchange rate that best fits their economic situations. In 1996, eleven different exchange rate regimes were chosen by different countries.

11.   The European Snake refers to the decision of the six original EU members to let their currencies float together against the U.S. dollar with a total fluctuation band of 2.25 percent.

12.   The European Monetary System (EMS) was established in March 1979. The objective set by the EMS members was "closer monetary cooperation leading to a zone of monetary stability in Europe."

13.   The merits of the flexible exchange rate system, according to its proponents, are that (a) it is more efficient than the fixed exchange rate system, and (b) it enables a nation to concentrate its resources on pursuing its internal economic goals rather than worrying about its external trade position.

14.   The main arguments advanced by proponents of the fixed exchange rate system are that (a) it leads to a lower degree of uncertainty than the flexible exchange rate system, (b) it causes speculators to have a less destabilizing effect on the exchange rate, and (c) it is not as prone to inflationary pressures as is the flexible exchange rate system.

Review Questions

1.   What two supporting institutions were established by the Bretton Woods agreement? List them and briefly describe their main objectives.

2.   Elaborate on the role of SDRs in the international monetary system. What purpose do they serve? What rights do they give their holders? How are their values determined today?

3.   Explain how exchange rates were established under the gold standard. How did the gold points determine the range within which foreign exchange rates fluctuated?

4.   Distinguish a fixed exchange rate system from a freely fluctuating exchange rate system. Explain how the BOP disequilibrium (deficit or surplus) is corrected under each of these systems.

5.   What theory provides the basis for the fixed exchange rate system? What are the assumptions of this theory? Explain.

6.   What is meant by an international monetary system? Ideally, what should the components of an international monetary system be? In practice, why have nations been reluctant to adopt an ideal international monetary system?

7.   Distinguish between a managed floating exchange rate system and a freely fluctuating exchange rate system. Elaborate on their relative advantages.

8.   What is the major goal of the European Monetary System? What is meant by the "European Snake?" What were the provisions of the Maastrich Treaty? How many phases did the Maastrich Treaty go through, and what was the objective of the last phase?

Problems

1.   Why do you think the managed floating exchange rate system has been chosen over the freely fluctuating exchange rate system or the fixed exchange rate system?

2.   Given the 1987 U.S. stock market crash and worldwide inflationary trends, what do you think is the possibility of returning to the gold standard and the resulting fixed exchange rate regime?

3.   Compare fixed exchange rate and flexible exchange rate systems. Which system do you think provides more freedom to governments in pursuing independent monetary policies? Explain.

4.   An international monetary system should ideally be composed of an international bank that handles an international money accepted by all nations. What do you think is the advantage of such a system? What is the disadvantage of such a system?

5.   One of the disadvantages of a flexible exchange rate is that it is prone to inflation. Explain why this is the case in general, and why it is especially true for countries that are heavily dependent on trade for their basic necessities.

6. Compare the overall status of U.S. BOP in the 1950s and 1960s. Why did the deficit not pose any problems in the early 1950s, but become problematic in the 1960s? Given the situation in the 1960s, do you think the dollar was overvalued or undervalued in the international market? Can you suggest alternatives that might have remedied the problem?

7. Distinguish between the present international monetary system and the Bretton Woods system.

8. Because under the present international monetary system, nations can choose the exchange rate system that best fits their economic conditions, the contemporary system could be described as a "nonsystem."

   Do you agree with this statement? Explain.

Notes

1. "The Soviets Consider Joining IMF, World Bank," The Wall Street Journal, 15 August 1986, 19.

2. "IMF's Russia Plan Could Speed Aid from World Bank, Debt Rescheduling," *The Wall Street Journal*, 26 June 1992, A14; "Russia, IMF Reach Pact Likely to Result in Flow of Western Aid," *The Wall Street Journal*, 6 July 1992, 8; "What's News," *The Wall Street Journal*, 6 August 1992, 1; "IMF Holds Aid to Russia, Citing Faltering Reforms," *The Wall Street Journal*, 10 September 1993, A13.

3. "World Bank Approves Loan to Nigeria to Aid Nation's Bid to Liberalize Trade," *The Wall Street Journal*, 17 October 1986, 33.

4. "IMF Approves 2-Loan Package for Philippines," *The Wall Street Journal*, 27 October 1986, 32.

5. "IMF Economic Plan for the Philippines Accepted by Aquino," *The Wall Street Journal*, 9 March 1989, A13.

6. International Monetary Fund, *Annual Report 1979* (Washington DC: International Monetary Fund, 1979), 40.

7. International Monetary Fund, *Annual Report 1985* (Washington DC: International Monetary Fund, 1985), 35-36.

8. "For Now, Central Bankers Regain Reins," *The Wall Street Journal*, 4 August 1993, C1.

9. Karl Habermeier and Horst Ungerer, "A Single Currency for the European Community," *Finance and Development* (September 1992): 26-29.

10. John Williamson, "Target Zones and the Management of the Dollar," *Brookings Papers on Economic Activity*, no. 1 (1986), 165-174.

Suggested Readings

Aliber, R. Z. *The International Money Game*. New York: Basic Books, 1973.

Artus, J. R., and J. H. Young. "Fixed and Flexible Rates: A Renewal of the Debate." *International Monetary Fund Staff Papers*. Washington, DC: International Monetary Fund, December 1979, 654-698.

Bordo, M. D., and Barry Eichengreen, eds. *A Retrospective on the Bretton Woods System*. Chicago: University of Chicago Press, 1993.

———. "The Classical Gold Standard: Some Lessons for Today. *Federal Reserve Bank of St. Louis Review* (May 1981).

Chrystal, K. Alec. *International Money and the Future of SDR*. Essays in International Finance Series, no. 128. Princeton, NJ: Princeton University Press, 1978.

Cohen, B. J. *The European Monetary System: An Outsider's View*. Essays in International Finance Series, no. 142. Princeton, NJ: Princeton University Press, December 1981.

De Uries, M. *The International Monetary Fund, 1966-1971*. Washington, DC: International Monetary Fund, 1976.

Eichengreen, Barry, ed. *The Gold Standard in Theory and History*. London: Methuen, 1985.

———. *Golden Fetters*. New York: Oxford University Press, 1992.

Eithier, W., and A. J. Bloosfield. *Managing the Managed Float*. Essays in International Finance Series, no. 112. Princeton, NJ: Princeton University Press, October 1979.

Frenkel, Jacob. "The International Monetary System: Should It Be Reformed?" *American Economic Review Papers and Proceedings* 77, no. 2 (May 1987): 205-211.

Frenkel, Jacob, and Moriss Goldstein. "Europe's Emerging Economic and Monetary Union." *Finance and Development* 28, no. 1 (March 1991): 2-5.

Habermeier, Karl, and Horst Ungerer. "A Single Currency for the European Community." *Finance and Development* 29, no. 3 (September 1992): 26-29.

Horne, Jocelyn, and Paul R. Masson. "Scope and Limits of International Economic Cooperation and Policy Coordination." *IMF Staff Papers* (June 1988): 259-296.

Hosefield, J. K. *The International Monetary Fund, 1945-1965.* Washington, DC: International Monetary Fund, 1969.

International Monetary Fund. *Annual Report.* Washington, DC: International Monetary Fund (published annually).

International Monetary Fund. *IMF Survey.* Washington, DC: International Monetary Fund (published bimonthly).

Krugman, P. "Target Zones and Exchange Rate Dynamics." *Quarterly Journal of Economics* (August 1991), 669-682.

Machlup, Fritz. *Remaking the International Monetary Systems: The Rio Agreement and Beyond.* Baltimore, MD: Johns Hopkins University Press, 1968.

McKinnon, R. I. *Money in International Exchange: The Convertible Currency System.* New York: Oxford University Press, 1979.

Solomon, R. *The International Monetary System, 1945-1976: An Insider's View.* New York: Harper & Row, 1976.

Triffin, R. *Our International Monetary System: Yesterday, Today, and Tomorrow.* New York: Random House, 1968.

Chapter 13

BALANCE OF PAYMENTS AUTOMATIC ADJUSTMENT MECHANISMS

13.1 INTRODUCTION

In Chapter 10, we elaborated on the balance of payments (BOP) and examined the meaning and measurement of a deficit and surplus in a country's BOP. As we explained, a deficit is measured by the excess of debits over credits in the nation's autonomous transactions; a surplus is the opposite. We learned that, depending on the type of transactions included in autonomous and accommodating items, different methods may be used for defining BOP surplus or deficit. For simplicity, in this chapter, we define a BOP surplus or deficit by the *current account* balance. A current account deficit is measured by the excess of imports over exports of goods and services, and unilateral transfers. A current account surplus implies the opposite.

A nation's BOP disequilibrium cannot continue indefinitely; it needs adjustment. A country can finance or cover its BOP deficits out of its international reserves, by borrowing abroad, or by attracting foreign direct investment. However, a nation's international reserves are limited, and other nations are generally reluctant to extend credit or invest indefinitely in a deficit nation.

The adjustment mechanism for correcting a BOP disequilibrium takes two different forms. The first is an **automatic adjustment mechanism** that corrects the BOP disequilibrium on its own, without any government action. Second, there are **adjustment policies** that are composed of specific measures adopted by the government with the primary objective of resolving the BOP disequilibrium.

Automatic adjustment mechanisms can be subdivided into the automatic price adjustment mechanism, the automatic income adjustment mechanism, and the automatic monetary adjustment mechanism. The **automatic price adjustment mechanism** works through price changes in the deficit and surplus nations to correct the BOP disequilibrium. The **automatic income adjustment mechanism** works through induced changes in national incomes of the surplus and deficit nations to bring about equilibrium in the BOP. Finally, the **automatic monetary adjustment mechanism** relies on money supply to adjust the BOP disequilibrium.

Theories of each of these adjustment mechanisms, developed during different time periods, reflect different philosophical approaches to economics and have their modern-day proponents. The automatic price adjustment mechanism stems from classical economic thinking that was linked to the gold standard and the resultant fixed exchange rate system of the 1800s and early 1900s. The income adjustment mechanism grew out of the Keynesian theory of income determination that flourished after the Great Depression of the 1930s. The automatic monetary adjustment mechanism, reflecting the monetary approach to the BOP, developed primarily by Harry Johnson and Robert Mudell, was initiated during the late 1960s and is identified with the University of Chicago.

In this chapter, we first explain all three of these adjustment mechanisms. We then discuss the purchasing-power-parity theory as a short-cut to estimating the equilibrium exchange rate when a country is in BOP equilibrium.

13.2 AUTOMATIC PRICE ADJUSTMENT MECHANISM

The automatic price adjustment mechanism operates differently under the flexible exchange rates than under the fixed exchange rates (the gold standard system). In this section, we examine the automatic mechanism under each of these exchange rate regimes.

13.2a Adjustment with Fixed Exchange Rates

As we explained in Chapter 12, under the gold standard system and the resultant fixed exchange rates, an automatic adjustment mechanism that corrected deficits or surpluses in the BOP trade account prevailed. Because under such a system each country's money supply was composed of either gold itself or paper money backed by gold, a surplus in a country's BOP trade account meant an inflow of gold and a rise in the money supply, resulting in higher domestic prices. This, in turn, caused exports to decrease and imports to increase, thus reducing the BOP trade account surplus. A deficit in a nation's BOP trade account meant an outflow of gold and a decrease in the money supply. The fall in the money supply, in its turn, resulted in lower domestic prices which caused exports to increase and imports to decrease, thus reducing the BOP trade account deficit.

This automatic adjustment mechanism is the same as the price-specie-flow mechanism described by David Hume in 1752. Recall from Chapter 2 that Hume used this concept to describe the irony of the mercantilist position that a country could continuously accrue gold by exporting more than it imported. He explained that as a country accumulated gold, domestic prices increased until the country's export surplus was eradicated. To make his point, he used the example of water levels in compartments. He explained that it is useless to try to raise the water above its natural level in one compartment as long as it is interconnected to other compartments. In the same manner, it is fruitless to try to enhance the amount of gold in one nation above its natural level, as long as nations are connected to each other through international trade.

The gold standard system is linked to classical economic theory. Consequently, the automatic adjustment in the BOP was based on the classical theory of income and employment which assumed the following:

1. There is full employment of resources, and thus a rise in the quantity of money ensures an increase in the general price level. In the same manner, a decrease in the quantity of money leads to a decrease in the general price level.
2. Prices and wages are flexible.

Given these assumptions, the price-specie-flow mechanism can be explained in terms of the quantity theory of money which comes from the *equation of exchange:*

$$MV = PQ, \qquad (13\text{-}1)$$

where

M   is the nation's money supply;
V   is the income velocity of money, defined as the average number of times per year that each unit of domestic currency is spent to purchase the economy's annual flow of goods and services (gross national product [GNP]);
P   is the general price index; and
Q   is the physical quantity of goods and services produced in a given year.

Classical economists presumed that V was constant because it was based on the long-run money-holding and money-disbursement habits of the public. These habits, according to classical economists, were relatively fixed. They also assumed that Q was fixed since the economy was self-correcting. This is because, according to classical economists, the economy was at, or was at least moving swiftly toward, full employment. They thus concluded that P depends directly on M. In other words, a given percentage change in the money supply causes an equal percentage change in the price level in the same direction.

With these assumptions in place, the price adjustment mechanism under classical theory is automatic, and it is triggered as soon as a BOP disequilibrium occurs and continues to operate until the disequilibrium is eliminated. As a country experiences a BOP deficit, it will lose gold, that is, its money supply declines. The fall in the money supply, in turn, leads to a proportional fall in domestic prices. For example, if a nation's BOP deficit reduces M by 20 percent, it also reduces P by 20 percent. The lower domestic prices encourage the deficit nation's exports and discourage its imports. The opposite occurs in the surplus nation. The increase in the money supply of the surplus nation leads to higher domestic prices. This, in turn, encourages its imports and discourages its exports. These adjustments continue until the surpluses or deficits are eliminated.

13.2b Adjustment with Flexible Exchange Rates

The automatic process of correcting a BOP deficit under flexible exchange rates is achieved by depreciation of the national currency. This process is shown in Figure 13-1. In the figure, it is assumed that (a) the United States and Germany are the only two countries in the world, and (b) there are no international capital flows, so that Germany's demand and supply curves for the U.S. dollar reflect only trade in goods and services.

Given these assumptions, S$ and D$ represent supply and demand for the U.S. dollar in Germany. The vertical axis measures the deutsche mark prices of the U.S. dollar. The horizontal axis measures the quantity of dollars. Equilibrium is established at DM 2.60 = $1 (point E). At point E, the quantity supplied and quantity demanded are equal at $4 billion a year. At any point lower than point E, quantity demanded is greater than quantity supplied, and

FIGURE 13-1
Balance of Payments Adjustment With Flexible Exchange Rates

S$ and D$ represent supply and demand for the U.S. dollar in Germany. The vertical axis measures the deutsche mark price of the U.S. dollar (DM/$). The horizontal axis measures the quantities of the dollar. Equilibrium is established at DM 2.60/$1 (point E). At this point, the quantity supplied and quantity demanded are equal at $4 billion a year. At any point lower than E, quantity demanded is greater than quantity supplied and a deficit exists in Germany's balance of payments, leading to depreciation of the deutsche mark (appreciation of the dollar). The deutsche mark continues to depreciate until the deficit is eliminated. At any point higher than E, a surplus exists in Germany's balance of payments, leading to an appreciation of the deutsche mark (depreciation of the dollar). The deutsche mark continues to appreciate until the surplus is eliminated.

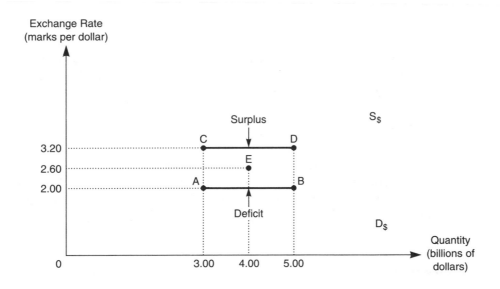

a deficit exists in Germany's BOP. The higher demand for the U.S. dollar will lead to a depreciation of the deutsche mark (appreciation of the U.S. dollar). The deutsche mark continues to depreciate until the deficit is eliminated. For example, at DM 2.00 = $1, the quantity of dollars demanded by Germany is $5 billion, whereas the quantity of dollars supplied is $3 billion. Thus, a deficit of $2 billion (line AB) exists in Germany's BOP. This deficit would be eliminated by a depreciation of the deutsche mark to the level of DM 2.60 = $1.*

At any point higher than equilibrium point E, a surplus in Germany's BOP exists leading to an appreciation of the deutsche mark (depreciation of the U.S. dollar). The deutsche mark continues to appreciate until the surplus is eliminated. For example at DM 3.20 = $1, a surplus of $2 billion (line CD) exists in Germany's BOP. This surplus would be eliminated by an appreciation of the deutsche mark to the level of DM 2.60 = $1.**

In summary, under a flexible (freely fluctuating) exchange rate system, the free movement of exchange rates, occurring in response to market forces of demand and supply, brings a nation's BOP into equilibrium. In other words, a country's BOP surplus or deficit is automatically resolved by appreciation or depreciation of its currency, respectively.

13.3 AUTOMATIC INCOME ADJUSTMENT MECHANISM

Classical economists basically held to the view described by Hume's price-specie-flow mechanism because the gold standard dominated for much of the nineteenth century. They relied primarily on the automatic price adjustment mechanism for restoring equilibrium in a nation's BOP. A main shortcoming of their theory was that they did not explain the effect of income adjustments. The theory of **income determination,** developed by John Maynard Keynes, provided such an explanation.

The Keynesian theory of income determination assumes the following:

1. Nations operate under a fixed exchange rate regime.
2. Prices, wages, and interest rates are inflexible (constant).

With these assumptions in place, the theory suggests that the impact of income changes in surplus and deficit nations leads to forces that automatically resolve the BOP disequilibrium. Given a persistent payments imbalance, the deficit country faces a decline in income, leading to a fall in imports. Conversely, the surplus country experiences an increased income level and, hence, increased imports. These income changes, affecting import levels, reverse a BOP disequilibrium.

The automatic income adjustment mechanism can be explained in terms of a closed economy and an open economy. We devote the next two sections to the examination of the income adjustment mechanism and the determination of the equilibrium national income in these two economies.

13.3a Income Determination in a Closed Economy

A **closed economy** is an economy in autarky, or an economy that does not engage in international trade. Assuming such an economy without a government sector, we proceed with a presentation of a simple Keynesian model. Recall from introductory economics courses that in such a model, national income (NI) is equal to consumption expenditure (C) plus desired or planned saving (S):***

---

* By decreasing the price of the deutsche mark in terms of the U.S. dollar, depreciation makes the value of Germany's exports (measured in terms of the dollar) cheaper, causing Germany's exports to rise. The depreciation of the deutsche mark also means that the value of Germany's imports are more expensive, causing imports to fall. The rise in exports along with a fall in imports decreases the BOP deficit.

** By increasing the price of the deutsche mark in terms of the U.S. dollar, appreciation makes the value of Germany's exports (measured in terms of the dollar) more expensive, causing Germany's exports to fall. The appreciation of the deutsche mark also means that the value of Germany's imports are cheaper, causing imports to rise. The fall in exports along with a rise in imports decreases the BOP surplus.

*** Although saving takes place in both the business and household sectors, for simplicity we assume that all savings are personal.

$$NI = C + S. \qquad (13\text{-}2)$$

Aggregate expenditure (AE) is equal to C plus desired or planned investment (I):

$$AE = C + I. \qquad (13\text{-}3)$$

Because at equilibrium NI = AE, we can set equations 13-2 and 13-3 equal to each other to get the following equation:

$$C + S = C + I. \qquad (13\text{-}4)$$

It follows from this that

$$S = I. \qquad (13\text{-}5)$$

Equation 13-5 represents equilibrium in a closed economy with no government sector. It shows that at any level of income or output (Y), desired investment is equal to desired savings.* Desired investment (I) is considered an "injection" into the system because it adds to total expenditures and stimulates output. Desired saving (S) is considered a "leakage" out of the system because it depicts income generated but not spent. Using these terms, we can say that equilibrium income (Y_E) occurs when injections into the income stream match leakages out of the stream.

Desired investment is exogenous, that is, it is independent of the level of Y. In other words, I is considered to be constant. On the other hand, desired consumption expenditure (C) is a positive function of Y; as Y rises, C also rises. The linear consumption function is given by C(Y). The change in consumption (ΔC) associated with a change in income (ΔY) is referred to as the **marginal propensity to consume (MPC).** It shows the fraction of each extra dollar of income that goes into consumption. Like consumption, saving (S) is a positive function of Y, that is, the linear saving function is given by line S(Y). The change in saving (ΔS) associated with a change in income (ΔY) is referred to as the **marginal propensity to save (MPS).** It shows the fraction of each extra dollar of income that goes into saving.

Graphical Determination of Equilibrium in a Closed Economy. The aforementioned relationships are portrayed in Figure 13-2 which presents the familiar income determination model taught in introductory economics courses. Panel (a) measures consumption (C) and investment (I) expenditures along the vertical axis; C(Y) is the consumption function. Desired consumption is equal to $25 billion when income is zero. In other words, when income drops to zero the nation has to spend (dissave) $25 billion out of its past savings. As income rises, desired consumption increases, but not as much as income. For example, as income increases by $400 billion (from $100 billion to $500 billion; line AB in the top panel), consumption increases by $300 billion (from $100 billion to $400 billion; line BC in the top panel). Thus, the MPC equals $\Delta C / \Delta Y = 300/400 = 3/4 = 0.75$. The equation for this linear consumption function is C = 25 + 0.75Y, where 25 is the vertical intercept and 0.75 is the slope.

The total expenditure function, C(Y) + I, is obtained by adding I to C(Y). Because I is constant, C(Y) and C(Y) + I curves are parallel to each other. Given an initial investment of $100 billion, the equilibrium level of income (Y_E) is defined at point E (Y_E = $500 billion), where C(Y) + I intersects the 45-degree line. Every point on the 45-degree line measures equal distances along horizontal and vertical axes. Accordingly, at point E, the level of income (measured along the horizontal axis) is equal to the total consumption and investment expenditures of $500 billion (measured along the vertical axis).

---

* We use the variable Y to represent both income and output. We assume that there is no depreciation. This assumption and our previous assumptions about saving and no government sector, allow us to treat GNP, net national product (NNP), gross national income (GNI), national income (NI), and personal income (PI) as equal to one another. In this context, the term output stands for GNP or NNP. In the same manner, the term income refers to GNI, NI, or PI.

FIGURE 13-2
Income Determination in a Closed Economy

In the top panel, C(Y) is the consumption function and C(Y) + I is the total expenditure function. The equilibrium level of income (Y_E) is defined at point E (Y_E = $500 billion), where C(Y) + I intersects the 45;dg line. In the bottom panel, the corresponding equilibrium point (E) occurs where the saving function S(Y) intersects the horizontal investment function I at $100 billion. If investment rises by $50 billion, from I to I', the equilibrium level of income increases from $500 billion at point E to $700 billion at point E', where C(Y) + I' intersects the 45;dg line or where I' intersects S(Y).

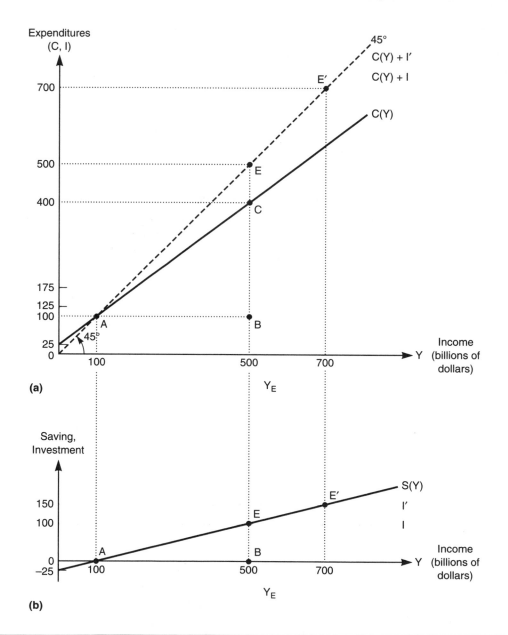

At any level of income greater than the equilibrium level of income (Y_E = $500 billion), output is greater than desired expenditure. This means that firms have an unplanned accumulation of inventories of unsold goods, and they reduce output.

At any level of income less than the equilibrium level of income, output is less than desired expenditure. Thus, firms have an unplanned reduction of inventories, and output is increased.

Thus, the equilibrium level of national income is stable. At any other level of national income, desired expenditures are either greater or less than the value of output, and the level of national income moves toward equilibrium. The equilibrium level of income does not have to be equal to the full-employment level of income, and we assume that it is not.

In panel (b), the vertical axis measures the level of saving and investment; the horizontal axis measures the level of income, as in panel (a). The level of desired investment is exogenous, that is, it does not depend on the level of income. However, the desired saving is a function of income. The saving function is given by the following equation:

$$S(Y) = Y - C(Y).$$

Desired saving is equal to -$25 billion when income is zero. In other words, when income drops to zero, the nation has to spend (dissave) $25 billion out of its past savings. As income rises, desired saving increases, but not as much as income. For example, as income increases by $400 billion (from $100 billion to $500 billion; line AB in the bottom panel), saving increases by $100 billion (from 0 to 100; line BE in the bottom panel. Thus, the MPS equals $\Delta S/\Delta Y = 100/400 = 1/4 = 0.25$. The equation for this linear saving function is $S = -25 + 0.25Y$, where -25 is the vertical intercept and 0.25 is the slope. Because any change in income is always equal to the change in consumption plus the change in saving, MPC + MPS = 1, so MPS = 1 - MPC. In our example, MPC + MPS = 0.75 + 0.25 = 1, and MPS = 1 - 0.75 = 0.25.

In panel (b), the corresponding equilibrium point E occurs when S(Y) intersects I at the level of $100 billion. At this point, the desired level of investment is equal to the desired level of saving (S = I = $100 billion). At any level of income greater than the equilibrium level of income (Y_E = $500 billion from panel [a]), desired saving is greater than desired investment, denoting an unplanned or unintended inventory investment. Accordingly, production and income fall toward Y_E = $500 billion.

At a level of income less than the equilibrium level of income, desired investment is greater than desired saving, representing an unintended or unplanned inventory disinvestment. As a result, income and output increase toward equilibrium.

In summary, the equilibrium level of national income is determined either at the intersection of the 45-degree line with C(Y) + I in panel (a) or by the intersection of S(Y) and I in panel (b). In either circumstance, the equilibrium level of national income is Y_E = $500 billion, and we conjecture that it is smaller than the full-employment level of income.

Now assume that in panel (b) the desired level of investment rises by $50 billion, from I = $100 billion to I' = $150 billion. The higher level of investment also leads to the upward shift of the expenditure function from C(Y) + I to C(Y) + I'. As the figure shows, this causes the equilibrium level of income to increase from $500 billion at point E to $700 billion at point E'. Thus, an increase of $50 billion in investment leads to a multiple (quadruple) increase in income, a result gained by the multiplier process. When investment expenditure increases, producers augment production and use more labor, capital, and other factors of production. Because the income generated in the process of production equals the value of output produced, increasing investment expenditure by a given amount has the immediate impact of also raising income by the same amount. Part of this extra income is spent by the income recipients on consumption, leading to further income. This further income leads to yet additional consumption, and so on. In summary, the original investment sets off a chain reaction that results in greater levels of spending, so that income increases by some multiple of the initial investment. But how is the multiplier determined? We answer this question in the next section.

The Closed Economy Multiplier. As we already know, the equilibrium level of income is established at the point where I = S. This implies that if investment increases by ΔI, equilibrium is re-established only when it is matched by an equivalent ΔS. Because saving is assumed to be a function of income, changes in saving are related to changes in income, or $\Delta S = (MPS)(\Delta Y)$, where MPS represents the marginal propensity to save out of additional income levels. Given an autonomous increase in investment, the equilibrium condition implies that

$$\Delta I = \Delta S = (MPS)(\Delta Y)$$

or

$$\Delta Y = 1/MPS (\Delta I).$$

Thus, the multiplier, k, is

$$k = \Delta Y/\Delta I = 1/MPS = 1/1-MPC \qquad (13\text{-}6)$$

Returning to our example in Figure 13-2, the MPS is equal to 0.25, indicating that out of every dollar of additional income, the nation saves $0.25. For example, an increase in income of $400 billion (from $100 billion to $500 billion) leads to an increase in saving of $100 billion (from 0 to $100 billion) in panel (b). Given that MPS = 0.25, the multiplier is equal to 4 (1/0.25 = 4), as indicated by equation 13-6.

13.3b Income Determination in an Open Economy

We now extend the discussion of income determination from a closed economy to an open economy. An **open economy** is an economy that engages in international trade. To extend our analysis to an open economy, we begin with the equilibrium equation for a closed economy, that is,

$$I = S$$

or

$$\text{Injections} = \text{Leakages}.$$

In an open economy, imports (M), like saving, represent a leakage out of income flow. Exports (X), like investment, constitute an injection into income flow. Thus, we can expand the equilibrium equation for a closed economy into an open economy by expanding injections and leakages to include X and M, respectively. Thus, we can write

$$I + X = S + M \qquad (13\text{-}7)^*$$

Equation 13-7 gives the condition for equilibrium in an open economy without a government sector; however, it does not imply that the balance of trade (and payments) is in equilibrium. This happens only if S = I, so that X = M. We can restate the condition for equilibrium level of income by rewriting equation 13-7 as

$$X - M = S - I \qquad (13\text{-}8)$$

This states that at equilibrium, the nation could have a surplus in its trade balance equal to the surplus of saving over domestic investment. On the other hand, a deficit in a country's balance of trade must be followed by an equal amount of extra domestic investment over saving at the equilibrium level of income.

As with investment, we assume that exports are exogenously determined, that is, they are unrelated to the level of income. As with saving, we assume that imports are a positive function of income, that is, the linear import

---

*   Equation 13-7 can be derived as follows:

$$Y = C + I + X - M$$

or

$$Y - C = I + X - M.$$

Because Y - C = S, we can write

$$S + M = I + X.$$

function is given as M(Y), and $\Delta M = (MPM)(\Delta Y)$, where MPM is the marginal propensity to import. The change in imports (ΔM) associated with a change in income (ΔY) is referred to as marginal propensity to import. It shows the fraction of each extra dollar of income that goes into imports.

Graphical Determination of Equilibrium in an Open Economy. Our algebraic assertion of equilibrium level of income in an open economy is shown in Figure 13-3. Panel (a) measures injections (I + X) and leakages (S + M) on the vertical axis and income (Y) on the horizontal axis. Panel (b) measures (X - M) and (S - I) on the vertical axis and Y along the horizontal axis. Note that S(Y) + M(Y) has a positive slope. This is because both S and M are positive functions of Y. The equation for the linear saving function is S = -25 + 0.25Y. The equation for the linear import function is M = 50 + 0.25Y, where 0.25 is the MPM and the vertical intercept (50) represents the nation's imports at zero level of income.* Thus, the equation for saving plus import is S + M = 25 + 0.5Y, where the vertical intercept is 25 and the slope is 0.5. The X - M(Y) has a negative slope because M is a positive function of Y, and X is constant (exogenously determined) and is assumed to be equal to $125 billion. Finally, S(Y) - I has a positive slope because S is a positive function of Y, and I is constant (exogenously determined) and is assumed to be equal to $50 billion. As both panels show, equilibrium level of income (Y$_E$) is equal to $300 billion. In panel (a), this equilibrium occurs where I + X ($50 billion + $125 billion = $175 billion) intersects S(Y) + M(Y) at point E, where S + M = $50 billion + $125 billion = $175 billion.** In other words, the equilibrium is determined where:

$$\text{Injections} = \text{Leakages}$$
$$I + X = S + M$$
$$50 + 125 = 50 + 125$$
$$175 = 175$$

As this equation shows, at equilibrium I = S = 50 and X = M = 125. In panel (b), the equilibrium level of income (Y$_E$) is given at the intersection of S(Y) - I and X - M(Y), so that equation 13-8 (S - I = X - M) is satisfied.*** Thus, panel (b) gives us the same results for equilibrium as panel (a). However, the advantage of constructing panel (b) and using equation 13-8 is that it allows us to read the trade balance directly from the figure. For example, at the equilibrium point, where X - M(Y) crosses the horizontal axis, the trade balance happens to be in equilibrium, that is X - M = 0.

How does a disturbance, such as a change in exports or investment, affect the nation's equilibrium level of income? To answer this question, first we need to recall the previously discussed multiplier process. Equipped with such knowledge, we then use algebraic and graphical techniques to demonstrate the impact of export and investment disturbances.

---

* This amount of imports is financed by either borrowing abroad or the nation's international reserves.

** The amounts of S and M are obtained by substituting 300 for Y in S and M equations

$$S = -25 + 0.25Y$$
$$S = -25 + 0.25(300) = 50;$$
$$M = 50 + 0.25Y$$
$$M = 50 + 0.25(300) = 125.$$

The linear equation for S(Y) + M(Y) is S + M = 25 + 0.5Y. Setting I + X function equal to this function, we get

$$I + X = S + M$$
$$50 + 125 = 25 + 0.5Y$$
$$0.5Y = 150$$
$$Y = 150/0.5 = 300.$$

*** Given that X = 125, I = 50, S = -25 + 0.25Y, and M = 50 + 0.25Y; at Y = 300, we have

$$S - I = X - M$$
$$-25 + 0.25(300) - 50 = 125 - 50 - 0.25(300)$$
$$0 = 0.$$

FIGURE 13-3
Income Determination in an Open Economy

The top panel measures injections (I + X) and leakages (S + M) on the vertical axis and income (Y) on the horizontal axis. The bottom panel measures X - M and S - I on the vertical axis and Y the horizontal axis. As both panels show, equilibrium level of income (Y_E) is equal to $300 billion. In the top panel, this equilibrium is determined where I + X ($50 billion + $125 billion = $175 billion) intersects S(Y) + M(Y) at point E, where S + M = $50 billion + $125 billion = $175 billion. In the bottom panel, the equilibrium level of income (Y_E) is given at the intersection of S(Y) - I and X - M(Y). Thus, both panels give us the same results in equilibrium.

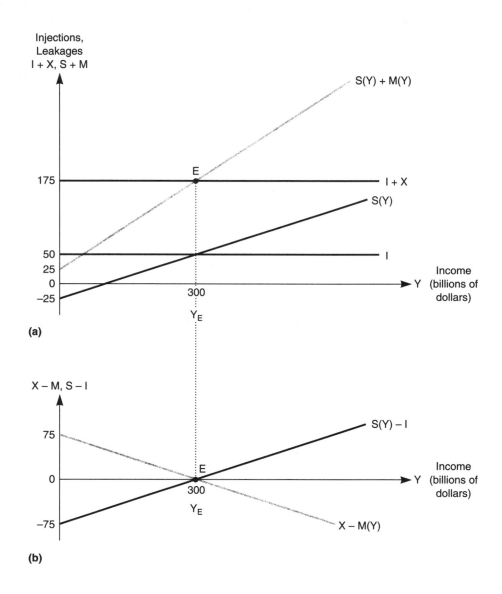

The Open Economy Multiplier. We can expand the closed economy multiplier to an open economy multiplier, deriving what is referred to as the **foreign trade multiplier**. We start with equation 13-7:

$$I + X = S + M$$

Letting both sides of the equation change by the same amount, we get

$$\Delta I + \Delta X = \Delta S + \Delta M$$

Substituting (MPS) (ΔY) for ΔS and (MPM) (ΔY) for ΔM in this equation yields

$$\Delta I + \Delta X = (MPS)\,(\Delta Y) + (MPM)\,(\Delta Y)$$

or

$$(MPS + MPM)\Delta Y = \Delta X + \Delta I \qquad (13\text{-}9)$$

Given that X is exogenously determined, that is, it is independent of the level of domestic income, we can write:

Foreign trade multiplier $- k' - \Delta Y/\Delta I = 1/(MPS + MPM)$ $\qquad$ (13-10)

As this formula shows, the foreign trade multiplier is smaller than the closed economy multiplier because the open economy has an extra leakage through imports.

Figure 13-4, which is a replica of panel (b) from Figure 13-3, illustrates the adjustment ramifications of the foreign trade multiplier. Beginning at the equilibrium level of income (Y_E), we first consider the impact of an autonomous increase in exports and then elaborate on an autonomous increase in investment.

Starting at an equilibrium income level of $300 billion, assume our autonomous exports increase by $100 billion. This causes the X - M(Y) schedule to shift upward by $100 billion, giving us the new schedule X'- M(Y). As a result, the level of income increases, leading to increases in imports and saving. The new equilibrium is established at point E', where equilibrium income = $500 billion, and S - I = X' - M = 50.[*] At point E', the balance of trade is no longer in equilibrium. There is a surplus of $50 billion in this account (X' - M = 50).[**] Note that this surplus is smaller than the initial increase of $100 billion in exports. This is because part of the surplus is offset by rises in imports caused by the increase in income from $300 billion to $500 billion.

To use the foreign trade multiplier concept to measure the impact of the rise in exports on the domestic economy, we need to plug the values of MPM and MPC into the foreign trade multiplier's equation (equation 13-10). As we mentioned earlier, MPS is given by the slope (rise/run) of S(Y) - I and is equal to 0.25; MPM, given by the slope of X - M(Y), is also equal to 0.25. Plugging these values into equation 13-10, we get

Foreign trade multiplier = $k' = 1/(MPS + MPM) = 1/(0.25 + 0.25) = 2$

---

[*] Equilibrium point E' can be obtained by setting S(Y) - I equal to X '- M(Y). Given that S = -25 + 0.25Y, I = 50, X` = 225, and M = 50 + 0.25Y, we can write:

$$S - I = X' - M$$
$$-25 + 0.25Y - 50 = 225 - 50 - 0.25Y$$

Solving this equation for Y, we get

$$Y = 250/0.5 = 500$$

[**] Given that X'= 225 and M = 50 + 0.25Y, X' − M (at the income level of 500) is

$$X' - (50 + 0.25Y)$$
$$225 - 50 - 0.25\,(500) = 50$$

FIGURE 13-4
Impact of an Autonomous Increase In Exports on Domestic Income

This diagram is a replica of the bottom panel of Figure 13-3. Beginning at the equilibrium level of income (Y_E), an autonomous increase in exports of $100 billion causes X - M(Y) to shift upward by $100 billion, giving us X' - M(Y). As a result, the level of income (Y) increases, leading to increases in imports (M) and saving (S). The new equilibrium is established at point E', where equilibrium income Y'_E = $500 billion, and S(Y) - I = X' - M(Y) = 50.

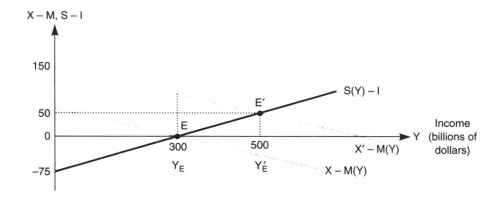

Thus, given a value of 2 for the foreign trade multiplier, an autonomous rise in exports of $100 billion causes a twofold ($200 billion) increase in income, that is, Y increases from $300 billion to $500 billion. Given an MPM of 0.25, this $200 billion rise in income generates a $50 billion increase in imports, leading to a balance of trade surplus of $50 billion. Thus, out of $100 billion initial autonomous rise in exports, half of it ($50 billion) is neutralized, decreasing it from $100 billion to $50 billion. The increase in imports will reduce the balance of trade surplus over time. However, the magnitude of this increase would not be sufficient to re-establish the BOP equilibrium.

Now consider the case of an autonomous increase in investment, as illustrated in Figure 13-5. Starting from an equilibrium income (Y_E) of $300 billion, assume that domestic investment (I) increases autonomously by $100 billion (line EF). This results in a shift of S(Y) - I to S(Y) - I'. Consequently, domestic income increases from $300 billion to $500 billion and leads to an increase in imports, generating a $50 billion balance of trade deficit at point G.[*]

As this analysis indicates, in comparison to an autonomous rise in exports that leads to a balance of trade surplus, an autonomous increase in domestic investment leads to a balance of trade deficit.

---

* The equilibrium level of income at point G can be obtained by setting S(Y) − I' equal to X − M(Y). Given that S = −25 + 0.25Y, I' = 150, X = 125, and M = 50 + 0.25Y, we can write

$$S - I' = X - M$$
$$-25 + 0.25Y - 150 = 125 - 50 - 0.25Y.$$

Solving this equation for Y, we get

$$Y = 250/0.5 = 500.$$

The balance of trade deficit is obtained by plugging 500 in X − M(Y):
$$125 - 50 - 0.25(500) = -50.$$

FIGURE 13-5
Impact of an Autonomous Increase in Investment on Domestic Income

Like Figure 13-4, this diagram is a replica of the bottom panel of Figure 13-3. Starting from the equilibrium income (Y_E) of $300 billion, assume that domestic investment (I) increases autonomously by $100 billion (line EF). This results in a shift of S(Y) - I to S(Y) - I'. Consequently, domestic income increases from $300 billion to $500 billion and leads to an increase in imports, generating a $50 billion balance of trade deficit at point G.

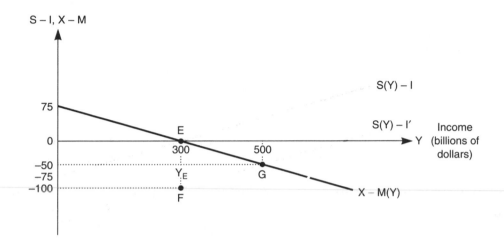

13.3c Foreign Trade Repercussions

In the preceding analysis, we assumed that imports are dependent on national income and exports are exogenously determined. These assumptions are plausible for a small country whose exports and imports are an insignificant percentage of the world's total output. However, for a large country, such as the United States, whose exports and imports are a significant percentage of the world's income, our analysis needs to be modified.

In an open economy, nations are economically interdependent. Accordingly, a nation's exports are the rest of the world's imports. In the same manner, a nation's imports are the rest of the world's exports. Thus, economic events, such as inflation or unemployment, in a large country affect the economies of the rest of the world. In the same manner, the existence of inflation and unemployment in the rest of the world affects the large country. For example, as we explained in Chapter 1, the crash of the U.S. stock market in 1987 affected most economies in the world. Also, the higher interest rates in Germany contributed to the depreciation of the U.S. dollar in the early 1990s. The depreciation of the dollar, in turn, has helped to promote U.S. exports to Europe, at the expense of the European exports.[1]

Assume that the world consists of two countries, the United States and Germany, and both countries' BOPs are initially in equilibrium. Now suppose that Germany's tastes for U.S. products increases suddenly. As a result, Germany experiences an autonomous rise in its imports from the United States. Because Germany's imports are the United States' exports, U.S. exports rise. According to the multiplier principle, Germany's income will decline, and the United States' income will increase. The lower level of income in Germany, in turn, leads to a fall in Germany's imports (U.S. exports).[*] In the meantime, the rise in the United States' income causes U.S. imports (Germany's

---

[*] Germany's income would fall because imports are substituted for domestically produced goods. Given the MPM, the fall in Germany's income will induce a reduction in its imports.

exports) to rise. This feedback mechanism is repeated over and over. The result of this mechanism is that both the increase in income of the United States (the surplus nation) and the fall in income of Germany (the deficit nation) are dampened. The significance of the foreign trade repercussion effect partially depends on the size of the countries in question. If a nation is small and its volume of trade is insignificant, its impact on a large nation is negligible. However, if a nation is large, the impact of foreign trade repercussion is probably important and should be considered in examining the income adjustment mechanism.

13.4 AUTOMATIC MONETARY ADJUSTMENT MECHANISM

As we explained earlier, the automatic **monetary adjustment mechanism**, reflecting the monetary approach to the BOP, was initiated during the late 1960s and is identified with the University of Chicago. This approach, stemming mainly from the work of Robert A. Mundell and Harry G. Johnson, considers a BOP disequilibrium as basically a monetary phenomenon.

The monetary approach to the BOP, as Harry Johnson puts it, is "basically Humean in spirit."[2] David Hume's analysis of the price-specie-flow mechanism illustrated that BOP surpluses and deficits lead to automatic forces that adjust a nation's supply of money to the demand for it. In the same manner, the monetary approach considers surpluses and deficits to be adjustment elements that establish equilibrium between the money supply and the money demand in an open economy. Thus, like Hume's theory, the monetary approach deals with a self-correcting mechanism based on monetary adjustments. However, the two theories differ in that Hume's mechanism works through commodity prices, whereas the monetary approach works through the demand and supply for money. Given a fixed exchange rate system, a nation's excess supply of money generates a deficit in its BOP. As the nation finances its deficit by using its international reserves, its money supply decreases. On the other hand, a country's excess demand for money leads to a surplus in its BOP. As other nations finance their deficits by using their international reserves, foreign exchange flows into the first country, thereby increasing its money supply. Equilibrium in the country's BOP is reestablished when the money supply is equal to the money demand.

To better comprehend the automatic monetary adjustment mechanism, we will first elaborate on the determinants of money demand and money supply and then use an example to illustrate how the mechanism works. The monetary approach assumes that, over the long run, a country's money demand is a stable function of real income, prices, and interest rates. Money demand depends positively on the level of income and prices and negatively on the level of real interest rates. If the economy expands and real income rises, the public's demand for money increases in order to finance growing transactions. If prices increase, the nominal value of transactions rises. As a result, the public demands more money to finance their transactions. Contractions in income and/or prices produce the opposite result. At high rates of interest, people try to minimize their money holdings by investing most of their money in interest-bearing assets. Conversely, a decrease in interest rates raises the quantity of money demanded.

A nation's monetary supply, defined as M_1, is some multiple (m) of its monetary base (B). The monetary base itself is composed of currency and international reserves. Thus, if international reserves increase (decrease), so does the money supply.

Given these assumptions regarding money supply and money demand, consider the case of the United States. Assume that this country's BOP is initially in equilibrium. Now suppose that in order to finance its budget deficit, the United States increases its money supply. Assuming that this money supply is in excess of the desired level of money U.S. residents wish to hold, they choose to increase their spending on goods and services. Given a fixed exchange rate regime, the increase in the United States' domestic expenditure on goods and services causes the prices of domestic goods and services to rise compared to foreign goods and services. Higher domestic prices encourages imports and discourages exports, thus leading to a BOP deficit in the United States. As the United States finances its deficit by the use of its intentional reserves (that is, by transferring foreign exchange to surplus nations), its money supply falls toward its desired level. The lower level of the money supply in turn leads to decrease spending and imports into the United States, re-establishing the BOP equilibrium.

GLOBAL INSIGHTS CASE 13.1

Economic Links among G-7 Countries

Given the increasing globalization of the world economy, the economic interdependence among nations continues to rise. In an empirical study, Roy C. Fair examined the links among nations in terms of price, interest rate, trade, and output. The table demonstrates the estimated final result of a sustained and autonomous increase of 1 percent in the U.S. GNP on the country's short-term interest rates, GDP deflator (a price index), exports, and imports. It also presents the effects that these changes have on the same variables in Great Britain, Canada, France, Germany, Italy, and Japan 18 months after the change in GDP takes place. As the table shows, the 1-percent rise in the U.S. GNP, working through the multiplier process, causes its GNP to rise even further (1.39 percent) 18 months after the change occurs. Short-term interest rates rise by 0.89 percent and the GDP deflator by 0.55 percent. Finally, exports increase by 0.65 percent and imports by 2.49 percent.

The rise in U.S. exports reflects the increase in other countries' GNP, which is stimulated by the increase in U.S. imports. As the table indicates, the 1-percent rise leads to an increase of 0.10 percent in Britain's GNP, 0.55 percent in Canada's GNP, -0.07 percent in France's GNP, 0.14 percent in (the former) West Germany's GNP, 0.21 percent in Italy's GNP, and 0.12 percent in Japan's GNP. It is interesting to note that the largest increase occurs in Canada. This reflect the relatively high interdependence of the Canadian and U.S. economies. The increase in U.S. GNP also results in an increase in short-term interest rates, exports, and imports for most of the other countries.*

Impact of a One-percent Increase in the United States Gross National Product (In Percentages)

Nation	Real GNP	Short-Term Interest Rate	GDP Deflator	Exports	Imports
United States	1.39	0.89	0.55	0.65	2.49
Great Britain	0.10	0.02	-0.11	0.20	0.23
Canada	0.55	0.60	0.56	2.66	1.14
France	-0.07	0.29	-0.14	0.20	0.25
Germany**	0.14	0.41	0.10	0.35	-0.60
Japan	0.12	-0.12	-0.10	0.92	1.04
Italy	0.21	-0.42	-0.27	0.39	0.43

*The negative signs in the table may reflect other changes occurring simultaneously in these countries, reversing the expected relationship.
** Denotes the former West Germany.

Source: Ray C. Fair, "Estimated Output, Price, Interest Rate, and Exchange Rate Linkages among Countries," *Journal of Political Economy* (June 1982): 507-535.

Considering a BOP disequilibrium as a temporary, self-correcting phenomenon, the policy implications of the monetary approach are clear. According to this approach, any measure to resolve the BOP problem is generally unnecessary. If the monetary authorities are tolerant and stay passive, the BOP disequilibrium eventually resolves itself automatically. The problem with this approach is that the correction mechanism might take a long time, during which the economy may endure unnecessary adjustment costs.

13.5 DISADVANTAGES OF AUTOMATIC ADJUSTMENT MECHANISMS

In the preceding section, we considered the automatic price, automatic income, and automatic monetary adjustment mechanisms. Starting with the automatic price adjustment mechanism, we learned that the automatic process for correcting a BOP deficit under flexible exchange rates is achieved by the depreciation of the national currency. The disadvantage of this process may be erratic fluctuations in exchange rates. Such fluctuations increase risk and uncertainty of engaging in foreign trade and foreign direct investment, and hence flexible rates may decrease the amount of such trade and investment. Additionally, erratic fluctuations in exchange rates cause frequent movement of factors of production in and out of tradable goods sectors. Such movement leads to costly adjustment burdens in terms of time wasted in the movement process, costs of moving, and, possibly, costs of retraining labor.

Under the fixed exchange rate regime, a BOP deficit tends to decrease a country's money supply, thus raising its interest rates.* The higher interest rates discourage domestic investment and decrease national income in the deficit nation.** This, in turn, causes its imports to decrease, thus reducing the deficit. The rise in interest rates also lures foreign capital, helping the country to finance the BOP deficit. The decline in national income and in the money supply also causes prices in the deficit country to decline relative to prices in surplus countries. This, in turn, helps to further correct the BOP deficit. The opposite happens in surplus countries.

Under the fixed exchange rate regime, most of the adjustment would have to come from the monetary adjustments we have examined unless the country devalues its money. However, the prospect of devaluation may lead to the destabilization of international capital flows, which could be disruptive. Thus, a fixed exchange rate system compels the country to depend basically on monetary adjustments.

Automatic income changes may also have serious disadvantages. For example, a country that is at full employment and is experiencing an autonomous rise in its exports must accept domestic inflation in order to eliminate its BOP surplus. Also, a country that experiences an autonomous increase in its imports at the expense of domestic production has to let its national income decline in order to eliminate its trade deficit.

Finally, the problem with the automatic monetary adjustment mechanism, as we mentioned before, is that the country has to passively let its money supply change following a BOP disequilibrium. In other words, a nation has to give up its employment of monetary policy as a tool to accomplish the major goal of domestic full employment without inflation.

Given the shortcomings associated with automatic adjustment mechanisms, most countries usually employ discretionary policies to correct a BOP problem rather than leave this correction to the automatic mechanisms. We examine these policies in the next chapter. In today's world, where inflation and unemployment occur frequently, their quick correction usually takes precedent over BOP equilibrium. Thus, in democratic modern countries, politicians are disinclined to make important internal concessions in order to achieve external equilibrium.

13.6 PURCHASING-POWER-PARITY THEORY

The purchasing-power-parity (PPP) doctrine, introduced by the Swedish economist Gustav Cassel, is based on the rudimentary concept that a given amount of money, when converted into different currencies, should buy the same basket of commodities in different nations. The motivation behind developing this theory was the desire to estimate the equilibrium exchange rate at which countries could return to the gold standard, following the interruption of international trade that led to vast changes in relative goods prices in different countries.

The estimation of the value of the long-run equilibrium exchange rate (that is, the value toward which the actual exchange rate tends to move) is important for effective exchange rate administration. For example, if a country's exchange rate (the price of foreign currency in terms of domestic currency) decreases below the amount allowed by economic conditions, that is, its currency becomes overvalued, the nation will no longer be competitive in the

---

* The nation's money supply decreases because the additional foreign exchange needed is acquired by exchanging domestic money balances with foreign exchange at the country's central bank. Given a fractional-reserve banking system, this loss of reserve makes the country's money supply decline by a multiple of the trade deficit.

** Reduction in national income occurs through the multiplier process.

international market, and a trade deficit will probably follow. In the same manner, an undervalued currency tends to induce a trade surplus.

There are two versions of PPP theory: the absolute version and the relative version. We devote the rest of this chapter to a discussion of these versions.

13.6a Absolute Version of the Purchasing-Power-Parity Theory

According to this theory, given two countries (X and Y), the equilibrium exchange rate between the currency of the two nations (E_{XY}) is equal to the ratio of the general price level (price of a basket of goods) in country X (P_X) divided by the general price level in country Y (P_Y). Presenting the absolute version of the PPP theory in terms of a formula, we have

$$E_{XY} = P_X/P_Y \qquad (13\text{-}11)$$

For example, assume that nation X is the United States and nation Y is Great Britain. Suppose the general price level in the United States (P_{US}) is twice the general price level in Great Britain (P_B). According to the formula, the absolute version of the PPP theory asserts that the equilibrium exchange rate (defined as the dollar price of pound) is 2 ($E = P_{US}/P_B = 2/1 = 2$). In other words, two United States dollars are equal to one British pound ($\$2 = £P1$).

Based on the absolute version of the PPP theory, the exchange rate should reflect the purchasing power of the currencies. In the preceding example, the same basket of goods costs twice as much in the United States as it does in Great Britain. This is because, according to the absolute version, the purchasing power of the British pound is two times greater than the purchasing power of the U.S. dollar. The absolute version of the PPP theory also implies that goods tend to have the same price worldwide when measured in the same currency. However, the absolute version of the PPP theory is subject to the following problems:

1. It does not take into account nontraded goods and services, that is, goods and services that are not traded internationally. Thus, it does not give the exchange rate that equilibrates trade in all goods and services (traded and nontraded).
2. It does not take transportation costs and trade barriers into consideration. The existence of these factors will keep prices from equalizing across different markets.
3. The two baskets of goods' prices may not be comparable because the general price in each country reflects the price of a basket of goods and services which may be unique to that nation. Hence, it is not directly comparable to another nation's price.

For these reasons, the absolute version of the PPP should be rejected, and the relative version is used instead.

13.6b Relative Version of the Purchasing-Power-Parity Theory

According to this theory, given two countries (X and Y), the percentage change in the exchange rate between the two currencies ($\%\Delta E_{XY}$) over any time period is equal to the percentage change in nation X's price level ($\%\Delta P_X$) minus the percentage change in nation Y's price level ($\%\Delta P_Y$). In other words,

$$\%\Delta E_{XY} = \%\Delta P_X - \%\Delta P_Y \qquad (13\text{-}12)^*$$

---

* Presented in more detail, equation 13-12 can be expressed as follow:

$$[F_{XY1} - F_{XY0}]/F_{XY0} = [(P_{X1} - P_{X0})/P_{X0}]/[(P_{Y1} - P_{Y0})/P_{Y0}]$$

Where, E_{XY1} and E_{XY0} represent the exchange rates between the currencies of nations X and Y in period 1 and the base period (0), respectively. P_{X1} and P_{X0} represent the general price levels in country X in period 1 and the base period, respectively. P_{Y1} and P_{Y0} represent the general price levels in country Y in period 1 and the base period, respectively.

For example, assume that the general price level in the United States increases by 12 percent in a given year while the level in Great Britain increases by 10 percent during the same time period. According to equation 13-12, $\%\Delta E$ = 2. In other words, the relative version of the PPP theory predicts that the exchange rate (defined as the U.S. dollar price of the pound) should be 2 percent higher, that is, the U.S. dollar should depreciate by 2 percent against the British pound. Depreciation of the U.S. dollar by 2 percent against the British pound nullifies the 2 percent by which U.S. inflation surpasses Great Britain, thereby keeping the relative domestic and foreign purchasing powers of both currencies intact. Thus, prices and exchange rates change in a way that preserves the ratio of each currency's domestic and foreign purchasing powers.

More formally, relative PPP between countries X and Y can be written as

$$E_{XY1}/E_{XY0} = (P_{X1}/P_{X0})/(P_{Y1}/P_{Y0}) \qquad (13\text{-}13)$$

or

$$E_{XY1} = [(P_{X1}/P_{X0})/(P_{Y1}/P_{Y0})]E_{XY0} \qquad (13\text{-}14)$$

Where, E_{XY1} and E_{XY0} represent the exchange rates between the currencies of nations X and Y in period 1 and the base period (0), respectively; P_{X1} and P_{X0} represent the general price levels in country X in period 1 and the base period, respectively; and P_{Y1} and P_{Y0} represent the general price levels in country Y in period 1 and the base period, respectively.[*]

Equation 13-4, suggested by Cassel, provides a method for calculating the equilibrium exchange rate between two countries in a year (E_{XY1}), given the data for the right-hand side of the equation. For example, using equation 13-14, let X and Y stand for the United States and Germany, respectively. Assume that the general price levels (indices) and the equilibrium exchange rate in a base year for these two countries are as follows: P_{X1} = 150, P_{X0} = 100, P_{Y1} = 100, P_{Y0} = 100, and E_{XY0} = \$0.50. Plugging these figures into equation 13-14, we can determine the new equilibrium exchange rate for period 1:

$$E_{XY1} = [(150/100)/(100/100)](\$0.50) = \$0.75.$$

Thus, the new exchange rate (\$0.75) between the U.S. dollar and the deutsche mark is 50 percent higher than the base exchange rate (\$0.50). This means that the maintenance of purchasing power parity between the two currencies requires the dollar to depreciate against the mark by an amount equal to the difference between the U.S. inflation rate and the German inflation rate, that is, by 50 percent. In other words, a change in the exchange rate reflects the change in relative purchasing power of the two currencies.

The absolute version of the PPP theory implies the relative version, but the reverse is not true. If the absolute version holds, the relative version must also hold. However, if the relative version holds, the absolute version may not hold. Given that the variables causing deviation from the absolute version are relatively stable over time, percentage changes in relative price levels can still approximate changes in exchange rates.

Although the relative version has some validity, its use presents some problems. One of these problems, as noted by B. Balassa, is related to the fact that the ratio of the price of nontraded to the price of traded goods and services is systematically higher in advanced countries than in developing countries.[**]

---

[*] Equation 13-12 provides a good approximation of equation 13-13. For more detail, see Maurice D. Levi, *International Finance: The Market and Financial Management of Multinational Business*, 2d ed. (New York: McGraw-Hill, 1990), 123-144.

[**] One possible explanation is that the level of wages paid in the production of traded goods might be quite similar between advanced countries and developing countries. However, the level of wages paid in the production of nontraded goods are higher in advanced countries than in developing countries. Because higher wages mean higher production costs, the ratio of the price of nontraded to traded goods and services in advanced countries turns out to be greater than the same ratio in developing countries.

GLOBAL INSIGHTS CASE 13.2

AN EMPIRICAL TEST OF PURCHASING-POWER-PARITY

One of the methods that frequently has been used to forecast exchange rate movements is the purchasing power parity (PPP). However, the forecasting record of the PPP was demolished by its complete failure to explain exchange rate movements starting with the late 1970s. This can be detected from the figure which represents data that can be used as a test of the purchasing-power-parity theory. Here P_{US} and P_B denote consumer price indexes for the United States and Britain, respectively; E denotes the exchange rate between the dollar and the pound, defined in terms of dollars per pound. Although deviations from the PPP can be clearly seen from before and after the onset of the freely fluctuating exchange rates in 1973, starting with 1977, the magnitude of these deviations increased significantly, attesting to the failure of the PPP in explaining the exchange rates movements. If the relative version of the PPP were to hold, changes in exchange rates would reflect changes in the two currencies' purchasing power. In other words, the two series had to move together.

Exchange Rate of U.S. Dollars Versus the British Pound and the Relative U.S.–British Prices

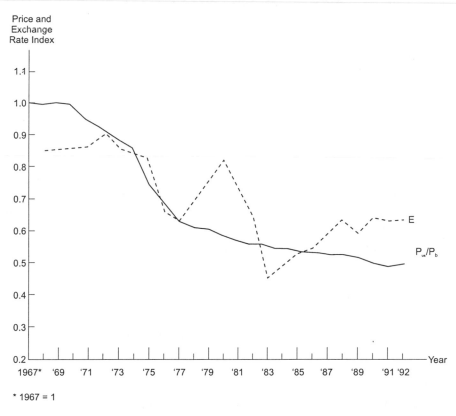

Source: *Economic Report of the President* (Washington D.C.: U.S. Government Printing Office, 1993).

As we already know, a general price index includes the prices of both traded and nontraded goods and services. International trade only equalizes the prices of traded goods and services. As a result, the prices of nontraded goods and services continue to remain relatively higher in advanced countries than in developing countries. Accordingly, the relative PPP theory tends to overestimate the predicted exchange rates for advanced nations and underestimate the predicted exchange rates for developing nations.

Another problem associated with the relative version of the PPP theory is that, in the presence of significant structural changes, it might produce erroneous results. For example, the relative version predicted that the British pound would be undervalued immediately after World War I. However, the opposite was true, and the British pound was overvalued. The reason was that Great Britain liquidated many of its foreign investments during the war. This led to a drop in its earnings on foreign investment. Because the relative version did not take this structural change into account, the equilibrium exchange rate predicted by this theory proved to be wrong.

Despite these problems, some empirical tests indicate that the relative version of the PPP theory provides us with a good approximation of equilibrium exchange rates, and it generally moves in the same direction as average exchange rates.

In closing this chapter, it must be emphasized that each of the theories concerning adjustment mechanisms discussed in this chapter were developed during different time periods. They reflect different philosophical approaches to economics and still have their modern-day proponents. In practice, given the shortcomings associated with the automatic adjustment mechanisms, most countries usually employ policies to correct their BOP problems rather than leave the correction to the automatic mechanisms.

13.7 SUMMARY

1. A nation's balance of payments (BOP) disequilibrium cannot continue indefinitely; it needs adjustment.
2. The adjustment mechanism for correcting a BOP disequilibrium takes two different forms. First, there is an automatic adjustment mechanism that corrects the BOP disequilibrium on its own, without any government action. Second, there are adjustment policies that are composed of specific measures adopted by the government with the primary objective of resolving the BOP disequilibrium.
3. Automatic adjustment mechanisms can be subdivided into the automatic price adjustment mechanism, the automatic income adjustment mechanism, and the automatic monetary adjustment mechanism.
4. The automatic price adjustment mechanism works through price changes in the deficit and surplus nations to correct the BOP disequilibrium.
5. The automatic income adjustment mechanism works through induced changes in national incomes of the surplus and deficit nations to bring about equilibrium in the BOP.
6. The automatic monetary adjustment mechanism relies on money supply to adjust the BOP disequilibrium.
7. The automatic price adjustment mechanism operates under both flexible exchange rates and fixed exchange rates (the gold standard system).
8. Under fixed exchange rates, the automatic adjustment mechanism is the same as the price-specie-flow mechanism described by David Hume in 1752.
9. The quantity theory of money can be explained by the equation of exchange:

$$MV = PQ,$$

   where M is the nation's money supply; V is the income velocity of money; P is the general price index; and Q is the physical quantity of goods produced.
10. The automatic process of correcting a BOP deficit under flexible exchange rates is achieved by a depreciation of the national currency.
11. The closed economy multiplier is given by the following formula:

$$k = \Delta Y/\Delta I = 1/MPS, = (1/1-MPC)$$

where k is the multiplier; ΔY is the change in output (income); MPS is the marginal propensity to save; and ΔI is the change in investment.

12. The condition for equilibrium in an open economy with no government sector is given by the following formula:

$$(I + X = S + M),$$

where I denotes desired investment; X denotes exports, S denotes desired saving; and M denotes imports.

13. The open economy multiplier is given by the following formula:

$$\text{Foreign trade multiplier} = k' = \Delta Y/\Delta I = 1/(MPS + MPM).$$

14. Foreign trade repercussion refers to the impact that a change in a large country's income and trade has on other countries, and the impact that other countries' changes have on the large country.

15. The automatic monetary adjustment mechanism, reflecting the monetary approach to the BOP, was initiated during the late 1960s and is identified with the Chicago school of thought.

16. The monetary approach considers surpluses and deficits to be adjustment elements that establish equilibrium between the money supply and the money demand in an open economy.

17. Given the shortcomings associated with automatic adjustment mechanisms, most countries usually employ discretionary policies to correct a BOP problem rather than leave this correction to the automatic mechanisms.

18. The purchasing-power-parity (PPP) doctrine, introduced by the Swedish economist Gustav Cassel, is based on the rudimentary concept that a given amount of money when converted to different currencies should buy the same basket of commodities in different nations.

19. According to the absolute version of the PPP theory, the equilibrium exchange rate (E_{XY}) between the currency of two nations is equal to the ratio of the general price level in country X (P_X) divided by the general price level in country Y (P_Y). Presenting the absolute version of the PPP theory in terms of a formula, we have $E_{XY} = P_X/P_Y$. Assuming the absolute version of the PPP theory is accurate, the exchange rate should reflect the purchasing power of the currencies. However, the absolute version of the PPP has limitations, and the relative version is often used.

20. According to the relative version of the PPP theory, the percentage change in the exchange rate between two currencies over a period of time must be proportional to the relative change in the price levels in the two countries. This theory can be presented in terms of a formula;

$$E_{XY1} = [(P_{X1}/P_{X0})/(P_{Y1}/P_{Y0})] \, E_{XY0}.$$

where E_{XY1} and E_{XY0} represent the exchange rates between the currencies of nation X and Y in period 1 and the base period (0), respectively; P_{X1} and P_{X0} represent the general price levels in country X in period 1 and the base period, respectively; and P_{Y1} and P_{Y0} represent the general price levels in country Y in period 1 and the base period, respectively. Although the relative version has some validity, its use presents some problems.

Review Questions

1. What are the main types of adjustment mechanisms for correcting a BOP disequilibrium? Explain, elaborating on the components of each of these mechanisms.
2. Under a flexible exchange rate system, what automatic adjustment eliminates a BOP disequilibrium? Explain.
3. Under a fixed exchange rate system, what automatic adjustment eliminates a BOP disequilibrium?
4. Given a fixed exchange rate system, how is a BOP disequilibrium corrected according to the Keynesian theory of income determination? Explain.
5. What is the equation of exchange? How did classical economists explain this equation?

6. What is meant by a closed economy? An open economy? What are a consumption function, a saving function, and an investment function? What are MPC, MPS, and MPM? How are they measured?

7. Assuming no government sector, what are the equilibrium equations for a closed economy and an open economy?

8. What is meant by a multiplier? What are the multiplier formulas for a closed economy and an open economy?

9. What are the major disadvantages of the automatic adjustment mechanism under (a) a flexible exchange rate system, and (b) a fixed exchange rate system?

10. What are the implications of the monetary approach for domestic economic policies?

11. Compare the relative and absolute versions of the PPP theory and elaborate on this theory's usefulness.

12. What is meant by foreign trade repercussions? What determines the significance of foreign trade repercussions for a country?

Problems

1. Assume the consumption and investment functions for a closed economy are given by the following equations:

$$C = 50 + 0.75Y \quad I = 100$$

Given this information; complete the following:

(a) What are the amounts of MPC and MPS?

(b) Derive the saving equation.

(c) Graphically demonstrate the equilibrium level of national income for this closed economy, and indicate the levels of consumption, saving, and investment.

(d) Graphically demonstrate the impact of an increase in autonomous investment expenditures (from $I = 100$ to $I = 200$) on equilibrium points.

(e) Calculate the multiplier for this hypothetical economy.

2. The following equations are given for a hypothetical economy:

$$
\begin{aligned}
C &= 100 + 0.6Y \\
M &= 50 + 0.3Y \quad I = 100 \\
X &= 200
\end{aligned}
$$

Given this information; complete the following:

(a) What are the amounts of MPC, MPS, and MPM?

(b) Derive the saving equation.

(c) Algebraically determine the equilibrium level of national income.

(d) Graphically demonstrate the equilibrium level of national income, as in panels (a) and (b) of Figure 13-3.

(e) Determine the value of the multiplier.

3. Given the algebraic and graphical results of problem 2, algebraically determine and graphically demonstrate the following:

(a) The effect on national income of an autonomous increase of 100 in X

(b) The effect of an autonomous increase in I of 100

4. Suppose that Israel's inflation rate is 80 percent in a given year, but the inflation rate in Canada is 20 percent over the same time period. According to the relative PPP theory, what should happen over the year to the exchange rate between the Canadian dollar and the Israeli currency (new shekel)?

5. Suppose the deutsche mark (DM) price of the U.S. dollar ($) was DM 1.850/$1 in 1993 and DM 1.790/$1 in 1983. If the price level for Germany (1983 = 100) was 125 in 1993, and the price index for the United States (1983 = 100) was 138 in 1993, according to the relative version of the PPP, was the dollar undervalued or overvalued in 1993? Explain.

6. The following table gives the prices of three goods in the United States and Germany.

	Briefcases	Watches	Jackets
U.S.	$80.00	$40.00	$80.00
Germany	DM 320.00	DM 120.00	DM 40.00

Suppose that a representative consumer basket of these goods contains 2 briefcases, 1 watch, and 3 jackets per period. Assuming that each product is the same in both countries, what is the exchange rate suggested by the PPP theory?

Notes

1. "Dollar's Plunge Worries U.S. and Europe," *The Wall Street Journal,* 25 August 1992, A2; "Dollar's Fall Is Expected to Continue," *The Wall Street Journal,* 24 August 1992, C1; "Dollar's Drop Cuts Likelihood of Lower Rates," *The Wall Street Journal,* 24 August 1992, C1.
2. H. G. Johnson, "The Monetary Approach to the Balance of Payments, *Journal of Finance and Quantitative Analysis* 16, no. 2 (March 1972):1556.

Suggested Readings

Balassa, B. "The Purchasing Power Parity Doctrine: A Reappraisal." *Journal of Political Economy* (December 1964); Reprinted in R. N. Cooper, *International Finance.* Baltimore: Penguin, 1969.

Bryant, R. C. *Money and Monetary Policy in an Open Economy.* Washington, DC: Brookings Institution, 1980.

Cassel, G. *Money and Foreign Exchange after 1914.* New York: Macmillan, 1923.

Cassel, G. *Postwar Monetary Stabilization.* New York: Columbia University Press, 1928.

Dornbusch, R. *Open Economy Macroeconomics.* New York: Basic Books, 1980.

Goldstein, M., and M. S. Khan. "Income and Price Effects in Foreign Trade." In *Handbook of International Economics,* vol. 2, edited by R. W. Jones and P. B. Kenen. New York: North Holland, 1985.

Hume, D. "Of the Balance of Trade." *Essays, Moral, Political and Literary,* vol. 1. London: Longmans Green, 1898.

Kravis, I. B. "Comparative Studies of National Income and Prices." *Journal of Economic Literature* 22 (March 1984): 1-39.

Kravis, I. B., and R. E. Lipsey. "Price Behavior in the Light of Balance of Payments Theories." *Journal of International Economics* (May 1978): 193-246.

Machlup, F. *International Trade and the National Income Multiplier.* Philadelphia: The Blakiston Company, 1943.

McDonald, R., and M. Taylor, eds. *Exchange Rates and Open Economy Macroeconomics.* New York: Basil Blackwell, 1989.

Officer, L. "The Purchasing-Power-Parity Theory of Exchange Rates: A Review Article." *International Monetary Fund Staff Papers* 23 (March 1976): 1-61.

Officer, L. H. "The Relation between Absolute and Relative Purchasing Power Parity." *Review of Economics and Statistics* (November 1978): 562-68

Robinson, R. "A Graphical Analysis of the Foreign Trade Multiplier." *Economic Journal* (September 1952): 546-564.

Chapter 14

BALANCE OF PAYMENTS ADJUSTMENT POLICIES

14.1 INTRODUCTION

In Chapter 13 we discussed the role of automatic adjustment mechanisms in promoting equilibrium in the balance of payments (BOP). As mentioned in that chapter, given the shortcomings associated with these adjustment mechanisms, most countries usually employ policies to correct their BOP problems rather than leave the correction to the mechanisms. However, **external balance,** or BOP equilibrium, is not the only economic objective a country has to achieve. Another significant economic goal is maintenance of its **internal balance,** or full employment and price stability. Usually countries give priority to their internal balance over their external balance. However, when faced with a persistent external balance, they may be compelled to change their priority.

To accomplish these goals, countries have the following policy tools available to them: (a) expenditure-adjusting policies, (b) general expenditure-switching policies, and (c) selective expenditure-switching policies, or direct controls. The purpose of this chapter is to elaborate these policy options and to provide a theoretical discussion of the effectiveness of devaluation in correcting a BOP disequilibrium.

14.2 EXPENDITURE-ADJUSTING POLICIES

Expenditure-adjusting policies, or policies that affect aggregate demand, include both fiscal and monetary policies. As discussed in introductory economics courses, **monetary policy** is the deliberate expansion or contraction of the money supply by a nation's monetary authorities. An expansionary monetary policy, that is, an increase in the nation's money supply (M_s), causes the interest rate (r) to fall. This generates an increase in the level of investment spending (I) and income (Y) in the country (through the multiplier process) and causes an increase in imports (M), worsening the current account of the BOP. In the meantime, the fall in interest rates generates a short-term capital outflow (CO) or decreases capital inflow (CI), worsening the capital account of the BOP. A contractionary monetary policy achieves the opposite.

Fiscal policy refers to an intentional increase or decrease in government expenditure and/or taxation. An expansionary fiscal policy (that is, an increase in government expenditure [G] or a decrease in taxation [T]) leads to an increase in domestic production and income (Y) through the multiplier process. This generates a rise in imports (M), depending on the nation's marginal propensity to import (MPM), worsening the current account of the BOP. But an increase in government spending also means bigger government budget deficits, or we could say reduced budget surpluses. The government has to borrow more money, driving up the interest rates (r). The higher interest rates in turn generate capital inflow (CI) or decrease capital outflow (CO), improving the capital account of the BOP. A contractionary fiscal policy achieves the opposite result.

Expansionary monetary and expansionary fiscal policies are portrayed in Figure 14-1. As the figure indicates, the effects of the two policies on the BOP are quite similar. Both policies can result in higher income that adversely affects the BOP in the short run. The main difference between the two policies is related to their impact on interest rates. Expansionary monetary policy leads to a fall in interest rates, worsening the BOP. However, expansionary fiscal policy induces a rise in interest rates, improving the BOP. But this difference in interest rate behavior and the resultant BOP effect is temporary. If one country attracts foreign funds from another country, its BOP improves at the expense of that other country. However, sooner or later the first country has to pay off the funds with interest. This leads to a worsening of its BOP and an improvement in the other country's BOP. Thus, the more permanent effect of either policy (monetary or fiscal) on the BOP is related to the income effect they share.

FIGURE 14-1
Expansionary Monetary and Fiscal Policies Flow-chart

An increase in a nation's money supply (M_s) causes the interest rate (r) to fall, generating an increase in the country's level of investment spending (I) and income (Y). This causes an increase in imports (M), worsening the current account of the balance of payments (BOP). In the meantime, the fall in interest rates generates a short-term capital outflow (CO) or decreases capital inflow (CI), again worsening the capital account of the balance of payments (BOP). A contractionary monetary policy achieves the opposite effect.

An increase in government expenditures (G) or a decrease in taxation (T) leads to an increase in domestic production and income (Y). This generates a rise in imports (M), worsening the current account of the balance of payments (BOP). But an increase in government spending also means the government must borrow more money, driving up interest rates (r). The higher interest rates in turn generate capital inflow (CI) or decrease capital outflow (CO), improving the capital account of the balance of payments (BOP). A contractionary fiscal policy achieves the opposite result.

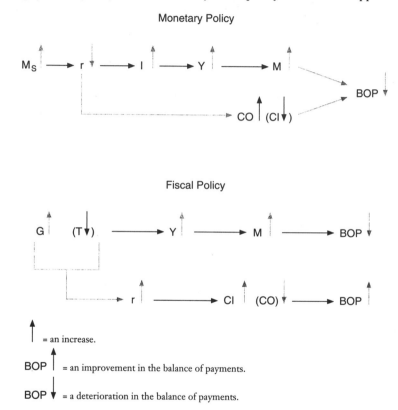

Setting aside the interest rate effect of monetary and fiscal policies and concentrating only on their income effects, we face a basic dilemma: It is often impossible to achieve both internal and external balance by using only aggregate-demand policy (in its monetary and fiscal version). This is because we have two objectives (internal and external balance) and essentially only one device, that is, aggregate-demand policy.

Historically, advanced countries have faced this dilemma. For example, the United States in the early 1960s and Great Britain in the late 1920s were faced with unemployment problems and BOP deficits. Resolving unemployment called for expansionary monetary or fiscal policy to stimulate aggregate demand, but this meant deteriorating the BOP. The problem was not resolved. Britain went into a depression, and the U.S. unemployment problem was resolved only after inflation was generated by, among other events, the United States' engagement in the Vietnam War. Also, Germany, Japan, and Switzerland, all of which enjoyed full employment during the post-World War II years of fixed exchange rates, regularly experienced rapid inflation and BOP surpluses. Which led these countries to an impasse. Reducing inflation calls for contractionary monetary or fiscal policy, but this means a further increase in the BOP surplus.

To get out of such dilemmas, a nation must either give up one of its two goals (internal or external) or manipulate its aggregate supply. Obviously, giving up one of its two goals is unpopular and unwise. Manipulating the aggregate supply, that is, adopting policies that create more income and employment by improving productivity, seems a logical way out of the dilemma. However, the problem is that productivity, which can be improved through advances in human skills and technology, reacts lethargically, if at all, to government maneuvering. In other words, a government may not be very effective in devising strategies to increase productivity. Additionally, it takes a long time to accomplish any significant technological progress. There is, however, a way to buy time and achieve both external and internal balance for some time, employing conventional demand-side policies and remaining on fixed exchange rates.

Robert Mundell and J. Marcus Fleming observed that monetary and fiscal policy exert different effects on internal and external balance. This implies that in fact we have two policy instruments (monetary policy and fiscal policy) rather than just one (aggregated-demand policy).* Given this observation, Mundell recommends mixing monetary and fiscal policy according to a guideline referred to as an **assignment rule.** According to this rule, each policy instrument should be assigned to the target on which it has the most impact. The mathematical foundation of this principle is beyond the scope of this book. We only need to know that monetary policy should be assigned to accomplish external balance and fiscal policy to accomplish internal balance, because monetary policy has a comparative advantage in manipulating external balance, whereas fiscal policy has a comparative advantage in manipulating internal balance. The policy implications of the assignment rule are presented in Table 14-1.

Advanced studies on this topic demonstrate that if policymakers implement the indicated policy changes smoothly and without lags, the assignment rule guides the economy to achievement of both external and internal balance.

14.2a Evaluation of Monetary-Fiscal Policy Mix

The strategy of mixing monetary and fiscal policies in order to achieve internal and external balance has been subject to the following criticisms.

First, short-run capital flows may not be as sensitive to international interest rate differentials as expected. Their response may be inadequate or even erratic rather than continuous as presumed by Mundell. Additionally, destabilizing speculators may complicate the issue enormously.

Second, policymakers do not know the precise impact of monetary and fiscal policies in advance. As a result, they may be reluctant to, for example, increase interest rates to high levels or decrease government spending to low levels.

Third, if either monetary policy or fiscal policy lags in receiving signals from the economy and reacting to them, Mundell's assignment rule may become unstable.**

TABLE 14-1
Assignment Rule: Policy Implications

State of the Economy	Monetary Policy	Fiscal Policy
Unemployment and surplus	Expansionary	Expansionary
Unemployment and deficit	Contractionary	Expansionary
Inflation and surplus	Expansionary	Contractionary
Inflation and deficit	Contractionary	Contractionary

---

* The key difference between the two policies, as we mentioned earlier, relates to their impact on interest rates. Expansionary monetary policy tends to decrease interest rates, and expansionary fiscal policy tends to increase them.

** For the proof of this theoretical proposition see Miltiades Chacholiades, *International Economics* (New York: McGraw-Hill Publishing Company, 1990), 575-577.

14.3 GENERAL EXPENDITURE-SWITCHING POLICIES

General expenditure-switching policies refer to changes in the exchange rate by means of devaluation and revaluation. A **devaluation** switches expenditures from foreign to domestic goods, improving a BOP deficit. On the other hand, a **revaluation** switches expenditures from domestic to foreign goods, reducing or eliminating a BOP surplus.

In this section, we first explain devaluation and revaluation. We then elaborate on approaches to devaluation to assess the conditions under which it is successful in resolving BOP problems.

14.3a Devaluation and Revaluation

Variations in exchange rates are referred to by different names depending on the type of exchange rate system used. Under the floating exchange rate system, an increase in the exchange rate (price of foreign currency in terms of domestic currency) is called **depreciation**; a decrease in the exchange rate is called **appreciation**. We refer to a deliberate increase in the par (peg) value of a currency as a **devaluation**; **revaluation** is an antonym, describing a deliberate decrease in the par value. Thus, devaluation and revaluation correspond to depreciation and appreciation, respectively, of a domestic currency. The distinct jargon reveals the exchange rate system used. Because the effects of a depreciation and a devaluation (or an appreciation and a revaluation) are generally the same, they are discussed together here and used interchangeably.*

Under the fixed exchange rate system, as we explained earlier, devaluation is achieved by increasing the par value of the currency in question. For example, the United States devalued the dollar in December 1971 by increasing the dollar price of gold from $35 per ounce to $38 per ounce. By increasing the par value of a currency, a devaluation makes the exchange rate rise. This makes the price of the home country's exports, measured in terms of the foreign currency, lower, causing exports to rise. The higher prices for foreign goods also mean that the value of the home country's imports are more expensive, causing imports to fall. Thus, if devaluation is successful, the increase in exports and decrease in imports improve the BOP.**

Under the managed floating exchange rate system, a nation can cause its currency to depreciate by simply buying another nation's currency through its central bank. Because this action raises the demand for the foreign currency, it causes the currency's price to increase in terms of the domestic currency. Additionally, because all currencies interact in the foreign exchange market, the decline in the price of one nation's currency in terms of another currency would lead to the depreciation of its price relative to other currencies. For example, since 1971, the Japanese government has repeatedly bought a tremendous volume of U.S. dollars in order to hold down the price of its currency, that is, the yen. The Japanese government apparently has used this policy to make U.S. exports relatively expensive abroad, giving Japanese exports an edge.

Since the 1980s, the popularity of devaluation as a policy tool has increased in many developing nations. In order to increase their exports and decrease their imports, many of these nations have cheapened their currencies. For example, from 1982 through 1986, Brazil devalued its currency by 99 percent, whereas Indonesia's was devalued by 62 percent and Mexico's by 97 percent.[1]

Devaluation or depreciation of country A's currency in terms of country B's currency means revaluation or appreciation of country B's currency in terms of country A's currency. For example, if the U.S. dollar is depreciated against the Japanese yen, making yen more expensive for U.S. residents to buy, Japanese yen would be appreciated against the U.S. dollar, making the U.S. dollar cheaper for the Japanese to buy. If this were the case, U.S. exports would increase (imports decrease), whereas Japanese exports would decrease (imports increase). As a result, the U.S. BOP would improve at the expense of the Japanese BOP. Thus, the stage is set for a "beggar-thy-neighbor" trade war between these two countries. For example, from 1931 through 1936, the world experienced numerous competitive devaluations as countries attempted to "export" their unemployment. Another example is the depreciation of the U.S.

---

* The news media uses the term devaluation to refer to an intentional increase in the exchange rate by its monetary authorities, regardless of the exchange rate system used.

** The condition necessary for successful devaluation is explained later in this chapter.

dollar on September 22, 1985, when the United States persuaded Japan, Germany, Great Britain, and France to agree to depreciate the U.S. dollar in an effort to pacify protectionist sentiment that existed in the U.S. Congress. Although the action was approved by this "Group of Five,"* the countries did not continue to cooperate with each other in practice. The U.S. dollar did decline, but the U.S. trade deficit continued to stay at a record high. At the same time, exporters in Japan and Germany continued to suffer from the cheap dollar, losing profits. Given this situation, Japan and European countries decided to fight back by causing their own currencies to depreciate. They did this by buying dollars to boost its price. The magnitude of their purchases can be inferred from the tremendous increase in the net foreign government purchases of U.S. government securities. This figure, which was $10 billion in the first quarter of 1986, rose to $52 billion in the second quarter.[2] Nevertheless, the magnitude of these purchases proved to be inadequate in changing the course the U.S. dollar was taking. The dollar continued to depreciate against major currencies, and, beginning in September 1987, the U.S. trade balance (exports − imports) started to show signs of improvement.[3]

14.3b Approaches to Devaluation

How does devaluation or depreciation affect a nation's BOP? In our previous discussion, we accentuated the impact that devaluation of a currency may have on a country's BOP. But we did not elaborate on conditions under which devaluation may be successful in bringing about the BOP equilibrium. Several approaches to devaluation can be considered. The **elasticity approach** stresses the *price effect* of devaluation and proposes that usually devaluation operates best when elasticities are high. The **absorption effect** emphasizes *income effects* and suggests that domestic expenditures must decline relative to income in order for devaluation to improve the BOP. The **monetary approach** emphasizes the impact devaluation has on the *purchasing power of money balances* and the ensuing effect on domestic expenditures. In this section, we explain these approaches to devaluation (depreciation), but the analyses are similarly applicable to revaluation (appreciation).

In explaining the elasticity approach, we also elaborate on the J-curve effect to explain why the initial effect of devaluation is to worsen a country's BOP before making it better.

The Elasticity Approach. A major course by which devaluation or depreciation of a currency affects a nation's BOP is through fluctuations in the relative prices of goods and services. As we explained earlier, by increasing the domestic price of foreign currencies, devaluation makes the value of the home country's exports, measured in terms of the foreign currency, cheaper, encouraging exports to expand. The higher prices for foreign goods mean that the value of the home country's imports are more expensive, thereby discouraging imports. The success of devaluation in curing a BOP disequilibrium depends on the price elasticity of demand for a country's exports and the price elasticity of demand for its imports.

Recalling microeconomics principles courses, elasticity measures the degree of responsiveness of a change in one variable with respect to a change in another variable, with responsiveness measured in percentage change. Thus, price elasticity of demand alludes to the responsiveness of the quantity demanded of a good to changes in price. It shows the percentage change in quantity demanded resulting from a 1-percent change in price. Mathematically, the price elasticity of demand (E_D) is measured by the ratio of percentage change in quantity demanded ($\Delta Q/Q$) to the percentage change in price ($\Delta P/P$):

$$E_D = -(\Delta Q/Q)/(\Delta P/P). \qquad (14\text{-}1)$$

Because the demand curve for a product has negative slope, E_D is negative. However, E_D is customarily expressed in absolute terms, that is, without regard for the algebraic sign. If a given percentage change in price causes a larger percentage change in quantity demanded, E_D is greater than 1, and we have a relatively elastic demand curve. If a given percentage change in price leads to an equal percentage change in quantity, E_D is equal to 1, and we have a unitary elastic demand curve. If a given percentage change in price results in a smaller percentage change in quantity, E_D is less than 1, and we have a relatively inelastic curve.

---

* The "Group of Five" consisted of the United States, Japan, and former West Germany, France, and Britain.

Having a knowledge of elasticity, we can use a general rule, known as the **Marshall-Lerner condition,** to assess the actual outcome of a devaluation. This rule gives conditions for improving the balance of trade. Defining BOP disequilibrium by the trade balance, improvements in the balance of trade implies improvements in the BOP. Thus, we use these terms interchangeably in this section.

Assuming the supply curves of imports and exports are both infinitely elastic (horizontal), according to the Marshall-Lerner condition, the following are true:

1. If the sum of the price elasticities of the demand for imports and the demand for exports is greater than 1 in absolute terms, devaluation will improve the balance of trade.
2. If the sum of the price elasticities of the demand for imports and the demand for exports is less than 1 in absolute terms, devaluation will worsen the balance of trade.
3. If the sum of the price elasticities of the demand for imports and the demand for exports is equal to 1 in absolute terms, devaluation will not affect the balance of trade.[*]

The Marshall-Lerner condition can be depicted in the context of either the country that is devaluing its currency or of its trading partner. However, the condition cannot be stated in terms of both countries' currencies at the same time.

To demonstrate the effects of devaluation on a country's balance of trade using the Marshall-Lerner condition, we present two hypothetical examples involving the United States and Oman. In these examples, we assume that Oman devalues its currency (the rial). Given this assumption, we present our analysis in terms of the rial, that is, the currency of the nation that undertakes devaluation.

Example 1: Improving the Balance of Trade. Assume that Oman's price elasticity of demand for imports is equal to 3.0, and the United States' price elasticity of demand for Omani exports is equal to 1.5. Now suppose Oman is facing a BOP deficit. To cure its deficit, Oman devalues its currency, the rial by 10 percent. This leads to a decrease in the price of the rial, in terms of the U.S. dollar. To determine the overall effect of devaluation on Oman's BOP, we need to assess the devaluation's impact on export receipts and import payments.

Assuming that import prices stay constant in terms of foreign currency, devaluation raises the domestic price of imported goods. Specifically, the import prices in Oman, measured in terms of the rial, will increase by 10 percent. Given the price elasticity of demand for imports (3.0), the devaluation precipitates a 30-percent (10 x 3) drop in the quantity of imports demanded. The 10-percent rise in price (P), along with a 30-percent quantity (Q) reduction, results in roughly a 20-percent decrease (10 - 30 = - 20) in Oman's import expenditure, reducing Oman's balance of trade deficit.[**]

The devaluation also affects Oman's export revenue. Assuming that Oman's export prices stay constant in terms of the rial, the devaluation of the rial causes Oman's export prices to decrease in terms of the U.S. dollar by 10 percent. This generates an increase in quantity demanded for Oman's exports to the United States. Given that the United States' price elasticity of demand for Oman's exports is equal to 1.5, the 10-percent devaluation of the rial will elevate foreign sales by approximately 15 percent (10 x 1.5). In other words, the export receipts in terms of the rial will increase by approximately 15 percent. This improves Oman's BOP trade account.

---

[*] Technically speaking, if the Marshal-Lerner condition is satisfied, balance of trade is improved. Defining BOP disequilibrium by the balance of trade, improvement in the former implies the latter.

[**] As you already know, total revenue (TR) is equal to price (P) times quantity (Q), that is,

$$TR = P \times Q.$$

Expressing this equation in logarithm, we have

$$\text{Log } TR = \text{Log } P + \text{Log } Q.$$

Taking the derivative of the logarithmic equation, we get

$$(1/TR)\, dTR = (I/P)\, dp + (1/Q)\, dQ$$

or

$$\%\Delta TR = \%\Delta P - \%\Delta Q.$$

Thus, our example uses this equation to get:

$$-20 = 10 - 30.$$

In summary, when the sum of elasticities is greater than 1, the devaluation effects of exports and imports reinforce each other, improving the balance of trade. In this example, the 20-percent decline in import expenditures coupled with a 15-percent increase in export receipts leads to a reduction in Oman's balance of trade deficit.

Example 2: Worsening the Balance of Trade. Given the same two countries, now assume that Oman's price elasticity of demand for imports is equal to 0.3, and the United States' price elasticity of demand for Omani exports is equal to 0.1. The 10-percent devaluation of the rial increases the rial price of Oman's imports by 10 percent, generating a 3-percent (10 x 0.3) decline in the quantity of imports demanded. Thus, in contrast to the first example, the devaluation contributes to a rise, rather than a decline, in import expenditures of about 7 percent (10 - 3).

Devaluation also affects Oman's exports. As in the previous example, the rial price of Oman's exports does not change, but the dollar price of exports falls by 10 percent. The United States' purchases of Omani exports increases by 1 percent (10 x 0.1), resulting in an increase of about 1 percent in Oman's export revenue, measured in terms of the rial.

Given a 7-percent increase in import expenditures and only a 1-percent increase in export revenue, Oman's balance of trade tends to deteriorate. This confirms the Marshall-Lerner condition of deterioration in the balance of trade when the sum of elasticities is less than 1. Both of our examples are summarized in Table 14-2.

TABLE 14-2
Hypothetical Examples of a Ten-percent Devaluation of the Rial

Example 1

Oman's price elasticities of demand for imports	3.0
The United States' price elasticity of demand for Oman's exports	1.5
Sum of the elasticities	4.5

Balance of Trade Outcome

Sector	Percentage Change in Rial Price	Percentage Change Quantity Demanded	Net Effect* (percentage)
Imports	+10	-30	-20
Exports**	0	+15	+15

Example 2

Oman's price elasticities of demand for imports	0.3
The United States' price elasticity of demand for Oman's exports	0.1
Sum of the elasticities	0.4

The Balance of Trade Outcome

Sector	Percentage Change in Rial Price	Percentage Change Quantity Demanded	Net Effect* (percentage)
Imports	+10	-3	+7
Exports**	0	+1	+1

* Net effect refers to either net change in import expenditures or net change in export receipts.

** Although the rial price of exports has not changed, the dollar price of exports falls, generating an increase in quantity demanded for Oman's exports to the United States and resulting in an increase in Oman's export revenue.

Estimates of import and export demand elasticities. The Marshall-Lerner condition underlines the significance of import and export demand elasticities in determining the effect of devaluation on a nation's balance of trade. If policymakers knew elasticities in advance, they could choose a suitable exchange rate policy to resolve the BOP problem.

During the 1930s and 1940s, an **elasticity pessimism** prevailed. A number of empirical studies suggested low-demand elasticities, implying that, according to the Marshall-Lerner condition, a devaluation does not improve a nation's BOP. However, a 1950 article by G. Orcutt, an economist, led to the belief that previous studies had grossly underestimated the true elasticities in international trade. Orcutt's findings paved the way for the gradual **elasticity optimism** that started in the 1960s. This optimism has been based, in part, on estimates such as those recently made by Jaime Marquez and presented in Table 14-3.[4] As the table shows, with the exception of Great Britain, the Marshall-Lerner condition is met in all cases (that is, the sum of import and export elasticities is greater than 1 in absolute terms). These estimates seem to be true for both advanced and developing countries. Furthermore, because these estimates are quarterly (short-run) estimates, and because long-run elasticities are greater than short-run elasticities, we can infer that devaluation has a long-run positive effect on the BOP.

J-Curve Effect. The most recent empirical estimates of elasticities, like those presented in Table 14-3, support the proposition that devaluation improves a nation's balance of trade (the Marshall-Lerner condition). A major problem in assessing world price elasticities, however, is that there tends to be a time lag between changes in exchange rates and their final impact on real trade. To elaborate on this time lag, we assume that the home country devalues or depreciates its currency with no offsetting devaluation by its trading partners, the result being an increase in the exchange rate (the price of foreign currency in terms of domestic currency).

TABLE 14-3
Price Elasticities of Demand for Imports and Exports (Quarterly, 1973I-1985II)

Country or Unit	Import Price Elasticity	Export Price Elasticity	Sum of Import and Export Elasticities
Canada	-1.02	-0.83	-1.85
Germany	-0.60	-0.66	-1.26
Japan	-0.93	-0.93	-1.86
Great Britain	-0.47	-0.44	-0.91
United States	-0.92	-0.99	-1.91
Other developed countries	-0.49	-0.83	-1.32
Less-developed countries	-0.81	-0.63	-1.44
OPEC nations	-1.14	-0.57	-1.71

Source: Jaime Marquez, "Bilateral Trade Elasticities," *Review of Economics and Statistics 72* (February 1990): 75-76.

Given this assumption, as we already know, devaluation of a currency affects a country's trade payments by its net impact on import expenditures and export receipts. If a country's national currency is devalued by 5 percent, its import prices (P_M) initially rise by 5 percent in terms of the domestic currency. As a result, the quantity of imports demanded (Q_M) falls according to domestic demand elasticities. If import demand is relatively elastic, total expenditure on imports ($P_M \times Q_M$) falls. At the same time, export prices (P_X) fall by 5 percent in terms of foreign currency. As a result, quantity demanded of exports (Q_X) increases according to foreign demand elasticities. If export demand is relatively elastic, total export revenue ($P_X \times Q_X$) will increase. Assuming that the Marshall-Lerner condition is satisfied, the mechanism by which devaluation affects import expenditures and export receipts and improves balance of trade is shown in Figure 14-2.

The difficulty with the preceding description is that for devaluation to have an effect, time is needed to enable consumers and producers to respond to changing relative prices. In other words, there is a time lag between a devaluation and its ultimate effect on the balance of trade. One popular explanation of this time lag is what is referred to as the **J-Curve effect.**

FIGURE 14-2
Devaluation Flow Chart

If a country's national currency is devalued or depreciated by 5 percent, its import prices (P_M) initially rise by 5 percent in terms of the domestic currency. As a result, the quantity of imports demanded (Q_M) falls according to domestic demand elasticities. If import demand is relatively elastic, total expenditure on imports (P_M x Q_M) falls. At the same time, export prices (P_X) fall by 5 percent in terms of foreign currency. As a result, quantity of exports demanded (Q_X) increases according to foreign demand elasticities. If export demand is relatively elastic, total exports revenue (P_X x Q_X) increase. Assuming that the Marshall-Lerner condition is satisfied, devaluation or depreciation, working through these mechanisms, improves the nation's balance of trade (BOT) deficit.

Devaluation (depreciation) and the Balance of Trade*

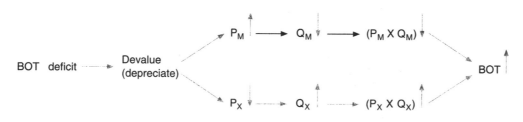

BOT   = balance of trade.

BOT $\uparrow$ = an improvement in the balance of trade.

* Assuming Marshel-Lerner condition is satisfied.

According to the J-Curve effect, devaluation worsens the balance of trade before improving it. This is, in fact, where the theory got its name. The letter "J" corresponds to the initial worsening of the balance of trade before the forthcoming improvements. This is because the initial effect of devaluation or depreciation is to increase import expenditures. Import expenditures (quantity of imports x price of imports) initially rise because there is an increase in import prices, while at the same time the quantity of imports remains unchanged due to prior commitments or established preferences. However, with the passage of time, the quantity of imports decreases while quantity of exports increases. In other words, the long-run price elasticities of demand for traded goods are not the same as the short-run elasticities. As a result, trade payments improve. Figure 14-3 illustrates a J-Curve, indicating the time path of the balance of trade's response to devaluation. As this figure indicates, the shape of the curve resembles the letter "J" (slightly askew).

FIGURE 14-3
J-Curve Effect

Devaluation or depreciation of a nation's currency, occurring at time T_0, initially results in a deterioration of the nation's balance of trade. Import expenditures (quantity of imports x price of imports) initially rise because there is an increase in import prices, while at the same time the quantity of imports remains unchanged due to prior commitments or established preferences. However, with the passage of time, the quantity of imports decreases and quantity of exports increases. As a result, the balance of trade starts showing a net improvement at time T_1.

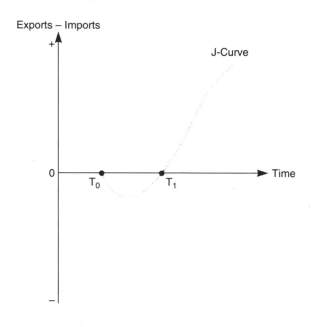

According to an empirical study, the factors that cause the time lags in the devaluation mechanism can be divided into the following categories:

1. **Recognition lag.** This lag refers to the length of time it takes for buyers and sellers to become aware of the changes in competitive position following a devaluation.
2. **Decision lag.** This lag refers to the period of time it takes for constituting new business relationships and setting new orders.
3. **Delivery lag.** This is the lag between the time new orders are set and the point at which they affect trade and expenditure patterns.
4. **Replacement lag.** This is the lag in depleting inventories and exhausting existing machinery before setting new orders.
5. **Production lag.** This represents the time it takes to shift from supplying one market to supplying another or enhancing capacity to supply the added market.

Given these time lags, the response of trade flows to relative price changes quite clearly seems to stretch over a period of about four to five years. Additionally, following a price change, approximately 50 percent of the full trade-flow reaction occurs within the first three years, and about 90 percent takes place during the first five years.[5]

One example of the J-Curve effect is the 1967 devaluation of the British pound. It took approximately two years before this devaluation had a significant effect on the British trade balance. Another example is the depreciation of the U.S. dollar in September 1985. After this depreciation, the U.S. trade balance continued to deteriorate for two years before it started to show signs of improvement in September 1987.[6]

In interpreting the J-Curve, we must note that it is often difficult to separate the currency-trade relationship, depicted by the curve, from other economic variables that affect a nation's trade balance.

The Absorption Approach. According to the elasticity approach, the improvement in a nation's BOP occurs because a devaluation encourages the nation's exports and discourages its imports. This stimulates domestic production. However, if a nation is operating near full employment, it needs to decrease its "absorption," or domestic expenditures, to eliminate a BOP deficit. This is the basic insight of the absorption approach. It takes into account the effect of devaluation on domestic expenditures and the influence of domestic expenditures on the trade balance. Defining BOP disequilibrium by the trade balance, an improvement in the balance of trade implies an improvement in the BOP. Thus, as in our previous discussion, we use these terms interchangeably in this section.

The **absorption approach**, introduced by Sidney Alexander, starts with the simple understanding that gross national product (GNP) or income (Y) is equal to consumption (C) plus domestic investment (I) plus government expenditure (G) plus net exports or the trade balance (X - M), where X represents the value of exports and M represent the value of imports. Presenting this identity in the form of an equation, we have

$$Y = C + I + G + (X - M). \quad (14\text{-}2)$$

Letting (C + I + G) represent domestic absorption (A) and (X - M) represent the trade balance (B), we have

$$Y = A + B \quad (14\text{-}3)$$

or

$$Y - A = B. \quad (14\text{-}4)$$

According to equation 14-4, the balance of trade is equal to the difference between gross national product or income and domestic absorption. Thus, if GNP exceeds domestic absorption, the nation's balance of trade is positive. A negative balance of trade suggests that the nation is spending beyond its capability to produce.

According to the absorption approach, for devaluation to improve a nation's trade balance and hence its BOP, GNP must increase and/or domestic absorption must fall.

Consider a nation that is facing both unemployment and a balance of trade deficit. Given that the economy operates below its capacity, the price incentives of devaluation encourages employment of the unused resources in the production of export commodities. It also encourages spending away from imports toward domestically produced substitutes. Thus, devaluation improves the nation's balance of trade. This is why policymakers have a tendency to consider devaluation as an effective instrument in resolving a nation's balance of trade when it is facing unemployment.

Now consider a nation that is at full employment. In this case, there are no idle resources available to expand the output. Thus, GNP is fixed and the only way that devaluation can improve the balance of trade is for the nation to somehow cut its domestic absorption. This releases resources needed for the production of additional exports and import substitutes. Although this could be achieved by restrictive monetary and fiscal policies, such a course may prove to be detrimental to those who endure the cost of such policies. As a result, devaluation may prove to be improper when a nation is at full employment.

The difference between the elasticity approach and the absorption approach can be viewed from the emphasis they put on either demand or supply. The elasticity approach emphasizes demand and tacitly assumes that there are idle resources in the economy that allow it to satisfy the added demand for import substitutes and exports. The absorption approach emphasizes supply and tacitly assumes that a sufficient demand for the country's import substitutes and exports exists. Both approaches are therefore significant and must be considered concurrently.

The Monetary Approach. The elasticity and absorption approaches both have a shortcoming, that is, they omit the monetary adjustments. Both of these approaches propose that the balance of trade does not have monetary effects. To the degree that such effects exist they can be sterilized (neutralized) by the nation's monetary authorities. The elasticity and absorption approaches concentrate on the BOP trade account, ignoring the consequences of capital movements. The monetary approach attempts to deal with this weakness.

Consider a nation whose money market is initially in equilibrium. Now suppose the nation devalues its currency. Following the devaluation, the domestic price level rises. Import prices rise because residents now require more units of domestic currency to buy a given amount of imported commodities. Export prices increase because, following devaluation, demand for exports rises. The rise in domestic prices increases the demand for money because more money is needed now for transaction purposes. If this added demand for money is not satisfied by domestic sources, foreign capital inflows increase. The rise in foreign capital inflows, in turn, lead to improvement in the BOP and an increase in the nation's international reserves. However, this surplus is temporary because foreign capital inflow adds to the international component of the nation's money supply, causing absorption (expenditures) to rise. The rise in absorption, in turn, reduces the surplus. This process continues until the surplus is wiped out and the equilibrium is re-established in the nation's money market. Thus, according to the monetary approach, devaluation generates a *temporary* improvement in the BOP. In the long run, devaluation only increases the domestic price level with no impact on real economic variables.

14.4 SELECTIVE EXPENDITURE-SWITCHING POLICIES OR DIRECT CONTROLS

Devaluation and revaluation present policymakers with general expenditure-switching policies. They are general in the sense that they influence the BOP indirectly (that is, they work on all BOP items at the same time). This section deals with **direct controls**, or **selective expenditure-switching** policies aimed at a specific BOP item. Direct controls can be classified as trade (or commercial) controls, capital flow controls, exchange controls, and other controls.

14.4a Trade Controls

Trade or **commercial, controls** include tariffs, taxes, subsidies, quotas, and advanced-deposit requirements. All of these instruments affect specific BOP items—mainly exports and imports of commodities. Generally, commodity exports and imports are more responsive than other BOP items to these instruments.

As we already know, tariffs, taxes, subsidies, and quotas can be used to encourage exports or discourage imports, thus improving the BOP. For example, an import tariff raises the price of imported goods to domestic consumers and induces domestic production of import substitutes, discouraging imports. Also, export subsidies make domestic commodities cheaper to foreigners, encouraging exports. A significant characteristic of tariffs, taxes, quotas, and subsidies, compared to general expenditure-switching policies, is in their operational flexibility. Such flexibility allows them to operate differently on exports and imports of specific goods or on exports to and imports from specific countries. Consider, for instance, the flexibility offered by ad valorem tariffs. Different ad valorem import tariffs may be imposed on different goods. For example, a 60-percent ad valorem tariff could be imposed on imported cosmetics with only a 10-percent tariff levied on imported foodstuffs. Also, different ad valorem import tariffs may be imposed on the same good imported from different nations. For instance, a 20-percent tariff might be imposed on cosmetics imported from Canada with only a 5-percent tariff on the same goods from France.

The flexibility of tariffs and subsidies allow policymakers to have more command over these variables, enhancing their effectiveness as a tool for BOP adjustment.

Imports may also be discouraged by an **advanced-deposit requirement (ADR).** This requirement, employed mostly by developing countries, demands that importers make an advance deposit in a commercial bank for an amount equal to a fraction of the imported commodities' value for a given period of time at no interest. This leads to a rise in the price of the imported good by an amount equal to the interest foregone on the funds deposited with the commercial bank. Thus, ADRs are similar to import taxes and discourage imports. These requirements offer the imposing nation great flexibility. For instance, a country can require an advance deposit of a different amount and time duration on each type of good. Although ADRs are relatively flexible instruments, they can be difficult and costly to administer. Nevertheless, they represent an attractive direct-control instrument, especially when international agreements make it difficult to use other direct-control devices.

14.4b Capital Flow Controls

Capital flow controls refer to restrictions imposed on capital inflows (imports) and capital outflows (exports) when a nation faces a BOP disequilibrium. Specifically, if a nation experiences a BOP deficit, it can impose restriction on capital outflows. On the other hand, if a country faces a BOP surplus, it can impose restrictions on capital inflows. The United States provides us with an example of a country that has tried to control its capital outflows in order to reduce its BOP deficit. This was done in 1963 when the United States levied the **Interest Equalization Tax** on portfolio capital exports and imposed voluntary restraints on direct investment abroad. These measures improved the U.S. capital account; however, they decreased U.S. exports and the consequent return flow of interest and profit on U.S. investments abroad. The net effect of these measures on the U.S. BOP was ambiguous.

The former West Germany and Switzerland present examples of countries that have tried to control their capital inflows in order to cure their BOP surpluses. To achieve their objectives they arranged for lower or no interest on foreign deposits in order to discourage capital imports and reduce their BOP surpluses.

A common strategy employed by advanced nations using changes in capital flows to deal with a BOP disequilibrium is to engage in forward transactions. Specifically, when facing BOP surpluses and large capital inflows, these countries frequently embark on forward sales of their currency in order to raise the forward discount and deter capital inflows. On the other hand, when facing BOP deficits and large capital outflows, they engage in forward purchases of their currency to raise the forward premium and prevent capital outflows. To finance their forward purchases, deficit countries commonly borrow from surplus countries. Such borrowing is facilitated for the major industrial nations by the **General Agreement to Borrow (GAB).** This agreement, negotiated within the framework of the International Monetary Fund in 1962, was renewed in 1979. Accordingly, a group of 10 major advanced countries consented to loan up to $6 billion to any member of the group experiencing huge short-term capital outflows.[*]

14.4c Exchange Controls

Exchange controls are limitations set on the supply of foreign exchange to potential buyers. The purpose of imposing exchange controls, like other direct controls, is to resolve a BOP problem. Exchange controls can be carried out at a *single official rate* or under a system of *multiple exchange rates.*

Under a **single official rate**, the control is implemented by subjective allocation of the fixed supply of foreign currency among possible purchasers at the current exchange rate. This may be achieved by establishing an exchange control authority in the deficit nation. Having this authority in place, the deficit nation may then demand that (a) foreign currency acquired by its citizens from abroad be sold to the authority at the current official exchange rate; and (b) foreign currency needed by its citizens to make payments abroad must be purchased from the authority.

Under a **multiple exchange rates system**, as we explained in Chapter 6, a country may assign separate official exchange rates to different commodities that are either imported to or exported from that country. Most developing countries today use this scheme to ensure that essential goods are imported and nonessential goods are discouraged. Thus, they assign a low exchange rate (price of foreign currency in terms of the domestic currency) for essential imports, such as raw materials or capital goods, and set high exchange rates for nonessentials, such as luxury goods.

In practice, the allocation of the right to buy foreign currency is very bureaucratic. To acquire foreign currency, one must go through an elaborate application process to justify the purchase at the official rate. To be effective, the administration of an exchange control calls for complicated postal control to deter foreign exchange transaction by mail. It also demands proper inspection procedures to ensure that travelers do not smuggle currency into or out of the country in violation of the statutory limits allowed.

---

[*]   In alphabetical order, the group of major advanced countries include Belgium, Canada, France, Germany, Great Britain, Italy, Japan, the Netherlands, Sweden, and the United States.

GLOBAL INSIGHTS CASE 14.1

Japanese Capital Flow Controls

In 1949, after World War II, Japan enacted a law that severely restricted foreign trade. This law was gradually liberalized over the years, allowing freer trade in goods and services. However, during the 1960s and 1970s, Japan continued to impose restrictions on capital outflows and inflows. These restrictions were primarily dismantled by the early 1980s under the Foreign Exchange and Trade Control Law.

With regard to capital outflows, Japanese residents were not allowed to buy foreign securities prior to 1970. In 1970, Japan's Ministry of Finance abolished the restriction and allowed the Asian Development Bank—an international development bank similar to the World Bank with its headquarters in Manila—to sell 6 billion yen in yen-denominated bonds to Japanese residents. These bonds, referred to as Samurai bonds, allowed nonresidents seeking finance sources to enter the Japanese financial market. However, selective restriction of investment remained throughout the 1970s.

With regard to capital inflows, foreigners were not allowed to buy numerous types of Japanese assets. The causes for the restrictions varied. One common reason was the Japanese government's fear that the capital inflows into Japan would increase the demand for the yen, leading to its appreciation. Such fear was not without basis. During the late 1970s, the yen significantly appreciated in value. The Japanese government was afraid that further appreciation would weaken Japan's competitive position in the world market. As a result, the government prohibited any significant capital inflows. In 1979, however, the yen depreciated against the U.S. dollar, prompting Japanese authorities to eliminate their restrictions on capital inflows. This allowed foreigners to buy a wide range of Japanese securities. In 1980, capital flows were liberalized further under the Foreign Exchange and Trade Control Law. This law abolished the constraint that foreigners acquire government permission before making investments in Japan.

The liberalization of investment flows in Japan significantly merged the Japanese financial system with the global financial market. This has resulted in the globalization of Japanese investment, as evidenced by the upsurge of Japan's investment in the United States and other nations. Today, the Japanese securities industry is both powerful and concentrated. The top four financial firms in that industry now rank among the world's chief and most profitable financial firms on the New York Stock Exchange and deal directly with the U.S. Treasury in treasury securities.

Sources: J. R. Lothian, "A History of Yen Exchange Rates," In W. T. Ziemba, W. Bailey, and Y. Hamao, eds., *Japanese Financial Market Research* (Amsterdam: Elsevier, 1991); J. Frankel, *The Yen/Dollar Agreement: Liberalizing Japanese Capital Markets* (Washington, DC: Institute for International Economics, 1984); F. McCall Rosenbluth, *Financial Politics in Contemporary Japan* (Ithaca, NY: Cornell University Press, 1989); H. Ueno, "Deregulation and Reorganization of Japan's Financial System," *Japanese Economics Studies* (Spring, 1988); Y Suziki, ed., *The Japanese Financial System* (Oxford: Clarendon Press, 1987).

The bureaucracy associated with exchange controls makes this device very costly. Additionally, it encourages transfer pricing and corruption. It often entices both exporters and importers to evade the law and acquire their foreign currency needs from black markets. **Black markets** are unregulated markets that allow foreign currency transactions to take place at unofficial rates determined by the supply and demand for foreign currency in these markets. In most developing countries, governments frequently impose foreign exchange controls in order to ration the amount of foreign currency. As a result, black markets have become a vital segment of the foreign exchange system. Such a system has allowed both individuals and commercial firms to meet their foreign exchange needs illegally or "unofficially." Examples of developing countries with well-developed black markets include Argentina, Bolivia, Brazil, Colombia, Ecuador, Iran, and Venezuela, among others.

GLOBAL INSIGHTS CASE 14.2

IMF Foreign Exchange Controls

Foreign exchange controls were very popular during the economic predicaments of the late 1930s and immediately following world War II. It was not until the late 1950s that advanced nations of the Western Europe found themselves financially secure enough to lift most controls, resulting to a high degree of freedom for many international transactions. However, the exchange controls continued to exist in one form or another and are still widespread today in both advanced nations and developing nations.

The table illustrates the extent to which foreign exchange controls are employed by member nations of the International the IMF. In 1998, out of 184 IMF nations 127 (79.3 percent) imposed controls on capital market securities. Additionally, 143 countries (80 percent) restricted FDI and 64 nations controlled personal capital movements. These restrictions suggest that capital is very immobile for many nations. In general, advanced countries, such as the United States, Canada, Germany, Japan, Sweden, Britain, and the Netherlands, impose fewer controls as compared to developing nations. Additionally, among the developing nations, the oil-rich nations such as Saudi Arabia, Kuwait, and Bahrain impose fewer restrictions relative to other developing nations. Although relative capital mobility exists for nations with well-developed financial markets, such as the United States, Canada, Germany, and Japan, various situations deter capital of being perfectly mobile between nations.

Foreign Exchange Controls Within IMF Membership, 1998

Type of Control	Number of Nations Using Restrictions	Percentage of Nations
Control on payments for invisible transactions and current transfers	102	55.43
Proceeds from exports and/or invisible transactions		
Repatriation requirements	111	50.32
Surrender requirements	85	46.19
Capital transactions		
Control on:		
Capital and market securities	127	69.02
Money market instruments	111	60.32
Collective investment securities	102	55.43
Derivatives and other instruments	82	44.56
Commercial credits	110	59.72
Financial credits	114	61.95
Guarantees, sureties and financial backup facilities	88	47.82
Liquidation of Direct investment	54	29.34
Real estate transactions	128	69.56
Personal capital movements	64	34.78
Provisions specific to :		
Commercial banks and other credit institutions	152	82.60
Institutional investors	68	36.56

Source: International Monetary Fund, *Exchange Arrangements and Exchange Restrictions Annual report 1998*, (Washington, D.C.: IMF), pp. 992-998.

GLOBAL INSIGHTS CASE 14.3

Black Market Premium/Discount for the Dollar

The black market gives rise to exchange rates that vary from the official rates, depending on supply and demand conditions in the market. The divergence between the black market and official exchange rates gives rise to a premium or discount. When the black market price of a dollar surpasses the official price, the dollar is sold at a premium in the black market. When the black market price of a dollar falls short of the official price, the dollar is sold at a discount (shown by a negative sign in the table) in the black market.

As the table indicates, the black market is especially prevalent in developing nations. Note that for most countries, the dollar was sold at a premium. The premium was especially high for communist countries like the former Soviet Union (1,095 percent) and Cuba (4,405 percent). This reflects the dollar's scarcity in these nations where the governments are unable to satisfy the excess demand for dollars at the official rates. Such excess demand is satisfied in the black market at a much higher exchange rate.

Black Market Premium/Discount for the U.S. Dollar, 1988*
(By Percentage)

Country	Premium/Discount	Country	Premium/Discount
Afghanistan	473	Iraq	328
Algeria	416	Ireland	2
Angola	6,083	Israel	18
Albania	400	Italy	1
Argentina	50	Jamaica	22
Bahamas, The	12	Jordan	10
Bangladesh	318	Kenya	13
Bermuda	25	Korea, North	1,516
Botswana	53	Lao P. D. Republic	6,600
Brazil	57	Libya	2,189
Bulgaria	691	Lesotho	5
Chile	29	Mexico	15
Chinese People's Rep.	169	Mozambique	60
Colombia	15	Nicaragua	416
Costa Rica	23	Nigeria	87
Cuba	4,405	Norway	−1
Egypt	248	Peru	240
El Salvador	195	Poland	537
Ethiopia	226	Romania	561
France	2	Somalia	48
German Dem. Rep	809	South Africa	5
Greece	8	Spain	2
Guinea	6	Sri Lanka	36
Guatemala	28	Taiwan	8
Hungary	56	U.S.S.R.	1,095
Iceland	5	Vietnam	65
India	14	Zaire	15
Iran	1,030	Zimbabwe	47

*Based on official or effective rate on December 31, 1988.

Source: Philip P. Cowitt, *World Currency Yearbook*, 1988-89 (Brooklyn, NY: International Currency Analysis, 1991):23. Reprinted by permission.

We should keep in mind that controls are protectionist devices that entail social costs. They are likely to appeal to government officials as a device for increasing their discretionary power over the allocation of resources. An altruistic interpretation is that the additional power helps policymakers reach social goals by extensive planning. A less altruistic interpretation, more compatible with reality, is that officials see the exchange controls as a vehicle for gaining personal power.

14.4d Other Direct Controls

Nations sometimes enact wage and price controls in order to accomplish a domestic objective such as inflation control, when more general policies have faltered. A case in point is the 1971 wage and price controls imposed by the Nixon administration to control inflation in the United States. However, as we explained in Chapter 12, these control measures were not very effective and were relaxed in 1973.

In closing this chapter, we should note that from the efficiency standpoint expenditure-adjusting and general expenditure-switching policies are preferable to direct controls (selective expenditure-switching policies). This is because direct controls usually disrupt the market mechanism, whereas the other policies work through the market. However, a nation may resort to direct controls as a temporary measure to accomplish certain goals. This may happen if (a) other policies take a long time to enforce; (b) the impact of other policies is dubious; or (c) the problem influences only one sector of the nation's economy. A case in point is the voluntary export restraint on Japanese automobiles, negotiated between the United States and Japan in 1981.

As a general rule, the effectiveness of BOP adjustment policies depends on international cooperation. In the absence of such cooperation, the impact of the adjustment policies may be nullified. For example, a nation's imposition of tariffs and quotas may lead to retaliation by other nations, making these restrictive measures ineffective. Also, a nation's effort to maintain a stable exchange rate may be nullified by retaliatory measures imposed by other nations. Finally, a nation's effort to attract foreign capital by supporting high interest rates may prove to be ineffective if other countries raise their interest rates by the same amount, thus leaving international interest rate differentials intact.

In summary, it is crucial for a nation's policymakers to ensure international cooperation before enforcing adjustment policies.

14.5 SUMMARY

1. External balance, or equilibrium in the balance of payments (BOP), is not the only economic objective a country has to achieve. Another significant economic goal is maintenance of its internal balance, or full employment and price stability.
2. Fiscal policy refers to an intentional increase or decrease in government expenditures and/or taxation.
3. The main difference between monetary and fiscal policies is related to their impact on interest rates. Expansionary monetary policy leads to a fall in interest rates, worsening the BOP. However, expansionary fiscal policy induces a rise in interest rates, improving the BOP. But this difference in interest rate behavior and the resultant BOP effect is temporary.
4. The more permanent effect of either policy (monetary or fiscal) on the BOP is related to the income effect they share.
5. One dilemma is that it is often impossible to achieve both internal and external balance by using aggregate-demand policies alone.
6. Robert Mundell recommends mixing monetary and fiscal policy according to a guideline referred to as an assignment rule. According to this rule, monetary policy should be assigned to accomplish external balance and fiscal policy to accomplish internal balance.
7. General expenditure-switching policies refer to changes in the exchange rate by means of devaluation and revaluation (depreciation and appreciation).

8. A devaluation switches expenditures from foreign to domestic goods, improving a BOP deficit. On the other hand, a revaluation switches expenditures from domestic to foreign goods, reducing or eliminating a BOP surplus.

9. Devaluation is a deliberate increase in the exchange rate (price of a foreign currency in terms of domestic currency) by a nation's monetary authorities under the fixed exchange rate system. Revaluation is a deliberate decrease in the foreign exchange rate (price of foreign currency in terms of domestic currency) of a nation's currency by its monetary authorities. Devaluation and revaluation correspond to depreciation and appreciation, respectively of a domestic currency. The distinct jargon reveals the exchange rate system used.

10. The elasticity approach stresses the price effect of devaluation and proposes that usually devaluation operates best when elasticities are high.

11. The absorption effect emphasizes income effects and suggests that domestic expenditures must decline relative to income in order for devaluation to improve the BOP.

12. The monetary approach emphasizes the impact devaluation has on the purchasing power of money balances and the ensuing effect on domestic expenditures.

13. Assuming the supply curves of imports and exports are both infinitely elastic (horizontal), according to the Marshall-Lerner condition, the following statements are true: (a) If the sum of the price elasticities of the demand for imports and the demand for exports is greater than 1 in absolute terms, devaluation will improve the balance of trade; (b) if the sum is less than 1 in absolute terms, devaluation will worsen the balance of trade; and (c) if the sum is equal to 1 in absolute terms, devaluation will not affect the balance of trade.

14. According to an empirical study, the factors that cause the time lags in the devaluation mechanism can be classified as recognition lag, decision lag, delivery lag, replacement lag, and production lag.

15. According to the absorption approach, for devaluation to improve a nation's trade balance, national income must increase and/or domestic absorption must fall.

16. Trade controls include tariffs, taxes, subsidies, quotas, and advanced-deposit requirements.

17. Capital flow controls refer to restrictions imposed on capital inflows (imports) and capital outflows (exports) when a nation faces a BOP disequilibrium.

18. Exchange controls are limitations set on the supply of foreign exchange to potential buyers. The purpose of imposing exchange controls, like other direct controls, is to resolve a BOP problem.

19. Exchange controls can be carried out at a single official rate or under a system of multiple exchange rates.

20. Under a single official rate, the control is implemented by subjective allocation of the fixed supply of foreign currency among possible purchasers at the current exchange rate.

21. Under a multiple exchange rates system, a country may assign separate official exchange rates to different commodities that are either imported to or exported from that country.

22. Nations sometimes enact direct controls in order to accomplish domestic objectives when general policies have faltered.

23. As a general rule, the effectiveness of BOP adjustment policies depends on international cooperation. In the absence of such cooperation, the impact of the adjustment policies may be nullified.

Review Questions

1. Explain how devaluation is achieved under the fixed exchange rate system. How can a nation depreciate its currency under a floating exchange rate system? Give an example of a recent devaluation or depreciation, explaining its possible impact on U.S. economy.

2. What is the relationship of the J-Curve to the time path of devaluation? Explain.

3. There are three approaches to devaluation. Elaborate on these approaches and distinguish among them.

4. What does the Marshall-Lerner condition suggest? Explain, elaborating on "elasticity optimism" and "elasticity pessimism."

5. According to the absorption approach, how does devaluation of a currency work (a) under the condition of unemployment and a BOP deficit, and (b) under the condition of full employment and a BOP surplus?

6. How does currency devaluation eradicate or decrease a country's BOP deficit? Explain.

7. Distinguish between expenditure-adjusting policies, general expenditure-switching policies, and selective expenditure-switching policies. What is meant by "switching?"

8. What are direct controls? Explain, briefly elaborating on each type of direct control. To be successful, what general rule should one follow when using a direct control?

9. According to an empirical study, there are different time lags in the devaluation mechanism. Identify these time lags and explain their impact on the devaluation process.

10. Setting aside the interest rate effect of monetary and fiscal policy and concentrating only on their income effects, we face a basic dilemma. What is this dilemma? According to Robert Mundell, how can we resolve this dilemma? Explain.

Problems

1. If two countries devalue their currencies at the same time, neither currency depreciates or appreciates in terms of the other currency.

   Do you agree with this statement? Discuss.

2. Assume that Libya's price elasticity of demand for imports is equal to 2.5, and Britain's price elasticity of demand for Libyan exports is equal to 1.5. Suppose Libya is facing a BOP deficit. To cure its deficit, Libya devalues its currency (the dinar) by 10 percent.

   (a)   What condition is necessary for the devaluation to be successful? Is such a condition met in this example? Explain.

   (b)   Determine the impact of the devaluation on Libya's balance of trade by completing the following table:

Sector	Percentage Change in Dinar Price	Percentage Change in Quantity	Net Effect (percentage)
Imports			
Exports			

3. Assume that Algeria's price elasticity of demand for imports is equal to 0.25, and Iraq's price elasticity of demand for Algerian exports is equal to 0.15. Suppose Algeria is facing a BOP deficit. To cure its deficit, Algeria devalues its currency (the dinar) by 20 percent. Given this information, answer the following questions

   (a)   What is the impact of devaluating the dinar on Iraq's import prices and export prices?

   (b)   What is the impact of devaluation on the quantities of imports demanded and quantities of exports supplied by Algeria?

   (c)   What is the impact of devaluation on Iraq's export receipts and import expenditures?

   (d)   Does the devaluation of the dinar improve Algeria's balance of trade? Explain.

4. A devaluation of a small nation's currency always improves its BOP.

   Do you agree with this statement? Discuss.

5. A devaluation is ineffective unless it is accompanied by higher domestic savings equivalent to any improvement in the BOP.

   (a)   Using the absorption approach, do you agree with this statement? Explain.

   (b)   Assuming that your answer to part a is affirmative, what do you think a government should do in order to enhance domestic savings and thereby make devaluation successful?

Notes

1. "Nation's Devaluation of Currencies Spark A Global War," *The Wall Street Journal*, 22 December 1986, 1, 15.

2. "Big-Five Attempt to Deflate the Dollar Is Losing Steam; Can They Win the War?" *The Wall Street Journal*, 12 December 1985, 34.

3. "Trade Deficit Shrank in Month," *The Wall Street Journal*, 13 November 1987, 3.

4. Jaime Marquez, "Bilateral Trade Elasticities," *Review of Economics and Statistics* 72 (February 1990): 70-77.
5. Helen Junz and Rudolf R. Rhomberg, "Price Competitiveness in Export Trade Among Industrial Countries," *American Economic Review* (May 1973): 412-419.
6. "Trade Deficit Shrank in Month," *The Wall Street Journal,* 13 November 1987, 3.

Suggested Readings

Alexandre, S. S. "Effects of a Devaluation on Trade Balance." *International Monetary Fund Staff Papers* (April 1952); Reprinted in R. E. Caves and H. G. Johnson. *Reading in International Economics.* Homewood, IL: Irwin, 1968.

Alexandre, Sidney S. "Effects of Devaluation on a Trade Balance." *IMF Staff Papers* (April 1952): 263-278.

Asheghian, Parviz. "Currency Devaluation: A Comparative Analysis of Advanced Countries and Less Developed Countries." *Quarterly Review of Economics and Business* (Summer 1988): 61-70. . "Impact of Devaluation on the Balance of Payments of Less Developed Countries: A Monetary Approach." *Journal of Economic Development* (July 1985): 143-151; Reprinted in *Portfolio: International Economic Perspectives,* no. 3 (1987).

Asheghian, Parviz, and Willian G. Foote. "Exchange Rate Devaluation: A Monetary Model and Empirical Investigation." *Eastern Economic Journal* (April-June 1988): 181-187.

Asheghian, Parviz, William G. Foote, and Reza Saidi. "Determinants of LDCs Devaluation Decisions: An Exploratory Investigation of Devaluation in Brazil." *Eastern Economic Journal* (October-December 1991): 491-497.

Bhagwati, J. N. *Anatomy and Consequences of Exchange Regimes.* Cambridge, MA: Ballinger, 1978.

Black, S. W. "The Relationship Between Exchange Rate Policy and Monetary Policy in Ten Industrial Countries." In *Exchange Rate Theory and Practice,* edited by J. F. O. Bilson and R. C. Martson. Chicago: University of Chicago Press, 1984.

M. Goldstein, and M. S. Khan. "Income and Price Effects in International Trade." In *Handbook of International Economics,* edited by R. W. Jones and P. B. Kenen. Amsterdam: North-Holland, 1985.

Gutowski, A. "Flexible Exchange Rates vs. Controls." In *International Monetary Problems,* edited by F. Machlup, A. Gutowski, and F. A. Lutz. Washington, DC: American Enterprises Institute, 1972.

Houthakker, Hendrik S., and Stephen P. Magee. "Income and Price Elasticities in World Trade." *Review of Economics and Statistics* (May 1969): 111-125.

International Monetary Fund. *Annual Report on Exchange Arrangements and Exchange Restrictions.* Washington, DC: International Monetary Fund (published annually).

Junz, Helen, and Rudolf R. Rhomberg. "Price Competitiveness in Export Trade Among Industrial Countries." *American Economic Review* (May 1973): 412-419.

Marquez, Jaime. "Bilateral Trade Elasticities." *Review of Economics and Statistics* (February 1990): 70-77. Michaely, M. *The Responsiveness of Demand Policies to Balance of Payments: The Postwar Patterns.* New York: NBER, 1971.

Mundell, Robert A. "The Appropriate Use of Monetary and Fiscal Policy for Internal and External Stability." *International Monetary Fund Staff Papers* (March 1962); Reprinted in R. A. Mundell, *International Economics.* New York: Macmillan, 1968. . "Should the United States Devalue the Dollar?" *Western Economic Journal* (September 1968): 247-259.

Mundell, Robert A., and A. Swoboda, eds. *Monetary Problems of International Economy.* Chicago: University of Chicago Press, 1968.

Stern, Robert M., Jonathan Francis, and Bruce Schumacher. *Price Elasticities in International Trade: An Annotated Bibliography.* London: MacMillian, 1975.

Tinbergen, Jan. *On the Theory of Economic Policy.* Amsterdam: North-Holland, 1952.

Tsiang, S. C. "The Role of Money in Trade Balance Stability: Synthesis of the Elasticity and Absorption Approaches." *American Economic Review* (December 1961); Reprinted in R. E. Caves and H. G. Johnson. *Readings in International Economics.* Homewood, IL: Irwin, 1968.

Ukpolo, Victor. "Currency Devaluation in Developing Countries: Some Lessons for Nigeria from Recent Experience." *Nigerian Journal of Economics and Social Studies* 29, no. 3 (1987): 257-268.

Part 4

INTERNATIONAL ECONOMICS AND DEVELOPING NATIONS

Conventional economic theory since Adam Smith and David Ricardo has accentuated the merit of comparative advantage and free international trade. It is maintained that adherence to free trade maximizes the world's welfare and the welfare of individual nations participating in global trade. However, this view is challenged by some economists who see over three quarters of the world's population living in poverty in developing countries. Torn by severe debt crises, most of these countries feel that free trade may not be the best policy for them at the present time. Given the degree of poverty and special obstacles facing developing countries, most of them feel that a laissez-faire approach is unsuitable and an alternative course of action should be explored.

The purpose of Part IV is to investigate the economic conditions in developing countries, elaborate on trade theory and economic development, examine international economic policies pursued by developing countries to achieve economic development, and discuss the external debt problems facing these nations. International Trade and economic development is explained in Chapter 15, followed by a discussion of developing countries' debt crises in Chapter 16.

Chapter 15

INTERNATIONAL TRADE AND ECONOMIC DEVELOPMENT

15.1 INTRODUCTION

Today, more than three quarters of the world's 5.3 billion inhabitants live in poverty, but they account for only about one quarter of the world's production and income. Occupying the vast regions of Africa, Asia, and Latin America, they have been referred to collectively as third-world countries, underdeveloped countries, developing countries, or less-developed countries (LDCs). These nations are primarily identified by low standards of living, high rates of population growth, low levels of per capita income, high illiteracy rates, unequal income distribution, and general economic and technological dependence on advanced (developed) countries.

Given the conditions existing in developing countries, some economists have questioned the wisdom of conventional trade theory based on the principle of comparative advantage. They believe that international trade has hampered rather than promoted the process of economic development in developing nations through deteriorating terms of trade and vast fluctuations in their export earnings. Such circumstances have prompted these economists to advise developing countries to place less reliance on international trade and to pursue **import-substitution policies**, that is, to engage in the domestic production of formerly imported manufactured goods.

The purpose of this chapter is to examine this issue and to elaborate on policies employed to promote the economic well-being of developing countries.

15.2 PROFILE OF DEVELOPING COUNTRIES

When the systematic study of economic development began in the late 1940s and early 1950s, it was conventional to divide nations into the two categories of rich and poor. The rich nations included Australia, Canada, Japan, New Zealand, and Western European countries. The poor nations encompassed Africa, Asia, and Latin America.

It is risky to attempt to generalize too much about these categories. The distinction between poor and rich countries, oversimplified before, has become more obscured in the 1990s. Today, the classification schemes used to define developing countries differ, depending on the agency providing the scheme. The United Nations (UN) distinguishes between three major classes of third-world countries: the least-developed, or poorest, nations; the non-oil-exporting developing nations; and the petroleum-rich OPEC (Organization for Petroleum Exporting Countries) nations.[*] The Organization for Economic Cooperation and Development (OECD) classifies developing nations into low-income countries, middle-income countries, newly industrialized countries (NICs), and members of OPEC. Finally, the World Bank divides all countries (both developing and advanced) into four categories: low-income, lower-middle-income, upper-middle-income, and high-income economies.

In spite of the diversity of classification schemes used to define developing countries, an examination of the characteristics of these nations is useful in demonstrating that they are very different from advanced countries. Table 15-1 provides data on selected indicators of development for both advanced and developing countries. In the table, nations are divided into four categories reported by the World Bank. Low-income economies are defined as those with a gross national product (GNP) per capita of $785 or less in 1997. Lower-middle-income economies include those countries with a GNP per capita of $786 to $3,125 in 1997. Upper-middle-income economies are those with a GNP per capita of $3,126 to $9,655 in 1997. Finally, high-income economies refer to countries with a GNP per capita income of $9,656 or more in 1997.

---

[*] The least-developed nations are sometimes referred to as fourth-world nations to identify them as the "poorest of the poor." See H. C. Low and J. W. Howe, "Focus on the Fourth World." In *World Development, Agenda for Action* 1975 Prager (New York: for the Overseas Development Council, 1974), 35-54.

TABLE 15-1
Selected Indicators of Development

	1997 GNP per Capita (U.S. $)	Population (Millions) 1997	Life Expectancy at Birth (years) 1996		Adult Literacy Rate % of People 15 and above 1995		Average Annual Population Growth Percentage Rate (1990-1997)	1997 Value Added as Percentage of GDP	
			Males	Females	Males	Females		Agriculture	Industry
Low Income	350	2,048	58	60	35	59	2.4	31	27
Lower Middle Income	1,230	22,85	66	71	12	27	1.2	14	40
Upper Middle Income	4,520	571	66	73	12	17	1.5	10	34
High Income	25,700	926	74	81	**	**	0.7	3*	36*

* 1980 data
** UNESCO estimates literacy to be less than 5 percent

Source: The World Bank, *World Development Report 1998/1999* (New York: Oxford University Press, 1999), 190-193, 212-213.

An examination of this data shows that, in general, as the level of GNP per capita rises, the life expectancy at birth rises; the adult illiteracy rate declines; the rate of population growth declines; the percentage of gross domestic product (GDP) allocated to the agriculture sector declines; and the percentage of GDP to the industrial sector rises. The relationship between income and some of these basic indicators is observed in most developing countries. Nevertheless, a high level of income alone is not sufficient to classify a country as an advanced nation. For example, in Table 15-1, high-income countries include Kuwait, which is considered a developing country.* In general, however, developing countries have low levels of per capita income, and they share a set of common problems in varying degrees. These include extensive and persistent absolute poverty; vast disparities in distribution of income; low and sluggish levels of agricultural productivity; high and growing levels of unemployment and underemployment; archaic, inappropriate educational and health systems; large and growing imbalances between urban and rural levels of living and economic opportunities; considerable and growing dependence on foreign, often inappropriate, technologies, institutions, and value systems; and intense balance of payments (BOP) and international debt problems.

15.3 TRADE THEORY AND ECONOMIC DEVELOPMENT

According to conventional trade theory, if each country specializes in the production of the commodity in which it is most efficient, not only does each nation gain from trade but world output also increases. The majority of Western economists support this theory and consider international trade an **"engine of growth."** To defend their position, they present historical evidence showing that in the nineteenth century, export-led growth in Great Britain and several other now-industrial nations propelled their economies into rapid growth and development. In other words, the majority of Western economists maintain that international trade served as an engine of growth for these nations during that period. This implies that today's developing nations could also benefit from international trade as the now-advanced countries did when they went through their development processes.

---

* Other developing countries that are included in the list of high-income countries are Israel, Hong Kong, Singapore, and the United Arab Emirates.

GLOBAL INSIGHTS CASE 15.1

Economic Development Strategies of East and Southeast Asia

During the 1960-1993 period, eight of the world's ten fastest-growing nations were in East and Southeast Asia. Japan's GDP per capita, adjusted for differences in relative prices, was only 30 percent of the United States' GDP per capita during 1960-1982. By 1994, it grew to the level of 82 percent of the United States' GDP per capita. The four Asian "tigers" (Hong Kong, Singapore, South Korea, and Taiwan) experienced growth in GDP per capita averaging over 6 percent a year during the period in which U.S. GDP per capita grew less than 2 percent a year. Malaysia and Indonesia's growth averaged about 4 percent a year. China, the world's most populous nation with more than a billion people, experienced astonishing growth in GDP per capita, averaging 8.1 percent since 1978.

Although these nations' economic development strategies have differed in various ways, they all followed a sound economic development strategy that included the following features:

1. **Investment in Human Capital.** All of these nations invested in nearly universal primary and secondary education, and developed their scientific and engineering skills.
2. **Investment in Physical Capital.** Given the relatively high rate of domestic saving rates in most of these nations, they were able to use domestic sources of financing to invest heavily in physical capital.
3. **The Complementary Role of the Government.** In most of these nations, the government adopted the strategy of complementing markets and making them work more efficiently, rather than trying to replace them.
4. **Outward Orientation.** Realizing the contribution of exports to their economies, the East and Southeast Asian economies adopted free trade policies. Accordingly, firms were compelled to compete in export markets and adhere to international standards and increase their efficiencies.

Source: U.S. Government Printing Office, *Economic Report of the President* (Washington DC: U.S. Government Printing Office, 1997), 238-242, Reprinted.

There are, however, some economists who do not share this view and present theories stating that international trade has hampered rather than promoted the development process. This has occurred through deterioration in terms of trade and vast oscillation in the export incomes of developing countries. Three theories that have attracted much attention are the dependency theory, the theory of immiserizing growth, and the Prebisch theory. In this section, we explain each of these theories and then elaborate on ways by which international trade can contribute to the process of economic development.

15.3a Dependency Theory

Dependency theory was developed by an influential group of writers sympathetic to Karl Marx. This theory attributes the sluggishness of economic growth and development in developing nations to their dependent relationships with advanced countries. The dependency literature is based primarily on Latin American experience and has been recognized as a method of study only since the mid-1960s.

A major contributor to dependency theory, Andre Gunder Frank, challenges the idea that developing countries resemble the now-advanced countries in their earlier stages. He criticizes the scholars who view the modernization of developing countries as simply the adoption of advanced countries' economic and political structures. He considers underdevelopment the outcome of modern capitalism permeating the antiquated economic systems of the third world. He perceives the upsetting of African communities by slave trade and resulting colonialism, the deindustrialization of India under British colonialism, and the total eradication of Incan and Aztec civilizations by Spanish conquistadors as cases of origination of underdevelopment.

According to Frank, Latin American countries and other developing nations have been assimilated into the global economy since the initial phases of their colonial periods. Such assimilation has transformed these nations into essentially capitalist economies. The integration of these presumably capitalist economies into the global economy is inevitably accomplished through an endless metropolis-satellite chain, in which surplus created by each satellite (developing nation) is absorbed by the metropolis (advanced) rations. According to Frank:

> *It is this satellite status that generates underdevelopment, then a weaker or lesser degree of metropolis-satellite relations may generate structural underemployment and/or allow for more possibility of local development.*[1]

Given this scenario, according to Frank's analysis, the only options available are to break with the metropolis-satellite network entirely, through socialist revolution, or to stay "underdeveloped" within this network.

Frank's ideas are echoed by Paul Baran, considered the father of dependency theory by some scholars, who writes:

> *What is decisive is that economic development in underdeveloped countries is profoundly inimical to the dominant interests in advanced countries.*[2]

To evade such development, advanced countries form coalitions with precapitalist native elites who will be unfavorably influenced by the metamorphosis brought about by capitalist development. The aim of these coalitions is to suppress the metamorphic process. Such an alliance allows advanced countries easy access to indigenous resources and preserves the traditional system of surplus extraction. Given these conditions, the prospect of economic growth in dependent nations would be unduly restricted. The surplus created by developing countries would be expropriated to a large extent by foreign capital and otherwise wasted on luxury consumption by traditional elites. Additionally, because capital goods would have to be purchased abroad, resources that could be set aside for investment significantly decline. This mechanism would essentially lead to economic stagnation, and the only solution would be political (that is, a socialist revolution). This is because, according to Frank, within the framework of capitalism there would be no alternative to underdevelopment.[3]

Criticism of Dependency Theory. The dependency theory has been subject to many criticisms, on both theoretical and empirical grounds. Most economic historians concede that economic dependency under foreign control and domination proved to be very costly for colonies. Under colonial power, production was guided toward foreign rather than indigenous requirements. Economic practices restrained regional industrial endeavors, leading to unbalanced national and regional economic development. This condition led to the rise of an elite that was oriented to foreign interests. Nevertheless, these sufferings were partially counterbalanced by the growth of roads, schools, railroads, and administrative services under colonial rule.

It is unjust to compare the experiences of countries under colonialism to what might have occurred in the absence of foreign rule. For example, Afghanistan, Ethiopia, and Thailand, which were not colonized although they were influenced by advanced countries, are severely underdeveloped. Additionally, the theory does not present a verifiable and independent explanation of the mechanism causing underdevelopment. Rather, dependence is defined in a circular fashion by saying the developing countries are underdeveloped because they are dependent. It is argued that the attributes usually ascribed to underdevelopment in dependent nations are not limited to these nations. Such attributes are also found in "nondependent" economies. Consequently, they are characteristics of capitalist development in general and not of dependent capitalism exclusively.

Today, most advanced nations are also dependent on foreign economies. Belgium and Canada are more dependent on foreign investment than India or Pakistan. However, according to dependency theory, they are not regarded as dependent nations. Thus, instead of dividing the world into dependent and independent nations, it seems more rational to consider a spectrum of dependence from the weakest developing country to the strongest capitalist nation.

In spite of the aforementioned criticism, dependency theory should not be totally dismissed. Developing countries have been subject to exploitation on a number of occasions. For example, economic growth in Indonesia was not very beneficial to the indigenous people during the Dutch colonial period. As another example, economic growth in

Mexico under foreign domination during the Porfirio Diaz rule (1876-1911) led to a decrease in living standards for the rural masses and fueled the revolution which began in 1910. Finally, there are several examples of nations that could have developed faster with less dependence on foreign countries. Bangladesh, Guatemala, Honduras, Pakistan, Zaire, and the Philippines were likely hindered by unreasonable economic dependence on advanced nations. The solution to these problems, however, is not necessarily detachment from the capitalist economic system, but the pursuit of more sensible policies when interacting with capitalist nations. Economic aid, trade, capital flows, and technology transfers from advanced countries must be conducted in a manner that directs investment to priority industries. Promoting domestic firms, deterring foreign monopoly power, evading significant technological dependence on foreigners, and avoiding excessive foreign investment should all be part of sensible policies. Also, as we study in Chapter 19, there are other policies that a country can employ when dealing with multinational corporations, allowing that country to enjoy the benefits of foreign investment without yielding to total control and ownership.

15.3b Theory of Immiserizing Growth

As we discussed in Chapter 2, according to the theory of comparative advantage, each country should specialize in and export the goods in which it is comparatively more efficient than its trading partners. Because the comparative advantage of most of the developing nations lies in the production of primary products, they should, according to the theory, specialize in and export these products. Around the mid-1950s, however, economists presented cases showing that the pursuit of comparative advantage dictates actually makes developing countries worse off; the pursuit "immiserizes" them. The possibility of *immiserizing growth*, which was emphasized by Jagdish N. Bhagwati, was later studied by Harry Johnson and Carlos Diaz Alejandro. Through their work, the concept of **immiserizing growth** came to be known as an expansion of the factor supply or productivity that makes a nation worse off. The possibility of immiserizing growth occurs when an increase in the supply of a tradable good tends to decrease its price in the world market. If the price decrease is large enough, it might have an adverse effect on the exporting country, thereby worsening its welfare.

Take the case of Brazil, which is the world's largest coffee-bean exporter. Assume that a technological advance in coffee-bean production is introduced to this country. This would encourage an individual coffee-bean grower to take advantage of the situation and increase production and sales. Because all farmers might behave in this fashion, their collective action may result in a considerable increase in output. Given that Brazil has a large share of the world's coffee-bean market, and given an inelastic demand for coffee beans, the expansion of Brazil's coffee-bean supply results in a lower world price for coffee beans. If this price decline is large enough to outweigh the increase in the quantity supplied, Brazil's revenue from coffee-bean exports will decrease. In this way, Brazil's own technological improvements and resulting increases in supply worsen its terms of trade (the amount of goods exported per unit imported). When this happens additional international trade will actually worsen Brazil's economic welfare rather than improve it.

Several conditions are necessary for immiserizing growth to occur:

1. The world's demand for the country's exports must be inelastic, such that an expansion in the quantity of exports results in a large decline in price.
2. The country's economic growth must be biased toward the export sector.
3. The country's economy must be dependent on international trade for national welfare to the extent that a decline in the terms of trade could outweigh the possible gains from increasing product supply.

Although immiserizing growth might have taken place for a developing country, like Brazil with its coffee-bean expansion, before the 1930s, it does not seem very prevalent in the real world although it is a possibility.[*] If it does occur, it brings unpleasant results. Because immiserizing growth takes place only in the presence of an inelastic demand, it is possible for a country to exploit this inelasticity by imposing optimum tariffs and taxes on exports. The

---

[*] Most developing nations are not large enough for export volume to significantly affect their terms of trade. As a result, immiserizing growth is not very prevalent in these nations.

success of such a strategy depends on the market power exercised by the country in question; and the market power, in turn, is limited by the existence of potential new entrants into the world market.

Graphical Illustration of Immiserizing Growth. Given our previous example of Brazil, Figure 15-1 portrays a case of immiserizing growth. The figure illustrates Brazil's production possibilities frontiers (PPFs) for coffee beans (export product) and steel (import product), both measured in terms of tons per year. Initially, before growth takes place, Brazil is producing at point P_0 on PPF_0 and consuming at point C_0 on its community indifference curve (I_0). It exports A_0P_0 tons of coffee for A_0C_0 tons of steel at the terms of trade ratio denoted by TOT_0.

FIGURE 15-1
A Case of Immiserizing Growth

Initially, before growth takes place, Brazil produces at point P_0 on its production possibilities curve PPF_0 and consumes at point C_0 on its community indifference curve I_0. It exports A_0P_0 tons of coffee for A_0C_0 tons of steel at the terms of trade ratio denoted by TOT_0. Assume that due to technological improvement, Brazil's ability to grow coffee beans increases much faster than its ability to produce steel. This causes Brazil's production possibilities frontier to shift right to PPF_1 and its term of trade to decline to TOT_1. At this new price ratio, Brazil produces at point P_1 on PPF_1 and consumes at point C_1 on. At this new terms of trade, Brazil exports A_1P_1 tons of coffee for A_1C_1 tons of steel. Because the consumption point moves from pregrowth position C_0 on community indifference curve I_0 to postgrowth point C_1 on the lower indifference curve I_1, Brazilian welfare decreases.

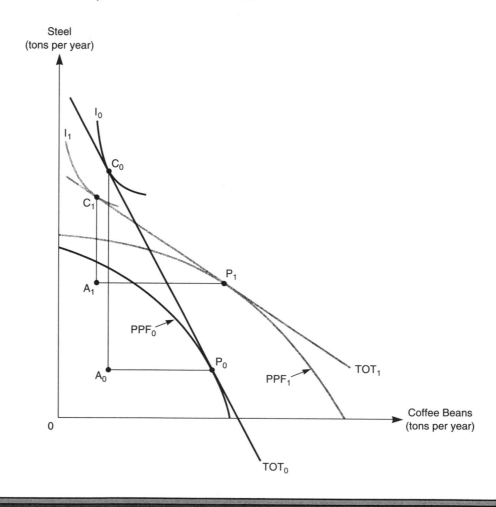

Now assume that due to technological improvement, Brazil's ability to grow coffee beans increases much faster than its ability to produce steel. This causes Brazil's production possibilities frontier to shift right to PPF_1. As the figure shows, the growth is "biased" toward Brazil's export product (coffee beans), indicating more favorable technological improvement in coffee-bean production than in steel production. Given that Brazil has a large share of the world market for coffee beans and the world demand for coffee beans is price inelastic, Brazil's expanded coffee-bean supply causes the world price for coffee beans to decline substantially. Thus, Brazil's terms of trade decline to TOT. At this new price ratio, Brazil produces at point P_1 on PPF_1 and consumes at point C_1 on curve I_1. At the new terms of trade (TOT.), Brazil exports A_1P_1 tons of coffee for A_1C_1 tons of steel. Because the consumption point moves from pregrowth position C_0 on curve I_0 to postgrowth point C_1 on curve I_1, Brazilian welfare decreases. In other words, Brazil's own advancement in supply ability makes it worse off, plunging it to a lower indifference curve.

15.3c Prebisch Theory

The possibility of immiserizing growth existing in developing countries gave rise to a new argument that questioned the wisdom of pursuing policies based on the theory of comparative advantage. In the early 1950s, Raul Prebisch, an Argentinean economist, and others argued that developing countries, primarily exporters of agricultural products and raw materials, faced an inelastic demand in their export markets and were not gaining (nor would they gain) from trade with advanced countries.[*] Because the prices of these products relative to manufactured goods had been declining and were unstable, Prebisch and others postulated a persistent, long-run tendency for developing countries' terms of trade to deteriorate. They also hypothesized that a developing country's initial export to an advanced country would bring a greater gain to the advanced country, alleging that the advanced country was in a more advantageous position.

Given these arguments, their policy recommendation to the developing countries was as follows:

1. Developing countries should decrease the resources used for the production and export of their primary product sectors.
2. They should expand the resources used in their modern and industrial sectors.
3. They should restrict the import of the industrial goods into their countries, replacing these imports with goods produced domestically.
4. They should demand a decrease in the trade barriers imposed against their industrial products by advanced countries.

The Prebisch theory created a great deal of controversy, especially regarding the validity of the facts presented to support it. The theory was based on data related to the long-run movements of the British terms of trade from the late 1800s to the end of the 1930s. Questions have been raised concerning the adequacy of such data. To be sure, the British terms of trade did improve, whereas the terms of trade of its trading partners declined during the period. However, it is argued that the British export and import structure was unique, and, as such, it does not lend itself to generalization about the deterioration of the terms of trade of today's developing countries. Additionally, such data do not allow for product quality changes. The evidence shows that the quality of primary products usually stays fairly constant, whereas the quality of manufactured products keeps improving as time goes by. For example, the quality of Brazilian coffee beans is almost the same as it was years ago, whereas a 1995 IBM computer is much more sophisticated than a 1970 model. Thus, if quality changes are taken into consideration, one could argue that developing countries' terms of trade may not have deteriorated over time. In other words, the reason that developing nations exported more primary products per unit of manufactured goods over time could be related to the rising relative value of the manufactured goods compared to the value of primary products over the same time. In our example, the quality of the Brazilian coffee beans has stayed fairly constant. Because in a competitive market a relatively higher-quality commodity commands a relatively higher price, more Brazilian coffee beans must be exported per unit of IBM computers imported into Brazil.

---

[*] Both income elasticity of demand and price elasticity of demand for primary products are low.

To date, the evidence indicates that periods of worsening terms of trade have alternated with periods of improving terms of trade. Thus, it is believed that policymakers should not discourage investment in primary products on the grounds that these sectors inevitably face unfavorable price trends; this may not happen. Research has also shown that, contrary to the Prebisch theory, in some cases, the gain from the initial opening of trade accrued mainly to primary-product exporters in developing countries as opposed to their trading partners in advanced countries. For example, when Thailand embarked on international trade in the 1850s, the price of rice, Thailand's newly growing export, increased significantly relative to the price of cloth and other imports. Most of the benefits accrued to Thai farmers. The opening of trade had a comparable impact in Japan during the 1850s and 1860s. During these periods, Japan exported massive amounts of tea and silk in exchange for imports of manufactured goods and rice. The evidence suggests that the gains from trade were mainly accrued to Japanese producers of tea and silk.

With all its controversies, the Prebisch theory has had an enormous impact on the economic policies of developing countries, especially those in Latin America. Many of these countries, such as Colombia, Peru, and Chile, have vigorously followed the policies of import substitution, replacing imports with domestically produced goods. Such policies, implemented by the imposition of taxes and tariffs on imported manufactured goods, have resulted in high production costs for domestically manufactured goods. For example, according to a 1970 study, in Colombia, Peru, and Chile, the production costs for motor vehicles runs about two to three times higher than the production costs for similar vehicles in the international market.[4] As we explained in Chapter 6, policies of indiscriminate import substitution have proven to be self-defeating. Such policies, which give rise to inefficient and costly production, result in losses for both consumers and producers, thereby reducing the world's welfare.

15.4 EXPORT INSTABILITY

The Prebisch theory postulated a persistent, long-run tendency for developing countries' terms of trade to deteriorate. Independent of this long-run phenomenon, developing countries may also experience short-run oscillations in their export prices and revenues. This can significantly hinder their economic development process. Export instability occurs because export earnings tend to fluctuate annually to a greater extent for developing countries than for advanced countries.

In this section, we elaborate on the factors that give rise to export instability. We then review empirical studies that have tried to assess the extent of these short-run oscillations and their real effects on the economic development process. Finally, we elaborate on policies employed by developing countries to stabilize their export prices or revenues.

15.4a Factors Giving Rise to Export Instability

The factors leading to export instability can be classified as price variability and a high degree of commodity concentration. In examining these two factors, we should keep in mind that developing countries are relatively more involved in the export of raw materials and primary products than of manufactured goods.

Price Variability. Price variability refers to dramatic fluctuations developing countries experience in the prices of their primary products. These fluctuations occur because demand for and supply of primary products produced by developing countries are both price inelastic and unstable. This situation is illustrated in Figure 15-2. D and S represent demand and supply curves, respectively, for a hypothetical developing country's primary-product exports. The equilibrium price is P. If D increases (shifts to the right) to D′ or S decreases (shifts to the left) to S′, the equilibrium price increases to P′. If both D and S shift simultaneously to D′ and S′, the equilibrium price rises even more, to P″. If the reverse case takes place, that is, D′ and S′ fall back to D and S, the equilibrium price declines significantly to P. Thus, given inelastic and unstable (shifting) demand and supply for developing countries' primary exports, one can expect wide oscillations in the prices these countries receive for their exports.

The inelasticity of demand for developing countries' primary-product exports is attributed to the fact that individual households in advanced countries allocate only a small proportion of their budgets to primary products, such as sugar, tobacco, tea, coffee, and bananas. In other words, each of these products is such a relatively small part of the consumer's total expenditures that changes in their prices lead to less-than-proportional changes in quantities demanded, resulting in a price inelastic demand.

FIGURE 15-2
A Case of Price Variability for a Developing Country's Primary Product Exports

D and S represent demand and supply curves for a hypothetical developing country's primary product exports. The equilibrium price is P. If D increases (shifts to the right) to D' or S decreases (shifts to the left) to S', the equilibrium price increases to P'. If both D and S shift simultaneously to D' and S', the equilibrium price rises even more to P". If the reverse takes place, that is D' and S' fall back to D and S, the equilibrium price declines significantly to P. Thus, given inelastic and unstable (that is, shifting) demand and supply for developing countries' exports, we can expect wide oscillations in the prices these countries receive for their exports.

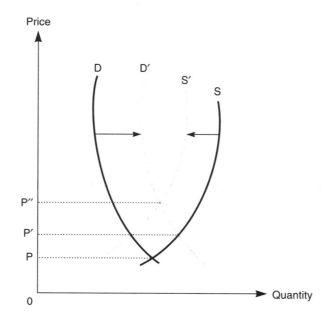

The inelasticity of supply of developing countries' primary-exports is attributed to the internal rigidities that exist in most of these countries regarding resource usage. As a result, changes in export prices lead to less-than-proportional changes in quantities supplied, resulting in a price inelastic supply.

High Degree of Commodity Concentration. One of the attributes of many developing countries is that their exports are concentrated in a small number of primary products. As Table 15-2 shows, in some developing countries, one or two commodities may contribute to the bulk of export earnings. This deficiency in diversification suggests that acute changes in the price of one or two commodities could lead to sharp changes in total export revenues. If the commodities exported were more diversified or less concentrated, a price increase in some commodities could be balanced by a price decrease in other commodities, leading to higher stability in total export revenue.

15.4b Empirical Studies of Export Instability in Developing Countries

One of the earliest investigations of export instability in developing countries was carried out by Alasdair MacBean. Using 1946-1958 data, he examined export instability for a sample of 45 developing countries and 18 advanced nations. His analysis suggested that export instability, measured by an index, was only slightly greater for the developing countries than for the advanced countries.[*] He thus concluded that the significance of short-term export

---

[*]   MacBean determined the instability index as the average percentage deviation of the dollar value of export earnings from a five-year moving average. Measuring the instability index on a scale of 0 to 100, he found the index value to be 18 for advanced nations and 23 for developing nations.

instability to developing countries had been overstated. In most cases, oscillations in income did not seem to be closely related at all to oscillations in export proceeds. Many nations with great export instability had relatively stable incomes, whereas many with high export stability experienced serious income instability.

TABLE 15-2
Percentage of Some Developing Countries' Major Primary Exports to Total Exports

Country	Major Exports	Percentage of Total Export Earnings
Bolivia	Tin	7
	Zinc	22
Colombia	Coffee beans	19
Ghana	Cocoa beans	22
Indonesia	Oil	17
Iraq	Oil	40
Kuwait	Oil	93
Libya	Oil	65
Oman	Oil	51
Saudi Arabia	Oil	91
Sri Lanka	Tea	14
Sudan	Cotton	43
United Arab Emirates	Oil	89
Venezuela	Oil	72

Source: International Monetary Fund, *International Financial Statistics* (Washington, DC: IMF, February 1994). Percentages were calculated by the author and are rounded to the nearest digit. For each country, the latest available yearly data were used.

MacBean's analysis also demonstrated that the greater oscillation in developing countries' export proceeds did not induce notable fluctuation in their macroeconomic variables of national income, savings, and investment. This, according to MacBean, may have been related to two factors. One is the relatively low absolute level of export instability; the other is the fact that the very low foreign-trade multipliers shielded the developing countries' economies from oscillations in their export proceeds.

MacBean rejected the commonly accepted explanations of export instability, such as specialization in primary products, commodity concentration, and geographic concentration. He explained that specialization, not simply in primary commodities, but in a specific commodity like natural rubber that is distinctively subject to instability, accounts for the oscillations in the export earnings.

MacBean's findings regarding the relative insignificance of export instability and its possible causes led him to make some policy rules. If export fluctuations did not inflict serious damage on most of the developing countries, he argued, the possible benefits of export stabilization may be negligible. Thus, according to MacBean, the costly international commodity agreements developing countries requested to stabilize their export proceeds were not defensible. The same resources could be employed more efficiently for genuine developmental objectives rather than for stabilizing export revenues that were stable at the outset.[5]

Further studies on the subject of export instability produced controversial results. Benton Massell, using 1950-1966 data and a sample of 36 developing countries and 19 advanced countries, showed that developing countries tended to experience higher export instability due to their higher product concentration. This instability, however, was mitigated by their dependence on food exports which tended to be more stable.[6]

Using 1950-1972 data and a sample of 123 developing countries and 26 advanced countries, Lancieri showed that developing countries were much more subject to fluctuations of export revenues than were advanced nations. His study supported the view that export instability is a significant obstacle to development.[7]

Love reexamined the effects of commodity concentration on instability in export earnings. Using time series data for 24 developing countries, he found a positive relationship between concentration and instability.[8] His findings, however, were rejected by Massell, who questioned whether Love employed a valid measure of export instability and whether his analysis supported his conclusions.[9]

In summary, empirical studies support the view that export instability is, in general, somewhat greater for developing countries than for advanced countries. However, the impact of export instability on economic development and its association with commodity concentration remain controversial. Nevertheless, the developing countries have continued to seek international commodity agreements in order to stabilize and enhance their export revenues.

15.4c Policies to Stabilize Export Prices or Revenues

The stabilization of a developing country's export prices or revenues can be achieved by either purely domestic strategies, such as establishing domestic marketing boards, or international strategies, such as engaging in international commodity agreements.

Domestic Marketing Boards. A domestic marketing board (DMB) is an agency that is set up by a developing country's government. The objective of this agency is to maintain price stability for the country's individual producers. To achieve this goal, the agency buys goods from individual domestic producers at a guaranteed price and then sells them on the global market at fluctuating world prices. In determining its guaranteed price, the board sets domestic prices below world prices in good years. This allows the board to accumulate funds needed in bad years to pay domestic producers prices that are higher than international prices. Examples of DMBs include the cocoa marketing boards of Ghana, the rice marketing board in Burma, and the Rice Export Corporation in Pakistan.

In practice, only a few of these agencies have met with some degree of success due to the corruption of agency officials and the difficulty in correctly forecasting domestic prices.

International Commodity Agreements. International commodity agreements (ICAs) refer to agreements between producing and consuming countries to stabilize and increase the prices and revenues of exports. The main types of ICAs are international buffer stock agreements, international export quota agreements, and multilateral agreements.

International Buffer Stock Agreements. This type of international agreement involves the establishment of an international agency by producing nations (often joined by consuming nations) to limit commodity price swings. To achieve this objective, the agency is provided with finances and supplies of a commodity to regulate its world price. If the supplies are abundant and the world price of the commodity falls below an agreed minimum price, the agency purchases the commodity, causing its price to rise to the desired level. On the other hand, if supplies are tight and the world price of the commodity rises above an agreed maximum price, the agency sells the commodity, causing its price to fall to the desired level.

The best-known example of an international buffer stock agreement is the *International Tin Agreement*. This agreement, reached in 1956, was successfully in force for a number of years before its eventual collapse in 1987. Other examples of international buffer stock agreements are the *International Cocoa Agreement* and the *International Natural Rubber Agreement*. Like the International Tin Agreement, these agreements are no longer operational.

Using the example of cocoa beans, Figures 15-3 and 15-4 illustrate how the agency regulates price. Assume that the cocoa-bean agreement calls for a minimum price of $2.50 per pound and a maximum price of $3.50 per pound. Starting at equilibrium point E in Figure 15-3, suppose the demand for cocoa rises from D to D', causing the equilibrium price to rise from $3.00 per pound to $3.75 per pound. To bring the price down to the maximum level of $3.50 per pound, the agency has to sell 10,000 tons of cocoa beans (line AE″, the excess demand at $3.50 per pound), causing the supply curve to shift to S'. This leads to the new equilibrium point E″, where the price is brought down to the maximum level of $3.50 per pound.

FIGURE 15-3
Buffer Stock Agreement: Price Setting In the Case of a Rise in Demand

Starting at equilibrium point E, suppose the demand for cocoa rises from D to D′, causing the equilibrium price to rise from $3.00 per pound to $3.75 per pound. To bring the price down to maximum level of $3.50 per pound, the agency has to sell 10,000 tons of cocoa beans (line AE″; the excess demand at the price of $3.50 per pound), causing the supply curve to shift to S′. This leads to the new equilibrium point E″, where the price is brought down to the maximum level of $3.50 per pound.

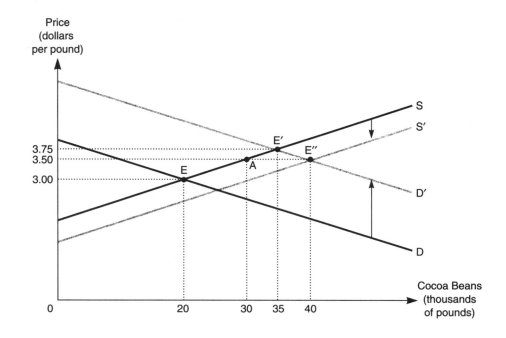

Conversely, starting at equilibrium point E in Figure 15-4, assume the supply of cocoa beans increases from S to S′, causing the price to fall from $3.00 per pound to $2.25 per pound. To raise the price to the minimum level of $2.50 per pound, the agency must purchase 10,000 pounds of cocoa beans (line AE″, the excess supply at the price of $2.50 per pound), causing the demand curve to shift to D′. This leads to the new equilibrium point E″, where the price is brought up to the minimum level of $2.50 per pound.

A buffer stock agreement is subject to the following disadvantages:

1. The extended maintenance of the minimum price level may deplete the funds needed to buy excess supplies at the lowest price. This may lead to a downward revision of the minimum price.
2. The extended maintenance of the maximum price level may deplete the agency's stockpile, destroying this price-stabilization strategy's effectiveness. This may lead to the upward revision of the maximum price.
3. Some goods can be stocked only at a very high cost.

International Export Quota Agreements. This type of agreement is aimed at regulating the quantity of an exported good in order to stabilize its price. In such an agreement, producing nations select a target price for the commodity and estimate the world demand for the coming year. Given the estimated demand, they ascertain the quantity of supply that generates the target price. They then divide up this quantity among the supplying nations and rule that no nation should export more than its assigned quota. If the estimated demand is accurate and if the participating nations honor their quotas, the target price is established for the coming year. If the price deviates from the target price, the quota is adjusted to reestablish the target price. This is illustrated in Figures 15-5 and 15-6, in which we assume that the agreement calls for the stabilization of the price of coffee at $1.00 per pound. S and D portray the estimated supply and demand, respectively, that yield this targeted price at equilibrium point E, where 40 million pounds of coffee are sold. Using Figure 15-5, assume that due to world recession the market demand for coffee decreases from D to D′, causing the price to fall to $0.75 (point E′). To re-establish the target price, the supplying nations' quotas must be tightened. This causes the supply curve to shift from S to S′, yielding the target price of $1.00 at equilibrium point E″.

FIGURE 15-4
Buffer Stock Agreement: Price Setting In the Case of a Rise in Supply

Starting at equilibrium point E, assume the supply of cocoa beans increases from S to S′, causing the price to fall from $3.00 per pound to $2.25 per pound. To raise the price to the minimum level of $2.50 per pound, the agency has to purchase 10,000 pounds of cocoa beans (line AE″, the excess supply at the price of $2.50 per pound), causing the demand to shift to D′. This leads to the new equilibrium point E″, where the price is brought up to the minimum level of $2.50 per pound.

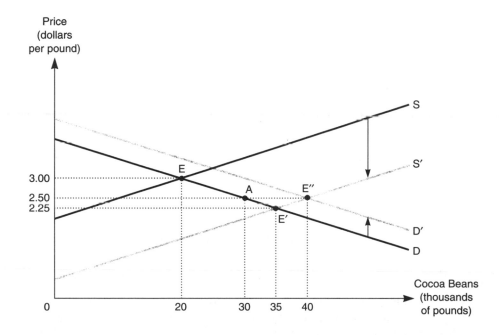

Conversely, starting from equilibrium point E in Figure 15-6, assume that demand shifts to the right, causing the equilibrium price to increase to $1.25. To re-establish the target price, the supplying nations' quotas must be relaxed. This causes the supply curve to shift from S to S′, yielding the target price of $1.00 at equilibrium point E″.

An example of an international export quota agreement is the *International Sugar Agreement*. This agreement, reached in 1954, has been generally ineffective in stabilizing and increasing sugar prices due to advanced countries' capability to enhance the production of their own beet sugar. Another example is the *International Coffee Agreement*, which was negotiated in 1962. Although this agreement succeeded in stabilizing coffee prices at a higher level, it was suspended in 1989. This led to a glut of coffee in the international market, causing its price to drop sharply. In 1994, the major producers negotiated a new International Coffee Agreement which contained provisions for regulation of exports and imports under certain price conditions, and for generic promotion of coffee.

Multilateral Agreements. A multilateral agreement is a long-term contract that determines a *minimum* price at which importing countries guarantee to buy a specified quantity of a good and a *maximum* price at which exporting countries guarantee to sell a specified quantity of a good. Thus, multilateral agreements are designed to set an upper limit (ceiling) and a lower limit (floor) on the prices of traded goods. Examples of multilateral agreements are the *International Sugar Agreement* and the *International Wheat Agreement*.

FIGURE 15-5
International Export Quota Agreement: Price Stabilization in the Case of a Fall in Demand

Assume that the agreement calls for the stabilization of the price of coffee at $1.00 per pound. S and D portray the estimated supply and demand that yield this targeted price at equilibrium point E, where 40 million pounds of coffee are sold. Now suppose that due to world recession the market demand for coffee decreases from D to D′, causing the price to fall to $0.75 (see point E′). To reestablish the target price, the quotas of the supplying nations will be tightened. This causes the supply curve to shift from S to S′, yielding the target price of $1.00 at equilibrium point E″.

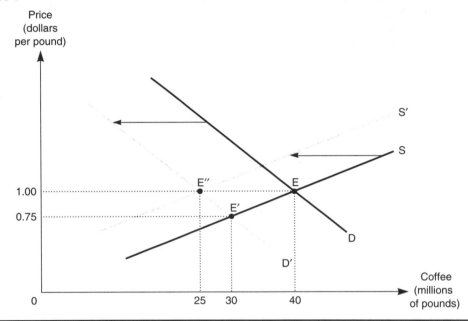

In comparison with buffer stock and export quota agreements, multilateral agreements lead to less distortion in the market mechanism and the allocation of scarce resources. This is because they usually do not impose output constraints on the commodity in question. As a result, they do not restrain the development of more efficient producers. However, given the relative ease of entry into and withdrawal from these contracts by participating nations, they tend to provide only limited market stability.

15.5 TRADE LIBERALIZATION IN DEVELOPING NATIONS

As we explained earlier, following the Prebisch theory, many developing nations, especially those in Latin American countries, pursued policies of import substitution. The 1950s and 1960s can be viewed as a period during which import-substitution industrialization was a popular trade strategy that was approved by many economists and pursued in many developing nations. Many of these nations initiated their import-substitution policies by protecting final stages of industry, such as food processing and automobile assembly. In some larger developing nations, domestic products almost entirely displaced imported consumer goods.

Although the import-substitution strategy succeeded in encouraging the growth of manufacturing, it did not promote economic development. The evidence shows that many developing nations that have followed import-substitution strategies have not shown signs of catching up with advanced nations. In some developing nations, the pursuit of import-substitution policies has led only to a marginal increase in per capita income. A case in point is India which, following the implementation of a series of economic plans between the early 1950s and the early 1970s, found itself with a per capita income that was only a few percent higher than before. In other developing nations, such as Mexico, the pursuit of import-substitution policies resulted in economic growth; however, it did not lead to narrowing the income gap between these nations and advanced countries.

FIGURE 15-6
International Export Quota Agreement: Price Stabilization in the Case of a Rise in Demand

This diagram is identical to Figure 15-5; however, starting from equilibrium point E, let us assume the demand shifts to the right (as opposed to the left in Figure 15-5). This causes the equilibrium price to increase to $1.25. To reestablish the target price, the quotas of the supplying nations will be relaxed. This causes the supply curve to shift to the right from S to S′, yielding the target price of $1.00 at equilibrium point E″.

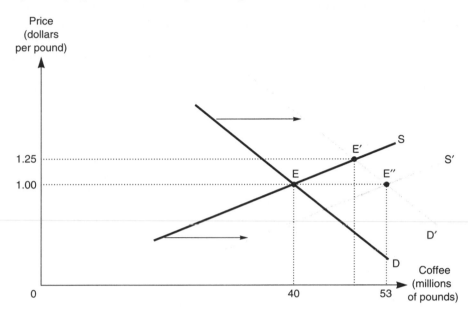

A number of empirical studies measured the welfare costs of developing countries' trade barriers that were imposed to promote industrialization in the 1960s and early 1970s. These studies showed that the trade barriers inflicted notable costs on Argentina, Chile, Colombia, Egypt, Ghana, India, Israel, Mexico, Pakistan, the Philippines, South Korea, Taiwan, and Turkey. The only exception was Malaysia, where the import barriers led to a small benefit due to favorable terms of trade.[10]

Given the shortcomings of import substitution in promoting economic development, such a strategy has come under increasingly harsh criticism by economists in recent years. As a result, since the 1960s, there has been a steady movement toward trade liberalization in some developing countries that previously followed import-substitution policies. In the 1960s, several trade liberalizations were carried out in Latin American countries, notably in Brazil and Chile from 1964 and in Colombia from 1967. By decreasing bias against manufactured exports, they improved export performance. Besides Latin American countries, a small group of initially poor countries pursued trade liberalization policies by combining rapid growth of output and living standards with industrialization directed primarily toward export markets instead of domestic markets. These countries, as we explain later in this chapter, have experienced impressive economic performance and have gained the status of NICs.

The most important trade liberalizations in the 1970s took place in Argentina, Chile, and Uruguay. These nations attempted to stabilize and liberalize their economies in the face of recession, inflation, declining terms of trade, and unstable capital flow which helped to induce the international debt crisis of the 1980s. Examples of other countries that have followed trade liberalization policies include Cameroon, Costa Rica, Cote d'Ivorie, Guatemala, Indonesia, Malaysia, Thailand, Tunisia, and Turkey.[11]

The road to trade liberalization, which started gradually in the 1960s and continues today, has not always been smooth. Import-substitution policies are still practiced in many developing nations that have rightly complained about the existence of import barriers against their exports of both manufactured and agricultural products to advanced nations. In fact, trade barriers against the manufactured products of developing countries have been higher than the tariffs on manufactured goods between advanced nations. Additionally, import barriers on manufactured goods from developing countries have risen since the 1960s.

Despite an increase in their manufactured goods, most developing nations' exports are still composed of raw materials and agricultural products. Yet advanced nations have kept and even increased their restrictions on imports and their subsidies to production and exports of agricultural products.[12]

Given the existence of trade barriers against the exports of developing countries, many nations that felt neglected by previous General Agreement on Tariff and Trade (GATT) rounds looked forward to the Uruguay Round of negotiation for dismantling trade barriers against them. The United States persuaded many of these nations to join the Uruguay Round of negotiation in 1986 with promises of significant concessions. Unfortunately, following the successful negotiation of this round on December 15, 1993, many developing nations felt they did not get all they hoped for. To be sure, trade barriers will fall as a result of the round, but not as much or as quickly as the developing nations had expected. In the area of agriculture, for example, developing nations expected that major industrial nations would entirely dismantle subsidies for their products, rapidly decrease tariffs, and open markets by reducing quotas. But the developing countries learned that they had to accept much less in all three areas. Nevertheless, despite their disappointment with the Uruguay Round, some developing nations, such as Chile and Brazil, believe that the agreement will lead to an overall net benefit for their economies due to relatively freer international trade.[13]

15.6 DEMANDS FOR A NEW INTERNATIONAL ECONOMIC ORDER

Skeptical about the possible advantages of the existing international trading system, developing countries have collectively demanded that advanced nations institute policies to improve the international trading system. Such a demand for a new international economic order (NIEO) led to the assembly of the United Nations Conference on Trade and Development (UNCTAD) in Geneva in 1964. Following this event, UNCTAD became a permanent organization of the United Nations that convenes every four years to discuss issues regarding trade between advanced and developing nations.[*]

Developing countries' demands for an NIEO, include a number of objectives, which are discussed subsequently.

1. **Dismantling of trade barriers on agricultural products in advanced countries.** Historically, the internal political power of agricultural interests in advanced nations has opposed the removal of trade barriers on agricultural products in those countries. However, as we explained in the previous section, some progress was made during the Uruguay Round of negotiations, resulting in a lowering of trade barriers against developing countries. However, as noted earlier, developing nations are not totally satisfied with the outcome of the Uruguay Round and feel that they were shortchanged by GATT.

2. **Creation of international commodity agreements to stabilize prices of primary products.** Over the years this objective has continued to be the centerpiece of developing nations' demand for an NIEO. Unfortunately, however, not much progress has been made in meeting this goal. Over time, international commodity agreements have resulted in uncontrollable goods inventory or have led to the use of export controls, contributing to existing inefficiencies.

3. **Enhancing advanced nations' aid to developing nations.** To fulfill this objective, developing nations have demanded that advanced nations increase their financial aid to 0.7 percent of their GNP. To date, little progress has been made in meeting this objective. The worldwide recession of the late 1980s and early 1990s has made it difficult for advanced nations to enhance their aid to developing nations. As Table 15-3 shows, the official development assistance, measured in terms of the percentage of GNP of the donor recipients, has decreased over the years . Additionally, according to Table 15-4 in every case, the amount of aid is still far from the target of 0.7 percent of the GNP of the donor nation.

---

* Other meetings of UNCTAD were held in New Delhi, 1968; in Santiago, 1972; in Nairobi, 1976; in Manila, 1979; in Belgrade, 1983; in Geneva, 1987; Cartegena, 1992; Midrand, South Africa, 1976; and Bangkok 2000.

TABLE 15-3
Total Official Development Assistance Received by the Developing Nations

Developing Countries	Dollars per capita		% of GNP of the Donor Recipients	
	1991	1996	1991	1996
Low Income	14	12	4.7	3.5
Lower Middle Income	10	8	0.8	0.4
Upper Middle Income	14	7	0.4	0.2

Source: World Bank, *World Development Report,* 1998/1999, 231.

TABLE 15-4
Aid from Advanced Nations to Developing Nations

Advance Countries	Aid as % of GNP of the Donor Countries 1995/1996
North America	0.02
Western and Southern Europe	0.11
OECD	0.06
European Union	0.09
Nordic Countries	0.24

Source: United Nations, *Human Development Report 1998* (New York: Oxford University Press, 1998), 196.

4. **Renegotiating developing countries' international debt and decreasing their interest payments.** Some steps, which we explain in the next chapter, were taken to meet this objective. Although some progress was made in defusing the international debt crisis, the debt dilemma continues in 2000.

5. **Increasing the transfer of technology from multinational corporations to developing nations.** As we explain in Chapter 17, although the positive role of multinational corporations (MNCs) has been met with skepticism from both advanced and developing countries, the role of MNCs has created more heated debate and has stirred more controversy in developing countries. So far, not much progress has been made in meeting the developing nations' demands for developing appropriate technologies, increasing the flow of technology from advanced nations, and adopting a code of conduct for MNCs to eradicate abuses.

6. **Permitting developing countries to have a greater role in the international decision-making process.** The participation of developing countries in international organizations, such as the International Monetary Fund, the World Bank, and the UN, has enhanced their role in the international decision-making process. Nevertheless, in spite of the fact that developing countries surpass advanced nations in sheer numbers, they are far from governing these critical organizations.

We may conclude this section by stating that although developing nations have succeeded in articulating their demands for an NIEO, they still have a long way to go before completely satisfying such demands. The worldwide recession of the late 1980s and early 1990s, which has forced many industrial nations to worry abut their own domestic economic problems, has put the NIEO on a back burner so to speak. Although some modest progress was made in the Uruguay Round in dismantling some of the trade barriers against developing nations, it is unlikely that any further progress will be made in meeting the overall demands for an NIEO in the near future.

15.7 NEWLY INDUSTRIALIZED COUNTRIES

Despite the negative view presented by dependency theory regarding the possible benefits of international trade for developing countries, an increasing number of these nations have been active in the international market. By promoting their manufacturing sectors, they have reached the status of NICs. **Newly industrialized countries** include Argentina, Brazil, Greece, Hong Kong, South Korea, Mexico, Portugal, Singapore, Spain, and Taiwan. These countries are at a relatively advanced stage of economic development. Each of these countries has a substantial and active industrial sector that is integrated into its international trade, finance, and investment systems.

Among the NICs, the four East Asian countries of South Korea, Hong Kong, Taiwan, and Singapore have achieved impressive economic performance and have been used as models for economic development by other developing countries. Table 15–5 provides selective data on the economic development performance of these nations. With a collective population of 75.9 million and a labor force of over 35 million, these countries possess substantial and formidable economic power. The unemployment rates in these nations are substantially below those of most advanced nations, ranging from 4.3 percent in Singapore to 1.69 percent in Taiwan. South Korea, the most dynamic of these countries, has even surpassed Japan in terms of rapid growth in a short time period. As a group, these nations have performed so well during the past three decades that they have sometimes been referred to facetiously as the "**Four Dragons**" or the "**Gang of Four**."

TABLE 15-5
Selective Indicators of Development of Newly Industrialized Pacific Rim Countries

	Hong Kong	Singapore	South Korea	Taiwan [*]
Population (1997)	7M	3M	46M	19.9M
Labor force (1997)	3M	2M	22M	8.25 M
Average annual GNP growth rate (1996-1997)	5.2%	8.8%	4.8%	7.33%
Unemployment rate	1.7% [*]	4.3% [*]	2.5% [*]	1.69% [*]
GNP per capita (1997)	$25,280	$32,940	$10,550	$6,053
Average annual inflation rate (1985-1995)	8.7%	3.9%	6.7%	1.28%
Exports (1996)	$211,680M [**]	$155,109M	$156,052M	$60,585M
Imports (1996)	$214,560M [**]	$175,763M	$142,461M	$46,770M
Average annual growth rate of exports (1990-1997)	14.4%	10.8%	12.0%	8.33%

M = millions.
** 1995 data

* 1988 data.

Source: The World Bank, *World Development Report 1998/99* (Washington DC: Oxford University Press, 1992); U.S. Department of Commerce, *Foreign Economic Trends and Their Implications for the United States* (Washington DC: International Trade Administration, 1989); *United Nations, Human Development Report 1998* (New York: Oxford University Press, 1992).

GLOBAL INSIGHTS CASE 15.2

U.S. Policy on Trade with Developing Countries

Much of the surge in the growth of U.S. exports in recent years is due to demand from developing countries. During the 1990s U.S. exports to advanced nations have grown at the rate of 5 percent per year in real terms. In the mean time, U.S. exports to developing nations have grown at about twice that rate. Among developing nations, the growth of U.S. exports to Latin America have been especially impressive, increasing from 0.9 percent of U.S. GDP in 1990 to 1.4 percent in the first three quarters of 1996. In the same period, exports to other developing and transition economies rose from 1.6 percent to 2.2 percent of GDP.

The United States' strategy has aimed at encouraging the involvement and integration of developing nations into a global trading system. To achieve this goal, a number of policies have been adopted that not only benefit U.S. consumers, but also provide special encouragement for developing nations to increase and diversify their exports.

One of the main U.S. programs for promoting trade with developing nations is the Generalized System of Preferences (GSP), instituted in 1976. Under this program, about 4,600 products from 148 developing nations and territories are eligible for duty-free entry into the United States. In 1995 the United States imported $18.3 billion in duty-free goods under the program, accounting for 16 percent of total U.S. imports from the GSP recipients. More than two-thirds of all GSP imports in 1995 originated in six developing nations, including Brazil, India, Indonesia, Malaysia, the Phillippines, and Thailand.

Under this program, as nations reach certain developmental stages they are graduated from the program, to allow lower income countries to take better advantage of available preferences. For example, Malaysia graduated in January 1, 1997.

The Caribbean Basin Economic Recovery Act, implemented in 1984, provides preferential access to the U.S. market for 24 Caribbean nations and territories. In 1991 the United States activated a similar program for four South American nations. This program is the cornerstone of U.S. strategy to lead these nations to curtail their production and exports of cocaine. These two programs help support growth and development in some of the globe's less developed nations, which in turn have become better consumers of U.S. goods.

Source: U.S. Government Printing Office, *Economic Report of the President* (Washington DC: U.S. Government Printing Office, 1997), 252-254

Given the shortages of natural resources and capital, these countries have tried to achieve development by pursuing a free-trade philosophy, creating a favorable investment climate and using a low-wage labor force that adheres to the Confucian ethic of emphasizing education and hard work. As a result, in recent years, their living standards have risen sharply, unemployment has stayed low, and their economies have continued to experience fast growth.

Although their GNPs remain lower than those of North America, Europe, and Japan, their overall economic growth is remarkable, ranging from about 5.2 percent a year in Hong Kong to 8.8 percent a year in Singapour. Their continuous growth has resulted in the development of strong domestic markets. Besides their striking growth performance, the most prominent feature of the Gang of Four is their adherence to free international trade. The NICs' relative share in the global market is still not large when compared to Japan's in most products. They continue, however, to experience a very strong export growth, ranging from 8.33 percent in Tawin to 14.4 percent in Hong Kong. Additionally, they are emerging as a formidable industrial force that advanced countries will have to compete with in the global market. Japan is already losing ground to the these nations in some industries, such as steel and textiles. In the international market for automobiles, Japan now has to reckon with South Korea, which has successfully eradicated Japan's position as the principal Asian automobile exporter.

Although the Gang of Four nations have been able to achieve remarkable economic success, their accomplishments have not come without problems. The philosophy of emphasizing industrialization at all costs has left these nations with major pollution problems. Labor unrest has become more common. South Korea, for example, recently faced pressure from workers to increase wages and bonuses, improve working conditions, and free labor unions which have been suppressed by the government.

In recent years, a new group of NICs (Indonesia, Malaysia, and Thailand) has begun to displace the Gang of Four as the "engine of growth" in the region. However, this trend seemed to change in 1991 when the growth of the Gang of Four surpassed that of the new group of NICs.

In concluding this chapter, we must emphasize that the road to economic development is not smooth and is imbued with uncertainty. A successful journey requires immense financial resources, technical expertise, and managerial know-how that are lacking in most developing countries. As a result, advanced countries have a crucial role in assisting developing countries to achieve their economic development goals. However, as NICs have demonstrated, the major effort should come from the developing countries themselves.

15.8 SUMMARY

1. Third world countries (also referred to as underdeveloped countries, developing countries, or less-developed countries) are primarily identified by low standards of living, high rates of population growth, low levels of per capita income, high illiteracy rates, unequal income distribution, and general economic and technological dependence on advanced countries.

2. Today, the classification schemes used to define developing countries differ, depending on the agency providing the scheme.

3. In general, developing countries have low levels of per capita income, and they share a set of common problems in varying degrees.

4. The majority of Western economists, supporting conventional trade theory, consider international trade an "engine of growth."

5. Dependency theory attributes the sluggishness of economic growth and development in developing nations to their dependent relationships with advanced countries.

6. The dependency theory has been subject to many criticisms, on both theoretical and empirical grounds.

7. Immiserizing growth is an expansion of the factor supply or productivity that makes a nation worse off when it exports the goods it specializes in producing.

8. According to the Prebisch theory, because world prices for primary products have been declining and unstable, developing countries' terms of trade have deteriorated over time. Thus, developing countries should restrict the import of industrial goods into their countries, replacing these imports with goods produced domestically.

9. The factors leading to export instability can be classified as price variability and a high degree of commodity concentration.

10. Price variability occurs because demand for and supply of primary products produced by developing countries are both price inelastic and unstable.

11. Empirical studies support the view that export instability is, in general, somewhat greater for developing countries than for advanced countries. However, the impact of export instability on economic development and its association with commodity concentration remains controversial.

12. The stabilization of a developing country's export prices or revenues can be achieved by either purely domestic strategies, such as domestic marketing boards (DMBs), or international strategies, such as international commodity agreements.

13. A DMB is an agency that is set up by a developing country's government. The objective of this agency is to maintain price stability for the country's individual producers.

14. International commodity agreements (ICAs) refer to agreements between producing and consuming countries to stabilize and increase the prices and revenues of their exports.

15. The main types of ICAs are international buffer stock agreements, international export quota agreements, and multilateral agreements.
16. Developing countries' demands for a new international economic order (NIEO) include a number of objectives.
17. Newly industrialized countries (NICs) are at a relatively advanced stage of economic development. Each of these countries has a substantial and active industrial sector that is integrated into its international trade, finance, and investment systems.

Review Questions

1. What are the major characteristics of developing countries? Is there a unified method for classifying a nation as a developing country? Explain.
2. Why do the majority of Western economists consider international trade an "engine of growth?" Is this assertion true for today's developing countries? Explain.
3. Why do some economists consider conventional international trade theory inappropriate for developing countries? Explain.
4. Elaborate on the dependency theory. What is a "metropolis-satellite chain?" What are the major criticisms of this theory? Should this theory be dismissed at face value?
5. What is "immiserizing growth?" What conditions are necessary for immiserizing growth to occur? Explain.
6. Explain the Prebisch theory. What is the basis of this theory? What are its policy implications? Give examples of countries that are somehow following the Prebisch recommendations.
7. What is "export instability?" What factors give rise to export instability?
8. What conclusions can be drawn from many empirical studies on the subject of export instability? Explain.
9. Commodity price stabilization has been a main goal of many developing countries. What are the major methods used to achieve this objective?
10. What are international commodity agreements? Give some examples of ICAs, and explain why many of them have failed over time.
11. Developing countries' demands for an NIEO include a number of objectives. Discuss these objectives.

Problems

1. Suppose a developing country produces only agricultural goods and manufacturing goods. Draw a production possibilities curve that displays increasing costs. Graphically illustrate and verbally explain the impact of a technological improvement in agriculture production.
2. Draw a hypothetical production possibilities curve for a developing country. Suppose the country produces only primary and manufacturing products. Analyze the impact of technological improvement in primary production on the country's terms of trade.
3. Using demand and supply analysis, show that when the supply of a good rises, its equilibrium price declines by a smaller amount, the more price elastic the demand curve for that good.
4. Graphically analyze and verbally explain how a buffer stock agreement can result in either the depletion of commodity stock or an unmanageable stock for the buffer authority.
5. Employing ordinary supply and demand curves, show that suppliers' revenue is subject to less fluctuation from a shift in the demand curve than from a shift in the supply curve.
6. Discuss the pros and cons of the argument that international trade can hamper economic development.
7. Import-substitution industrialization is more effective for a large developing country than for a small one. Do you agree with this statement? Discuss.

Notes

1. Andre G. Frank, *Capitalism and Underdevelopment in Latin America: Historical Studies of Chile and Brazil* (New York: Monthly Review Press, 1967), 11.
2. Paul Baran, *La Economica Politica del Crecimiento, Mexico.* (Mexico: F.C.E., 1957), 28.
3. Andre G. Frank, *Capitalism and Underdevelopment in Latin America: Historical Studies of Chile and Brazil.* (New York: Monthly Review Press, 1967).
4. Bernard Munk, "The Colombian Automobile Industry: The Welfare Consequences of Import Substitution," *Economic and Business Bulletin* (Fall 1970): 6-22.
5. A. I. MacBean, *Export Instability and Economic Structure.* (Cambridge, MA: Harvard University Press, 1966).
6. Benton F. Massell, "Export Instability and Economic Structure," *American Economic Review* 40 (September 1970): 618-630.
7. E. Lanceri, "Export Instability and Economic Development," *Banca del Lavoro Quarterly Review* (June 1978): 135-152.
8. J. Love, "Commodity Concentration and Export Earnings Instability: A Shift from Cross-Section to Time Series Analysis," *Journal of Development Economics* 24 (1986): 239-248.
9. Benson F. Massell, "Concentration and Instability Revisited," *Journal of Development Economics,* 33 (1990): 145-147.
10. Bela Balassa, *The Structure of Protection in Developing Countries,* (Baltimore: John Hopkins Press, 1971); Jagdish N. Bhagwati and Anne Krueger, *Foreign Trade Regimes and Economic Development,* multiple volumes (New York: Colombia University Press for the National Bureau of Economic Research, 1973-76).
11. The World Bank, *World Development Report 1987* (New York: Oxford University Press, 1987), ch. 5.
12. For a discussion on reasons for the pursuit of protectionist agricultural policies by advanced nations, see The World Bank, *World Development Report 1986* (New York: Oxford University Press, 1986), ch. 6.
13. "Developing Nations Feel Shortchanged by GATT," *The Wall Street Journal,* 15 December 1993, A6.

Suggested Readings

Balassa, B. *Comparative Advantage, Trade Policy and Economic Development.* New York: New York University Press, 1989.

Baran, P. A. *The Political Economy of Growth.* New York: Monthly Review Press, 1957.

Bhagwati, J. N. "Immiserizing Growth." *Readings in International Economics.* Homewood, IL: Irwin, 1967.

———. *Dependency and Interdependence.* Cambridge, MA: MIT Press, 1985.

———. *Foreign Trade Regimes and Economic Development: Anatomy and Consequences of Exchange Control Regimes.* Cambridge, MA: Ballinger, 1978.

———. *The New International Economic Order: The North-South Debate.* Cambridge, MA: MIT Press, 1977.

Cline, W. R., ed. *Policy Alternatives for a New International Economic Order.* New York: Praeger, 1979.

Finlayson, J. A. *Managing International Markets: Developing Countries and the Commodity Trade Regime.* New York: Columbia University Press, 1988.

Frank, A. G. *Capitalism and Underdevelopment in Latin America: Historical Studies of Chile and Brasil.* New York: Monthly Review Press, 1967.

———. *Latin America: Underdevelopment or Revolution?* New York: Monthly Review Press, 1978.

Greenway D., ed. *Economic Development in International Trade.* London: MacMillian, 1987.

Gwin, C. *Integration of Developing Countries into the World Trading System.* Cambridge, MA: Ballinger, 1989.

Hecksher, E. "The Effects of Foreign Trade on Distribution of Income." *Economisc Tidskrift* 21 (1919): 497-512.

Johnson, H. G. *Economic Policies Toward Less Developed Countries.* New York: Praeger, 1967.

Krueger, A. D. *Trade and Employment in Developing Countries.* Chicago: University of Chicago Press, 1983.

Lewis, J. P., ed. *Development Strategies: A New Synthesis.* Washington DC: Overseas Development Council, 1985.

Little, I., et al. *Industries and Trade in Some Developing Countries.* London: Oxford University Press, 1970.

MacBean, A. I. *Export Instability and Economic Development.* Cambridge, MA: Harvard University Press, 1966.

Martin, M., et al. *Studies of Development and Change in the Modern World.* New York: Oxford University Press, 1988.

Meier, G. *The International Economics of Development.* New York: Harper & Row, 1968, ch. 3.

Nurkse, R. "Patterns of Trade and Development in International Trade." In *Problems of Capital Formation in Underdeveloped Countries and Patterns of Trade and Development,* edited by R. Nurkse. New York: Oxford University Press, 1970.

Prebisch, R. *Toward a New Trade Policy for Development.* New York: United Nations, 1964.

Purcell, R. B., ed. *The Newly Industrializing Countries in the Third World.* Boulder, CO: Lynne Rienner, 1989.

Skully, M. T. *Financing East Asia's Success.* New York: St. Martin's Press, 1988.

Taylor, L. *Varieties of Stabilization Experience.* New York: Oxford University Press, 1988.

Turner, L. and N. McMullen. *The Newly Industrializing Countries: Trade and Adjustment.* London: George Allen & Unwin, 1982.

Chapter 16

DEVELOPING COUNTRIES AND THE DEBT CRISIS

16.1 INTRODUCTION

One of the major problems that has plagued developing countries in recent years is a precarious debt dilemma. During the past two decades, developing countries have accumulated a total international debt amounting to $1.76 trillion in 1997. Although the seeds of the debt crisis were planted during the energy crisis of the early 1970s, it did not became apparent to the world until August 12, 1982. On that date, Mexico declared that it could no longer observe its formerly scheduled payments on its foreign debt. Subsequently, many other developing countries, especially those in Latin America, announced similar problems.

The debt crisis has had far-reaching implications for both developing countries and advanced nations. From the developing countries' standpoint, it has seriously hampered their economic development process because money that could have been used to finance development projects had to be set aside for servicing external debts. From the advanced countries' standpoint, the debt crisis has threatened the stability of the international banking system. Given this situation, many solutions have been suggested to mitigate the potential threats of the debt crisis.

Although no widespread default has erupted yet, the debt problem is by no means over. In this chapter, we first elaborate on the magnitude of the debt crisis and discuss its origin. Then, we explain the debt crisis in Mexico and other developing countries. Next, we define sovereign default and examine the impact of the debt crisis on the International Monetary Fund (IMF) and the United States. Finally, we review resolutions to the debt crisis and discuss the challenge ahead.

16.2 MAGNITUDE OF THE DEBT CRISIS

Tables 16-1 and 16-2 portray the extent of the developing countries' debt burden. Table 16-1 indicates the rate of growth of the developing countries' debt from 1990 through 1999. As this table shows, the total combined debt of developing countries $1.76 trillion in 1997. This figure is more than 17 times larger than the $100 billion total of these same countries debt in 1973. Measuring debt as a percentage of exports of goods and services, the developing countries' debt fell from its 1990 level (178.2 percent) to 140.9 percent in 1997. Thus, as the table illustrates, although the debt keeps on rising in absolute terms, the debt to export ratios have been declining in recent years.

According to Table 16-1, the debt is concentrated in two regions, Asia and the Western Hemisphere (Latin America). One striking difference between these two regions is how their external debt has been financed. In general, Latin American countries have been much more dependent on bank financing than Asian countries, which owe the bulk of their debts to official agencies and governments. Additionally, most private loans given to Latin American nations are made by a few major U.S. banks.

Table 16-2 shows the **debt-service ratios,** that is, payments of interest on total debt plus amortization as a percentage of total exports. The debt-service ratio is an indicator of indebted countries' burden. As this table indicates, there are noticeable differences among regions with regard to the debt burden. More specifically, Latin America's burden is much larger than Asia's, and has not declined nearly as fast as Asia's. Asia's debt burden decreased by 24.09 percent (from 8.3 percent in 1990 to 6.3 percent in 1997). However, Latin America's debt burden did not change during the same period (1990–1997).

TABLE 16-1
Total External Debt of Developing Countries (In Billions of U.S. $)*

	1990	1991	1992	1993	1994	1995	1996	1997	1998**	1999**
Total Debt	1,182.4	1,250.4	1,330.2	1,445.5	1,573.5	1,706.6	1,768.4	1,764.0	1,838.5	1,918.1
Debt by Region	(178.2)	(186.4)	(181.1)	(188.7)	(179.8)	(165.0)	(153.3)	(140.9)	(141.5)	(135.4)
Africa	234.7	241.7	242.1	250.0	272.6	290.9	292.1	283.6	287.0	295.7
	(225.4)	(237.1)	(235.1)	(256.1)	(270.0)	(246.3)	(220.9)	(209.5)	(216.8)	(205.2)
Asia	332.6	365.8	407.8	454.5	509.5	558.9	600.4	581.2	605.7	622.0
	(164.3)	(160.8)	(154.7)	(152.8)	(138.0)	(123.1)	(118.5)	(103.6)	(101.1)	(94.8)
Middle East & Europe	174.3	179.9	182.2	203.1	210.8	215.5	216.5	217.0	229.3	241.9
	(91.2)	(102.1)	(96.9)	(108.7)	(108.1)	(99.5)	(89.0)	(84.8)	(91.3)	(89.9)
Western Hemisphere	440.8	463.0	492.1	537.8	580.7	641.4	659.54	682.2	716.5	758.5
	(256.6)	(280.1)	(283.3)	(292.3)	(276.7)	(260.6)	(242.7)	(227.8)	(226.1)	(218.4)

*FIGURES IN PARENTHESES INDICATE DEBT AS A PERCENTAGE OF EXPORTS OF GOODS AND SERVICES.
**Estimated data.
Source: International Monetary Fund, *World Economic Outlook* (Washington, DC:IMF, May 1998) 204-205, table A38.

Although the total amount of debt in Africa is the second smallest among the regions (see Table 16-1), as Table 16-2 shows, Africa's debt-service ratio is the second largest among the regions. In other words, like Latin American nations, African nations have also been suffering from a severe debt problem. However, unlike Latin American countries, which have been dependent on bank financing, the bulk of African nations' debt is owed to official agencies and governments.

TABLE 16-2
Debt-Service Ratios of Developing Countries
(As a Percentage of Exports of Goods and Services)

	1990	1991	1992	1993	1994	1995	1996	1997	1998*	1999*
Total Percentage	9.1	9.3	9.0	9.1	8.5	8.6	8.4	8.3	8.7	8.1
Africa	10.2	10.5	9.8	10.0	10.5	10.1	10.2	10.6	11.9	10.3
Asia	8.3	8.1	7.6	7.0	6.4	6.1	6.1	6.3	6.0	5.6
Middle East & Europe	4.0	3.7	4.6	4.9	3.9	3.8	4.0	3.5	3.8	3.6
Western Hemisphere	15.4	16.3	15.6	16.3	15.6	16.7	15.7	15.4	16.1	15.6

*Estimated data.
Source: International Monetary Fund, *World Economic Outlook* (Washington, DC: IMF, May 1998) 211, Table A42.

The magnitude of the debt problem can also be observed by a closer look at the "Group of 15" (or G-15) heavily indebted countries, including Argentina, Bolivia, Brazil, Chile, Colombia, Cote d'Ivoire, Ecuador, Mexico, Morocco, Nigeria, Peru, the Philippines, Uruguay, Venezuela, and the former Yugoslavia. For these nations, the average ratio of external public debt to gross domestic product (GDP) increased by about 15 percentage points during the 1980s. Moreover, for the largest debtors—Argentina, Brazil, Mexico, and Venezuela—this ratio rose more than 9 percent during the same period.[1] Given the magnitude and the nature of debt in Latin American countries, it is no surprise that these countries have attracted so much attention in recent years. Yet, the debt crisis is obviously not limited to Latin America, but embraces most of the third-world nations.

16.3 ORIGIN OF DEVELOPING COUNTRIES' DEBT CRISIS

In hindsight, researchers have suggested a number of factors as having a significant role in the developing countries' debt crisis. These factors include advanced countries' tighter monetary policies, the second oil shock of the late 1970s, poor public-sector investment in developing countries, the worldwide recession (1980-1982), capital flight from developing countries, the appreciation of the dollar, and excess loanable funds in advanced countries. Attempting to assign appropriate weights to each of these factors is highly subjective and debatable. The relative significance of each factor differs depending on the nation under consideration. As a result, it is very hard to make generalizations. In this section, we elaborate on each of these factors, keeping in mind that each played a crucial role in fueling the debt crisis.

16.3a Tight Monetary Policies of Advanced Countries

To combat inflation in the late 1970s, the Federal Reserve Bank of the United States (the Fed) initiated a tight monetary policy in 1979. This led to a rise in the U.S. prime rate, which eventually peaked at 20.5 percent in 1981. It also caused the London Interbank Offered Rate (LIBOR) to increase sharply, from 9.5 percent in 1978 to 16.6 percent in 1981 (see Table 16-3).*

In the late 1970s, a large percentage of the developing countries' debt, especially that of Latin American countries, was based on adjustable interest rates that were tied to LIBOR. Thus, the sharp rise in LIBOR not only made new borrowing more expensive for developing countries, but also caused the interest payments on old loans to rise sharply. As a result, the debt-service ratio of the developing countries' rose significantly (see Table 16-2).

TABLE 16-3
Changes in Six-month Dollar Libor

	1978	1979	1980	1981	1982	1983	1984	1985
Percent	9.5	12.1	14.3	16.6	13.3	9.9	11.2	8.7

Source: The World Bank, *World Development Report 1986* (Washington, DC: Oxford University Press, 1986), 32.

16.3b The Second Oil Shock

One of the factors that might have contributed to the debt crisis at the start of the 1980s is the second oil shock of 1979-1980. The first oil shock occurred in 1973 and 1974, and resulted in the transfer of billions of dollars (or "petrodollars") from oil-importing nations to oil-exporting nations. This led to huge balance of payments (BOP) surpluses in the Organization of Petroleum Exporting Countries (OPEC). For example, in 1974 alone, the OPEC nations, taken as a whole, had a current account surplus of about $60 billion. Surely, given the limited capacity of OPEC nations, they could not absorb the tremendous influx of funds into goods and services; hence, they had to search for alternative ways to spend the massive funds.

---

* As we explained in Chapter 10, LIBOR is the rate of interest used between banks when they provide Eurocurrency loans to each other.

As oil-exporting nations examined options for spending their surpluses, other countries searched for means to finance their deficits. More specifically, developing countries were hard stricken by the oil price hike and desperately needed new sources of capital. This situation eventually led to the recycling of petrodollars, as illustrated in Figure 16-1. The OPEC nations exported oil to advanced countries (arrow 1) in exchange for dollars (arrow 2). These dollars were deposited in the Eurocurrency market (arrow 3) and then were loaned to developing countries (arrow 4). In turn, the developing nations used the loans (arrow 5) for net imports of goods and services from advanced countries (arrow 6).

The recycling of petrodollars provided developing nations with easy access to badly needed funds. As a result, they continued to increase their borrowing in order to finance their additional import expenditures. The second oil shock only exacerbated this situation and ignited the debt crisis in 1982. Some writers concede that oil shocks serve to explain the timing of the crisis for oil-importing developing countries, such as Argentina, Brazil, and Poland. However, the same oil shocks could have made it simpler for oil exporters, like Mexico, Nigeria, and Venezuela, to reimburse their debtors in the early 1980s. Instead, these exporters were in the same predicament as the oil importers. As a result, according to these writers, it is doubtful that the oil shocks played a significant role in touching off the debt dilemma in 1982.[2]

FIGURE 16-1
Petrodollar Recycling

The OPEC nations exported oil to advanced countries (arrow 1) in exchange for dollars (arrow 2). These dollars were deposited in the Eurocurrency market (arrow 3) and then were loaned out to developing countries (arrow 4). In turn, the developing nations used the loan proceeds to pay for (arrow 5) the net imports of goods and services from advanced nations (arrow 6).

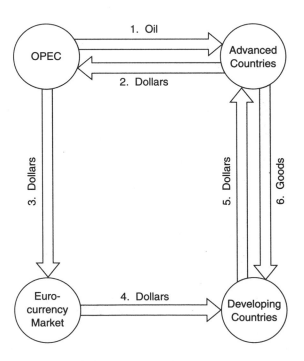

16.3c Poor Public Sector Investment in Developing Countries

Evidence indicates that the borrowed petrodollars were not invested wisely. First, a large percentage of loans went toward consumption and extravagance on the part of corrupt officials. Second, the funds were poorly invested in inefficient public enterprises. For example, the Las Truchas Steel complex in western Mexico, built with the help of loans from suppliers and from the World Bank, sustains production costs that are reportedly twice as large as those of the South Korean steel mills.[3] Finally, many of these investments were made with the expectation that domestic growth would continue at the same expansionary rate as in the 1970s. Consequently, some of the borrowed money was used for investment in energy production sources, especially hydroelectricity. The fact that the expected growth did not materialize made these investments, for the most part, fruitless.

16.3d The World Wide Recession

Fueled by the 1973-1974 quadrupling of oil prices, a short, sharp recession hit the world economy from 1974 through 1975. Table 16-4 illustrates the changes in key world economic indicators from 1973 through 1982. Besides the oil price hike, other factors that contributed to this recession included the 1972-1974 food crisis, the realignment of currencies following the collapse of the Bretton Woods system, and advanced countries' anti-inflationary policies. After three years of recovery, the world was hit by yet another oil shock. The oil prices doubled from 1979 through 1980, setting the stage for the 1980-1982 recession. Although this recession was milder than the previous one, it lasted longer due to the contractionary monetary policies employed by advanced countries to combat inflation. As a result, unemployment, which had remained at about 5 percent after the first recession, rose to more than 8 percent in advanced countries while real GDP growth became negative (see Table 16-4). This can be detected from Figure 16-2 (page 316) that illustrates growth, inflation, and unemployment rates in seven major industrialized countries. As Figure 16-3 (page 318) shows, for developing countries, growth in GDP followed an analogous pattern. The world recessions decreased the income of developing countries for two reasons: (a) The recession made their exports grow slowly or decline; and (b) the lower demand for developing countries' exports caused export prices to decline which, given a relatively inelastic demand for these exports, led to declining export revenues. With declining export revenues, developing countries were forced to increase their borrowing in order to meet their import requirements.

TABLE 16-4
Key Economic Indicators, 1973-1982 (By Percentage)

Indicators	1973	1974	1975	1976	1977	1978	1979	1980	1981	1982[a]
World trade growth (volume)[b]	12.5	4.0	-4.0	11.5	4.5	5.0	6.5	1.5	0.0	-2.0
Advanced Countries										
GDP growth	6.3	0.6	-0.7	5.1	3.6	3.9	3.2	1.3	1.0	-0.2
Unemployment	3.4	3.7	5.5	5.5	5.4	5.1	5.0	5.6	6.5	8.0
Inflation rate	7.7	11.6	10.2	7.3	7.4	7.3	7.3	8.8	8.6	7.5
Developing Countries										
Oil importers										
GDP growth	6.5	5.3	4.0	5.3	5.6	6.6	4.2	5.0	2.2	2.0
Debt—service ratio[c]	12.6	11.4	13.3	12.6	12.7	15.7	14.7	13.9	16.6	21.5
Oil exporters[d]										
GDP growth	9.1	7.2	3.7	8.2	4.8	2.4	1.2	-1.3	1.5	1.9
Debt—service ratio	12.2	6.7	7.8	8.4	11.1	14.9	15.5	13.0	15.7	19.1

[a] Estimated data.

[b] IMF data for 1973 to 1981; GATT data for 1982.

[c] Service of medium- and long-term debt as a percentage of exports of goods and services.

[d] Excludes China.

Source: The World Bank, World Development Report 1983 (Washington, DC: Oxford University Press, 1983) 1.

FIGURE 16-2
Growth, Inflation, and Unemployment in Seven Major Industrial Countries,* 1965-1985

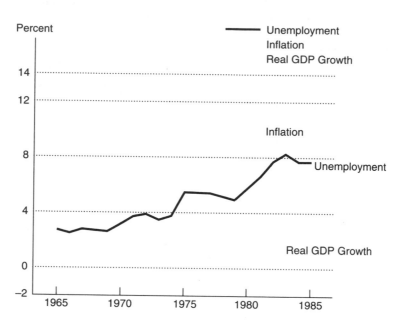

* Data are for Canada, France, Germany, Italy, Japan, Great Britian, and the United States.

Source: The World Bank, *World Development Report 1986* (New York: Oxford University Press, 1986), 16. Copyright © 1986 by The International Bank for Reconstruction and Development/The World Bank. Reprinted by permission of Oxford University Press, Inc.

16.3e Capital Flight from Developing Countries

Capital flight refers to the transfer of funds from one nation to another by firms or individuals. It happens when the expected returns from keeping funds abroad are higher or more secure than from keeping them at home. During the early 1980s, a large-scale capital flight occurred in many developing countries, contributing to their debt crisis. Unfortunately, it is extremely difficult to estimate the amount of capital flight because it often goes unreported. Nevertheless, as Table 16-5 indicates, capital flight from developing countries has been relatively large and has clearly fueled the debt crisis in these countries. From 1976 through 1985, the ratio of capital flight to debt growth ranged from 13 percent for Brazil to 115 percent for Venezuela. Given such estimates, some economists think it is useless to lend money to developing countries. They maintain that flight deepens foreign exchange shortages. This may force the developing country to devalue its national currency. As a result, it would be more expensive to import the equipment and machinery needed for the economic development process.[4] Although reversing capital flight will not eradicate the debt, it can diminish it and help to strengthen commercial bankers' basis for avoiding enhanced exposure to debtor nations.[5]

TABLE 16-5
Estimated Net Capital Flight from Developing Countries, 1976-1985

Country	Capital Flight (billions of U.S. $)	Changes in External Debt	Flight as Percentage of Debt Growth
Argentina	26	42	62
Bolivia	1	3	33
Brazil	10	80	13
Ecuador	2	7	29
India	10	22	45
Indonesia	5	27	19
Korea	12	40	30
Malaysia	12	19	63
Mexico	53	75	71
Nigeria	10	18	56
Philippines	9	23	39
South Africa	17	16	106
Uruguay	1	4	25
Venezuela	30	26	115

Source: Morgan Guaranty Trust Company of New York, *World Financial Markets,* March 1986, 13, table 10.

Capital flight is caused by several factors. Chief among these are the following:

1. **Currency overvaluation.** As we already know, a nation's overvalued domestic currency may lead to a rise in imports and a decline in exports, deteriorating the BOP. This raises the possibility of devaluation of the currency to resolve the BOP problem. Such a possibility encourages financial investors to transfer their capital abroad in order to decrease the risk and to profit from devaluation when it transpires.
2. **Interest-rate ceilings.** To encourage the development process, many developing countries impose ceilings on interest rates. Such a repressive financial policy encourages financial investors to move their funds out of the country in order to gain from higher interest rates abroad.
3. **High and variable inflation.** This leads to uncertainty and discourages investment activities. It also causes real interest rates to decline. The higher uncertainty and lower real interest rates at home encourage financial investors to transfer their money out of the country.
4. **Taxation.** If the tax rate on either investment income or wealth is lower on assets held abroad than those held at home, investors are encouraged to transfer their funds abroad.

Other factors that contribute to capital flight are slow growth, default on government obligations, limitations on currency conversion, poor investment climate, and political instability at home.

FIGURE 16-3
Growth Rate of Real GDP in Developing And Industrial Countries, 1961-1985

The diagram shows that developing countries have followed an analogous pattern with regard to the growth of their GDP.

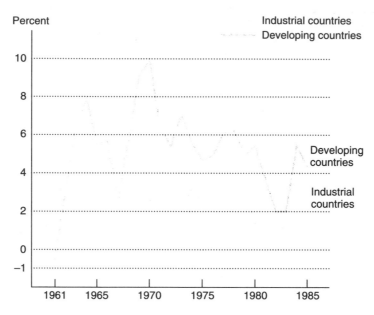

Source: The World Bank, *World Development Report 1986* (New York: Oxford University Press, 1986), 16, figure 2v1. Copyright © 1986 by The International Bank for Reconstruction and Development/The World Bank. Reprinted by permission of Oxford University Press, Inc.

16.3f Appreciation of the Dollar

As we explained in Chapter 1, 'the U.S. budget deficit, induced by tight monetary policies, caused U.S. interest rates to rise during the 1980s. The higher U.S. interest rates compared to those of other industrial nations, encouraged the movement of short-term funds from those countries to the United States. The increase in the inflow of short-term funds to the U.S. caused the U.S. dollar to appreciate.

The higher interest rates, along with appreciation of the dollar, intensified the debt problems of developing countries in two ways. First, the rising interest rates caused developing countries' interest payments on debt to escalate. Second, because the developing countries' debt was denominated in U.S. dollars, the appreciation of the dollar caused the real value of the debt to rise.

16.3g Excess Loanable Funds in Advanced Countries

Although the oil shocks of the early 1970s (1973-1974) and the late 1970s (1979-1980) resulted in a large increase in the oil-import expenditures of many developing countries, it also provided OPEC members with ample money to spend. Most of this money was invested in predominantly Western banks, providing them with excess loanable funds. This was accompanied by deregulation of U.S. financial institutions, enhancing banks' power in managing their operations. Given the excess cash and deregulation, banks found themselves anxious to expand their loans. As a result, they invested, often recklessly, in developing countries. Loans were often made without sound economic analysis or adequate assessment of risk factors. In many instances, the developing countries' expanding debt problem was practically overlooked as their governments were lured into accepting more debt than the countries could handle.

16.4 THE MEXICAN DEBT CRISIS

As we already mentioned, the debt crisis, rooted in the 1970s, became apparent to the world in August 12, 1982. On that date, Mexico, which had been regarded as one of the most credible developing countries, declared that it could no longer service its debt. Mexico's debt, amounting to more than $80 billion at the time, made it the world's second-largest developing country debtor after Brazil. During the "Mexican Weekend," Mexico had to come up with $3 billion to meet a servicing payment due on Monday, August 16. Unable to service its debt, Mexico requested and was granted the following: (a) a rescheduling of the debt's principal; (b) a moratorium on payments of principal to commercial banks; and (c) a loan from various international sources (foreign governments, central banks, and the IMF).

The timely intervention of the IMF proved to be crucial in preventing an immediate crisis. In return for the new loans, Mexico agreed to follow a stringent austerity program, demanding a cut in its massive public-sector deficits and improvement in its balance of trade.

The Mexican debt crisis resulted in part, from the discovery of an estimated 72 billion barrels of oil reserves in 1977. This made Mexico a major oil exporter, generating additional revenue for its government to spend. By the mid-1980s, about 60 percent of Mexico's export revenue was attributed to oil. This sudden influx of income encouraged rapid public investment. Funds were used to finance subsidies, social programs, and public works. In fact, government spending increased more rapidly than oil revenue. To supplement the oil revenue, some spending was financed through **seigniorage,** that is, the benefit from printing money. Other spending was financed by borrowing abroad. Aided by the fiscal stimulus, Mexico managed to attain a high rate of economic growth. In the meantime, oil prices continued to rise, providing the country with additional revenues. Given the high rate of economic growth and the rising oil revenue, foreign commercial banks, especially U.S. banks, rushed to lend money to Mexico. By 1982, about 92 percent of Mexico's loans originated from commercial banks and the rest from official lenders. As Mexico continued its borrowing from private banks, the terms of borrowing became more unfavorable. *Floating interest rates,* which rose with the growth in market rates, were increasingly employed by the commercial banks lending money to Mexico. As a result, the percentage of Mexico's loans that was based on floating rates increased from about 47 percent in the mid-1970s to 82 percent in 1982.

The rapid increase in government spending, supported by oil revenues and borrowed money, led to inflation (too much money chasing too few goods), which reached the rate of 30 percent in 1981. The worldwide recession in 1981, accompanied by rising interest rates and falling oil prices, put additional strain on the Mexican economy. The increasing interest rates raised Mexico's cost of borrowing. Falling oil prices decreased export revenues from $20 billion in 1981 to $6 billion in 1986. As a result, Mexico experienced a BOP deficit. To resolve the deficit, the Mexican authorities devalued the peso in 1982. However, they failed to reduce the government budget deficit or employ other policies that would control the deficit and thus diminish the nation's demand for additional foreign loans. Consequently, devaluation resulted in further domestic inflation without much gain to domestic employment or the BOP.

Given events described, commercial banks started to question Mexico's creditworthiness. In the summer of 1982, the country learned that its conventional foreign credit lines were drying up. By 1986, it became evident that Mexico could not meet its loan obligations. As a result, Mexican authorities entered negotiations with various commercial banks, the IMF, the World Bank, the Inter-American Development Bank, and the U.S. government. Together, they agreed on a new loan package. According to the agreement, commercial banks and multilateral institutions would increase their loans to Mexico for a two-year period. Furthermore, the United States committed a $1.5 billion contingency fund to assist Mexico for the oil revenue lost to declining prices. Accordingly, the United States pledged to make funds available to Mexico any time oil prices decreased to between $5 and $9 a barrel for 90 days or more during the first nine months of the agreement. After nine months, Mexico would have to bear the burden of falling oil prices. Additionally, if oil prices rose above $14 per barrel, Mexico would have to pay back some of its loans. The agreement proposed a number of measures to foster economic growth in Mexico. These included trade liberalization, export promotion, reduction of government subsidies and price controls, increased reliance on the private sector, and policies to enhance domestic investment.

GLOBAL INSIGHTS CASE 16.1

DEBTS OF TRANSITIONAL ECONOMIES

Like developing countries, Eastern Europe and the former Soviet Union have suffered from the debt burden. These former nonmarket economies borrowed substantially from the West before the outbreak of the debt crisis in 1982. As a result, like developing countries, they encountered debt problems in the 1980s. As the table shows, the former Soviet Union, Poland, and the former Yugoslavia were among the major debtors in the Eastern block countries. With the exception of Poland and Romania, these nations have been rated as above-average risks by the West in recent years.

The most dramatic drop ever recorded in a nation's credit rating was that of the former Soviet Union. In 1989, the international banking community placed the creditworthiness of the former Soviet Union below that of developing countries Greece, Portugal, and Saudi Arabia. After the demise of the Soviet Union, the governments of the Russian Federation, Ukraine, and most of the other newly independent states announced their intent to pay the debts owed by the Soviet Union. Although this announcement reassured creditors initially, there was considerable difficulty in establishing a mechanism for distributing the debt burdens among the independent states.

Today, world leaders realize that the smooth transition of the Eastern European countries and the former Soviet Union to market economies cannot be achieved without assistance from the West. Given this fact, in addition to humanitarian assistance, financial assistance is granted on the basis of adjustment and development plans approved by the World Bank and the IMF. Membership in these international organizations is perceived as part of the process leading to a market economy. As a result, all transitional economies have either become members or are in the process of joining these organizations.

Today, the World Bank and the IMF have become significant sources of funds for Eastern block countries. For example, in 1991, Bulgaria, Czechoslovakia, Hungary, Poland, and Romania received a combined loan of $3.6 billion and $2 billion from the IMF and the World Bank, respectively. In April 1992, the Group of Seven (Canada, France, Germany, Italy, Japan, Great Britain, and the United States) provided a multilateral financial assistance package for the Russian Federation, which included the following:

- ◆ National bank of Bulgaria.
- ◆ Approximately $18 billion in financial assistance to help the Russian Federation reform its economy
- ◆ Six billion dollars to help stabilize the ruble exchange rate
- ◆ Early membership in the IMF

In April 1993, Russian and Western governments agreed to reschedule $15 billion of the nation's $20 billion debt to its creditors. How long will the West continue to provide financial assistance to the transitional economies? Only time will tell.

EXTERNAL DEBTS OF THE SOVIET UNION AND EASTERN EUROPE, 1987

	Debt*	Debt/Exports**
Bulgaria	7.6	205
Czechoslovakia	5.1	59
East Germany	19.9	98
Hungary	17.3	310
Poland	38.9	427
Romania	2.7	19
Yugoslavia	22.5	113
Soviet Union	40.0	48

*Convertible currency debt in billions of U.S. dollars.
**Ratio of external debt to exports to the market economies.
Source: Rudiger Dornbush, *Stabilization, Debt, and Reform* (Endlewood Cliffs: NJ: Prentice Hall, 1993).
Sources: Rudiger Dornbush, *Stabilization, Debt, and Reform* (Englewood Cliffs, NJ: Prentice Hall, 1993); United Nations, *World Economic Survey 1992* (New York: United Nations, 1992).

The Mexican agreement set the stage for a new approach to dealing with the international debt crisis. Formerly, the IMF and other creditors had demanded that debtor nations employ austerity measures, which essentially required these nations to reduce their public-sector expenditures and improve their merchandise trade balances. However, starting with this agreement, creditors became more flexible and realized that austerity measures alone might be self-defeating in the long run.

16.5 DEBT CRISIS IN OTHER DEVELOPING COUNTRIES

As Mexico began to struggle with the debt crisis and search for a solution, other developing countries in Latin America found themselves in the same predicament. Notable among them were Argentina (with a total debt of about $40 billion in 1982) and Brazil (with a total debt of about $88 billion in 1982). Together, the debts of Argentina, Brazil, and Mexico ranked highest among developing countries, accounting for about one third of the total debt. Unfortunately, the debt crisis was not limited to Latin American countries but encompassed other developing countries in Africa, Asia, Europe, the Western Hemisphere, and the Middle East. As Table 16-6 indicates, at the outbreak of the debt crisis in 1982, the total debt of developing countries reached the level of $747 billion and continued to grow thereafter. In contrast to Latin American nations that owed most of their debts to commercial banks, African nations owed their debts to official agencies and governments. This provided an opportunity for the resolution of the African debt problem through the Paris Club. The **Paris Club** refers to an informal group of creditor governments who meet in the French Treasury to assure that all creditor governments grant comparable concessions. The Paris Club granted debt relief to the poorest and most heavily indebted nations, such as those in sub-Saharan Africa. However, given that most of the Latin American nations' debt was owed to commercial banks, a framework for rescheduling these debts did not yet exist. Numerous banks around the globe had invested heavily in Latin America, including major U.S. banks, such as Bank of America and Citicorp. A rampant Latin American default would have jeopardized the survival of these large banks and some of the smaller banks, threatening international financial stability. The stage was set for the international financial community to seek a solution to the debt crisis in order to prevent a potential international financial disaster.

TABLE 16-6
Summary of Developing Countries' External Debts by Regions
(In Billions of U.S. Dollars)

	1977	1978	1979	1980	1981	1982	1983	1984	1985	1986
Africa	60.9	72.2	84.0	94.1	102.8	117.2	123.3	126.8	130.0	131.5
Asia	83.4	93.8	110.2	134.3	155.0	179.8	197.1	210.9	230.9	250.1
Europe	38.2	47.3	55.3	67.0	71.5	72.7	75.3	79.1	81.4	82.2
Nonoil Middle East	25.8	30.7	36.3	41.9	46.8	52.0	56.0	59.7	65.8	69.1
Western Hemisphere	124.1	154.4	185.2	227.8	284.3	325.3	338.9	351.1	357.1	363.6
Total	332.4	398.4	471.0	565.0	660.4	747.0	790.6	827.6	865.2	896.5

Source: International Monetary Fund, *World Economic Outlook* (Washington, DC: IMF, April 1985, 262, table 45.

16.6 SOVEREIGN DEFAULT

Because developing countries are sovereign, that is, independent of all other nations, they cannot be forced to pay their debts. A nation's decision to default on its external debt is known as **sovereign default.** Most of the debt of developing countries is *sovereign debt,* composed of loans that are either borrowed or guaranteed by these nations' governments. Given this fact, some economists have suggested that debtor nations should default on their external obligations. On the surface, this action seems to be very tempting for the debtor developing countries, and its immediate impact is to relieve the country of its external obligations. However, the potential costs associated with sovereign default have made developing countries reluctant to embark on such an action. The three main costs related to sovereign default are as follows:

1. **Confiscation of assets.** An easy option open to a creditor government is to impound the debtor nations' assets that are within its jurisdiction. However, given the small size of a developing country's assets held abroad, relative to its total external debt, confiscation of assets does not seem to be a significant obstacle to sovereign default. It may, however, serve as a minor deterrent to a country that may be contemplating the default. For example, in 1986, the government of Peru repatriated almost $700 million worth of gold and silver from abroad, fearing that these assets might be confiscated by creditor governments.

2. **Exclusion from new borrowing.** A defaulted nation may be excluded from the international capital market. Such an exclusion does not even have to be orchestrated by creditor nations. If a nation defaults, prospective lenders will view that country as a bad risk, and they will be unwilling to extend new loans to that country. Even if the country succeeds in securing an external loan, it is possible that the loan's proceeds would be impounded by the country's creditors. Given the inadequacy of domestic savings in developing countries, most of these nations count on external borrowing to finance badly needed domestic investment projects. Thus, excluding these countries from the international capital market may prove to be very damaging to their process of economic development.

3. **Trade restrictions and reductions in gains from trade.** A creditor nation may ban all trade with the defaulting nation or impose trade restrictions. In practice, such a ban or restriction may be not be very effective because a country may default on loans to banks in some countries but not in others. As a result, it could maintain its ability to engage in international trade.

The most significant cost of default, resulting from reductions in gains from trade, is related to the first two costs discussed. As noted earlier, creditor nations may confiscate the assets of the debtor nations. They may also exclude the debtor nations from new borrowing. The combined effect of these actions would be a significant reduction in the volume of and gains from trade for the debtor nation.

16.7 THE INTERNATIONAL MONETARY FUND AND THE DEBT CRISIS

As we explained in Chapter 12, the IMF was set up to achieve two main goals: (a) to make sure that countries follow the agreed-on set of rules for engaging in international business, and (b) to help countries with temporary BOP problems. These objectives put the IMF in the position of a watch dog or a manager of international finance. From its inception in 1947 until the early 1970s, the IMF appeared as a powerful institution that dominated the international monetary system. This power stemmed from its ability to finance BOP deficits of member countries. However, with the breakdown of the Bretton Woods system and adoption of the managed floating exchange rate system by IMF members in 1973, the fund lost most of its power over the international monetary system. The first oil shock that hit the world in 1973 led to the influx of petrodollars from the oil-exporting nations to commercial banks. This event led to excess liquidity in such banks, enabling them to offer loans on much easier terms than the high-conditionality credit offered by the IMF. Commercial banks rushed to lend their excess reserves in order to boost their profits. A study of 13 major U.S. banks reports that from 1970 through 1976, earnings on domestic transactions increased by $40 million, while foreign earnings hit the level of $700 million. The study also finds that in 1975, 52 percent of total earnings were derived from international transactions. Such enormous profits encouraged commercial banks to become the major source of financing in developing countries, increasing their exposure in these countries.[6] As a result, the IMF became an insignificant source of BOP financing.

Aware of the situation, the IMF tried to make some adjustment to reestablish its dominance in the international monetary system. This included creation of the Extended Fund Facility (EFF) in 1974, and the Supplementary

Financing Facility (SFF) in 1979.[7] However, only a few developing countries took advantage of these facilities during the 1970s.

The international debt crisis renewed the IMF's power in managing international finance. Lending and conditionality by the IMF became more noticeable. The IMF's **conditionality,** a quid pro quo for borrowing, requires a close economic surveillance of a nation as a prerequisite for borrowing from the Fund (the IMF). This often requires borrowing developing countries to engage in budget-deficit reduction through tax revenue enhancements and decreased social spending, trade liberalization, currency devaluation, abolishment of price controls, restrictions on public-sector employment and wage rates, and restraints on credit creation. These steps are often referred to as *austerity policies.* The IMF monitors the debt targets, the exchange rate, and domestic credit for compliance.

The IMF responded to the debt crisis by increasing its own resources and enhancing its lending to developing countries. It used its power to lead debtors and creditors in the "required direction." From August 1982 through December 1984, the IMF lent $22 billion to 70 countries to support their economic adjustment programs. Beginning in 1984, almost every prominent debtor had either secured or was in the process of negotiating a stabilization package with the IMF.[8]

By the late 1980s, the IMF's image as the manager of international finance was clearly tarnished by the failure of the stabilization programs. Such failure was either due to the refusal of officials to implement austerity policies at the level demanded by the IMF or simply to the fact that the program did not work. During the 1980s, many countries that had implemented IMF stabilization programs experienced contraction in their economies, inflation, and insignificant improvement in their current accounts. By 1987, it was evident that the assets of commercial banks were lost in Latin America, and the IMF's major management strategy of influencing and coercing commercial lending had met with scant success. This is evident from the following statement made by the seven largest Latin American nations in their Declaration of Uruguay, October 27-29, 1988:

> *The conditionality of adjustment programs, sector lending, and restructuring agreements often entail measures that are inadequate and contradictory, making the economic policies more difficult in an extremely harsh economic climate.*[9]

The IMF's failure in managing the debt crisis may have been related to its lack of power in implementing its strategies. The debt crisis of the 1980s strengthened its managerial position but did not provide the IMF with the necessary power. As a result, the Fund continued to rely mainly on short-term strategies of reacting to unpredictable events instead of taking initiative on long-run issues.[10]

16.8 THE UNITED STATES AND THE DEBT CRISIS

The debt crisis has had significant implications for the United States. The decrease in the growth of Latin American economies and their suppressed demand for imports means fewer exports for the United States, leading to a decline in the U.S. gross national product (GNP). Using 1985 data, a study of U.S. exports to Argentina, Brazil, Mexico, Venezuela, and the Philippines revealed that debt-related austerity programs lowered U.S. net exports in 40 out of 61 industries studied. As a result, U.S. net trade was $13.7 billion lower than what it could have been in the absence of such programs. Additionally, the study reports that overall U.S. production fell by $21.9 billion, or 0.5 percent of the 1985 GNP.[11]

The decline in developing countries' ability to pay their debts meant trouble for creditor banks in general and the United States in particular. A default by one of the larger debtors or a group of the smaller debtors could create substantial liquidity problems in the world financial system. Given the magnitude of investment by U.S. giants in Latin America in 1983 (see Table 16-7), the United States considered the responsibility of deterring default, even by a single nation, crucial. A default by even one country, such as Mexico, could have generated a chain reaction of bank failures affecting many nations. The United States and other nations did not want a replay of the rampant banking disaster that started the Great Depression.

TABLE 16-7
Top U.S. Bank Loans to Major Latin American Debtor Nations, December 1983
(In Millions of U.S. Dollars)

Bank	Argentina	Brazil	Mexico	Venezuela	Total
Citicorp	1,090	4,700	2,900	1,500	10,190
Bank of America	300	2,484	2,741	1,614	7,139
Manufacturers Hanover	1,321	2,130	1,915	1,084	6,441
Chase Manhattan	775	2,560	1,553	1,226	6,114
J. P. Morgan	741	1,785	1,174	464	4,164
Chemical	370	1,276	1,414	776	3,836
Bankers Trust	230	743	1,286	436	2,695

Source: Brian Kettell and George Magunus, *The International Debt Game* (Cambridge: Ballinger Publishing Company, 1986), x.

These considerations led the United States to get seriously involved with the debt crisis, searching for viable solutions. In the next section, we study the resolutions to the debt crisis and elaborate on the plans that were suggested by the United States to deal with this dilemma.

16.9 SOLUTIONS TO THE DEBT CRISIS

During the 1970s and early 1980s, creditors took a case-by-case approach in dealing with the debt crisis. By the mid-1980s, it was evident that this approach had not greatly relieved the problem. As a result, several solutions were proposed. Although some of these solutions have proven unworthy, others have helped to alleviate the problem, though not to the degree necessary. In this section, we concentrate on some of the widely discussed proposals.

16.9a Debt-Equity Swap

Debt-equity swaps are methods used to transform some of the existing debt to equity. A foreign buyer, usually a multinational corporation (MNC), purchases a country's debt at a discount and sells it back to the debtor country in return for its domestic currency. The buyer is then required to use this currency to purchase shares of stock in a domestic enterprise or to make a direct investment in the country. As a result, the developing country's external debts and interest obligations decrease. Additionally, the creditor disposes a bond whose repayment is questionable, but instead carries shares of stock in an existing enterprise in the developing country.

Examples of MNCs that have engaged in debt-equity swaps include Fiat, Dow Chemical Company, and Nissan Corporation. Fiat purchased Brazilian debt at a discount and exchanged it for the cruzado (the Brazilian currency). It then used the proceeds to augment its plant in Brazil. Dow Chemical Company and Nissan Corporation engaged in similar arrangements with Chile and Mexico, respectively.

The United States supported the debt-equity swaps and proposed that the World Bank promote this arrangement. This encouraged countries such as Argentina, Brazil, Mexico, Chile, and the Philippines, to participate in debt-equity swaps.

GLOBAL INSIGHTS CASE 16.2

Trade Liberalization and the Debt Crisis

Many debt-stricken developing nations have reacted to their dilemma by trying new policies that strive to stimulate long-term economic growth and reduce fiscal debts. Many of these nations have adopted policies that aim at promotion of free markets and elimination of government restrictions of domestic and international trade. For example, soon after his inauguration in July 1989, Carlos Menem, the president of Argentina, introduced new policies to achieve the following three objectives:

1. Increasing market orientation
2. Encouraging freer international trade
3. Privatizing state-owned enterprises

These policies were a reversal of Argentina's strategies for inward-oriented development and concentrated intervention in the market mechanism that had existed for more than a decade. Other countries that have embarked on market-oriented reforms include Mexico, Venezuela, and Poland. Market-oriented reforms have been identified with the restoration of sustained growth in Chile, Mauririus (after 1984), and Mexico (after 1988). However, the new reforms have not yet eliminated economic and political instability in these nations. Efforts to execute the reforms have elicited great resistance and have not yielded fast improvement.

It seems that the worst is over for the debt-stricken countries. In many of these nations, debt-exports and deb-GNP ratios have substantially decreased. Data show that a large percentage of debt owned by affected nations in 1982 has already been paid. For example, it is estimated that from 1983 to 1989, Argentina has paid 40 percent of its debt; Brazil, 38 percent; Mexico, 62 percent; Nigeria, 30 percent; and Venezuela, 75 percent.

Sources: D. Cohen, "The Debt Crisis: A Postmortem," in O. J. Blanchard and S. Fischer, eds, *NBER Macroeconomics Annual 1992* (Cambridge, MA: The MIT Press, 1992), 70-71; L. B. Krause and K. Kihwan, eds., *Liberalization in the Process of Economic Development* (Berkely, CA: University of California Press, 1991); World Bank, *World Development Report 1991* (New York: Oxford University Press, 1991).

16.9b The Baker Plan

During the early 1980s, the United States insisted that debtor developing countries pay the full interest owed to U.S. banks. By 1985, however, it was evident that the austerity policies of the previous few years had not greatly reduced the debt problem. Latin American nations found themselves deeper in debt, and U.S. policymakers realized the restraints the debt crisis inflicted upon the growth of these nations and thus their demand for U.S. exports. In the fall of 1985, the U.S. Secretary of Treasury, James Baker, presented a plan to deal with the continuing dilemma. The plan called for a number of measures to alleviate the problems of the highly indebted developing countries. These measures included:

1. Additional funding by commercial banks
2. Provision of credit by the IMF and the Inter-American Development Bank
3. World Bank structural assistance
4. Subsidies from trade surplus nations, such as Japan
5. Promotion of a world economic environment that supports continued and enlarged market access for everyone and supplements debtors' sustained growth

In summary, the Baker Plan emphasized growth over austerity in developing countries, based on funds generated by trade surplus nations, the IMF, the World Bank, the Inter-American Development Bank, and commercial banks. The plan called for $20 billion in loans from commercial banks, and $9 billion in additional loans from multilateral agencies over and above the money that was normally lent to the 15 most-indebted nations. Unfortunately, however, the large commercial banks were very reluctant to go along with the plan. In fact, these banks actually withdrew $2 billion instead of lending the additional $20 billion called for. As the debt problem persisted into 1988, it was evident that the Baker Plan was inadequate to resolve the crisis. This resulted in a major alteration of the plan and gave birth to the Brady Plan.

GLOBAL INSIGHTS CASE 16.3

Tied-Aid Agreements

Tied aid is officially supported concessional financing linked to procurement in the donor country. It distorts trade when used to win contracts for capital goods exports rather than to provide true aid. Tied aid can misallocate resources from more efficient to less efficient producers whose governments offer such financing.

When used for exports promotion, tied aid can also distort aid flows by directing scarce resources away from high-priority development projects to projects of interest to industries in donor countries. Traditionally, tied aid has directed donor support toward, for example, large electric power generation and telecommunication projects and away from social sector projects. This skewing of resources allocation in developing countries increases the capital intensity of development and burdens the recipient country with high maintenance expenditures in the future.

In response to complaints from exporters that they often faced tied-aid competition for capital goods projects, the United States negotiated rules in the OECD to govern tied-aid programs. The rules, dubbed the Helsinki Package, became effective in February 1992. They apply to nonconcessional financing and stipulate that higher income developing countries (those with per capita above $3,035) are ineligible for all tied aid. The least developed countries remain eligible for all types of financing because of their desperate shortage of capital. For countries in between, such as China, Indonesia, and India, tied aid is prohibited for projects that can generate cash flows sufficient to repay debt on commercial terms.

It is hoped that the Helsinki rules will reduce dislocations and maximize the total resources—aid and commercial financing—available to promote economic development. Last year the OECD issued guidelines for the use of tied aid, to draw the line between projects that should receive tied aid. Since 1992, under the Helsinki Package, annual tied aid has declined from $10 billion to about $4 billion. The tied aid that remains has been shifted away from major capital projects capable of supporting financing on commercial terms to legitimate aid projects such as water and sewerage, and health and other social services.

Source: U.S. Government Printing Office, *Economic Report of the President* (Washington DC: U.S. Government Printing Office, 1997), 275, Box 7-5, Reprinted.

16.9c The Brady Plan

The Brady Plan was an extension of the Baker Plan. It took shape in March 1989 and enhanced the Baker Plan by augmenting debt reduction and multilaterally financed loan guarantees. The plan was unclear about how its suggestions were to be implemented. However, one thing was clear: The market-based debt reduction (the decrease in nations' external debts through "voluntary" market transactions) had to be promoted by official agencies. The plan targeted a 20-percent, or $70 billion, reduction in the $350 billion that developing countries owed to commercial banks in advanced countries. The World Bank, the IMF, and Japan committed a combined total of $29.5 billion from 1989 through 1992. Although these strategies succeeded in alleviating the debt crisis to some degree by the early 1990s, the dilemma still lingers on.

16.10 PHASES OF THE DEBT CRISIS

In the last section, we elaborated on the most widely discussed proposals for resolving the debt crisis. Equipped with this knowledge, we now look at the debt crisis from an historical perspective. The debt crisis has gone through several phases since 1982. In the first phase, commercial banks put together short-term emergency packages that extended the maturity of some loans that were due over the next two years or over five to seven years. Additionally, they committed new money to cover any immediate needs, such as the 1982-1983 restructuring of Argentina, Brazil, and Mexico. Bank lending under these situations is known as *concerted lending,* a tactful terminology for lending that was, in many circumstances, involuntary. Under this arrangement, banks had to contribute new money in proportion to their loan exposure at the beginning of the crisis.

The second phase was a period aimed at buying time. Concerted lending, conceived as an emergency measure, was designed to give nations time to achieve reforms and banks time to raise reserves and capital. It was agreed that the IMF would oversee a nation's economic accomplishment and provide the resultant information to commercial banks. During this phase, in 1984, Mexico agreed with its creditor banks on the first multiyear restructuring agreement. The Mexican restructuring also highlighted the first use of debt-equity swaps.

The third phase began with the announcement of the Baker Plan in October 1985. As we mentioned earlier, this plan emphasized growth-oriented reforms for debtor countries in return for new loans from banks. Until then, the debt-relief strategy was dominated by the IMF. Beginning with this phase, however, the World Bank joined the IMF in combating the debt crisis. Also, with this phase, Mexico and Chile started to emphasize structural adjustment in the areas of privatization and trade.

The fourth phase started with the introduction of the Brady Plan in March 1989. As we explained earlier, the Brady plan built on the Baker Plan by enhancing debt reduction and multilaterally financed loan guarantees. The plan was employed to restructure the commercial bank debts of Costa Rica, Nigeria, Venezuela, the Philippines, and Uruguay. Additionally, the plan provided the basis for debt agreements with Argentina and Brazil.

16.11 THE CHALLENGE AHEAD

The debt crisis hit the world in 1982 and attracted a great deal of attention during the 1980s. Some observers suggested that the crisis would be over almost exactly 10 years after it began. As the 1980s wore on, it became apparent that these observers were overly optimistic. Debtors continued to experience problems in fully servicing their debts, and banks increasingly treated their loans to debt-stricken nations as "value impaired." In much of Africa and some segments of Latin America today, access to world capital markets is either nonexistent or remains impaired. The former communist nations of Eastern Europe and the new Commonwealth of Independent States (CIS) are in need of resource transfers from abroad as they attempt to establish market economies in the face of heavy foreign debt burdens.

Nevertheless, to date, there has been a significant amount of progress. In October 1992, Brazil agreed to restructure the $44 billion it owed to foreign banks.[12] In April 1992, Argentina reached an accord with its creditor banks, covering $23 billion of medium-term debt and $8 billion of overdue interest. The Philippines completed the second phase of a two-part agreement with its creditor banks in February 1992, providing a framework for "debt and debt-service reduction."[*] For its part, the U.S. government has continued to follow several multilateral and bilateral initiatives to decrease the debt burden of the poorest developing nations. In mid-December 1994, the Paris Club of creditor countries, including the United States, agreed on more favorable debt reduction terms, referred to as "Naples Terms." Naples Terms aimed at lowering the debts of heavily indebted poor nations by up to 67 percent. During the

---

[*] The first part was signed in January 1990.

1996 fiscal year, the United States negotiated debt-reduction agreements with seven nations under Naples Terms. In February 1996, the United States' Congress commissioned a pilot debt buyback and swap initiative for lower income Latin American and Caribbean nations that are active in economic reforms, particularly investment reforms. Countries must also meet certain political principles, including democratic governments, and good records in the areas of human rights, narcotics, and terrorism. Such progress has convinced some observers that the debt crisis is over. To others, however, the assertion that the situation has improved is questionable. Nonetheless, it is clear there are still nations, such as Peru and Ecuador, that have yet to put the problem behind them. Additionally, the debt crisis has caused policymakers in developing countries to shift economic discussion away from income distribution and poverty, which are the crucial problems that exist in many of these countries. If the debt crisis were under control, there would be enormous pressure on policymakers in both developing and advanced countries to address these problems. This is a challenge that policymakers will have to deal with in the future.[13] A new challenge to officials in advanced countries is the growing debt burden in Russia. A solution to this problem is a prerequisite to Russia's smooth transition from communism to a free market.[14]

Today's international debt strategy reflects a realization that many of the heavily indebted developing countries cannot resolve their debt problems by themselves, and some of the debt must be written off as uncollectible. Given this fact, creditors have been increasingly willing to write off these debts as uncollectible subject to implementation of the required structural changes for adjustment by the debtor developing countries.[15]

Although the employment of the new strategy has not resulted in a significant decrease in the debt itself, progress toward resolving the problem seems well on its way. Some heavily indebted nations, chiefly in Latin America, that had been closed out of financial markets are again considered creditworthy. However, the conditions in smaller nations look less optimistic.

The vast increase in the inflow of funds to heavily indebted developing countries in 1991 underlined the major gain of the "debt-regularization process"—new lending, foreign portfolio investment, the return of capital flight, and new investment advancement. What seems to be needed in the years ahead is for the inflow of funds to continue. This, in turn, depends on the following factors: the growth of the world economy, leading to higher export earnings for developing countries; continued progress in adjustment reforms with greater social equality in developing countries; political tranquility; and an open market that is free from protectionist measures against developing countries. The likely outcome is a long, painful period in which indebted developing countries endure more economic hardships than they would prefer.

16.12 SUMMARY

1. During the past two decades, developing countries have accumulated a total international debt amounting to $1.76 trillion in 1997.

2. Although the seeds of the debt crisis were planted during the energy crisis of the early 1970s, it did not become apparent to the world until August 12, 1982, when Mexico declared it could no longer service its debt.

3. In general, Latin American countries have been much more dependent on bank financing than Asian countries. Additionally, most private loans given to Latin American nations are made by a few major U.S. banks.

4. Researchers have suggested a number of factors as having a significant role in the developing countries' debt crisis. These factors include advanced countries' tighter monetary policies, the second oil shock of the late 1970s, poor public-sector investment in developing countries, the worldwide recession (1980-1982), capital flight from developing countries, the appreciation of the dollar, and excess loanable funds in advanced countries.

5. Capital flight refers to the transfer of funds from one nation to another by firms or individuals. It happens when the expected returns from keeping funds abroad are higher or more secure than from keeping them at home.

6. Capital flight is caused by several factors. Chief among these factors are currency overvaluation, interest-rate ceilings, high and variable inflation, and high domestic tax rates.

7. Starting with the Mexican agreement, creditors became more flexible and realized that austerity measures alone might be self-defeating in the long run.

8. Together, the debts of Argentina, Brazil, and Mexico ranked highest among developing countries, accounting for about one third of the total debt in 1982.
9. Unfortunately, the debt crisis was not limited to Latin American countries, but encompassed other developing nations in Africa, Asia, Europe, the Western Hemisphere, and the Middle East.
10. A nation's decision to default on its external debt is known as sovereign default.
11. The three main costs related to sovereign default are (a) confiscation of assets; (b) exclusion from new borrowing; and (c) trade restrictions and reductions in gains from trade.
12. The international debt crisis renewed the IMF's power in managing international finance.
13. The decline in developing countries' ability to pay their debts meant trouble for creditor banks in general and the United States in particular.
14. Debt-equity swaps are methods used to transform some of the existing debt to equity.
15. The Baker Plan emphasized growth over austerity in developing countries, based on funds generated by trade surplus nations, the IMF, the World Bank, the Inter-American Development Bank, and commercial banks.
16. The Brady Plan enhanced the Baker Plan by augmenting debt reduction and multilaterally financed loan guarantees.

Review Questions

1. What factors caused the debt crisis of developing countries to occur in the 1980s? Explain.
2. Why did the debt crisis of the 1980s jeopardize the stability of the world's financial system? Explain.
3. What have been the implications of the debt crisis for both advanced and developing countries? Explain.
4. What factors give rise to capital flight? Explain.
5. What is "sovereign default?" What factors are associated with sovereign default? Explain.
6. What is the major difference between the nature of the debt crisis in Latin America and Asia?
7. What factors caused the Mexican debt crisis to occur? Explain.
8. What has been the major impact of the debt crisis on the IMF? Explain.
9. What implications has the debt crisis had for the United States? Explain.
10. What is the difference between the Baker Plan and the Brady Plan? Explain.
11. What phases has the debt crisis gone through? Explain.

Problems

1. Why do you think a debtor nation prefers to borrow from a commercial bank rather than from the IMF? Explain.
2. Given the Japanese position as the United States' largest foreign creditor, the U.S. government should default on its foreign debt to Japan in order to resolve its debt problem.
    Do you agree with this statement? Discuss.
3. In choosing a lender, should developing countries take into consideration the currency in which the loan is denominated? Discuss.
4. The debt problem is caused by developing countries themselves. Thus, it is their responsibility to resolve the debt problem on their own, rather than involving advanced countries.
    Do you agree with this statement? Discuss.
5. Capital flight is one of the major factors responsible for the debt burden in some developing countries. Because capital flight creates a large debt for a government but generates a countervailing foreign asset for citizens who carry funds abroad, the overall net debt of the nation as a whole does not change. Thus, nations whose external debts are mainly due to capital flight should encounter no debt problem.
    Do you agree with this statement? Explain.
6. Developing countries' debt was frequently undertaken by state-owned companies. Some of these nations have embarked on privatization by selling state-owned companies to the private sector. Do you think the amount

of borrowing by these nations would have been higher or lower if they had moved on privatization earlier? Discuss.

7. What is the possible impact of lifting trade barriers on a nations's ability to borrow in the international financial market? Explain.

Notes

1. Pablo Guidotti and Manmohan S. Kumar, "Managing Domestic Public Debt," *Finance and Development* (September 1992): 9-12.
2. Peter H. Lindert, *International Economics,* 9th ed. (Homewood, IL: Irwin, 1991), 555.
3. Pedro P. Kucznski, *Latin American Debt* (Maryland: Johns Hopkins University Press, 1988), 64,
4. John T. Cuddington, *Capital Flight: Estimates, Issues, and Explanations.* Princeton Studies in International Finance, no. 58 (Princeton, NJ: Princeton University, 1986).
5. Donald R. Lessard and John Williamson, eds., *Capital Flight and Third-World Debt* (Washington, DC: Institute for International Economics, 1987); John Williamson and Donald R. Lessard, *Capital Flight: The Problem and Policy Responses* (Washington, DC: Institute for International Economics, 1987).
6. L. R. Bernal, "Resolving the Global Debt Crisis," *Economica Internazionale* 40 (May-August 1987): 155-171.
7. Jonathan D. Aronson, *Money and Power* (London: Sage Publications, 1977), 178.
8. "Muddling Through," *The Economist,* (6 February 1988), 80.
9. "Latin American Declaration Deplores Adverse Impact of Debt, Projectionism," *IMF Survey* (November 14, 1988), 354-355.
10. Parviz Asheghian, "International Banking Management and the Debt Crisis," *International Academy of Management and Marketing, 1991 Proceedings,* 716-735.
11. Gerald Berg, "The Effects of External Debts of Mexico, Brazil, Argentina, Venezuela, and the Philippines on the United States," *Applied Economics* 20 (1988): 939-956.
12. "Brazilian Accord Puts End to Debt Crisis in Region, But Not to Economic Troubles," *The Wall Street Journal,* 10 July 1992, A12.
13. *Ibid;* U.S. Government Printing Office, *Economic Report of the President* (Washington DC: U.S. Government Printing Office, 1998), 275.
14. "Debt Burden Is Very Perilous, Russian Warns," *The Wall Street Journal,* 14 July 1993, A9.
15. United Nations, *World Economic Survey 1992* (New York: United Nations), 157-164.

Suggested Readings

Bergsten, Fred, and William Cline. *Bank Lending to Developing Countries: The Policy Alternatives.* Washington DC: Institute for International Economic, November 1987.

Bouchet, M. H. *The Political Economy of International Debt.* Westport, CT: Greenwood Press, 1987.

Clark, John, and Eliot Kalter. "Recent Innovation in Debt Restructuring." *Finance and Development* (September 1992): 6-8.

Cline, William. "International Debt: Progress and Strategy." *Finance and Development* (June 1987): 9-11. "International Debt: From Crisis to Recovery." *American Economic Review, Papers and Proceedings* 75, no. 2 (May 1985): 185-190. *Mobilizing Bank Lending to Debtor Countries.* Washington, DC: Institute for International Economics, 1987.

Corden, W. Max. "Debt Relief and Adjustment Incentives." *International Monetary Fund Staff Papers* 35, no. 4 (December 1988): 628-643.

Darity, W. L., and B. Horn. *The Loan Pushers: The Role of Commercial Banks in the International Debt Crisis.* Cambridge, MA: Ballinger, 1988.

Dornbusch, Rudiger. "Latin American Debt Problem: Anatomy and Solutions." In *Debt and Democracy in Latin America,* edited by Barbara Stallings and Robert Kaufman. Boulder, CO: Westview Press, 1989.

Dornbusch, Rudiger, and Stanley Fischer. "The World Debt Problem: Origins and Prospects." *Journal of Development Planning* (1984): 57-81.

Fisher, Stanley, and Ishrat Husain. "Managing the Debt Crisis." *Challenge: The Magazine of Economic Affairs* 28, no. 2 (June 1990): 24-27.

Felix, David. "How to Resolve Latin America's Debt Crisis." *Challenge: The Magazine of Economic Affairs* 28, no. 5 (November/December 1985): 44-51.

Foxely, Alejandro. "Latin American Development After the Debt Crisis." *Journal of Economic Development* 27 (1987): 201-225.

Kenen, Peter. "Organizing Debt Relief: The Need for a New Institution." *Journal of Economic Perspectives* (Winter 1990): 7-18.

Lancaster, Carol, and John Williamson, eds. *African Debt and Financing.* Washington, DC: Institute for International Economics, 1986.

Nowzad, Bahman. "Lessons of the Debt Decade." *Finance and Development* 27, no. 1 (March 1990): 9-13.

Orlando, Frank, and Simon Tietel. "Latin America's External Debt Problem: Debt Servicing Strategies Comparable With Long-Term Economic Growth." *Economic Development and Cultural Change* (April 1986): 641-671.

Rhode, William R. "Third-World Debt: The Disaster that Didn't Happen." *The Economist* (12 September 1992): 21-23.

Sachs, Jeffrey D. "The Debt Crisis at a Turning Point." *Challenge* (May-June 1988): 17-26.

Sachs, Jeffrey D., ed. *Developing Country Debt and the World Economy.* Chicago: University of Chicago Press, 1989.

Trebat, Thomas. "Latin American Debt in the Eighties: A Case Study of Brazil." In *Foreign Debt and Latin American Development,* edited by Antonio Jorge, et al. New York: Pergamon Press, 1983.

Ukpolo, Victor, "Foreign Debt and Economic Development: The Case of Sub-Sahran African Economies." *Journal of Third World Studies* 9, no. 1 (1992): 199-214.

Williamson, John, *Voluntary Approaches to Debt Relief.* Washington DC: September 1988, revised June 1989.

Part 5

FOREIGN DIRECT INVESTMENT AND MULTINATIONAL CORPORATIONS

In the first three parts of this book, we described and analyzed international economic relations in the context of trade in goods and services. However, economic relations between nations are not limited to trade in goods and services, but also include investment of capital in tangible and intangible assets.

Multinational corporations (MNCs) are the major source of capital investment across national boundaries. Today, large MNCs hold the financial and market power to make decisions that influence the amount, configuration, and course of international trade and investment. These corporate giants have become autonomous players in the international economic scene and exert significant influence on government decision-making processes. With the increasing importance of MNCs to the world economy, questions are being raised about the fundamental roles these corporations are expected to perform in society. Although MNCs have met with resistance in both home and host countries, they have stirred more controversies in developing countries than in advanced countries. Such controversies have added to the uncertainty of the future events MNCs must deal with.

The purpose of this part is to provide an overview of MNCs and elaborate on the role they play in the global economy. Chapter 17 investigates the nature and scope of MNCs. Chapter 18 elaborates on theories of international factor movements and multinational corporations; it also covers labor migration. Finally, Chapter 19 discusses controversies surrounding MNCs.

Chapter 17

NATURE AND SCOPE OF MULTINATIONAL CORPORATIONS

17.1 INTRODUCTION

Our attention so far has been devoted to international trade, that is, the export and import of goods and services. However, trade in goods and services is only part of international business.

International business can be defined as those business transactions among individuals, firms, or other entities (both private and public) that occur across national boundaries. These activities include the movement of goods (the importing and exporting of commodities); the transaction of services, such as management, accounting, marketing, finance, and legal services; the investment of capital in tangible assets, such as manufacturing, agriculture, mining, petroleum production, transportation, and communications media; and transactions in intangible assets, such as trademarks, patents, and the licensing of manufacturing technology.

A multinational corporation (MNC) is the principal player in international business. To engage in international business, MNCs rely heavily on foreign direct investment (FDI), that is, the acquisition of a controlling interest in a company or facility. Although their history goes back a long way, the mid-nineteenth century can be marked as an important period in the development of MNCs. During this period, a number of companies began expanding their operations by establishing branch offices in foreign countries. Alfred Nobel, the Swedish entrepreneur, started his first foreign plant in Hamburg, Germany, in 1866. The Singer Company established a plant in Glasgow, Scotland, in 1867. Fredrick Bayer founded dye factories in Russia in 1876, in France in 1882, and in Belgium in 1908.

The proliferation of MNCs and their emergence as a pivotal global economic force had to await the significant postwar advancement in transportation and communications and enormous liberalization of international trade and payments that began to gather momentum in the late 1950s. During the 1960s, U.S. direct investment in foreign countries grew rapidly—mainly in Canada and Europe—accounting for roughly 70 percent of the net FDI in the world during the post-World War II period through the 1960s. However, following this period, the share of U.S. net FDI relative to the total amount of FDI by advanced countries in the world gradually declined, reaching the approximate levels of 63 percent in 1970, 54 percent in 1975, 44.5 percent in 1980, 39 percent in 1991, and 23.33 percent in 1997.[*1]

Starting with the 1970s, the picture of international business began to change. Advances in communications media, speedier worldwide travel made possible by jet-age technology, and lower costs of production in developing countries resulted in the expansion of international business. During this period, the former West Germany, Great Britain, other European countries, Canada, and Japan started catching up with the United States. Japan's rapid growth in the automobile and steel industries, for example, placed that country's corporations on the list of the 50 largest corporations in the world.

The international business activities of developing countries have increased in recent years as well. Many companies from developing countries (such as Argentina, Brazil, Hong Kong, India, South Korea, and Taiwan) have engaged in FDI, mainly in manufacturing in other developing countries. Because of their "scaled-down," relatively more labor-intensive technology and their lower managerial and overhead costs, these companies have been able to produce relatively low-cost products. These products have successfully competed in the world market, mainly on the basis of their low prices.

---

* As we explain later in this chapter, foreign direct investment involves an investment in the equity securities of a foreign firm that is large enough to exert effective control over the firm.

All of these events have contributed to the weakening position of the United States as the world leader in international business. Later in this chapter we use data to provide further explanations regarding the United States' position in the world of international business.[2]

Today, the yearly sales of such MNCs as General Motors, Exxon, and Ford Motor Company, surpass the total national income of all but a handful of nations. It is estimated that the sales between foreign subsidiaries of the same company may account for roughly 25 percent of global trade. Such estimates emphasize that the competitiveness of business in this age is beyond the grasp of any purely domestic company. In such a competitive environment, the life cycles of different products are getting shorter, and it is costlier and harder to develop new products. This makes the jobs of today's corporate managers more challenging. To turn these challenges into opportunities, today's managers need to develop products and bring them to global markets much faster than ever before.

The purpose of this chapter is to provide an understanding of the nature and scope of MNCs. First, we define the concept of MNC and present the world's major MNCs. Next, we differentiate between FDI and portfolio investment, providing some statistics for FDI. We also elaborate on MNCs' channels of entry into international business. Finally, we discuss technology transfer by MNCs.

17.2 DEFINITION OF MULTINATIONAL CORPORATION

There is no consensus among scholars regarding the definition of MNC. Differences in definitions stem from the different types of MNCs, each type following a specific purpose. Consequently, each definition is based on a given criterion that is considered indicative of the purpose and type of MNC. Three major criteria have been used: (a) a structural criterion, (b) a performance criterion, and (c) a behavioral criterion.

Using the **structural criterion,** an MNC can be defined by two approaches. In the first approach, multinationality is defined by the number of countries in which a firm is operating. This means that a firm has its base in one country, such as the United States, and operates in a number of other countries. In the second approach, ownership characteristics are used as the basis for definition. Since the term "multi" means "many," the multinational firm refers to a firm that is owned or operated by individuals from many nations. Thus, an MNC can be defined either by the nationality of its owners or by the nationality of its top management.

If the first definition is adopted, an MNC is a firm that makes its stocks available to all the countries in which it is operating. If the second definition is adopted, a firm could be considered an MNC if its top management is composed of people from various countries. It is assumed that such individuals would have a worldwide outlook and would be less prone to follow the interest of any specific nation.

Using the **performance criterion,** the MNC can be defined on the basis of the absolute amount or the relative share (percentage) of assets, number of employees, sales, or earnings in a foreign country. According to the absolute measure, a firm is considered an MNC if it has allocated a "certain amount" of its resources to its foreign operations. By the relative measure, a firm is considered an MNC if it allocates a "significant portion," that is, a very large percentage, of its resources to foreign operations. This measure implies that the magnitude of the firm's foreign operations is so significant that it depends on other countries for its growth and financial stability.

Using the **behavioral criterion,** a firm can be classified as multinational if its top management "thinks internationally." In this definition, it is assumed that because the MNC is concerned with more than one country, its top management sees the entire world as the domain of their operation. Thus, the international manager is considered a person who searches for investment opportunities in the world market rather than being confined to the domestic market.[3]

In this book, we define a multinational corporation as a group of corporations that is operating in different countries but is controlled by its headquarters in a given country. We refer to the country that houses the headquarters of an MNC as the home country and to other countries as host countries. We maintain that the ownership of MNCs can be public, private, or mixed.

17.3 THE WORLD'S MAJOR MULTINATIONAL CORPORATIONS

Table 17-1 shows the 50 largest corporations, ranked on the basis of their total sales in 1995. Table 17-2 indicates, for each country, the number of firms, total sales, and the percentage sale of the world's largest corporations among the major investing countries in 1995.

TABLE 17-1
The World Fifty Largest Corporations Ranked by Sales

Rank 1995	1994	Company	Headquarters	Sales $Millions	Profits $Millions
1	1	Mitsubishi	Japan	184,365.2	346.2
2	2	Mitsu	Japan	181,518.7	314.8
3	3	Itochu	Japan	169,164.6	121.2
4	5	General Motors	U.S.	168,828.6	6,8880.7
5	4	Sumitomo	Japan	167,530.7	210.5
6	6	Marubeni	Japan	161,057.4	156.6
7	7	Ford Motor	U.S.	137,137.0	4,139.0
8	11	Toyota Motor	Japan	111,052.0	2,662.4
9	8	Exxon	U.S.	110,009.0	6,470.0
10	10	Royal Dutch/ Shell Group	Brit./Neth.	109,833.7	6,904.6
11	9	Nissho Iwai	Japan	97,886.4	(259.5)
12	12	Wal-Mart Stores	U.S.	93,627.0	2,740.0
13	13	Hitachi	Japan	84,167.1	1,468.8
14	14	Nippon Life Insurance	Japan	83,206.7	2,426.6
15	16	Nippon Telegraph & Telephone	Japan	81,937.2	2,209.1
16	15	AT & T	U.S.	79,609.0	139.0
17	20	Daimler-Benz	Germany	72,256.1	(3,959.3)
18	21	Intl. Business Machines	U.S.	71,940.0	4,178.0
19	17	Matsushita Electric Industrial	Japan	70,398.4	(589.2)
20	19	General Electric	U.S.	70,028.0	6,573.0
21	18	Tomen	Japan	67,755.8	46.2
22	22	Mobil	U.S.	66,724.0	2,376.0
23	23	Nissan Motor	Japan	62,568.5	(916.1)
24	34	Volkswagen	Germany	61,489.1	247.0
25	30	Siemens	Germany	60,673.6	1,268.0
26	26	Dai-Ichi Mutual Life Insurance	Japan	58,052.4	1,732.2
27	31	British Petroleum	Britain	56,981.9	1,770.7
28	.	Metro Holding	Switzerland	56,459.0	403.5
29	33	U.S. Postal Service	U.S.	54,293.5	1,770.3
30	29	Chrysler	U.S.	53,195.0	2,025.0
31	28	Philip Morris	U.S.	53,139.0	5,450.0
32	36	Toshiba	Japan	53,046.9	936.5
33	32	Tokyo Electric Power	Japan	52,361.5	536.9
34	52	Daewoo	South Korea	51,215.3	N.A.
35	24	Nichimen	Japan	50,841.9	44.3
36	35	Sumitomo Life Insurance	Japan	50,710.5	1,871.6
27	25	Kanematsu	Japan	49,838.5	3.5
38	37	Unilever	Britain/Netherlands	49,738.0	2,324.7
39	39	Nestle	Switzerland	47,780.4	2,468.4
40	43	Sony	Japan	47,581.5	562.1
41	41	Fiat	Italy	46,467.6	1,318.0
42	44	Veba Group	Germany	46,279.9	1,336.3
43	40	Deutsche Telekom	Germany	46,148.7	3,678.8
44	42	Allianz Holding	Germany	46,044.9	592.4
45	48	NEC	Japan	45,557.3	799.5
46	45	Honda Motor	Japan	44,055.6	733.5
47	46	Elf Aquitaine	France	43,618.4	1,009.2
48	59	Electronic De France	France	43,507.8	246.8
49	54	Union Des Assurances De Paris	France	42,004.2	(413.9)
50	38	IRI	Italy	41,903.2	391.7

According to Table 17-2, Japan, with 22 firms, has the largest number of MNCs in the world, accounting for about 51.20 percent of the total sales of the fifty largest corporations . Other advanced nations on the list are the United States, Germany, Great Britain, France, Switzerland, and Italy. Among these nations, the United States, with 11 firms, is second to Japan in its number of MNCs. As the table indicates, the majority of the top MNCs are headquartered in advanced nations. The list includes only one newly industrialized country (NIC), South Korea.

17.4 FOREIGN DIRECT INVESTMENT AND PORTFOLIO INVESTMENT

One must differentiate between the terms portfolio investment and foreign direct investment. The main criterion for differentiating between the two is control. **Portfolio investment** is merely a financial investment that does not give the owner the power to exert control over the assets of the firm in question. This can involve investment in debt securities (bonds) or a small amount of investment in equity securities (stocks of a firm). **Foreign direct investment** is an investment that results in control of a firm by the investor. This can involve an investment in a firm's equity securities large enough for the investor to exert effective control over the firm.

The amount of equity securities needed to classify an investment as either portfolio or FDI is a subject that is open to debate. In practice, the amount is arbitrarily set by different countries, depending on their perception of effective control. The U.S. Department of Commerce, for example, considers FDI as any investment by an individual or a firm in a foreign company that represents more than 10 percent of the outstanding stock of that company. The percentage chosen by other nations varies and is usually higher than 10 percent.

It should be noted that FDI does not necessarily involve the movement of capital from a host to a home country. In fact, FDI can be financed in a number of other ways. As a foreign investor, one could finance an investment by (a) selling technology to affiliates in a foreign country and investing the proceeds in that country, (b) raising the needed capital locally, (c) reinvesting the firm's foreign earnings in that country, or (d) using the management service fees that are earned in a foreign country. Thus, the important characteristic of FDI is not how the investment is financed but the control that it confers. As we already mentioned, it is the word "control" that differentiates FDI and portfolio investment. Portfolio investment does not involve control and is undertaken solely as a means of obtaining capital gain, rather than engaging in entrepreneurial activities.

TABLE 17-2
Number of Firms, Total Sales, and the Percentage Share of the World's Fifty Largest Corporations among the Major Investing Countries, 1995

Rank	Country	Number of Firms	Total Sale (Millions of U.S. $)	Percentage Share
1	Japan	22	1,974,654.8	51.20
2	The United States	11	958,530.1	24.90
3	Germany	6	332,892.3	8.63
4	Great Britain	3	216,553.6	5.62
5	France	3	129,130.4	3.35
6	Switzerland	2	104,239.4	2.70
7	Italy	2	88,370.8	2.70
8	South Korea	1	51,215.3	1.33

Source: Calculated by the author from Table 17.1 data.

As we explained in Chapter 1, international trade is dominated by the world's advanced industrial nations, so FDI also is led by these countries. Table 17-3 shows the outflows and inflows of foreign direct investment by major industrial countries.

TABLE 17-3
Distribution of Major Industrial Countries' Foreign Direct Investment at Home and Abroad
(Millions of dollars)

Country	1990 Investment		1995 Investment		Percentage Change	
	Abroad	Home	Abroad	Home	Abroad	Home
Canada	4.725	7.855	5.761	10.789	21.93	37.35
France	34.823	13.183	18.734	23.735	-46.20	80.04
Germany	24.200	2.530	34.890	8.940	44.17	253.36
Great Britain	19.200	32.430	40.330	32.210	110.05	-0.68
Italy	7.394	6.411	6.925	4.875	-6.34	-23.96
Japan	48.050	1.760	22.660	0.060	-52.84	-96.59
Netherlands	15.388	12.349	12.419	10.689	-19.29	-13.44
United States	29.950	47.920	95.530	60.230	218.96	25.69

Source: International Monetary Fund. *Direction of Trade Statistics* (Washington, DC: International Monetary Fund, February 1997).

As this table indicates, according to 1995 data, the United States is the major investor and the major recipient of foreign direct investment in the world. The U.S. position as the major investor of FDI abroad followed by Great Britain, Germany, Japan, France, Netherlands, Canada, and Italy. A comparison of data for 1990 and 1995 reveals that the position of the United States as the world's leading foreign investor has been improving. It is interesting to note that the growth rate of FDI abroad (218.96 %) is about eight-and -a-half time greater than thc ratc of growth of FDI at home (25.69%).

The growing amount of U.S. FDI abroad, can be attributed, among other factors, to the economic recovery of the United States in the early 1990s, and the growth of the market economies in the world. Such growth has been aided by the collapse of the former Soviet Union, Eastern European countries' economic reforms, and the unification of Germany. As Table 17-3 indicates during the 1990-1995, Germany experienced the highest rate of growth of FDI than any other countries.

The growing amount of FDI in the United States can be attributed, among other factors, to the relative market size in the United States, the declining labor costs relative to other rich nations, the relative abundance of raw materials, and the restrictions on the importation of certain products to the United States. These factors, which encourage a firm to invest in another country, will be more fully discussed in later chapters.

Table 17-4 provide us with more detail on the activities of the United States with regard to FDI. As the column entitled "Abroad " shows , Great Britain is the major recipient of U.S. FDI abroad, accounting for 16.85 percent of the total. The next largest recipient is Canada, which accounts for 11.44 percent. It is interesting to note that the total combined shares of Canada, Australia, Japan, and Europe of the U.S. FDI abroad is 71.5 percent. This mean that the U.S. FDI is predominantly directed toward advanced nations as is U.S. trade. The column entitled "Home" shows the FDI activities of other countries in the United States. According to the data presented in this column, Great Britain is the major investor in the United States, accounting for 23.62 percent of the total. A comparison of the total combined investment of Canada, Australia, Japan, and Europe (93.40%) in the United States, and the total combined investment of the rest of the countries, shows that advanced countries have by far greater amount of investment in the United States than do developing countries, which account for only 6.60 percent of the total.

TABLE 17-4
Percentage Distribution of U.S. Foreign Direct Investment Abroad and at Home,
Year End 1995*

Countries	Abroad	Home
All Countries	**100.00**	100.00
Canada	**11.44**	8.21
Europe	**51.08**	64.41
France	4.59	6.83
Germany	6.04	8.55
Netherlands	5.26	12.08
Great Britain	16.85	23.62
Latin America and Other Western Hemisphere	**17.25**	**4.06**
Africa	**0.92**	**0.17**
Middle East	**1.12**	**0.90**
Asia and Pacific	**17.70**	**22.25**
Australia	3.47	1.39
Japan	5.51	19.39
International	**0.53**	**0.00**

Source: *The Survey of Current Business* (January 19 97): D-2, D-4.

17.5 CHANNELS OF ENTRY INTO INTERNATIONAL BUSINESS*

Multinational corporations conduct their overseas operations in a variety of ways. An MNC with a full global orientation usually makes use of many channels of entry to get involved in international business. The choice of different channels of entry depends on the corporation's specific product and service lines, the foreign environment in question, and the firm's operating characteristics.

The possible channels of entry from which an MNC may choose include exporting, licensing, franchising, MNC-owned foreign enterprises, joint ventures, wholly owned subsidiaries, management contracts, and turnkey operations. In the following section, we elaborate on these channels of entry.

17.5a Exporting

Exporting is the most traditional mode of entry into international markets. Exporting and trading have been the subject of different theories of international trade, as we discussed in previous chapters.

Exporting is still the most important entry strategy for many companies. The majority of international marketing is carried out by firms that sell domestically produced goods in foreign markets. Exporting is favored by small and large companies as an initial entry strategy or as the most effective means of continuously serving foreign markets.

There are a number of motives behind exporting domestic production. Among these motives are the following:

---

* This section is a condensed version of "Foreign Market Entry," that was written by professor Bahman Ebrahimi of the University of Denver for inclusion in Parviz Asheghian and Bahman Ebrahim, *International Business*, (New York: Harper Collins, 1990), Chapter 12, 316-331.

1. The desire to use excess production capacity at home. For example, small-scale steel mills in the United States export excess supply to overseas markets. This is because they do not want to sell off excess inventory at depressed prices in home markets since doing so might depress the domestic market even further.
2. The desire to overcome problems of domestic market saturation.
3. The desire to explore new avenues for growth.
4. The desire to gain from the effects of economies of scale, thereby realizing competitive cost advantages both domestically and internationally.

Many firms lack the resources to acquire factories in foreign countries, or they fear the problems and risks associated with production abroad. As a result, these companies find some way to serve foreign markets with the products they produce in their domestic factories. Exporting takes advantage of operating leverage from domestic operations because fixed costs may already have been covered by domestic operations. Exporting also helps a firm become experienced in foreign markets. Such experience may help further expansion through other channels of entry.

17.5b Licensing

Although a firm may decide to manufacture its product abroad, this does not mean that it has to carry out the production activities itself. Foreign production can be performed by a firm in a host country through a licensing agreement. In other words, **licensing** is the process of entering a foreign market by selling technology to an independent foreign firm. This is in contrast to FDI which takes place by the "internalization" of technology, that is, using the technology in company-owned affiliates. Through licensing, a firm provides a combination of technology, brand-name use, the right to use certain patents or copyrights, and management services to another firm that produces the product in a foreign country. The supplier is called the **licensor.** The firm receiving the know-how and the right to manufacture in the host country is called the **licensee.**

By engaging in licensing, a firm avoids investing in production facilities, as well as the difficulties of producing and marketing in a foreign environment. Therefore, the licensor is only minimally involved internationally. In return for its minimal involvement, the licensor receives a modest return, perhaps 2 percent to 5 percent of sales, from the licensee. For example, Disney receives a 5-percent royalty on its licensed amusement park in Japan. Usually, the licensing agreement stipulates each party's responsibilities, the markets to be served, the rights granted, the control specifications, and the provisions for royalty payments.

Licensing has been an easy route for producers in developing countries as well as some advanced nations, such as Japan, to establish themselves as new global competitors by accessing technology from foreign MNCs. For example, after World War II, the Japanese government restricted domestic industries to local participants. As a result, exporting and the licensing of technology to Japanese firms became the only two alternatives for foreign producers to enter the Japanese market. Japanese companies thereby gained access to otherwise unavailable and valuable technologies that helped the country's industrialization after World War II.

In summary, licensing is an "arm's length" pattern of international involvement that plays an important role in international business. The choice of licensing versus FDI is influenced by a country's environmental factors, industry conditions, and company preferences. Usually, licensing decreases in relative importance as a host country's per capita gross national product (GNP) and industrialization rises. In countries with restrictions on FDI, such as post-World War II Japan, licensing becomes more important. On the other hand, in the presence of incentives for FDI, licensing is pursued less and less. Licensing also requires the presence of certain indigenous technical capabilities in the host country. Licensing is used more often when a firm's technology is not research intensive and when it can be codified, patented, and transferred.[4]

17.5c Franchising

Franchising is a form of licensing, and it is the fastest-growing segment of international licensing. Franchises involve giving permission to a foreign firm to produce a product and to use its name, trademark, or copyright. In producing the product, the **franchisee** (the receiver of the rights) is usually required to use a specific set of procedures and methods and to follow a set of quality guidelines. In return, the **franchiser** (the supplier of the rights) receives a franchise right fee and royalties. The franchisee, which is the local (host country) partner, provides the capital and knowledge of the local environment. The local partner also operates the business using operational and marketing strategies provided by the franchiser.

GLOBAL INSIGHTS CASE 17.1

Pizza Hut Goes to Brazil

Brazil is a land of enormous opportunity and is one of the fastest growing developing countries in the world. Yet, the country continues to face significant economic and social upheavals. The state plays a central role in the economy, and privatization has been difficult. The huge gap between poor and rich has grown in recent years, and there are problems with affordable housing, clean water, and adequate sewage systems. However, trade restrictions have plummeted, and Brazil is luring a large amount of foreign investment.

Pizza Hut, a company with more than 10, 000 restaurants worldwide, entered the Brazilian market in 1988 through franchisee operations . At that time, the country was suffering from high inflation and economic instability. Initially, Pizza Hut did not have a well thought-out strategy for Brazil. In 1991, the company opened up an office in Brazil with the purpose of establishing a plan for its Brazilian operations. Pizza Hut decided to follow the strategy of corporate franchises as opposed to a unit-by-unit franchise that had been adopted by other U.S. companies such as Kentucky Fried Chicken. In a unit-by-unit franchise, an individual restaurant is franchised to a certain franchisee, but in corporate franchise, the corporate franchisee is provided with a whole territory. The strategy of using strong corporate franchises was based on Pizza Hut's desire to have franchisees with strong financial backing and experience in operation in an inflationary economy.

In 1995, Fernando Henrique Carsoso was elected as the president of Brazil. Pizza Hut learned that it had to adopt to a new Brazilian economic condition, characterized by price stabilization and a significant drop in the exchange rate between the U.S. dollar and the Brazilian Real. This situation led to a significant decline in Pizza Hut's sales volume. To deal with this problem, the company instructed its franchisees to reduce their prices by 25 percent in order to meet its competition. In January 1992, McDonald's, the leading fast-food franchise in Brazil, raised its prices by 40 percent in order to keep up with inflation, but later decreased them by 40 percent and publicized the drop as a vote of confidence in Brazil. The strategy was very successful and contributed to McDonald's market growth. Many Pizza Hut units, on the other hand, decreased prices in the last week of October 1995. However, this strategy proved to be a failure. The news media portrayed the move as a desperate attempt by Pizza Hut to compete with the McDonald's.

As 1996 was coming to an end, Pizza Hut was continuing to grapple with its problems, and in 1997 PepsiCo (Pizza Hut's parent company) declared that it was planning to sell its restaurant division. It remains to be seen if Pizza Hut would continue its expansion in Brazil under new ownership, and if it will be successful.

Source: J.R. Whitaker Penteado, "Fast Food Franchises Fight for Brazilian Aficionados,"*Business week* June 7, 1993, pp. 20-24; "Pizza-Hut Cooks in Brazil," *Advertising Age*, April 4, 1994, p.45; Jeanne Whalten, "PepsiCo Restaurants Cook With Enrico," *Advertising Age*, June 5, 1995, p.4.

In addition to the right to use its name, the franchiser generally sells the franchisee some array of products and services. For example, one can make a franchise contract with Hilton Hotels to buy its supplies, receive its training for staff, and connect with its reservation system. Hilton maintains the right to control the quality of services provided by the franchisee. This right is maintained so the franchisee cannot tarnish the company's image. In return for using the Hilton name and receiving its services, the franchisee pays the company a fee based on the volume of sales. The technology that is transferred includes a well-known name, an established reputation, a management system, some marketing skills, and certain supplies.

Today, franchise operations in retailing and the restaurant business are popping up all over the world. You can see familiar McDonald's and Kentucky Fried Chicken restaurants next to Hilton hotels in countries such as Japan, Britain, Canada, Malaysia, and Mexico.

17.5d MNC-Owned Foreign Enterprise

If an MNC chooses to have its production and marketing facilities in a certain country, it creates an entity under the local law of the host country. The production facilities may be in the form of assembly plants or complete manufacturing plants.

An assembly plant requires less capital investment, and it is less expensive and less complicated to operate. As a result, it may be preferable to a complete manufacturing plant. Not only does an assembly plant provide for control of operations by the MNC, but it also benefits the home country by keeping some jobs and the value-added at home.* Because most of the vital elements of the MNC's technologies stay out of the host nations, assembly plants are less likely to be nationalized by a host government. This type of foreign involvement may be preferred for satisfying a host government's requirements that a foreign firm be established under its local laws, or it may be used as a strategy to improve goodwill or prevent hostile actions by host nations.

A complete manufacturing plant, however, reduces both the cost of the transportation of parts and the cost of import duties and tariffs. It can also improve marketing by providing better adaptation of a firm's products and services to the host nation's local market conditions.

MNC-owned foreign manufacturing may be 100 percent company owned (wholly owned), or it may be a joint venture with another firm. The firm with which an MNC enters a joint venture agreement may be a local firm or a firm from another country.

Joint Venture. A *joint venture* is a corporate entity or partnership created under a host country's law between an MNC and other parties. If the joint venture parties are local, it is called a **foreign-local joint venture**. If all the parties involved are foreign to the host country, the arrangement is called a **foreigners' joint venture**. For example, General Motors (the United States) and Isuzu (Japan) have a foreigners' joint venture to produce automobiles in Egypt. In order to entice the two companies to operate in their country, Egyptian officials offered a number of incentives, including an extension of the usual five-year income tax "holiday" to eight years.[5]

Formation of a joint venture with local partners may be required by a host government. A joint venture may also be desirable to improve local goodwill and to reduce the chance of possible hostile actions from local customers, the local government, or local labor. For instance, when faced with the threat of a protectionist move from the U.S. Congress and the "Buy American" campaign, Japanese automobile makers voluntarily limited their auto exports to the United States and sought joint venture partners among U.S. automakers. For example, Toyota entered a joint venture agreement with General Motors to produce cars in the United States.

Joint ventures are also used to phase out foreign ownership over a period of time. Instead of demanding an immediate sale of a foreign MNC's affiliate to locals, a number of developing countries require the sale of 51 percent or more of the ownership to locals over a period of 10 to 20 years. For example, such a policy is followed by India (60 percent local ownership) and Nigeria (40 or 60 percent local ownership, depending on the industry). These

---

*   *Value-added* is the increase in the value of a product contributed by each producer or distributor as the product progresses through the stages of production and distribution. Value-added may also be defined as the value of the product (sales price) minus the cost of its inputs purchased from other firms.

phasing-out policies are considered partial nationalization of the industry in question, since the intent of the developing countries is to pass ownership and control away from the foreign MNC to local investors.[6]

Increased nationalistic sentiments in some developing countries have encouraged many MNCs to hide their identity by seeking joint ventures with local partners. In such cases, the local partner simultaneously publicizes local ownership and a foreign technology link. The foreign technology used in the production may be indicative of superior product quality to local customers.

Joint ventures are usually less expensive to establish than wholly-owned subsidiary. An MNC may provide technology and management, and the joint venture partner may raise the necessary capital. Joint ventures can make entry into new markets easier and quicker than wholly owned subsidiaries. Using a local partner with its knowledge of the local environment and with local business contacts may be advantageous for the MNC. The local partner may know of existing product facilities and distribution capabilities that will reduce the MNC's time and effort. The local partner also can serve as a potential cushion against mishap and help the MNC avoid mistakes. It may make the MNC's presence less visible and troublesome. Lower overall investment risks make the joint venture an appealing option to some MNCs. For example, Pepsico has a joint venture bottling plant in Minatitlan, Mexico.

On the negative side, joint ventures mean less control and flexibility for the MNC. Control is shared at best, especially if the MNC's interest is less than 50 percent. However, minority involvement by foreign MNCs may be required by local law. The MNC and its partners may have differing objectives. An MNC's global objectives are organizing operations and getting returns on an international basis. Such objectives may be meaningless to a local partner who is interested in his/her own objectives.

Joint ventures may mean revealing exclusive technology to other firms. These firms may use the technology in the future to compete with the MNC, making such technology disclosure expensive to the MNC. Thus, many MNCs are reluctant to enter into joint venture agreements. For example, Coca-Cola decided to pull out of India rather than share its long-kept secret syrup formula with the Indian government through a required joint venture.

The methods and philosophies of the MNC and the local partner may be different enough to lead to conflicts over the way the affiliate is run. Product lines and marketing approaches may not be transferable to the host country. This may cause difficulties in teaching the partners the MNC's preferred methods. Further product choices may be limited because of such difficulties.

Another disadvantage of the joint venture is the sharing of profits with a partner. Profits are shared in proportion to ownership. An MNC that needs to show a large profit from a risky venture may find this a problem. Joint ventures tend to be unstable. One obvious reason is the conflict between partners. Another less obvious, but more frequent, reason is the MNC's shifting interests and priorities. By virtue of their global orientation, MNCs must balance product and market diversification against concentration on the local area. This may lead to shifts in priorities among production facilities, product choices, market coverages, and market concentrations. Such shifts may require pulling out of a joint venture contract.

Wholly Owned Subsidiary. *Wholly owned subsidiary* may be the preferred type of foreign production ownership because it provides the MNC with a great deal of control and flexibility. Under this arrangement, coordination among multinational operations can be easier, and conflicts with joint venture partners are nonexistent. At the same time, 100 percent ownership means more investment and greater commitment by the MNC. It also increases the risk associated with greater involvement in a host nation that may have a different and potentially hostile environment.

Some international markets may be closed if the MNC insists on complete ownership of a subsidiary. For instance, IBM was forced to leave India when the firm insisted on full ownership of its facilities. Strong attachments to full ownership may need modification in order to open certain markets to MNCs. The advantages and disadvantages of the wholly owned subsidiary form of foreign involvement are the opposite of those of the joint venture, discussed in the previous section.

17.5e Management Contract

A **management contract** is an arrangement by which a company provides managerial assistance to another company in return for a fee. Such managerial help can be provided for other independent companies, joint venture partners, or an MNC's wholly owned subsidiaries in foreign nations. In providing help to a wholly owned subsidiary under a management contract, the MNC is trying to extract a larger proportion of its subsidiary's profits out of a host country. This strategy can combat limitations set on the repatriation of profits for the host nation.

Contracts to manage can also be used in nationalized operations. In addition to the normal compensation, an MNC receives fees for providing vital expertise needed in operations. Such contracts may be for a specific time period or on an ongoing basis. Management contracts can also be used in combination with turnkey contracts. An example of a management contract is the operation of many U.S. hotel chains in foreign countries. Under a management contract arrangement, these hotel companies agree to operate, for a fee, hotels owned by foreign investors or governments. A management contract can also be used in combination with a franchise agreement. A franchisee can arrange for a third party to manage the franchised operation.

17.5f Turnkey Operation

A **turnkey operation** is an arrangement by which an MNC agrees to construct an entire facility or plant, prepare it for operation, and then turn the key of the plant over to the local owners. The essence of turnkey is the construction and equipping of the facility rather than the future use of its technology and operations, as is the case in licensing agreements. Typical turnkey projects include large-scale construction projects, such as dams, nuclear power plants, or airports. The operation of such projects is less complex than the initial construction. Operation of the project may also require expertise that an MNC lacks. In a licensing agreement, the purpose is the use of technology in operations. By contrast, a turnkey operation consists of the construction of facilities that can be turned over to another firm for operation. For example, many telecommunications firms, such as Siemens of Germany, NEC of Japan, and AT&T of the United States, construct telephone installations in foreign countries which are turned over to local operators on completion.

If an MNC has the expertise for operating such projects, and if the local firm or government chooses, a management contract can be arranged. If a management contract is agreed on with the turnkey project, the MNC provides the expertise to enable the project to be operational when construction is completed. The MNC provides training and instruction for local individuals to make the local firm self-sufficient. The MNC receives additional monies for providing management assistance and training services.

Turnkey operations fit the plans of some countries, such as the People's Republic of China, India, Iran, and Turkey. These countries can speed up their development process by contracting with foreign firms to build much-needed projects for these nations. For example, in 1980, the former Soviet Union contracted with firms from Germany, France, Britain, and Italy to build its $4 billion natural gas pipeline. Other examples of turnkey operations include the building of steel mills by the former Soviet Union in Iran and the building of fertilizer and chemical plants by the Japanese in Iraq and Iran.

17.6 APPROPRIATE TECHNOLOGY AND TECHNOLOGY TRANSFER

In the past, most technologies have been developed by advanced industrial nations, spreading to other countries only after different time lags. For example, the Industrial Revolution that started in Britain in the eighteenth century later spread to North America and Western Europe in the nineteenth century, and finally to Japan and Russia in the early twentieth century. However, this process has not yet been completed, and many developing countries in Africa, Asia, and South America are still using pre-Industrial Revolution technologies. As a result, developing countries have become technologically dependent on advanced nations for their economic growth and development. To obtain the needed technology, many developing countries have turned to the international market as a channel for modern technology transfer.

Theoretically, FDI in developing countries is perceived not only as a source of capital inflow but also as a vehicle for acquiring modern technology and the necessary managerial know-how these countries require for their development. Following World War II, when a shortage of capital existed, FDI was emphasized as a significant source for providing the needed funds to developing countries. As the shortage of capital was slowly resolved, however, and as many development efforts based solely on capital failed, the technology transfer role of FDI became the center of attention.

Given the importance of FDI as a vehicle for technology transfer, it has become evident that much of the success of investment projects depends on the selection of **appropriate technology,** or a technology that fits the economic and social environment of the country in question. What may be an appropriate technology for the capital-abundant United States may be totally inappropriate for a labor-abundant country like India. Thus, it is necessary for an MNC to adapt its technology to the national environment of the country in which it operates. In general, however, MNCs in developing countries have used capital-intensive technologies that are inappropriate for labor-abundant developing countries. This tendency can be attributed to the following factors:

1. **Engineering mentality.** Engineers who design a plant for an MNC are usually trained according to an advanced country's curricula. Thus, an engineer's interest is in **technical efficiency**, that is, to produce the maximum amount of output from a given amount of input. Given such an orientation, machines are often considered more efficient than humans, a capital-intensive technology is chosen.[7]
2. **Fixed factor proportions.** In some industries, such as chemicals, petroleum refining, and steel, capital-labor ratios are not alterable to a significant degree. Thus, capital and labor should be combined in a relatively fixed proportion. As a result, there may be no substitute for a highly capital-intensive technology.
3. **Scarcity of skilled workers.** In many developing countries, the technical, administrative, and managerial resources needed to implement labor-intensive technology are scarce. As a result, it may be cheaper for an MNC to use a capital-intensive technology, conserving expensive personnel.
4. **High cost of adaptation.** Corporations may find that modifying their capital-intensive technology is more expensive than employing it without modification.
5. **Factor market distortions.** The policies of some developing countries may make capital cheaper than its equilibrium price, that is, the price determined by market forces of demand and supply. The cheaper capital, in turn, may encourage the use of capital-intensive technology. Policies that lead to factor market distortions include minimum wage legislation, capital subsidization, and artificially low foreign exchange prices. The minimum wage legislation, resulting from organized labor pressure, artificially raises the level of wages in a developing country and discourages the use of a labor-intensive technology. On the other hand, capital subsidies and low foreign exchange prices, designed to promote industrialization, encourage the use of a capital-intensive technology.

The purpose of this section is to provide a broad understanding of the issues raised when technology is transferred through MNCs. First, we elaborate on technology transfer by MNCs and discuss the controversies surrounding this issue. We then explain the modes by which technologies are transferred. Finally, we study the pricing of technology transfer.

17.6a Technology Transfer

One of the potential benefits of MNCs to host countries, especially developing countries, is their ability to generate and transfer technology to these countries. Aware of the importance of technology in the process of economic development, many developing countries have deemed it to be an important consideration in deciding in favor of FDI. For example, a government official in prerevolutionary Iran stated:

> *Since our development plan reserves a high place for the private sector, the role of foreign private investment in this sector is very important. For it should also bring with it administrative and managerial skills, innovations, and entrepreneurship to our private sector, creating a true and genuine partnership, but also laying the foundation for self-sustained and sound expansion.*[8]

Technology transfer is a complex, time-consuming, and costly process that is composed of many stages. This process ranges from research and development to product planning and design. It includes labor training, quality control, management practices, marketing skills, and service supports. The successful implementation of such a process demands continuous communication and requires close cooperation between the parties involved. Unfortunately, however, both home and host countries have raised questions regarding the potential benefits of technology transfers to developing countries. This has led to controversy and conflict between home and host countries, further complicating MNC management.

GLOBAL INSIGHTS CASE 17.2

Gillette's Blunder

When the Gillette Company developed a superior stainless steel razor blade, it feared that such a superior product might mean fewer replacements and sales. Thus, the company decided not to market it. Instead, Gillette sold the technology to Wilkinson, a British garden tool manufacturer. Because Gillette thought that Wilkinson would use the technology only in the production of garden tools, it did not restrict its use in the razor blade market. However, when Wilkinson Sword Blades were introduced they sold quickly, and Gillette realized the magnitude of its mistake. Only superior marketing skills and experience enabled Gillette to eventually recover .

Source: David A. Ricks, *Big Business Blunders: Mistakes in Multinational Marketing* (Homewood, Ill.: Dow Jones-Irwin, 1983), p.21.

Home Countries' Reactions to Technology Transfer. Home countries have often reacted against the export of technology on the grounds that it is harmful to their economic base. They argue that the establishment of production facilities by MNCs' subsidiaries abroad decreases their export potential. Additionally, they claim that because some of the MNCs' imports come from their subsidiaries abroad, the volume of imports to the home country increases. Given the decrease in exports and increase in imports, it is argued that the availability of jobs in the home country will be diminished. It is also argued that by providing technological know-how to foreign nations, a country might lose its international competitiveness. This, in turn, would reduce its rate of economic growth.

These arguments have caused some groups, especially labor unions, to oppose the expansion of MNCs to foreign countries. In the United States, this has been a sensitive issue especially in recent years. Many U.S. MNCs have chosen to set up plants in countries such as Mexico, Singapore, and Taiwan in order to take advantage of the cheaper labor costs in these countries. These plants are used to assemble American-made components into products that are then exported back to the United States. For example, in 1982, some U.S. automobile manufacturers set up assembly plants in Mexican border towns to make cars using U.S. parts and inexpensive Mexican labor.[9] As another example, Zenith Radio Corporation closed its television plant in Sioux City, Iowa in 1979 and set up plants in Mexico and Taiwan.[10] Such incidents have caused a bitter confrontation between MNCs and labor unions, whose members have been asked to accept wage cuts in order to keep jobs at home. The labor unions have blamed MNCs not only for exporting jobs abroad, but also for exploiting foreigners by paying them low wages.

Host Countries' Reactions to Technology Transfer. The subject of technology transfer by MNCs has been a more sensitive issue in host countries than it has been in home countries. Suspicion of MNCs, fueled by the fear of technological dependency, has caused the residents of many host countries, especially laborers, to persuade their governments to enact regulations that control the activities of these corporations. For example, in the hope of upgrading the skill levels of jobs in Canada, the country's government has encouraged MNCs to locate all production phases for at least one of their product lines in Canada. As another example, Japan has feared that MNCs, through their superior technology, might dominate local firms. As a result, Japan has restricted the flow of technology through

MNCs by "taking the foreign investment package apart;" that is, by buying capital, management, and technology separately, rather than acquiring them together through the MNC.

Although the positive role of MNCs in technology transfer has been met with skepticism from both advanced and developing countries, the role of these corporations has created more heated debates and stirred more controversy in developing countries. This has led some economists to question the possible advantages of MNC's technology transfers to these countries. Two types of criticisms can be differentiated concerning MNC transfers of technology.

The first is related to the monopolistic nature of MNCs. It is argued that an MNC that is transferring technology to a developing country can dictate conditions that are favorable to its own interests. This is due to the MNC's monopolistic power over the technical and managerial know-how, the capital, and the foreign exchange (currency) transferred to the developing country through its investment. Consequently, it is argued, the real cost to a developing country of obtaining foreign private technical knowledge may well be higher than it first appears. For example, a study of U.S. subsidiaries abroad found that these subsidiaries were established mostly in industries that were oligopolistic in nature, and that their purpose was to protect the United State's interest in a market that previously was served by U.S. exports.[11]

The second criticism is related to the type of technology that is transferred. It is argued that the technology transmitted through MNCs is inappropriate for conditions that exist in developing countries. Compared to advanced countries, most developing countries are located in tropical and subtropical zones and, therefore, have a different climate from advanced countries. Their local factors of production are available in quite different proportions. Educated managers, skilled workers, technicians, and professionals are relatively scarce. Given these conditions, if a technology designed for an advanced country is transferred to a developing country, it will have a distorting effect on that country's economy as a whole. To avoid this problem, the MNC must adapt its technology to the conditions that exist in the developing country. However, it must be realized that technology is not transferred in a vacuum. The successful transfer of technology and its adaptation to a developing country's environment depends not only on the willingness and ability of the MNCs, but also on the absorptive capacity of the recipient host country and its relationship with the MNC. The lack of technical and managerial skills needed to operate a successful manufacturing process, the existence of small and stagnant markets, and the restrictive government policies in developing countries are among the factors providing serious obstacles to the process of technology transfer and adaptation. Consequently, although MNCs have been the means of some technology transfer in a few cases, they have not, in general, performed this task up to their potential.[12] For example, a study of U.S. MNCs in developing countries found that every U.S. MNC operating an industrial plant in a developing country employed basically the same technology used in plants in advanced countries. Given the limited markets in developing countries, however, the plants were often "scaled-down" versions of those in advanced countries.[13] As another example, a study of Latin America illustrated that the Latin American companies usually took the same approach as foreign firms in selecting a production technique. These companies often used capital-intensive techniques developed in advanced countries. The use of these techniques, according to the study, was related mostly to the lack of skilled labor in Latin America. The study also emphasized that the MNCs had not tried to design labor-intensive techniques that could solve, at least partially, Latin America's unemployment problem.[14] A similar study of Brazil found that MNCs were reluctant to fully adapt their technology to the prevailing local conditions. According to the study, the MNCs' failure in this area was related to their unwillingness to do an adequate search to understand prevailing conditions in Brazil's "permissive environment," that is, an environment that allowed them to operate profitably without fully adapting their technologies.[15]

Reconciling Host and Home Countries' Reactions. The question to ask at this point is whether the host and home countries are both correct in their negative views of technology transfer. Theoretically speaking, as our discussion of trade theories throughout this book has indicated, free trade would lead to a maximization of the world's economic welfare. Thus, we could argue that as long as technology flows from the donor country to the recipient country in a perfectly competitive market, free from government intervention, both countries should benefit. However, because in actual market settings both government intervention and market imperfections exist, disturbing the free flow of technology, there is reason to believe that both the recipient and donor countries might not benefit from the transfer process. Thus, what seems to be needed is the absence of government intervention, allowing the free forces of market demand and supply to direct the flow of technology transfer as dictated by the precepts of the comparative advantage theory of trade. Unfortunately, however, what seems to be theoretically correct is not often implemented due to noneconomic variables, such as xenophobia, nationalistic ideology, and labor union demands, that affect the decision-making process and play a significant role in the process of technology transfer.

17.6b Modes of Technology Transfer

The transfer of technology through MNCs depends on their channels of entry into international business, which were fully described at the beginning of this chapter. These channels provide us with the modes of technology transfer. These modes of transfer include the export of goods and services, licensing, turnkey operations, management contracts, franchising, joint ventures, and wholly owned subsidiaries. Among these modes, wholly owned subsidiaries are potentially the best means of technology transfer to developing countries because they provide not only the technology needed for successful operation, but also the knowledge and skills required for actual production to take place.

Given that the international transfer of technology can take different modes, the question now is what mode does the MNC choose? The answer depends on the relative cost and feasibility of technology transfer. These, in turn, are determined by four interrelated factors: (a) the sophistication of the technology, (b) the national environments of the home and host countries, (c) the MNC's characteristics, and (d) the characteristics of the domestic firms.

Sophistication of the Technology. If a product is relatively new or it involves a highly sophisticated technology, an MNC is more apt to establish a wholly-owned subsidiary rather than choose other modes of technology transfer. This is because the MNC has full ownership and, therefore, full control over its subsidiary. This enables the corporation to better protect and internalize those technologies that have been obtained through its own substantial research and development expenditures.

Home and Host Countries' Environments. Existing laws and the competitive environment in both the home and host countries have a bearing on the technology transfer mode chosen. Many MNCs move their production facilities abroad to protect a market that is in danger of being lost either due to a market takeover by competitors or because the tax structure of the host or home country makes such a move profitable.

The MNC's choice of technology transfer modes is especially limited in developing countries. These countries usually lack technical and managerial know-how, yet they often insist on national ownership and staffing. Consequently, most developing countries, such as Kuwait and the United Arab Emirates, do not even allow the establishment of wholly owned subsidiaries in their countries. These nations usually set percentage ceilings on the foreign equity that can be invested in each firm of an industry. They also may limit FDI in joint ventures.

Characteristics of the Multinational Corporation. The financial capability of an MNC and its top executive strategy regarding long-run profit maximization are important elements that affect the choice of technology transfer methods. If top executives view technology as an essential ingredient of the MNC's marketing-manufacturing package, and if they believe that such a strategy would lead to long-run profit maximization, a wholly-owned subsidiary is preferred over other modes of technology transfer. The top executive view of long-run profit maximization can be formulated in terms of cost-benefit analysis.

Different investment projects are expected to generate different costs and revenues, leading to different profits. At one extreme, the exporting mode could be chosen. This alternative is relatively cost-free because it does not require investment in equipment and machinery in a foreign country. At the other extreme, the wholly-owned subsidiary could be used, involving the commitment of financial and managerial resources for a long period of time. Which alternative should be chosen? This depends on the expected profit from these projects and the attitudes of top executives with regard to risk. If the top executives are risk takers, they would choose the mode that is expected to have the higher risk and the higher profit. On the other hand, if they are risk averters, they would select the mode that is expected to involve lower risk and lower profit.

GLOBAL INSIGHTS CASE 17.3

Matsushita's Forecast of the Growth of Electronics and Related Technologies

Matsushita Electric Industrial Company is the largest of Japan's electronics manufacturers. In 1983 Matsushita implemented a three-year corporate strategy. The major thrust of this strategy was a "metamorphosis from a manufacturer of home-appliance products to a manufacturer of consumer and industrial electronics." The reason for this shift in strategy was the slow rate of growth in the home-appliance industry. If Matsushita had continued as a manufacturer of home-appliance products after 1986, they might have had less than 5 percent average sales growth per year.

Matsushita's strategic shift to consumer and industrial electronics is based on their belief that electronics and related technologies will be key to their survival and growth through the year 2000. The Japanese Association for Electronics Industries Development forecast the average annual growth rate for the whole industry at 12.6 percent. Matsushita responded by establishing a semiconductor laboratory in the summer of 1985. This exemplifies Matsushita's strong strategic planning capabilities.

Source: Gen-Ichi Nakamura, "Strategic Management in Major Japanese High-Tech Companies," *Long Range Planning*, vol 19, no. 6 (December 1986), pp. 82-91.

Characteristics of Domestic Firms. The size, degree of competitiveness, and ability of domestic firms to absorb the imported technology are among the factors that affect the MNC's choice of technology transfer mode. For example, when an MNC plans to invest in a developing country, FDI might be the preferable mode of technology transfer, due to problems in exporting technology to such countries. However, in advanced countries, where domestic firms are capable of imitating an imported technology, licensing arrangements might be preferable to FDI. Additionally, licensing might be suitable for relatively small corporations that do not have the necessary capital, management, or experience to get involved in FDI.

17.6c Pricing of Technology Transfer

Because the market for technology is highly imperfect and pricing information is not readily available, the pricing decisions for technology transfer represent a complex issue. This complexity is further amplified by the different compensation packages an MNC can choose. These packages range from simple royalties and licensing fees to more comprehensive agreements that include additional payments to the licensor for technical assistance and other services rendered. Other payments to the licensor might be made based on profits, on goods supplied by the licensor, on dividends from an equity share granted by the licensee, and on tax savings resulting from the agreement.

Given the complexity of pricing international technology transfer and the lack of a standard model for negotiation, the success of an MNC's manager in dealing with a nonaffiliated foreign buyer depends on his or her negotiating skills and bargaining power.

Transfer Pricing. The issue of pricing technology transfer is further complicated by what is known as transfer pricing. **Transfer pricing** refers to the pricing of goods and services that pass between either a parent company and its subsidiaries or the subsidiaries themselves. Because transfer prices are set by the corporate family when dealing with each other, the prices may not reflect market prices. Often a market price for a particular good or service may not even exist. As a result, an MNC may use transfer pricing to minimize taxes or to overcome foreign exchange controls that prohibit the repatriation of funds.

Because tax rates are different between nations, a parent company exporting goods and services to a subsidiary in a high-tax nation (compared to the taxes charged in the home country) could set a high transfer price. This has the effect of decreasing the profits of the foreign subsidiary and lowering taxes in the host country. In the same manner, if the subsidiary is located in a low-tax nation, an MNC could minimize taxes by charging a low transfer price. However, if import tariffs are present, the MNC will consider both taxes and tariffs in formulating the transfer pricing policy because a high transfer price means a high value for the goods and services sold. Similarly, a low transfer price means a low value for the goods and services sold. Because import tariffs are imposed on the declared value of imports, this leads to a higher or lower tariff cost depending on the case, an MNC should measure the tax benefit of a higher or lower transfer price against the resulting higher or lower tariff cost. A high transfer price will be charged if the savings on the host country's taxes are greater than the additional tariff costs. A low transfer price will be used if the savings on tariffs are greater than the additional taxes.

Foreign exchange controls prevent repatriation of funds by MNCs. To circumvent such controls, an MNC can charge high transfer prices to its subsidiaries, thus repatriating profits from those host countries that impose foreign exchange controls.

Other circumstances in which an MNC may use transfer pricing to minimize its costs occur when taxes are imposed on dividends or when a host country's currency is rapidly depreciating. Because dividend taxes, in essence, tax the MNC's profit twice, the firm can transfer funds using a high transfer price instead of repatriating dividends. If a host country's currency is rapidly depreciating, the MNC can protect itself by adopting a high transfer pricing policy. This allows the MNC to exchange the depreciating currency for stronger currencies, thus minimizing the exchange losses that may result from the weaker currency.

To modify the impact of MNCs' transfer pricing practices, many host country governments have tried to intervene in the negotiations on agreements for technology payments. In the United States, the government is given the right to reallocate gross income, deductions, credits, or allowances between the parent company and its subsidiaries if arbitrary pricing or allocation of expenses may have taken place to avoid taxes. If the taxpaying company is not happy with the government reallocation procedure, it has to prove that the reallocation was not warranted and that a refund is in order. An example of the tax implication of transfer pricing is seen in the case of Eli Lilly & Company in the 1950s. In this case, the Internal Revenue Service ended up collecting $4 million from the company. Although the company appealed the decision, it did not win the case. The tax court maintained that the company's pricing policy had resulted in "tax avoidance and [did] not clearly reflect the income of the related organizations."[16]

In closing this chapter, we may note that the controversies surrounding the question of technology are going to be with us for a long time. At the national level, environmentalists and consumer advocates have continued to raise questions regarding the environmental effects and safety aspects of technologies that are being introduced. At the international level, developing countries have passionately pressed MNCs for the transfer of appropriate technology to their countries. What seems to be needed in the midst of such controversies is more cooperation among home countries, host countries, and MNCs. To this end, numerous observers have recommended an international code of conduct that governs international technology transfers. Such a code should take into account the legitimate rights of the parties involved.

17.7 SUMMARY

1. International business can be defined as those business transactions among individuals, firms, or other entities (both private and public) that occur across national boundaries.
2. There is no consensus among scholars regarding the definition of multinational corporation (MNC). Different definitions are based on different criteria that are considered indicative of the purpose and type of MNC.
3. Using the structural criterion, the MNC can be defined by the number of countries in which a firm is operating or by the nationalities of its owners and/or top management.
4. Using the performance criterion, an MNC can be defined on the basis of the absolute amount or the relative share (percentage) of assets, number of employees, sales, or earnings in a foreign country.
5. Using the behavioral criterion, a firm can be classified as multinational if its top management "thinks internationally."
6. In this book, an MNC is defined as a group of corporations that is operating in different countries but is controlled by its headquarters in a given country.

7. The main criterion for differentiating between portfolio investment and foreign direct investment (FDI) is the amount of control the investment allows the company to retain.

8. Foreign direct investment can be financed by (a) selling technology to affiliates in a foreign country and investing the proceeds in that country, (b) raising the needed capital locally, (c) reinvesting the firm's foreign earnings in that country, or (d) using the management service fees that are earned in a foreign country.

9. International business is dominated by the world's major industrial countries. The United States is the world's major exporter, the major investor, and the major recipient of FDI.

10. The United States' position as the world's leading foreign investor has weakened over the years, losing ground to countries such as Japan and Western Europe.

11. The possible channels of entry into international business include exporting, licensing, franchising, MNC-owned foreign enterprises, (joint ventures and wholly owned subsidiaries), management contracts, and turnkey operations.

12. An MNC can manufacture products in a foreign country by signing a licensing agreement with an independent foreign firm that obtains the right to produce and sell the product in return for a modest fee.

13. Franchising involves granting permission to a foreign firm to produce a product and to use its name, trademark, or copyright, in return for a fee and royalties (based on a contract).

14. An MNC may have part ownership (a joint venture) or complete ownership (a wholly owned subsidiary) of its foreign production and marketing operations.

15. In a management contract, a company provides managerial assistance to another company in return for a fee.

16. A turnkey operation is an arrangement by which an MNC agrees to construct an entire facility or plant, prepare it for operation, and then turn the key over to the local owners, for a fee.

17. Technology transfer is a complex, time-consuming, and costly process that is composed of many stages. This process ranges from research and development to product planning and design. It includes labor training, quality control, management practices, marketing skills, and service supports.

18. The successful transfer of technology requires close cooperation between the parties involved. In practice, however, both home and host countries have raised questions regarding the potential benefits or drawbacks of technology transfers to their nations.

19. Home countries have argued that the establishment of production facilities abroad decreases their export potential and increases their imports. This leads to the loss of jobs and a decrease in the GNP in the home country.

20. Suspicion of MNCs, fueled by the fear of technological dependency, has caused the residents of many host countries, especially laborers, to persuade their governments to enact regulations that control the activities of these corporations.

21. Technology transfers to host countries have met with more criticism in developing countries than in advanced countries. Two major criticisms that are raised by developing countries regarding technology transfers are (a) that the MNCs are monopolistic in nature, and (b) that the type of technology transferred by the MNCs is inappropriate for developing countries.

22. It is argued that the technology transmitted through MNCs is inappropriate for the conditions that exist in developing countries. To avoid this problem, an MNC must adapt its technology to developing countries' requirements.

23. It has been argued that as long as technology flows from the donor country to the recipient country in a perfectly competitive market, free from government intervention, both countries should benefit.

24. Modes of technology transfer include exporting, licensing, turnkey operations, management contracts, franchising, joint ventures, and wholly owned subsidiaries.

25. The factors that determine the mode of technology transfer chosen by an MNC are (a) the sophistication of the technology, (b) the national environments of the home and host countries, (c) the MNC's characteristics, (d) the characteristics of the domestic firms.

26. Transfer pricing refers to the pricing of goods and services that pass between either a parent company and its subsidiaries or the subsidiaries themselves.

27. Because transfer prices are set by the corporate family when they are dealing with each other, the prices may not reflect market prices. Often a market price for a particular good or service may not even exist.

28. An MNC may use transfer pricing to minimize taxes or to overcome foreign exchange controls that prohibit repatriation of funds.

Review Questions

1. What is the difference between international trade and international business?
2. What are the three criteria used in defining the MNC? Explain.
3. What are the different ways a foreign investor can finance an investment? Explain.
4. Differentiate between portfolio investment and FDI.
5. What are the different channels through which an MNC may enter international business? Discuss.
6. What factors determine the mode of technology transfer an MNC chooses? Explain.
7. What are the motives behind exporting domestic production? Is exporting favored by small firms or large firms? Explain.
8. What is the difference between licensing and franchising? Explain.
9. Explain the home countries' and host countries' reactions to the issue of technology. Why is technology transfer a source of conflict between host and home countries? Are both host and home countries correct in their opposing views of technology? Explain.
10. What is transfer pricing? Why might transfer prices not reflect market value? Explain.
11. How can an MNC minimize its costs through transfer pricing? What are the reactions of the governments in host and/or home countries to transfer pricing?

Problems

1. International business has a long history that dates back to ancient times. Why has so much attention been directed to this subject in recent years?
2. Explain the changing pattern of the United States' overall international business position in the last two decades. In your answer include a discussion of the growth of FDI in the European countries and Japan. What do you think the patterns of FDI will look like in the future?
3. To maintain its competitive position in the world market and protect jobs, the U.S. government should ban the transfer of U.S. technology to any other country.

    Do you agree with this statement? Discuss.
4. To alleviate some of the problems raised in the international transfer of technology, it is believed that a code of conduct is needed to govern such transfers. Whose rights do you think should be incorporated into such a code? What do you think the major objectives of such a code should be?
5. You are the manager of an MNC that is planning to install a new plant in India (a labor-abundant country) to manufacture prefabricated housing units. You have been advised by the production manager that the production process can range from a very labor-intensive to a very capital-intensive technology. How do you choose the correct technology? Why is your choice the correct one? Would your answer to these questions change if the plant were to be built in an advanced country, such as Canada? What would happen if you were dealing with a different type of industry?
6. As the manager of an MNC that enjoys a technological edge in the domestic market, what factors would you consider in selecting your method for expansion into the international market?
7. Compare and contrast management contracts and turnkey arrangements. Can these two be combined? How? Give examples.
8. The major objective of all firms, whether domestic or international, is to make a profit. To achieve this goal, can we apply the same techniques and concepts we use for domestic firms to the MNCs? Discuss.

9. Compare the different criteria used to define international business. Refer to Table 17-1 and explain what criterion is used in identifying firms as MNCs. Why do you think such a criterion is used as opposed to others?

10. What are the advantages and disadvantages of exporting compared with foreign production?

Notes

1. United Nations Center on Transnational Corporations, *Transnational Corporations in World Development* (London: Graham & Trotman, 1985), 207; International Monetary Fund, *Balance of Payments Statistics Yearbook* (Washington DC: IMF, 1992); The World Bank, *The World Development Report 1999-2000* (Washington, DC: Oxford University Press, 2000), 271.

2. Franklin R. Root, "Some Trends in the World Economy and Their Implications for International Business," *Journal of International Business Studies* (Winter 1984): 19-23; William A. Dymsza, "Trends in Multinational Business and Global Environment: A Perspective," *Journal of International Business Studies* (Winter 1984): 25-46.

3. Yair Aharoni, "On the Definition of a Multinational Corporation," *The Quarterly Review of Economics and Business* 11 (Autumn 1971): 27-37.

4. J. Farok, "Choosing Between Direct and Licensing: Theoretical Considerations and Empirical Tests," *Journal of International Business Studies* 15, no. 3 (Winter 1984): 167-188.

5. *IL&T Egypt.* Business International Corporation, (October 1986): 4.

6. Robert Grosse and Duane Kujawa, *International Business: Theory and Managerial Applications* (Homewood, IL: Irwin, 1988), 612-613.

7. James Pickett, D. J. C. Forsyth, and N. S. McBain, "The Choice of Technology," *World Development* 2 (March 1974): 47-54.

8. Mehdi Samii, "The Role of Foreign Private Investment in Iran's Economic Development," *Bank Markazi Iran, Bulletin* (January/February 1971): 531.

9. "American Auto Makers Using More Mexico Assembly Lines," *The New York Times*, 25 July 1982, 1.

10. "Sioux City Still Suffers After Its Top Employer Moves Business Abroad," *The Wall Street Journal*, 5 April 1979, 1.

11. Raymond Vernon, *The Multinational Spread of the U.S. Enterprise* (New York: Basic Books, 1971).

12. R. S. Eckaus, "Technological Change in the Less Developed Countries," in Stephen Spiegelglas and Charles J. Welsch, eds., *Economic Development: Challenge and Promise* (Englewood Cliffs, NJ: Prentice-Hall, 1970); see also, ch. 2, 18-23 of this publication for a summary of other empirical studies in the area of technology transfer.

13. Roy B. Helfgott, "Multinational Corporations and Manpower Utilization in Developing Nations," *Journal of Developing Areas* 7 (January 1973): 225-246.

14. Doug Hellinger and Steve Hellinger, "The Job Crisis in Latin America: A Role for Multinational Corporations in Introducing More Labor-Intensive Technologies, *World Development* 3 (June 1975): 399-410.

15. Samuel A. Morely and Gordon W. Smith, "Limited Search and Technology Choices of Multinational Firms in Brazil," *Quarterly Journal of Economics* 31 (May 1977): 263-287.

16. "Elli Lilly and Company v. the United States," *U.S. Tax Cases,* vol. 67-1 (Chicago: Commerce Clearing House, 1967), 9248-9249

Suggested Readings

Aharoni, Yair. "On the Definition of a Multinational Corporation." *The Quarterly Review of Economics and Business* 11 (Autumn 1971): 27-37.

Asheghian, Parviz. "The Comparative Capital Intensities of Joint Venture Firms and Local Firms in Iran." *Journal of Economic Development* 7 (December 1982): 77-86.

———. "The R&D Activities of Foreign Firms in a Less Developed Country: An Iranian Case Study." *Journal of Business and Economic Perspectives* 10 (Spring 1984): 19-28.

————. "Technology Transfer by Foreign Firms to Iran." *Middle Eastern Studies* 21 (January 1985): 72-79.

Baranson, Jack. *Technology and the Multinationals: Corporate Strategies in a Changing World Economy.* Lexington, MA: Lexington Books, D.C. Heath, 1978.

Benvignati, Anita M. "International Technology Transfer Patterns in a Traditional Industry." *Journal of International Business Studies* 16 (Winter 1983): 63-75.

Casson, M., ed. *Multinational Corporations.* Aldershot, England: Edward Elgar Publishing Ltd., 1990.

Casson, M., et al. *Multinationals and World Trade.* Winchester, MA: Allen and Unwin, 1986.

Caves, Richard E. *Multinational Enterprise and Economic Analysis.* Cambridge: Cambridge University Press, 1982.

Daniels, John P., and Fernando Robles. "The Choice of Technology and Export Commitment: The Peruvian Textile Industry." *Journal of International Business Studies* 13 (Spring/Summer 1982): 67-87.

Davidson, W. H. "Key Characteristics in the Choice of International Technology Transfer Mode." *Journal of International Business Studies* 16 (Summer 1985): 5-21.

Dunning, John H. *International Production and the Multinational Enterprise.* London: Allen & Unwin, 1981, ch. 12.

————. *International Production and the Multinational Enterprise.* London: Allen & Unwin, 1981, ch. 1.

————. "Technology, United States Investment and European Economic Growth." In *The International Corporation: A Symposium,* edited by Charles P. Kindleberger. Cambridge, MA: Massachusetts Institute of Technology Press, 1970.

Eckaus, Richard. "The Factor Proportions Problems in Underdeveloped Areas." *American Economic Review* 45 (1955): 539-565.

Fishwick, Frances. *Multinational Companies and Economic Concentration in Europe.* New York: Praeger, 1982.

Freeman, Orille L. *The Multinational Company: Instrument for World Growth.* New York: Praeger, 1981.

Hart, Thomas, Michael E. Porter, and Eileen Rudden. "How Global Companies Win Out." *Harvard Business Review* 60 (September-October 1982): 98-108.

Kindleberger, C. P., and D. B. Audretsch, eds. *The Multinational Corporations in the 1980s.* Cambridge, MA: MIT Press, 1983.

Kujawa, Duane. "Technology Strategy and Industrial Relations: Case Studies of Japanese Multinationals in the United States." *Journal of International Business Studies* 16 (Winter 1983): 9-22.

Magee, Stephen P. "Multinational Corporations, the Industry Technology Cycle and Development." *Journal of World Trade Law* 11 (1977): 297-321.

Mansfield, Edwin. *The Economics of Technological Change.* New York: Norton, 1968.

Mason, Hal H. "The Multinational Firm and the Cost of Technology to Developing Countries." *California Management Review* 15 (Summer 1973): 5-13.

————. "Some Aspects of Technology Transfer: A Case Study Comparing U.S. Subsidiaries and Local Counterparts in the Philippines." *The Philippine Economic Journal* 9 (September 1970): 83-108.

Morley, Samuel A., and Gordon Smith. "Limited Search and the Technology Choices of Multinational Firms in Brazil." *Quarterly Journal of Economics* 91 (1977): 263-287.

Pavitt, Keith. "The Multinational Enterprise and the Transfer of Technology." In *The Multinational Enterprise,* edited by John H. Dunning. London: Allen & Unwin, 1971.

Peck, Morton J. "Technology." In *Asia's New Giant: How the Japanese Economy Works,* edited by Hugh Patrick and Henry Rosovsky. Washington, DC: Brookings Institution, 1978, ch. 8.

Pickett, James D., J. C. Forsyth, and N. S. McBain. "The Choice of Technology, Economic Efficiency and Employment in Developing Countries." *World Development* 2 (1974): 47-54.

Pitelis, Christos N., and Roger Sugden, eds. *The Nature of Transnational Firms.* New York: Routledge, 1991.

Steward, Frances. *Technology and Underdevelopment.* Boulder, CO: Westview Press, 1977.

————. "Choice of Technique in Developing Countries." *Journal of Development Studies* 9 (October 1972): 99-122.

Teece, David J. *The Multinational Corporation and the Resource Cost of International Technology Transfer.* Cambridge, MA: Ballinger, 1976.

United Nations Commission on Transnational Corporations. *Transnational Corporations in World Development: A Re-examination.* New York: United Nations, 1978.

Vernon, Raymond. *Sovereignty at Bay: The Multinational Spread of United States Enterprises.* New York: Basic Books, 1971.

———. *The Technology Factor in International Trade.* New York: National Bureau of Economic Research, 1970.

Vernon, Raymond, and Louis T. Wells, Jr. *Manager in the International Economy,* 5th ed. Englewood Cliffs, NJ: Prentice-Hall, 1986, ch. 2.

Wilkins, Mira. *The Emergence of Multinational Enterprise: American Business Abroad from the Colonial Era to 1914.* Cambridge, MA: Harvard University Press, 1971.

———. *The Maturing of Multinational Enterprise: American Business Abroad from 1914 to 1970.* Cambridge, MA: Harvard University Press, 1971.

Chapter 18

THEORIES OF INTERNATIONAL FACTOR MOVEMENTS AND MULTINATIONAL CORPORATIONS

18.1 INTRODUCTION

So far, the bulk of the theories presented in this book have provided us with an explanation of international trade, that is, export and import of goods and services. In developing these theories, we have assumed no international factor movements. However, as we saw in the previous chapter, capital, labor, and technology move across national boundaries.

The economic factors that lead to the movements of productive resources across national boundaries are identical to those underlying international trade in goods and services. As in the case of international trade, productive factors move from nations with relative abundance and low returns (for example, wages and interest) to nations with relative scarcity and high returns. In fact, international trade and factor movements can be considered substitutes for one another. For example, a relatively labor-scarce and capital-abundant nation, such as the United States, could either import labor-intensive products or permit the immigration of workers from nations with an abundance of labor. Alternatively, it could export capital-intensive goods or export capital itself.

The inadequacy of international trade theories to explain all the facets of international factor movements and the multinational corporation (MNC)—an important instrument for the international movement of capital, labor, and technology—has led some economists to develop theories that deal specifically with these subjects.

In this chapter, we first review the main theories of international capital movements. Then we discuss some of the major theories concerning MNCs. These theories have been developed in the free-market, capitalist economies by economists who are receptive, for the most part, to both foreign direct investment (FDI) and MNCs. Next, we provide an explanation of the Marxist theory that is used to oppose both FDI and MNCs. Finally, we elaborate on international factor mobility and immigration, and discuss their theoretical and practical implications.

18.2 THEORIES OF INTERNATIONAL CAPITAL MOVEMENTS

Before the emergence of multinational corporations, private capital crossed national boundaries only in the form of portfolio investment. The real drive toward FDI started in the 1920s. During the Great Depression, FDI experienced some setbacks but recovered somewhat in the late 1930s. World War II was an important stage in its development. As we explained in Chapter 17, the United States emerged from the war as the world's main economic power. The U.S. FDI grew rapidly, accounting for roughly 70 percent of the net FDI from the postwar period through the 1960s. Following this period, the relative share of the U.S. FDI in the world declined, reaching the level of 23.33 percent in 1997. Rapid expansion in other countries' FDI did not occur until about 1965, because these countries were busy rebuilding their domestic economies after World War II and did not have sufficient funds to invest significant amounts outside their borders.

In the previous chapter, we differentiated between portfolio investment and FDI. The question now is, "Why does capital cross national boundaries?" In answering this question, we first present the theory of international portfolio investment and then elaborate on the market imperfections theory.

18.2a Theory of International Portfolio Investment

Capital moves across national boundaries in different ways. International capital movements can occur through purchases and sales of outstanding bonds and stocks, through different short-term credit instruments, and through FDI. The earliest theoreticians, who assumed that a perfectly competitive market exists, relied on a model of portfolio investment to explain the international movement of capital. According to this model, the rate of return on capital is the cause of international capital movement among countries. In other words, capital moves from nation X to nation Y because the rate of return on capital is higher in nation Y than in nation X, indicating the comparative abundance of capital in the latter.

To be sure, the earliest theoreticians did not differentiate between the determinants of portfolio investment and FDI. Foreign direct investment was considered a form of capital movement which, like international portfolio investment, could be explained in terms of differential rates of return. In other words, the theory postulated that a firm crossed its national boundaries to earn a higher rate of return in a foreign country than it could earn at home. Foreign direct investment was considered different, from international portfolio investment, however, in that it was accompanied by different degrees of control, technology, and management brought by the foreign investor.[*]

In 1960, economist Stephen Hymer wrote a groundbreaking doctoral dissertation and laid the foundation for the modern theories of FDI.[1] In his dissertation he made the first systematic presentation of the market imperfection theory, asserting that the investing firm has monopolistic advantages that make it possible to run subsidiaries abroad more profitably than domestic competing firms. A few years later, in the late 1960s, Charles Kindleberger provided the first comprehensive survey of the literature for FDI along the lines explained by Hymer. Kindleberger elaborated on the inadequacy of the assumption of perfect competition in the analysis of FDI, and he asserted that FDI could not exist under such an assumption. He explained that, in a perfectly competitive market, domestic firms could purchase needed capital through capital markets that specialize in capital movements. This is preferable to purchasing needed capital through firms that specialize in the production and distribution of goods and services. Thus, for a firm to undertake FDI, it must possess an advantage over domestic firms operating in the host countries. In other words, there must be some imperfections in the market. He concluded that "in a world of perfect competition for goods and factors, direct investment cannot exist."[2]

Today, Hymer's early insights into the determinants of FDI remain unshaken. Although contributions by different specialists in the fields of industrial organization, management, and international finance have increased our understanding of FDI in general and MNCs in particular, the assumption of market imperfections remains an integral part of theories regarding FDI and MNCs. We devote the rest of this section to an explanation of this important theory.

18.2b Market Imperfections Theory

This theory provides a further step in the understanding of FDI. The market imperfections theory asserts that an MNC's decision to undertake FDI stems from its desire to capitalize on certain advantages that are not available to domestic firms operating in the host country.

An MNC beginning operations in a foreign country is at a disadvantage compared to indigenous (local) firms. The managers of an indigenous firm are familiar with their national environment. They know their country's economy, politics, history, laws, geography, and culture. The managers of a foreign firm can obtain the same knowledge, but only at a cost. In addition, managers of foreign firms face added risks that are not shared by the indigenous firms. These risks include the uncertainty of operating in a foreign exchange market, the fears of a political takeover of the business, and the additional costs of operating outside the firm's home country, such as higher insurance premiums and transportation costs.

---

[*] The rate of return on investment is the ratio of annual receipts to original cost.

Despite these disadvantages, a foreign firm enjoys a number of advantages that are not shared by local firms. These advantages may include superior management skills, better technology, better economies of scale, a greater knowledge of the world market, and a better financial network.*

According to the market imperfections theory, the advantages must be greater than the disadvantages or the foreign firm will incur losses and decide not to operate in a host country. Furthermore, advantages must be transferable within the firm and across national boundaries.

Theoretically, these advantages stem from imperfections in the market (this is where the theory gets its name). Market imperfections arise when some of the underlying assumptions of perfect competition are violated. In the theoretical world of perfect competition, it is assumed that (a) a large number of firms are producing homogeneous products, (b) both buyers and sellers have free entry to and exit from the industry, (c) perfect and free knowledge prevails in the market, and (d) all factors of production are perfectly mobile. In the real world, however, these assumptions do not hold true, and, as a result, some firms acquire competitive advantages over others. These advantages are referred to as **ownership-specific advantages** or **firm-specific advantages.** Such advantages are internal to the firm and consist of tangible and intangible assets that are under the firm's control. Two examples of tangible assets are (a) the availability of specific markets or raw materials not accessible to other firms, and (b) a larger firm that leads to economies of scale and lower production costs, which in turn hamper competition. Intangible assets include trademarks, brand names, patents, management skills, marketing skills, and so forth, which give a firm a competitive edge over others and enables it to achieve greater market power.

The market imperfections theory helps us to speculate about industries that are likely candidates for the expansion of either indigenous or international operations. This approach alone, however, cannot answer many questions raised in the area of foreign investment. For example, it does not tell us why a firm has to invest in a foreign country in order to take advantage of its competitive edge. As we explained in Chapter 17, other forms of international business, such as licensing, franchising, management contracts, and so forth, also allow a firm to exploit its advantages.

One application of the market imperfection theory is its use in explaining horizontal and vertical integration. **Horizontal integration** means the merger of firms that are producing similar products under one ownership. The products may be close substitutes, such as gasoline produced by different plants, or comparable products, such as aluminum cans and bottles. The purpose of integration is to form a line of products that can be sold through the same selling and distribution channels, thereby increasing profit. On an international scale, horizontal integration means the production, in foreign countries, of goods that are similar to those manufactured at home. The motive for integration is to gain from the firm-specific advantages. Chrysler, General Motors, Volkswagen, Toyota, Honda, General Tire and Rubber, and Pfizer are examples of firms that produce products in foreign countries similar to those products manufactured at home.

Vertical integration is a merger of firms engaged in different stages of production and distribution under one ownership. Vertical integration can be either forward or backward. **Forward integration** means extending operations into the buyer's market. For example, a potato grower could vertically integrate by extending its activities to include the selling, marketing, and distribution of potatoes. **Backward integration** means expanding operations into the suppliers' market. Using the same example, a firm engaged in selling potatoes could take over production of potatoes as well. Internationally, as with horizontal integration, the motive behind vertical integration is to augment firm-specific advantages. The oil industry is a prime example of vertical integration. This industry is dominated by a small number of international firms, such as Exxon, Mobil, and Texaco. The firms in this industry frequently engage in vertical integration to bring extraction, transportation, refining, and distribution under their control. This allows them to fully use their firm-specific advantages and also provides them with a secure source of both supply and demand. Such security permits them to operate refineries to their potential, minimizing costs that arise from an underused capacity.

---

* Economies of scale refers to decreases in a firm's long-run average costs as the size of its plant is increased.

GLOBAL INSIGHT CASE 18.1

Investment Climate in Poland

Following the drastic reforms launched in January 1990, Poland gradually turned to the fastest growing economy in Europe. To survive, restructured its organization. New accounting rules emerged that helped improve management quality, and Polish workers began to realize that foreign direct investment (FDI) could bring with it the new technology that they needed to strengthen their economic development process.

Today, Polish workers no longer consider foreign capital as a tool of imperialism or an instrument of capitalism to exploit their resources. They now believe that foreign direct investment plays an important role in the modernization of the Polish economy and can rationalize the economic activity in accordance with the market mechanism. Today, Poland's major objectives are to become an industrial free trade system, to harmonize legislation, and to develop economic cooperation that supports its goal of becoming a member of the European Union (EU).

Two actions that are indicative of Poland's openness to FDI are the Foreign Investment Act of 1991, and its accession to the OECD. The Foreign Investment Act of 1991 provides the basis for opening the Polish economy to FDI. Poland's accession to the OECD in mid 1996, has accelerated procedural changes that should help enhance foreign investment. This includes equal treatment of foreign and domestic investors, thus making it more efficient to purchase land, and easing restrictions on capital flows.

Although Poland has welcomed FDI in many business sectors, the road to FDI in Poland has not been a smooth one. Currently, foreign investors face potential discrimination in public procurement contracts. Poland's public procurement law allows for a 20 percent price advantage for domestic firms, and there is a 50 percent domestic material and labor content minimum for all bids. In some cases, the Polish authorities have reverted to protectionism to preserve its national sovereignty. This has resulted in the control of some business sectors by the government. These sectors include telecommunications, mining, steel, defense, transportation, energy, and banking. One of the countries that has been a major beneficiary of Poland's privatization efforts is the United States. In 1995, the U.S. was the top foreign investor in Poland, accounting for 25 percent of the total foreign investment. The top 20 U.S. investors include: Polish American Enterprise Fund, International Paper Corp, Philip Morris, Proctor and Gamble, Curtis, Epstein, D. Chase Enterprises, Schooner Capital, Ford Motor, Goodyear Tires, Mars, McDonald's, Ameritech, RJ Reynolds, Airtouch, Liquid Carbonic, Citibank, General Motors, and Gerber.

Currently, trade regulations and standards of doing business in Poland have become a concern for the U.S. Tariff rates are subject to frequent change as Poland moves toward becoming a market economy. Customs duties apply to all products imported into Poland ranging from 0 to 90 percent with the average between 8 and 12 percent. In 1992, Poland signed the European Community Association Agreement with the EU which lowered or eliminated tariffs on many EU produced goods imported into Poland, while tariffs on U.S. products remained the same. This has put the United States in a disadvantageous position relative to the EU, in trading with Poland.

Sources: "Poland Emerges As The Test Case For EU Expansion," *The Wall Street Journal* 30 Oct. 1996, B9A; Graham Field, "A Guide to Poland," *Euromoney (*September 1996): 248; Gene. Koretz, "Paths Forward A Free Market," *Business Week*, (January 1997): 27; "Polish Program of Privatization Shows Progress, *Wall Street Journal*, 8 July 1996, "Poland Allows Foreign Buyers For Some Banks," *Wall Street Journal* , 1 July 1996, B7F; "Booming Economy In Poland Brings Jobs, Wealth, and Apathy," *Wall Street Journal* 25 November 1996, A1; "For Polish Firms, Mass Privatization Moves Glacially, " *Wall Street Journal*, 6 January 1997, A7C; *National Trade Data Bank.*

18.3 THEORIES OF THE MULTINATIONAL CORPORATION

According to our discussion of FDI theories, a firm's decision to invest can be explained in the context of market imperfections. Although market imperfections still represent the basis for the theoretical development of the MNC, theoreticians have recently shifted their attention toward developing a global theory of the MNC that also accounts for the firm's internal organization.[3]

In this section we study three of the major theories of the MNC.

18.3a Internalization Theory

The **internalization theory** is an extension of the market imperfection theory. For a firm to have a competitive edge in an imperfect market, it must have advantages over other firms. Internalizing means keeping those advantages within the firm in order to maintain the competitive edge. Externalizing, on the other hand, means making those advantages available to others in return for some gain, usually money. As an example, assume you are the manager of a local restaurant, and your success in business is due to your knowledge of a special recipe. Obviously, one way for you to capitalize on this knowledge is to externalize it; that is, you can make the knowledge available to others in return for money. As you know, however, if such an action is taken, your competitive position naturally will be weakened and your profits will decline. Additionally, it is very difficult for you to estimate the monetary value of your knowledge. Because of this uncertainty, you may decide to internalize your knowledge, that is, keep it to yourself. Methods for internalization include secrecy, patents, copyrights, or family networks. As we explain later, internalization also explains vertical and horizontal integration when they are used to reduce risk and to increase the efficiency of an MNC's operation.

On an international level, MNCs regularly engage in internalization to more fully capitalize on their firm-specific advantages. Chief among these advantages is knowledge. An MNC obtains knowledge by either experience or research and development. Knowledge may include skills or technologies that are used in the MNC's management and production processes. In this case, knowledge is considered an intermediate good that is used in the production of final goods. As such, it is an intangible asset to the firm. To be competitive in the world market, MNCs try to establish property rights over their acquired knowledge. In other words, they internalize their knowledge rather than sell it. This prevents potential rivals at home or abroad from having access to the MNC's knowledge. With such knowledge, rivals could threaten the competitive advantage of the MNC.

Besides knowledge, other factors induce a firm to internalize. Among these factors are transaction costs, buyers' uncertainty, quality control, foreign exchange control, taxes and tariffs imposed by the government, and regulations governing FDI. For example, some MNCs engage in internalization by vertical integration in order to reduce risks and to increase efficiency. In fact, many European and U.S. MNCs have integrated backward to minimize risks of variation in quantity, quality, and price of their inputs. They have also engaged in internalization by forward integration to reduce the risks associated with sales volume and price. Consider the Iranian revolution of the late 1970s that drastically reduced the outflow of oil from that country. Multinational corporations involved in that part of the world survived because their integration simply allowed them to adjust to the situation, thus preventing disruption in their worldwide activities.

18.3b Appropriability Theory

This theory is based on the assumption that the eminent feature of MNCs is their ability to specialize in the creation of technology. Technology is created by MNCs at five different stages: (a) discovery of a new product, (b) development of a product, (c) generation of the production function, (d) market generation, and (e) appropriability.[*][4]

---

*   The term appropriability comes from the word "appropriable," which means "can be appropriated to take for one's own or exclusive use." *Webster's New Dictionary of the American Languages*, 2d ed. (New York: Simon & Schuster, 1980), 68.

According to the appropriability theory, after generating a technology, a firm should be able to appropriate the resulting benefits. If this were not possible, the firm would not be able to bear the cost of generation and thus would have no incentive to create new technology. The theory also asserts that MNCs specialize in creating technologies that are transmitted more efficiently through their internal channels than through market mechanisms. The use of internal channels enables firms to appropriate the technology they generate—technology that would otherwise be lost to other firms. Furthermore, MNCs prefer to produce sophisticated technologies to the extent that they may be detrimental to the technology users. This is because MNCs are more successful in appropriating returns from sophisticated technologies than from simple technologies. Ultimately, however, there is a decline in the production of new technology. This situation creates a technology cycle at the industry level. In this cycle, industries producing information at a fast rate are considered young. As the industry ages and matures, the amount of information and the rate at which it is generated decline. As a result, the optimum industry size diminishes.

The appropriability theory provides an explanation for MNCs' tendency to engage in takeover activities. This approach considers takeovers of a host country's plants and equipment as the normal result of an MNC's growth to optimum firm size at the beginning stage of an industry's life cycle.

In summary, the appropriability theory is similar to the internalization theory in terms of creating an internal market (internal channels) for exploiting firm-specific advantages. The appropriability theory accentuates the potential returns from technology generation and the ability of the MNC to appropriate such returns.

18.3c Eclectic Theory of International Production

This theory was developed by John Dunning in an attempt to build a general theory based on firm-specific advantages and location-specific advantages. More specifically, this theory maintains that for an MNC to invest abroad, three advantages must be present. These are (a) firm-specific advantages, (b) internalization advantages, and (c) location-specific advantages.

Firm-specific advantages, as we explained earlier, result from tangible and intangible resources that are owned by a firm. These resources, exclusive to the firm, give it a comparative advantage over other firms. For a firm to become an MNC, however, it should possess **internalization advantages** as well. This means that the firm must have a desire and an ability to internalize (use) its firm-specific advantages rather than externalizing (selling) them through licensing, management contracts, and so forth. This, of course, is achieved by serving a foreign market. But a firm can serve a foreign market by extending its activities to include either exportation or production in a foreign country. For production to take place, the foreign country should have some **location-specific advantages**. In other words, some natural resources, or perhaps a low-cost labor force, should exist to make it profitable for a firm to locate its production facilities abroad instead of at home.

The **eclectic theory** suggests that, given a firm-specific advantage, internalization and competitiveness are positively correlated. This means that MNCs that are able to internalize their activities the most are more competitive in the world market. Multinational Corporations usually engage in the kinds of internalization that are most appropriate to their market conditions, their input combination, and the policies of the countries with which they are dealing. For example, the theory predicts that internalization would be greater for MNCs headquartered in countries with minimal raw materials than from those with abundant materials.

In summary, the eclectic approach suggests that knowledge alone does not give the MNC a competitive edge over rivals. Instead, the firm's willingness to internalize its knowledge rather than sell it to others contributes to its success. The use of this knowledge in a host country is a prerequisite for FDI to take place.

The eclectic theory provides an explanation of the pattern of international production on a country-by-country basis. For an MNC to invest in a foreign country, both firm-specific and location-specific advantages must be present. The MNC favors investment in the country where it is most profitable to internalize its monopolistic advantages. Otherwise, it would be preferable for the corporation to serve the foreign country through exports or licensing.

18.4 MARXIST THEORY

Karl Marx considered history a logical process that changes mainly in response to economic activities. In providing his economic interpretation of history, he distinguished among three stages of a capitalist enterprise's development: the investment expansion, the concentration of power, and the growth of the world market.

Marx believed that the economic environment in a capitalist society is such that it forces capitalist entrepreneurs to constantly expand their operations. He wrote the following:

> *Moreover, the development of capitalist production makes it constantly necessary to keep increasing the amount of the capital laid out in a given industrial undertaking, and competition makes the imminent laws of capitalist production to be felt by each individual capitalist, as external coercive laws. It compels him to keep constantly extending his capital, in order to preserve it, but extend it he cannot, except by means of progressive accumulation.*[5]

As the process of capital expansion continues, Marx explained, it gives rise to an increasing concentration of capital in the hands of fewer and fewer capitalists. In the meantime, such a concentration alone calls for more capital accumulation. The process of concentration, he maintained, appears in two different shapes which are interrelated. The first is the dissemination of large-scale production, and the second is the enlargement of enterprise via takeover and expansion. Marx explained that the organizational structure most appropriate to capital expansion is a joint-stock company—what we call a corporation today.

Marx maintained that the world market is vital to the existence of capitalists and provides the basis for capitalist production. Capitalism rose in the commercial revolution of the sixteenth and early seventeenth centuries. It provided an international market in the world. The expansion of this market, which was based on the needs of Western European countries, fueled further expansion of capitalist enterprises and facilitated the transition from feudalism to capitalism.

Having explained the three stages of capitalist enterprise development, Marx considered MNCs the final chapter of this development process. The three stages of investment expansion, concentration of power, and growth of the world market lead to the monopolization of capital, which is the result of increasing competition among capitalists. At this stage, the small capitalist either weakens or is taken over by a few larger ones, or as Marx put it, "one capitalist always kills many."[6] He implied that a final stage follows the monopolization of capital. It was left to V. I. Lenin, however, the founder of Russian communist ideology in the early twentieth century, to elaborate on this stage. Lenin argued that concentration and monopolization of capital lead to an economic system that is controlled by "finance capital." This is the stage at which large banks, in cooperation with huge monopolies, control and manipulate the masses. The expansion of these giants necessitates their penetration into foreign markets. This is achieved by crossing national boundaries and forming international companies (MNCs), which then control the market and resources of other nations. When this happens the economy has reached the highest and final stage of capitalism, which is called "capitalistic imperialism."

Marx's followers, such as Paul Baran, Paul Sweezy, Harry Magdoff, and Stephen Hymer, have all considered FDI a vehicle for transferring riches from poor nations to wealthy countries. They believe that MNCs will tear the social and political fabrics of developing countries and destroy the possibility of their self-sufficiency, making them dependent on advanced countries. This is achieved by the hierarchical division of labor and a tendency to centralize the decision-making process in a few key cities located in the advanced countries. As a result, the rest of the world is confined to a lower level of activity and income. Thus, the present pattern of income inequality and dependency worsens, and the relationship between different countries is based on "superior" and "subordinate," and "head office" and "branch plant."

In analyzing the political consequences of MNCs, Stephen Hymer takes a very pessimistic view. He sees that MNCs are faced with unavoidable nationalistic rivalry among the major capitalist countries, with the economic challenge of the socialist bloc countries, and with threats from developing countries. He specifically emphasizes that "one could easily argue that the age of multinational corporations is at its end rather than its beginning."[7]

The Marxist theory has attracted the attention of many political groups as a rationale for opposing MNCs. Consequently, some countries, such as Cuba, have gone so far as to break their economic ties with Western capitalist economies. Evidence shows, however, that as a result of their actions, these same countries have suffered from stagnation by reducing or severing their economic relations with the West.

GLOBAL INSIGHTS CASE 18.2

McDonald's In Russia

When the world's biggest McDonald's first opened in Moscow in January 1990, it was hard to believe that a symbol of American capitalism would ever be profitable in a former communist nation. It turned out that since McDonald's opened its doors for the first time it had to serve 35,000-45,000 customers a day. Customers were willing to wait in a three-hour line to get their favorite food from McDonald's. Some Russians even got into the business of buying sandwiches for resale at a slight profit. It was evident that McDonald's had problems in meeting such a high demand.

Historically, Russians have always been very curious about life in America and McDonald's gave them a taste of American culture. It seems ironic that McDonald's demand continued to stay strong despite the fact that inflation kept rising with Russian salaries averaging about 10,000 rubles ($16.95) a month, failing to keep up with inflation. Yet, McDonald's experienced no significant change in its sales revenue.

Given the growing demand for its product, McDonald's decided to expand its domain of operation in Russia by opening additional restaurants at the rate of one per month. At this rate, McDonald's was expected to have 100 restaurants in Russia by the year 2000.

By the mid-1990s, the demand for McDonald's product in Russia started to weaken. The long lines began to disappear as the number of customers dwindled to a more manageable size than the 35,000-45,000 daily that once waited for 3 hours for a Big Mac. It seems that inflation had finally taken its toll. Several customers found that they were no longer able to afford to "eat out". Many citizens were locked into state jobs and while inflation increased, their salaries stayed the same forcing them to cut back on their discretionary spending.

In response to this weakening demand, McDonald's marketing department had to come up with some innovative ideas for advertising in order to stimulate demand and accept the fact that future inflation related incidents can hardly guarantee the same sales growth rate when operating in an unstable economy like Russia.

Currently, McDonald's offers a streamlined menu. It does not include breakfast, Happy Meals, chicken or many other items that are offered in America. However, the menu does cater to the Russian market. The menu includes Russian favorites such as pirogi, mushroom soup, sugary tea, Kvas (a Russian drink that is made from fermented bread), blini (thin pancakes), and of course McDonald's in Russia would not be complete without serving Russia's favorite drink: vodka. Two new products that McDonald's is planning to add to its menu are chicken sandwiches, and a fish sandwich that is made of Alaskan pollack fillet.

Given McDonald's effort in adapting its products to the Russian environment, it is expected that its sales will increase in the future. McDonald's ability to run a profitable operation in a country that does not offer much political and economic stability is indicative of its ability to adapt to the environment of the country in which it operates. Having proved to be profitable in Russia, McDonald's future plans include expansion into the rest of Russia and other former Soviet Republics.

Sources: Gribanov, Valeri., "Fast Food St. Petersburg Style," *Kommersant-Food* 11 April 1997, p.2;   "Five McDonald's Outlets To Be Built In Nizhny Novgood," *Finansovye Izvestia* September, 1996, p 2; Plotnikova, Tatyana. "McDonald's Picks Out An Advertiser In Russia," *Kommersant* 4 March 1997, p.10;   RICA News Agency. "American Investments Into Russian Economy," *Rica BiznesYezhenedelnik* 24 January 1994; Vardanyan, Raznik. "The Impact of Economic Reform On International Migration," *Sotsis,* 20 October 1995, p58-67.

Marx's economic thoughts have been criticized on many grounds. With regard to large corporations specifically, one economic historian writes, "Marx failed to recognize. . .that the large corporation, while facilitating the concentration of control, has at the same time been instrumental in diffusing property among many capitalists."[8] In fact, evidence shows that countries such as Taiwan and South Korea have experienced a healthy economic growth and a more equitable income distribution while they have been highly dependent on the United States and other capitalist countries for their trade and investment.[*]

In today's world, pragmatism has undermined the philosophical ideologies of Marxist sympathizers. This is evident by the operation of multinational enterprises in nonsocialist countries by the former Soviet Union and the former socialist countries of Eastern Europe. Even more important, a significant shift in the People's Republic of China's economic policies followed the demise of Mao Tse-tung in 1976. Since then the Chinese have reversed their policies with regard to FDI, openly inviting Western entrepreneurs to invest in their country.

The economic reform of the Eastern European countries, the collapse of the Soviet Union, and the reunification of Germany are among the events that make the practical application of the Marxist theory questionable.

18.5 INTERNATIONAL LABOR MOBILITY AND IMMIGRATION

Although labor is generally less mobile than capital across national boundaries, it represents one of the most sensitive issues of our time. For some countries, having natives migrate to other nations could tarnish national dignity and lead to economic losses for those who are left behind. In receiving nations, immigration might raise nationalist fervor and fuel xenophobia and ethnic prejudice, mainly among those who fear that competition from immigrants could lead to loss of their jobs and economic well-being. For migrants themselves, the road to another nation with a different culture has its cost and is filled with uncertainty. The costs consist of transportation expenses and loss of income during the transitory stage of resettling and looking for a job in the new country. A migrant leaving friends and family behind has to endure the "cultural shock" of adjusting to a new culture and, often, a new language. Also, subject to new potential ailments and possible exploitation by others, a migrant may fail to find a better income in the new nation and return home frustrated. Nevertheless, on average, migrants should benefit from migration; if this were not the case, they would not decide to migrate.

The purpose of this section is to shed some light on the main issues surrounding labor migration. First, we describe the causes of international labor migration. Second, we provide a theoretical explanation of labor migration by examining its welfare effects in the context of demand and supply analysis.

18.5a Causes of International Labor Migration

The factors giving rise to international labor migration are both economic and noneconomic in nature, and often the two are interconnected. In some instances, noneconomic factors, such as political, religious, and physical freedom, gained by refugees who escape oppressive governments constitute the major reason for migration. This was certainly the case for some of the migrations that occurred in the nineteenth century and earlier in Europe. In other cases, the expectation of higher real wages and income constitute the main cause of migrating to another country. In fact, most international labor migration, especially following World War II, has been inspired by the possibility of securing higher earnings abroad. Highly educated professionals from developing countries have increased their income substantially by migrating to countries such as Australia, Great Britain, Canada, Germany, and the United States.

The United States has been an especially attractive place for migration, admitting more than 57 million migrants from 1820 through 2000. Western Europe was the chief origin of migrants during this period; Britain, Germany, and Italy were among the major contributors. In recent years, however, the percentage of immigrants from developing countries has increased, whereas the percentage of European migrants has declined. This can be seen from Table 18-1. As this table indicates, in 1995, out of 720,500 immigrants, 128,200 (17.79 percent) were European, whereas 267,900, (37.18 percent) were Asian. In other words, the number of Asians that migrated to the United States was

---

[*] Both Taiwan and South Korea have experienced a real per capita income growth of over 6 percent per year during the 1960s, 1970s, while highly dependent on trade, assistance, and investment from the United States and other capitalist nations.

more than two times greater than the number of European immigrants. As Table 18-2 shows, in 1995 the most popular state for immigration was California, followed by New York, Florida, Texas, New Jersey, Illinois, Massachusetts, Virginia, and Arizona.

TABLE 18-1
Immigrants Admitted to the United States by Country of Birth: 1981-1995
(In thousands)

COUNTRY OF BIRTH	1981-90, total	1991-93, total	1994	1995
All Countries	7,338.1	3,705.4	804.4	720.5
Europe	705.6	438.9	160.9	128.2
Asia	2,817.4	1,073.5	292.6	267.9
North America	3,125.0	3,125.0	272.2	231.5
South America	455.9	455.9	47.4	45.7
Africa	192.3	192.3	26.7	42.5

Source: U.S. Bureau of Census, *Statistical Abstracts of the United States: 1997,* 117th ed. (Washington, DC: Government Printing Office, 1997), 11.

TABLE 18-2
Immigrants Admitted, by Leading Country of Birth and State: 1995
(In thousands)

STATE	Total	Mexico	Soviet Union, former	Philippines	Vietnam	Dominican Republic	China	India	Cuba
California	166,482	34,416	10,045	22,584	16,755	71	10,256	6,646	428
New York	128,406	848	19,227	3,216	963	21,471	11,254	4,859	331
Florida	62,023	1,922	1,021	1,086	1,194	2,090	639	1,141	15,112
Texas	49,963	22,792	824	1,997	4,251	101	1,002	2,400	131
New Jersey	39,729	375	1,631	2,626	435	4,136	1,134	3,958	805
Illinois	33,898	6,500	3,384	2,690	583	102	986	3,051	96
Massachusetts	20,523	89	2,253	229	1,247	1,970	1,287	873	54
Virginia	16,319	318	575	1,219	1,236	69	455	931	36
Arizona	7,700	3,640	215	294	396	15	270	218	13

Source: U.S. Bureau of Census, *Statistical Abstracts of the United States: 1997,* 117th ed. (Washington, DC: Government Printing Office, 1997), 11.

To be sure, an intricate mesh of elements affects a person's decision to emigrate. For simplification of the analysis, however, in the next section we focus on economic causes and assume that an individual's decision to emigrate is only motivated by higher wages in the country of his or her destination.

18.5b Effects of International Labor Migration

The effects of international labor migration can be investigated in terms of output effect and income distribution effect. Let us first study these effects in the context of demand and supply analysis. Next, we elaborate on other effects of international labor migration that are not apparent from the demand and supply analysis.

The Output Effect. In Figure 18-1, assume the world is composed of only two countries, the United States and Mexico; there are only two factors of production, capital and labor. O_U represents the origin of the United States, and O_M represents the origin of Mexico. The length of the horizontal axis ($O_U O_M$) represents the fixed supply of labor in the world. The initial allocation of this supply between the two countries is shown by the intersection of the entirely inelastic supply curve (S) with the horizontal axis at L_0.

FIGURE 18-1
Output and Income Distribution Effects of International Labor Migration

Given a supply of $O_U L_0$ units of labor, the United States has a wage rate of $O_U W_U$, and the value of its total output is measured by $O_U CAL_0$, or areas h + g + f. Given a supply of $O_M L_0$ units of labor, Mexico has a wage rate of $O_M W_M$, and the value of its total output is measured by $O_M DBL_0$, or areas a + b + c + d + e. The migration of $L_0 L_1$ labor from Mexico to the United States equalizes wage rates in both nations at $L_1 E$. This increases total output by areas d + e + j + i in the United States and reduces Mexico's total output by areas d + e. Thus, immigration leads to a net gain in the value of world output as shown by areas j + i.

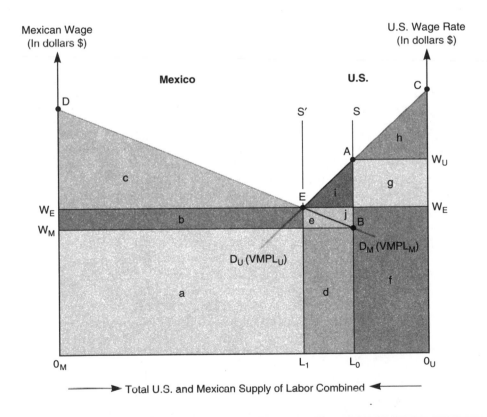

GLOBAL INSIGHTS CASE 18.3

The Push and Pull of U.S. Immigration Policy

The elements that give rise to international migration can be classified into "push" and "pull" forces. The extent of migration depends on the interaction of these two forces. Push forces are those factors that drive many persons to decide to emigrate, leaving their nation of origin. These factors may be major events causing widespread civil disorder and disruption of lives and a nation's economy—war with other countries, civil war, or large-scale ethnic persecutions. Examples of such situations can be seen in the refugee flows leaving Haiti, Bosnia, and Rwanda; the 800,000 Cuban refugees who have fled to the United States; and the tens of thousands of Russian Jews fleeing the former Soviet Union. Other push factors of significance may be natural disasters, including floods, earthquakes, and massive crop diseases, such as the infamous potato famine of the 1840s. Sometimes a nation's economy falters to the extent that droves of residents seek employment elsewhere, as in the case of the estimated millions of undocumented Mexicans coming to the United States.

Pull forces are those factors that attract large waves of immigration to a specific country. They are often linked in some way to push forces. In times of civil unrest and war, a nation that promises political and social stability draws people from the fighting countries. In times of religious and ethnic persecution, a country where freedom of religion is an important value again attracts the persecuted. And in times of economic disruption, a nation with a strong economy and the hope of jobs will, like a powerful magnet, draw millions of migrants.

Figure A traces the immigration patterns in the United States from 1820 to 1990. It clearly illustrates the ebb and flow of immigration and briefly highlights some of the major push and pull forces that have contributed to the process over the years.[1]

United States immigration policy responds to the ebb and flow of immigration by attempting to influence the push and pull forces. Two recent policy initiatives exemplify an attempt to control the immigration flow into the nation by influencing the push and pull forces perceived to be causing the influx.

The North American Free Trade Agreement (NAFTA) is first and foremost a matter of economic policymaking, not of immigration policy (as we discussed in Chapter 9). But by having a positive impact on Mexico's economy by creating jobs there, it will reduce the push forces driving millions of Mexican nationals to the United States. More jobs will result in people remaining in Mexico rather than flowing across the over-2,000 miles of border between the two nations.

In 1986, the United States enacted the most sweeping immigration laws reform in 20 years—the Immigration Reform and Control Act (IRCA). This law exemplifies an attempt to influence pull forces. A major provision was the enactment of a new device to control immigration, employer sanctions. The most significant immigration problem of the 1970s and 1980s was perceived to be the annual flow of hundreds of thousands of illegal aliens into the United States, drawn by the economy. The IRCA was conceived as a way to "demagnetize" the draw of the U.S. economy by making every employer an agent of the Immigration and Naturalization Service (INS); the act made it illegal to hire an undocumented alien. While initially successful in causing a nearly 30-percent decline in the number of illegal aliens apprehended at the nation's borders, the impact of IRCA clearly has been largely temporary. As Figure B shows, the number of illegal aliens apprehended at U.S. borders has gradually risen back to pre-IRCA levels. Perhaps the ineffectiveness of IRCA to control the flow of illegal aliens is in large measure due to the fact that push forces are as strong or stronger than the pull forces influencing international migration in the 1990s.[2]

Notes

1. Michael LeMay, *From Open Door to Dutch Door: An Analysis of U.S. Immigration Policy Since 1820.* New York: Praeger, 1987.
2. Michael LeMay, *Anatomy of a Policy: The Reform of Current U.S. Immigration Policy.* Westport, CT: Praeger, 1994.

Source: This case was written by Professor Michael LeMay of California State University, San Bernardino.

Global Insights Case 18.3 (Continued)

FIGURE A
Trends in Immigration by Phrases, 1820-1990

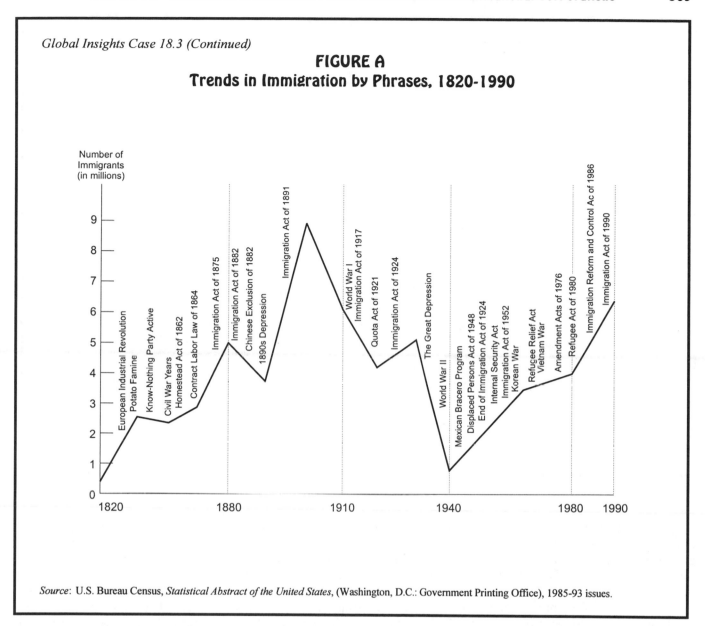

Source: U.S. Bureau Census, *Statistical Abstract of the United States*, (Washington, D.C.: Government Printing Office), 1985-93 issues.

Accordingly, the United States has $O_U L_0$ units of labor, and Mexico has $O_M L_0$ units of labor. The demand schedule for each nation is represented by the value of the marginal product of labor (VMPL) in that nation. The United States demand for labor (D_U) is denoted by $VMPL_U$; Mexico's demand for labor (D_M) is denoted by $VMPL_M$.

As we know from microeconomics courses, VMPL is equal to the marginal physical product of labor (the amount of output associated with the last unit of labor hired) multiplied by the price of the product produced. In other words, VMPL measures the amount of money producers receive from the sale of the output produced by the last unit of labor hired. As the quantity of labor in a given nation increases, the marginal physical product of labor decreases and VMPL declines. Because under competitive conditions VMPL is equal to the wage rate, it follows that an increase in the quantity of labor leads to a decline in the wage rate. In other words, the VMPL curve in each country is the labor demand schedule, portraying a negative relationship between the wage rate (W) and the quantity of labor employed.

The premigration equilibrium wage rate in each country is found at the intersection of labor demand and supply curves for that country. In the United States, this equilibrium occurs at point A where S and D_U intersect. At this point, the U.S. wage rate is $O_U W_U$, and the value of total output is measured by $O_U CAL_0$ (areas h + g + f). Out of this

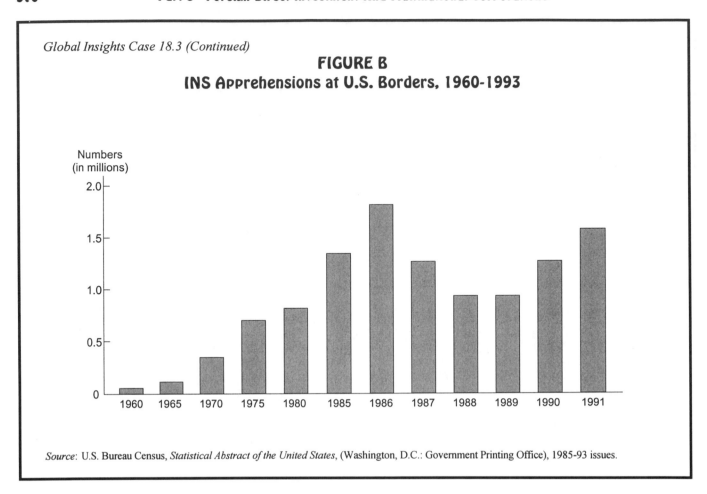

Global Insights Case 18.3 (Continued)

FIGURE B
INS Apprehensions at U.S. Borders, 1960-1993

Numbers
(in millions)

Source: U.S. Bureau Census, *Statistical Abstract of the United States*, (Washington, D.C.: Government Printing Office), 1985-93 issues.

total, areas g + f represents total labor income, that is, the wage rate ($O_U W_U$) multiplied by the quantity of labor ($O_U L_0$). The rest (area h) represents the share of national income collected by the owners of capital.[*] In Mexico, the equilibrium occurs at point B where S and D_M intersect. At this point, the equilibrium wage rate in Mexico is $O_M W_M$, and the value of total output is measured by $O_M DBL_0$ (areas a + b + c + d + e). Out of this total, areas a + d measures total labor income ($O_M L_0 \times O_M W_M$). The rest (areas b + c + e) denotes the share of income collected by the owners of capital.

Now assume free international labor migration, meaning that labor can move freely between the two nations solely in response to wage differentials. Because wages are higher in the United States than in Mexico, there is an incentive for Mexican workers to migrate to the United States to compete for the higher wages. This process continues until the wage differential between the two nations is eliminated. Graphically, this is represented by the shift of the supply of labor from S to S′, where it intersects both D_U and D_M at equilibrium point E. At this postmigration equilibrium point, the wage rate in both countries is equal ($O_U W_E = O_M W_E$), and the quantity of labor employed in the United States and Mexico is $O_U L_1$ and $O_M L_1$, respectively. Thus, wage rates rise in Mexico and fall in the United States. However, the value of total output falls from $O_M DBL_0$ (areas a + b + c + d + e) to $O_M DEL_1$ (areas a + b + c) in Mexico, and rises from $O_U CAL_0$ (areas h + g + f) to $O_U CEL_1$ (areas h + g + f + d + e + j + i) in the United States. These results are summarized in Table 18-3. As this table indicates, free immigration leads to a net gain in the value of world output shown by areas i + j.

Income Distribution Effect. Migration also alters the income distribution in both nations. As Table 18-3 indicates, the United States' total gain in output is measured by areas i + j + e + d. Out of this total, areas d + e + j represent total labor income ($O_U W_E \times L_1 L_0$) paid to Mexican migrant workers, and the rest (area i) represents the extra earnings

---

[*] In our analysis, we are assuming capital and labor are the only two productive factors for production.

TABLE 18-3
The Output Effect of Migration

	Before Migration	After Migration	Gains (+)/Loss (-)
U.S. output	Areas h + g + f	Areas h + g + f + d + e + j + i	Areas i + j + e + d
Mexican output	Areas a + b + c + d + e	Areas a + b + c	− e − d
Net gain in world output			Areas i + j

gained by U.S. owners of capital due to the availability of additional labor. However, immigration causes wage rates to go down in the United States from $O_U W_U$ to $O_U W_E$. As a result, the earnings of native U.S. workers decrease by area g, which is transferred to U.S. owners of capital.

In the case of Mexico, as our analysis showed, labor emigration causes its output to fall by areas d + e. This total represents a transfer from Mexico to the United States. The remaining workers in Mexico gain area b at the expense of the owners of capital due to higher wage rates following emigration.

To summarize, under competitive conditions, labor migration causes overall world output to increase. It also causes a redistribution of income from capital to labor in the sending country (Mexico) and from labor to capital in the receiving country (the United States).

Other Effects. In the preceding analysis, we tacitly conjectured that workers are unskilled. However, in real-world settings, migrants are people with different skills and educational backgrounds. The effect of skilled workers' migration is likely to be significantly different from that of unskilled workers. Economically speaking, highly skilled workers are considered human capital, obtained by incurring great cost in education and training. Thus, the departure of these workers from developing countries to advanced countries results in a gain in the advanced countries' capital stock at the expense of developing countries. This limits the growth potential of a developing country, retarding its economic development process. Given the scarcity of capital in most developing countries, the emigration of highly skilled workers from these countries to advanced countries has continued to be a sensitive issue and has been referred to as **brain drain.**

Brain drain is often encouraged by national immigration laws (like those in the United States, Canada, Great Britain, Australia, and other advanced countries) that encourage immigration of skilled workers while discouraging the immigration of unskilled workers. This has resulted in the exodus of a large number of highly skilled workers, such as medical doctors, scientists, engineers, and nurses, from developing countries and Europe to the United States, especially since the 1950s. For example, during the 1980s, more than 200 well-known scientists left Britain to accept positions in the United States' top universities. As another example, following the collapse of the Soviet Union, a large number of scientists continued to emigrate to the United States.

To be sure, the brain drain inflicts clear costs on the sending nations. Closing borders to unskilled migrants causes more of the globe's work force to be trapped in less-efficient economies, contributing to the divergence of income between developing and advanced countries. A case can be made for a brain drain tax that remunerates sending nations for their human capital investment in emigrants.

In our demand and supply analysis of labor migration, we also implicitly assumed that the decision of Mexican workers to migrate to the United States was essentially permanent. In the real world, however, a large number of workers migrate to another country on a temporary basis. This has been the case especially for the European Union (EU). Members of the EU, such as France and Germany, permit migration of foreign workers, referred to as *guest workers,* on a temporary basis, depending on the members' domestic economic conditions. In a recessionary period, when foreign workers are no longer needed, these countries refuse to issue work permits. During a recovery period, however, they issue new work permits or renew the old ones. Such a practice tends to shield their economies and their labor forces from labor shortages during recovery periods and labor surpluses in recessionary periods. The pursuit of such a practice shifts the labor adjustment problem to the labor-emigrating nations, such as Turkey, Portugal, and Spain, which are relatively poorer and less prepared to handle the problem.

Given the low wages paid to guest workers, in 1991 the EU commission called for new regulations regarding pay levels and social conditions for guest workers.[9]

Another issue that is not apparent from our demand and supply analysis is the question of illegal immigration. This has been especially problematic for the United States. Today, millions of illegal immigrants work in the "underground economy" in the United States at below minimum wages. Many of these workers coming from Mexico to southwestern states (especially California), join the ranks of unskilled workers and provide a cheap supply of workers for the U.S. agricultural, restaurant, and garment industries. Although these workers receive few, if any, social benefits in the United States, they have been subject to resentment by low-skilled U.S. workers, mainly for depressing the wage level. This has made the subject of immigration, both legal and illegal, a "political hot potato" in the United States and has put pressure on policymakers to come up with a viable solution. One outcome of this pressure has been the passage of the U.S. Immigration Reform and Control Act in 1986. According to this act illegal aliens who could prove they had lived in the United States since before January 1, 1982, would be granted amnesty and the chance to obtain legal status and, ultimately, citizenship. Also, employers would be subject to fines, ranging from $250 to $10,000, for every illegal alien they employed. May 4, 1988, was set as the registration deadline. This act resulted in granting legal status to 3 million illegal immigrants of all nationalities. However, the act does not seem to have either slowed down the flow of illegal immigrants to the United States or significantly deterred employers from hiring undocumented immigrants. According to a report by the U.S. Immigration and Naturalization Service (INS), the number of illegal immigrants entering California seems to be increasing overall. In fact, the apprehension of illegal immigrants along the California and Arizona borders has increased 30 percent over the last decade, from 970,000 in 1982 to 1,258,000 in 1992. Additionally, according to random audits of all businesses by the INS, one third of them are in violation of the act. Violations encompass both the employment of illegal immigrants and shoddy documentation of workers' citizenship status.[10]

Unfortunately, there are no definite empirical studies to assess the impact of illegal immigrants on the U.S. economy. However, according to a report by Los Angeles County, illegal immigrants cost the county government $308 million, primarily in education and public assistance expenses, in 1991-1992. But the same group paid about $904 million in local and federal government taxes. In other words, illegal immigration provided a net gain of $596 million ($904 million - $308 million).[11] Thus, judging from the available data, the popular belief that illegal immigrants are a financial burden is apparently inaccurate. Overall, legal and illegal immigrants taken as a whole are likely to induce a net gain in the receiving country.

We conclude this chapter by stating that theories of international factor movements and MNCs, like those of trade theories, are abstractions from reality. As such, they help us to understand the "why" and "how" of factor movements and MNCs. One must be careful, however, not to read too much into theories. We should keep in mind that these theories provide only some comprehension of the general elements that explain FDI and MNCs. These theories should be employed along with additional data gathered in the real world when trying to answer the questions that are raised by FDI, MNCs, and immigration.

18.6 SUMMARY

1. According to the theory of international portfolio investment, the rate of return on capital is the cause of international capital movement among countries.
2. In the late 1960s, the inadequacy of the assumption of perfect competition in the analysis of foreign direct investment (FDI) was recognized. It was concluded that market imperfections is the prerequisite for FDI.
3. According to the market imperfections theory, for a firm to undertake FDI, it must have a comparative advantage over domestic firms in the host country.
4. The competitive advantages of a foreign firm, compared with those of a domestic firm, might be found in superior managerial skills, better technology, better economies of scale, a greater knowledge of the world market, and a better financial network.
5. A firm's competitive advantages are referred to as "ownership advantages" or firm-specific advantages. Such advantages are internal to the firm and consist of the tangible and intangible assets that are under the firm's control.
6. Horizontal integration means the merger of firms that are producing similar products under one ownership.

7. Vertical integration is the merger of firms engaged in different stages of production and distribution under one ownership.

8. Vertical integration can be either forward or backward. Forward integration means extending operations into the buyer's market. Backward integration means expanding operations into the supplier's market.

9. The internalization theory is an extension of the market imperfections theory. This theory assumes that a firm will capitalize on its knowledge by internalizing it, that is, keeping it to itself.

10. On an international level, multinational corporations (MNCs) regularly engage in internalization to more fully capitalize on their firm-specific advantages.

11. According to the appropriability theory, MNCs prefer to produce sophisticated technologies instead of simple ones, because they are more successful in appropriating returns from sophisticated technologies.

12. According to the eclectic theory, knowledge alone does not give an MNC a competitive edge over its rivals; the firm's willingness to internalize its knowledge rather than sell it to others contributes to its success.

13. Karl Marx distinguished among three stages of capitalist enterprise development. These stages are investment expansion, concentration of power, and growth of the world market.

14. According to Marxist theory, the three stages of capitalist enterprise development would eventually result in monopolization of capital, which in turn leads to an economic system that is controlled by "finance capital." When this happens, the economy has reached the highest and final stage of capitalism—capitalistic imperialism—in which MNCs come into existence.

15. Marx's economic thoughts have been criticized on many grounds. In today's world, pragmatism has undermined the philosophical ideologies of Marxist sympathizers.

16. The factors giving rise to international labor migration are both economic and noneconomic in nature, and often the two are interconnected.

17. The impact of international labor migration can be studied in terms of output effect, income distribution effect, and other effects. Other effects include brain drain, temporary migration, and illegal migration.

18. Theoretically, labor migration causes overall world output to increase. It also causes a redistribution of income from labor to capital in the receiving country and from capital to labor in the sending country.

19. Overall, immigrants are likely to induce net gain in the receiving country.

Review Questions

1. Are the economic factors leading to the movements of productive resources across national boundaries identical to those underlying international trade in goods and services? Explain.

2. Discuss the major shortcomings of trade theories in explaining FDI and MNCs.

3. Distinguish between portfolio investment and FDI.

4. Distinguish between the market imperfection theory and the internalization theory.

5. Compare the appropriability theory and the internalization theory.

6. According to the eclectic theory of international production, for an MNC to invest abroad, three advantages must be present. What are these advantages? Explain.

7. According to Marxist theory, what are the three stages of capitalist enterprise development? Explain.

8. According to this chapter, the impact of international migration can be studied in terms of three effects. What are these effects? Explain.

Problems

1. Choose a capital-abundant country and a labor-abundant country and assume that (a) the world consists only of these two countries, and (b) there are only two factors of production, capital and labor. Given your choice of countries, answer the following questions:
   (a) What are the output effects of labor migration?
   (b) What are the income distribution effects of labor migration?
   (c) What is the net effect of labor migration on the world?

2. As an MNC manager, how can you benefit from the eclectic theory when investing in a foreign country?
3. Distinguish between horizontal integration and vertical integration, and give examples of industries that have experienced integration. Are the motives behind horizontal and vertical integration the same? Explain.
4. The existence of superior managerial and marketing skills is a necessary, but not a sufficient, condition for international integration.
     Do you agree with this statement? Discuss.
5. Compare Marxist theory with the theories of FDI and MNCs as they have developed in the free-market, capitalist economies. How does the Marxist view of FDI and MNC differ from the free-market view? What are the implications of each of these views regarding international business?
6. Given the demise of the Soviet Union, the reunification of Germany, and the collapse of communist power in Eastern Europe, how do you perceive the usefulness of Marxist theory? Discuss.
7. Update Table 18-1 for the most recent years for which data is available, and interpret the data.

Notes

1. Stephen H. Hymer, "The International Operation of National Firm." Ph.D. diss. Massachusetts Institute of Technology, 1960.
2. Charles P. Kindleberger, *American Business Abroad: Six Lectures on Direct Investment* (New Haven, CT: Yale University Press, 1969), 13.
3. A. V. Calvet, "A Synthesis of Foreign Direct Investment Theories and Theories of the Multinational Firm," *Journal of International Business Studies* (Spring/Summer 1981): 43-59.
4. Stephen P. Magee, "Technology and the Appropriability Theory of the Multinational," in Jagdish Bhagwati, ed., *The New International Economic Order* (Cambridge, MA: Massachusetts Institute of Technology Press, 1976).
5. Karl Marx, *Capital,* 3 vols. (Moscow: Progress Publisher, 1975), vol. 1, 555.
6. *Ibid,* 714.
7. Stephen H. Hymer, "The Multinational Corporation and the Law of Uneven Development," in Jagdish Bhagwati, ed., *Economics and World Order: From the 1970s to the 1990s* (London: Macmillan, 1972), 131.

8. H. William Spiegel, *The Growth of Economic Thought* (Englewood Cliffs, NJ: Prentice-Hall, 1971), 475.
9. "Temporary Workers in Europe, " *The Wall Street Journal,* 21 June 1991, A8.
10. "The Day-Laborer Bottom Line: Demand Fuels Phenomenon," *Inland Valley Daily Bulletin,* 8 August 1993, A1.
11. *Ibid.*

Suggested Readings

Agarwall, Ray. "Investment Performance of U.S. Based Multinational Companies: Comments and a Perspective on International Diversification of Real Assets." *Journal of International Business Studies* (Spring/Summer 1980): 98-104.

Agarwall, Sanjeev, and Sridhar N. Ramaswami. "Choice of Foreign Market Entry Mode: Impact of Ownership, Location and Internalization Factors." *Journal of International Business Studies* (First Quarter 1992): 1-27.

Aliber, Robert Z. "A Theory of Direct Foreign Investment." In *The International Corporation,* edited by Charles P. Kindleberger. Cambridge, MA: Massachusetts Institute of Technology Press, 1970.

Asheghian, Parviz. "Foreign Direct Investment and Its Economic Impact in a Less Developed Country: The Case of Iran." *Managing International Development* (July/August 1984): 38-51.

Brewer, Thomas L. "Government Policies, Market Imperfections and Foreign Direct Investment." *Journal of International Business Studies* (First Quarter 1993): 101-120.

Calvet, A. L. "A Synthesis of Foreign Direct Investment Theories and Theories of the Multinational Firm." *Journal of International Business Studies* (Spring/Summer 1981): 43-59.

Caves, Richard E. *Multinational Enterprise and Economic Analysis.* Cambridge, MA: Harvard University Press, 1982.

Chiswick, Barry R. "Illegal Immigration and Immigration Control." *Journal of Economic Perspectives* (Summer 1988): 101-116.

Dunning, John H. *International Production and the Multinational Enterprise.* London: Allen & Unwin, 1981, ch. 2.

Errunza, V. R., and L. W. Sanhet. "The Effects of International Operation on the Market Value of the Firm: Theory and Practice."*Journal of Finance* (May 1981): 401-417.

Greenwood, Michael J., and John M. McDowell. "The Factor Market Consequences of U.S. Immigration." *Journal of Economic Literature* 24 (December 1986): 1738-1772.

Hirsch, S. "An International Trade and Investment Theory of the Firm." *Oxford Economic Papers* 28 (July 1976): 258-270.

Hood, Neil, and Stephen Young. *The Economics of Multinational Enterprise.* New York: Longman, 1979.

Hymer, Stephen H. *The International Operations of National Firms: A Study of Direct Investment.* Cambridge, MA: Massachusetts Institute of Technology Press, 1976.

Hymer, Stephen H., and Robert Rowthorn. "Multinational Corporations and International Oligopoly: The Non-American Challenge." In *The International Corporation: A Symposium,* edited by Charles P. Kindleberger. Cambridge, MA: Massachusetts Institute of Technology Press, 1970.

Knickerbocker, Frederick T. *Oligopolistic Reaction and Multinational Enterprise.* Boston: Division of Research, Graduate School of Business Administration, Harvard University, 1973.

Kogut, Bruce, and Udo Zander. "Knowledge of the Firm and Evolutionary Theory of Multinational Corporation." *Journal of International Business Studies* (Fourth Quarter 1993): 625-640.

Levy, Haim, and Marshall Sarnat. "International Diversification of Investment Portfolio." *The American Economic Review* (September 1970): 668-675.

Magdoff, Harry. "The Multinational Corporation and Development-A Contradiction." In *The Multinational Corporation and Social Change,* edited by David E. Apter and Louis W. Goodman. New York: Praeger, 1976.

Magee, Stephen D. "Information and the Multinational Corporation: An Appropriability Theory of Direct Investment." In *The New International Economic Order,* edited by Jagdish N. Bhagwati. Cambridge, MA: Massachusetts Institute of Technology Press, 1977.

Rugman Alan, M. *International Diversification and the Multinational Enterprise.* Lexington, MA: Lexington Books, 1979.

———."Internalization as a General Theory of Foreign Direct Investment." *Welwirtschaftliches Archiv* 116 (June 1980): 365-379.

Schoening, Niles C. "A Slow Leak: Effects of the U.S. Shifts in International Investment. *Survey of Business* (Spring 1989): 21-26.

Schorath, Fredrick W., Michael Y. Hu, and Haiyang Chen. "Country-of-Origin Effects of Foreign Investments in People's Republic of China." *Journal of International Business Studies* (Second Quarter 1993): 277-290.

Simon, Julian L. *The Economic Consequences of Immigration.* Oxford: Basil Blackwell, 1989.

Suzuki, Katshido. "Choice Between International Capital and Labor Mobility of Diversified Economies." *Journal of International Economics* (November 1989): 347-361.

Chapter 19

CONFLICTS SURROUNDING MULTINATIONAL CORPORATIONS

19.1 INTRODUCTION

The rapid growth of multinational corporations (MNCs) in recent years has given rise to heated debates regarding the usefulness of these corporations for both host and home countries. Nations differ in their attitudes toward the presence of foreign corporations, and they display different degrees of tension about this situation. In general, MNCs have met with more resistance in developing countries than in advanced countries.

Some writers in advanced countries consider MNCs the chief instrument in abolishing poverty in developing countries. Others in developing countries, however, refer to MNCs as the main device used by advanced nations to achieve "economic imperialism." These writings have fueled tensions and contributed to the imposition of governmental restrictions on MNC activities.

Although objections to the presence of MNCs has an economic tone, political and nationalistic considerations have played a significant role in shaping conflicting views toward these corporations. Xenophobia and the fear of economic dependence have lured some politicians to suggest economic confinement of foreign interests and the reservation of certain sectors for exclusive exploitation by local entrepreneurs.[1]

The purpose of this chapter is to provide a general understanding of the major opposing views on the MNC activities in host countries. First, we list the major criticisms of MNCs. Second, we study the sources of conflict. Third, we elaborate on host countries' reactions to MNCs. Finally, we raise the question as to who is right—MNCs or the countries in which they do business.

19.2 MAJOR CRITICISMS OF MULTINATIONAL CORPORATIONS

The subject of MNCs is imbued with a variety of complaints raised by host countries against these corporations. The criticisms dealing with technology transfer were discussed in Chapter 17. Some other major criticisms aimed at MNCs are as follows:

1. They raise needed capital locally, contributing to the rise in interest rates in their host countries.
2. The majority (sometimes even 100 percent) of the stocks of an MNC's subsidiary is owned by the parent company. Consequently, the host country's residents do not have much control over the operations of these corporations within their borders.
3. They reserve the key managerial and technical positions for expatriates. As a result, they do not contribute to the "learning-by-doing" process in host countries.
4. They do not provide training for host countries' workers.
5. They do not adapt their technology to the conditions that exist in host countries.
6. They concentrate their research and development activities in their home countries. As a result, they restrict the transfer of modern technology and know-how to host countries.
7. They give rise to demands for luxury goods in host countries at the expense of essential consumer goods.
8. They start their foreign operations by the purchase of existing firms, rather than by developing new productive facilities in host countries.
9. They do not contribute to host countries' exports.
10. They worsen the income distribution of host countries.

11. They do not observe the objectives of the host countries' national plans for development.
12. They earn excessively high profits and fees, due to their monopoly power in host countries.
13. They dominate major industrial sectors.
14. They are not accountable to their host nations, only to their home governments.
15. They contribute to inflation by stimulating demand for scarce resources.
16. They recruit the best personnel and the best managers from host countries at the expense of local entrepreneurs.
17. They form alliances with corrupt developing country elites.
18. They interfere with the political conditions of developing host countries.
19. They disregard the impact of their actions on consumer safety and environmental conditions.
20. They disregard the cultural and social impact of their actions on host countries.

To understand the elements that give rise to these criticisms, we should look at the sources of conflicts.

19.3 SOURCES OF CONFLICTS

Conflicts arise from a clash of goals between constituencies. A firm must satisfy different groups of people, each group with its own specific goals. Employees, customers, stockholders, and the governments of home and host countries have different objectives that may not be compatible. Employees strive for a higher compensation package and better working conditions. Customers expect high-quality goods at a low price. Stockholders would like higher rates of return on their investment. Governments in both host and home countries may want higher exports or strive for certain social goals.

Thus, the incompatibility of objectives of the parties involved in international business may set the stage for confrontation among them.

19.3a Multinational Corporations' Objectives

The main objective of an MNC is to maximize its global profit. The pursuit of this goal leads the MNC to (a) choose the type of operation that best suits its objective, (b) improve efficiency by allocating its resources within its corporate family, and (c) retain as much of its profit as possible.

Because MNCs operate in different host countries, each with its own governmental jurisdiction, they are not accountable to these nations for most aspects of their operations. Each nation controls only that part of the MNC's activities that fall within its borders. This gives the MNC more power than local firms when dealing with the host country's demands. Multinational Corporations can counter the pressure of any given host country by simply threatening to curtail their activities or to shut down their operations in that country. This unique characteristic of MNCs goes against a host country's economic and social objectives. For example, a host government might be interested in export promotion; however, the MNC may find exporting unprofitable and hence does not cooperate with the host government in achieving this goal. This may lead to a conflict of interests and can raise tensions between the MNC and the host government.

19.3b Home Countries' Objectives

Conflicts between MNCs and their home countries can arise from both economic and noneconomic goals.

Economic Goals. Economically speaking, there is not often much conflict between the goals of MNCs and the objectives of their home countries. In striving for profit maximization, an MNC generates earnings for (a) its stockholders in terms of dividends and capital appreciation; (b) its employees in the form of wages and salaries; and (c) its home government through the payment of corporate profit taxes. Because increases in their residents' earnings is an economic objective of all host countries, there seems to be no conflict of interest between these countries and MNCs on that score.

Because most managers and owners of an MNC are residents of the MNC's home country, they tend to identify their interests with those of their home country. As a result, they may try to fuse the corporate interest with the home country's interest. For example, an MNC may try to buy most of its resources at home, as long as it is compatible with its profit maximization objectives.

GLOBAL INSIGHTS CASE 19.1

Fears and Facts about Foreign Direct Investment

In the 1980s concerns arose in the United States that the rapid rise in inward FDI would have adverse effects on American workers. Some feared that foreign-controlled affiliates that displaced U.S. firms might change the composition of employment, moving "good" jobs to the home country and offering only "bad" jobs in the United States. In fact, foreign multinationals in the United States pay higher than average wages, suggesting that they provide good jobs. When net FDI flows turned outward during the 1990s, the concern became that U.S. companies would begin outsourcing much of their production to other countries, again at the expense of jobs and wages at home. This seeming contradiction—that inward and outward FDI would have similar effects on U.S. workers—may reflect how little was actually known about the effects of FDI.

Unlike trade, which has been studied for hundreds of years, FDI has been subjected to little rigorous study until recently. As more has been learned about FDI, many of these fears have subsided. The following are some fears that have been recently expressed about FDI, and the facts that we now know.

Fear: Won't U.S. industries leave for low-wage developing countries?

Fact: During the NAFTA debate, some voiced concern that lower barriers to investment in Mexico would result in large movement of U.S. industry there, as firms exploited low Mexican wages. But since the passage of NAFTA in 1993, Mexico's share of the U.S. outward FDI position has decreased. The reason there has been no mass exodus of U.S. industry to Mexico or to other low-wage countries is simple: there is no free lunch-for multinationals as for the rest of us. Real wages may vary significantly across countries, but studies show that these differences are linked to productivity differences, just as economic theory would predict. Low wages are not a sufficient reason to move production to a foreign country, if low productivity there raises the labor cost per unit of output to a level close to that of the United States. The vast majority of U.S. FDI continues to be with other high-wage countries, so clearly other motivations than the potential for low-wage outsourcing are behind the greater part of FDI.

Fear: Are U.S. firms that invest abroad exporting jobs?

Fact: It may seem reasonable to suppose that a U.S. firm that hires workers in an overseas affiliate is contributing to U.S. unemployment, since the firm could be hiring U.S. workers to do the same job here. Evidence shows, however, that generally this is not the case: increases in employment in foreign affiliates of U.S. firms are often associated with increases in employment at the parent as well. What employment substitution there is seems to be occurring entirely offshore, between countries competing for U.S. FDI, not between U.S. parents that creating jobs at home as well.

Fear: Doesn't U.S. FDI abroad represent domestic investment forgone?

Fact: With the surge in outward FDI in recent years, FDI outflows now amount to more than 10 percent of gross private nonresidential fixed investment. However, when a U.S. firm invests abroad, that does not necessarily mean it would have invested here instead if FDI had not been an option. It might then have chosen not to invest at all. Moreover, two-thirds of recorded outflows in 1996 were actually the reinvested earnings of foreign affiliates, into capital originating in the United States. Considering only actual capital outflow, a recent study estimated that outward FDI averaged only 0.9 percent of nonresidential fixed investment between 1970 and 1990-and the share has been trending downward. Capital outflows are also largely compensated by foreign investment inflows. Evidence suggests that complementarity may exist between the investment decisions of domestic and foreign firms, which would imply that reciprocal direct investment between the Untied States and other industrial countries increases total investment in all countries that participate.

In short, opponents of FDI have incorrectly framed it as a zero-sum venture, where for one country to gain, another must lose. Both the theoretical arguments of the benefits of FDI and the evidence now available suggest that FDI can provide net gains for all parties.

Source: U.S. Government Printing Office, *Economic Report of the President* (Washington DC: U.S. government Printing Office, 1998), Box 7-5, pp. 251-252, Reprinted.

However, in spite of this tendency, an MNC cannot ignore world economic conditions when allocating its resources. Thus, if labor costs are high at home, or if the home country's economy is weak, the MNC may close its factories at home and invest its capital abroad, helping increase employment in a foreign country rather than at home. Such an action leads to higher unemployment at home and may cause depression in areas where the MNC's factories have been closed. For example, when General Electric moved its plant from Ashland, Massachusetts, to Singapore, it caused the loss of 1,100 jobs in Ashland. In another example, 4,000 jobs were lost at home when RCA closed its Memphis, Tennessee, facilities and moved them to Taiwan.[2]

Such incidents lead to tension between unemployed workers and the MNCs. This might cause the home government to step in and restrict the activities of MNCs abroad. For example, U.S. labor's opposition to MNCs contributed to the passage of the Trade and Investment Act of 1972, known as the "Burke-Hartke Bill" after its original cosponsors. This bill introduced certain measures that have restricted both U.S. imports and foreign direct investment (FDI) by U.S. corporations. According to the bill, the president of the United States has the right to forbid any person within U.S. jurisdiction from making transfers of capital to or within any foreign nation if, in the president's judgment, the transfer would lead to a net increase in unemployment in the United States.

Noneconomic Goals. Conflicts between MNCs and home governments can also stem from noneconomic goals that are set by the government. Chief among these goals is national defense. A home government might impose restrictions on (a) the exportation of certain products, such as computer hardware and electronic devices, that might be strategically significant to hostile nations; (b) the licensing and technology needed to produce such goods; and (c) the investment in host countries' facilities needed to produce these goods. While these restrictions might be necessary from the home country's national security standpoint, they may prove detrimental to the MNC's profit maximization process.

19.3c Host Countries' Objectives

The subject of MNCs is a more touchy issue in host countries than it is in home countries. While home countries perceive MNCs as an integral part of their economic systems, host countries may view them as foreign agents whose benefits are not worth their costs. Such a negative attitude toward MNCs is especially strong in developing countries. The notion that large MNCs somehow undermine the independence of these countries raises their nationalistic ferver and invites emotional reaction against MNCs. Nevertheless, host countries' responses vary, depending on (a) the relative dominance of MNCs in their economy, (b) their perceived degree of dependence on the MNCs, and (c) the extent to which MNCs' activities are subsidized by the host government.

The sources of conflict between MNCs and host countries can be traced not only to the economic goals of the host countries, but to their noneconomic goals as well. A new area of conflict between host countries and MNCs is the transborder data flow (TDF) problem. Given the increasing importance of this issue, with its economic and noneconomic implications, a separate discussion of this topic is included in this section.

Economic Goals. The economic objectives of a host country in allowing MNCs to operate within its borders can be stated as three separate goals: (a) the economic growth goal, (b) the distributive and allocative goal, and (c) the balance of payments (BOP) goal.

Economic Growth Goal. The increase in the rate of economic growth is the primary reason for a country to open its doors to MNCs. It hopes that foreign investment will augment national resources, contributing to the growth of gross national product (GNP). It also hopes that MNCs will transfer their technology and provide training for the local workers. This is critical to a country's economic growth, because it allows the nation to become technologically independent in the long run, achieving its economic growth goals without foreign help. However, because MNCs have obtained their superior knowledge and technology through their investment in research and development, they do not have any incentive to transfer their technology and know-how completely to their host countries. Such a transfer would cause these corporations to lose their competitive edge over local firms. The MNC's unwillingness to transfer its technology to its host country leads to that country's technological dependence on MNC, setting the stage for future conflicts.

Distributive and Allocative Goal. The second economic goal of host countries is related to (a) the distribution of profits earned by MNCs, and (b) control over the allocation of resources by these corporations.

Host countries wish to maximize the benefits that accrue to them from MNCs' activities in their countries. To achieve this goal, they believe they should have control over the allocation of resources flowing across their borders. This belief is based on the contention that MNCs' profits in host countries arise from the employment of local resources and access to domestic markets. However, MNCs challenge this view. They maintain that their profits in host countries stem from the efficient use and allocation of their firm-specific advantages. Because they have property rights over these advantages, MNCs argue, the profits generated by their operations should accrue to them alone. Additionally, they should have the right to control their own scarce resources.

The controversy over control of resources and distribution of profit is a major issue that has not yet been resolved, and it continues to intensify the tension between MNCs and their host countries.

Balance of Payments Goal. The third economic goal of a host country in allowing MNCs to operate within its borders is to improve its BOP. Because foreign exchange is a scarce resource, especially in developing countries, many countries look to MNCs as a source for financing their foreign currency needs.

The impact of an MNC on a host country's BOP changes with the passage of time. Initially, an MNC may bring in capital to a host country and contribute to the BOP position. This is because payment for this capital is usually made in a foreign currency, strengthening the country's holding of international reserve assets. However, if a well-developed capital market exists in the host country, an MNC might raise the demand for capital in the local market, causing the home country's interest rates to rise. If this happens, the MNC's initial investment is not helpful to the BOP. For this reason, most countries, especially developing countries, insist that an MNC pay for the initial cost of its new investment with foreign currencies that have been obtained outside the host country's national borders.

After the initial investment is made and the plant becomes operational, there is a second impact on the BOP. If the plant produces goods that can effectively compete with commodities imported from foreign countries, there is a decrease in payments for imports. This results in a decline in the outflow of foreign currencies, causing improvement in the BOP. If the plant also produces goods that can be exported, there is an increase in the inflow of foreign exchange, leading to further improvement in the BOP.

There is a third impact on the BOP that results from an MNC's initial investment in a host country. If the investment is profitable, the foreign owners may wish to repatriate their capital in the form of royalties, licensing fees, and eventually dividends. This results in an outflow of foreign currencies from the host country, worsening the BOP. Aware of this negative outcome on their BOP, many countries have established ceilings on the amount of profits, licensing fees, and royalties that can be repatriated by MNCs. Unfortunately, however, this has caused some MNCs to engage in deceptive policies, such as transfer pricing, to circumvent restrictions imposed by their host governments on their repatriation of capital. Other MNCs have preferred to plow their earnings into future investment and further growth. This, in turn, has caused additional complaints from host countries, who relate the size of MNCs in their countries to the degree of foreign domination imposed on them.

A major way in which MNCs can contribute to the BOP position of their host countries is through the export of goods and services. However, many MNCs feel that the conditions that exist in developing countries are not conducive to exporting from those countries. This is because production in many of these countries is supported by protectionist policies, such as import tariffs. As a result, the goods produced by these nations are relatively expensive and, hence, incapable of competing with the cheaper, better-quality goods abroad.

Noneconomic Goals. The main noneconomic goal of a host country in dealing with MNCs is to maintain its independence. Another is to maintain a social, political, and cultural atmosphere that is free from friction.

GLOBAL INSIGHTS CASE 19.2

Historical Evidence Against Multinational Corporations

There is historical evidence that the actions undertaken by some MNCs have in the past led to undesirable, often disastrous, outcomes for the societies in which these MNCs have operated. The following examples are cases in point:

1. Some MNCs have formed alliances with corrupt Third World elites. This has led many observers to believe that MNCs, whether they know it or not, are siding with the elites and promoting inequalities in these societies.[1]

2. MNCs' excessive interference in the political conditions of host countries in the Third World is a sore issue that has been documented on many occasions. The well-publicized alleged role of ITT in the 1973 coup d'etat against Salvador Allende's regime in Chile is a prime example. Another example is Gulf Oil's political involvement in Angola.[2]

3. The increase in African infant mortality that resulted from the introduction of Western-style baby formula into that continent by Nestle and a number of other MNCs is seen as an example of their irresponsibility.[3]

4. The excessive use of transfer pricing, tax havens, and the manipulation of currency fluctuations by some MNCs exemplify the abuse of both home and host country laws. Examples of these abuses include the Hoffman-LaRoche use of transfer pricing and Lonrho's use of tax havens.[4]

5. The MNCs are also seen as disregarding the impact of their actions on consumer safety and environmental conditions. This is especially true when host government regulations to protect the consumer or the environment are absent. These activities can take different forms, such as the dumping of industrial wastes and pollutants, the use of harmful pesticides, and the sale of unsafe products. A well-publicized example is the leakage of a deadly gas at Union Carbide's chemical plant in Bhopal, India, in 1984. The accident caused the death of approximately 2,500 people, exposed 200,000 people to the gas, and made about 50,000 people sick. It killed thousands of animals and destroyed vegetation.[5] Another example is the case of a U.S. children's wear manufacturer. The sale of its sleep wear that was treated with a particular carcinogenic fire retardant has been banned in the United States, but the company continues to sell the banned product in other countries.[6]

6. There have been unfair labor practices by some MNCs in some host countries. For example, Kodak, Nestle, and IBM have been associated with abuses in trade union recognition.[7]

7. Reports of illegal payments, bribery, and other corrupt practices by MNCs have been frequently written about in the press. Aircraft manufacturers and oil companies have been implicated in these illegal dealings. For example, Lockheed has been accused of trying to influence the Japanese government military purchases through multimillion dollar "commissions." Overall, the company has been accused of giving $25 million in bribes to government officials in different countries in order to win orders for its new aircraft. Similarly, Exxon was accused of making payoffs of $28 million in the form of political contributions. United Brands was accused of attempting to alter a tax law in Honduras by making a $1.25 million payoff in political contributions to influential individuals. And there have been bribery convictions against Imperial Chemical Industries of the United Kingdom and Marubeni Trading Company of Japan.[8]

The above examples illustrate why MNCs, which use the most sophisticated public relations services in the world, have gained such dubious reputations.

Notes

1. L. M. Turner, "There's No Love Lost between Multinational Companies and the Third World, "*Business and Society Review*, vol.11, no.2 (autumn 1974), pp. 75-78.
2. Michael Z. Brook, and H. Lee Remmers, *International Management and Business Policy* (Boston: Hohghoton Mifflin, 1978), p. 311.
3. Ibid., p.310.
4. Ibid., p.311.
5. *The New York Times*, 6 December 1984, p.1.
6. James Brady, "An Export Trade in Death," *Advertising Age*, vol. 49, patt 2, 15 May 1978, p. 99.
7. Brook and Remmers, *International Management*, p. 311.
8. Annat Negandhi, *International Management* (Boston: Allyn and Bacon, 1987) p. 55.

Many developing countries view MNCs with suspicion, and they fear that interaction with these corporate giants will lead to a loss of control over their political, cultural, and economic lives. They feel that in dealing with MNCs they will become subservient, providing raw materials and cheap labor to these corporations, but never playing a crucial role in a production process based on advanced technology controlled by the MNCs. These nations feel that the intention of MNCs in investing in their countries is to serve the local markets exclusively. They charge that MNCs reserve exporting functions only for their parent companies or for some of their advanced subsidiaries. Such a negative view toward MNCs is based on both hard evidence and pure fantasy. The following examples, highlighted in Global Insights Case 19.2, are cases in point:

1. Accusations were made against ITT of taking an active role in the 1973 coup d'état against Salvador Allende's regime in Chile.[3]
2. Gulf Oil had controversial involvement in the political process of Angola.[4]
3. Nestle and a number of other MNCs introduced Western-style baby formula into Africa, resulting in increased infant mortality on that continent.[5]
4. Kodak, Nestle, and IBM engaged in unfair labor practices associated with abuses in trade union recognition.[6]
5. Lockheed attempted to influence the Japanese government's military purchases through multimillion dollar "commissions." The company was accused of handing over $25 million in bribes to government officials in different nations to secure orders for its new aircraft.[7]
6. Exxon was accused of making payoffs of $28 million in the form of political contributions.[8]
7. United Brands was accused of trying to alter a tax law in Honduras by giving a $1.25 million payoff in political contributions to influential officials.[9]
8. Imperial Chemical Industries of Great Britain and Marubeni Trading Company of Japan were convicted of bribery.[10]

These examples illustrate why MNCs are viewed with suspicion in developing countries. Such suspicion, in turn, causes some of these countries to eventually pursue policies aimed at the curtailment of MNCs' activities within their borders.

Even in an advanced country, such as the United States, MNCs cannot escape resistance. For example, in 1987 when a Japanese company gave in to pressure from the U.S. government and abandoned its bid to take over a semiconductor company, a U.S. politician stated: "We have won one for America's national security."[11] Worried about the ever-increasing size of foreign investment in the United States, another politician was wondering if Americans would lose ". . . control over our economic destiny."[12] Yet such views are not shared by many economists, who believe the inflow of FDI to the United States will provide the country with know-how and capital. The restriction of FDI is detrimental, they argue, to a nation that has assumed a new role as the world's largest debtor, requiring roughly $150 billion a year from overseas to finance its growth.[13]

Pessimistic attitudes toward MNCs, to a large extent, come from (a) developing countries' experience with colonialism, (b) the income distribution effect of MNCs' investments, and (c) environmental effect of MNCs.

Colonialism. In the past, colonialism in many developing countries crippled their efforts to industrialize. Colonies were forced by their mother countries, who made all resource allocation decisions, to specialize in the production of primary and intermediate goods. As a result, colonies did not develop an industrial base conducive to economic independence. Today, some developing countries see a close resemblance between the former mother countries of colonialism and present-day MNCs. They believe that if the resource allocation decisions are made at the MNC's headquarters, subsidiaries in developing countries will end up producing goods that will not make any significant contribution toward host countries' economic development.

Income Distribution Effect. The activities of an MNC may disturb a host country's income distribution, leading to social and political unrest. An MNC's investment may cause the emergence of new entrepreneurs, whose fortunes may increase at the expense of those in power. The reverse may also be true; that is, an MNC may further intensify the strength of the group already in power. It is also possible that an MNC may pay higher wages than those paid by local firms. Any of these scenarios would cause one group to gain wealth and power at the expense of another group, at least in the short run. This may cause those who benefit from an MNC's operations to lobby their government in support of such corporations. Those who lose from the MNCs' activities, however, may demand that their government restrict the activities of these corporations. Those who lose from MNCs' activities may be supported by others who feel a sense of subservience, weakness, and inferiority in dealing with these corporate giants. These feelings may stem from a suspicion that they may not be able to invent, produce, or market a product on their own without the help of MNCs. Whatever the reasons, this situation leads to social and political unrest and sets the stage for governmental intervention that leads to more restrictive policies toward MNCs.

Environmental Effect of Multinational Corporations. Another noneconomic goal that may lead to conflict between an MNC and its host country's government is the government's objective of environmental protection. A host government may desire an environment that is free from water pollution, air pollution, and toxic wastes. Yet the MNC might not take these problems seriously because of the high cost of alleviating them. This may cause the host government to step in and force the MNC to take responsibility for cleaning up the environment.

Transborder Data Flow. Transborder data flow (TDF) refers to the flow of electronically transmitted information across national boundaries. The immense growth in the computer and telecommunications industries since the 1970s has tremendously facilitated the storage and transmission of massive amounts of information across national boundaries. This has enabled MNCs to collect information in different host countries and transmit it to their home countries for use in worldwide operations. For example, an MNC with its headquarters in New York can build a computerized marketing data file in Europe and transfer this information electronically to its New York headquarters.

Information collected by MNCs in host countries covers a wide range of subjects, including data on production, distribution, research and development, finance, marketing, personnel, and payroll. Europe is the end point for many MNCs transmission of information. Data is transmitted from Europe for storage and processing in the United States, and the results are then transmitted back to Europe.

Given the large volume of information collected by MNCs and the significance of this information in shaping today's global markets, host countries (both advanced and developing) have come to realize the impact of TDF on their countries' economic and noneconomic goals.

Economically speaking, information is an economic resource, and as such it is a marketable, transferable, and exportable commodity. The ability of one country to store and process information may give that country a technological advantage over other countries. A case in point is the United States, which has derived immense benefits not only from processing and storing data in American-based computer systems, but also by exporting sophisticated computer equipment.

From a noneconomic standpoint, host countries are worried that the collection and storage of certain types of data may give home countries a political advantage and may jeopardize the host countries' national sovereignty. Indeed, it has been argued that in times of war or national emergency, host countries might not be able to gain access to vital information stored in hostile home countries.

Given the economic and noneconomic implications of TDF, European countries have decided to deal with the problem through a new form of privacy protection legislation. In addition, due to the diversity of laws in different countries and the global importance of this issue, the Organization of Economic Cooperation and Development (OECD) devised guidelines on TDF in 1980. These voluntary guidelines, adopted by Canada in 1984, are to encourage the cooperation of member nations regarding the exchange of information. Adherence to these guidelines means that OECD member countries will consider the guidelines equivalent to their own privacy laws. This may result in the relaxation or removal of barriers to the free flow of information between OECD members and the United States.

Legislation regarding TDF can be considered a form of nontariff trade barriers. The effects of these trade barriers can be viewed from two perspectives—international and domestic. Internationally, the decrease in the flow of information increases the uncertainty felt by potential importers and exporters. As a result, the volume of international trade in goods and services decreases. Service-sector industries that are heavily dependent on TDF, such as airlines, banking, financial services, and tourism, are especially affected by barriers against TDF. Domestically, as the flow of information into a country diminishes, the prices charged by data-processing industries rise. Also, as the foreign cost-cutting technological information is denied to domestic producers, their production costs rise. Thus, the legislation over TDF, like tariff barriers, may result in losses for business on both the national and international levels. We must stress that the abuse of TDF is a serious problem that would be best resolved by international cooperation rather than by protectionist barriers that retard the free flow of international trade.

GLOBAL INSIGHTS CASE 19.3

The Role of Copyright in an Electronic Global Economy

The growth of telecommunications, computing power, and their joint progeny, the Internet, is revolutionizing the way in which information is created and shared. Whether by satellite or by fiber-optic cable, electronic telecommunications networks today transmit vast amounts of scientific and commercial information, and entertainment around the globe in a heartbeat.

Since the 18th century, markets for the products of creative expression and technical innovation have been supported through copyright and patent laws, which extend private property rights to intellectual property. These laws have historically attempted to strike a balance between enhancing economic incentives to create and promoting widespread use of the thing created. By preventing unauthorized copying, intellectual property laws allow creators and innovators to profit from their original works and inventions.

Strong copyright and patent protection can help provide the appropriate incentives to create, by allowing creators to capture a greater share of the marginal benefit of their efforts. The cost of strong protection, however, is that prices to use copyrighted works or patents may remain high for some period of time. Ironically, because patents and copyrights build on the work of others, overly strong intellectual property protection today could discourage innovation and creativity in the future.

An increasingly important policy question is whether these traditional legal means for striking the balance between incentives to create and incentives to use will continue to apply in a global information-based economy. Difficult issues to resolve include:

✦ rights to display copyrighted information on computer screens
✦ the applicability of copyright to electronic data bases
✦ "fair use" rights and other traditional exceptions for the educational and research community, and
✦ competition within broad-based collective copyright licensing organizations.

The need to coordinate our efforts with other nations makes the resolution of these crucial questions even more complex.

Source: U.S. Government Printing Office, *Economic Report of the President* (Washington DC: U.S. Government Printing Office, 1997), 193, Reprinted.

19.4 HOST COUNTRIES' REACTION TO MULTINATIONAL CORPORATIONS

Given the conflicting goals of MNCs vis-a-vis the goals of host countries, different nations' reactions to these corporations vary considerably. The factors that determine the intensity of these reactions are (a) the perceived degree of foreign domination and control, and (b) the extent to which the MNC's activities are subsidized by the host country's government.

Suspicions concerning the presence of foreigners have led some countries to go so far as to confiscate foreign enterprises within their borders. For example, after the downfall of the Shah of Iran in 1979, the new Islamic Republic government of that country confiscated all U.S. companies. Other countries, however, have been indecisive about the presence of MNCs and have gone from one extreme to the other. For example, the French government has shifted its policies regarding FDI three times within a five-year period.

Some countries have developed different policy measures with the intention of lessening the effects of FDI on their economic systems without banning it altogether. They hope such policies will provide them with the benefits of FDI—technology, managerial know-how, labor training, needed capital, and access to foreign markets—without forcing them to yield completely to foreign ownership and control.

Some of the major policies host countries employ in dealing with MNCs are requiring joint venture arrangements; controlling entries and takeovers; excluding foreigners from specific activities; controlling the local content and local employment; imposing export requirements; controlling the local capital market; establishing debt equity requirements; taking the foreign investment package apart; requiring disinvestment; and controlling remittances, rates, and fees.

19.4a Joint Venture Arrangements

As we explained in Chapter 17, a joint venture arrangement calls for a partnership involving an MNC with either private entrepreneurs or the government of a host country. There are two advantages for an MNC engaging in a joint venture arrangement (rather than having a wholly owned subsidiary). First, by making a host country's residents part owners of the operation, it minimizes the control measures used by that country's government against the foreign operation. Second, by placing indigenous partners on the board of directors, the MNC is better equipped to deal with the cultural elements existing in the host country. For example, American Telephone and Telegraph (AT&T), the world's largest communication company, began to expand into the European market. After spending millions of dollars to figure out a European strategy, the company decided to try local partnership. This decision was based on the realization that the European market was crowded, governments were hostile, and trade barriers were formidable. In 1983, AT&T began to form joint ventures with different European companies to gain local expertise, political power in Europe's protected market, and faster growth. Accordingly, joint ventures were arranged with Phillips for producing communication gear, Olivetti for producing computers, and Cia. Telefonica Nacionale de Espara for producing microchips. There are signs that AT&T's strategy has paid off, and the company plans to form more partnerships with other European countries.[14]

The advantages of joint venture arrangements for host countries' residents are (a) their ability, as partial owners, to make decisions about the operations of the firm, and (b) their ability to share in the profits resulting from the firm's activities in their country.

However, joint venture arrangements, like any other kind of partnership, are not without problems. First, a joint venture is composed of partners with different cultural backgrounds and different objectives. This can lead to disagreements regarding different aspects of the firm's day-to-day operations. For example, foreign partners are more likely to opt for putting their earnings back into the company, whereas local partners might prefer higher dividends. The time may also come when the corporation needs to build up its capital, but the local partners are unwilling to contribute their share. As another example, a host government might desire a more equitable income distribution. However, the MNC might have entered into partnership with the host country's wealthy class. If such a partnership is successful, the high profit earned by the joint venture would further increase the power and wealth of the wealthy class, thereby worsening the income distribution in the country as a whole.

Given the problems associated with joint ventures, some MNCs have gone so far as to shut down their existing operations rather than engage in such arrangements. For example, in response to India's demand that IBM and Coca-Cola sell 60 percent of the equity in their Indian subsidiaries to domestic interests, both companies pulled out of that country.[15]

Today, joint venture arrangements are still popular in some countries, such as Japan and South Korea. Such arrangements have given these host countries access to advanced Western technology without yielding complete ownership and control to foreign interests. Unfortunately, however, cultural gaps between partners have diminished the potential benefits of joint venture arrangements. For example, in a move to acquire aerospace technology, a group of Japanese companies negotiated a joint venture with Boeing, the U.S. aerospace company. From the beginning of negotiations there were signs of disagreements between the two sides. For instance, the Japanese complained that

"Boeing assigns to the project too many young executives who don't understand Japanese business practice."[16] Americans complained about "the Japanese negotiator's lack of technical knowledge."[17]

Joint venture arrangements are not only popular in market economies, but they are also encouraged in nonmarket economies, such as the People's Republic of China. However, due to difficulties that have afflicted Western joint venture projects in the former Soviet Union, in Eastern Europe before its recent economic reform, and in China, Western entrepreneurs have remained reluctant to expand their investments into nonmarket economies.[18] Following the economic reforms of the Eastern European countries and the collapse of the Soviet Union, the activities of MNCs in these nations have increased. As a result, countries such as Hungary and Russia have become popular sites for joint ventures.[19]

19.4b Controlling Entries and Takeovers

In most developing countries and some advanced countries, the entry of foreign firms into the country is controlled. Such firms are required to obtain approval for a new investment venture or for the takeover of an existing firm. In Canada, for example, the Foreign Investment Review Agency (FIRA) is in charge of screening FDI. In India, a foreign investment board is given the responsibility of reviewing FDI.

Although different countries have different requirements for approving FDI, most nations demand a detailed description of the applicant's operations and financial position. Additionally, they require the potential investor to explain how the investment project would contribute to national objectives. The approval process puts the country's review board in the driver's seat so to speak, enabling the board to approve only those projects that are potentially beneficial to the country.

Many countries tend to prohibit the purchase of existing plants, requiring a foreign investment project to start from scratch. This tendency arises from the argument against monopoly. It is felt that an MNC's takeover of an existing firm keeps the number of firms in an industry constant and does not contribute to market competition. Thus, for example, if an industry is composed of 10 firms, the takeover of an existing firm by an MNC leaves the total number at 10. A new entry, however, raises the number to 11, increasing the degree of competitiveness in the industry.

Although this argument is theoretically strong, practically speaking, it loses its appeal when an industry is already competitive and when the government feels, for no good reason, that a new investment is somehow preferable to the takeover of an existing one. Suppose an ailing domestic firm is operating in a relatively competitive situation, and its operators are not capable of running it efficiently. In this situation, the plant and equipment are worth more to foreign entrepreneurs who wish to invest in that country than to the domestic entrepreneurs who are sustaining losses. Thus, both parties would gain from a takeover by the foreign entrepreneurs. In this situation, a policy of forcing foreign entrepreneurs to start from scratch and causing domestic entrepreneurs to scrap their plants seems unproductive.

Today, countries that are open to foreign investment gladly hand over control of their troubled companies in the hope of acquiring as much foreign investment and technology as they can. For example, in pursuing its new policy of openness to foreign investment in 1986, Spain allowed four takeovers of domestic firms by foreign firms: SEAT group was taken over by Volkswagen AG of West Germany; a locally known maker of natural cosmetics was taken over by Gillette; a local meat packer was taken over by Unilever; and a canner was taken over by Pillsbury.[20]

19.4c Excluding Foreigners from Specific Activities

A host country may reserve certain business fields for domestic entrepreneurs only, prohibiting foreign involvement in those areas. The business activities usually prohibited are banking, insurance, public utilities, communications and the media, and the exploitation of certain natural resources.

Banking, insurance, and other financial institutions in general are prohibited as investments by foreigners because some host countries, such as Canada and Mexico, fear that these institutions could provide foreigners with influence and control over their economic system. Such control, it is argued, may be in conflict with the economic policies of the host country.*[21]

Public utilities are prohibited as foreign investments by many host governments because such businesses are considered an inseparable part of national development.

Host governments usually restrict the operation of communications and the media—radio, television, and newspapers—to local entrepreneurs or to the host government itself. It is argued that they represent a vital national interest that should not be entrusted to foreign hands.

Involvement of foreigners in the exploitation of certain natural resources in many host countries, such as Brazil, Finland, Mexico, and Morocco, is very limited because these resources are considered a gift of nature that should be exploited only for public use, rather than for private gain. Many developing countries limit foreign involvement and investment in their mineral deposits, oil reserves, and forestry resources to purchases of concessions by foreigners. Such concessions provide foreign firms with the exclusive rights to explore a given resource, but only for a limited time. In return for these rights, the host governments receive royalties on the extracted resource and income taxes on the net profits of the foreign firms.

19.4d Controlling the Local Content and Local Employment

To ensure that MNCs' operations are conducive to the industrialization process of and increase employment in host countries, many developing countries demand that foreign firms continually increase the amount of locally produced goods used to make their final products. Additionally, they require that a certain percentage of the foreign firm's employees be citizens of the host country. The local content policies are widely used by Latin American countries where MNCs are engaged in automobile manufacturing. Mexico has gone so far as to require foreign firms to employ a labor force that is 90 percent Mexican.

Nations that impose local content requirements in a new industry hope to improve their economy not only through that industry, but also via that industry's links with the suppliers of component parts and materials. Unfortunately, the local content requirement may prove costly if the local market is not large enough to allow economies of scale in producing the related component parts and materials.

19.4e Export Requirements

Foreign exchange is scarce in many countries, especially in developing countries. It provides these countries with the needed funds for the importation of items they need in their industrialization process. Exports are the surest way of acquiring the necessary foreign exchange, and foreign investment projects are often evaluated on the basis of their potential contribution to the host country's exports.

Many nations have learned that MNCs' overall strategies may not permit or inspire their new subsidiaries to compete against old subsidiaries in securing markets for their exports. This has led host countries to be skeptical of the MNC's role in enhancing their exports. As a result, some countries have considered a subsidiary's ability to export freely a prerequisite for its approval as a foreign investment.

Unfortunately, many developing countries' markets are protected with high tariffs and quotas. If a foreign firm's subsidiary is forced to operate in a protected industry, its high production cost will erode its competitiveness in the world market. Thus, the ability of the subsidiary to export freely should be weighed against the government's desire to engage in protectionist policies.

19.4f Controlling the Local Capital Market

Because most developing countries lack the needed capital and technology for their own development process, they look on MNCs as a major source of financing. However, the foreign exchange authorities of these countries often

---

* None of these prohibitions apply to trade between the United States, Mexico, and Canada. As explained in Chapter 9, trade between these countries is covered under the provisions of the North American Free Trade Agreement.

fear that an MNC might raise all or some of its capital in the host country, further draining capital out of that country. To ensure against this possibility, many developing countries exclude foreigners from their local capital market, requiring that all capital funds be raised outside their national boundaries. The impact of this requirement is to increase the inflow of foreign exchange into the host country, improving its BOP at the time of investment.

The policy of forcing foreign investors to bring in their own money, without furnishing any local capital, must be exercised with caution. Such a policy may discourage some prospective investors who might potentially be a significant source of technology transfer to the developing country.

19.4g Debt Equity Requirements

Some countries provide guidelines on debt equity ratios. The purpose of such guidelines is to ensure that the investing firm has sufficient financial resources to minimize the possibility of bankruptcy. For example, a regulation by the People's Republic of China requires the following: (a) For joint ventures with an investment of $3 million or less, there can be no debt; (b) for investments of $3 million to $10 million, the amount of debt cannot be greater than the equity investment; (c) for investments of $10 million to $30 million, the amount of debt cannot be greater than twice the equity; and (d) for investments greater than $30 million, the debt cannot exceed triple the equity investment. The problem with this requirement is that it might discourage some small potential investors from entering the marketplace. In China's case, it was predicted that many firms that had hoped to set up electronics assembly plants there would be forced out of business in that country.[22]

19.4h Taking the Foreign Investment Package Apart

One way for host countries to resist foreign investment, yet enjoy foreign capital and foreign technology, is by "taking the foreign investment package apart." This means buying the needed technology, management, and capital separately, rather than acquiring them in one package through an MNC's investment.

Although this is a sound strategy and has been successfully implemented in Japan, its application in other countries is questionable. This is because many countries, especially developing countries, do not have the necessary skill to imitate foreign technology and adapt it to their national requirements as the Japanese did. Additionally, many corporations are reluctant to break their package apart and leave control of their technology in foreign hands. As a result, the opportunity for most developing countries to pursue such a strategy is relatively limited. Nevertheless, it pays off for a host country to explore the possibility of purchasing only those parts of an investment package that are needed. For example, South Korea has attempted to follow Japan's lead by importing technology from Europe and the United States. To explain such a strategy, the head of South Korean technology transfer stated that "We're very weak in designing technology. We're very weak in process technology, so we import what we can't create."[23]

Although South Korea's strategy for technology transfer has been relatively successful, it has met with some problems. For example, South Korea has been unable to transfer robot technology from Japanese robot makers. The Japanese have refused to provide South Korea with the software that controls robot operation, stating that South Koreans are not ready for such technology.[24]

A more current example involved the People's Republic of China and Chrysler Corporation. According to a contract, Chrysler had agreed to the transfer of engine equipment to China's First Automotive Works. However, it remains to be seen if Chrysler can overcome the market pitfalls that other Western investors have experienced in China.[25]

19.4i Requiring Disinvestment

According to this policy, the host government requires the potential foreign investor to disinvest over a period of time by transferring the corporation's ownership to the host country at a specified time for a predetermined price.

The problem with this strategy is the determination of a price both parties can agree on, given the uncertainty of future events. Even if an agreement is reached, it may still lead to a distortion of incentives by the foreign firm and the host country. Assume that an MNC invests in a host country and agrees to surrender its ownership to that country at a predetermined price of $1 billion at the end of a 10-year period. Under the agreement, the MNC has the incentive to devise strategies to ensure that it will not have more than $1 billion worth of assets in its investment at the end of the 10-year period. However, at the same time, the host country tries to ensure that the value of the corporation's assets does not fall below $1 billion. Thus, the stage is set for a conflict between the MNC and the host country. As a result, the company might follow strategies in the next 10 years that are not helpful to its future when its ownership is reverted to the host country.

19.4j Controlling Remittances, Rates, and Fees

Some of the policies that host countries can use to improve their BOPs, fulfill national domestic policies, or prevent MNCs from reaping excess profits involve the restriction of remittances, the imposition of ceiling rates on royalties, and the imposition of limits on fees paid for technology. However, the problem with these policies is that an MNC may be in a position to circumvent these restrictions through extra charges for training, research and development, machinery, advice, use of overhead facilities, corporate overhead, interest, and other services. An MNC also has the power to circumvent the system by altering its transfer prices for raw materials, component parts, and final products. All these actions have the effect of increasing the flow of funds from the host country to the corporation's headquarters in the home country, thus dampening the host government's effort to diminish the foreign exchange outflow.

19.4k Other Policies

Other policies used by host countries in securing some of the benefits of MNC investments are requiring foreign firms to engage in labor training, requiring that certain key managerial positions be held by nationals, prohibiting foreign firms from engaging in technologically stagnant industries, and demanding that foreign firms engage in research and development in the host countries.

Host countries hope that these measures will contribute to the internalization of the firm's technological and managerial know-how within the nation, thereby improving the country's BOP. Empirical studies suggest that host countries have been at least partially successful in implementing such measures. These studies show that MNCs usually train local labor. Studies also show that MNCs' training budgets might be greater than those of domestic firms.[26] However, MNCs' research and development activities carried out in developing countries seem to be of an elementary nature, and these efforts usually do not lead to these corporations' adaptation of technology. Additionally, there seems to be no significant difference between the amount of research rendered by foreign firms and that rendered by domestic firms.[27]

19.5 WHO IS RIGHT?

Our prior discussion suggests that all MNC activities do not have the same impact on either host or home countries. Additionally, it is difficult to measure these effects and to reach a general conclusion that can be applied to all countries and all MNCs. In fact, much of the literature in the area of FDI is composed of studies that deal with the isolated problems of individual countries. As a result, any generalization about the conclusions reached by these studies is questionable.

GLOBAL INSIGHTS CASE 19.4

U.S. Tobacco Exports: A Health-Trade Controversy

Since January 11, 1964, when *the Surgeon General's Report documented* the health problems associated with smoking U.S. cigarette and other tobacco products, consumption has been steadily declining. Such a decline is not only related to the public awareness of the adverse health effects of smoking, but other factors as well, such as government restriction on where smoking is permitted, and higher local and federal taxes. This resulted in higher cigarette prices, affecting the decline of the sale of tobacco-related products in the U.S.

Considering the diminishing sales in its domestic market, the U.S. tobacco industry has been actively promoting cigarette export in the international market. As a result, U.S. export of tobacco has continued to experience a rapid growth overseas, leading to more than $2 billion trade surplus in cigarettes. Such a surplus could be attributed to the opening of new overseas markets in Asia to American tobacco products. The opening of these markets was achieved with the help of United States Trade Representative (USTR).

Under the banner of free trade, the USTR engages in negotiations that are aimed at the removal of unfair trade practices against U.S. goods. Japan, South Korea, Taiwan, and Thailand are examples of countries that have negotiated with USTR regarding their high import tariffs, discriminatory taxes and unfair marketing and distribution practices. For example, in 1985 USTR was successful in getting Japan to agree to remove cigarette tariffs, as well other discriminatory barriers directed against import of cigarettes.

Besides USTR efforts to ensure fair treatment for U.S. cigarettes abroad, the U.S. government funds three specific programs that are designed to promote tobacco exports: the Department of Agriculture's Cooperator Market Development Program, the Targeted Export Assistance Program, and the Export Credit Guarantee Programs.

Ironically, the government continues to vigorously support the sales of tobacco companies abroad, even though it appears to be a powerful supporter of the global antismoking movement. This is evident by the activities of the Department of Health and Human Services. This organization acts as a collaborating headquarters for the United Nation's World Health Organization and maintains close relationships with other health organizations around the globe in disseminating information regarding the adverse effects of smoking. It is obvious that the U.S. trade policy of promoting tobacco exports is clearly in conflict with its stated health policy of reducing the use of tobacco products.

Sources: United States General Accounting Office, "Trade and Health Issues: Dichotomy between U.S. Tobacco Export Policy and Antismoking Initiatives," May 1990; "Tobacco Industry: Stubbed Out," *The Economist*, August 20, 1994, 26.

One thing is clear: Many host countries believe that there are gains to be made from MNC operations within their borders, and they continue to receive these corporations with open arms. This is especially true for countries with market economies. For example, Brazil offers a number of incentives to attract foreign investment, including tax rebates for MNCs that reinvest corporate earnings into the economy, convertibility of earnings into the dollar, fiscal incentives, and free repatriation of corporate earnings up to 12 percent of the invested capital. But even in the case of nonmarket economies, the most unlikely countries, such as the People's Republic of China and Nicaragua, are not reluctant to seek foreign investment. China has gone so far in receiving FDI that it offers incentives to MNCs to engage in the exploration of one of its most precious resources, oil.[28] In 1986, the former Marxist government of Nicaragua hosted about 60 MNCs, which contributed approximately 13 percent of its GNP.[29]

Much of the conflict between MNCs and nations seems to be political. The sheer size of MNCs is indicative of their power. For example, data show that the sales of General Motors and Exxon are greater than the GNPs of Switzerland and Saudi Arabia.[30] As a result, these corporations can negotiate business contracts that may have a greater impact on the negotiating countries than many treaties would have.

There is considerable concern that MNCs can be used by home countries to impose their political wills on host countries. For example, the U.S. government has forbidden affiliates of U.S. MNCs to sell to certain communist nations. This goes against the laws of both France and Canada, which require that sales be made. Enforcement of this law could thus be considered an intrusion by the United States into French and Canadian sovereignty. Another example is the case of South Africa. The foreign affiliates of some U.S. MNCs, such as IBM and GM, under pressure at home, have reluctantly pulled out of this country because of its past racial policies.[31] Some observers doubted that such a political move was significant in changing South African racial policies. The move resulted in economic hardship for many South Africans, who had to face the loss of jobs and fringe benefits from the operations of these companies.[32]

As this example indicates, the curtailment of MNCs' operations does not seem to resolve political problems. A useful means of reaching agreements might be a forum for discussing controversial issues that give rise to conflicting views between parties involved in international business.

19.6 SUMMARY

1. Multinational corporations (MNCs) have been criticized by host countries for many reasons.

2. An MNC must satisfy different groups. These groups include employees, customers, stockholders, and the governments of its home and host countries. Because the objectives of these different groups are not necessarily compatible, conflicts among groups involved in international business are bound to arise.

3. The pursuit of the profit maximization goal leads an MNC to (a) choose the type of operation that best suits its objective, (b) improve efficiency by allocating its resources within its corporate family, and (c) retain as much of its profit as possible.

4. Economically speaking, there are few conflicts between the goals of MNCs and the objectives of their home countries. Conflicts do arise, however, if an MNC closes its factory at home and invests money abroad, leading to higher unemployment at home.

5. Conflicts between the MNC and its home country can also stem from noneconomic goals that are set by the government. Conflicts may arise over exports and over the licensing and production of certain products in certain host countries.

6. A host country's objectives in allowing MNCs to operate within its borders can be divided into economic goals and noneconomic goals.

7. The economic goals of a host country in receiving MNC investment are to (a) achieve economic growth, (b) achieve better distribution and allocation of resources, and (c) improve its balance of payments (BOP).

8. The main noneconomic goal of a host country is to maintain its independence. Another noneconomic goal is the maintenance of a social, political, and cultural atmosphere that is free from friction.

9. Transborder data flow (TDF) refers to the flow of electronically transmitted information across national boundaries. TDF is an economic resource and as such is a marketable, transferable, and exportable commodity. The legislation regarding TDF may be considered a form of nontariff trade barriers. The effects of these trade barriers may be viewed from two perspectives—international and domestic.

10. The factors that determine the intensity of a host country's reactions to an MNC are (a) the perceived degree of foreign domination and control, and (b) the extent to which the MNC's activities are subsidized by the host country's government.

11. Some of the major policies host countries employ to make use of FDI without yielding to complete foreign ownership and control are requiring joint venture arrangements; controlling entries and takeovers; excluding foreigners from specific activities; controlling the local content and local employment; imposing export requirements, controlling the local capital market; establishing debt equity requirements; taking the foreign investment package apart; requiring disinvestment; and controlling remittances, rates, and fees.

12. A joint venture arrangement calls for a partnership involving an MNC with either private entrepreneurs or the government of a host country.

13. Controlling market entries and takeovers of foreign firms is achieved by requiring these firms to have approval for a new investment venture or for the takeover of an existing firm. In most countries the purchase of an existing firm is not allowed.

14. Excluding foreigners from certain business activities is usually achieved by prohibiting their engagement in banking, insurance, public utilities, communications and the media, and in the exploitation of certain natural resources.

15. To control the local content of products and local employment, host countries can require foreign firms to continually increase the amount of locally produced goods used to make their final products. Additionally, they can require that a certain percentage of the foreign firm's employees be citizens of the host country.

16. According to the export requirement policy, the approval of a potential foreign investment project is contingent on its contribution to the host country's exports.

17. The policy of controlling the local capital market calls for the exclusion of foreigners from the host country's local capital market, requiring that all capital funds be raised outside the host's national boundaries.

18. A host government's control of debt equity provides guidelines on the debt equity ratio of the MNC's potential investment project in the host country.

19. "Taking the foreign investment package apart" means that a host country buys the needed technology, management, and capital in separate business deals, rather than acquiring them in one package through an MNC investment.

20. A policy of disinvestment calls on the investing MNC to disinvest over a period of time by transferring the corporation's ownership to the host country at a specified time for a predetermined price.

21. The policies of controlling remittances, rates, and fees are used by host countries to improve their BOPs positions, fulfill national domestic policies, and prevent MNCs from reaping excess profits.

22. Other policies used by host countries in securing some of the benefits of MNC investments are requiring foreign firms to engage in labor training, requiring that certain key positions be held by nationals, prohibiting foreign firms from engaging in technologically stagnant industries, and demanding that foreign firms engage in research and development in the host countries.

Review Questions

1. What are some of the major criticisms aimed at MNCs?
2. What elements give rise to the criticisms aimed at MNC?
3. What are the main objectives of MNCs? Why does the pursuit of these objectives lead to conflicts of interest between MNCs and their host country governments?
4. Economically speaking, there is often little conflict between the goals of MNCs and the objectives of their home countries. Why are there conflicts between MNCs and their home countries?
5. What effects do MNCs have on the balance of payments of their host countries? Explain.
6. What noneconomic factors underscore host countries' pessimistic attitude toward MNCs? Explain.
7. What is TDF? Economically speaking, how do you perceive the legislation of TDF?
8. What factors determine the intensity of a host country's reaction to an MNC? Explain.
9. Given the major criticisms aimed at MNCs, what policy measures can a host country adopt to lessen the effects of FDI on its economic system without banning it altogether? Explain.

Problems

1. In order to dampen the effects of foreign ownership and control, some host developing countries have forced MNCs to share their ownership with the host country's nationals. Such policies have reduced the amount of capital inflow that MNCs can transfer to host countries. Given the scarcity of capital in developing countries, why do you think they continue to press for joint foreign-local ownership?

2. Some countries prohibit the purchase of an existing firm by an MNC, requiring a foreign investment project to start from scratch. What theoretical justification is given for such a prohibition? Explain. Does this theoretical justification hold true in practice? Explain.

3. Given the conflicts between MNCs and their home and host countries, who do you think is correct—MNCs, home countries, or host countries? Explain. What is one possible way of alleviating the conflicts? Explain.

4. Suppose you are responsible for attracting FDI to your country. Which incentives do you use to attract FDI, and why? How do you deal with possible resistance to FDI in your country? Under what conditions do you prevent foreign firms from acquiring domestic firms in your country?

5. Choose an advanced country and a developing country and undertake a research project to determine the following:
   (a) The restrictions imposed by the developing and advanced countries' governments on foreign ownership
   (b) The incentives both countries offer to attract FDI
   (c) Which country seems to be pro-foreign investment and why

6. Some host countries have objected to the presence of MNCs inside their borders on the grounds that MNCs impinge upon their national independence. What factors have contributed to such an attitude? Explain.

7. Given the presence of hostility toward the United States in some developing countries, do you think the U.S. government should take any action against developing countries that expropriate the investments of U.S. MNCs? Discuss.

Notes

1. Thomas W. Allen, "Industrial Development Strategies and Foreign Investment Policies of Southern Asia and South Pacific Developing Countries," in R. Hal Mason, ed., *International Business in the Pacific Basin* (Lexington, MA: Lexington Books, D.C. Heath, 1978), 51-92.

2. California Newsreel, *Controlling Interest: The World of Multinational Corporation* (San Francisco: California Newsreel, 1978), video tape.

3. Michael Z. Brooke and H. Lee Remmers, *International Management and Business Policy* (Boston: Houghton Mifflin, 1978), 311.

4. *Ibid.*

5. *Ibid,* 310.

6. Brooke and Remmers, *International Management.*

7. Anant Negandhi, *International Management* (Boston: Allyn and Bacon, 1978), 55.

8. *Ibid.*

9. *Ibid.*

10. *Ibid.*

11. "U.S. Efforts to Deter Foreign Investor View with Need for Capital," *The Wall Street Journal,* 5 August 1987, 1.

12. *Ibid,* 13.

13. *Ibid,* 1, 13.

14. "AT&T Finding Success in Europe Elusive, So It Tries Local Partners New Strategies," *The Wall Street Journal,* 19 December 1985, 33.

15. "IBM Shuts Down Operations in India," *The New York Times,* 2 June 1978, D5; "India Demands `Know-How' and 60% Share of Coca-Cola Operation," *The New York Times,* 9 August 1977, 45.

16. "Venture with Boeing Is Likely to Give Japan Big Boost in Aerospace," *The Wall Street Journal,* 14 January 1986, 22.

17. *Ibid.*

18. "Capitalists Wary of Moscow's Hard Sell to Invest in Joint-Venture Enterprises," *The Wall Street Journal,* 6 April 1987, 25; "Joint Ventures in China Get Clobbered By Beijing's Draconian Credit Squeeze," *The Wall Street Journal,* 29 March 1989, A10.

19. "Progress in Work: Joint Ventures Raise Hungary's Hope for Future," *The Wall Street Journal,* 5 April 1990, A14. "Space Race Becomes a Joint Venture," *The Wall Street Journal,* 11 November 1992, A10; "The Pioneers A Small Joint Venture is Leading the Way in Getting Russian Oil," *The Wall Street Journal,* 29 January 1992, 1.

20. "Spain's New Openness to Foreign Investment Is a Boon to Consumers," *The Wall Street Journal,* 29 July 1987, 1.

21. "Foreign Ownership and Structure of Canadian Industry," *Report of the Task Force on the Structure of Canadian* (Ottawa: Queen's Printer, 1968), 389.

22. "China Sets Equity Requirement for Its Partners in Joint Ventures," *The Wall Street Journal,* 19 December 1985, 33.

23. "Weak in Technology, South Korea Seeks Help from Overseas," *The Wall Street Journal,* 7 January 1986, 1.

24. *Ibid,* 1, 14.

25. "Chrysler Corp. to Enter Chinese Market with Major Sale of Engine Equipment," *The Wall Street Journal,* 21 July 1987, 12.

26. Parviz Asheghian, "Joint Venture Firms and Labour Training in Iran," *Management Research News,* no. 3 (1983): 16-19.

27. Parviz Asheghian, "The R&D Activities of Foreign Firms in a Less Developed Country: An Iranian Case Study," *Journal of Business and Economic Perspectives* (Spring 1984): 19-28.

28. "China to Give Foreign Companies Better Terms in Oil Exploration," *The Wall Street Journal,* 3 December 1985, 34.

29. "Multinational Corporations Continue to Be Crucial to Nicaraguan Economy," *The Wall Street Journal,* 14 November 1986, 34.

30. John Heim, "The Top 100 Economies," *Across the Board* (May 1980): 8-11. This study uses data from 1978.

31. "GM, IBM, and Others Departing South Africa Are Faulted for Plans to Continue Sales There," *The Wall Street Journal,* 24 October 1986, 2.

32. "South Africans Face Pain in Life Without U.S. Firms," *The Wall Street Journal,* 24 October 1986, 24; "U.S. Exodus Touches Many South Africans," *The Wall Street Journal,* 6 November 1986, 36.

Suggested Readings

Agmon, Tamir, and Seev Hirsch. "Multinational Corporations and the Developing Economies: Potential Gains in a World of Imperfect Market and Uncertainty." *Oxford Bulletin of Economics and Statistics* 41 (November 1979): 333-344.

Asheghian, Parviz. "Comparative Efficiencies of Foreign Firms and Local Firms in Iran." *Journal of International Business Studies* 13 (Winter 1982): 113-120.

———. "Joint Venture Firms and Labour Training in Iran." *Management Research News,* no. 3 (1983): 16-19.

Asheghian, Parviz, and William G. Foote. "Capital Efficiency, Capital Intensity and Debt-Equity: A Comparison of U.S.-Owned and Canadian-Owned Firms in Canada." *Midwestern Journal of Business and Economics* 2 (Fall 1986): 39-48.

———. "The Productivities of U.S. Multinationals in the Industrial Sector of the Canadian Economy." *Eastern Economic Journal* 11 (April/June 1983): 123-133.

———. "X-Inefficiencies and Interfirm Comparison of U.S. and Canadian Manufacturing Firms in Canada." *Quarterly Journal of Business and Economics* 24 (Autumn 1985): 3-12; abstract printed in *Journal of Economic Literature* 24 (June 1986): 1085.

Banai, Moshe, and William D. Reisal. "Enterprise Manager's Loyalty to the MNC: Myth or Reality? An Exploratory Study." *Journal of International Business Study* (Second Quarter 1993): 233-248.

Behrman, Jack N. *National Interests and the Multinational Enterprise: Tensions Among the North Atlantic Countries.* Englewood Cliffs, NJ: Prentice-Hall, 1970.

Behrman, Jack N., and Robert E. Grosse. *International Business and Governments.* Columbia, SC: University of South Carolina Press, 1990.

Bergstan, C. F., and T. Moran. *American Multinationals and American Interests.* Washington, DC: Brookings Institution, 1978. Brash, D. T. *American Investment in Austrian Industry.* Cambridge, MA: Ballinger, 1976.

Buss, Martin D. J. "Legislative Threat to Transborder Data Flow." *Harvard Business Review* 62 (May/June 1984): 111-118.

Cassers-Gomes, Benjamin. "Firm Ownership Preferences and Host Government Restrictions: An Integrated Approach." *Journal of International Business Studies* (First Quarter 1990): 1-22.

Casson, Mark. *Alternatives to the Multinational Enterprise.* London: Macmillan, 1979.

Dunning, John H. *American Investment in British Manufacturing Industry.* London: Allen & Unwin, 1958.

————. "Multinational Enterprises and Nation States." In *The Multinational Enterprise in Transition,* edited by A. Kapoor and Philip D. Grulb. Princeton, NJ: Darwin Press, 1972, ch. 28.

Forsyth, David J. C. *U.S. Investment in Scotland.* New York: Praeger, 1972.

Garg, Arun Kumar. *Multinational Corporations in India: Export Promises.* Mearut, India: Friends Publications, 1992.

Gedicks, Al. *The New Resource Wars: Native and Environmental Struggles Against Multinational Corporations.* Boston: South End Press, 1993.

Globerman, Stephen. "Technological Diffusion in the Canadian Tool and Die Industry." *Review of Economic Statistics* 57 (November 1975): 428-434.

————. "Foreign Direct Investment and Spillover Efficiency Benefits in Canadian Manufacturing Industries." *Canadian Journal of Economics* 12 (February 1979): 42-56.

Johnson, Harry G. "The Efficiency and Welfare Implications of the International Corporation." In *The International Corporation,* edited by Charles P. Kindleberger. Cambridge, MA: Massachusetts Institute of Technology Press, 1970.

Kindleberger, Charles P. *American Business Abroad.* New Haven, CT: Yale University Press, 1969.

Lafalce, John J. "TDF Barriers to Service Trade." *International Data Report* 8, no. 4 (1985): 190-193.

Lall, Sanjaya. "Performance of Transnational Corporations in Less Developed Countries." *Journal of International Business Studies* (Spring 1983): 13-33.

Langlois, Catherine C., and Bodo B. Schlegelmilch. "Do Corporate Codes of Ethics Reflect National Character? Evidence from Europe and the United States." *Journal of International Business Studies* (Fourth Quarter 1990): 519-539.

Mansfield, Edwin, J. Teece, and S. Wagner. "Overseas Research and Development by U.S.-Based Firms." *Review of Economics and Statistics* 46 (May 1979): 187-196.

Organization for Economic Cooperation and Development. *Trade, Investment, and Technology in the 1990s.* Paris: OECD, 1991.

Rearden, John J. *America and Multinational Corporation: The History of a Troubled Partnership.* Westport, CT: Praeger, 1992.

Rugman, Alan M. *Multinationals in Canada: Theory, Performance and Economic Impact.* Boston: Martinus Nijhoff, 1980.

Safarian, A. E. *The Performance of Foreign Owned Firms in Canada.* Washington, DC: Canadian-American Committee, National Planning Association, 1969.

————. *Storm over the Multinationals.* Cambridge, MA: Harvard University Press, 1977.

Sethi, S. Prakash. *Multinational Corporations and the Impact of Public Advocacy on Corporate Strategy: Nestle and Infant Formula Controversy.* Boston: Kluwer Academic, 1994.

Streeten, Paul. "Costs and Benefits of Multinational Enterprises in Less Developed Countries." In *The Multinational Enterprise,* edited by John H. Dunning. London: Allen & Unwin, 1971, ch. 9.

Tsanacas, Demetri. "The Transborder Data Flow in the New World Information Order: Privacy or Control." *Review of Social Economy* 43 (December 1985): 357-370.

Twomey, Michael J. *Multinational Corporations and the North American Free Trade Agreement.* Westport, CT: Praeger 1993.

United Nations. *Transnational Corporations in World Development: Trends and Prospects.* New York: United Nations, 1988, overview, part 1.

Vaistos, Constantine V. "Income Distribution and Welfare Considerations. In *Economic Analysis and the Multinational Enterprise,* edited by John H. Dunning. New York: Praeger, 1974, ch. 12.

Vernon, Raymond. *Sovereignty at Bay: The Multinational Spread of U.S. Enterprise.* New York: Basic Books, 1971.

———. *Storm Over Multinationals.* Cambridge, MA: Harvard University Press, 1974.

Part 6

COMPREHENSIVE CASES

This part contains ten comprehensive case studies and includes questions for discussion at the end of each case. These real cases describe situations faced by a nation or an organization whose identities are known. They typically include a chronology of significant events, summaries of important financial and nonfinancial data, and information about competitors and industry. Cases provide students with an opportunity to use the principles and theories presented in the text in decision-making situations.

Case 6:1

CHINA OPENS ITS DOORS TO THE WEST

INTRODUCTION

During the last few decades we have seen the world become a smaller, more interdependent place. With the advancement of technology and the expansion of the communications industry, international trade has become easier and much more manageable. With the rapidly growing world population and the ever increasing scarcity of the world's raw materials, international trade has become of fundamental importance to future global economic growth and international political stability. Given the scarcity of the world resources the importance of the People's Republic of China as a country that holds one of the most untapped resources for international trade and modernized development becomes apparent. The People's Republic of China (PRC) will prove to be an oasis for many multinational corporations as it gradually opens its doors to foreign trade.

History

The year 1949 marked the formal establishment of the People's Republic of China. The communists seized power and brought with them radical reforms and an ideology unprecedented in the history of Chinese culture. During the 1950s, China was greatly dependent on the former Soviet Union, its communist brother. Mao Tse-tung, chairman of the Central Communist Party (CCP), stated in his famous address to the Soviet Union's Seventh CCP Central Committee that it was China's purpose to approach the international arena from an anti-imperialist stance by following the leadership of the Soviet Union, their only genuine friend. "Dependence on the Soviet Union during the 1950s produced one of the most remarkable technology transfers in modern history."[1] With the help of the Soviets, large-scale socialist construction was undertaken to industrialize a country whose semifeudal, semicolonial society had been dominated by stagnant productive forces that for centuries had been based on primitive agriculture and handicraft industries.

The period of harmony between the Soviets and the Chinese did not last long, however. Differences over ideology, politics, and policies on economic reform and development reached a peak in 1958-1959, bringing about an almost overnight withdrawal of the former Soviet Union influence from China.

In the wake of the Sino-Soviet split, a radically new approach was taken by the Chinese concerning international involvement. Being left on the brink of economic collapse by the Soviets was a bitter experience for the Chinese and dramatized to them the high potential costs of dependence on any one country or any one source of supply.[2] The doctrine of self-reliance was instituted and became the new guideline. Self-reliance did not construe complete or absolute self-sufficiency. Self-reliance called for China to rely primarily on its own efforts, manufacturing the products needed by society whenever and wherever possible. And self-reliance meant continued economic growth, given the country's human, material, and financial resources.

The doctrine of self-reliance paralleled the ultra-left-wing movement known as the "Cultural Revolution," which peaked in 1967. The radical policies and actions by Lin Biao and the Gang of Four, who led the revolution, caused already strained foreign relations to become worse. The radicals in power supported strong economic nationalism, resistance to foreign influences, and reliance on domestic innovations for economic and technical development. This led to China's failing to fulfill export contracts, to attacks on foreign embassies, and to outbreaks of antiforeign hysteria, further damaging economic relations.

The beginning of the 1970s saw normality finally return to China as the government began to realize that the costs of continued isolationism would hurt economic growth. The policies of self-reliance became modified to coincide with the new goals of accelerated economic growth and industrialization. In 1972, President Nixon visited China and began the "opening" of China. The Chinese put forth a new trade offensive, and relations between China and the West steadily improved. The new policy of trade expansion, however, did not proceed without debate. The radicals held that increasing foreign dependence and relaxing the self-reliance policies were actions promoted by profiteers and were a sellout to foreign capitalism and imperialism.

In October of 1976, the Gang of Four were arrested, and the pragmatists came to control China's destiny. Deng Xiaoping's push for rapid modernization embarked China on a massive acquisition of Western technology and machinery. An initial trickle of business contracts in mid-1977 was followed by an upsurge of contracts, which began in May 1978 and continued through December. This resulted in the importation of $6.9 billion worth of plants and equipment in 1978 alone.[3] However, the deficit and lack of capable technicians to handle the massive influx of technology led the overzealous Ministry of Finance to suspend many late 1978 contracts while they reevaluated their open door policy. This resulted in major cancellations including a $14 billion Jidong steel project with West Germany and two nuclear power plants from France.[4]

By early 1979 the government reaffirmed its commitment to modernization through an open door policy of trade liberalization and expansion. The underdeveloped state of China's foreign trade was due primarily to the underdeveloped state of her economy, which limited the amount of merchandise available for export and, consequently, the amount China could import from other countries due to balance of payments concerns. To cope with the problems involved with foreign investment in China, the government established an array of organizations to control and monitor trade. The Foreign Investment Control Commission was established to supervise approval of foreign trade offers. The Chinese International Trust and Investment Corporation was founded to act as a goodwill agency and promote international commerce in the PRC. Also established were the Import-Export Control Commission and the State General Administration of Exchange Control.

International Arrangements

China has made a substantial move toward furthering its international economic involvement. Its most recent endeavor is the establishment of the Foreign Trade Law of the People's Republic of China on May 12, 1994. Accordingly, "This law is formulated with a view to developing the foreign trade, maintaining of the foreign trade order and promoting a healthy development of the socialist market economy."[5]

The main arrangements used in China to conduct international business can be categorized as joint venture, cooperative enterprise, and compensation trade.

Joint Venture

By 1981, 28 joint ventures had been approved and established. China strictly followed a policy of import substitution, purchasing plants and equipment that produced goods that had been imported from abroad. This policy, coinciding with that of self-reliance, was aimed at making China less dependent upon the "outside" world. The Chinese government promoted joint ventures by doing the following:

1. The government required only a minimum of 25 percent financing of a project by a foreign entity, much lower than the traditional 50 percent required by some countries, such as Japan.
2. The government set no upper limit to the percentage being financed by the foreign entity.
3. The government granted two to three year tax holidays to encourage investment.

By the end of 1981, total investments in joint ventures had risen to $240 million.[6]

Since 1981, China has worked with the United Nations Industrial Development Organization (UNIDO) to advertise over 130 investment opportunities for small- to medium-size joint ventures, bringing an expected $900 million in foreign investment into the country.[7] An example of these joint ventures is the Shanghai Volkswagen Corporation, a Sino-German joint venture, which plans to merge with the Shanghai Automobile Factory. Its annual production capacity is set to increase from 60,000 to 150,000 cars.[8] It also plans to setup a large factory, producing engines for the German Volkswagen Corp.

An important industry that relies on joint venture arrangements in China is oil prospecting and exploration. The movement for modernization in China has created enormous demands for foreign exchange, and the Chinese are looking toward the petroleum industry to play a critical role in financing their balance of payments problems through the sales of petroleum products. The costs of developing an efficient petroleum industry are staggering, and China has relaxed its self-reliance policies and invited Japanese and Western oil companies to participate in China's oil development, especially in areas of prospecting and exploration. The China Petroleum Company, a government-run organization that oversees the oil industry in China, has signed several joint prospecting and exploration contracts with major world oil companies. China's offshore oil deposits in the Bohai Gulf and the Northern Gulf of the South China Sea are expected to produce hundreds of millions of barrels of oil annually once they are developed. Some 300 field joint ventures are presently being negotiated by businesspersons from over 30 countries.[9]

The historical problems with joint ventures in China have been price controls implemented by the government and preset wage levels. However, the Chinese are slowly granting greater freedom in the marketplace, and these issues are being addressed.

Cooperative Enterprise

A cooperative enterprise, also known as contractual ventures, differs from a joint venture in that it is owned and operated by the Chinese. An investor from another country contributes whatever resources he or she wants and draws a percentage of the profits according to the value of what has been invested.

Compensation Trade

This is an arrangement under which the Chinese produce goods with the equipment and technology supplied by foreign corporations. The Chinese pay off the value of the equipment and technology by selling the goods produced back to the suppliers.[10] This type of investment has brought over $300 million in investment in China from foreign entities, including such American corporations as the Boston-based Gillette Company.[11]

CHINA'S MAIN TRADING PARTNERS

China's significant trading partners are Japan, the United States, and Western Europe.

Japan

Japan has benefited from China's open door policy more than any other nation in the world. China buys more goods from its island neighbor than from any other country, accounting for Japan's 26 percent control of China's nearly $50 billion worth of world trade in 1984.[12] Anti-Japanese sentiments are prevalent throughout China ever since the occupation of China by Japan during the war years of the 1930s and 1940s. It is therefore surprising that Japan's control of the Chinese market is so strong. Several reasons for this, however, can be pointed out. First, the Japanese have made extensive efforts in filling China with corporate offices and personnel. Compared with the fewer than 100 U.S. corporate offices in Beijing, there are more than 250 Japanese companies and banks, many with dozens of salespersons, engineers, and support staff.[13] In addition, the Western MNCs have typically limited their offices in China to the major cities, whereas Japan has made great efforts to have offices throughout the country.

Among other Japanese advantages are their efficient use of trading companies to organize package deals when trading with China. ""If China wants to modernize a plant, it would take 10 to 20 American companies offering different machines to close the deal. The Japanese utilize a trading company who puts the whole package together, including financing, shipping, insurance and engineering."[14] It is no wonder that the Japanese are able to negotiate many trade contracts using this efficient method.

There also exists a cultural tie that links these two countries. Japan's location and its cultural affinity with China through religion, language, and customs offer an advantage with which the rest of the world is unable to compete. Intangibles, such as proper seating arrangements at business meetings and bowing manners when greeting someone, are new and unfamiliar to Western business society, but are familiar to the Japanese and have contributed to their success.

The future of the Sino-Japanese trading relations is not clear. Continued trade will enhance China's modernization prospects, but there is increasing sentiment that Japan must increase actual investment in China or retaliatory sanctions against the Japanese may result.

The United States

Unlike the Japanese domination, the United States has not been able to capture a significant percentage of China's foreign trade.[15] The historic visit of President Nixon to China in 1972 laid the foundation for the present Sino-American relations.[16]

With the opening of China, many U.S. businesspersons envisioned extremely rapid U.S. integration into their markets. China's growth has been substantial, but it has fallen short of the original expectations of many Western businesspersons. Although the initial surge of U.S. investment in China was tremendous, things cooled off as U.S. businesses realized that China was short on cash for purchases, had a low ability to manage the vast technological transfer programs planned, and had a reputation for quick decisions to cancel already signed contracts. China and the United States formed the Joint Commission on Commerce and Trade to focus on these trade problems and to search for their solutions. In addition to the previously mentioned issues, other problems being addressed are the following:

1. China's lack of copyright laws
2. China's lack of patent control in the chemical industry
3. China's profit limit laws
4. China's lack of commercial law.

Many of these issues have been addressed and reforms have been implemented. As a result, U.S. trade volume expanded from a relatively small amount in 1971 to $58.5 billion in 1995. In recent years, China's exports to the United States have accounted for most of the growth in bilateral trade causing the U.S. merchandise deficit with China to reach the level of $36 billion for 1995. Key U.S. products that have held a dominant position in China include chemical fertilizer, timber, cotton, food grains, computers, air craft parts and oil production equipment. The trade in these products exceed $ 100 million annually[17].

It is likely that Sino-American trade will further expand throughout the 2000s. The U.S. Congress, through its 1982 Export Trading Company Act, is attempting to ease antitrust policies to encourage more investment in China. The Chinese government is also making strides in freeing the market place to encourage modernization, which will expand their international trade involvement. In September 1993, President Clinton propelled a policy of comprehensive engagement with China in order to protect U.S. interests through continued high level dialogue with Chinese officials.[18]

Western Europe

During the 1960s and 1970s, four of China's 12 leading trading partners were in Western Europe.[19] Chinese exports to Western Europe were mainly foodstuffs, textiles, and light manufactured goods; while their imports from Western Europe were predominantly machine tools, chemicals, and finished steel products. China views Western Europe as an alternative to its traditional major trading partners, the United States and Japan. They have worked diligently to enhance relations with the Western European nations, and they have a strong desire to continue increasing trade in this sector.

BALANCE OF PAYMENTS

Unlike many countries in the world, China managed from 1949 to 1979 to maintain a balance of trade from a gross perspective. They experienced trade deficits during the years of 1951-1955, 1960, 1974-1975, and 1978-1979, but these were offset by surpluses during 1956-1973 and 1976-1977.[20] China's requirements for modernization and industrialization demand massive expenditures abroad to import the necessary goods and technology. These massive expenditures place great strain on their balance of payments. China's main hope is for successful, rapid expansion of its petroleum industry to significantly counteract the balance of payments trend toward deficits.

LOOKING INTO THE FUTURE

China seems to be the "wild card" of the new global economy. Its emergence as a modernizing, industrial nation shall have profound effects on the rest of the world. It appears that before long China will become one of the global leaders in the export of energy. Their petroleum reserves have been estimated at 50 to 80 billion barrels (compared to Saudi Arabia's reserves of 163 billion and the U.S. reserves of 27 billion).[21] In April 1996 Premier Li Peng announced the approval of a major oil deal in South China with the Anglo-Dutch oil group, Shell. The project is expected to run $6 billion with 50% going to Shell [22].

Today, China has a quarter of the world's population and its market-oriented reforms have contributed to the generation of a very rpaidly growing economy. It was predicted that the China's economy will grow 8% a year until the year 2000.[23] China's huge population and abundant, untapped natural resources give it much potential for tremendous future economic growth.

It seems clear now that the ultimate success of China's development program depends on modifying guidelines and principles of communist ideology.

CONCLUDING REMARKS

Since 1979, China has distanced itself from its Maoist past and instituted free market reforms and free trade zones. Nevertheless, as indicated by the 1989 Tiannamen Square massacre, it still represents one of the most repressive regimes in existence today.

On June 30, 1997 the control of Hong Kong reverted from the British government back to Chinese government, allowing it to control what has been to many a city that is the symbol of capitalism. Hong Kong is now a Special Administrative Region within the People's Republic of China. Its constitution, called the Basic Law, ensures that Hong Kong's way of life, especially its economy and judicial system, will continue for another 50 years. It remains to be seen if China's " one nation two system " approach will succeed in Hong Kong or if the world will experience another repeat of the 1989 Tianemen Square massacre.

QUESTIONS

1. Why does a communist country like China open its door to capitalist entrepreneurs? Discuss.
2. Suppose you are the manager of an MNC that is planning to open a plant in China. What factors do you consider?
3. Why do you think the Japanese are more successful in China than the Americans?
4. What are the principle arrangements employed in China for conducting international business? Explain.
5. What do you think will happen in China, and how will it affect that country's relations with the West?

Notes

1. Chu-yuan Cheng, *China's Economic Development: Growth and Structural Change* (Boulder, Colo.: Westview Press, 1982), p. 448.
2. Ibid., p. 449.
3. Ibid., p. 451.
4. Ibid., p. 452.
5. "Foreign Trade Law of the People's Republic of China (Adopted at the Seventh Sexxion of the Standing Committee of the Eight National People's Congress on May 12, 1994), Chapter I Principles," in The U.S. Bureau of Public Affairs, *Fact Sheet: U.S.-China Relations*, April 15, 1996.
6. Arnold Chao, "Economic Readjustment and the Open-Door Policy," in Lin Wei and Arnold Chao, eds., *China's Economic Reforms* (Philadelphia: University of Pennsylvania Press, 1982), p. 209.
7. "China Thinks Small to Woo Investors Back," *Business Week*, 17 May 1982, p. 44.
8. LiMin, "Future Development for Shanghai Volkswagen," *Beijing Review* (June 3-9 1991): 40.
9. Arnold Chao, "Economic Readjustment and the Open-Door Policy," p. 211.
10. Ibid., p. 210.
11. "China Thinks Small ... ," Business Week, p. 44.
12. Barry Kramer, "Master Merchants: Japanese Dominate the Chinese Market with Savvy Trading," *The Wall Street Journal*, 18 November 1985, p. 1.
13. Ibid.
14. Ibid.
15. Percy Timberlake, "China as a Trading Nation," in Nelville Maxwell, ed., *China's Road to Development* (Oxford: Oxford University Press, 1982), pp. 575-586.
16. Cheng, *China's Economic Development*, p. 468.
17. Ibid., p. 34; The U.S. Bureau of Public Affairs, *Fact Sheet: U.S.-China Relations*, April 15, 1996, p. 2..
18. The U.S. Bureau of Public Affairs, *Fact Sheet: U.S.-China Relations*, April 15, 1996, p.1.
19. Cheng, *China's Economic Development*, p. 468.
20. Ibid., p. 474.
21. Hunter Lewis and Donald Allison, *The Real World War* (New York: Coward, McCann, and Geoghegan, 1982), p. 132.
22. Bruce Arnold, "Slippery Slope, " *Far Eastern Economic Review* (March 28, 1996): 20.
23. The U.S. Bureau of Public Affairs, *Fact Sheet: U.S.-China Relations*, April 15, 1996, p. 2.

Suggested Readings

Anders, Stephen. *China's Industrial Revolution*. New York: Pantheon Books, 1977.
"Arco's Deal with China Is a Tough Act to Follow." *Business Week*, 4 October 1984, pp. 44-44.
Cheng, Chu-yuan. *China's Economic Development*. Boulder, Colo.: Westview Press, 1982.
"China Begins A New Long March." *Business Week*, 5 June 1989, p. 38.
"China Thinks Small to Woo Investors Back." *Business Week*, 17 May 1982, p. 44.
"China Unloads a Pile of Surplus Imports." *Business Week*, 6 September 1982, p. 44.
"China Update." *Business Week*, 14 May 1984, p. 44.
"Communism in Turmoil: Special Report on China and the Soviet Union," *Business Week*, 5 June 1989, pp. 52-87.
Editor, "Constructive attitude Essential For Sino-US Economic Relations " *Beijing Review* (May 20, 1991).
Elliot, Dorinda, and Maks Westerman. "Why Beijing Is Hungry for U.S. Food Companies." *Business Week*, 24 December 1984, p. 43.
Gallery, Bruce "Slippery *Slope,"Far Eastern Economic Review (March 28 1996)*.
"The Greatest Leap Yet Toward a Free Market." *Business Week*, 14 November 1984, p. 45.
Ho, Sam P. China's Open Door Policy: The Quest for Foreign Technology and Capital. Vancouver, B.C.: University of British Columbia Press, 1984.

Ignatius, Adi."People's Republic: Chinese Communism Faces a Crossroads as the Masses Speak." *TheWall Street Journal*, 19 May 1989, pp. A1, A6.

Keidel, Albert. "China: Gaining Efficiency Through Western Ways." *Business Week*, 24 May pp. 172-174.

Kramer, Barry. "Japanese Dominate the Chinese Market with Savvy Trading." *The Wall Street Journal*, 18 November 1985, pp. 1, 26.

Lewis, Hunter, and Donald Allison. *The Real World War*. New York: Coward, McCann, and eoghegan, 1982.

Maxwell, Nelville. *China's Road to Development*. Oxford: Oxford University Press, 1975.

Min, Li   "Future Development For Shanghi Volkswagen "*Beijing Review* (June 3-9, 1991).

Office of the Group of 30 for the Study Group on Foreign Direct Investment. *Foreign Direct Investment 1973-1987: A Survey of Foreign Direct* Investment. Washington, D.C.: U.S. Government Printing Office, 1984.

Sterba, James P. "Whither China? Bungled Effort to End Protests Leaves Nation in Danger of Anarchy." *The Wall Street Journal*, 30 May 1989, pp. A1, A12.

Sterba, James P., Adi Ignatius, and Robert S. Greenberger."Class Struggle: Chinas's Harsh Actions Threaten to Set Back 10-Year Reform Drive." *The Wall Street Journal*, 5 June 1989, pp. A1, A8.

U.S. Department of Commerce. International Trade Administration. *Investment Climate in Foreign Countries*. Washington, D.C.: U.S. Government Printing Office, 1983.

Wang, George C. *Economic Reform in the PRC*. Boulder, Colo.: Westview Press, 1982.

Wei, Lin, and Arnold Chao. *China's Economic Reforms*. Philadelphia: University of Pennsylvania Press, 1982.

Zhiping "Guandong to attract more investment " *Beijing Review* (June 3-9, 1996).

TO PROTECT OR NOT TO PROTECT:
THAT IS THE QUESTION

INTRODUCTION

When President Reagan was first elected, he strongly promoted a free foreign trade policy. For example, in the 198
Economic Report of the President, Mr. Reagan wrote:

> I remain committed to the principle of free trade as the best way to bring the benefits of competition to American
> consumers and businesses. It would be totally inappropriate to respond by erecting trade barriers or by using taxpayers'
> dollars to subsidize exports.[1]

Although President Reagan preached this hands-off policy, his political and legal actions showed that he intende
to protect U.S. industries that he felt were important to the economic and social well-being of the United States. Trad
legislation in the steel, textile, and motorcycle industries were prime examples of the Reagan administration'
protectionist actions.

One main argument of the administration for protectionism was its desire to sustain a diversified economy in th
United States. An example of this type of protection of an industry by the Reagan administration is the legislatio
passed in the motorcycle industry. Harley-Davidson is the only American motorcycle maker still in productior
During the late 1970s and early 1980s its profits continued to fall greatly because Japanese heavy motorcycl
producers were dumping their cheaper products on the U.S. market. Japanese could produce the motorcycles mor
cheaply, mainly because of their lower labor costs. As Harley-Davidson was just about to fold, the company mad
a request to the administration for some type of protection. Because Reagan felt it was important to keep motorcycle
in production in the United States and to keep the U.S. economy more diversified, he imposed a 49.9 percent tarif
on heavy motorcycles entering the nation. The result of the tariff was a 10 to 15 percent rise in the price of importec
motorcycles.[2] Harley-Davidson has since managed to keep up production and stay competitive in the motorcycl
market because of Reagan's protectionist act. In 1997, the company shipped over 132,285 motorcycles to it
worldwide dealership and planned to increase its output to ship 200,000 motorcycles annually by 2003.

National security was another Reagan argument for protectionism. National security was a high-priority objectiv
in the Reagan administration, as was evidenced by the continual increases in military spending witnessed during hi
administration. Mr. Reagan advocated protection of several industries that he felt were important to Americar
national security. The U.S. steel industry is indispensable with respect to national security. Steel is a material used
in the production of almost all weaponry and other military-related commodities. Competition from the former Wes
Germany, the Netherlands, Japan, and several other nations had been taking its toll on the U.S. steel industry. The
president, feeling this industry to be vital to the United States' security, initiated several protectionist actions to allow
U.S. steel producers to stay competitive in the international market. In 1984, the U.S. carbon steel industry filed
several petitions to the government explaining its persistent losses and their effects on the country, such as an increase
in unemployment if the industry were to fold. Reagan responded by sending Commerce Secretary Malcolm Baldrige
to negotiate with European steel producers. This resulted in the imposition of quotas on imported carbon steel into
the United States. Reagan also continued the protection that the Ford administration induced in 1976 in the form of
tariffs for the specialty steel industry.[3] Following this protectionist measure, the U.S. steel industry has continued
to survive, and the Reagan administration believed that such policies strengthened the U.S. national security.

Reagan argued for protectionism as necessary for maintaining wages and full employment. A case in point is the
U.S. automobile industry. During the 1970s and the early 1980s the U.S. auto industry experienced a large decrease
in its sales. One factor contributing to the sales decline of the U.S.-produced cars was the supply of cheap labor

available in competing foreign nations. Japan is a prime example, where lower wages allow the Japanese producers to lower the selling price of their cars in the U.S. market. In 1984, to deal with these situations, the Reagan administration negotiated a three-year trade agreement with Japan in which Japan agreed to abide by the restraints that were requested by the Reagan administration.[4] Reagan's motive in this agreement was to keep the U.S. car industry competitive with foreign competition. He also wished to avoid high unemployment levels that would occur if U.S. automobile plants were shut down.

Finally, an important Reagan argument for protectionism was the desire to lessen the U.S. trade deficit. Given the huge balance of payments deficit in the United States, the Reagan administration protectionist policies aimed to restrict imports from countries such as Japan in order to restore the equilibrium in the balance of payments.

QUESTIONS

1. What theoretical arguments supported President Reagan's commitment to free trade? Explain.
2. The Reagan administration used different arguments to impose protectionist measures. Are these arguments justifiable? Discuss. What are other arguments that call for protectionist policies? Explain.
3. Give examples of products that you know have enjoyed protection by the United States or another government. Can you pinpoint the reasons for the imposition of such protection?

Notes

1. Lee Hamilton, "Free Trade: Rhetoric vs. Reality," *Christian Science Monitor*, 25 April 1984, p. 14.
2. Ibid.
3. M. Weidenbaum, and M. Munger, "Protectionism: Who Gets Protected," *Consumers Research Magazine* 66 (October 1983): 16-17.
4. John Destler, "Why Reagan Is a Free Trade Villain," *New York Times*, 18 March 1984, p.

Suggested Readings

Destler, John. "Why Reagan is a Free Trade Villain." *New York Times*, 18 March 1984, p. F3.

Forsythe, David. *American Foreign Policy in an Uncertain World.* Lincoln: University of Nebraska Press, 1984, p. 203.

Friedman, Milton. Free to Choose, New York: Harcourt Brace Jovanovich, 1980.

Garten, Jeffrey. "America's Retreat from Protectionism." *New York Times*, 16 June 1985, p. F3.

Hamilton, Lee. "Free Trade: Rhetoric vs. Reality." *Christian Science Monitor*, 25 April 1984, p. 14.
    "How to Foil Protectionism." *Fortune*, 21 March 1983, p. 76.

Kinsley, Michael. "Keep Trade Free." *The New Republic*, 11 April 1983, p. 10.

McKenzie, Richard. "Low Wages in Foreign Countries Do Not Fully Explain Imports." *Consumer Research Magazine*, October 1983, pp. 18-19.

Mouat, Lucia. "Reagan Nominee Sees Danger in Rising Trade Protectionism." *Christian Science Monitor*, 11 April 1985, p. 3.

Pine, Art. "Can Reagan Resist Protectionist Forces?" *The Wall Street Journal*, 30 July 1984, p. 1.

"The Protection Racket." *The Wall Street Journal, 20 December 1984*, p. 26L.

Putka, Gary. "Western Europe Sees U.S. Protectionism Looming, and Warns It Would Retaliate." *The Wall Street Journal*, 13 March 1985, p. 38.

Richey, Warren. "U.S. Trade Commissioner Urges U.S. Industries to Forego Protectionism." *Christian Science Monitor*, 12 October 1984, p. 6.

Weidenbaum, M., and M. Munger. "Protectionism: Who Gets Protected?" *Consumers Research Magazine*, October 1983, pp. 16-17.

Case 6:3

DOLEFIL

INTRODUCTION

Dole Philippines, Inc., which operates under the name Dolefil, is a subsidiary of Castle & Cooke, Inc., which has its headquarters in Hawaii. Castle & Cooke, Inc., is the world's largest producer of pineapples.[1] In 1995, the company's gross sales was $3,803.8 million and its net income was $119.8 million.[2] The Dolefil subsidiary is wholly owned by Castle & Cooke, and is located on the island of Mindanao, the largest of the 7,000 Philippine islands.

The Philippines, like many Third World countries, has welcomed foreign corporations. American companies, in particular, have always found favorable conditions in the Philippines, even as far back as the colonial days.

> The colonial relationship with the United States and the so-called free-trade policy tended to concentrate Philippine trade with the United States. By the late interwar period the Philippines was sending three-quarters of its exports (by value) to the United States....[3]

Tariff policy is one of the critical determinants in the success of the Philippine export industries. U.S. tariff policy permits Philippine products to have special access to the U.S. marketplace.[4]

OPERATIONS

The operation of Dolefil is located mainly in Polomolok municipality, but there are some fields in Tupi and General Santos. This region is comparatively underdeveloped.

The operation commenced in 1963 on a 6,000 hectare plantation. It is now one of the largest plantations and processing operations in the world, with 10,000 hectares of land under its control. Out of these 10,000 hectares, 8,000 are leased from the National Development Corporation, which is a government agency. The lease is for a 25-year period, subject to renegotiation for renewal. Rent is based on production, with a minimum guarantee that is reviewed periodically. The remaining 2,000 hectares have individual owners and are obtained through Farm Management Arrangement contracts. Dolefil can use this land for ten years with a renewal option. Individual owners receive a set annual rent per hectare plus a premium based on production.[5] Production is based on a three-year cycle. The first crop is ready for picking between 14 and 17 months after planting. The maturation of pineapples is chemically controlled so as to maintain the cycle. A year later a second crop is produced. After knocking down the plants, the land is left fallow for two to three months before it is tilled and then replanted. Waste from the cannery is incorporated back into the soil to increase its organic content and fertility. The degree of labor-intensive production varies with the scheme used. Planting and harvesting are labor-intensive, whereas the rest of the agricultural operations is more mechanized, using bulldozers, tractors, and spraying mechanisms for pest control.[6]

In addition to plantations, Dolefil owns a highly mechanized cannery, which is considered to be the best in the world. Every part of the pineapple is used, including the shell, which is used for cattle feed and field emulsion.[7] The company participates in comprehensive training programs in an effort to educate Filipino employees, thus enabling them to move upward in the company organization.[8]

Initially, the entire output was shipped to the United States; now it is shipped mainly to Japan and the United States. Some of the product also goes to the rest of the world.

The company also has its own support services, which provide it with electrical generation, repair services, maintenance, and engineering facilities. Water used in the area is treated at the company's water treatment plant. Paper cartons that are used for packing are built by Dolefil at its plant at Calumpang Wharfin. In addition to building and maintaining hundreds of kilometers of dirt roads throughout the plantation, Dolefil also maintains many of the provincial roads that run through the plantation. Finally, it owns the warehouse, which is fully equipped for storage at the shipping dock. Transportation to and from the field is provided by the company. Workers are picked up from specific locations in uncovered cargo trucks, which have no provisions for rain or sun.[9]

EMPLOYMENT PRACTICES

In the early 1980st the company was employing 9,000 workers. Half were in agricultural operations; a third in industrial operations; and the rest in administrative and general service activities. Of the 9,000, less than ten were permanent non-Filipino executive staff; all were in top management. Between 1963 and 1980 there was a large increase in the Polomolok population. In 1963, the population was only 15,000. It reached 59,200 in 1980, a 294.6 percent increase. This increase was largely due to Dolefil's creation of jobs that were made available not only to local residents but also to immigrants from the northern part of the Philippines.

Today, the company employs more than 12,000 workers. Well-established unionization of labor exists, but the effectiveness of unions is questionable due to internal squabbles. Furthermore, martial law has been in effect since 1972, banning strikes in "vital industries." These industries include companies engaged in foreign exports, such as Dolefil. The workday consists of 10- to 12-hour shifts, and there is compulsory work on Sundays during peak seasons.[10]

Housing in Polomolok and the cannery area is scarce and overcrowded. In order to resolve this problem, Dolefil has engaged in housing development schemes. The scheme is controlled through a real estate agency, and plots may be purchased by employees of the company. Dolefil has subsidized the loans needed for the completion of the project, thereby exerting control over the quality of the structures constructed. Workers who cannot be accommodated by the subsidized housing scheme must seek housing from local residents. This generally means exorbitant rents, with no electricity and a limited water supply. However, the mid-level managers are provided with housing at the residential compound near the cannery site. This compound has several sports and recreational facilities, which are subsidized by Dolefil. About five kilometers north of the cannery on a mountain slope is Kalsangi, the housing area for top management. It is an exclusive housing complex with suburban-style homes. Invitation is required for entrance. The area has 55 executive homes. It also has its own school (the elementary grades through high school), a well-maintained golf course, a swimming pool, tennis courts, and a clubhouse that is used as a center for community activities. A small number of people own their own homes, but they must pay rent for the land.[11]

As with any MNC, Dolefil has its own interests to serve, namely, to make a profit. In the pineapple business in the Philippines, where Dolefil faces stiff competition from another MNC, Del Monte, the question that is often raised is whether or not it is possible to simultaneously serve the interests of the local community and also to continue to make a profit and prosper as a business?

COMMUNITY RELATIONS

Dolefil has taken a number of steps in the overall development of the local community of Polomolok. It provides a 99-bed hospital, serviced by eight doctors and one dentist. In an emergency situation, up to 120 beds may be accommodated by taking advantage of all available space. The company has also improved water availability, health, sanitation, and educational and recreational facilities. Total aid to the community from 1973 to 1979 amounted to $754,666. Dolefil's extensive training programs in management, mechanics, and engineering have enabled Filipinos to start their own businesses or find employment elsewhere. Agricultural workers are paid approximately 40 percent more and industrial workers approximately 55 percent more than the required minimum wage. They also receive fringe benefits, such as hospital care and the use of recreational facilities. The average annual wage paid by Dolefil to its workers in Polomolok is inadequate to provide the average family with the necessities of life. The average wages are also far less than the average wages at the company's operation in Hawaii. With regard to the land, Dolefil has made some attempts to combat soil erosion by contour plowing of fields across rather than down the slopes of hills. Dolefil has also reorganized and reshaped dry creeks, and it has extensively planted, ipil-ipil trees on the creek banks. Contours are placed at regular distances and at a given slope to carry away surplus water through natural waterways across the plantation.[12]

In Polomolok, the host of this highly mechanized and modern industrial plant, there are no paved roads, no street lights, inadequate health care, and a very poor garbage and waste disposal system. Although taxes from the corporation have contributed millions of pesos to the local government, the government administration does not use these funds for community development. Furthermore, the use of numerous chemical additives in the soil in an effort to increase its fertility is causing the gradual deterioration of the land. If Dolefil were to pull out, the soil would be unproductive and thus useless to local farmers. The presence of Dolefil and Del Monte has discouraged local entrepreneurs from trying to penetrate the pineapple market. They accuse both of these corporations of dumping, and thus monopolizing, the market. Finally, constitutional questions have been raised concerning Dolefil's sublease agreement with the government-owned National Development Corporation for Dolefil's use of the land in Mindanao. The constitution imposes a 1,024 hectare limitation on foreign corporate land holdings.[13]

QUESTIONS

1. Lee A. Tavis, *Multinational Managers and Poverty in the Third World* (Notre Dame, Ind.: University of Notre Dame Press, 1982), p. 199.
2. "Dole Food Company, Inc.," in *Moody's Handbook of Common Stocks, Winter 1996-1997* (New York: Moody's Investors Service, 1996), pp. 194-195.
3. What can the government of the Philippines do to enhance the potential benefit of FDI in that country?
4. What mistakes do you think have been made by Dolefil? Could Dolefil have prevented its mistakes in the Philippines?

Notes

1. "Dole Food Company Inc.," in *Moody's Handbook of Common Stocks, Winter 1996-1997* Ed., New York: Moody's Investors Service, 1996.
2. Ibid., pp. 194-195.
3. Ibid., p. 195.
4. Ibid.
5. Frank H. Golay, *The Philippines: Public Policy and National Economic Development* (Ithaca, N.Y.: Cornell University Press, 1961), p. 47.
6. Tavis, *Multinational Managers*, p. 195.
7. Ibid., pp. 199-203.
8. Ibid., pp. 201-202, 204.
9. Ibid., pp. 205-206.
10. Ibid., pp. 195, 209-216.
11. Ibid., pp. 215-217.
12. Ibid., pp. 195, 209.
13. Ibid., pp. 215-217.

Suggested Readings

Frank, Isaiah. *Foreign Enterprise in Developing Countries*. Baltimore, Md.: Johns Hopkins University Press, 1979.

Golay, Frank H. *The Philippines: Public Policy and National Economic Development*. Ithaca, N.Y.: Cornell University Press, 1961.

Moody's Industrial Manual. Moody's Investors Service, 1986. p. 2673.

Nafziger, Wayne P. *The Economics of Developing Countries*. Belmont, Calif.: Wadsworth, 1984. Ch.16.

Steinberg, David Joel. *The Philippines, a Singular and a Plural Place*. Boulder, Colo.: Westview Press, 1982.

Case 6:4

ALUMINUM INDUSTRY OF JAMAICA AND REYNOLDS METALS COMPANY

INTRODUCTION

There exists an ongoing conflict who's center is in Jamaica. The nature of the conflict is not to be described as open warfare; yet there are many battles. The gains and losses are not measured by body counts, but in dollars and cents. The struggle is between the government of Jamaica and the North American aluminum companies, and the battles are played out in the halls of government and the boardrooms of the aluminum producers. Gains and losses are measured by the level of governmental revenues, taxes, and royalties in the case of the Jamaican government, and by the level of net income or loss in the case of the aluminum producers.

THE ALUMINUM INDUSTRY IN JAMAICA

Jamaica is a nation in the West Indies. It is the third largest island in the Caribbean (after Cuba and Hispaniola), with a population of approximately 2.5 billion. Jamaica covers an area of 4,244 square miles.[1] This country has vast reserves of bauxite.

Bauxite is the natural ore from which aluminum is extracted. In 1994, 11,760 metric tons of bauxite were mined in Jamaica, making that country the third largest source of bauxite after Australia and Guinea (see Table 6:4.1). Today, bauxite and its derivative, alumina (aluminum oxide), accounts for more than 50 percent share of Jamaica's earnings. Four aluminum companies dominate bauxite mining in Jamaica. All are North American metals and mining companies that are classified as MNCs. Table 6:4.2 illustrates the relative performance of these companies.

TABLE 6:4.1
The Relative Amount of Bauxite by Produced by the Three Major Producing Countries in the World in 1994 (Thousands of Metric Tones)

Country	1992	1993	1994
Australia	34,788	41,180	41,286
Guinea	15,997	na	na
Jamaica	11,370	11,200	11,760

na. Data not available.
Source: *The European World Yearbook 1996*, Vol. 1, London: European Publication Limited, 1996.

TABLE 6:4.1
The Relative Performance of the Four Major Aluminum Companies

Financial Data	Alcoa	Alcan	Reynolds	Kaiser
Revenue (million of U.S. dollars)	12,499.7	9,387	1,1004	886
Net Income (million of U.S. dollars)	790.5	543	93.7	122,586

Source: *Moody's Handbook of Common Stocks Winter 1996-97 Edition*, New York: Moody's Investor's Service Inc., 1996.

In addition to mining, all of these companies have operations in Jamaica for the conversion of bauxite into alumina. Alumina is the intermediary product in the production process whose end product is aluminum. Alcan Aluminum, the most important of the MNCs in Jamaica, provides an example of the size and the extent of the operation of these corporations.

The importance of the aluminum industry to Jamaica is well known and acknowledged. This can be inferred from a 1982 report on Latin America by the Inter-American Development Bank stating that "the aluminum industry is critical to the economic growth, foreign exchange earnings, and government revenues in Jamaica."[2] Bauxite and alumina led the country's list of export products and contributed an average of $300 million per year to merchandise export earnings during the period from 1978 to 1982. Exports fell 20 percent to $240 million in 1982, reflecting the severe effects of the 1982 recession on the aluminum industry.[3]

THE JAMAICAN BUSINESS ENVIRONMENT

The relationship that has existed between the industry and the government of Jamaica since the industry's first presence in the 1940s has been tested many times, but never more so than in the 1970s. The confrontation is between a sovereign nation and MNCs over the control, the price, and the distribution of the nation's raw materials.

In 1972, Michael Manley, a U.S.-educated leftist leader was swept into office as Jamaica's Prime Minister. He had promised to free the former British Colony from colonialism and create a new economic order. In 1980, a journalist vividly described what happened next:

> *He promptly installed his aggressive brand of democratic socialism, expropriating private farms, taxing business heavily, abolishing private education, and spending huge sums of mostly borrowed money on social programs. Abroad he nuzzled up to the Soviet bloc nations and railed against Western imperialism in fiery eloquent speeches from Moscow, Baghdad, and Havana. The results for Jamaica were disastrous. If a country could be declared bankrupt, it would be among the first to go.[4]*

If Manley's efforts alone were not sufficient to cripple the economy, most certainly the effects of the OPEC oil price hikes would. Oil prices began rising in 1972. "OPEC's quadrupling of oil prices in 1973-74 was an expensive shock: it pushed Jamaica's oil bill up from $73 million (11% of its imports) in 1973 to $195 million (21%) in 1974."[5] Unfortunately for Jamaica, the nation imports almost 100 percent of its energy needs. The Inter-American Development Bank observes that "The oil crisis dealt a severe blow to Jamaica's industrialization strategy and helped reduce its imports capacity sharply through the second half of the decade [1970s]."[6]

To finance the trade deficits, the government of Jamaica borrowed heavily from anyone who would lend. In addition to international commercial banks (that have long considered Jamaica a poor risk), the government relied on supranational institutions and the International Monetary Fund. In 1982, it was observed that "on a per capita basis, Jamaica's foreign debt of $2.1 billion is nearly as large as Mexico's and debt service of $300 million will swell its total payments deficit to an estimated $500 million."[7]

Looking elsewhere for hard currency revenues, two traditional sources held little potential. The agricultural sector was badly managed and disorganized; and tourism revenues were poor because of the threat of economic chaos and political violence.

Mr. Manley turned his attention to the bauxite and alumina industry, upon whose shoulders he felt the government of Jamaica could ride out of the storm. It was in 1974, after the initial oil price hikes, that the government sought a different relationship with the industry. Manley raised a "7.5% levy on aluminum prices. The levy increased total government revenues by over 60% in a single year." This first step by Manley seemed as if it would help Jamaica. But the five MNCs in Jamaica decreased the volume of their production. As a result, the volume of bauxite and aluminum production decreased by 38 percent during the 1974-1976 period.[8]

In addition, the government of Jamaica acquired nearly all the land that the companies had owned and 50 percent of their assets, which the government then leased back to the companies. Instead of cash, the companies were given promissory notes to be repaid over 10 years—presumably out of the proceeds of the new levies. The Jamaican government was also instrumental in organizing the International Bauxite Association (IBA), a cartel of 11 bauxite-producing nations which sought to set minimum prices and production quotas for the ore.[9]

The attempts of the International Bauxite Association to develop a unified pricing and levy structure throughout its membership have proven unsuccessful for a number of reasons. First, there has been no essential unanimity among its members concerning the pricing and levy structure. This problem is aggravated by Australia's competitive edge in the production and exports of bauxite and alumina.[10] Australia was the leading bauxite producer by a wide margin (27.8 million tons in 1980) and its actions had a great impact on the cartel's influence.[11] Second, the IBA had tried to operate during a period of economic recession without realistic flexibility. Third, the association did not take into account the already occurring shift of production from member countries to nonmember countries prior to the development of the levy structure. Finally, and most important, historically speaking cartels have had relatively short lives. When dealing with entities operating in a competitive environment, the attempt to maintain unanimity within a cartel seems doomed to failure.[12]

REYNOLDS METAL COMPANY

At the level of the individual firm, Reynolds Metals Co. suffered significantly as a result of its heavy investment in Jamaica. It was fortunate, however, that the years from 1975 to 1986 were years of strong demand for aluminum with the growth of new markets—particularly in the beverage can market industry. This helped offset the drain of the bauxite levy on Reynolds resources.

Since the imposition of the levy, Reynolds has undertaken substantial negotiation efforts to reduce the magnitude of the tax. As first imposed, the levy was 7.5 percent of the average realized price of a ton of primary aluminum. In terms of a ton of bauxite, the cost of production doubled.[13]

It is important to note the reasons that Reynolds had not chosen to sell, or abandon, its operation in Jamaica. Chief among these reasons were: (1) the large write-off of capital investment that would have been necessary, (2) the problem of raw materials replacement to supplant the Jamaican bauxite ore at a reasonable cost, and (3) the high capital cost of building replacement facilities.

From the introduction of the levy, Reynolds management has had a desire to lower this tax burden. An agreement was signed in 1975 between the Jamaican government and Reynolds that outlined levy relief covering bauxite mining operations, subject to finalization in formal agreements. This formal agreement was signed in 1977. It was a plan of lower taxation coupled with joint venture participation.[14]

The agreement of 1977 had not yet become effective in late 1978 so Reynolds stepped up its efforts to obtain levy relief. Meetings between the government of Jamaica and a Reynolds representative occurred to outline the severe problem that Reynolds was facing and its need to reduce the production levy in order to make the Jamaican operations more competitive. Reynolds arguments for lower production levies did not insist upon immediate action, but only upon agreements on steps that would bring Jamaican bauxite cost to competitive levels within a reasonable time period. Reynolds added, however, that immediate levy relief was essential to eliminate the disparity between the levy costs and the costs of other procedures, both in Jamaica and in other countries.

Many more meetings were held with the government of Jamaica. During 1979 a new levy compromise was reached, placing a levy of about 7 percent on the primary aluminum ingot price. Additional concessions, for using lower grade bauxite and for increasing production, were later added, as well as a cap on the primary ingot prices. Each year brings additional negotiations based primarily upon industry market conditions.

The battles referred to here do not promise to abate soon, nor is it to be expected that they should. The executives of Reynolds have planned a continued geographical diversification program that promises to add additional clout to their arguments for lower taxes.

QUESTIONS

1. Why are aluminum companies investing in Jamaica? Why did the Jamaican government allow these firms to invest there? Explain.
2. What is an international cartel? Who benefits from a cartel? Is it the firms or the countries in which the cartel is operating? Explain, using the Jamaican case as an example.
3. To curve its foreign debt the host country should impose heavy taxes on the subsidiaries of MNCs that are operating in that country. Do you agree with this statement? Discuss.
4. Given the levy of 7.5 percent in Jamaica on aluminum production, do you think that Reynolds should have abandoned its operation in that country? Discuss.

Notes

1. The European Year Book 1996, Vol. 1, London: European Publication Limited, 1996.
2. Inter-American Development Bank, *Economic and Social Progress in Latin America: The External Sector, 1982 Report* (Washington, D.C.: Inter-American Development Bank, 1982), p. 278.
3. Ibid., p. 184.
4. "For Socialist Jamaica, Big Capital Infusion May Be Only Salvation," *The Wall Street Journal*, 25 February 1980, p. 1.
5. "Jamaica: Island in the Soup," *Economist* (21 June 1980) p. 51.
6. Inter-American Development Bank, *Economic and Social Progress in Latin America*, p. 278.
7. "Why Jamaica's Economy May Run Aground," *Business Week*, 18 October 1982, p. 162.
8. "Jamaica: Island in the Soup," p. 51.
9. "Bauxite Producers to Meet," The New York Times, 14 February 1974, p. 62; "International Bauxite Association," *Yearbook of International Organizations* 1983/1984, Union of International Associations, ed. Vol. 1, 20th ed. (New York: K. G. Sam Muchen, 1983), p. C4625.
10. "Australia Exploits Edge in Aluminum," *The New York Times*, 20 February 1979, p. D1.
11. Kaufman, *Jamaica Under Manley*, p. 25.
12. Ibid., pp. 83-85.
13. Ibid., pp. 8-9.
14. "Reynolds Unit in Pact on Jamaica Bauxite," *The New York Times*, 1 April 1977, p. D12.

Suggested Readings

"Australia Exploits Edge in Aluminum." *The New York Times*, 20 February 1979, p. D1.

"Bauxite Producers to Meet." *The New York Times*, 14 February 1974, p. 62.

"For Socialist Jamaica, Big Capital Infusion May Be Only Salvation." *The Wall Street Journal*, 25 February 1980, p. 1.

Hurwitz, Samuel J. *Jamaica: A Historical Portrait*. New York: Praeger, 1971.

Inter-American Development Bank, *Economic and Social Progress In Latin America: The External Sector*. Washington, D. C., Inter-American Developmental Bank, 1982.

"Jamaica: Island in the Soup." *Economist*, 21 June 1980, pp. 51-53.

Kaufman, Michael. *Jamaica Under Manley: Dilemmas of Socialism and Democracy*. London: Zed Books, 1985.

The New Encyclopedia Britannica, 15th ed., vol. 6. Chicago: *Encyclopaedia Britannica*, Inc., 1985. pp. 478-479.

"Reynolds Unit in Pact on Jamaican Bauxite." *The New York Times*, 1 April 1977, p. D12.

"Why Jamaica's Economy May Run Aground." *Business Week*, 18 October 1982, pp. 162-163.

THE SONY CORPORATION

INTRODUCTION

When Akio Morita was browsing in a Tokyo antiques shop one day shortly after World War II, he saw a customer pick up an ivory figurine and proceed to buy it for a huge sum of money. "I learned," Morita said, "that if a thing has quality, and people know its value, they will be willing to pay the price for it."[1] Morita then took this valuable lesson and used it to help him build Sony, the highly successful multinational corporation.

Whether it be a Trinitron, a Betamax, a Walkman, a word processor, or even life insurance or spaghetti, Sony's got it, but why the name Sony? Looking through several dictionaries in 1958, Mr. Morita and his partner, Masaru Ibuka, came up with two terms. Sonus, a Latin word meaning sound, and sonny boy, meaning a young boy. These founders of the company decided that since they were a couple of sonny boys in the sound business, they would call their business "Sony." It was just what they were looking for: a short name that was international and sounded the same all over the world.[2]

In 1946, Morita started his business with $528 and seven employees in a small, boarded-up room in a Tokyo department store. Sony is now a huge multinational corporation, boasting an annual sales level of more than $45 billion, owning 20 plants worldwide, and providing jobs for about 180,000 employees.[3]

It is hard to say that it has been smooth sailing for Sony throughout its existence. Sony has had setbacks, some major and some minor. Sony's management has always been optimistic in a crisis situation, and although Sony may have occasionally stumbled, it has never fallen.

COMPANY HISTORY

Akio Morita, founder and chairman of Sony until 1993, was working in a business with his father in 1945 when he read in a newspaper about a small telecommunications laboratory that had recently opened up. Morita wrote to Masaru Ibuka, an old friend of his, who was founder of the newly opened Tokyo Telecommunications Laboratory. A few days later, Morita received a letter from Ibuka asking Morita to join him, and they started working together.[4]

In 1946, they decided to incorporate and became Tokyo Telecommunications Company, making communications equipment for the Japanese telephone and telegraph companies and also for the national railroads.[5]

They started research for the production of consumer goods in 1947, and they put their first tape recorder on the market in 1950. They started doing research on their first transistor radio in 1953 and subsequently marketed it in 1955. In 1957 they made their first big impact in the world market by marketing their first export product, the world's first pocket radio, which was very successful in the United States and other advanced countries. In the beginning of 1958 they adopted their present name of Sony, because they needed a shorter, more universal name for international business. At the end of 1959, after much research, Sony introduced the world's first all-transistorized television, and was very successful in doing so.[6]

In 1960, Sony Corporation of America in New York and Sony Overseas S.A. in Switzerland were established. In 1965, Sony formed a joint venture with Tektronix, Incorporated, to produce electronic measuring devices in Japan. In 1968, Sony established a subsidiary in the United Kingdom called Sony (U.K.) Ltd. In 1970, Sony formed a fifty-fifty joint venture with Columbia Broadcasting System in Japan to make, sell, and promote musical equipment. This new company was originally named CBS/Sony Records Corporation but is now called CBS/Sony Group Incorporated. In 1970, Sony established a subsidiary in the former West Germany called Sony GmbH. This subsidiary's name was changed in 1980 to Sony Deutschland GmbH.[7]

In 1972, Sony established the Sony Trading Company, a wholly owned subsidiary that takes products that were made in the United States and Europe and then markets them in Japan.[8]

In 1993, Akio Morita collapsed on a tennis court with a brain hemorrhage, and consequently completely removed himself from working at Sony. He died in Tokyo of pneumonia in October, 1999, at the age of 78. Sony Corporation is now headed by Norio Ohga, as the Chairman and Chief Executive Officer, and Nabuyuki Icki, the President and Chief Operating Officer.

In August 1972, Sony opened up a manufacturing facility in San Diego, California. This television assembly plant was its first manufacturing facility outside the Orient. In fall of 1972, Sony changed its management characteristics by appointing Harvey L. Schein, an American, president of Sony Corporation of America.[9]

In 1973, Sony established a subsidiary in France (Sony France S.A.). In 1975, Sony formed a joint venture with Union Carbide Corporation and called it Sony Eveready Incorporated. This fifty-fifty joint venture enabled the import and eventual sale of Union Carbide's high performance dry cell batteries to Japan. This was done under the trademark of Sony-Eveready.[10]

Also in 1975, Sony had to lower its inventories by cutting production; it therefore gave one-half of its labor force five extra holidays for the year.[11]

In 1978, there were some problems with communications between the parent company and its U.S. subsidiary. Sony made some shifts in management to speed decision making. Harvey Schein resigned after five years with Sony. Akio Morita, president of the parent company, replaced him.[12]

In 1979, Sony formed a joint venture with Prudential Life Insurance Company of America Ltd. This enabled Sony to start selling group and individual life insurance in Japan. Prudential owns 50 percent plus one share of Sony Prudential Life Insurance Company Ltd.[13]

In 1979, Sony formed a joint venture with PepsiCo Incorporated to produce Wilson Sporting Goods products in Japan.[14]

In May 1982, Sony started manufacturing Betamax VCRs in West Germany.[15]

In December 1982, Sony had to remove its VCRs from France because of import restrictions on VCRs that had been imposed by France.[16]

In April 1984, Sony bought hard disc technology from Apple Computer Incorporated so that it could produce hard disks in Japan and market them in the United States.[17]

In October 1985, Sony bought out Columbia Broadcasting System's half interest in the joint venture that had been set up in 1970. This move gave Sony a wholly owned subsidiary that would manufacture compact disks in Indiana. The disks had previously been produced in Japan and imported into the United States.[18]

In November 1985, Sony raised its prices on electronic products by 5 percent to 12 percent. This price increase was due to the strengthening of the yen.[19]

In March 1986, Sony's U.S. subsidiary formed a medical data firm to make products that analyze and display medical products.[20]

INDUSTRY DESCRIPTION

Sony is classified as a Japanese diversified company. Sony's sales are mainly in consumer electronics. In 1993 Sony's total sales amounted to $34,766.million. Out of this total $28, 585 or about 82 percent was in consumer electronics. In 1993, Sony was ranked 5 In the list of Japan's top 50 electronic companies ranked by sales. Table 6:5.1 shows comparative sales and ranking of Sony's major Japanese competitors in electronic industry in 1994.

TABLE 6:5.1
Comparative Sales of Sony and its Competition
(Millions of Dollars) in 1994

Rank	Company	Electronic Sales
1	Matshshita	41,882
2	NEC	34,775
3	Toshiba	32,200
4	Fujistu	30,479
5	Sony	28,585

Source: Patrick J. Spain and James R. Talbot., eds., *Hoover's Handbook of World Business 1995-1996* (Austin, Texas: The Reference Press Inc, 1995), pp.332 and 482.

COMPANY DESCRIPTION

Sony is a leading producer of consumer electronics, but it is concentrating more and more on broadcasting equipment, office equipment, and computer chips. Sony has a total of 16 plants worldwide, nine of which are in Japan, three in the United States, and four in Europe. Foreign sales represent 74 percent of its total sales. Sony spends 18 percent of its sales on labor, and 9.2 percent on research and development. In the fiscal year ended March 31, 1997, consolidated sales and operating revenue rose to an all-time high of 5,663 billion yen ($45,670 million). This was the result of higher sales in all business segments—Electronics, Entertainment, and Insurance and Financing—combined with the progressive weakening of the yen.[21]

In addition to its factories, Sony owns a research center, an audio/video technology center, the Sony Development Center, and their headquarters, all of which are located in Japan. Sony's management is made up of a seven-man executive board, with nine managing directors, 14 directors, and four statutory auditors. Sony and all of its subsidiaries use the accounting principles that are generally accepted in the host countries (for example, Sony Corporation of America uses accounting principles that are generally accepted in the United States). At year-end, Sony sums up all of the asset and liability accounts and expresses these figures in terms of Japanese yen at the appropriate year-end current rates.[22]

SONY GOES MULTINATIONAL

Sony had always been a corporation that depended on its exports, but in 1972 it decided to start producing its products in the United States. In 1973, Sony made some management changes and appointed an American to be in charge of its U.S. subsidiary. These key moves made Sony a true multinational corporation.

Sony management felt that they were better off going multinational because of two upward revaluations of the Japanese yen and because the world market was flooded by Japanese products.

Sony began planning to go multinational in 1971, after President Nixon put economic controls into effect. The president had imposed a price freeze and a surcharge on all imports. Nixon also put an end to the conversion of the U.S. dollar into gold.[23] Sony was plagued by a similar problem in France in 1982, when the French put up custom barriers against Japanese makers of VCRs because of their opposition to Japanese exports.[24]

When Sony analyzed Nixon's policies, it realized that it could not continue to make its products in Japan but had to start manufacturing them in the different countries where markets for its goods existed. Sony also had to start thinking multinationally, and it began hiring foreign nationals to manage its foreign subsidiaries.[25] Sony responded to France's custom barriers in 1982 by cutting its shipments to France.[26]

Another reason why Sony went multinational is because the United States was moving more toward protectionism. Sony came to the conclusion that it would not cost more to manufacture its products in the United States and other advanced countries. Sony came to this conclusion by taking into account the higher costs of labor in the United States, the upward revaluation of the yen, and the newly increased shipping charges and custom duties.

Although it seems that Sony became multinational solely to cut costs, the company claims that it went multinational in order to change its management philosophy. Sony did not want anything, such as trade barriers or currency problems, to get in the way of its production.

Sony prices were raised by about 5 percent after the dollar was devalued in February 1973. This brought Sony's price increases to an average of 10 percent to 12 percent following the first revaluation of yen in December 1971.

Sony insisted that its problem in the United States has always been a shortage of merchandise rather than price competition from other companies. It contended that, even though it had announced the price increases, there had been no order cancellations and that, in fact, orders had been backlogged since the end of February 1973.[27]

QUALITY

Sony could easily have taken advantage of cheap labor by opening up manufacturing subsidiaries in developing countries instead of in the United States. A developing country such as Mexico would be inclined to invite a company like Sony to open up a factory and create both employment and income. But Sony is, and always has been, turned off to the idea of manufacturing in developing countries.

Sony would still have to contend with the trade barriers and currency problems by producing in a developing country, and Sony has always taken pride in the quality of its products, its innovations, and its progress in the industry. If Sony moved to a developing country, the factor of quality in its products might be greatly reduced.

Sony has always been a pioneer in its industry, having spent a large percentage of its revenues on research and development. At one time, Akio Morita stated that "we don't market products that have already been developed. Rather, we develop markets for products we make."[28] Such a philosophy has led Sony to plan way in advance in developing its products. An example of this attitude is shown in Sony's research for Betamax, which began in 1960, 16 years before the product was introduced in the United States.[29]

Sony's innovation and research had always paid off because it had always had a monopoly of its products for two or three years. But in the late 1970s and early 1980s, Sony's competitors started closing the technological gap. Sony could no longer charge a high price for its quality products. Other manufacturers have started producing products of comparable quality at a much lower price. In October 1982, Sony introduced its first compact laser disk player. It had taken Sony six years and $25 million to develop this product. This move paid off at first, but only ten months later Sony's major competitors, Matsushita and Hitachi, were selling disk players of the same quality at a price that was as much as 35 percent lower.[30]

LIFETIME EMPLOYMENT SYSTEM

Why are competitors catching up to Sony so quickly? It may be, in part, because Japan's lifetime employment system has put quite a burden on Sony. During slow years, instead of laying off workers, Sony has been committed to putting its employees into meaningless positions where they do nothing but busy work, but where they still receive the same wages. Former computer chip makers might be transferred to work in the company's cafeteria. Some 2,100 employees, who had previously been working on the production lines in a Betamax factory, spent their time putting together suggestions to improve productivity. These workers were efficient, putting together 8,000 ideas (close to their target of 12,000). But many feel that these maneuvers were not good for Sony. One competitor, Sharp Incorporated, had cut production of their calculators, and, instead of laying off people, Sharp had sent almost half of its production people out to sell overstocked calculators that had accumulated when the calculator market collapsed in 1972.[31]

Is Sony spending too much on labor? Looking at the 1994 statistics in Table 6:5.1, it is clear that compared with its competitors, Sony is making the most amount of sales per employee.

TABLE 6:5.1
Comparative Sales per Employee of Major Sony's Competitors on Consumers electronics in 1994

Company	Sales per Employee
Matsushita	253,118
NEC	237,279
Toshiba	26,462
Fujista	19, 141
Sony	$278,864

Source: Calculated by the author from the data provided by Patrick J. Spain and James R. Talbot., eds., *Hoover's Hand-book of World Business 1995-1996* (Austin, Texas: The Reference Press Inc, 1995), various pages.

DIVERSIFICATION

Since Sony had been facing a lot of competition in its consumer electronics business, it has decided to concentrate on other market targets, such as nonconsumer electronics and other businesses, some of which are related to the electronics business. Sony wanted to concentrate on the tape and disk business because of the high profit margin (50 percent) and because people will keep buying tapes and disks even after they buy their VCRs, tape recorders, and disk players. Morita uses the example of Kodak, which is making much more money from selling film than from selling its cameras.[32]

Sony surprised a lot of people in the late 1970s when, instead of getting into promising electronics markets, it opened up some unrelated businesses, selling such products as cosmetics, sporting goods, life insurance, and even spaghetti. Morita stated, "If we have enough money and know-how to create new businesses around our main business, it has to improve our long term outlook."[33]

Another example of this diversification came in 1972 when Sony, having a reputation as an exporter, decided to get into the import business. Sony opened up 8,000 of its retail outlets to imported products. This gave manufacturers with products that were suitable to Sony the opportunity to deal with the final retailer in Japan, instead of a merchandising house. Sony gained on this deal by getting a commission and increasing the variety in its outlets. This also went against the worldwide belief that Japan was exporting too much and not importing enough. This move may have encouraged other nations to cut back on their trade restrictions against Japan as it began some importing.[34]

In the late 1990s, Sony was trying to enhance its involvement in the entertainment business. Although the company's original reason for such involvement was to promote its hardware line of CDS, cassette players, TVS, VCRs, it's addition of a complementary line of records, tapes, and films has become a significant source of revenue. [35]

LOOKING INTO THE FUTURE

Sony has always been known as a firm that concentrated on the consumer electronics business, but according to Sony's management times are changing. In the mid 1980s Sony started to shift from the consumer electronics market to the communications industry. Today this communications company concentrates on such products as computers, telecommunications, air navigation equipment, and broadcasting equipment.

Why this change in philosophy? Sony was plagued by a profit slump that started in 1980 and continued until 1983. For the first time in Sony's history, it had to go against the lifetime employment philosophy by offering incentives for workers to quit. Sony had to change its thinking.

Sony now sells 80 percent of its products to consumers. Today, executives at Sony want more than 50 percent of its products to be sold to businesses because these sales represent bigger profits and more faithful customers.[36]

Having celebrated its 50th anniversary, in describing the future of the company, the president of Sony stated that "The Digital Dream Kids concept defines the future direction of our product development activities. We aim to fulfill the dreams of customers worldwide who are captivated by the potential of digital technology. To do so, we must strive to supply products that are unique and fun to use. This is why we at Sony have to become digital dream kids mesmerized by new technologies. All of our hardware and software must be based on the premise of providing enjoyment."

QUESTIONS

1. What factors should be considered when an MNC chooses a name? Explain.
2. What motivates a firm to go international? Explain. What motivated Sony?
3. Why does an MNC diversify its business? Explain. Why did Sony?
4. Since labor is cheaper in LDCs than in advanced countries, it always pays off for an MNC to locate its production facilities in those countries. Do you agree with this statement? Explain. Do you think that Sony's decision not to operate in developing countries is correct? Explain.
5. What is the impact of revaluation of the home country's currency on an MNC? How did Sony deal with yen's revaluation? Explain.

6. What are the major reasons behind Sony's success? Explain.
7. A policy of lifetime employment by a company breeds a sense of loyalty in employees, causing them to work harder. As a result, in such companies efficiency rises and profits increase. Do you agree with this statement? Explain.
8. What are the major elements of Sony's global strategy? Explain.

Notes

1. "Akio Morita of Sony Corp.," *Nation's Business*, December 1973, p. 45.
2. Ibid., p. 48.
3. Sony Corporation, *Global Corporate Information Services*, 1997.
4. "Akio Morita of Sony Corp.," p. 45.
5. Ibid., p. 46.
6. *Moody's Industrial Manual*, p. 4401.
7. Ibid.
8. "Sony Marketing Subsidiary Attacks U.S. Applications," *The New York Times*, 4 July 1972, p. 25.
9. Gerd Wilke, "The Americanization of Sony," *The New York Times*, 18 March 1973, sec. III, p. 1.
10. *Moody's Industrial Manual*, p. 4401
11. "Sony Adds 5 Holidays to Reduce Production," *The New York Times*, 11 January 1975, p. 41
12. "Sony's U.S. Operation Goes in for Repairs," Business Week, 13 March 1978, p. 31.
13. "Prudential and Sony in Insurance Accord," The New York Times, 14 August 1979, sec. IV, p. 4.
14. "Sony: An Incongruous Search for Greener Pastures," *Business Week*, 11 February 1980, p. 105.
15. "Sony to Manufacture VTRs at German Plant," *The Wall Street Journal*, 1 April 1982, p. 31.
16. "Japanese Makers of VTRs Cut Shipments to France as Customs Barriers Take Hold," The Wall Street Journal, 2 December 1982, p. 32.
17. "Apple Sets Accord to Sell Hard-Disk Technology to Sony," *The Wall Street Journal*, 6 April 1984, p. 12.
18. Laura Landro, "Sony Set to Buy CBS Inc.'s Stake in Disk Venture," *The Wall Street Journal*, 17 October 1985, p. 8.
19. "Sony's U.S. Affiliate Plans a Price Boost of 5% to 12% for Electronic Products," *The Wall Street Journal*, 6 November 1985, p. 5.
20. " Sony U.S. Unit Forms Medical Data Firm: Pollack Is President," The Wall Street Journal, 21 March 1986, p. 34.
21. Sony, *Annual Report 1997.*
22. *Moody's Industrial Manual*, pp. 4401-4404.
23. Wilke, "The Americanization of Sony," p. 1.
24. "Japanese Makers of VTRs Cut Shipments to France," p. 32.
25. Wilke, "The Americanization of Sony," p. 1.
26. "Japanese Makers of VTRs Cut Shipments to France," p. 32.
27. Wilke,"The Americanization of Sony," p. 9.
28. "The Surge in Sony," *Financial World*, 1 October 1980, p. 43.
29. Ibid., pp. 42-44.
30. Michael Cieply, "Sony's Profitless Prosperity," *Forbe*s, 24 October 1983, pp. 129-130
31. Ibid., p. 133.
32. "Sony, A Diversification Plan Tuned to the People Factor," *Business Week*, 9 February 1981, p. 88.
33. Ibid.
34. "Sony'll Sell for You," *The Economist*, 21 October 1972, pp. 86-89.
35. Sony Corporation, Hoover's Profile Database, Copyright (C), 1995, The Reference Press, Inc., Austin, TX (internet).
36. E. S. Browning, "Japan's Sony, Famous for Consumer Electronics, Decides that the Future Lies in Sales to Business," *The Wall Street Journal*, 9 October 1984, p. 33.

Suggested Readings

"Akio Morita of Sony Corp." *Nation's Business*, December 1973, pp. 45-48.

Browning, E. S. "Japan's Sony, Famous for Consumer Electronics, Decides that the Future Lies in Sales to Business." *The Wall Street Journal*, 9 October 1984, p. 33.

"Chinese-Hong Kong Venture to Produce Sony VTR's in China." *The Wall Street Journal*, 6 April 1984, p. 12.

Cieply, Michael. "Sony's Profitless Prosperity." *Forbes*, 24 October 1983, pp. 129-130, 133.

Landro, Laura. "Sony Set to Buy CBS Inc.'s Stake in Disk Venture." *The Wall Street Journal*, 17 October 1985, p. 8.

Moody's Industrial Manual, 1986. vol. 2, pp. 4401-4404.

"Sony Marketing Subsidiary Attacks U.S. Subsidiary Application." *The New York Times*, 4 July 1972, p. 25.

"Sony Adds 5 Holidays to Reduce Production." *The New York Times*, 11 January 1975, p. 41.

"Prudential and Sony in Insurance Accord." *The New York Times*, 14 August 1979, sec. IV, p. 4.

"Sony, a Diversification Plan Tuned to the People Factor." *Business Week*, 9 February 1981, p. 88.

"Sony: An Incongruous Search for Greener Pastures." *Business Week*, 11 February 1980, p. 105.

"Sony U.S. Unit Forms Medical Data Firms: Pollack Is President." *The Wall Street Journal*, 21 March 1986, p. 34.

"Sony U.S. Operation Goes in for Repairs." *Business Week*, 13 March 1978, p. 31.

"Sony'll Sell for You." *The Economist*, 21 October 1972, pp. 86-89.

"The Surge in Sony." *Financial World*, 1 October 1980, pp. 42-44.

"Sony to Manufacture VTRs at German Plant." *The Wall Street Journal*, 1 April 1982, p. 31.

"Japanese Makers of VTRs Cut Shipments to France as Custom Barriers Take Hold." *The Wall Street Journal*, 2 December 1982, p. 32.

"Sony's U.S. Affiliate Plans a Price Boost of 5% to 12% for Electronic Products." *The Wall Street Journal*, 6 November 1985, p. 5.

Wilke, Gerd. "The Americanization of Sony." *The New York Times*, 18 March 1973, sec. III, pp. 1, 9.

Case 6:6

POLAROID: THE INSTANT IMAGE AND THE SUN CITY

INTRODUCTION

Polaroid Corporation, a Delaware-based company founded in 1937, and its 23 subsidiaries are a worldwide enterprise with annual sales of more than $1.8 billion. The company designs, manufactures, and markets a variety of products primarily in the "instant" photography field. These products include "instant" photograph cameras and their films, light polarizing filters and lenses, and other diversified chemicals and optical products.

For the past half a century, Polaroid has continually dominated its niche in the photography market. Initially, the concept of "instant" photography, in which the film is developed quickly inside the camera, was difficult for consumers to understand. Today, the "instant" photograph camera is used in millions of households around the world.

Polaroid uses a highly specialized marketing and business strategy for each country. A heated controversy that occurred between South Africa and Polaroid three decades ago shows the corporation's stylish attack in conquering the marketing problem, thus enabling them to remain the dominant pioneer of their industry.

THE PROBLEM

In the fall of 1970, the Polaroid Corporation was stuck with a thorn in its side that would bother it for the next seven and a half years. Upon arrival at his Cambridge, Massachusetts, office on October 7, Dr. Edwin Land, founder, chief executive officer, and president of Polaroid discovered leaflets tacked to numerous company bulletin boards proclaiming: "Polaroid Imprisons Black People in 60 Seconds."[1] Taking a closer look into the matter, Land found that the memos were distributed by the Polaroid Revolutionary Workers Movement (PRWM; Land had never heard of such a group), who claimed that the corporation was guilty of "grave moral offenses for its involvement-through the sale of identification equipment and other Polaroid products—with the white supremacist regime of South Africa."[2]

Naturally, this development was quite a shock to the entire company. The following day, another memo was distributed throughout the offices, only this time the assistant secretary of the corporation was doing the handing out. His note stated that Polaroid did not sell any film, cameras, or identification equipment to the government of South Africa. He did point out that the company's identification equipment had been sold to its distributor in the country, Frank and Hirsch, Ltd., but that to their knowledge none of the identification equipment had been resold to the South African government. His last point in his note stated that their distributor in South Africa had, in fact, taken a strong public stand against apartheid.

The next day there was a protest rally staged outside the Polaroid building in Cambridge. The Polaroid Revolutionary Workers Movement, led by activist Kenneth Williams, made clear-cut demands of Polaroid. They insisted on an immediate halt to all sales in South Africa, a severing of all Polaroid's ties with that nation, and the turning over of all profits earned there to groups combating the racist system of apartheid.[3]

In most MNCs, this problem would be seen as mundane. But with Dr. Land and his company, this situation was treated quite differently from the start. Land had run Polaroid as an extension of his own beliefs. He believed in smooth operations with no surprises and no tricks. This was one of the reasons for Polaroid's total success. Land was always by the corporation's side to lead it through any problem it might encounter. Other multinational companies might have just passed the problem to someone else to worry about it. But this was not one of those wheeler-dealer corporations with no personal involvement—this was Polaroid!

Why was there so much protest against Polaroid? The entire problem evolved around South Africa's Pass Laws, which had been revised in 1952. Under these laws, all "nonwhite" citizens in the country were forced at all times to carry a "passport" bearing their photograph and showing where the bearer lived and worked. Although it was initially unaware of it, Polaroid discovered that its film was being used to make many of the negatives, for these "passport" photographs.

Strangely enough, it was necessary to try to understand how a country such as South Africa, whose contribution to Polaroid's total income was less than 1 percent, could have had such a major effect on a large corporation.[4] The problem was that unlike their other dealings in foreign nations, where Polaroid had set up profitable subsidiaries, the company in South Africa was selling to a distributor, Frank and Hirsch. But at first glance, it did not seem as though this distributor was selling directly to the government of South Africa. If Polaroid wanted to really make a profit, they probably would have sold to the ruling white class, but they had chosen not to do so.

The tension in Cambridge grew over the weeks, but still no solutions were forthcoming. It was a very delicate matter, and although both the corporation and the protesters abhorred apartheid, there was no unanimity as to what to do about it.

THE SOLUTION

Positive momentum on the issue was achieved in late October when an ad hoc committee, consisting of seven black and seven white employees was set up by executive vice-president William McCune.[5] Through weeks of meetings, the committee discussed the idea of completely boycotting South Africa. But would this actually accomplish anything? It was felt by the committee, as well as by Dr. Land himself, that his company was being watched by many other multinational firms that had a much greater stake in South Africa. Polaroid was pulled out of a basket of hundreds of corporations to be used as an example of the "unprecedented position" of many American businesses in South Africa.[6]

Finally, a decision was reached. It was concluded that a fact-finding team, consisting of four Polaroid employees, should be sent to South Africa. This group was to consult experts in economics, African history, and other related areas to try and determine the possible outcomes of the many options that the company could pursue in South Africa.

While this was taking place, other uproars, as expected, began to erupt all over the United States. After Polaroid, many other large corporations found themselves in the same boat. Only this time, church groups were telling the other firms to boycott South Africa, and the influence of these groups caused boycott campaigns at IBM, at a few airline companies, and at several automobile factories in Detroit.[7]

On November 25, 1970, in The Boston Globe, Polaroid ran an ad trying to explain why they were doing business with South Africa in the first place. The advertisement asked the question, "Why was Polaroid chosen to be the first company to face pressure (handbills, pickets, a boycott) about business in South Africa?"[8] The answer stated, "Perhaps because the revolutionaries thought we [Polaroid] would take the subject seriously. They were right. We do."[9] The gist of the ad was that the company was dealing with the ethical questions of its involvement in South Africa, and that Polaroid would make a sound decision on what it felt would be right for the future.

During their ten-day stay in South Africa, the Polaroid inquiry group interviewed close to 150 individuals involved with Frank and Hirsch. They found that nonwhite workers for the company were paid considerably less wages than their white co-workers in the same level jobs. But most nonwhite workers felt that Polaroid could do more to upgrade their socioeconomic conditions by staying in South Africa than by boycotting the country.[10] Upon returning, the inquiry group submitted their suggestion to Polaroid. All four members of the group unanimously agreed that the company should stay and take specific steps to upgrade the working situation not only at Frank and Hirsch, but also in the rest of the country as well. A few weeks later, on January 13, 1971, Polaroid Corporation ran an ad that appeared in *The Boston Globe*, *The Wall Street Journal*, *The Washington Post*, *The Chicago Tribune*, *The Los Angeles Times*, *The Christian Science Monitor*, and *The New York Times*. The ad stated the company's decision about South Africa. The advertisement was a page in length and was entitled, "An Experiment in South Africa." The company declared that they would continue their business relationship with South Africa, except for sales to the government, which their distributor would discontinue, but only under an experimental basis for the next year. If things were running smoothly in 1972, then the company would continue its business with the country. There were three major reforms that the company hoped to successfully accomplish within the next year in South Africa. They were as follows:

1. Polaroid would drastically improve the benefits and salaries of its nonwhite employees.
2. Polaroid would require their South African distributor and suppliers to initiate a program to train a significant number of nonwhite employees for the more responsible jobs within the company.
3. Polaroid would make a commitment toward the education of nonwhites at all levels, with a grant to underwrite the educational expenses for about 500 nonwhites. Also included would be a donation to assist all teachers of various levels.[11]

Land's program, known as the "South African Experiment," gained support from a wide range of respected institutions and leaders. Among them was Ulric Haynes, a former African affairs specialist with the State Department. In a *New York Times* article, Haynes pointed out that South Africa had an abundant shortage of skilled labor and that "conscious attempts" to upgrade the capabilities of nonwhite workers would have eventually enabled these peoples to assume more responsible positions in the industry. Haynes said that "attacking apartheid by shoring up the weaknesses in the South African economy is both beneficial to nonwhites and the most effective way of highlighting the senseless contradictions of apartheid and ultimately destroying it."[12]

Polaroid's lead was eventually followed by other top multinational firms. Several of these companies were influenced by Polaroid's breakthrough in management technique. After Polaroid's experience, there was a new willingness for employers to utilize nonwhites in jobs that were previously reserved for white workers only. Other companies found that increased training and preparation for any particular job brought the nonwhite worker up to the same level as his or her fellow white worker.[13] Although nonwhites were forbidden by law to supervise whites in South Africa, there was a much greater respect for the senior nonwhites among many of the junior white employees. Only in the sales department were nonwhites not able to rise in rank, and this was because white customers refused to deal with nonwhite salesmen.

In December of 1971, the entire program was evaluated. Because it seemed as though the experiment was an important factor in creating new awareness of the oppressed situation of nonwhites in South Africa, Polaroid agreed to continue with its monumental reforms. These reforms continued for six more years, until they were overshadowed by a dark cloud.

RECURRENCE OF THE PROBLEM

The Boston Globe printed an article in November 1977 claiming that Polaroid's distributor, Frank and Hirsch, had violated the 1971 agreement with the parent company and were selling company products to the South African government. The Globe reporter claimed that the Polaroid products were being delivered in unmarked boxes to various military stations around the country. When a Polaroid representative was sent from Cambridge to investigate the situation, he found the unfortunate truth. Hans Jensen found concrete evidence showing that Polaroid products were, in fact, being used to promote apartheid. With no other alternatives available, Dr. Land and his Board of Directors decided to withdraw their business from South Africa. Polaroid had been the first U.S. company to remain in South Africa for ideological reasons, and they became the first to vacate for ideological reasons.[14]

QUESTIONS

1. What was Dr. Land's management philosophy? Explain.
2. Do you think that Dr. Land's decision to implement the "South African Experiment" program was a good choice? Explain.
3. Overall, do you think Polaroid's strategy in dealing with South Africa was a success? Explain.
4. Is there anything that the company could have done to prevent its eventual downfall in South Africa? Explain.
5. Do you think that Polaroid acted in a socially responsible way in the case of South Africa? Explain.

Notes

1. Mark Olshacker, *The Instant Image* (New York: Stein and Day, 1978), p. 147.
2. Ibid.
3. Murray Illson, "Polaroid, Under Attack, Plans to Aid Some South African Blacks," *The New York Times*, 13 January 1971, p. 9.
4. Olshacker, *The Instant Image*, p. 149
5. Ibid., p. 152.
6. Ibid., p. 153.
7. Kathy Tetsch, "Wide Drive Against U.S. Trade with South Africa Is Expected," *The New York Times*, 7 February 1971, p. 2.
8. "What Is Polaroid Doing in South Africa?" The Boston Globe, 25 November 1970, p. 15.
9. Ibid.
10. Olshacker, *The Instant Image*, p. 156.
11. Illson, "Polaroid Under Attack," p. 9.
12. Ulric Haynes, "Church Action Plan Ill-Conceived," *The New York Times*, 28 March 1971, Sec. 3, p. 14.
13. Olshacker, The Instant Image, p. 161.
14. Ibid., p. 162.

Suggested Readings

Illson, Murray. "Polaroid, Under Attack, Plans to Aid Some South African Blacks." *The New York Times*, 13 January 1971, p. 9.
Keegan, Warren J. *Multinational Marketing Management*. Englewood Cliffs, N.J.: Prentice-Hall,   1974.
Madden, Carl. *The Case for the Multinational Corporation*. New York: Praeger, 1977.
Olshacker, Mark. *The Polaroid Story*. New York: Stein and Day, 1978.
Rodwin, William. "Polaroid Outlook." *The Boston Globe*, 25 November 1970, p. 17.

Case 6:7

THE INGERSOLL-RAND CORPORATION

INTRODUCTION

The Ingersoll-Rand Corporation is analogous to a wise old grandfather who has learned certain lessons through experience. The first lesson learned was that a top-quality product at a premium price will sell well. The second lesson was that diversifying products will ensure substantial profits in good times and serve as a cushion in bad times. The third lesson was that making acquisitions instead of using profits to improve products with advanced technology meant larger profits. Consequently, this wise old grandfather of a company became very rich and powerful through the years, and Ingersoll-Rand kept to its staunch conservative beliefs because they were producing considerable profits. Eventually, the company was selling its products more than anyone else in the market. But then the competition began to catch up. New young blood entered the market, like Caterpillar Tractor, Clark Equipment, Gardner Dever, Dresser Industries, and Cooper Industries. These producers sold products that were more technologically advanced than Ingersoll-Rand's old products. In addition, these new companies reinvested their profits back into their products in order to improve them and to increase efficiency. However, Ingersoll-Rand continued to invest in other companies so as not to put all of its eggs in one basket. As a result the new companies began to catch up, and eventually they surpassed Ingersoll-Rand which had kept its conservative views. That is the basic story of Ingersoll-Rand.

HISTORY

This mass producer of industrial machinery was born on June 1, 1905, as a result of the consolidation of the Ingersoll-Sergeant Drill Company and the Rand Drill Company. From that point on, its history consists of the acquisitions of numerous other companies that all produce industrial machinery. These acquired companies became subsidiaries, and today, Ingersoll-Rand conducts its manufacturing and assembly operations in 63 plants in the United States and 59 plants outside the United States.[1]

Throughout most of its history, Ingersoll-Rand has been in the forefront of selling capital goods. In 1968, the company was called "the most profitable, best managed company, the closest thing to a blue chip in the industry."[2] Indeed, Ingersoll-Rand was the largest and most diversified of any of its competitors, and because of this it usually made most of the profits. However, this position was not always reflected in the stock market prices for the company.

Although Ingersoll-Rand has consistently topped the market for the production and sale of industrial machinery, its price per share in the stock market has usually fluctuated. For example, in 1968 its shares sold at $43.00 per share. This was 20 percent lower than the 1954 mark of $53.00. This also decreased the company's price-earning ratio over that time period from 27 to 11. Ingersoll-Rand reasoned that it had been the "victim of changing stock market fads."[3] In 1976, after the company announced that earnings would be off for the year, its stock dropped 9¼ points to 75⅜ in one month. Moreover, the drop in the price of its stock carried many other machinery stocks, like Caterpillar Tractor, Clark Equipment, and Cooper Industries, down with it. Ingersoll-Rand's reason for decreased earnings was the "unanticipated slowdown in demand for capital goods and problems with its capital spending."[4] Finally, in 1983, Ingersoll-Rand's average return on equity decreased to 14.4 percent, well behind Dresser Industries' 17.9 percent, or Cooper Industries' 24.2 percent. Ingersoll-Rand expected a boom in capital spending that year, but it never happened. As a result, Ingersoll-Rand was burdened with overcapacity in production. Also, the wildly fluctuating dollar hurt Ingersoll-Rand, whose foreign sales amounted to 35 percent of total sales.[5]

Ingersoll-Rand still remains one of the largest manufacturers of industrial equipment to this date. However, according to a statement made in 1979 by William L. Wearly, chairman and chief executive officer of the company, since Ingersoll-Rand depends heavily on the lagging demand for capital goods, its earnings had been about 5 percent lower than what they could be. Moreover, Wearly thought this loss of profitability reflected a tremendous increase in competition. For example, portable compressors, which Ingersoll-Rand had made and sold successfully for years, were manufactured by only six companies in 1940. By 1960, however, there were 13 and by 1968 there were 18 companies manufacturing the product.[6]

Today, Ingersoll-Rand owns 51 percent of Dresser-Rand , a gas compressor and turbo machine company . It also owns Clark Equipment Company that was acquired in May 1995. Aided by the continued growth within domestic market, and stronger international operations , The company's sales continue to grow and its margins strengthen. The company's growth in recent years can be detected form the major financial data, as shown in Table 6:7.1

Company Description

Portable compressors are just one of the many industrial products that Ingersoll-Rand manufactures. Through the years the company has supplemented its original business, which had mainly consisted of the manufacture and sale of rock-drilling equipment. Additional products had been developed internally, or through acquisitions, until three major production segments were created by the company.

The first segment is the standard machinery division. Products made in this division include air compressors, which are mainly used to supply pressurized air to chemical plants, industrial plants, and electrical utilities. Construction equipment is also manufactured within this division. This division also serves the construction and metal mining industries as well as well-drilling contractors. Mining machinery is the last group served by the standard machinery division. It serves the underground coal-mining industry by supplying coal haulers, crushers, and roof-stabling equipment.[7]

TABLE 6:7.1
Ingersoll-Rand Company
Selected Financial Data, 1986-1995

Year	Gross Revenue ($million)	Net Income ($million)	Shares (000)	Earing Per Share $
1986	2,799.5	100.6	95,716	0.96
1990	3,737.8	185.3	107,122	1.78
1995	5,729.0	270.3	109,705	2.55

Source: Moody's Handbook of Common Stocks Winter 1996-97, New York: Moody's Investors Service, 1996.

The second segment is the engineered equipment division. Three major products are made in this division. First, gas compressors, which are used in the oil, gas, and petrochemical industries, are manufactured. Turbo machinery is the second group of products made. These products include gas and steam turbines, positive-displacement compressors, and axial flow compressors. These are products used in the oil and gas production, refining and transmission, as well as in chemical and other processing industries. The third segment is the bearings, locks, and tools division. This consists of three broad production groups: bearings and their components, which are used primarily in the automotive and aerospace industries; professional tools, which are sold to the appliance, aircraft, construction, and automotive industries; and door hardware, which includes locks, electronic access systems, and exit devices, which are used in the commercial and residential construction industries. Table 6:7.2.shows the contribution of the company's three major production segment to sales.

TABLE 6:7.2
The Contribution of Ingersoll Rand Company's Major Production Segments to its sales ▬▬▬

Production Segment	Sales	Profit
Standard Machinery	31%	27%
Engineered Equipment	23%	9%
Bearnign, Locks& tools	46%	64%

Source: *Standard & Poor's 500 Guide* 1995 edition , New York: McGraw-Hill, Inc, 1995.

Ingersoll-Rand's competition consists of companies that specialize in one of the many industries in which it does business. Hence, the company is like a large whale who must compete with many little fish for its food. In the process of eating so much food (profits), it devours (acquires) some of the smaller fish (other companies). In the long run, this whale realizes that it should not have eaten so many fish.

INTERNATIONAL OPERATIONS

One cannot talk about Ingersoll-Rand's production and operations without discussing its international operations. The company originally went overseas in 1885 in order to serve the mining industry in Africa, South America, and Australia. However, as time went on, management realized that it was more profitable to manufacture most of its products in the United States and use foreign countries primarily as markets for its sales and service. Today, Ingersoll-Rand manufactures 70 percent of its products at home and only 30 percent abroad. Ingersoll-Rand's strategy regarding international marketing can be inferred from the statement made by William L. Wearly, the company's chairman: "In the export field, you have to have your service organization over there, and at least the standard products on the shelf."[8] In short, investing in foreign sales and service organizations helps support exports from the United States as well as production abroad. In 1978, Ingersoll-Rand exported $408 million worth of goods out of a total sales of $2.1 billion—a 20 percent export ratio that is relatively high for an American multinational corporation.[9]

In the past, Ingersoll-Rand was managed by people who were supply oriented. That is, they were very conscious of manufacturing enough industrial products to supply the market. For example, in 1968 the company was concerned more with turning their profits into acquisitions than with turning out a better product. Wayne Hallstein, then-president of Ingersoll-Rand, exemplified this by saying: "Our people overseas tell us that their market shares are such that they can just about guarantee yearly increases no matter what the economy does—if they can get more product."[10] As a result, management had inventories increased substantially until, in 1978, Ingersoll-Rand's assets reached to $723 million outside the United States, of which inventories and receivables accounted for $561 million, nearly 80 percent of the total.[11] Things were going well, and in 1981, Ingersoll-Rand reported record earnings of $9.71 per share, a 21 percent gain over 1980. President Holmes predicted a capital spending boom as a result. Inventories and stock prices began to increase considerably, until in 1983 inventory was up to a $1.1 billion high. Then things began to fall apart. The capital spending boom never came, and Ingersoll-Rand was stuck with huge inventories and, as a result, major losses. For the first time in 40 years, the directors cut the common dividend-from $0.85 to $0.65. Holmes was shocked at the collapse: "In the past, there was always some part of business going up when something else was going down."[12]

Since then Ingersoll-Rand has seen some growth potential. A new management has been formed called Hapton and Johnson, and they have begun to address the problems of overcapacity, overdiversification, and lack of efficiency. First, they have cut inventory costs, which is one of the biggest expenses for most manufacturing companies. They decreased the number of inventory warehouses from eight to two. To cut down on inefficiency, more than $100 million in unprofitable or unpromising businesses have been sold, using that money to pay off short-term debts. Thomas Holmes, president of Ingersoll-Rand in 1983, admitted the inefficiency with which the company had been run in the past.[13]

To deal with the lack of technology, the company began using its profits to address this problem. Today, for example, their entire pneumatic tool line has been redesigned. Also, their tools are now bioengineered for the world market. According to Gene Driscoll, president of the Ingersoll-Rand Tools Group, engineering has always been an important factor and the "majority in management have technical backgrounds."[14]

An intelligent step that has been taken by Ingersoll-Rand in order to catch up with its competitors is the development of Advanced Research Centers in Princeton and in Liberty Corners, New Jersey.[15] The sole purpose of the centers is research and development, having as its main objective the transformation of industrial machinery into high-tech products. One of the results of R & D is the X-Flow compressor. It is designed to increase efficiency by 5 percent, while decreasing installation and maintenance costs because it has fewer moving parts.[16]

QUESTIONS

1. What are the implications for other MNCs of the lessons learned by the Ingersoll-Rand Corporation?
2. How critical is technology to the survival of an MNC? Explain.
3. Where did Ingersoll-Rand go wrong, and what can the company do to improve its sales in the future?
4. Is a "supply-oriented" strategy an efficient way of selling products to foreign markets? Explain.

Notes

1. Ingersoll-Rand Company, *Facts at a Glance* 1999.
2. "We'll Be the Best of the Bad Guys," *Forbes*, 1 February 1968, p. 18.
3. Ibid.
4. "Guilt by Association," *Forbes*, 15 October 1976, p. 156.
5. John A. Byrne, "... And Then the Bottom Fell Out," *Forbes*, 14 February 1983, p. 142.
6. Jean A. Briggs, "Like Capital Goods? You'll Love Ingersoll-Rand," *Forbes*, 16 April 1979, p. 81.
7. "Ingersoll-Rand Company," p. 436.
8. "Ingersoll-Rand's Secret of Success," *Business Week*, 10 April 1978, p. 66.
9. Ibid.
10. "We'll Be the Best of the Bad Guys," p. 18.
11. "Ingersoll-Rand's Secret of Success," p. 66.
12. Byrne, "... And Then the Bottom Fell Out," p. 142.
13. Ibid.
14. Ernest Raia, "Litmus Test for 80's: Top Quality, Low Costs," *Purchasing*, 27 January 1983, p. 25.
15. "Supplier Profiles," *Automotive Industries*, June 1984, p. 145.
16. "New Turbo Compressor Called Major Advance," Machine Design, 8 August 1985, p. 2.

Suggested Readings

Briggs, Jean A. "Like Capital Goods? You'll Love Ingersoll-Rand." *Forbes,* 16 April 1979, p. 81.

Byrne, John A. "... And Then the Bottom Fell Out." *Forbes*, 14 February 1983, p. 142.

"Guilt by Association." *Forbes*, 15 October 1976, p. 156.

"Ingersoll-Rand Company." *Moody's Industrial Manual*, vol. 1, New York: Moody's Investors Service, 1988, pp. 436-447.

"Ingersoll-Rand: Is Price Pressure Ending?" *Forbes*, 31 August 1981, p. 144.

"Ingersoll-Rand's Secret of Success." *Business Week*, 10 April 1978, p. 66.

"New Turbo Compressor Called Major Advance." *Machine Design*, 8 August 1985, p. 2.

Raia, Ernest."Litmus Test for 80's: Top Quality, Low Costs." *Purchasing*, 27 January 1983, p. 25.

"Supplier Profiles." *Automotive Industries* (June 1984), p. 145.

"We'll Be the Best of the Bad Guys." *Forbes*, 1 February 1964, p. 18.

Case 6:8

CITICORP

INTRODUCTION

Citicorp is the largest multinational financial institution in the world. It operates approximately 3,100 offices and other facilities in 94 countries, employing over 88,000 people.[1] In 1995, it generated $31,690 million gross income and 3,646 million net income.[2] Its home office, known as Citicorp Center, is located in New York City. It has a highly diversified offering of financial services, including commercial banking, investment banking, venture capital financing, insurance, brokerage houses, and industrial lending. Each of these services offers several lines of financial products. For example, Citicorp Industrial Credit-Citicorp's industrial lending subsidiary-offers the following product lines: Asset Based Lending, Corporate Asset Funding, Equipment Finance and Leasing, and Citicorp Business Loans. These specialized products have been developed so that clients can be easily identified, categorized, and serviced.*

TABLE 6:8.1
Citycorp's Selected Financial Data (1980-1996)

Year	Deposits ($milllion)	Loans ($millions)	Gross Income ($million)	Net Income ($million)	Shares (ooo)	Earning per Share ($)
1986	114,689	129,206	23,496	1,058	275,230	3.57
1990	142,452	151,857	38,385	318	336,513	0.57
1995	167,131	160,253	31,690	3,646	427,289	7.21

Source: *Moody's Handbook of Common Stocks Winter 1996-97* New York: Moody's Investtors Service, Inc, 1996.

INTERNATIONAL OPERATIONS

In 1914, Citicorp became the first foreign bank in Buenos Aires, Argentina, and a year later purchased a private banking network, with offices in Shanghai, Yokohama, Hong Kong, Manila, Singapore, Calcutta, and London. Seventy years later, it had increased its multinational holdings to $128.3 billion in assets within 94 foreign countries.[3]

Citicorp's management philosophy has emphasized the grouping of assets and earnings by geography, currency, customer, and product. Its international hierarchy is contrived of five banking groups identified as North America (NA); Caribbean, Central, and South America (CCSA); Europe, Middle East, and Africa (EMEA); and Asia/Pacific (AP) and Other. The North American banking group contribute about 46 percent of Citicorp's net income, while the EMEA banking group contributes about 19 percent, the CCSA contributes about 25 percent, and the AP contributes about 10 percent.[4]

---

* For a summary of some of the important financial data on Citicorp, see Table 6:8.1.

LATIN AMERICAN OPERATIONS

Brazilian subsidiaries are responsible for almost half of the newly industrialized countries' (NICs') and developing countries' profit contributions to Citicorp.[5] Citicorp in Brazil employs about 6,000 people, which is almost 10 percent of the financial services workforce of the entire corporation.[6] Brazilian holdings include 11 branches and a 49.9 percent stake in Crefisul, a financial service holding company that is composed of an investment bank, a brokerage firm, a data processing company, and a credit card operation.[7]

In the early 1980s many U.S. banks in Brazil were failing. This was due to the state governors' liberal use of the banks to fund their election campaigns. Banks were failing also because of the country's weakening economy. Citicorp has managed to avoid these pitfalls by establishing strong relations with the Brazilian private sector and by designating its funds to them. The majority of profits were earned from investment banking, insurance brokerage, and fund management.[8]

Nearly 15 percent of the total U.S. bank exposure to the Latin American debt belongs to Citicorp. They have taken advantage of these countries' nonrestricted financial worlds and have experienced large gains, as seen in the Brazilian reports, but they have also realized substantial losses in Mexico and in Argentina. Citibank has been cooperative with its host country governments. For example, in 1997the Citibank froze $26 million in the New York bank account of a Chilean businessman who was suspected of money laundering by Mexican authorities for Mexico's largest cocaine cartel by Mexican authorities. A Citibank spokesman stated, "The bank is firmly committed to efforts to prevent money laundering and has in place rigorous programs designed to keep our accounts and facilities from being used for such illegal activities and cooperates fully with official investigation"[9]. It should be noted that U.S. money-laundering regulations require banks to be familiar with the source of clients' money and to report "suspicious" transactions. Although Citicorp reported one suspicious transaction related to the owner of the frozen account, but it is not clear when that occurred or which account was blocked.

UNITED KINGDOM'S OPERATIONS

In the late 1990s, Citibank was investing in 13 countries in Europe, encompassing 464 branches and generating $2.0 billion.[10] Citicorp has shied away from making large loans to governments and corporations in Europe and, instead, concentrated on "going native" by lending in local currencies to consumers and small businesses.[11] The United Kingdom is no exception. Citibank Business Loans (CBLs), specializing in loans of between $1 million and $25 million, have been introduced into the British market and have successfully adapted to the market in a relatively short period of time. Most foreign banks within the United Kingdom support their own investors and usually with their own form of currency. Citicorp is not exclusive when choosing its clients, and in order to attract domestic (British) clients it simplifies the currency conversion procedure by converting from the dollar to the pound only once.[12]

Citicorp enjoys several advantages from its presence in the British market. London has seasoned and experienced financiers from whom young Citicorp employees can learn much. Minute by minute communications of currency valuations are at the bank's fingertips. Government restrictions are more relaxed than in the United States. The Bank of England has a liberal policy toward the banking and investment world in order to try to limit intrusive regulation, as it supports the freedom of the Euromarket businesses.[13]

By positioning itself in an atmosphere so conducive to growth, Citicorp has been given the opportunity to expand experimentally with new financial services, such as investment banking, stock brokering, underwriting, life insurance, and other insurance selling. These activities are heavily regulated in the United States, but are possible in the United Kingdom. In the mid 1980s, Citicorp purchased the stocks of Scrimgeour Vickers, Seccombe, Marshall and Campion. These firms specialize in investment banking and venture capital. Market gains and the bank's domination of certain markets are expected in the future.[14]

Another strategic advantage enjoyed by Citicorp in this location is its aggressive and unpolished manner of doing business. The British traditional banking atmosphere is characterized by seasoned financiers making low-risk, high-cost decisions behind heavy oak desks. This way of doing business is being challenged by Citicorp. The market seems to be jumping right into their hands as Citicorp cuts costs and gets the deal signed, sealed, and delivered in half the time it has taken in the past. Not only does Citicorp benefit from this environment, but the British consumers also benefit from decreased borrowing costs due to this heightened competition between the old banks and Citicorp. As a result, Citicorp continues to penetrate the British banking system. For example, in January 1985, Citicorp became the first foreign bank in England to join the "circle of British clearing banks." In February of the same year, it became the first bank, British or foreign, to purchase a "discount house."[15]

ADAPTATION

Because Citicorp is not a manufacturing firm, the marketing and advertising of Citicorp's service products are not so necessary for the creation of business as they would be for most manufacturing firms. After the initial notification to the consumer of Citicorp's service offerings, most prospective clients seek out Citicorp because they are in need of its services and there are few substitutes available due to the reasons described earlier. It is seldom that Citicorp participates in "cold call" campaigns to attract business. Thus, the entry of Citicorp into a foreign market has been made that much easier by the relative unavailability of substitutes for its services.

Banking, like any service, is people oriented. Communication is essential for successful business. Often cultural barriers interfere with a multinational's endeavors. Two of these barriers are language and religion. Citicorp has been sensitive to this issue. Its German-based subsidiary, KKB Bank in Dusseldorf, is operated entirely by Germans and German-speaking personnel so that it resembles a local bank.[16] To better facilitate the adaptation process, Citicorp has often taken over existing firms upon entering a country for the first time. By buying into a ready-made firm, usually one that is in a turnaround transition, Citicorp has acquired a trained workforce with knowledge not only of financial services but also of the host country's culture, which aids Citicorp in its relationships with employees and the public.

QUESTIONS

1. Why does a bank go international? Why did Citicorp?
2. Given the debt crisis of some of its major clients in Latin America, how can Citicorp protect itself? Explain.
3. What are the differences between operating a subsidiary bank in an advanced country, like the United Kingdom, and operating in a developing country, like Brazil?
4. Describe Citicorp's management strategy with regard to international banking.
5. What are the differences between the operations of multinational manufacturing companies and the operations of multinational service companies?

Notes

1. *Moody's Bank and Finance Manual*, 1987, p. 142.
2. *Moody's Handbook of Common Stocks Winter 1996-97 Edition*, New York: Moody's Investors Service, Inc., 1996.
3. "Citibank's Pervasive Influence on International Lending," *Business Week*, 16 May 1983, p. 124.
4. Citicorp, *Annual Report 1984*, (New York: Citicorp).
5. Moody's Bank and Finance Manual, 1987, p. 143.
6. "The Booty from Brazil," *The Economist*, 5 May 1984, pp. 89-91.
7. "Citibank's Pervasive Influence on International Lending," p. 126.
8. "The Booty from Brazil," pp. 89-91.
9. "Citicorp Freezes Suspected Drug-Fund Account," *The Wall Street Journal*, 12 September 1997, p. A18.
10. Citicorp, *Annual Review, 1997*.
11. "Citicorp's Gutsy Campaign to Conquer Europe," *Business Week*, 15 July 1985, p. 46.
12. "Citibank's Pervasive Influence on International Lending," p. 125.
13. Gunter Dufey and Ian H. Giddy, *The International Money Market* (Englewood Cliffs, N.J.: Prentice-Hall, 1978), p. 40.
14. "What Are Britons Doing Patronizing a New York Bank?" p. 18.

15. Ibid., pp. 18, 20.
16. "Citicorp's Gutsy Campaign to Conquer Europe," p. 47.

Suggested Readings

"The Booty from Brazil." *The Economist*, 5 May 1984, pp. 89-90.

"Citibank's Pervasive Influence on International Lending." *Business Week*, 16 May 1983, pp. 124-127.

Citicorp. Annual Report. New York: Citicorp, 1984.

Dufey, Gunter, and Ian H. Giddy. *The International Money Market*. Englewood Cliffs, N.J.: Prentice-Hall, 1978.

Jensen, Michael C. *The Financiers*. New York: Weybright and Talley, 1976.

Moody's Bank and Finance Manual, 1984.

Sampson, Anthony. *The Money Lenders: Bankers and a World of Turmoil*. New York: Viking Press, 1982.

Wilson, Andrew B."Citicorp's Gutsy Campaign to Conquer Europe." *Business Week*, 15 July 1985, pp. 46-47.

FORD: "QUALITY IS JOB ONE"

INTRODUCTION

As the first automaker in the world, Ford has been a leader in the automotive industry. Its history has been filled with accomplishments that pioneered the way for manufacturers throughout the rest of the world. Henry Ford's development of the assembly line radically changed the auto industry, but, more important, it changed the whole manufacturing process.

Unfortunately, Ford has been plagued by numerous liability suits over the years. These suits have led to questions regarding Ford's goals and aspirations. Ford has pulled through these rough times and has since reorganized and changed its motto. Along with these changes, Ford has turned to its operations overseas for guidance. It will be only through cooperation, not only with its overseas subsidiaries but also with its competitors, that Ford will gain the knowledge and know-how that will keep it in the forefront of the automobile industry.

THE HISTORY OF FORD

In 1903, the Ford Motor Company was incorporated into the business world in Michigan "to produce automobiles designed and engineered by Henry Ford."[1] Initially Ford was but a tiny operation located in a converted wagon factory in Detroit. Today, Ford is an MNC with a worldwide operation. It is one of the largest industrial enterprises with active manufacturing, assembly, and sales operations in 30 countries and on six continents. More than 345,000 men and women in 200 countries work for Ford every day. The company's annual sales are greater than the gross national products of many industrialized countries.[2] Ford cars and trucks are manufactured and assembled by its subsidiaries in Germany, Great Britain, Canada, Spain, Brazil, Australia, Argentina, and other countries. In 1999, Ford's sales reached the level of $162,558 million, which was 12.6% higher than the previous year. For the same year, it earned a net income of $7,237 million, which was 5.1% higher than the previous year.[3] Ford held 25.6 percent of the total car and truck market share in the United States in 1995. In Europe it held a 12.3 percent total market share.[4]

In its first year, the Ford Motor Company was a big success. Sales for the first three and one-half months totaled $132,482, and resulted in a net profit of $36,958.[5] A dividend of 2 percent was paid on October 1, 1903; a month later the dividend was 10 percent. In January, 1904, it was 20 percent, and six months later it was 68 percent.[6] In the first 15 months 1,700 cars-early Model As-were produced.[7] Between 1903 and 1908, Henry Ford, chief engineer and later president, used the first 19 letters of the alphabet to designate his cars, although some of the cars never reached the public.

The most successful Ford car was the Model N.[8] It was a small, light, four-cylinder luxury car which sold for $500.[9] The Model K was a six-cylinder luxury car for $2,500, but it sold poorly.[10] Because of the Model K's failure, Mr. Ford insisted that the company's future lay in the production of inexpensive cars for a mass market. This caused conflict between Mr. Ford and Alexander Malcomson, a Detroit coal dealer, who had helped finance the company. Because of these problems, Mr. Malcomson left the company, allowing Mr. Ford to acquire enough of his stock to become president in 1906. In 1908 the Model T was produced, and it became an immediate success because of improvements in its quality. Within 19 years, more than 15,000,000 Model Ts were sold, making Ford Motor Company a giant industrial corporation throughout the world.[11] Ford revolutionized manufacturing with wages of $5 a day-very high for that time.

By 1927, however, people were ready for a more stylish and powerful car. The Model T had been basically unchanged for two decades, and it was losing ground to its competitors. A vastly improved Model A was designed, and 4,500,000 of them were produced between 1927 and 1931.[12]

Eventually people again wanted a more luxurious and powerful car, so the Ford V-8 was designed in 1932. Ford was the first company in history to successfully cast a V-8 engine block in one piece, and it was many years before Ford's competitors learned how to mass-produce a reliable V-8 engine.[13] As a result, Ford continued to expand rapidly its production of the V-8 engine, producing its 30 millionth V-8 engine in 1962.[14]

In the post-World War II period, Ford experienced a definite decrease in the sales of its automobiles. It halted civilian car production and shifted to military production. Ford was losing money at a rate of several million dollars per month. Ford was in no position at that time to resume its role as a major competitor in the automobile industry. In 1943 Ford reopened civilian automobile production. At that time, In response to the World War II demand, Ford had already built 8,600 bombers, 278,000 jeeps and 57,000 aircraft engines.[15] Henry Ford II reorganized the company, and an expansion plan was designed, restoring the company to prosperity.

Along with Ford's domestic growth, there was also foreign expansion. Ford Motor Company of Canada was formed by Gordon McGregor, who negotiated a contract with the Michigan company and Henry Ford on August 10, 1904.[16] According to this contract the Canadian corporation was to be established with the capital of $125,000, of which 51 percent was to be distributed pro rata to stockholders in the parent Ford Company. Thus, Ford could gain majority control of the Canadian branch.[17] A branch of Ford Motor Company was established in London in 1908. Since then, Ford has continued to expand, establishing subsidiaries in a number of nations.[18] In 2000, Ford had "active manufacturing, assembly and sales operations in 30 countries on six continents."[19]

LEGAL ACTIONS

The Ford Motor Company's slogan is "Quality Is Job One." Its customer research concluded that the quality of Ford's 1986 cars and trucks was more than 50 percent better than that of their 1980 models.[20] Ford claimed that it was the leader in quality among major domestic producers. For example, Louis Ross, executive vice president, stated that "Our goal of customer satisfaction dictates that quality is, and will remain, our number one priority. We are already the leader in quality among major North American manufacturers and our efforts now are aimed at being the best in the industry."[21]

The need for emphasis on quality had arisen from lawsuits against Ford over the quality of its products in recent years, particularly involving the Ford Pinto. In June of 1978, the Ford Motor Company recalled 1.9 million Pintos in order to improve the safety of the fuel tanks. This was done at the request of the government and because of public pressure.[22] The next year the company was brought to court to face three charges of reckless homicide in connection with the deaths of three young women in a fiery crash in August of 1978.[23] The prosecution claimed that Ford knew that the gasoline tanks of the subcompact Ford Pinto tended to explode when struck from behind. And the prosecution claimed that the company did nothing to correct this problem. Harley Copp, the chief witness for the prosecution, stated that "Ford knew about the problem, and that Ford failed to do anything about it because it would have cut into profits."[24] The prosecutor, Michael Cosentino, described the Pinto as being poorly designed and the only car that the government had ever asked an automaker to recall.[25]

Ford denied the charges against it, arguing that its vehicles were as safe as its competitors' vehicles. Ford was found not guilty on three charges of reckless homicide on March 13, 1980.[26] On Thursday, April 10, 1980, the case of the *State of Indiana v. Ford Motor Company* was officially closed after 19 months.[27] Ford had won, but the fact still remained that quality was not "job one" in the design of the Pinto.

Ford has been a defendant in various other actions for damages arising out of automobile accidents where injuries resulted from alleged deficiencies in the fuel systems. It has also been a defendant in cases involving defective automatic transmissions. In August 1981, owners of vehicles produced between the years 1976 and 1979 that were equipped with certain automatic transmissions claimed to have had property damage, personal injury, economic losses, or liability losses because of the tendency of the vehicles to slip from the parking gear into reverse.[28] Ford has also been a defendant in cases involving the failure to provide an air bag and in cases where injuries were alleged to have resulted from contact with certain Ford parts and other products containing asbestos.

In June 1986, Ford recalled 162,000 1985-model and 1986-model Ranger light trucks because the vapor emissions of these trucks were above federal standards. Tests indicated that vapor return lines may have been pinched during assembly.[29] Again, in February 1988, Ford announced that it would recall 103,000 1985-model through 1987-model Ford Ranger trucks for "... a defect that could cause them to exceed federal pollution guidelines."[30]

These documented cases seem to show the lack of social responsibility on Ford's part. But many improvements have been demonstrated since its major problems with the Ford Pinto during the late 1970s and the early 1980s. During this period of time Ford was the last U.S. automaker to adjust to the new demand for fuel-efficient cars. This resulted in decreased sales and a large loss of market share in the United States. Since the implementation of "Quality Is Job One," Ford's strategy had deviated from traditional ideas. It now looks to its European divisions for design and engineering ideas and management talent.[31] These changes have brought Ford success over recent years. Through the introduction of designs developed in Europe, Ford cars have taken on a new image. Ford is looking for greater fuel efficiency through improved aerodynamics, adapting a rounded, overtly aerodynamic appearance.

To make the Ford Bronco better, the company has installed robots, other automated equipment, and statistical controls. The Bronco's design has been improved and there are tougher inspection systems.[32] In Louisville, Kentucky, an employee involvement strategy has been implemented. The workers now have a voice in how the truck is put together. This is expected to increase morale, leading to better-quality automobiles. The Louisville assembly plant demonstrates that U.S. industry can achieve huge improvements in quality and productivity, but only when circumstances force labor and management to get together and work more intelligently.[33]

FORD OVERSEAS OPERATIONS

Ford's operations span the world, but one must wonder why this U.S. automaker turned to foreign operations. Four main reasons seem to be the driving force for Ford's foreign direct investment abroad. First, car and truck sales in overseas markets are large, and although these markets can be served through exports, transportation costs are high. Additionally, servicing those exports would be difficult. The establishment of foreign facilities lowers the transportation costs and reduces the service of subsidiaries in those areas. Second, certain foreign governments do not allow participation in their markets without local investment. Third, some of these foreign markets have certain advantages economically over the U.S. market. For example, Korea and Mexico offer substantially lower costs to Ford since labor costs in those countries are relatively cheap. Thus, parts and even final products can be produced at a substantially lower unit cost in some foreign countries as compared with similar operations in the United States. Lastly, through diversification of investments, Ford has become less dependent on economic conditions in the United States. The idea of diversification definitely aided the company during the period from 1978 to 1982 when Ford in the United States began to take on heavy losses.

Ford's most important subsidiary has been its Ford of Europe division. Until 1967, the foreign operations were independently owned and run.[34] They even made their own product lines of cars, which were different from the parent company's product lines.[35] In 1967, Henry Ford II brought these independent operations of Europe together to form Ford of Europe.[36]

It is interesting to note that Ford of Europe does not own any assets, nor does it directly run any of the plants. It acts as a high-level service center that coordinates and supervises all operations. The goal that Henry Ford II had behind this Ford of Europe concept was to foster competition between Ford in the United States and Ford of Europe.[37] How could this help? Europe is known for its preferences for high-performance, sporty cars. By learning and developing technology to suit the preferences of European consumers, Ford could gain this new technology and then transfer it to the United States. This would set up a network through which information and new developments could be shared between the Ford companies in Europe and Ford in the United States. This would then allow Ford to be producing products with the latest technology. Unfortunately, this strategy was not carried out to its full potential until 1981.

Prior to 1981, the parent company in the United States made all the decisions for Ford of Europe. Instead of sharing information, the parent company dictated the styles and product types for the European market. This was a big marketing flaw, because it did not take into consideration the different tastes and preferences of the Europeans. Because of this flaw, Ford, during the 1970s, did not perform very well. But in 1981, under the leadership of Robert Lutz, Ford of Europe broke away from previous policies and began manufacturing cars that would be competitive in the European market.[38] What is interesting to note is not only did Europe break from U.S. leadership, Ford's headquarters in the United States began looking to Europe for development of Ford's models for the world market.[39] In other words, "The parent is drawing on its subsidiary for design and engineering ideas and management talent."[40] Ford's European operations were saving the parent company from real difficulties and cash flow problems, which had left Ford in the United States with losses of $3.9 billion during the 1978—1982 period.[41] Coinciding with the losses, Ford was the slowest to react to the new demand for fuel-efficient, economical cars. This caused Ford's sales to drop to their lowest levels in two decades and lose 6.6 percent of its market share during the 1978—1982 period. Eventually Ford's market share was down to a mere 17 percent of the automobile market.[42]

During this period of slumping sales and large losses in the United States, Ford of Europe was doing very well. As the fifth largest automaker in 1981, Ford of Europe was one of the only two automakers to turn a profit. Net profits generated in Europe from 1978 to 1982 came to over $2 billion for the parent company.[43] Also, Ford of Europe loaned the parent company an additional $1.2 billion to ease the losses in the U.S. market.[44] Thus, the European operations were not only breaking from tradition but also were aiding the company in avoiding financial disaster.

The major strategy that Ford of Europe undertook under the leadership of Robert Lutz was called the "After Japan" strategy.[45] The first priority that faced Ford of Europe was to gain back the market share which the Japanese had penetrated to the greatest extent, notably the markets in the Nordic countries and in Ireland.[46] Ford designed and manufactured cars that were specifically equipped to demonstrate to buyers that Ford cars were offering more value for their money.

To make such a statement, Ford had to be competitive with the Japanese in manufacturing efficiency. Lutz, through studying the Japanese automakers, began to reshape operations, and he copied some of the Japanese techniques. Many changes had to be made, but they seemed to have been implemented with few disruptions. The benefits of these changes have become very noticeable. Some statistics that prove the success of the "After Japan" strategy (the AJ strategy) are the following:

+ Body defects per 100 cars decreased from 835 in 1980 to 650 in 1982.
+ The average rate of growth of manufacturing productivity was 4.8 percent in 1981 and about 6.0 percent in 1982.
+ Reduction of the break-even point from 80 percent of capacity prior to the AJ program to 60 percent of capacity in 1982.[47]

These statistics demonstrated Ford's new commitment to producing quality built cars. They had abandoned some old ideas and replaced them with radically new ideas that were necessary to get Ford back on its feet again. The result of the AJ program paid off in 1984 when Ford became the number-one automaker in Europe.[48] But this distinction was not held for long. Competition in the European market has been heating up since 1984, locking its six major automakers in "a loss making battle for a larger share of stagnant sales." This caused great increases in the amount of money spent on advertising, and these added costs have effectively reduced the profit levels in Europe. Once again Ford was faced with changing conditions in Europe. The reduction in profits put pressure on top management. The predictions for the European market looked so bleak that in the early months of 1985, Ford of Europe began talks with Fiat of Italy on a possible merger. The possibilities of the linkup seemed endless. The merger would create a giant with a 25 percent share of the 10 million car market and would cause the other car makers to scramble. With a 25 percent share of the market, Ford could then specialize on its more profitable mid-sized models, while Fiat would pick up the small car market. With this type of specialization both companies would gain because they would be focusing on the models in which they have comparative advantages.

Unfortunately, the talks were curtailed toward the end of September 1985.[49] Reasons for the breakdown of talks were basically due to a power struggle. Neither company wished to surrender control to the other, but they did agree to merge their truck operations in Europe in March 1986. The hopes of another merger with the British government-owned BL and PLC car and truck divisions were struck down as a wave of anti-Americanism swept through Parliament.[50]

Because of these setbacks, Ford again changed its strategy. It would now focus its efforts on joint venture projects with other car manufacturers. Talks showed possible areas of development in the manufacture of engines, transmissions, and other parts. There was even a possibility of joining with a European rival to design a car with common parts, keeping only the exterior styling of the car different.[51] Such plans were being suggested since plant closings could be difficult.

Plant closings, however, were one option that Ford used successfully in the United States. In 1978, Ford in the United States was selling roughly 2.8 million cars, but at a loss. From 1978 to 1983, Ford decreased the number of jobs and cut down on the volume of cars sold. The result was a substantial increase in profits. This strategy of reducing the amount of production and the number of jobs made many European workers nervous. Possible plant closing of Ford's Dagenham plant near London alone could place 2,000 out of work.[52] But while these fears were well warranted, Ford faced problems in initiating plant closings because it was dealing with a dozen different countries, each with its own unions and government policies, which in some cases would make plant closings almost impossible.[53]

Outside the U.S. and European markets, Ford was also making some adjustments. Decreasing sales in Argentina caused Ford and Volkswagen to begin merger talks.[54] Similar to what Henry Ford II did in Europe, Ford management restructured its operations in Brazil. Its 13 subsidiaries joined together to form one single holding company. In so doing it took advantage of some tax breaks, and also was able to increase efficiency. By centralizing operations, it could help solve some of the cash flow problems that existed in the past. With interest rates at 20 percent, and inflation at 210 percent annually, the cash-poor divisions could then be aided by some of the more cash-rich divisions. Even under these adverse economic circumstances, and even with very complicated government restrictions, Ford saw a great potential for the development of vertically integrated operations in Brazil. Labor is cheap, and there is an abundant supply of energy and raw materials. And there is also a large potential market. But because of the restrictions placed on high-tech manufacturing areas by the nationalistic military government, it was difficult for Ford to integrate its operations in Brazil.[55]

In 1991, Ford purchased 50% of Mazada Motor Manufacturing and renamed the company Auto Alliance International.[56] Mazda then began working with Ford's affiliates in the Asian-Pacific region to develop, with Ford, a minicar to be built by Kia of South Korea.[57] In 1996, Ford owned 90% of Kia Motor Company.[58] Here again is an example of Ford's strategy of using joint ventures with some of its leading competitors as a way of keeping abreast of the latest developments in technology. In return, Ford agreed to purchase a significant portion of the production from Mazda's new assembly plant that was being built in Flat Rock, Michigan.[59]

Overall, Ford is searching for ways to ensure that the vehicles that it produces meet customer requirements and are competitive in cost and in quality. And it is through the new strategy of sharing information and technology with competitors and among its divisions that Ford will continue to be a forerunner in the auto industry.

There are now indications that Ford's strategy is paying off. The analysis of the existing data indicates that Ford's share of the car market and its share of the truck market have risen both in the United States and in some other countries in recent years. Table 3:6.1 shows Ford's sales, net income, and earning per share has risen in recent years.

TABLE 3:6.1
Ford's Five Year Summary of Financial Data

Years	Sales (000$)	Net Income	Earning per Share
1995	137,137,000	4,139,000	3.58
1994	128,439,000	5,308,000	4.97
1993	108,521	2,529,000	2.27
1992	100,132,000	-7,385,000	-7.81
1991	88,286	-2,258,000	12.40

Source: Ford Motor Company, *Annual Reports* (various years)

Today, Ford is the world's largest automaker and number 2 maker of cars and trucks combined, behind General Motors. In October of 1993, Alex Trotman became Chairman and Chief Executive Officer of Ford Motor company. He launched a series of studies and development efforts to globalize the company. As a results, the Ford 2,000 initiative came to existence. Accordingly, Ford consolidated its North American and European operations in 1994, and continued with a commitment to bring the entire Ford global organization into a single operations by the year 2,000. So far, the program has enabled the company to abolish duplication, launch best practices, employ common components and designs, and allocate resources in order to best satisfy the market demands for its products.[60] In elaborating on its new global strategy in its 1995 annual report, Ford stated that: "We're focused on fundamentals: lowering our costs, growing profitably in both mature and new markets, developing excellent products and satisfying our customers in every way."

QUESTIONS

1. What was Henry Ford's marketing strategy? Explain.
2. How do you perceive the Ford strategy during World War II? Explain.
3. Ford claims that "Quality Is Job One." Has it lived up to its promise? Explain.
4. Is the pursuit of short-run profit the only purpose of a business firm? Has Ford acted in a socially responsible manner throughout its history? Discuss.
5. Why does a firm engage in foreign direct investment? What are Ford's major reasons for doing so? Explain.
6. What degree of centralization has Ford utilized in controlling its foreign operation during its history? Explain. What have been the implications of Ford's centralization philosophy on its overseas operations?
7. Why does an MNC engage in a joint venture arrangement? Discuss the pros and cons of joint ventures, using Ford as an example.

Notes

1. *Ford Motor Company Annual Report on Form 10-K for the Year Ended December 31, 1985* (Dearborn, Mich.; 1985), p. 1
2. *News from the World of Ford: An American Legend* (Dearborn, Mich.: Corporate News Department, March 1988), p. 1.
3. Hoover's On Line, *Ford Motor Company*, p. 1.
4. Ibid., p. 2.
5. Lawrence Seltzer, *A Financial History of the American Automobile Industry* (Boston: Houghton Mifflin, 1928), p. 91.
6. Ibid.
7. *News from the World of Ford: An American Legend* (Dearborn, Mich.: Corporate News Department, 1988), p. 2.
8. Ibid.
9. Ibid.
10. Ibid.
11. Ibid., p. 3.
12. Ibid., p. 4.
13. Ibid.
14. Ford Motor Company, *Ford Motor Company: Histroic Milestoned* (Detroit: Ford Motor Company, 1997).
15. Ford Motor Company, *Ford Motor Company: Histroic Milestoned* (Detroit: Ford Motor Company, 1997)
16. A. Nevins, *Ford: The Times, The Man, The Company* (New York: Scribner, 1954), p. 357.
17. Ibid.
18. Ibid., p. 362.
19. *News from the World of Ford: An American Legend* (Dearborn, Mich.: Corporate News Department, 1988), p. 1.
20. *Ford Motor Company Annual Report 1985* (Dearborn, Mich.: Corporate News Department, 1985).
21. Ibid.

22. "Ford Motor Company Cleared in Three Deaths," *The New York Times*, 14 March 1980, p. A1.
23. Ibid.
24. Lee Patrick Strobel, *Reckless Homicide? Ford's Pinto Trial* (South Bend, Ind.: And Books, 1980), p. 177.
25. Ibid., p. 157.
26. "Ford Auto Company Cleared in Three Deaths," p. D12.
27. Strobel, *Reckless Homicide?* p. 272.
28. *Ford Motor Company Annual Report on Form 10-K for the Year Ended December 31, 1985* (Dearborn, Mich., 1985), p. 22.
29. "Ford Announces Recall of 162,000 Ranger Trucks," *The Wall Street Journal*, 23 June 1986, p. 2.
30. "Ford Motor to Recall 103,000 Ranger Trucks," *The Wall Street Journal*, 10 February 1988, p. 4.
31. "Ford Is on a Roll in Europe," *Fortune*, 18 October 1982, p. 182.
32. "Ford's Drive for Quality," *Fortune*, 18 April 1983, p. 62.
33. Ibid.
34. "Ford Is on a Roll in Europe," p. 182.
35. Ibid.
36. Ibid., p. 191.
37. Ibid.
38. Ibid., p.182.
39. Ibid.
40. Ibid.
41. Ibid.
42. Ibid.
43. Ibid.
44. Ibid.
45. Ibid., p. 184.
46. Ibid.
47. Ibid., p. 185.
48. "Ford Rolls Out the Profits," *Business Week*, 4 March 1985, p. 40.
49. "Ford-Fiat: How Their Contest of Wills Prevented a "Perfect Marriage' in Europe," *The Wall Street Journal*, 21 November 1985, p. 34.
50. "Yanks, Go Home: Furor over Selling BL," Business Week, 24 March 1986, p. 50.
51. "Ford Moderates European Strategy with New Focus on Profitability," *The Wall Street Journal*, 27 March 1986, p. 37.
52. "Brits Out, Mexicans In," *The Economist*, 14 January 1984, p. 60.
53. "Ford Moderates European Strategy with New Focus on Profitability," p. 37.
54. "Ford-VW Talks," *The New York Times*, 27 August 1986, p. D3.
55. "Ford Revamps for an Export Push," *Business Week*, 27 February 1984, pp. 47-50.
56. Ford Motor Company, *Ford Motor Company: Historic Milestoned* (Detroit: Ford Motor Company, 1997)
57. Ford Motor Company Annual Report, 1985, p. 5
58. Ford Motor Company, *Ford Motor Company: Historic Milestoned* (Detroit: Ford Motor Company, 1997).
59. *Ford Motor Company Annual Report* 1985 (Dearborn, Mich., 1985).
60. Ford Motor Company, *Ford Motor Company: Historic Milestoned* (Detroit: Ford Motor Company, 1997).

Suggested Readings

"Either We're Crazy or They're Crazy." *Forbes*, 29 July 1985, pp. 64-66.

"Ford Announces Recall of 162,000 Ranger Trucks," *The Wall Street Journal*, 23 June 1986.

"Ford Auto Company Cleared in Three Deaths," *The New York Times*, 14 March 1980, p. A1.

"Ford's Drive for Quality." *Fortune*, 18 April 1983, p. 62.

"Will Fiat and Ford of Europe Tie the Knot?" *Business Week*, 29 April 1985, p. 44.

"Ford-Fiat: How Their Contest of Wills Prevented a "Perfect Marriage' in Europe." *The Wall Street Journal*, 21 November 1985, p. 34.

"Ford Is on a Roll in Europe." *Fortune*, 18 October 1982, pp. 182-191.

"Ford Moderates Europe Strategy with New Focus on Profitability." *The Wall Street Journal*, 27 March 1986, p. 37.

Ford Motor Company Annual Report. Dearborn, Mich., 1985.

Ford Motor Company Annual Report on Form 10-K for the Year Ended December 31, 1985. Dearborn, Mich., 1985.

"Ford Motor Names Benton to Head International Lines." *The Wall Street Journal*, 18 March 1986, p. 14.

"Ford Revamps for an Export Push." *Business Week*, 27 February 1984, pp. 47-50.

"Ford Rolls Out the Profits." *Business Week*, 4 March 1985, p. 40.

"Ford-VW Talks." *The New York Times*, 27 August 1986, p. 3.

"A Japanese Beat for the Motown Sound." *The Economist*, 14 January 1984, pp. 59-60.

Marsden, D., T. Morris, P. Willman, and S. Wood. *The Motor Industry*. London: Hertford and Harlow, Simpson Shand, 1956.

Maxcy, D., T. Morris, P. Willman, and S. Wood. *The Car Industry*. London and New York: Tavistock, 1955.

Nevins, A. Ford: *The Times, The Man, The Company*, New York: Scribner, 1957.

News from the World of Ford: An American Legend. Dearborn, Mich.: Corporate News Department, April 1986.

Seltzer, L. *A Financial History of the American Automobile Industry*. Boston: Houghton Mifflin, 1928.

Strobel, Lee Patrick. *Reckless Homicide? Ford's Pinto Trial. South Bend*, Ind.: And Books, 1980.

"What's Good for Ford." *New Statesman*, 1 February 1985.

"Yanks, Go Home: The Furor over Selling BL." *Business Week*, 24 March 1986.

Case 6:10

UNION CARBIDE AND THE BHOPAL ACCIDENT

INTRODUCTION

Union Carbide is a long-established MNC that has many subsidiaries across the globe. It produces a diverse range of materials, from batteries to plastic bags, with the emphasis on the production of plastics and chemicals. This wide range of products has made this large organization a very stable company in the international market. Since 1984, however, there has been a change in Union Carbide's stability. This is mostly due to a severe chemical accident that occurred in Bhopal, India, in early December of 1984.

HISTORY

The corporation's history has been one of consistent increases in production and in rapid diversification. Union Carbide Corporation was incorporated in 1917 with the name Union Carbide and Carbon Corporation.[1] Management soon realized its growth potential, and decided to go abroad to get needed materials and technology. Gradually Union Carbide became established in almost every area of the world. Today, the corporation has 11,500 employees, working in factories, mills, and labs in over 40 countries.[2]

Beginning in the late 1970s business started to slow down for the large corporation. In an effort to restore profit levels to where they had been in the early 1970s, Union Carbide tried to diversify its operation (like many other large chemical corporations had done), but this time it did not work.[3] It then decided to decrease diversification and to emphasize the production of chemicals, plastics, and gas-the products which had been most profitable.[4] In 1980 it sold two of its subsidiaries, Jaques Seeds Company and Amchem Products, Inc.[5] It also sold a water treatment business and a metals business.[6] The sale of some businesses did not increase profits either, so, in 1984, Union Carbide put emphasis on the sale of patented technology and formed a group to help in the maintenance and the operations of its chemical plants.[7] In December 1984, as we will explain later, a disastrous chemical leak accident occurred at the Union Carbide India, Ltd. subsidiary in Bhopal, India. This incident has damaged the financial stability and public image of the corporation since that date.

OPERATIONS

Union Carbide organization includes five industry units: petrochemicals; industrial gases; metals and carbon products; consumer products; and technology, services, and specialty products.[8] Chemicals and plastics are the products with which the company has been most competitive, but in the late 1980s those industry segments have not been doing so well.

The major competitors of Union Carbide are the big chemical producers. One of these is Rhom and Hass Company, which has 39 chemical plants worldwide. Chevron Chemical, Olin Corporation, Shell Oil, and Dow Chemical are some other major chemical producers that compete against Union Carbide.[9] Another chemical firm that has been in competition with Union Carbide is GAF. GAF is a small but aggressive company. It was going to buy out Union Carbide, sell all of its assets, and start another business with the cash. Union Carbide defended itself by selling its automotive and home products division to First Boston Corporation. It also sold the battery products division to Ralston Purina. The two sales generated over $800 million. This made Union Carbide too expensive for GAF to buy.[10] Although Union Carbide survived the GAF takeover bid, the Bhopal accident still lingers as a problem for the company.

UNION CARBIDE IN INDIA

In 1961 the Indian government wanted to eliminate chronic food shortages, and they felt the production of pesticides and fertilizers would provide more efficient farming.[11] That led to a joint venture between Union Carbide and Union Carbide India Ltd. According to Indian law, Union Carbide was required to engineer, design, build, and operate the Bhopal plant by using local Indian labor, materials, equipment, and staff. Union Carbide India was not controlled by the parent company. There was no monitoring or control of plant safety or of environmental protection measures. The plant was built under India's 1973 Foreign Exchange Regulation Act, which generally limits foreign investors to a 40 percent equity stake in operations in India.[12] At a later date, Union Carbide persuaded the Indian government to let the parent company have a larger stake (50.9% ownership) in the plant because of Union Carbide's large export volume and the technological expertise needed for the operation of the plant. Relations between the town of Bhopal and Union Carbide had always been good since the large corporation had brought jobs, wealth, and many more people to that area of India.

THE BHOPAL ACCIDENT

The Problem

During the night of December 3, 1984, methyl-isocyanate (MIC) gas leaked out of the Union Carbide India subsidiary pesticide plant in Bhopal, India. The toxic gas leak initially killed approximately 1,600 people, and as many as 700 more died of aftereffects.[13] Some of the medical problems included lung problems, shortness of breath, depression, eye irritation, and stomach pains. Iswar Dass, the state official in charge of relief efforts, stated that the death toll continues to rise due to the lingering effects of the gas.[14]

The suffering that the Indian people endured caused them to file lawsuits against the American-based Union Carbide Corporation. The major questions to be settled by the lawsuits were the following: (1) Was a Union Carbide engineer responsible for the design of the ill-fated Bhopal subsidiary plant? (2) Did Union Carbide officials know that safety equipment at the plant was not up to par? If so, were steps taken to remedy the problem?[15] The answers to these questions would determine the extent of the liability of Union Carbide in the Bhopal tragedy.

The Company's Reaction

The immediate problems faced by company executives of Union Carbide as a result of the Bhopal accident required management decisions. Led by Chairman Warren M. Anderson, management had to decide how to help the survivors of Bhopal, how to ensure that this type of accident could never happen again, how to keep up employee morale, how to keep investors' attitudes positive about Union Carbide's financial stability, and how to protect the corporation from undue legal liability.[16] Chairman Anderson and management set a precedent in their handling of the Bhopal incident. As a journalist put it, "How Chairman Anderson and his team deal with the aftereffects will influence managers elsewhere who are imagining the unimaginable happening to them."[17]

On the morning of December 3, 1984, Van Den Ameele, Union Carbide's manager of press relations, and William Lutz, chairman of Union Carbide Eastern, gathered the other senior executives together to give India the quick response it needed to deal with the crisis situation.

The committee decided to immediately send food, shelter, and medical aid to help the survivors. Union Carbide also sent a doctor to India with knowledge of the effects of methyl-isocyanate (MIC) gas. A team of technical advisors was sent to inspect the Bhopal plant and make recommendations. Shortly thereafter, Chairman Warren Anderson flew to Bhopal to see what he could do. He was arrested upon arrival in Bhopal and was then asked to leave the country. Anderson offered the Indian government $1 million in cash for immediate aid, as well as use of the company's guesthouse to house orphans of the tragedy. India refused both gestures.[18] The total immediate relief offered by Union Carbide to India was about $8 million. India accepted $1 million, but declined the rest because it felt there were too many strings attached to the use of the money. In return for the money, Union Carbide wanted records kept on what the money was used for and who it helped.[19]

While Union Carbide was desperately seeking to deal with the tragic gas leak in Bhopal, back in the United States, the worldwide publicity was taking its toll on Union Carbide as a corporation. Union Carbide stock fell sharply below $33 per share. This made Union Carbide a takeover target. As a result of the stock price fall and the Bhopal accident, Union Carbide reorganized, eliminating 4,500 staff positions. Union Carbide maintains that no one was directly fired as a result of the Bhopal accident.[20]

Bhopal's Reaction

Union Carbide maintains that there were no U.S. jobs eliminated as a result of the Bhopal accident, but India claims that the world's largest industrial accident touched all but a few lives in Bhopal and has rendered almost the entire population of the city unable to work. There are still many dying from the aftereffects of the gas leak, and at least 60,000 people cannot work a full day because they are disabled.[21]

As to the questions to be settled in the lawsuit, India maintained that a Union Carbide engineer was responsible for the design of the Bhopal plant. The question that had to be answered was whether the engineer, L. J. Couvaras, a Union Carbide employee, was under the Indian subsidiary's jurisdiction or whether he was under the jurisdiction of Union Carbide U.S.A.[22]

The Carbide Strategy of Containment

Union Carbide, faced with a disaster of truly historic proportions which seems to have been caused by its own negligence, adopted a carefully orchestrated strategy of containment. "The objectives of the strategy are clear: downplay the seriousness of the situation, to minimize the adverse impacts, especially on health, and seek to implicate others."[23] It seems that the goal of such strategy was to protect the assets of the company at whatever cost. "It also appears to be a typical, if not standard, industry response to situations in which industry actions have inflicted great personal injury, suffering, and even death on their own workers, users of their products, and residents of communities nearby their industrial installations."[24]

""Life is cheap in India. That, at least, was the foundation of Union Carbide's legal strategy. ..."[25] If the accident had happened in the United States, the cost of settling lawsuits on behalf of the more than 3,300 who died and the tens of thousands who were injured as a result of this incident might have run into billions of dollars. Such large settlement would have almost surely sent the Connecticut-based multinational company into bankruptcy court.[26]

In India, however, the value of life established by courts is a fraction of the amounts set by the juries in the U.S. courts. That was the main reason for Carbide attempting to move the suits to the Indian courts.

Today, Union Carbide's strategy is to portray itself as an environmental corporation. The company's advertising is embedded with slogans such as "cleaner air, purer water, and less waste." In various cases corporate safety precautions have been tightened. [27]

Settlement Talks

There were more than 130 lawsuits filed in the United States, and over 2,700 lawsuits filed in India, in connection with the Bhopal tragedy. The United States tried to consolidate most of the U.S. lawsuits into the court system of New York. India rejected Union Carbide's offer of $30 million to be paid out over a 30-year period.[28]

One of the main issues was whether the lawsuits should be tried in Indian courts or whether they should be tried in American courts. Bud Holman, the chief attorney for Union Carbide, demanded that the trials be conducted in India because he felt it would be easier to see firsthand the results of the tragic gas leak, to interview witnesses, to inspect documents, and so forth. However, Michael Ciresi, a Minneapolis lawyer hired by the Indian government, requested that the trials be kept in the United States because U.S. courts offer "the most expeditious hearings."[29]

A brief filed by Union Carbide before Judge Keenan implied that the preferred forum for the trial was the Indian Courts; however, Union Carbide found the Indian courts undesirable as well. Interestingly, Union Carbide could not hope to be clear of the case simply because no court could be found as a suitable forum for the trial. And yet, legal experts believed Union Carbide had implied just that fact. "Union Carbide, it would appear, finds no court suitable, arguing in fact that it is beyond the law."[30] Ultimately, Judge John Keenan would rule that the United States District Court did not have jurisdiction over the case. The Bhopal accident trial would be moved directly into India's Supreme Court.

After three years to reflect on the problem, Union Carbide thoroughly investigated the Bhopal accident. It concluded that a large amount of water was added to the tank which contained the methyl-isocyanate (MIC) gas. It believed that a disgruntled employee deliberately added water to the tank, resulting in the chemical reaction that caused the disaster. Union Carbide continued to investigate the alleged sabotage, and shared the information with the Indian government.[31]

Indian officials rejected the company's claims of sabotage.[32] The Indian government continued to attack Union Carbide's negligence, wishing to ""save face" and not wanting to appear to be "selling out." Both sides seriously negotiated for an out-of-court settlement. Neither side wished to endure a lengthy Indian trial, and both sides were afraid of damaging information that the trial would bring out. An out-of-court settlement was difficult to reach because both sides felt the need to "save face."[33]

India Settles Lawsuit

On February 14, 1989, the Indian government reached its historical settlement with the Danbury, Connecticut, based Union Carbide. According to the terms of this settlement, which outraged many people, the Indian Supreme Court ordered Union Carbide to pay $470 million in damages to the Indian government on behalf of victims of the Bhopal toxic gas tragedy. As a part of the settlement, all criminal charges and civil suits in India against Union Carbide and Warren Anderson the company's chairman at the time of the accident would be dropped.[34] When the Indian Federal Minister for Industries presented the settlement to the Parliament, opposition members, shouting "Shame, Shame," walked out of the house in protest.[35]

The Indian Supreme Court did not address the issue of whether Union Carbide or the Indian government was to blame for the accident.[36] However, the court did agree to determine how the $470 million settlement would be distributed to the victims. According to the court, Union Carbide were to pay the compensation award to the Indian government. Government officials indicated that the court would decide on the distribution of the award.[37] Many experts, however, believed that the Bhopal victims would get very little of the money. In the past, the Indian government had been accused of corruption and mismanagement of the funds that had been set to aid the victims. Kenneth Ditkowsky, a former Carbide lawyer indicated, "Most of the money would end up in the pockets of Indian government officials."[38]

Many members of the Parliament who belong to the minority Janata Party and the Communist Party and activists on behalf of Bhopal victims believe that the final judgement is an outrage and "ludicrously low."[39] Activists in Bhopal denounced the settlement as the betrayal of the 20,000 victims who still suffer from exposure to the deadly gas.[40]

On February 23, 1989, India's Supreme Court agreed to hear petitions from the activist group, the Association for Socio-Legal Literacy, demanding $600 million in civil liability. There was confusion as to whether the group wants either an additional $600 million in liability or $130 million added to the current monetary agreement. An Indian Supreme Court lawyer, however, warned the petitioners that the court has issued its order which legally binds all the parties involved and concludes the lawsuit.[41]

Beginning with February of 1989, several other victims' groups and public-interest lawyers also argued that the settlement was unconstitutional. Surprisingly, the Indian Supreme Court took these claims seriously enough to hear their arguments. In July of 1989, the court was expected to rule on these challenges to the settlement. If any of these challenges were considered valid, the settlement might become null and the case open once again.[42]

It was believed that if the settlement would hold, the financial effects would be minimal on Union Carbide. Of the $470 million, $250 million would be paid by Carbide's insurance company; another $200 million would be paid by a reserve fund which is already established by Union Carbide. Therefore, Union Carbide had to pay the balance of $20 million out of its 1989 revenues. For a company with revenues of just over $8 billion in 1988, this was a very minimal amount.[43]

Many analysts believed that the settlement was psychologically good and financially reasonable for Union Carbide. On February 15, 1989, just one day after the settlement was announced, Carbide stock rose $2 to $31⅛ and was the

New York Stock Exchange's most active issue. However, a few analysts thought that the settlement could increase Union Carbide's attractiveness as a takeover target.[44] In April 1999, Union Carbide Corporation (UCC) established an independent charitable trust for Bhopal hospital and announced plans to sell its interest in Union Carbide India Limited (UCIL). In February 1994, India Supreme Court announced that it would allow UCC to sell its shares in UCIL so the assets can be used to build the Bhopal hospital with $20 million turned over to the charitable trust. Groundbreaking for the hospital began in mid October 1997. According to Indian Press reports, the hospital was expected to be completed and operational in year 2000.[45]

CONCLUSION

There is no agreement on the effects and the implications of the settlement to the worst industrial incident in the history. Legal experts cannot agree whether this hybrid settlement actually represents a successful conclusion to the unprecedented tragedy. Unlike earlier attempts to settle this international dispute, which were based on direct U.S.-style payments to the victims, it is not clear who will finally receive the money. The direct payment of damages to the Indian government raises concern over whether the money will reach the victims or whether it will be wasted in the inefficient and sometimes corrupt government bureaucracy.[46]

More fundamentally, it seems that the strategy of containment pursued by Union Carbide as described earlier had worked. The strategy was to value human life based on a Third World rather than a Western standard. The result was to pay about $10,000 per victim of the disastrous methyl isocyanide gas leak.[47] The settlement based on the Third World standard of human life is not even close to tragedies of lesser severity in the Western World. For example, Manville Corp. paid $3 billion to its asbestos victims, and $2.38 billion was paid by A.H. Robins to its Dalkon Shield users.[48] Generally, industry observers and legal experts praise the company's handling of the case. They believe that Robert D. Kennedy, who replaced Anderson as Carbide's chairman, effectively contained the damage from the accident.[49]

A number of analysts consider this case as a test of multinational corporations' social responsibilities in host nations and in industrial disasters. Again there is no agreement on this issue either. A trial lawyer indicated that this accident forced many companies to increase quality control in their foreign plants. He stated that, "Prior to Bhopal, few people thought American parents had to assume the liability for the problems of their subsidiaries. If Bhopal had gone the full route, it would have been interesting to see how that issue would have played out."[50] Another lawyer retained by the Indian government stated that, "This outcome sends a message to the world that these companies are responsible."[51]

Opponents, however, consider the settlement a victory for Union Carbide, and state that the Indian government had "surrendered before the multinational."[52] In the words of David Dembo, of the Bhopal Action Resource Center in New York, "We thought that enough pressure had been mounted in India itself against an inadequate settlement. I guess we were wrong."[53]

Professor Thomas Gladwin of New York University sees the effect of the Bhopal tragedy as relatively fewer plant investments in developing nations and a trend in building "hazardous substance plants in regulatory climates where there are inspections and educated workforce."[54]

QUESTIONS

1. Why did Union Carbide go international? Explain.
2. How do you describe Union Carbide's management philosophy—centralized or decentralized? Explain.
3. Who do you think is responsible for the Bhopal incident—the engineer who designed the plant, Union Carbide Corporation, or the Indian government? Discuss.
4. Are there any indications that Union Carbide officials knew that the Bhopal plant was unsafe?
5. Should the lawsuits have been tried in American or Indian courts?
6. How has Union Carbide's attitude toward litigation with India changed over time?
7. How has the Bhopal accident affected relations between the United States and India?
8. How can Union Carbide improve its tarnished image?

9. Do you agree with the settlement? Why? Why not?
10. What are the implications of this tragedy and subsequent settlement for MNCs in host nations?

Notes

1. *Moody's Industrial Manual*, vol. 2 (New York: Moodys Investors Service, 1986), p. 4519.
2. Ibid., p. 4521.
3. Barry Meter and Ron Winslow, "Union Carbide Faces Difficult Challenge Even Without Bhopal," *The Wall Street Journal*, 27 December 1984, pp. 1, 6.
4. Ibid.
5. *Moody's Industrial Manual*, p. 4519.
6. Ibid.
7. Winslow Meter, "Union Carbide Faces Difficult Challenge," pp. 1, 6.
8. *Moody's Industrial Manual*, p. 4521.
9. Winslow Meter, "Union Carbide Faces Difficult Challenge," pp. 1, 6.
10. Barry Meter, "Carbide to Sell Consumer Lines for $800 Million," *The Wall Street Journal*, 22 April 1986, p. 4.
11. Mark Whittacker, "It Was Like Breathing Fire," *Newsweek*, 17 December 1984, p. 26.
12. Thomas Gladwin, "Bhopal and the Multinational," *The Wall Street Journal*, 16 January 1985, p. 28.
13. M. Miller, "Two Years After Bhopal's Gas Disaster, Lingering Effects Still Plague Its People," *The Wall Street Journal*, 5 December 1986, p. 34.
14. Ibid.
15. B. Meier, "India Says a Union Engineer Was Responsible for Bhopal Site Design," *The Wall Street Journal*, 8 January 1987, p. 10.
16. R. J. Kirkland, Jr., "Union Carbide: Coping with Catastrophe," *Fortune*, 7 January 1985, pp. 50-53.
17. Ibid., p. 50
18. Ibid., p. 52.
19. L. Helm, "Bhopal, a Year Later: Union Carbide Takes a Tougher Line," *Business Week*, 25 November 1985, pp. 96-101.
20. Ibid., p. 97.
21. Ibid., p. 96.
22. Meier, "India Says a Union Engineer Was Responsible," p. 10.
23. Ward Morehouse and M. Arun Subramaniam, *The Bhopal Tragedy: What Really Happened and What It Means for American Workers and Communities at Risk, A Preliminary Report for the Citizens Commission on Bhopal* (New York: The Council on International and Public Affairs, 1986), pp. 40-41.
24. Ibid.
25. Malcolm Gladwell, "American vs. Indian Value of Life Molded Bhopal Suit Strategy," *Dallas Times Herald*, 19 February, 1989, p. A-6.
26. Ibid.
27. Norman, James "A New Union Carbide is Slowly Starting to Gel," *Business Week* April 18, 1988, pp. 68-69.
28. Helm, "Bhopal, a Year Later," p. 97.
29. J. Nolan, "Insurers Bear Brunt of Bhopal," *The Journal of Commerce*, 6 January 1986, pp. 1, 12.
30. Ward Morehouse and M. Arun Subramaniam, The Bhopal Tragedy, pp. 81-83.
31. Wil Lepkowski, "Efforts Toward Settlement Pick Up Steam," *Chemical and Engineering News*, 15 September 1986, pp. 14-15.
32. Meier, "India Says a Union Engineer Was Responsible," p. 10.
33. Lepkowski, "Efforts Toward Settlement," p. 14.
34. Sanjay Hazarika, "Bhopal Payments by Union Carbide Set at $470 Million," *The New York Times*, 15 February 1989, p. 1.
35. "More Sought in Bhopal Settlement," *Dallas Times Herald*, 24 February 1989, p. A-8.

36. Sanjay Hazarika, "Bhopal Payments."
37. Sheila Tefft and Siddharth Dube, "Settlement Is Reached on Bhopal," *The Washington Post*, 15 February 1989, p. 1.
38. Wayne Beissert and Andrea Stone, "Lawyers: Bhopal Victims to Get Little," *USA Today*, 15 February 1989, p. 1.
39. Paul Richter, "$470-Million Settlement for Bhopal OKd," *Los Angeles Times*, 15 February 1989, p. 1.
40. Ibid., p. 13
41. "More Sought in Bhopal Settlement."
42. Stephen J. Adler, "New Litigation Is Imperiling Bhopal-Disaster Settlement," *The Wall Street Journal*, 22 June 1989, pp. B1, B4.
43. Malcolm Gladwell, "Settlement Won't Hurt Carbide: Insurer, Fund Will Pay Most of Costs," *The Washington Post*, 15 February 1989, pp. D1, D5.
44. Andrea Stone, "Union Carbide up $2 after Bhopal Settlement," *USA Today*, 15 February 1989, p. 3B.
45. Union Carbide Corporation, *Bhopal Fact Sheet*, January 2000.
46. Malcolm Gladwell, "American vs. Indian Value of Life Molded Bhopal Suit Strategy."
47. Ibid, p. A-7.
48. Wayne Beissert and Andrea Stone, "Lawyers: Bhopal Victims to Get Little," p. 4A.
49. Malcolm Gladwell, "Settlement Won't Hurt Carbide: Insurer, Fund Will Pay Most of Costs," p. D5.
50. Stephen Lebatan, "Bhopal Outcome: Trial Is Avoided," *The New York Times*, 15 February 1989, p. D3.
51. Paul Richter, "$470-Million Settlement for Bhopal OKd," p. 13.
52. Stephen Lebatan, "Bhopal Outcome: Trial Is Avoided."
53. Malcolm Gladell, "Settlement Won't Hurt Carbige: Insurer, Fund Will Pay Most of Costs," p. D 5.
54. James Flanigan, "Bhopal a Hard Lesson in Value of Safety Rules," *Los Angeles Times*, 15 February 1989, pp. IV-1, IV-9.

Suggested Readings

Adler, Stephen J. "New Litigation Is Imperiling Bhopal-Disaster Settlement." *The Wall Street Journal*, 22 June 1989, pp. B1, B4.

Beissert, Wayne, and Andrea Stone. "Lawyers: Bhopal Victims to Get Little." *USA Today*, 15 February 1989, p. 1.

Eichenwald, Kurt. "Lead Lawyers for Carbide Relieved by End of Case." *The New York Times*, 15 February 1989, p. D3.

Flanigan, James. "Bhopal a Hard Lesson in Value of Safety Rules." *Los Angeles Times*, 15 February 1989, pp. IV-1, IV-9.

Gladwell, Malcolm. ""American vs. Indian Value of Life Molded Bhopal Suit Strategy." *Dallas Times Herald*, 19 February, 1989, p. A-6.

———. "Settlement Won't Hurt Carbide: Insurer, Fund Will Pay Most of Costs." *The Washington Post*, 15 February 1989, pp. D1, D5.

Hazarika, Sanjay. ""Bhopal Payments by Union Carbide Set at $470 Million." *The New York Times*, 15 February 1989, p. 1.

Helm, L. "Bhopal, a Year Later: Union Carbide Takes a Tougher Line." *Business Week*, 25 November 1985, pp. 96-101.

Hicks, Jonathan P. "After Bhopal, the Company Rebuilds." *The New York Times*, 15 February 1989, p. D3.

"Indian Court Orders Bhopal Settlement," *Dallas Times Herald*, 14 February 1989, pp. A-1, A-8.

Kirkland, R. I., Jr. "Union Carbide: Coping with Catastrophe." *Fortune*, 7 January 1985, pp. 50-53.

Lebatan, Stephen. ""Bhopal Outcome: Trial Is Avoided." *The New York Times*, 15 February 1989, p. D3.

McMurray, Scott. "Wounded Giant: Union Carbide Offers Some Sober Lessons in Crisis Management, " *The Wall Street Journal*, 28 January 1992, p.1.

Meier, B. "India Says a Union Engineer Was Responsible for Bhopal Site Design." The Wall Street Journal, 8 January 1987, pp. 10.

Miller, M. "Two Years After Bhopal's Gas Disaster—Lingering Effects Still Plague Its People." *The Wall Street Journal*, 5 December 1986, p. 34.

Morehouse, Ward, and M. Arun Subramaniam. *The Bhopal Tragedy: What Really Happened and What It Means for American Workers and Communities at Risk, A Preliminary Report for the Citizens Commission on Bhopal.* New York: The Council on International and Public Affairs, 1986.

"More Sought in Bhopal Settlement." *Dallas Times Herald*, 24 February 1989, p. A-8.

Nolan, J.""Insurers Bear Brunt of Bhopal." *The Journal of Commerce*, 6 January 1986, pp. 1, 12.

Richter, Paul.""$470-Million Settlement for Bhopal OKd." *Los Angeles Times*, 15 February 1989, p. 1.

Ritcher, Paul. "Settlement Leaves Bhopal Mystery Unresolved." *Los Angeles Times*, 15 February 1989, p. IV-1.

Stone, Andrea. "Union Carbide up $2 after Bhopal Settlement." *USA Today*, 15 February 1989, p. 3B.

Tefft, Sheila, and Siddharth Dube. "Settlement Is Reached on Bhopal." *The Washington Post*, 15 February 1989, p. 1.

Tripathi, S."After Bhopal." *Canadian Forum*, December 1985, pp. 12-14.

Varma, Vijaya Shankar. "Bhopal: The Unfolding of a Tragedy." *Alternatives*, July 1986, pp. 133-145.

Visvanathan, Shiv. "Bhopal: The Imagination of a Disaster." *Alternatives*, July 1986, pp. 147-165.

GLOSSARY

Absolute advantage
A theory developed by Adam Smith that states that two countries could benefit from trade if, due to natural or acquired endowment, they could provide each other with a product cheaper than they could produce it at home.

Absolute version of the purchasing power parity (PPP) theory
A version of the PPP theory, postulating that the equilibrium exchange rate between the currency of two nations is equal to the ratio of their general price levels. This version of the PPP theory should be rejected.

Absorption approach to devaluation
An approach that emphasizes income effects and suggests that domestic expenditure must decline relative to income for devaluation or depreciation to improve the balance of payments.

Accommodating (below-the-line) items
Transactions that are viewed as items that could be used to finance the balance of payments surplus or deficit.

Ad valorem tariff
A tariff expressed in terms of a percentage of the total value of a commodity. For example, 10 percent of the value of baseball gloves, or 20 percent of the value of plywood imported.

Adjustable peg system
The system by which a country may change its par value in order to correct its fundamental disequilibrium.

Adjustment policies
Specific measures adopted by a government with the primary objective of resolving a balance of payments disequilibrium.

Advanced countries
See Developed countries.

Advanced-deposit requirements (ADR)
A requirement, employed mostly by developing countries, demanding that importers make an advance deposit in a commercial bank for a fraction of the value of imported commodities. The deposit is made for a given period of time at no interest.

Andean Common Market (ANCOM)
A common market that was established by Bolivia, Colombia, Chile, Ecuador, and Peru in 1969. Venezuela joined this market in 1973, and Chile left in 1976. This market is a subgroup of the Latin American Free Trade Association, and its main policy is to restrict foreign-owned investment.

Antidumping argument
An argument for protection stating, that because dumping a product into a country puts that country's import-competing firms at a disadvantage, it is justifiable to impose a remedial tariff to offset the dumper's price advantage.

Applied technology
The transformation of general basic technology into new products and processes applicable to a specific firm.

Appreciation
A decrease in the exchange rate (prices of foreign currencies in terms of the domestic currency) in a floating exchange rate system.

Appropriability theory
A foreign direct investment stating that multinational corporations prefer to produce sophisticated technologies instead of simple ones, because they are more successful in appropriating returns from these technologies.

Appropriate technology
A technology that fits the economic and social environment of a specific country.

Arbitrage
The simultaneous purchase of foreign exchange in one market, where it is cheaper, and sale in another market, where it is more expensive, to profit from differences in spot exchange rate.

Association of Southern Asian Nations (ASEAN)
A major trading association among developing countries, established by Indonesia, Malaysia, the Philippines, Singapore, and Thailand in 1967.

Autarky
The absence of trade.

Automatic adjustment mechanism
An adjustment mechanism that corrects a balance of payments disequilibrium on its own without any government intervention.

Automatic income adjustment mechanism
An adjustment mechanism that works through induced changes in national incomes of surplus and deficit nations to bring about adjustment in the balance of payments.

Automatic price adjustment mechanism
An adjustment mechanism that works through price changes in deficit and surplus nations to correct a balance of payments disequilibrium.

Autonomous (above-the-line) items
Transactions that take place for their own sake, irrespective of balance of payments position, including all transactions that respond to business conditions at home and abroad.

Backward integration
Expansion of a firm's operations into a supplier's market.

Baker Plan
A plan presented in 1985 by James Baker, the U.S. Secretary of the Treasury, to deal with the debt crisis of developing nations. The plan emphasized growth over austerity in developing countries, based on funds generated by trade surplus nations, the International Monetary Fund, the World Bank, the Inter-American Development Bank, and the commercial banks.

Balance of payments (BOP)
An accounting statement that shows the summary of all transactions between the residents of one nations and the residents of all other nations during a given period of time (usually a calendar year).

Balance of trade argument
An argument for protection stating that tariffs or quotas are necessary because they encourage a favorable balance of trade, that is, a surplus of exports over imports.

Bank acceptance
A bill of exchange that has been accepted by a bank.

Bank draft
Similar to a commercial bill of exchange, a written order by a drawer to a drawee instructing him or her to pay on demand or at a certain date a specified amount of money to a payee. The major difference between the two financial instruments is that in the case of a bank draft, the drawee is a bank rather than an importer.

Behavioral criterion
A criterion used to define a multinational corporation as a firm whose top management "thinks internationally."

Bilateral agreement
An agreement between two countries concerning the quantities and terms of a specific transaction.

Bilateral or multilateral export quota
An export quota that is established by agreement between the trading nations.

Bilateral or multilateral quota
A quota that is imposed by an importing country after consultation or negotiation with the exporting country.

Bill of lading
A document that provides evidence that a commodity was shipped.

Black market
An unregulated market that allows foreign currency transactions to take place at unofficial rates.

Brady Plan
A plan proposed by Nicholas Brady, former U.S. Secretary of the Treasury, to deal with the developing countries' debt crisis. The Brady Plan enhanced the Baker Plan by augmenting the debt reduction and multilaterally financed loan guarantees.

Brain drain
The migration of highly skilled workers from developing countries to advanced countries.

Bretton Woods System
An international monetary system established in 1944 by agreements between the United States, Great Britain, and 42 other nations who met at Bretton Woods, New Hampshire.

Bulk purchasing
An agreement to purchase a given amount of a good for a period of one year or several years.

Buy back
A form of countertrade that involves the export of a technology package, the construction of an entire project, or provision of services by a firm.

Cable transfer
An order that is transmitted by a bank in one country to its foreign correspondent in another country instructing the corresponding bank to pay out a specific amount of money to a designated person or account.

Capital account
Part of a country's balance of payments accounts; includes those transactions that involve future obligations. These transactions include: investing in foreign nations; providing loans to foreigners; and depositing money in foreign banks.

Capital flight
The transfer of funds from one nation to another by firms or individuals. This occurs when the expected returns from keeping funds abroad are higher or more secure than keeping them at home.

Capital flow controls
Restrictions imposed on capital inflows (imports) and capital outflows (exports) when a nation faces a balance of payments disequilibrium.

Capital inflow
An increase in foreign assets within a country, or a decrease in a country's assets abroad.

Capital outflow
An increase in a country's assets abroad, or a decrease in foreign assets within a country.

Caribbean Free Trade Association (CARIFTA)
A major trade association among developing countries established in 1968 by Antigua, Barbados, Bolivia, Colombia, Dominica, Ecuador, Grenada, Guyana, Jamaica, Montserrat, Peru, St. Lucia, St. Vincent, Trinidad, Tobago, and Venezuela. In 1973, this was changed into the Caribbean Common Market (CARICOM) and was extended to include the Bahamas, Belize, and St. Kitts-Nevis-Angullia.

Central American Common Market (CACM)
A customs union established by Costa Rica, El Salvador, Guatemala, Honduras, and Nicaragua in 1960.

Centralized cartel
A cartel that operates as a single profit maximizing monopolist.

Commercial bill of exchange
A written order by an exporter (the drawer) to an importer (the drawee) instructing the importer to pay on demand or at a certain date a specified amount of money to a designated party (the payee).

Commercial controls
See Direct controls.

Commodity terms of trade
A ratio portraying the relationship between the price a nation pays for its imports and acquires for its exports. Commodity terms of trade is calculated by dividing a nation's exports price index by its import price index. Also referred to as net barter terms of trade.

Common market
A more complete form of customs union combining the characteristics of a customs union with the elimination of barriers on the movement of capital and labor among member countries.

Community indifference curve
A curve that is the locus of points representing combinations of two goods that give the same level of satisfaction to the community or nation. Community indifference curves are convex to the origin, have negative slopes, and do not intersect.

Comparative advantage
A theory first presented by David Ricardo that two nations can benefit from trade even when one of the nations has an absolute advantage in the production of all commodities.

Compensating (reserve) account
Part of a country's balance of payments accounts; includes a nation's holdings of foreign convertible currencies, gold, and special drawing rights that are used by its monetary authorities to intervene in the foreign exchange market to resolve balance of payments problems.

Compound tariff
A tariff that includes a specific portion and an ad valorem portion.

Concerted lending
A tactful terminology for lending, describing often involuntary bank lending to developing nations during the first phase of the debt crisis. Under this arrangement, banks had to contribute new money in proportion to their loan exposure.

Constant opportunity costs
The relative cost of one product that is constant in terms of another product. Under constant costs, a nation's transformation cost is a straight line.

Constant return to scale
The production condition whereby doubling of all factor inputs results in doubling the output of a specific commodity.

Consumer surplus
The difference between what a buyer pays for a good and the maximum amount that he or she would have been willing to pay for that good.

Consumption distortion loss of a tariff
See Consumption effect of a tariff.

Consumption effect of a tariff
A loss resulting from domestic consumption due to a rise in the import price following imposition of a tariff.

Council of Mutual Economic Assistance (CMEA or COMECON)
An organization formed in January 1949 by the former Soviet Union and the former communist bloc countries in Eastern Europe. Besides the Soviet Union, the original members of the council included Bulgaria, Czechoslovakia, Hungary, Poland, and Rumania. Late in 1949, Albania and East Germany joined the council. In 1962, Mongolia and Cuba joined, and Albania withdrew. The purpose of the council was to divert trade away from Western market economies and achieve a higher level of self-sufficiency among its members.

Countertrade
The process by which an importing nation imposes conditions linking imports to exports and, as a result, minimizes its net outflow of foreign exchange.

Crawling peg system
An exchange rate system under which the par rate changes frequently but by very small amounts each time. Changes take place at clearly specified periods, such as every year, until the desired exchange rate is achieved, correcting the balance of payments of disequilibrium.

Credit items
Those items in the balance of payments that involve the receipt of payments from foreigners. These items give a nation more foreign currencies or reduce a foreign nation's holdings of domestic currency. They include exports of goods and services, unilateral transfers received from foreigners, and capital inflows.

Credit swap
An arrangement between a firm and a foreign central or commercial bank to exchange one currency for another, reversing the exchange at a future date.

Culture
A set of beliefs, values, attitudes, and practices held by a group of people who live in a given environment.

Currency swap
An arrangement between two firms to exchange one currency for another, reversing the exchange at a future date.

Current account
Part of a country's balance of payments accounts; includes those transactions that do not result in any future obligations. These transactions include: purchases of goods and services from foreigners; and unilateral transfers, that is, remittances and grants given to foreigners for free.

Customs union
An organization that allows the lowering or abolishment of trade barriers between member countries and adopts a unified system of tariffs against nonmembers.

Debit items
Those items in the balance of payments that involve payments to foreigners. These are transactions that use up a nation's foreign currencies or increase foreign holdings of the domestic currency. They include imports of goods and services, unilateral transfers given to foreigners, and capital outflows.

Debt-equity swaps
Methods used to transform some of an existing debt to equity.

Debt-service ratio
A ratio showing the payments of interest on total debt plus amortization as a percentage of total exports.

Decision lag of a devaluation
The period of time it takes to constitute new business relationships and set new orders, following a devaluation.

Demand lag of a devaluation
The time needed to develop a demand for newly exported goods.

Delivery lag of a devaluation
The lag between the time new orders are set and their effects are seen on trade and expenditure patterns.

Dependency theory
A theory that attributes the sluggishness of economic growth and development in developing nations to their dependent relationships on advanced countries.

Depreciation
An increase in the exchange rate (price of foreign currencies in terms of the domestic currency) in a floating exchange rate system.

Destabilizing speculation
The sale of a foreign currency when its domestic price falls, in anticipation that it will decrease even more in the future. Destabilizing speculation also refers to the purchase of a foreign currency when its domestic price rises, in anticipation that it will increase even more in the future.

Devaluation
A deliberate increase in the foreign exchange rate (the price of foreign currencies in terms of the domestic currency) by a country's monetary authorities from one pegged or fixed level to another.

Developed countries
The industrialized market economies of Western Europe, North America, South Africa, Australia, and New Zealand.

Developing countries
See Third-world countries.

Direct controls
See Selective expenditure switching policies.

Diversification argument
An argument for protection stating that countries that are dependent on a single commodity for their economic survival should follow protectionist policies to encourage the establishment of different industries.

Documentary-acceptance (D/A) draft
A draft that provides for the release of supplementary documents to an importer upon his or her acceptance of the draft. These documents give the importer the right to claim the imported goods at the port of entry.

Documentary-on-payments (D/P) Draft
A draft that provides for the release of supplementary documents to an importer upon his or her payment of the draft. These documents give the importer the right to claim the imported goods at the port of entry.

Domestic distortion argument
An argument for protection based on the theory of the second best. According to this theory, if the presence of distortion in an economy prevents the achievement of pareto optimality, it may be justifiable for the government to employ policies that add more distortions (such as tariffs).

Domestic marketing board (DMB)
An agency that is set up by a developing country's government. The objective of this agency is to maintain price stability for individual producers in a developing country.

Domestic production argument
An argument for protection stating that domestic producers have rights to the domestic market. The protection of these rights requires reduction or abolishment of imports.

Domestic production subsidy
A subsidy granted to the domestic producers of an import-competing good in order to increase domestic production of that good and decrease imports.

Double factoral terms of trade
The ratio of the price index of a nation's exports to the price index of its imports times the ratio of its export productivity index to the import productivity index times 100. Double factoral terms of trade indicate how many units of foreign factors of production contained in a country's imports are exchanged per unit of domestic factors of production contained in its exports.

Dumping
The practice of selling a commodity in a foreign market at below cost or at a cheaper price than that charged in the domestic market.

East African Community (EAC)
A major trade association among developing countries established by Kenya, Tanzania, and Uganda in 1967. Due to the ideological, economic, and political upheavals in Uganda, this association lost its effectiveness and was dissolved in 1977.

Eclectic theory of international production
A theory stating that for a multinational corporation to invest abroad three advantages must be present: firm-specific advantages, internalization advantages, and location-specific advantages. Accordingly, it is not the possession of knowledge alone that gives the corporation a competitive edge over its rivals, but its willingness to internalize this knowledge rather than sell it.

Economic Community of West African Nations (ECOWAS)
A major trade association among developing countries established by the Treaty of Lagos (Nigeria) which was signed in May 1975. Its membership includes the following 16 countries: Benin, Burkina Faso, Cape Verde Islands, Cote d'Ivoire, Gambia, Ghana, Guinea, Guinea-Bissau, Liberia, Mali, Mauritania, Niger, Nigeria, Senegal, Sierra Leone, and Togo.

Economic exposure
The risk resulting from the total impact of fluctuating exchange rates on a multinational corporation's profitability.

Economic integration
An agreement among nations to decrease or eliminate trade barriers. Depending on the terms and intensity of agreements, economic integration can be classified as a preferential trade arrangement, a free trade area, a customs union, a common market, or an economic union.

Economic union
The most complete form of economic integration. This kind of integration goes one step further than a common market and calls for harmonization or unification of the fiscal, monetary, and tax policies of the member nations.

Edge Act
An act passed in 1919 in the United States that permitted the organization of the "Edge Act Corporation" of U.S. banks. This allowed Edge Act corporations of U.S. banks to engage in banking activities that were not permitted in foreign countries' local markets.

Effective exchange rate
The exchange rate that measures the value of a given currency in terms of the weighted average of a basket of major currencies. The rate considers factors such as the size of trade flows and the relevant price elasticities of exchange rate changes.

Effective rate of protection
The percentage increase in the domestic value added of a product as the result of tariffs.

Elasticity approach to devaluation
An approach that stresses the price effect of devaluation and proposes that devaluation or depreciation operates primarily when elasticities are high.

Elasticity optimism
A belief, stemming from the empirical studies started in the 1960s, that demand elasticities are high. As a result, according to the Marshall-Lerner condition, a devaluation improves a country's balance of trade.

Elasticity pessimism
A conviction, stemming from the empirical studies of the 1930s and 1940s, that demand elasticities are low. As a result, according to the Marshall-Lerner condition, a devaluation does not improve a country's balance of trade.

Employment-protection argument
An argument for protection stating that the imposition of tariffs or other forms of import restrictions is desirable in periods of unemployment because they reduce imports and stimulate domestic production. Increased domestic production, in turn, leads to a reduction in unemployment.

Engine of growth
The idea that export-led growth in Great Britain and several now-industrial nations propelled their economies into rapid growth and development.

Equalization of production costs argument
An argument for protection that calls for the imposition of a "scientific tariff," that is, a tariff specifically devised to neutralize the cost advantage enjoyed by foreign producers of a tariffed product.

Erroneous arguments for protection
Those arguments that are not based on economic reasoning, but hinge on nationalistic fervor and emotion. The domestic production, prevent-money-outflow, wage protection, and equalization of production costs arguments are conventional erroneous arguments.

Errors and omissions (statistical discrepancy)
An item incorporated into the balance of payments to make the sum of debit items equal to the sum of credit items.

Eurocurrencies
Currencies that are deposited outside their country of origin.

Eurocurrency market
The market where eurocurrencies are transacted.

European Common Market (ECM)
See European Union.

European Community (EC)
See European Union.

European Economic Community (EEC)
See European Union.

European Exchange Rate Mechanism (ERM)
Exchange rate mechanism that fixes exchange rates among the currencies of European Union—member countries. *See* also Joint floating exchange rate system.

European snake
The decision of the original six members of the European Union to let their currencies float jointly against the U.S. dollar within a range of 2.25 percent around the par value.

European Monetary Corporation Fund (EMCF)
A corporation established by the European Union to allocate European Currency Units (ECUs) to member nations in return for 20 percent of their gold and dollar reserves.

European Monetary System (EMS)
An organization formed by the European Union in 1979 to provide "closer monetary cooperation leading to a zone of monetary stability in Europe."

European Union (EU)
Previously referred to as the European Community (EC), the European Economic Community (ECC), and the European Common Market (ECM). The EU provides an example of a customs union that developed into a common market and, in 1994, was evolving into an economic union. The EU was formed in 1958 by Belgium, France, Italy, Luxembourg, West Germany, and the Netherlands. In 1973, Denmark, Ireland, and Great Britain joined; Greece joined in 1981; and Portugal and Spain joined in 1986.

Exchange controls
Limitations set on the supply of foreign exchange to potential buyers. Exchange controls can be carried out at a single official rate or at multiple exchange rates.

Exchange rate
See Foreign exchange rate.

Excise tax
A sales tax that is collectable when a good enters through customs.

Expatriate
A person working in another country other than his or her own.

Expenditure-adjusting policies
Policies that affect aggregate demand and include both fiscal and monetary policies.

Export instability
Short-run oscillations in export prices and revenues. The factors giving rise to export instability can be classified as price variability and a high degree of commodity concentration.

Export quota
See Quota.

Export subsidy
A subsidy granted to domestic producers of an export industry to enhance its exports, increasing its foreign exchange earnings.

External balance
The goal of equilibrium in a country's balance of payments.

External diseconomy
An externality that imposes costs on third parties. Pollution is an example of external diseconomy.

External economy
An externality that induces gains for third parties. The Apple blossoms of an apple orchardist which provides nectar to the bees of a neighboring beekeeper, provides an example of external economy.

Externality
Effects of a firm's production of a good on external parties that are not reckoned in the production decision. Externality can be divided into external economy and external diseconomy.

Factor-price equalization theorem
A theory deduced from the Heckscher-Ohlin theory. According to this theorem, free international trade leads to equalization of both goods prices and factor prices.

Firm-specific advantages
Advantages that result from tangible and intangible resources that are owned by a firm. These resources, exclusive to the firm, enables a firm to have a comparative advantage over other firms. Also referred to as ownership-specific advantages.

First oil shock
Oil price increases in 1973—1974.

Fixed exchange rate system
An exchange rate system in which the exchange rate is fixed and can only fluctuate within a very limited band.

Foreign direct investment (FDI)
An investment that results in control of a firm by the investor. This can involve an investment in equity securities that is large enough to exert effective control over the firm.

Foreign exchange instruments
Written or printed financial documents that allow the payments of funds from one country and one currency to another country and another currency. Chief among these instruments are cable (telegraphic) transfers, commercial bills of exchange (commercial drafts), bank drafts, and letters of credit.

Foreign exchange market
A market within which individuals, business firms, and banks purchase and sell foreign currencies and other debt instruments.

Foreign exchange rate
The price of one currency in terms of another measured by: the price of the foreign currency in terms of the domestic currency; or the price of the domestic currency in terms of the foreign currency.

Foreign exchange risk exposure
The risk resulting from fluctuations in the values of the currencies used in evaluating multinational corporations' assets, liabilities, and profits.

Foreign trade multiplier (k')
The ratio of a change in income to change in export and/or investment; $k' = 1/(MPS + MPM)$.

Forward integration
Extension of a firm's activities into a buyer's market.

Forward market
A type of foreign exchange market in which foreign currencies are purchased and sold for future delivery.

Four Dragons
See Gang of Four.

Franchisee
The receiver of rights to produce a product or use a name, trademark, or copyright.

Franchising
A form of licensing; includes permission to produce a product or use a name, trademark, or copyright. A franchiser, that is, the supplier of the rights, receives a franchise right fee and royalties.

Free trade area
An agreement between nations that removes trade barriers among members, while allowing each nation to define its own barriers on trade with nonmembers.

Freely fluctuating exchange rate system
An exchange rate system in which the exchange rate is set by the free market forces of demand and supply.

Gang of Four
A term used facetiously to refer to the group of four East Asian countries of South Korea, Hong Kong, Taiwan, and Singapore. As a group, these newly industrialized countries have achieved impressive economic performance. Also called Four Dragons.

General Agreement on Tariffs and Trade (GATT)
An organization created to promote freer international trade. Established in 1947 by 23 countries, including the United States, GATT has expanded over the years. In early 1994, it had 117 contracting parties from virtually all the advanced countries, many developing countries, and several former communist countries in Eastern Europe. An updated version of GATT is now part of WTO.

General Agreement to Borrow (GAB)
An agreement negotiated within the framework of the International Monetary Fund in 1962 and renewed in 1979. Accordingly, the group of ten advanced countries (Belgium, Canada, France, Germany, Great Britain, Italy, Japan, the Netherlands, Sweden, and the United States) consented to loan up to $6 billion to any member of the group experiencing huge short-term capital outflows.

General expenditure switching policies
Changes in exchange rates by means of devaluation and revaluation of a nation's currency.

Gold bullion standard
A monetary standard similar to the gold coin standard. Under this system, a nation's unit of currency was defined in terms of a fixed weight of gold. However, unlike the gold coin standard, gold did not circulate within the domestic economy. Thus, the impact of gold on the monetary system was largely neutralized, that is, gold was demonetized.

Gold coin standard
A monetary standard that defined a country's unit of currency in terms of a fixed weight of gold. Gold metals were permitted to be exported or imported without any restriction, and the national currency and gold could be converted to each other at the defined rate. There were no restrictions imposed on the coinage of the gold, and gold coins were considered full legal tender for all debts.

Guest workers
A term used by European Union members to refer to foreign workers.

Heckscher-Ohlin (H-O) theory
A theory holding that each country should export those commodities that use its abundant factor most intensively and import goods that use its scarce factor most intensively.

Hedging
Making sure that one neither owns nor owes a foreign currency. Hedging can take place in either a spot market or a forward market.

Horizontal integration
A merger of firms that are producing similar products under one ownership.

Imitation lag
A concept introduced by Posner in 1973 to elaborate on the possibility of international trade between two nations. The lag is divided into two components: demand lag and reaction lag. *See* Demand lag; Reaction lag.

Immiserizing growth
An expansion of factor supply or productivity that makes a nation worse off when it exports the goods it specializes in producing.

Import quota
See Quota.

Income terms of trade
The ratio of the price index of a nation's exports to the price index of its imports times its export volume index. Income terms of trade indicate a country's export-generated capacity to import.

Increasing opportunity costs
The increasing amount of one good that a nation must sacrifice to produce an additional unit of another good. Under opportunity costs, a nation's transformation curve is concave to the origin.

Indifference map
An entire set of indifference curves.

Individual's indifference curve
A curve that is the locus of points representing combinations of two goods that give the same level of satisfaction to the individual consumer. Individual indifference curves are convex to the origin, have negative slopes, and do not intersect.

Industry
A group of firms that produce products and services that are close substitutes for each other.

Infant industry argument
An argument for protection stating that because a new and underdeveloped industry cannot survive competition from abroad, it should be protected temporarily with high tariffs and quotas on imported goods.

Infant government argument
An argument for protection stating that a nation that is young and has no alternative means of raising needed funds for its economic development could revert to import and/or export duties as a crucial source of public revenue.

Interest equalization tax (IET)
An excise tax introduced in the United States in 1963 and eliminated in 1974. It imposed a tax on the purchase of foreign securities by U.S. citizens, discouraging the outflow of funds from the United States to foreign countries.

Internal balance
The goal of full employment with price stability in a nation's economy.

Internalization advantages
Advantages that result from a firm's desire and ability to internalize (use) its specific advantages, rather than externalizing (selling) them through licensing, management contracts, and so on.

International banking
Those banking activities that cross national boundaries, facilitating the flow of money between different countries.

International buffer stock agreement
An agreement that calls for the establishment of an international agency by producing nations (often joined by consuming nations) to limit commodity price swings.

International business
Those business transactions among individuals, firms, or other entities (both private and public) that occur across national boundaries.

International cartel
An organization composed of firms in the same industry from different countries who agree to limit their outputs and exports in order to influence the prices of commodities and maximize their profits.

International commodity agreements (ICAs)
Agreements between producing and consuming countries to stabilize and increase the prices and revenues of their exports.

International Development Association (IDA)
One of the two major supporting institutions of the World Bank created in 1960 to make "soft loans," that is, loans on much easier terms than the World Bank would normally make.

International export quota agreement
An agreement among producing nations to regulate the quantity of a good exported by a country in order to stabilize its price.

International economics
Like other economics subjects, international economics is the study of the allocation of scarce resources to satisfy human alternative wants. However, the distinctive feature of international economics is that it approaches this basic problem at the international level, as opposed to the national level.

International Finance Corporation (IFC)
One of the two major supporting institutions of the World Bank established in July 1956 to provide capital and man-

agerial assistance to private businesses in developing countries.

International investment position (IIP)

A statement that presents the total amount and distribution of a country's foreign assets at given points in time (the end of a year). Also referred to as the balance of international indebtedness.

International monetary system

The rules, procedures, customs instruments, and organizational setting that provide a workable system of international payments between different countries and facilitates international trade among them.

International price discrimination

See Persistent dumping.

International reserves.

Foreign exchange and other assets that act as international mediums of exchange and are set aside (reserved) by a nation in settling its balance of payments deficit.

J-curve effect

A curve showing that with devaluation or depreciation the trade balance worsens before it gets better. The shape of the letter "J" corresponds to the initial worsening of the trade balance before the forthcoming improvements take place.

Joint floating exchange rate system

An exchange rate system in which currencies of member nations are tied closely to each other but are allowed to fluctuate against a given currency. This system was adopted by the six original members of the European Union in March 1972 and was referred to as the European exchange rate mechanism (ERM).

Joint venture

A corporate entity that is created between a multinational corporation and other parties under a host country's law.

Kennedy Round

The multilateral trade negotiations formally opened in 1964 and concluded in 1967. This round led to agreement for the reduction of tariff rates on industrial products by a total of 35 percent from their 1962 level, with tariffs to be phased out in five years.

Latin American Free Trade Association (LAFTA)

A free trade association established by Argentina, Bolivia, Brazil, Chile, Colombia, Ecuador, Mexico, Paraguay, Peru, Uruguay, and Venezuela in 1960. This association was relatively successful in extending tariff reductions to its members until the mid-1960s. Following that date, however, the nationalist views of some of its members made further tariff reductions difficult. In 1980, the members of LAFTA signed a treaty to form a new association called the Latin American Integration Association (LAIA). This association established new objectives for tariff reductions and other policies that are to be followed in integrating the economies of its members.

Latin American Integration Association

See Latin American Free Trade Association.

Leading and lagging

An intracompany transfer in which fund transfers are deliberately timed so as to delay (lag) some payments or accelerate (lead) other payments.

Leontief Paradox

An empirical study suggesting that the United States export goods that are relatively labor intensive and import goods that are capital intensive. This is contrary to the Heckscher-Ohlin theory which predicts that, as a capital-abundant nation, the United States should export capital-intensive commodities.

Less developed countries (LDCs)

See Third-world countries.

Letter of credit

A document issued by an importer's bank declaring that payments will be made to an exporter regarding a specific shipment of commodities, accompanied by the shipment documents.

Licensee

A firm that receives know-how and the right to manufacture in a host country.

Licensing

An agreement through which production is performed by a firm in a host country.

Licensor

The supplier of technology, a brand name, the right to patents or copyrights, or management services to another firm which produces the product in a foreign country.

Linder thesis

See Theory of overlapping demand.

Location-specific advantages

The existence of some natural resources, or perhaps a low-cost labor force, in a foreign country that makes it profitable for a firm to locate its production facilities in that country instead of at home.

London Interbank offered rate (LIBOR)

The rate of interest used between banks when they provide Eurocurrency loans to each other.

Maastricht Treaty

A treaty providing the blueprint for monetary union and closer cooperation among European Union members.

Managed floating exchange rate

The exchange rate system that has been in effect since March 1973. Under this system, the exchange rate of a currency is determined by the market forces of demand and supply. However, a nation is allowed to intervene in the market to smooth out short-run fluctuations without trying to change the long-run pattern of the exchange rate.

Management contract

An arrangement by which a company provides managerial assistance to another company in return for a fee.

Marginal propensity to consume (MPC)

The ratio of change in consumption (;tdC) to change in income (;tdY), or ;tdC/;tdY.

Marginal propensity to import (MPI)

The ratio of change in imports (;tdM) to change in income (;tdY), or ;tdM/;tdY.

Marginal propensity to save (MPS)

The ratio of a change in saving (;tdS) to a change in income (;tdY), or ;tdS/;tdY.

Marginal rate of substitution (MRS)

The rate at which commodities are substituted for each other by an individual or nation while keeping the level of satisfaction unchanged. In other words, MRS shows the amount of a good that an individual or nation must give up in exchange for an additional unit of another good and still enjoy the same level of satisfaction. This is shown by the slope of the individual's (community) indifference curve at the point of consumption and decreases as the individual (nation) continues to substitute one good for another.

Marginal rate of transformation (MRT)

The amount of a good that a nation must forgo to produce each additional unit of another good. In other words, the opportunity cost of a good measured in terms of another good. This is measured by the absolute value of the slope of the transformation curve.

Marine insurance certificate

A document showing that shipped merchandise has insurance coverage.

Market imperfection theory

A theory asserting that a multinational corporation's decision to undertake foreign direct investment stems from its desire to capitalize on certain advantages that are not available to domestic firms operating in the host country.

Marshall-Lerner condition

A general rule used to assess actual devaluation or depreciation. According to this rule, if the sum of the price elasticities of demand for imports and the demand for exports is greater than one in absolute value, devaluation or depreciation would improve the balance of trade. If the sum is less than one, devaluation or depreciation would worsen the balance of trade. If the sum is equal to one, devaluation or depreciation would not affect the balance of trade.

Maquiladoras

Manufacturing plants located along the U.S.—Mexican border. These plants assemble components that are produced in the United States and shipped to Mexico duty-free. The assembled components are then shipped back to the United States for resale.

Marxist theory

The theory that three stages of capitalist enterprise development eventually results in monopolization of capital, which in turn leads to an economic system that is controlled by "finance capital." When this happens, the economy has reached the highest and final stage of capitalism—capitalistic imperialism—in which multinational corporations come into existence.

Mercantilism

A theory holding that wealth is a necessary condition for national power. National power is enhanced in turn by the increase in species (gold and silver). Thus, for a country that lacks gold and silver mines, the only means of acquiring gold and silver is by encouraging exports and discouraging imports.

Model

A means for explaining the relationship between different variables. Models can be presented in three different forms: tables, graphs, and equations.

Modes of technology transfer

Investment methods by which a multinational corporation transfers technology. Modes of technology transfer include exports of goods and services, licensing, turnkey operations, management contracts, franchises, joint ventures, and wholly-owned subsidiaries.

Monetary approach to devaluation

An approach that emphasizes the impact devaluation or depreciation has on the purchasing power of money balances and the ensuing effect on domestic expenditure amounts.

Most-favored nation (MFN)

A principle stating that changes in tariff rates agreed on between two GATT countries must also be applied to other GATT countries.

Multilateral agreements

A long-term contract that determines a minimum price at which importing countries guarantee to buy a specified quantity of a good.

Multinational corporation (MNC)

A group of corporations operating in different countries but controlled by a headquarters in a given country.

Multiple exchange rates

Separate official exchange rates assigned by a country for different commodities that it imports or exports.

Multiplier (k)

The ratio of change in income (ΔY) to change in investment (ΔI). in a closed economy, without government sector, this is shown by $k = 1/MPS$.

Mundell's assignment rule
A guideline for mixing monetary and fiscal policy stating that each policy instrument should be assigned to the target on which it has the most impact.

National security argument
An argument for protection stating that a country needs to impose tariffs on crucial goods that are needed for war and defense in order to promote their domestic production and ensure their continued availability.

Net barter terms of trade
See Commodity terms of trade.

New international economic order (NIEO)
Demands made by developing nations as a group at the United Nations for advanced countries to institute policies to improve international trading systems.

Newly industrialized countries (NICs)
Developing countries at a relatively advanced stage of economic development. Each of these countries has a substantial and active industrial sector that is integrated into the international trade, finance, and investment system. Such countries include Argentina, Brazil, Greece, Hong Kong, South Korea, Mexico, Portugal, Singapore, Spain, and Taiwan.

Nominal tariffs rates
Tariff rates published in a country's tariff schedule.

North American Free Trade Agreement (NAFTA)
Agreement reached in 1990 by U.S. and Mexican officials to negotiate a free trade area between the two nations. Later, Canada declared that it would participate in negotiations, setting the stage for the formation of NAFTA, the largest free trade area in the world, which was established August 12, 1992.

Offer curve
A curve indicating the relationship between a nation's exports and imports at different relative commodity prices. Each point on an offer curve shows the maximum (minimum) amount of its export (import) commodity that a nation is willing to offer (accept) in exchange for a certain amount of import (export) commodity at a given relative price level.

Opportunity cost
The value of the benefits foregone when one alternative is chosen over another.

Optimum tariff
A tariff rate that maximizes a nation's welfare.

Organization for Economic Cooperation and Development (OECD)
An organization that currently provides an important channel for multilateral cooperation in the world; established in Europe in 1961. Although most members of this organization are European, it also includes major industrial countries—Australia, Canada, Japan, New Zealand, and the United States.

Organization of Petroleum Exporting Countries (OPEC)
An international cartel formed in 1960. Today, it is composed of 12 oil-producing nations.

Ownership specific advantages
See Firm-specific advantages.

Pareto optimal
A social organization in which no one can be made better off without making someone else worse off.

Paris Club
An informal group of creditor governments who meet in the French Treasury to assure that all creditor governments grant comparable concessions to debtor nations. Paris Club granted debt relief to the poorest and most heavily indebted nations, such as nations in Sub-Saharan Africa.

Performance criterion
A criterion used to define multinational corporations on the basis of absolute amount or relative share of assets, number of employees, sales, or earnings in a foreign country.

Persistent dumping
Consistently selling a firm's product abroad at below cost or at lower prices than at home.

Prebisch theory
A theory stating that because world prices for primary products have been declining and unstable, the terms of trade for developing countries have deteriorated over time. Thus, developing countries should restrict their imports of industrial goods, replacing these imports with domestically produced goods.

Preferential trade arrangement
An agreement among participating nations for lowering trade barriers.

Portfolio investment
A financial investment that does not exert control over the assets of the firm in question. This can involve investment in debt securities (bonds) or small investment in equity security (stock in the firm).

Predatory dumping
The practice of pricing a product at below cost or at lower price than competitors charge for a similar product in order to weaken or drive the competitors out of the market.

Prevent-money-outflow argument
An argument for protection stating that imports of goods into a nation will result in an outflow of money from that nation. To stop such an outflow, the nation must resort to protectionism to substitute domestic production for imports.

Price-specie-flow mechanism
An automatic adjustment mechanism under the gold standard system. It functions by the surplus country gaining gold and

experiencing an increase in its money supply. This in turn increases domestic prices, stimulating imports and discouraging exports until the surplus is eliminated. A deficit is resolved by the opposite process.

Producer surplus
The difference between the amount a producer receives for a good and the minimum amount that he or she would have been willing to accept for that good.

Product life cycle
A theory pioneered by Raymond Vernon which holds that manufactured goods pass through a product life cycle composed of five stages: new, expansion, maturity, sales decline, and demise.

Production distortion loss of a tariff
See Production effect of a tariff.

Production effect of a tariff
A measure of the loss to a nation that is imposing a tariff. This loss results from wasted resources employed to produce additional domestic goods at increasing unit costs.

Production lag of a devaluation
The time period it takes to shift from supplying one market to supplying another or to enhance capacity to supply the added market.

Production possibilities frontier (curve)
A curve showing all possible combinations of two products that a country can produce with its available technology and full employment of all resources.

Protective tariff
A tax imposed on the importation of a foreign product with the intention of protecting the home industry from foreign competitors.

Purchasing power parity (PPP) theory
A theory stating that a given amount of money, when converted into different currencies, should buy the same basket of commodities in different nations.

Qualified arguments for protection
Arguments for protection that can be justified based on either noneconomic origin, such as national security, or the anticipation that long-run economic gains will more than offset the short-run protection costs. The infant industry, national security, diversification, and infant government arguments are traditional qualified arguments.

Questionable arguments for protection
Arguments for protection that are not totally erroneous, but exemplify poor policies that have abusive potentials. The antidumping, balance of trade, and employment protection arguments are typical questionable arguments.

Quota
A limitation set on the amount of a commodity that crosses national boundaries. Depending on whether a good is exported or imported, the quota is referred to as an export quota or an import quota.

Reaction lag
The time it takes for a local entrepreneur to react to competition from abroad by starting local production.

Real exchange rate
The nominal exchange rate divided by the ratio of the consumer price index in one country to the consumer price index in another country.

Reciprocal demand curve
See Offer curve

Recognition lag of a devaluation
The period of time it takes for buyers and sellers to become aware of changes in competitive position following a devaluation or depreciation.

Regulation Q
A regulation that imposed a ceiling on the interest rates U.S. banks could pay on time deposits.

Relative commodity prices
The price of one good divided by the price of another good. This measures the opportunity cost of the first good and is given by the absolute value of the slope of the transformation curve.

Relative version of the purchasing power parity (PPP) theory
A version of the PPP theory stating that the percentage change in the exchange rate between two nations' currencies over any time period is equal to the relative percentage change in their price levels. This version of the PPP theory has some validity.

Replacement lags of a devaluation
Lags in depleting inventories and exhausting existing machinery before setting new orders.

Reserve tranche
The 25 percent of a country's quota in the International Monetary Fund that a nation is required to pay either in acceptable currencies or in special drawing rights.

Revaluation
A deliberate decrease in the foreign exchange rate (price of foreign currencies in terms of the domestic currency) by a country's monetary authorities from one pegged or fixed level to another.

Revenue tariff
A tariff imposed by a government to raise tax revenues.

Scientific tariff
A tariff specifically devised to neutralize the cost advantage enjoyed by foreign producers of a tariffed product.

Second oil shock
Oil price increases in 1979—1981.

Seigniorage
The gains accruing to a country from printing its currency or when its currency is employed as an international currency and reserve.

Selective expenditure switching policies
Polices aimed at a specific item in the balance of payments. Also referred to as direct controls.

Sight bill
A bill of exchange that is payable on demand to the drawee.

Simple barter
An arrangement through which imported goods are traded for domestically produced commodities of equal value.

Single factoral terms of trade
The ratio of the price index of a nation's exports to the price index of its imports times its export productivity index. Single factoral terms of trade indicate the amount of imports a country acquires for each unit of domestic factors of production contained in its exports.

Smithsonian Agreement
An agreement reached by the representative of the "big ten" trading nations at the Smithsonian Institution in Washington, DC in December 1971. This agreement, which was an attempt to shape the international monetary system, resulted in the devaluation of the dollar from $35 to $38 per ounce of gold.

Sovereign default
A nation's decision to default on its external debt.

Specific tariff
A tariff expressed in terms of a fixed amount of money per unit of the imported product, such as 2 cents per chicken or $500 per automobile.

Speculation
The opposite of hedging; purposely undertaking risk in expectation of profit. Like hedging, speculation can occur in either a spot market or a forward market.

Sporadic dumping
Selling the product of a firm with surplus inventories in a foreign market at a price that is lower than that charged in the domestic market.

Spot market
A type of foreign exchange market in which foreign currencies are purchased and sold for immediate delivery, that is, within two business days after the day the transaction is agreed on.

Stabilizing speculation
Purchase of a foreign currency when its domestic price (the exchange rate) is declining, in anticipation that it will soon increase, thus generating a profit. Stabilizing speculation also refers to the sale of a foreign currency when its domestic price is rising, in anticipation that it will soon decline.

State trading companies
Organizations that control all international transactions in command economies.

Strategic trade policy argument
An argument for protection stating that high-technology industries are crucial to a nation's future growth and should be protected temporarily with subsidies, tariffs, and other forms of protection.

Subsidy
An indirect form of protection granted by a government to domestic producers. Subsidies are given either to export industries or import-competing industries.

Structural criterion
A criterion used to define multinational corporations as firms that make their stocks available to all countries in which they operate and firms whose top management are composed of people from various countries.

Swap
An arrangement by which two parties exchange one currency for another and agree that, at a certain future date, each party receives from the other the amount of the original currency that was given up at the time of the swap.

Target zone approach
An approach calling on major industrialized countries to establish mutually consistent targets for their real effective exchange rates. Each nation would allow its real exchange rate to vary within a narrow band of fluctuation around the target rate.

Tariff
A tax or custom duty imposed on the importation or exportation of a product that is crossing national boundaries.

Tariff quota
A combination of tariff and quota setting a limit on the amount of a commodity that can enter a country at a given rate of or zero duty. Any additional quantities that are imported are subject to higher duty rates.

Technological gap theory
A theory that relates the trade between nations to the existence of a technological gap among them. According to the theory, a country's technological superiority gives it an advantage in securing export markets.

Terms of trade (TOT)
The relative prices at which two products are traded in the international market; measured as the ratio of the price of exports to the price of imports.

Terms of trade argument
An argument for protection stating that a nation's restrictive trade policy can increase the ratio of export price index to import price index and, hence, improve its welfare.

Theory

An abstraction from reality based on certain simplifying assumptions.

Theory-based arguments for protection

Arguments for protection derived from the models of international trade theories, including terms of trade argument and optimum tariff, domestic distortion argument, and strategic trade policy argument.

Theory of international portfolio investment

A model of portfolio investment explaining the international movement of capital. According to this model, the rate of return on capital is the cause of international capital movement among countries.

Theory of overlapping demand

A theory stating that international trade in manufactured goods is undertaken by countries that have similar demand and income level. Thus, the more similar two countries are with respect to demand and income, the greater the potential for trade in manufactured products between them.

Theory of the second best

If the presence of distortion in an economy prevents the achievement of pareto optimality, it may be justifiable for a government to employ policies that add more distortions (such as tariffs).

Third-world countries

Nations occupying the vast regions of Africa, Asia, and Latin America. These nations are primarily identified by low standards of living, high rates of population growth, low levels of per capita income, high illiteracy rates, and general economic and technological dependence on advanced (developed) countries. Also referred to as underdeveloped countries, developing countries, or less-developed countries.

Three-party arbitrage

See Triangular arbitrage.

Time bill

A bill of exchange that is payable at some future date.

Tokyo Round

The multilateral negotiations formally opened in Tokyo in 1973 and concluded in 1979. The primary goal of the Tokyo Round was the elimination of nontariff trade barriers. It ruled that industrial countries' tariffs had to be cut by an average of 33 percent over an eight-year period. This included tariff cuts of 31 percent for the United States, 27 percent for the European Common Market, and 28 percent for Japan.

Trade controls

Direct control measures, such as tariffs, taxes, subsidies, quotas, and advance deposit requirements, that are aimed at a specific item in the balance of payments. Also referred to as commercial controls.

Trade creation

A change in the trade pattern that arises when a domestically produced good of a customs union member is replaced by a lower-cost import from another customs union member.

Trade diversion

A change in the trade pattern that occurs when lower-cost imports from a country that is not a member of the customs union are replaced by higher-cost imports from a member country.

Transaction exposure

The determination of actual losses or gains that occur due to fluctuations in exchange rates in transferring funds across national boundaries.

Transborder data flow (TDF)

The flow of electronically transmitted information across national boundaries.

Transfer pricing

The pricing of goods and services that pass between either a parent company and its subsidiaries or subsidiaries themselves.

Transformation curve

See Production possibilities frontier (curve).

Translation exposure

A risk associated with the impact of exchange rate fluctuations on the recording and reporting of a company's financial position in its financial statements. This is basically an accounting exposure.

Triangular (three-party) arbitrage

An arbitrage that involves three currencies traded between financial centers.

Turnkey operation

An arrangement by which a multinational corporation agrees to construct an entire facility or plant in a host country, prepare it for operation, and then "turn the key" over to the host country.

Two-party arbitrage

An arbitrage that involves only two currencies traded between two financial centers.

Underdeveloped countries

See Third-world countries.

Unilateral export quota

An export quota established by an importing country without the prior consent of the trading nations.

Unilateral quota

A quota imposed by an importing country without negotiation or consultation with exporting countries.

United States—Canada Free Trade Agreement (FTA)

A free trade agreement between the United States and Canada signed in 1988 and enforced a year later (1989). The factors that contributed to the eventual enforcement of the FTA include the weakening U.S. international position and Canada's increasing dependence on the United States.

Uruguay Round
The multilateral trade negations that started in 1986, concluded in December 1993, taking effect in July 1995.

Value added
The price of a final product minus the cost of its imported inputs.

Value-added tax
A tax imposed on the value that is added at each stage of a given good's production.

Velocity of money
The average number of times per year that each unit of domestic currency is spent to purchase the economy's flow of goods and services.

Vertical integration
A merger of firms engaged in different stages of production and distribution, under one ownership.

Voluntary export restraint
A quota that is voluntarily imposed by an exporting nation. The imposition of this type of quote implies that the importing nation has threatened to impose even tougher restrictions if exporters do not cooperate voluntarily with the restraint.

Wage protection argument
An argument for protection, stating that high-wage countries, such as the United States or Great Britain, cannot effectively compete with low-wage countries; hence, they should impose tariffs or quotas to protect their workers from products made by low-wage workers overseas.

White Paper
A document endorsed by European Union members at their 1985 summit in Milan. The White Paper established a detailed legislative program for complete economic integration by 1992. Its basic thrust was the removal of a whole series of trade barriers—physical barriers, technical barriers, and fiscal barriers.

Wholly-owned subsidiary
A firm established by multinational corporation in a foreign country under the host country's laws. The firm is wholly owned by the corporation, that is, all of its stock is owned by the corporation.

World Bank
An international bank that was initially set up by the International Monetary Fund to provide loans for post-war reconstruction. Today, the bank's major function is to provide financial resources for implementation of development projects in developing countries.

World Trade Organization (WTO)
The WTO is an organization that is set up to facilitate international trade and investment. By May 1997 the WTO had 131 members.

Zollverein
A customs union established in 1834 by a number of sovereign German states. This preceded the political union of Germany in 1870. By removing trade barriers through much of the country, zollverein was an important factor in German reunification.

INDEX

A

Above-the-line items, 191
Absolute advantage, theory of, 20-21
Absorption approach to devaluation, 268
Absorption effect, 269
Accommodating items, 191
Accounting exposure, 208
Adjustable peg system, 225
Adjustment policies, 241
Administrative and technical regulations, 107
Advanced countries
    excess loanable funds in, 313
    tight monetary policies of, as cause of debt crisis, 313
Advanced-deposit requirement (ADR), 276
Alejandro, Carlos Diaz, 291
Alexander, Sidney, 275
Allocative goal, as source of conflict, 381
American Telephone & Telegraph (AT&T), 337, 386
Ancillary facilities, development of, 62
Andean Common Market (ANCOM), 145
Anti-dumping Act (1921), 105
Antidumping argument, 120
Appreciation, 206, 268
Appropriability theory, 361
Arbitrage, 216
Asian-Pacific Economic Cooperation (APEC) group, 167, 168
Assignment rule, 267
Association of Southeast Asian Nations (ASEAN), 145
Autarky, 25
    equilibrium in, 40–42
Automatic adjustment mechanism, 241
Automatic income adjustment mechanism, 241
Automatic monetary adjustment mechanism, 241
Automatic price adjustment mechanism, 241
Autonomous items, 191

B

Backward integration, 359
Baker, James, 325
Baker Plan, 325-326
Balance of goods and services, 191
    and remittances, 191
Balance of international indebtedness, 192
Balance of payments (BOP), 241
    accounting for, 181
    credit items, 182
    debit items, 182
    double-entry bookkeeping, 181
    major accounts in, 183
    automatic adjustment mechanisms, disadvantages of, 254
    automatic income adjustment mechanism
    foreign trade repercussions, 253
    income determination in closed economy, 244
    income determination in open economy, 248
    automatic monetary adjustment mechanism, 254
    automatic price adjustment mechanism

    adjustment with fixed exchange rates, 242
    adjustment with flexible exchange rates, 243
    definition of, 181
    direct controls, 276-281
    expenditure-adjustment policies, 265
    evaluation of monetary-fiscal policy mix, 267
    general expenditure-switching policies, 268
    approaches to devaluation, 268-276
    devaluation and revaluation, 268-269
    goal of, as source of conflict, 265
    and gold standards, 223
    measures of deficits and surpluses in, 191
    purchasing power-parity theory, 257
    absolute version of, 257
    empirical test of, 259
    relative version, 257
    selective expenditure-switching policies, 276
    United States, 181
    usefulness of, 181, 195
Balance of trade argument, 121
Balassa, Bela, 142
Bank acceptance, 201
Bank drafts, 201
Banking, international, 199
Banks. *See* Central banks; Commercial banks
Baran, Paul, 290
Basic balance, 191
Bayer, Fredrick, 335
"Beggar Thy Neighbor" policies, 78
Behavioral criterion, in defining multinational corporations, 336
Below-the-line items, 191
Benelux, 143
Berlin Wall, fall of, 169
Bhagwati, Jagdish N., 291
Bharadwaj, R., 62
Bilateral agreement, 151
Bilateral export quota, 93
Bilateral quota, 93
Bill of lading, 202
"Black Friday," 2
Black markets, 278
    premium/discount for dollar in, 280
"Black Monday," 2
Blough, Roger, 123
Boeing, 386
BOP. *See* Balance of payments
Bowmar Corporation, 67
Brady Plan, 326-328
Brain drain, 371
Brazil
    and immiserizing growth, 291-294
    liberalization program in, 300-302
Bretton Woods system
    breakdown of, 233
    demise of, 229
    and the Gold Exchange Standard, 225
British Commonwealth Preference scheme, 137
British Petroleum, 337

Bulk purchasing, 151
Burke-Hartke Bill, 380
Bush, George, and demise of Soviet Union, 172
"Buy American" campaign, 343
By-products, use of, 62

C

Cable transfers, 200
Calculator, product life cycle of, 65
Canada, and imposition of antidumping tariffs, 105
Capital flight, 174
    from developing countries,
        316-318
Capital flow controls, 278-279
Capital inflows, 182
Capital-intensive industries, 6
Capital outflows, 182
Caribbean Common Market
    (CARICOM), 145
Caribbean Free Trade Association (CARIFTA), 145
Cartels
    centralized, 134
    international, 133
Carter, Jimmy, 127
Cash payment, 202
Casio, 67
Central American Common Market (CACM), 145
Central banks, participation in foreign exchange market, 199
Centralized cartels, 134
China, renewal of MFN status of, 146
Chrysler Corporation, 389
    bail out of, 17
    British investment in, 183
Classical economic theory, gold standard system link to, 242
Clean-floating exchange rate system, 204
Clinton, Bill
    and aid to Russia, 174
    and renewal of China's MFN status, 146
Closed economy
    definition of, 244
    income determination in, 244
Closed economy multiplier, 247
Coca-Cola, 344, 387
Colonialism, as source of conflict, 383
Command economies, state trading in, 133
Commercial banks
    functions of, in foreign exchange market, 199
    and minimizing of foreign exchange risk, 208
    participation in foreign exchange market, 199
Commercial bills of exchange, 200
Commercial controls, 276
Commercial invoice, 202
Commodity concentration, and export instability, 302
Commodity terms of trade, 45-48
Common markets, 142
Commonwealth of Independent States (CIS), 6, 170
    formation of, 226
Community indifference curve, 35-39
Comparative advantage
    empirical test of, 22-24
    theory of, 22
Compensating account, 197

Compensation principle, 39
Compensation trading, 194
Competition, increased, as benefit of customs union, 141
Complete specialization, 30
Compound tariff, 76
Confirmed letter of credit, 202
Constant costs assumption, basis for, and gains from international
    trade under, 30-31
Constant opportunity costs, production possibility frontier
    under, 30-31
Consumers, effect of tariffs on, 80
Consumer surplus, 79
Consumption distortion loss, 86
Consumption effect, 86
Consumption gains from trade, 28
Council of Mutual Economic Assistance (CMEA or
    COMECON), 151
Counterpurchase agreement, 194
Countertrade, 194
Crawling peg system, 234
Credit items, 182
Credit swap, 215
Cultures, in distinguishing international trade from domestic
    trade, 5
Currency swap, 215
Current account, 183
Current account balance, 190, 241
Customs procedures and valuation, 108
Customs union, 137
    dynamic welfare effects of, 141
    empirical investigations of, 142
    static welfare effects of, 137
    trade-creating, 137
    trade-diverting, 139

D

Daewoo, 337
Daimler-Benz, 337
Deadweight loss, 86
Debit items, 182
Debt crisis
    and developing countries, 313, 321
    challenge ahead, 327-328
    and international monetary fund, 322-323
    magnitude of, 311-313
    in Mexico, 319, 321
    origin of, 313
    phases of, 327
    solutions to, 324-326
    sovereign default, 322
    and the United States, 318
    trade liberalization and, 325-327
Debt-equity requirements, 387
Debt-equity swap, 244
Debt-service ratios, 311
Decision lag, 274
De Gaulle, Charles, mercantilist policy of, 21
Delivery lag, 274
Demand
    community indifference curves, 35-39
    individual indifference curves, 35-39
    and measurement of terms of trade, 47-52

and offer curves, 45
and taste differentials, 43
Demand lag, 65
Dependency theory, 289
criticism of, 290
Depreciation, 206, 268
Destabilizing speculation, 217
Devaluation, 206, 268, 269-270
absorption approach to, 275
elasticity approach to, 269-272
monetary approach to, 276
price effect of, 269
Developing countries
advanced nations' aid to, 302
black markets in, 278
capital flight from, 316-317
debt crisis in, 312-313
challenge ahead, 327-328
and international monetary fund, 322-323
magnitude of, 311-313
in Mexico, 319, 321
origin of, 313-319
phases of, 327
solutions to, 324
sovereign default, 322
and the United States, 323
debt of, 17
defining characteristics of, 1
demands for new international economic order, 302-304
export instability, 295
empirical studies of, 295
factors giving rise to, 294
policies to stabilize export prices or revenues, 297-300
external debt of, 7
importance of, in global markets, 1
international business activities of, 335
labor costs in, 2
major trade associations among, 143
migration of professionals from, 357
newly industrialized countries, 304
poor public sector investment in, 314
profile of, 287
renegotiating international debt, 303
role in international decision-making process, 303
trade liberalization in, 300
trade theory and economic development, 288-290
dependency theory, 289-291
immiserizing growth theory, 291-293
Prebisch theory, 293
use of revenue tariffs in, 75
Diaz, Porfirio, 291
Direct controls, 276
Direct investment, foreign, 333, 338-339
Disinvestment, requiring, 389
Distortions, 116
Distributive goal, as source of conflict, 381
Diversification argument, 123
Documentary-acceptance (D/A) draft, 202
Documentary draft, 202
Documentary-on-payment (D/P) draft, 202
Dollar
appreciation of, 318
black market premium/discount for, 280

Domestic distortion argument, 113
Domestic firms, characteristics of, and technology transfer, 350
Domestic marketing boards, 297
Domestic production argument, 118
Domestic production subsidy, 101
Domestic trade, versus international trade, 4-5
Double-entry bookkeeping, 181
Double factorial terms of trade, 47, 52
Douglass, Gordon, 65
Dow Chemical Company, 324
Dumping
and antidumping argument, 120
definition of, 104
persistent, 105
predatory, 105
sporadic, 104-105
Dunning, John, 362
Dutch disease, 207
Dutch guilders, 216
Dynamic Random Access Memory (DRAM), 118

E

East African Community (EAC), 145
Eastern European countries
economic reforms in, 168
Economic Union and, 157, 168
political independence of, 6
Eclectic theory of international production, 362
Economic Community of West African States (ECIWAS), 145
Economic exposure, 208
Economic goals as source of conflict, 378
Economic integration
common markets, 142
customs unions, 137
economic union, 143
free-trade areas, 137
preferential trade arrangements, 137
Economic sanctions, 125
Economic Union (EU), 137
and Eastern European countries, 153
Economies of scale, 359
as benefit of customs union, 136
Edge Act, 218
Edge Act Corporations, 218
Effective exchange rates, 235
Effective rate of protection, 75
Elasticity approach, 269
to devaluation, 269-272
Elasticity optimism, 272
Elasticity pessimism, 272
Electronics market, currency hedging and exchange rate fluctuations in,
Elf Aquitaine, 337
Employment, controlling local, 381-382
Employment protection argument, 121-122
Engine of growth, 288
Entries, controlling, 387
Environmental effects of multinational corporations, 384
Environmental protection argument, 125
Equalization of production costs argument, 120
Equilibrium relative commodity price, with offer curves, 45
Errors and omissions, 182

Eurobond market, 217, 220
Eurocurrency market, 199
    financial activities of, 216, 220
Eurodollars, 216
Europe, changes in, 6
European Common Market (ECM), 143
European Community (EC), 143. *See also* European Union (EU)
    and oilseed disputes, 144
European Currency Unit (ECU), 233, 234
European Economic Community (EEC), 142, 143
European Exchange Rate Mechanism (ERM), 232
European Free Trade Association (EFTA), 137
European Monetary Corporation Fund (EMCF), 233
European Monetary System (EMS), 232
European Snake, 232
European Union (EU)
    economic integration in, 6
    establishment of, 63
    Milan summit, 143
    subsidization of oilseed producers, 148
Eurosterling, 216
Evidence accounts, 195
Excess loanable funds, in advanced countries, 318
Exchange controls, 277-279
Exchange rate, 108
Exchange rate systems
    alternative, 233
    crawling peg, 233
    target zone approach, 233
    fixed versus flexible exchange rates, 235
    Latin American exchange rate systems, 234
Excise taxes, 104
Expenditure-adjusting policies, 265-267
    evaluation of monetary-fiscal policy mix, 267
Export and import price indexes, and terms of trade, 45
Export duties, 75
Export-Import Bank of the United States, 101
Exporting, 340
Export instability, 294
    empirical studies of, 295-296
    factors giving rise to, 294
    policies to stabilize export prices or revenues, 297-300
Export quotas, 94
Export requirements, 387
Export shipment process, 199
Export subsidy, 101
External balance, 265
External diseconomy, 116
External economy, 116
Externality, 116
Exxon, 336, 337

F

Factor mobility, in distinguishing international trade from domestic trade, 4
Factor-price equalization theorem, 58-59
Fair, Roy C., 255
Federal Reserve System's "Regulation Q," 216, 220
Fees, controlling, 387
Fiat, 324, 337
Financial sanctions, 126
Firm-specific advantages, 359

First-best world, 87
Fiscal policy
    definition of, 265
    expansionary, 266
Fixed exchange rate
    automatic price adjustment with, 241
    versus flexible exchange rate, 235
Fixed exchange rate system, 204
    devaluation in, 268
Fleming, J. Marcus, 267
Flexible exchange rate
    automatic price adjustment with, 243
    versus fixed exchange rate, 235
Flexible exchange rate system, 204
Floating dollar, 235
Floating exchange rate system, 204
Floating interest rates, 319
Ford Motor Company, 336
Foreign direct investment (FDI), 333, 338-340
    concentration of U.S. firms in, 10
    in developing countries, 335, 346
    distribution of major industrial countries, ?
    as form of capital movement, 358
    during the Great Depression, 357
    involvement of developing countries in, 5
    percentage distribution of United States, 340
Foreigners
    excluding from specific activities, 387
    joint venture, 386
Foreign exchange
    growth of Eurodollar market, 219
    transactions, 199
    arbitrage, 216
    foreign exchange risks, 208
    forward market, 211
    hedging, 212
    speculation, 212
    swaps, 214
Foreign exchange instruments
    bank drafts as, 201
    cable transfers as, 200
    cash payments as, 202
    commercial bills of exchange as, 200
    definition of, 200
    letters of credit as, 202
    open account as, 202
Foreign exchange market
    commercial banks in, 204
    definition of, 204, 205
    functions of, 204, 205
Foreign exchange rate, determination of, 204
Foreign exchange risk, 208
    exposure, 208
Foreign Investment Review Agency (FIRA), 387
Foreign-local joint venture, 343
Foreign trade multiplier, 251
Foreign trade repercussions, 253
Forward contracts, 211
Forward discount, 212
Forward integration, 359
Forward market, 207, 211
Forward premium, 212

Forward rate, 211
"Four Dragons," 304
Franchisee, 342
Franchiser, 342
Franchising, 342
Frank, Andre Gunder, 289-290
Freely floating exchange rate system, 204
Freely fluctuating exchange rate system, 204, 231
Free-trade agreements, affecting global economy, 157
Free-trade areas, 137
    economic effects of, 164
    and North American Free Trade Agreement (NAFTA), 162
French francs, 208
Fundamental disequilibrium, 206, 225

G

G-7 nations, 174, 208
    economic links among, 255
"Gang of Four," 304
General Agreement on Tariffs and Trade (GATT), 87, 93, 126
    Dillion Round, 148
    and environmental policy, 126
    as forum for discussion in resolving trade disputes, 150
    Kennedy Round, 105, 147, 148
    and nondiscrimination, 147
    and reduction of tariffs by negotiation, 147
    Tokyo Round, 147, 148
    Uruguay Round, 143, 148, 302
General Agreement to Borrow, 277
General Electric, 337, 380
    move to Singapore, 2
General expenditure-switching policies
    approaches to devaluation, 269-276
    devaluation and revaluation, 268-269
General Motors, 336, 337, 343, 359, 360
General Tire and Rubber, 359
German deutsche marks, 210
Germany
    unification of, 6
    Zollverein as factor in reunification, 137
Gillette Company, 162, 387
Glasnost, 6
Global economy. See International economics
Global markets, growth in, 1
Global resource endowments and trade patterns, 60
Global sugar market, 97
Gold bullion standard, 225
Gold coin standard, 223
Gold exchange standard, 225
    and Bretton Woods system, 225
Gold export point, 223
Gold import point, 223
Gold standard system, link to classical economic theory, 241
Gold tranche, 226
Gorbachev, Mikhail S., 172
Government health and safety standards, 107
Government purchasing policies, 107
Government revenue, effect of tariffs on, 85
Great Britain, oil and deindustrialization in, 209
Gross national product (GNP),
    absorption by foreign trade, 1

Group of 15 (G-15), 313
Group of Seven (G-7), 210
Guest workers, 371

H

Hamilton, Alexander, 122
Haufbauer, Gary, 65
Health and safety violations, at Lockheed, 382, 383
Heckscher, Eli, 55
Heckscher-Ohlin theory, 55-56
    assumptions and implications of, 57
    empirical studies of, 61
    extensions of and alternatives to, 62
    graphical illustration of, 57
Hedging, 212
Helleman Brewing Company, 151
Hewlett-Packard, 67
High-income economies, 288
High-technology industries, characteristics of, 116
Hilton Hotels, 343
Hitachi, 337
Home countries
    environment of, and technology transfer, 346
    objectives of, as source of conflict, 378-380
    reactions to technology transfer, 347
Honda Motor Company, 105, 337, 359
Hong Kong, and diversity in industrial policy, 304
Horizontal integration, 359
Hornick, Phillip Von, 20
Host countries
    environment of, and technology transfer, 346
    objectives of, as source of conflict, 377, 380-385
    reactions to technology transfer, 347
    reaction to multinational corporations, 385-390
    reconciling with reactions, 348-349
Hume, David, 19, 242, 254
Hymer, Stephen, 358, 363

I

Iacocca, Lee A., 98
IBM, 8, 382, 383
Ichimura, 62
Illegal immigration, question of, 372
Imitation lag, 65
Immigration
    international labor mobility and, 365-372
    push and pull of U.S. policy, 368
    question of illegal, 372
    trends in, by phrases, 369
    to United States, 365, 366, 372
Immiserizing growth theory, 291-293
Import duties, 75
Import quotas, 93
Import-substitution policies, 287
Income determination
    in open economy, 248
    theory of, 244
Income determination in closed economy, 244
Income distribution effect
    of international labor migration, 365, 370-371

of international trade, 59
 as source of conflict, 383-384
Income terms of trade, 47-51
Increasing costs, 27
Increasing costs assumption
 basis for and gains from international trade under, 28-29
 basis for and gains from trade under, 40-41
 production possibility frontier under, 24-27
Increasing returns to scale, as basis for international trade, 62–63
India, Bhopal accident in, 382
Indifference curve
 community, 35-39
 definition of, 38
 implications of convexity of, 37
 implications of upward-sloping, 36
 individual, 35-39
 intersecting, 38
Indifference map, 38
Individual indifference curves, 35-39
Industrial policy, diversity in, 304
Infant government argument, 124
Infant industry argument, 116
Inter-American Development Bank, 325-326
Interest Equalization Tax (IET), 218
Internal balance, 265
Internalization advantages, 362
Internalization theory, 361
International Bank for Reconstruction and Development
 (IBRD), 225
International banking, 199
International banking facilities (IBFs), 218
International buffer stock agreements, 297-300
International business
 changes in, 335
 channels of entry into, 340
 exporting, 340-341
 franchising, 342-343
 joint ventures, 343-344
 licensing, 340-341
 management contract, 340-345
 turnkey operation, 340-345
 wholly owned subsidiary, 344
 definition of, 335
 in developing countries, 335
International Business Machines (IBM), 344
International capital movements, theories of, 357-360
International cartels, 133
International Cocoa Agreement, 297
International Coffee Agreement, 299
International Commodity Agreements (ICAs), 297
 creation of, to stabilize prices of primary products, 302
International debt crisis, 7
International Development Association (IDA), 229
International economics
 changes in, 1
 definition of, 3-4
 importance of, 1
 recent free trade agreements affecting, 162
 recent political events affecting, 169
 significance of international trade in, 8-12
International Export Quota Agreement, 298-300
International Finance Corporation (IFC), 229

International investment position (IIP), 192
International labor migration
 causes of, 365-367
 effects of, 365, 367-370
International labor mobility, and immigration, 365-372
International migration, and global market for health professionals,
 368
International Monetary Fund (IMF), 213, 234
 conditionality, 323
 and debt crisis, 322-323
 foreign exchange controls, 279
 and international debt crisis, 7
 International monetary system, 223
 Bretton Woods system and the Gold Exchange Standard, 234
 demise of Bretton Woods system, 229
 European, 226
 gold bullion standard, 225
 gold coin standard, 223
 international monetary fund, 225
 Smithsonian agreement, 230
 World Bank, 225
International Natural Rubber Agreement, 297
International portfolio investment, theory of, 357-358
International price discrimination, 93-105
International production, eclectic theory of, 362
International reserve, 206
International Sugar Agreement, 299
International Tin Agreement, 297
International trade
 basis for and gains from
 under constant costs assumptions, 24
 under increasing costs assumptions, 29
 and community indifference curves, 35-39
 versus domestic trade, 4-7
 effects of transportation costs on, 68-69
 income distribution effects of, 59
 increasing returns to scale as basis for, 62-64
 significance of, in world economy, 8-12
 taste differentials as basis of, 43-44
 theories of, 17-31
International trade theories
 demand
 community indifference curves, 35-39
 community indifference curves and international trade, 35-39
 individual indifference curves, 35-39
 and measurement of terms of trade, 47
 and offer curves, 35-45
 and taste differentials, 43-44
 effects of transportation costs, 68
 factor-prime equalization theorem, 58
 Heckscher-Ohlin, 55-62
 income distribution effects, 59
 overlapping demand theory, 64
 product life cycle, 65
 real-world relevance of, 69
 supply
 and absolute advantage, 20-21
 and comparative advantage, 22-24
 and mercantilism, 19-21
 and production possibilities frontier, 24-27
 and specialization, 20-21
 technological gap, 64

International Wheat Agreement, 299
Intervention in foreign exchange market, 107-108
Iran-Iraq war (1980--1988), 17
IRI, 337
Isuzu, 343

J

Jamaica Accords, 231
Japanese capital flow controls, 278
Japanese yen, 208
J-Curve effect, 272-275
Johnson, Harry G., 139, 241, 254, 291
Joint floating exchange rate system, 232
Joint venture, 343-344
    arrangements, 386-387
    foreigners', 343
    foreign-local, 343
    U.S.-Mexican, 347

K

Kawasaki Heavy Industries, 105
Kemp, Jack, 237
Keynes, John Maynard, 244
Keynesian theory of income determination, 241, 244
Khrushchev, Nikita, 172
Kindleberger, Charles, 358
Knowledge/service-intensive industries, 6
Kongsberg Vaapenfabrikk, 95
Kravis, Irving, 64

L

Labor productivity, in determining unit labor costs, 21
Lag
    decision, 274
    delivery, 274
    production, 274
    recognition, 274
    replacement, 274
Lancieri, 296
Latin America
    crawling peg system in, 233
    debt crisis in, 1
    debt-service ratios, 11
    exchange rate systems in, 233
Latin American Free Trade Association (LAFTA), 145
Latin American Integration Association (LAIA), 145
Leontief, Wassily, 61
Leontief paradox, 61
Letter of credit, 202
    confirmed, 202
Licensee, 341
Licensing, 341
Licensor, 341
Lincoln, Abraham, 119
Linder, Staffan, 64
Linder thesis, theory of, 64
Liquidity, 191
Liquidity balance, 191
Local capital market, controlling, 388-389

Lockheed, health and safety violations at, 382, 383
London Interbank Offered Rate (LIBOR), 217, 313
Long position, 214
Love, 296-297
Lower-middle-income economies, 288
Low-income economies, 288

M

Maastricht Treaty, 160, 161, 171, 233
*MacBean, Alasdair, 295-296
MacDougall, G. D. A., 22-24
Magdoff, Harry, 363
Managed-floating exchange rate system, 230-231
    adoption of, 215
    devaluation in, 268
Management contract, 340-345
Mao Tse-tung, 365
Maquiladoras, 166
Marginal private cost (MPC), 116
Marginal propensity to consume (MPC), 245
Marginal propensity to save (MPS), 245
Marginal rate of substitution, 37
Marginal rate of transformation (MRT), 25
Marginal social cost (MSC), 116
Marine insurance certificate, 202
Market imperfections theory, 358-360
Marketing and packaging standards, 107
Market-oriented economies, state trading in, 152
Marquez, Jaime, 272
Marshall-Lerner condition, 270-273
Marx, Karl, 363-365
Marxist theory, 363-365
Massell, Benton, 296-297
Matsushita Electric Industry, 337
*McBean, 142
Meade, James, 139
Medium-term Eurocurrency loan, 217
Menem, Carlos, 325
Mercantilism, 19-21
Mexico
    debt crisis in, 319-321
    and need for North American Free Trade Agreement (NAFTA), 164
MNCs. *See* Multinational corporations (MNCs)
Mobil, 337
Monetary approach, to devaluation, 269
    to devaluation, 269
Monetary policy
    definition of, 265
    expansionary, 266
Monopolistic nature of MNCs, 348
Monopsony power, 413
Most-favored nation (MFN) status, 147
    U.S.-Chinese standoff over, 146
Multilateral Agreements, 299-300
Multilateral quota, 93
Multinational corporations (MNCs), 7
    appropriate technology and technology transfer, 345-351
    channels of entry into international business, 340
    exporting, 340-341
    franchising, 342-343

joint venture, 343-344
licensing, 341
management contract, 345
owned foreign enterprise, 343-344
turnkey operation, 345
wholly owned subsidiary, 344
characteristics of, and technology transfer, 349
code of conduct for operations of, 145
definition of, 336
environmental effects of, 384
and foreign direct investment and portfolio investment,
        338-340
foreign enterprises owned by, 340
home countries' reactions to, 347
host countries' reactions to, 347-348, 385-390
increasing transfer of technology from, to developing
        nations, 303
major criticisms of, 377-378
move of plants to developing countries, 2
nature and scope of, 336
objectives of, as source of conflict, 378-385
and opportunities offered by European Union, 157
production by, 67
proliferation of, 335
reconciling host and home countries' reactions, 348-349
sources of conflicts involving, 377-385
theories of, 361-362
and theories of international factor movements, 357-372
and use of credit swaps, 215
and use of currency swaps, 215
world's major, 336-338
Multiple exchange rates system, 277
        in controlling flow of trade, 109
Mundell, Robert A., 241, 254, 267
Murayma, Tomiichi,

N

National currencies, in distinguishing international trade from
        domestic trade, 4
National policies, in distinguishing international trade from
        domestic trade, 4
National security argument, 123
Nations Conference on Trade and Development (UNCTAD), 302
Natural endowment, 21
NEC, 337
Neoclassical economists, 4
Nestle, 337
Net barter terms of trade, 47
Net international investment position (NIIP), 192
Net national loss, from tariffs, 79, 85-87
New international economic order (NIEO), demands for, 302-304
Newly industrialized countries (NICs), 304-306
        and economic reforms, 157
        international business in, 335
        share of world market, 1
Nissan Corporation, 324
Nixon, Richard, and breakdown of Bretton Woods system, 230
Nobel, Alfred, 335
Nominal tariff, 77
Noneconomic goals as source of conflict, 378, 380, 381, 382-383
Nontariff trade barriers, 93
        administrative and technical regulations as, 107
        dumping as, 93
        government purchasing policies as, 107
        intervention in foreign exchange market as, 107
        quotas as, 93
        subsidies as, 100
        taxes as, 104
        voluntary export restraints, 96
North American Free Trade Agreement (NAFTA), 7, 126, 148,
        161–165, 368
        arguments against formation of, 166
        highlights of, 164

O

OECD. See Organization for Economic Co-operation and
        Development (OECD)
Offer curves, 45
        derivation of, 46
        equilibrium relative commodity price with, 45-47
Official reserve transactions balance (ORT), 191
Offset trading, 194
Offshore assembly provisions, 84
Ohlin, Bertil, 55
Oil market
        and deindustrialization in Britain, 207
OPEC's power in controlling, 133
Oilseed disputes, 144
Oil shock
        second, as cause of debt crisis, 313-314
        and terms of trade, 50
Open account, 202
Open economy
        definition of, 248
        income determination in, 248-253
Open economy multiplier, 251
Opportunity cost, 21
Optimum tariff, 113
Orcutt, G., 272
Organization for Economic Cooperation and Development
        (OECD), 145, 287
        guidelines on transborder data flow, 384
Organization of Petroleum Exporting Countries (OPEC), 133, 287
        control of oil prices by, 17
        erosion of power in global market, 136
        growth of, 133
        member countries in, 133
        objectives of, 133
        role of, in controlling price of oil, 95
        and second oil shock, 313
Output effect, of international labor migration, 367-370
Overlapping demand, theory of, 64
Ownership-specific advantages, 359

P

Pareto optimal, 116
Paris Club, 321
Partial specialization, 30-32
Par value, 206
Pepsico, 342, 344
Perestroika, 6, 170

Performance criterion, in defining multinational corporations, 336
Persian Gulf War, 17-18
    and OPEC, 434
Persistent dumping, 405
Petrodollar recycling, 313-314
Pfizer, 359
Pillsbury, 387
Political argument for protection, 126
Pollution, as example of externality, 116
Portfolio investment, 336, 338
Prebisch, Raul, 293-294
Prebisch theory, 293-294, 300
Predatory dumping, 105
Preferential trade arrangements, 137
Prevent-money-outflow argument, 119
Price discrimination, international, 93-105
Price-specie-flow mechanism, 19, 254
Price variability, and export instability, 294-295
Processing taxes, 104
Producers, effect of tariffs on, 83
Producer surplus, 79
Production distortion loss, 85
Production effect, 85
Production gains from trade, 25
Production lag, 274
Production possibilities frontier (PPF), 24
    under constants assumption, 24
    under increasing costs assumption, 27
Productive equipment, 62
Product life cycle theory, 65
    of pocket calculator, 65
Profit maximization
    by centralized cartel, 435
    role of multinational corporations in, 388
Protection
    environmental protection argument, 125
    political, 126
    erroneous arguments
    domestic production, 118
    equalization of production costs, 120
    prevent-money-outflow, 119
    wage protection, 119
    qualified arguments, 122
    diversification, 123
    infant government, 124
    infant industry, 116
    national security, 122
    questionable arguments
    antidumping, 120
    balance of trade, 121
    employment protection, 121
    theory-based arguments for, 128
    domestic distortion argument, 116
    strategic trade policy argument, 113
    terms-of trade argument and optimum tariff, 113
Protective tariff, 75, 79 102
Purchasing-power of money balances, 269
Purchasing-power-parity theory, 256-257
    absolute version of, 257
    empirical test of, 259
    relative version of, 257-260

Q

Quota
    bilateral, 93
    comparison of tariffs and, 100
    definition of, 93
    export, 94
    import, 93
    multilateral, 93
    tariff, 93
    unilateral, 93
    welfare effects of, 95

R

Rates, controlling, 390
RCA, 380
Reaction lag, 65
Reagan, Ronald, protectionist arguments of, 121
Real-world relevance, of international trade theories, 69
Reciprocal demand curve. See Offer curves
Recognition lag, 274
Relative commodity price, 25
Remedial tariff, 105
Remittances, controlling, 390
Replacement lag, 274
Reserve tranche, 226
Revaluation, 206, 207
Revenue Canada, 107
Revenue tariffs, 75
Ricardo, David, 19, 22, 55, 285
Roosa bonds, 229
Royal Dutch/Shell Group, 337
Russia. See also Soviet Union
    climate for foreign investment in, 360
    and the International Monetary Fund, 230

S

Samuelson, Paul, 58
Samurai bonds, 278
Sanctions
    economic, 125
    financial, 126
    trade, 126
Scientific tariff, 120
Selective expenditure-switching policies, 276-281
Semiconductor accord, 118
Short position, 214
Short-term capital, 183
    short-term Eurocurrency loan, 217
Siemens, 337, 345
Sight bill, 200, 202
Simple barter, 194
Singapore, and diversity in industrial policy, 304
Singer Company, 335
Single factorial terms of trade, 47
Single official rate, 277
Small-country case, with constant opportunity costs, 31
Smith, Adam, 19, 20, 285
Smithsonian Agreement, 230-231
Smoot-Hawley tariff, 78

*Snowden, 142
Sony Corporation, 337
Sovereign debt, 322
Sovereign default, 322
Soviet Union. *See also* Russia
    collapse of, 6, 168, 226
Special Drawing Rights (SDRs), 183, 226, 227–228
Specialization, 56
    complete versus partial, 30
Specific advantages, 359
Specific tariff, 76
Speculation, 206–212
Spillover effects, 116
Sporadic dumping, 104, 105, 121
Spot market, 210
Stabilizing speculation, 214
Statement of changes in financial
    position (SCFP), 181
State trading, 152
State trading companies, 152
Static welfare effects, of customs union, 137
Statistical discrepancy, 182
Stimulus to investment, as benefit of customs union, 141
Strategic trade policy argument, 113-117, 128
Stroh Company, 151
Structural criterion, in defining multinational corporations, 336
Subsidiary, 102
    domestic production, 95
    export, 93
    welfare effects of, 98
    wholly owned, 344
Sugar market, global, 97
Sunlock Comptometer Corporation, 67
Supply
    and absolute advantage, 20-22
    and comparative advantage, 22-27
    and mercantilism, 19-20
    and production possibilities frontier, 24-29
    and specialization, 20-22
Suzuki Motor Company, 105
Swaps, 214
Sweezy, Paul, 363
Swiss francs, 216
Switch trade, 194

T

Takeovers, controlling, 386-387
Target zone approach, 233
Tariff Act (1922), 120
Tariff Act (1930), 120
Tariff factories, 142
Tariff quota, 93
Tariffs
    ad valorem, 76-77, 87
    comparison of quotas and, 100
    compound, 76
    definition of, 76
    and effective rate of protections, 75
    effect of, on consumers, 79
    effect of, on government revenue, 75

    effects of, on producers, 83-85
    net national loss from, 85
    nominal, 77
    and offshore assembly provisions, 84
    optimum, 113
    and terms-of-trade argument, 113
    protective, 75, 179
    remedial, 105
    revenue, 75
    scientific, 120
    specific, 76
    welfare effects of, 75
Taste differentials, trade based on, 43-44
Tatemoto, 62
Tax, 104
    excise, 104
    interest equalization, 208, 277
    processing, 104
    value-added, 104
Technological gap theory, 64
Technology
    acquisition and adaptation of, 348
    internalization of, 341
    joint ventures in revealing exclusive, 344
    selection of appropriate, 346
    sophistication of, 349
Technology transfer, 346-349
    modes of, 349-350
    pricing of, 350-351
Tehran Agreement, 133
Terms of trade (TOT), 26, 42
    commodity, 42
    double, 47
    and export and import price indexes, 45
    and growth in advanced nations, 52
    and imposition tariffs, 113
    income, 42
    measurement of, 47
    and oil shocks, 50
    and optimum tariff, 113
    and relative cost equalization, 29-30
    single factorial, 47
Texas Instruments, 67
Textile industry, and comparative advantage, 22
Theory, definition of, 19
Three-point arbitrage, 216
Time bill, 201
Time draft, 201
Toshiba Machine Company, 95, 337
Toyota Motor, 337, 359
Trade, switch, 194
Trade acceptance, 201
Trade barriers
    dismantling of, on agricultural products in advanced
        countries, 302
    removal of, in European Union, 157
Trade controls, 276-277
Trade-creating customs unions, 137
Trade-creation, 137
Trade-creation effect, 139
Trade-diversion, 140

Trade-diversion effect, 140
Trade-diverting customs unions, 140
Trade liberalization
    and debt crisis, 325
    in developing nations, 300-302
Trade sanctions, 126
Trade theory and economic development, 288-294
Trade-weighted exchange rate (TWEX), 208
Trading
    buy-back, 194
    compensation, 194
    offset, 194
Transaction exposure, 208
Transborder data flow (TDF), 7, 384-385
    as source of conflict, 377-374
Transfer pricing, 350
Transitional economies, debts of, 320
Translation exposure, 208
Transportation costs, effects of, on trade, 59
Triangular arbitrage, 216
Turnkey operation, 345
Two-point arbitrage, 216

U

Unilateral export quota, 93
Unilateral quota, 93
Unilever, 337, 387
Union Carbide, 382
United States
    automobile industry until 1970s, 17
    balance of payments, 179-196
    budget deficit, 2
    collapse of stock market, 2
    and debt crisis, 322-324
    depreciation of dollar in, 2-3
    immigration to, 365, 368
    push and pull of immigration policy, 368
United States—Canada Free Trade Agreement (FTA), 162
U.S. Immigration and Naturalization Service (INS), 368, 372
U.S. Immigration Reform and Control Act (1986), 372
U.S.—Mexico—Canada free-trade agreement, 162
Upper-middle-income economies, 288

V

Value-added tax, 104
Value of the marginal product of labor (VMPL), 369
Vernon, Raymond, 65
Vertical integration, 359
*Viner, 169, 137, 139, 169
Volkswagen, 359, 337, 387
Voluntary export restraints, 93
    welfare effects of, 98

W

Wage level in determining unit labor costs, 23
Wage protection argument, 119
Wahl, D. F., 62
Welfare effects

of a customs, 137
of customs union, 137
of quota, 98
of subsidy, 100
of tariff, 75
of voluntary export restraints, 98
Wells, Louis, 65
White Paper, 9, 157
Wholly owned subsidiary, 344
Williamson, John, 235
World Bank, 229, 324
World economy. *See* International economics
World wide recession, as cause of debt crisis, 313

X

Xenophobia, 377

Y

Yamaha Motor Company, 105, 106

Z

Zenith Radio Corporation, 347
Zollverein, 137